THE ORGANIZATIONAL BEHAVIOR READER

SEVENTH EDITION

Edited by:

Joyce S. Osland
UNIVERSITY OF PORTLAND

David A. Kolb
CASE WESTERN RESERVE UNIVERSITY

Irwin M. Rubin
TEMENOS, INC.

Prentice
Hall

Upper Saddle River, New Jersey 07458

Library of Congress Cataloging-in-Publication Data

The organizational behavior reader / edited by Joyce S. Osland, David A. Kolb, Irwin M. Rubin.—7th ed.
     p. cm.
  Includes bibliographical references.
  ISBN 0-13-026554-3
  1. Psychology, Industrial. 2. Organizational behavior. I. Osland, Joyce. II. Kolb, David A., -III. Rubin, Irwin M.,

HF5548.8 .K552 2001
158.7—dc21

                                00-032397

Executive Editor: David Shafer
Managing Editor (Editorial): Jennifer Glennon
Editorial Assistant: Kim Marsden
Assistant Editor: Michele Foresta
Media Project Manager: Michele Faranda
Executive Marketing Manager: Michael Campbell
Managing Editor (Production): Judy Leale
Production Editor: Cindy Spreder
Production Assistant: Keri Jean
Production Manager: Arnold Vila
Associate Director, Manufacturing: Vincent Scelta
Permissions Supervisor: Suzanne Grappi
Design Manager: Patricia Smythe
Designer: Michael Fruhbeis
Cover Design: Michael Fruhbeis
Cover Art/Photo: David Madison/Tony Stone Images 1999
Associate Director, Multimedia Production: Karen Goldsmith
Manager, Multimedia Production: Christina Mahon
Formatter: Ashley Scattergood
Composition: Preparé, Inc.

10 9 8 7 6 5 4 3 2 1

ISBN 0-13-026554-3

CONTENTS

▲▲

PREFACE

▲▲▲

This book is a primer on human behavior in organizations for students of management at three different levels—undergraduate, graduate, and executive education. Our goal in this volume is to prepare employees and managers to diagnose and understand organizational issues and be more effective. The reader includes writings by scholars and practitioners in the key areas of organizational behavior, which have been divided into four sections: "Understanding Yourself and Other People at Work," "Creating Effective Work Groups," "Leadership and Management," and "Managing Effective Organizations." This edition contains basic ideas and concepts, new research findings and practical applications, as well as emerging perspectives that suggest the future shape of the field. In contrast with previous editions, there is more emphasis on international topics, teams, commitment, creativity, diversity, e-commerce, and global business.

Our aim was to compile an exciting collection of significant, theoretical, and practical work that is both reader-friendly and topical. We have read hundreds of articles to find "just the right ones," which can be classified in one or more of the following categories:

1. Classic, ground-breaking articles that, while written years ago, still provide the definitive treatment of a subject and deserve to be read in the scholar's original words
2. Lucid overviews of research findings and theories on a particular topic
3. Descriptions of cutting-edge research
4. Practical guides for managers based on research findings.

For the first time, this edition contains brief chapter introductions to set the stage for readers and provide a glimpse of what they can expect. This book is designed to be used with the text/workbook *Organizational Behavior: An Experiential Approach to Organizational Behavior Seventh Edition*, by the same authors. The articles contained herein form a complete package with the exercises and theory contained in the workbook, allowing the student to go through all the phases of the experiential learning process.

Although designed as a companion volume, this collection of readings stands on its own and should be useful to teachers, managers, and consultants for the breadth of viewpoints and the wealth of data that it provides about the field of organizational behavior.

When it comes to acknowledging contributions to this edition, our greatest debt of gratitude goes to Susan Mann, research assistant extraordinaire. Innumerable colleagues have suggested their favorite readings. In particular, we would like to thank Suzanne Adams, Bruce Drake, Howard Feldman, Tom Howe, Asbjorn Osland, Robert Peterson, and Susan Schor for their contributions and opinions. The reviewers of the previous edition were extremely helpful and thorough: John Dopp, Gene Hendrix, Avis Johnson, and Dennis O'Connor. The reference librarians at the University of Portland—Tony Greiner, Susan Hinken, Pam Horan, Torie Scott, Heidi Senior, as well as the director, Rich Hines—all went well above the call of duty in tracking down articles and citations. Carol Henson, Susan Mann, Jessica Osland and Debra Stephens deserve thanks for their proof readings contributions. Ron Hill, dean at the University of Portland's business school, and the Robert B. Pamplin, Jr. Foundation have provided support for this project. Finally, we're very grateful to Melissa O'Neill, Gwynn Klobes, Michael Kuchler, and the student workers at the University of Portland business school who cheerfully lent a helping hand to this project.

It was pleasure, as always, to work with the Prentice Hall crew: David Shafer, Jennifer Glennon, Michele Foresta, Judy Leale, Kim Marsden, and the unflappable Cindy Spreder.

In addition to colleagues and publishing staff, an effort like this reader is also the culmination of numerous family sacrifices, favors, and opinions. We owe a special debt of gratitude, in partyicular, to Asbjorn, Jessica and Carol, and also to Michael, Katrina, Ellie and Anna.

Joyce S. Osland
David A. Kolb
Irwin M. Rubin

The goal of the first section is to help you become aware of your mental maps or models, as well as those of people with whom you work. Although the concept has existed since ancient times, the term *mental models* was coined by Kenneth Craik, a Scottish psychologist in the 1940s. It refers to "the images, assumptions, and stories that we carry in our minds of ourselves, other people, institutions, and every aspect of the world. Like a pane of glass framing and subtly distorting our vision, mental models determine what we see and then how we act."[1] One way to understand our behavior is to make these usually tacit maps visible. In this section, you will have an opportunity to examine mental maps about psychological contracts, theories of management, learning styles, ethics, and values. We hope you will finish the section with more self-knowledge and a greater appreciation for the differences you will discover in other people.

CHAPTER 1

THE PSYCHOLOGICAL CONTRACT

PSYCHOLOGICAL CONTRACTS: VIOLATIONS AND MODIFICATIONS
Denise M. Rousseau

HOW 'GEN X' MANAGERS MANAGE
Jay A. Conger

HOW TO EARN YOUR EMPLOYEES' COMMITMENT
Gary Dessler

The first mental map we are going to examine concerns the psychological contract, an individual's beliefs, shaped by the organization, regarding the terms and conditions of a reciprocal exchange agreement between individuals and their organization. People frame events at work, such as promises, expectations, and future payoffs for their contributions, according to their own mental model and past history. There are negative consequences when psychological contracts are violated; understanding this concept can prevent managers from making mistakes and harming their relationship with employees.

Denise Rousseau, one of the foremost experts on psychological contracts, describes what happens when people fail to comply with the terms of a contract in "Psychological Contracts: Violations and Modifications." Rousseau identifies common sources of contract violation and typical responses. In a rapidly changing environment, it is sometimes impossible to avoid modifying psychological contracts. Rousseau explains how to change psychological contracts with the least possible disruption.

Psychological contracts are the link between the individual and the organization, but we cannot assume all generations have the same expectations or attitudes about the workplace. Jay Conger profiles the distinct generations in the U.S. workforce and the historical events that shaped their values and worldviews in "How 'Gen X' Managers Manage." Different generations operate with distinct mental maps; understanding these maps makes it easier to get along in the workplace. Conger, known for his work on leadership, dispels some of the myths about Generation X, children of the Baby Boomers, and explains what motivates this group.

---

[1] P. Senge, A. Kleiner, C. Roberts, R. Ross, and B. Smith, *The Fifth Discipline Fieldbook: Strategies and Tools for Building a Learning Organization* (New York: Currency, 1993) 235.

The final article in this section, Gary Dessler's "How to Earn Your Employees' Commitment," responds to a business challenge that resulted from major modifications in the psychological contract. Before the 1980s, employees expected their competence and loyalty to be rewarded with long-term employment and advancement. Globalization and rapid changes in the business environment, however, produced massive terminations resulting from downsizing, reengineering, and mergers and acquisitions. Many employees had to accept a new psychological contract consisting of increasing demands for performance, flexibility, and innovation *without* the promise of job security. Not surprisingly, less commitment on the part of employers was matched by less commitment on the part of employees; putting individual career needs ahead of the company's needs became more common as did frequent job-hopping. The commitment challenge was compounded in the United States by the tightest labor market since the 1950s; as a result more companies are competing for workers, devoting more effort to retaining them, and worrying about commitment. Dessler, an authority on human resources, explains why committed employees are so crucial and provides practical lessons from organizations that are good at building commitment.

THE PSYCHOLOGICAL CONTRACT:
VIOLATIONS AND MODIFICATIONS*

Denise M. Rousseau

> *"They promised me a job in marketing and here I am doing telephone sales."*
> *"The company promised that no one would be fired out of the training program—that all of us were 'safe' until placement. In return for this security, we accepted lower pay. The company subsequently fired four people from the training program."*
> *"Original representations of the company's financial and market strength (were) clearly fraudulent."*

The common thread found in these quotations from recently hired employees is a violation of the psychological contract, which is defined as individual beliefs, shaped by the organization, regarding terms of an exchange agreement between individuals and their organizations. A contract is a mental model that people use to frame events such as promises, acceptance, and reliance. The promises that make up contracts have no objective meaning. Promises ultimately are perceptions of what was sent and what was meant. Perceptions, however, are not simply passive interpretations of reality; people create their own meaning for many events. The close supervision one person sees as controlling may seem supportive and helpful to her coworker. Yet reality is not constructed wholly in the minds of individuals. Groups sometimes do agree on events and their meaning. Investment bankers, for example, may share a belief that their firm rewards those who make profitable deals.

Contract violation erodes trust. It undermines the employment relationship, yielding both lower employee contributions (e.g., performance and attendance) and lower employer investments (e.g., retention and promotion) in employees. Therefore, it's important for managers to understand how to avoid violating psychological contracts unnecessarily and how to modify them without eroding trust when change is essential.

---

*Excerpted and reprinted with permission from D. M. Rousseau, *Psychological Contracts in Organizations* (Thousand Oaks, CA: Sage, 1995).

Psychological contract violation can run the gamut from subtle misperceptions to stark breaches of good faith. In organizations, violated contracts are at the heart of many lawsuits brought by customers and employees. Although potentially damaging to reputations, careers, and relationships, violations also appear to be both frequent and survivable.

The basic facts of contract violation are these:

- Contract violation is commonplace.
- Violated contracts lead to adverse reactions by the injured party.
- Failure to fulfill a contract need not be fatal to the relationship.

WHAT IS CONTRACT VIOLATION?

In the strictest sense, violation is a failure to comply with the terms of a contract. But, given the subjective nature of psychological contracts, how people interpret the circumstances of this failure determines whether they experience a violation. Violation takes three forms (Table 1). *Inadvertent violation* occurs when both parties are able and willing to keep their bargain, but divergent interpretations lead one party to act in a manner at odds with the understanding and interests of the other. Two people who misunderstand the time of a meeting will inadvertently fail to honor their mutual commitment to attend. *Disruption* to the contract occurs when circumstances make it impossible for one or both parties to fulfill their end of the contract, despite the fact that they are willing to do so. A plant closing forced by a hurricane can prevent an employer from providing work. Similarly, a car accident can keep an employee from showing up to work on time. Reneging or *breach of contract* occurs when one side, otherwise capable of performing the contract, refuses to do so. A bank manager who wants to spend more time with his family leaves a high demand/high pay job with one bank for another with a smaller financial institution. The major attraction of the new bank for the manager is its low pressure environment, which is played up by the officers who recruit him. Within two weeks of taking the job, the manager learns that the smaller firm is starting an aggressive marketing campaign he is expected to head, which will keep him away from his family for even longer hours than before. Damages include increased stress and family conflict along with loss of reputation if he tries to change jobs again soon. The sense of betrayal and entrapment this manager feels exacerbates his personal costs from the organization's actions. Whether the victim understands the source of violation to be unwillingness or inability to comply has a tremendous impact on how violation is experienced and what victims do in response (Bies and Moag, 1986).

Although contracts can be violated in innumerable ways, there are a number of common forms (Table 2). Recruiters may overpromise a job's opportunity for challenge, growth or development, while at the same time, eager job seekers may read into a promise what they want to hear. Managers, coworkers, or executives who say one thing and do another all can engender violation. A common cause of violation for many employees involves a change in superiors. When one's boss or mentor is promoted, terminated, or retired, old deals may be abrogated. Similarly, changes in human resource practices, even with constructive intent (e.g., to align with a new business strategy) can appear to break old

TABLE 1   Sources of Experienced Violation

Inadvertent	Able and willing (divergent interpretations made in good faith)
Disruption	Willing but unable (inability to fulfill contract)
Breach of contract	Able but unwilling (reneging)

TABLE 2   Sources of Violation by Contract Makers and Systems

Sources	Violations
Contract makers:	
recruiters	■ unfamiliar with actual job ■ overpromise
managers	■ say one thing, do another
coworkers	■ failure to provide support
mentors	■ little follow-through ■ few interactions
top management	■ mixed messages
Systems:	
compensation	■ changing criteria ■ reward seniority, low job security
benefits	■ changing coverage
career paths	■ dependent on one's manager ■ inconsistent application
performance review	■ not done on time ■ little feedback
training	■ skills learned not tied to job
documentation	■ stated procedures at odds with actual practice

commitments (e.g., introducing new results-based performance criteria among veteran employees used to a seniority system). Then there is the phenomenon of mixed messages, where different contract makers express divergent intentions. A mission statement can convey that the organization rewards based upon merit ("commitment to excellence") while the compensation system is based on seniority. Different contract sources may each convey mutually exclusive promises.

WHEN IS VIOLATION MOST LIKELY?

• When there is a history of conflict and low trust in the relationship.
• When social distance exists between the parties such that one does not understand the perspective of the other.
• When an external pattern of violations exists (e.g., an era of business retrenchment).
• When incentives to breach contracts are very high or when perpetrators perceive themselves to have no alternatives (e.g., organizational crises).
• When one party places little value in the relationship (e.g., alternative parties are relatively available and there are few sunk costs).

WHEN A CONTRACT IS VIOLATED

Responses to violation take many forms. Violated contracts promote mistrust, anger, and attrition and change the way people behave in subsequent interactions. The aftermath of contract violation can be seen in declining corporate loyalty and increased litigation. Managers decry the decline of employee loyalty, while at the same time, the workforce has been counselled to eschew reliance on job security and employee commitments, and to "pack its own parachute" instead. In both instances there is the suggestion of contract violation, and the implication that at least one party has failed to keep its side of the bargain.

TYPES OF RESPONSES

Whether organizations and individuals choose to end their relationship, resolve their dispute, sue, or suffer in silence is a function of both situational factors and the predispositions of the parties. Previous research on responses to the more general phenomenon of dissatisfaction has largely focused on four courses of action: exit, voice, loyalty, and destruction. Although studied in various combinations (e.g., Hirschman, 1970's *Exit, Voice, and Loyalty*) and labels (e.g., Farrell's, 1983, *Exit, Voice, Loyalty and Neglect*), these courses of action reflect two essential dimensions: active-passive and constructive-destructive (Figure 1).

Personal characteristics predisposing the victim to believe that the relationship is valuable or can be saved should promote either relationship-building behaviors of voice or loyalty. Without this belief, behaviors that undermine the relationship, exit or destruction, are more likely. Research on individual reactions to inequitable situations suggests that people differ in terms of their willingness to tolerate unfair or inequitable exchanges (Berscheid and Walster, 1973). "Equity-sensitives" are people who tend to monitor their exchanges with others very carefully. "Beneficient" individuals are those who tend to be other-oriented, or comfortable when exchanges benefit others more than themselves. There is some evidence that men are more likely to be equity-sensitive and women more beneficient, although personality and other factors also enter in.

Situational factors promoting certain behaviors and inhibiting others also affect responses to violation. Social learning and the presence of behavioral role models tend to induce certain types of behaviors. Thus, employees in organizations where other victims have left might be inclined to leave themselves. Similarly, individuals who have observed others successfully complain about their treatment might themselves be inclined to complain (Robinson, 1992). It is likely that the culture of the organization shapes the type of violation responses people make. A very bureaucratic organization that stifles communication and deviant behavior probably engenders little voice and more neglect and disloyalty. An open, communal organization might foster more overt complaints, as well as attempting to repair the contract by communicating with superiors.

Exit is voluntary termination of the relationship. Employers can terminate workers whose performance does not meet standards (e.g., too frequently tardy, absent, or careless), while workers can quit an untrustworthy or unreliable employer (e.g., who fails to deliver promised training or promotions). Exit is most likely in employment with transactional terms, where its costs are relatively low. Transactional terms are exemplified by *a fair day's work for a fair day's pay*—focusing on short-term and monetizable exchanges. Employment agencies such as Manpower, Kelly, Nursetemps, and other temporary employment services offer organizations the opportunity to create purely transactional agreements with workers. Transactional contract terms include: specific economic conditions (e.g., wage rate) as the primary incentive, limited personal involvement in the job, closed-ended time frame (e.g., seasonal employment), commitments limited to well-specified conditions (e.g., union contract), unambiguous terms readily understood by outsiders, and the use of existing skills (no development).

Both active and destructive, exit terminates the relationship. The vast majority of people quitting jobs within the first two years of employment report that their employer had violated commitments it had made (Robinson and Rousseau, 1994).

FIGURE 1   Responses to Violation

	Constructive	Destructive
Active	Voice	Neglect/Destruction
Passive	Loyalty/Silence	Exit

Exit is most likely following violation when:

1. the contract is transactional;
2. many other potential jobs or potential employees are available;
3. the relationship is relatively brief;
4. other people are also exiting; and
5. attempts to remedy a violated contract have failed.

However, it should be pointed out that violations don't always lead to exit. Robinson and Rousseau (1994) found that although 79 percent of leavers reported violated contracts, so too did 52 percent of stayers. While enduring violation, stayers can manifest three forms of response: voice, loyalty, or neglect.

Voice refers to the actions victims take to remedy the violation. Any attempt to change the objectionable features in the situation, such as complaints to one's boss or to human resources, or the filing of a grievance, are efforts made to remedy or compensate for the violation while remaining in the relationship. As a means of expressing general dissatisfaction, voice has received wide study in terms of grievance filing (Allen and Keaveny, 1981), willingness to vote for unions (Getman, Goldberg and Herman, 1976), and whistleblowing (Near and Miceli, 1986). However, as a means of remediating a contract violation, voice has distinct features from reparations for dissatisfaction. Voice in contract violation focuses on (1) reducing losses and (2) restoring trust.

As a response to dissatisfaction, voice often has been associated with relationship-threatening alternatives, where members in effect burn their bridges (e.g., whistleblowing). Voice in response to contract violation is an active, constructive effort and is manifest in a number of ways. In a study of MBA alumni, there were three major types of employee voice behaviors: talking with superiors, threats, and changes in behavior (Rousseau, Robinson and Kraatz, 1992).

Talking with superiors was the most frequent type of voice:

I discussed my disappointment with my boss and also with my mentor. I was assured that, although I did not receive a bonus, my performance was above average. I was promoted and received a salary increase six months later.

Some complaints obtain some sort of substitution:

They said the situation was out of their hands and gave me a substantial salary increase.

Some complaints elicit no response:

My boss paid lip service to making changes, but nothing actually occurred.

Voice can take the form of a threat in a smaller number of cases:

I threatened to leave based on my work assignment, training, and development opportunities. I was given new assignments, more training, and was allowed to stretch for development...however, I believe that happened primarily because of my director; another director probably would have let me leave.

In a few instances, a change in the victim's behavior generates a response:

I was unhappy with the situation and my performance reflected it. The decision was made by (my) managers to reverse the situation. I now report to the marketing manager with a dotted line reporting relationship with the financial manager (a reversal of the previous situation).

Exit was the final resort for some:

First there was a confrontation on my part to bring the problem forth, then following further unkept promises, I left the company (giving over a month's notice).

Voice is most likely when:

1. A positive relationship and trust exist.
2. Voice channels exist.
3. Other people are using voice.
4. People believe that they can influence the other contract party.

Silence is a form of non-response. Manifest as loyalty or as avoidance, silence reflects a willingness to endure or accept unfavorable circumstances. Silence can imply pessimism, in terms of believing that one has no available alternatives. Or, silence can reflect loyalty—optimistically waiting for conditions to improve (Rusbult, Farrell, Rogers, and Mainous, 1988). As a passive, constructive response, silence serves to perpetuate the existing relationship:

I started spending more time with my family and worrying less about what was happening at work.

Silence is likely when:

1. there are no voice channels, or established ways of complaining or communicating violations, and
2. no available alternative opportunities exist elsewhere.

Neglect, which entails passive negligence or active destruction, is a complex form of response. It can involve neglect of one's duties to the detriment of the interests of the other party. Passive-aggressive employee behavior, as in work slowdowns or providing customers with poor service, is a form of neglect, as is an organization's failure to invest in certain employees while developing others. Even when passive, neglect reflects erosion of the relationship between the parties. Destruction involves more active examples of counterproductive behaviors, including vandalism, theft, and interpersonal aggression (e.g., violence at work).

VIOLATION ISN'T THE END OF THE CONTRACT

Exit is only one of many results of contract violation. The fact that so many people with violated contracts remain with their employer suggests although violation may be based on a discrete event (e.g., a willful breach of contract terms), a contract's fulfillment is more a matter of degree. When Robinson and Rousseau (1994) asked employees to indicate whether their contract had been violated using a yes/no format, a total of 59 percent indicated *Yes*. However, when respondents were asked if their contract had been ultimately fulfilled by their employer, a large proportion (73 percent) indicated that their employer had honored its commitments at least moderately well. Among those employees reporting a violation at some point in the first two years of employment, 48 percent indicated that their contract had been honored at least somewhat by their employer. The major difference was that for victims of violation, the model rating of fulfillment was 3 on a 5 point scale (mean = 2.65) while for non-victims it was 4 (mean = 3.93). Extent of contract keeping was affected by what benefits the employee received (e.g., if not the promotion as scheduled, then a later promotion) as well as whether the violation was an isolated incident or part of a larger pattern. These findings suggest that although violation is a discrete event, contract fulfillment is not. Rather, fulfillment is a continuum shaped by both the quality of the relationship and post-violation behavior of both the victim and perpetrator.

How people respond to violation is largely a function of attributions made regarding the violators' motives, the behavior of the violator, and the scope of losses incurred. To understand how events are experienced as violations, it is necessary to take into account the perspective of the victim and the behavior of the perpetrator. For the prospective victim, the experience of violation is heightened when:

• Losses seem greater; experienced violation is a matter of degree rather than a discrete event (all or nothing).

- The event occurs in a context where it poses a threat to the relationship between the parties (e.g., a history of previous breach or conflict).
- The violation event appears to be voluntary, as opposed to inadvertent, accidental, or due to forces beyond the violator's control.
- No evidence of good faith efforts to avoid violation (the appearance of irresponsibility or neglect) is perceived by the victim.

The strength and quality of the relationship affects not only the extent to which violation is tolerated or leads to dissolution of the contract, but also affects the ability of the parties to repair the relationship. How people are treated following violation can repair the relationship or exacerbate its problems.

The dynamics of psychological contract violation offer some lessons for both managers and workers. Perceptions are facts to the person who shares them and must be taken into account in a successful worker-manager relationship. When changes are introduced it is quite possible that workers will believe that new practices will violate old promises. Rather than merely accepting the inevitability of violation, a number of steps spell the difference between a well managed employment relationship and violation, anger, and mistrust.

Actively seek to understand what the people we work with interpret to be our and the organization's commitments to them. This understanding makes it easier to both honor existing commitments as well as to know how to effectively change a deal or create a new one.

Recognize that any departure from the status quo can involve losses, painful consequences for the people who have enjoyed its benefits. Managing these losses, first by recognizing what forms they might take, and then taking steps to offset or accommodate them, can spell the difference between successful management and a breach of trust.

Even when complaints and anger indicate a violation has been experienced, a sense of good faith can be restored when the issues are directly addressed through a joint problem-solving process. Such actions can make a so-so relationship far stronger by showing commitment to joint agreement and respect for the people involved.

REFERENCES

R. Allen and T. Keaveny, "Correlates of Faculty Interests in Unionization: A Replication and Extension," *Journal of Applied Psychology 66* (1981): 582–588.

R. Bies and J. Moag, "Interactional Justice Communication Criteria of Fairness," M. Bazerman, R. Lewicki, and B. Shephard (eds.) *Research on Negotiations in Organizations 1* (Greenwich, CT: JAI Press, 1986): 43–45.

D. Farrell, "Exit, Voice, Loyalty, and Neglect as Responses to Job Dissatisfaction: A Multidimensional Scaling Study," *Academy of Management Journal 26* (1983): 596–607.

J. Getman, S. Goldberg, and J. Herman, *Union Representation Elections: Law and Reality* (New York: Russell Sage, 1976).

A. O. Hirschman, *Exit, Voice, and Loyalty* (Cambridge, MA: Harvard University Press, 1970).

J. Near, and M. Miceli, "Retaliation Against Whistleblowers: Predictors and Effects," *Journal of Applied Psychology 71* (1986): 137–145.

S. L. Robinson, *Responses to Dissatisfaction.* Unpublished dissertation, Northwestern University, Kellogg Graduate School of Management, 1992.

S. L. Robinson and D. M. Rousseau, "Violating the Psychological Contract: Not the Exception But the Norm," *Journal of Organizational Behavior 15* (1994): 245–259.

D. M. Rousseau, S. L. Robinson, and M. S. Kraatz, "Renegotiating the Psychological Contract," Paper presented at the Society for Industrial Organizational Psychology meetings, Montreal, May 1992.

C. Rusbult, D. Farrell, G. Rogers, and A. Mainous, "Impact of Exchange Variables on Exit, Voice, Loyalty and Neglect: An Integrative Model of Response to Declining Job Satisfaction," *Academy of Management Journal 31* (1988): 599–627.

E. Walster, E. Bercheid, and G. Walster, "New Directions in Equity Research," *Journal of Personality and Social Psychology 25* (1973): 151–176.

How 'Gen X' Managers Manage*

Jay A. Conger

If you want to witness the power of demographics, simply take a drive through the garage of my parents' retirement complex. There you will see row after row of Buicks, Cadillacs, Lincolns, Oldsmobiles, and Chryslers. You will see few Toyotas, Nissans, Mazdas, and Audis.

The absence of foreign brands seems at first peculiar. So you need to know one thing about my parents and their peers. They are in their 80s, products of the World War II generation, one that was fiercely loyal to America and to the products it makes. Through the ups and downs of the American automobile industry, they stayed true to a belief in "Buy American." They are just one small example of how history shapes the attitudes and tastes of a generation.

In this article, we will turn our attention to the newest adult generation, Generation X, and specifically its attitudes toward the workplace and toward managing. Originally called the *Slackers* or the *MTV generation*, Generation X'ers were at first thought to be a somewhat unmotivated, cynical group of nihilists. After all, Beavis and Butthead were their cultural icons.

Coca-Cola thought so, too, when it introduced a soda with the name OK in 1994. With cans colored in gray, the label read, "Don't be fooled into thinking there has to be a reason for everything," and "What's the point of OK soda? Well, what's the point of anything?" To Coke's surprise, the campaign failed, and the product was withdrawn.

Coke and the rest of the world discovered that certain myths about this generation are grossly inaccurate. What we are now realizing is that Generation X'ers are very much in sync with the new rules of the workplace and with America's love affair with financial success. At the same time, they are indeed different from previous generations. For example, 61 percent of Generation X women answering a Gallup poll said they would prefer to work for a woman, compared with 26 percent of the women surveyed in a group of older baby boomers.[1]

And if Madonna was the "material girl," she was certainly the forerunner to the "material generation." The term *slacker* doesn't apply to this generation when it comes to making money. Financial well-being is very important to Gen X'ers—even more than it was for the boomers in their earlier years. For example, the Roper Organization found that 69 percent of today's 29-year-olds are interested in a high-paying job.[2] This contrasts with 58 percent of a comparable group in 1978 who pined for a job that "pays a lot more than average." When the University of California at Los Angeles asked freshmen in 1993 whether "to be very well off financially" was an objective they considered essential or very important, 74.5 percent responded in the affirmative. The figure in 1971 was just 40.1 percent. When asked why it was very important to go to college, 75.1 percent of freshmen in 1993 said "to make more money." Only 49.9 percent said so in 1971[3] (see Exhibit 1).

What we are seeing in Generation X'ers is a different set of attitudes about the workplace. In a nutshell, they distrust hierarchy. They prefer more informal arrangements. They prefer to judge on merit rather than on status. They are far less loyal to their companies. They are the first generation in America to be raised on a heavy diet of workplace participation and teamwork. They know computers inside and out. They like money, but they also say they want balance in their lives.

What we are experiencing is a remarkable historical event—a pivotal change between the workplace generations in their attitudes toward authority and toward organizations. Many of these changes began with the baby boomers and continue today with Generation X, setting these two groups distinctly apart from innumerable generations that went before them.

*Reprinted with permission from *Strategy & Business* (First Quarter 1998): 21–29.

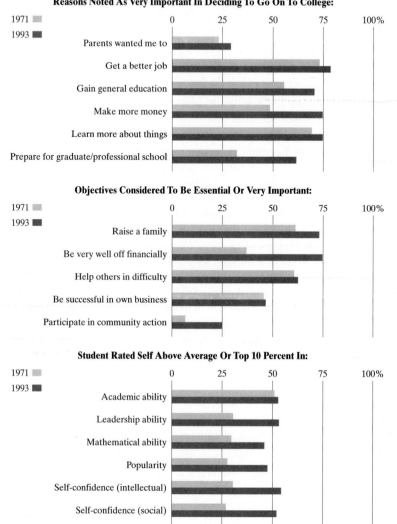

Reasons Noted As Very Important In Deciding To Go On To College:

1971
1993

- Parents wanted me to
- Get a better job
- Gain general education
- Make more money
- Learn more about things
- Prepare for graduate/professional school

Objectives Considered To Be Essential Or Very Important:

1971
1993

- Raise a family
- Be very well off financially
- Help others in difficulty
- Be successful in own business
- Participate in community action

Student Rated Self Above Average Or Top 10 Percent In:

1971
1993

- Academic ability
- Leadership ability
- Mathematical ability
- Popularity
- Self-confidence (intellectual)
- Self-confidence (social)

EXHIBIT 1   How the Generations Compare
Source: Higher Education Research Institute, U.C.L.A.

WHY GENERATIONS DIFFER

To understand how generations come to differ from one another, we have to see each as a product of historical events that have profoundly shaped its members' values and views of the world. These events leave emotional memories that are far more potent than the mental impressions derived from reading about events that have never been experienced. These emotional memories deeply shape our feelings about institutions, authority, materialism, family and careers.

For example, the Silent Generation—composed of those born between 1925 and 1942—was filled with the children of families that went through the Great Depression; they were influenced by their parents' hardships to treasure employment and to be obedient employees, and by their parents' military service in World War II to be command-oriented in their leadership style.[4] Following the Silent Generation came the well-publicized Baby Boomers, the group born between 1943 and 1964. Raised on rock and rebellion in an era of phenomenal national wealth, they became a somewhat indulged and narcissistic tribe nicknamed Yuppies. Their views were shaped by events such as Watergate and Vietnam, which exposed the vulnerability of authority and the follies of a powerful nation. They were also witnesses to striking contrasts in leaders—some inducing hope and idealism, like Martin Luther King Jr. and John F. Kennedy, and others promoting cynicism and apathy, such as Lyndon Johnson and Richard Nixon.

The most recent generation—born between 1965 and 1981—is called *Generation X* (after the title of a novel about them), or sometimes the busters because of the drop-off or "bust" in births following the boomer generation. They are the children of dual-career parents and of parents whose marriages produced record divorce rates. In contrast to the boomers, who in college tended to major in liberal arts, this group chose majors in business and economics. In short, they spurned the idealism that their parents had embraced when young for a more pragmatic and cynical realism. The shaping events in their lives were Ronald Reagan, the crash of the *Challenger* space shuttle, and the Gulf War.

To understand how Generation X managers may prove to be different from yesterday's flock, we need to take a step backward and look briefly at the Silent Generation managers for whom the term the *organization man* was coined. They are our point of contrast—after all, they were the managers of the 1950s, 1960s and 1970s. They were loyal to their organizations and given loyalty in return.

Nowhere was this world of the organization man more in evidence than in America's banking industry, where I conducted interviews with managers who began their careers in the 1950s and 1960s. There I discovered a startling contrast with the world of management today. The comments of one senior executive at a New York bank who started out in the 1960s are representative of the command era of just a generation ago:

> As a junior man, I didn't even have an office, of course. I was out on what we then called a platform. Having an office was a sign of having really arrived. We wore white shirts only. We wore hats to and from the office; hats were considered part of the uniform. And, of course, we would never dare take our suit coats off. Not even in our offices, if we had one. That was totally taboo. Instead, we wore them all day—even if our door was closed.
>
> It was easy to manage in a strictly hierarchical setting like that, because that was the system that was in place and that was the system that was honored, revered, feared—all of the above— both by those managing the hierarchy on top and by those who were on the rungs below. You always knew exactly where you stood. There was a built-in sort of incentive to go level by level by level. You would go one at a time.
>
> There were sharp divisions of labor. Vice presidents and senior vice presidents discussed policy matters only among themselves. It was absolutely off-limits for them to talk about policy with junior people. The decisions of the senior people were never questioned by the juniors. You would never say, 'Does the president really know what he is doing with this particular thing?' That stuff was in the exclusive domain of the senior people.
>
> Relationships with bosses were much more formal than they are today. You would work many, many years before referring to the vice president and certainly the senior vice president by their first names. There was always a very formal overtone to the whole thing. Seniority almost always meant age as well as rank; your bosses were older than you were. I think the formality was necessary to support the hierarchical system.
>
> Sharing of secrets was much more restricted then. Your discussions with a boss would be confined to the matter of the day. If you happened to be working on a project for U.S. Steel, your

discussions with your seniors would usually be limited quite narrowly to discussions about U.S. Steel. Usually the senior's standard question at the end was 'How are things going?' The expected response was 'Things are going very well, sir.'

The world our banker describes is one that, until fairly recently, shaped most managers' actions and values. But by the mid-1970s, this world of the organization man started to erode. The changes began as soon as the baby boomers entered the workforce.

THE BRIDGE TO A CHANGING WORKPLACE: THE BABY BOOMERS

To understand Generation X, we need to begin with their older brethren, the Baby Boomers. The trends that started with the boomers have become only more pronounced with Generation X.

First of all, what separates both generations from earlier ones are important changes in the world of business. Competition has become much more intense; companies have been forced to speed up their responsiveness to the marketplace as never before. The hierarchical chain of command of the past has proved too slow. It took too long for decisions to move up and down the levels in their ordained sequence. In response, cross-functional and special project teams have been introduced as the new organizing units.

As the command model has weakened and teamwork increased, working relationships have become more informal. Employees assert themselves more. They have less patience with the restrictions of a hierarchical system and are less likely to defer to their bosses automatically. A command boss can no longer manage with the ease of just a decade ago. Loyalty has diminished sharply—at first, on the side of the corporation, but this has been followed by employees. The Number 1 book on the *Business Week* best-seller list—*The Dilbert Principle*—mocks managers and their half-hearted and sometimes deceptive attempts to garner employee loyalty.

Collapsing at the same time is the traditional aura that surrounded positions of authority. In part, this is due to the flattening of organizational hierarchies. More profoundly, it is due to societal events. Unlike their parents, boomers as children saw the vulnerability of authority in society at large. Instead of watching a victorious battle with Nazi Germany, they witnessed a failed war in Vietnam, a series of assassinations of national leaders, the disgrace of several presidents, an economic breakdown following the OPEC oil crisis and environmental disasters like Three Mile Island.

For this generation, authority looked increasingly unreliable and often just plain wrong. So, in their music and manners, they displayed contempt for leadership. They took to the streets and invaded college administration offices to protest. This kind of challenge to authority would have been unimaginable to their Silent Generation parents. Both the Silents and their own parents served in the military, where they learned great respect for the effectiveness of the command model. After all, they had seen strong and admired military and political leaders win a world war and overcome an economic depression.

Tied to these crumbling perceptions of the legitimacy of authority is a steep rise in the importance of individual independence. For example, throughout this century, independence has become more and more desirable to parents as a character attribute for their children, as evidenced by historical surveys. In 1890, for example, only 16 percent of parents believed that independence was an important quality; but by the end of the 1970s, approximately 75 percent felt that independence was the most important character trait.

As independence has grown in importance, its antithesis—obedience—has diminished steadily as a valued trait. For example, 64 percent of parents in 1890 cited obedience as one of the three most important characteristics in child-rearing. This fell to 17 percent by 1978.[5] This gap between the two traits has only grown further with Generation X.

The heightened importance of independence is, in part, related to the nation's growing affluence. People have more money for the services and machinery needed to run a household. That has made them less dependent on family and community. Fathers were transferred by their companies across the nation, and this mobility further encouraged self-sufficiency. A book, *Dr. Spock's Baby and Child Care*, published in 1946, put a strong emphasis on teaching children the value of independence. Over the next decade, the book became hugely influential—the bible for child-rearing.

In the 1960's came the commercial introduction of the contraceptive pill, which gave women a greater sense of control and aided the emergence of the women's movement. Women also began to enter the workforce in ever-growing numbers. For many women, these events spelled autonomy.

Education, too, undercut traditional authority. The baby boomers and Generation X'ers were beneficiaries of the greatest surge in education in history. Since 1960, the percentages of men and women graduating from high school have doubled and, from college, considerably more than doubled.[6] The new hordes in college and graduate school found themselves encouraged to critique the books and ideas they were studying. They were actually graded on their ability to challenge one another's thinking, and often the professor's.

These changes created a new breed of businessperson among boomer managers. One editor of *Fortune*, Walter Kiechel, caught it perfectly. "As managers," he wrote, "and with remarkable consistency across the group, they espouse values that any progressive organization would endorse: lots of communication, sharing of responsibility, respect for each other's autonomy…They are also thoroughly uncomfortable with much of what has traditionally…been thought of as the leader's role. They don't like telling others what to do any more than they like being told. As bosses, they can be just as controlling as prior generations…but they're sneakier about it. [They are] no respecters of hierarchy."[7]

I will use Paul as a paradigm of today's boomer executive. Just 40, Paul is the chief executive of a subsidiary of one of the world's largest pharmaceutical companies. He is also at the forefront of a wave of baby boomer bosses now filling the executive suites of North American corporations. A former hockey player, Paul stands tall and is physically imposing. Perfectly groomed, he looks the part of a young CEO. As he speaks, you hear the confidence in his voice, yet there is also a reflectiveness that hints at a different breed of company president. Deeply concerned about teamwork and participation, Paul believes in the egalitarian organization:

> *I grew up with autocratic leadership—top-down management. I found in those situations that there are always winners and losers and that it doesn't necessarily resolve issues effectively or move an organization forward. For me, there's a lot wrapped up in the word* boss. *People of my generation are negative on the word. We don't want to be a 'boss.'*
>
> *When people ask me what I do, I say I'm with so-and-so company. I don't say I'm the president. You don't take pride in being a boss over people. What you take pride in is the accomplishments of your organization and how you help people's daily lives.*
>
> *So my style is to be very involved with other people. I prefer to get expert opinions before having to impose a decision. I'm not afraid to impose one if I have to, but I like to involve others in the decision process. You'll get a better solution that way.*

Within the space of a single generation, then, words like *boss* and *president* have completely changed their meanings. No longer positive signs of accomplishment and authority, they now symbolize distance from others, an unreasonable toughness, and other unattractive attributes.

Compared with executives of previous generations, Paul and his peers are distinctly different in style and attitude, and it shows in small ways as well as large. After a luncheon interview with Paul, I watched him climb into the front seat of his chauffeured company car so that he could be "up front" with the driver he knew. In the simple choice of where to sit, he had made a not-so-subtle statement about how he regarded his relationship to employees far down the line.

These generational shifts characterizing the baby boomers are now becoming more magnified with Generation X. Like their older brothers and sisters, the X'ers possess a strong sense of independence and a desire to be masters of their own destiny.

GENERATION X'ERS: WHAT SETS THEM APART?

Four prominent character traits of Generation X'ers have implications for today's workplace. First, they quest for a real balance between work and private life. Second, they are deeply independent, following in the footsteps of the boomers. Third, they are the first real Information Age generation. Finally, they yearn for workplaces that feel like communities.

QUEST FOR CAMELOT: WORK/LIFE BALANCE

There is a greater search among this generation for a balance between work and private life. This quest is rooted in the childhood homes of X'ers and in the organizations where their parents work.

For one thing, Gen X'ers tend to be the children of parents who both held jobs. Indeed, the share of women participating in the labor force who had children under the age of six jumped from 18.6 percent in 1960 to 59.9 percent in 1992.[8] The X'ers benefited from the extra family income these dual careers produced, but they felt deprived of their parents' company, a situation aggravated by the fact that a very high percentage of them were the children of divorce.

It was during their growing-up years that the divorce rates soared—roughly doubling between 1965 and 1977, the biggest jump ever. This was mainly because more of their mothers had an income of their own, and so had fewer worries about the poverty that can come with divorce. As a result, more than 40 percent of this generation spent time in a single-parent home by age 16.[9]

Generation X'ers appear not to want the sort of lives their parents led. They want to build more traditional families and to be more available to their children. As a 25-year-old manager explained, "You really need to be careful not to give 100 percent of yourself to the job, or else there will be nothing left over for your partner when you get home at the end of the day."

Having time at home with the family is a priority they felt their parents set too low. Consistently in interviews, I have heard the comment, "We are not living to work, but working to live. We are choosing a life, as opposed to just bringing home a paycheck."

They also want families. The Roper Organization found that between the late 1970s and late 1980s, the share of 29-year-olds who said they expected to have no children fell to 8 percent, from 21 percent.[10]

Marie is a good example of this new attitude. She is fresh from college and now training to become a corporate banker. Well educated, a child of divorced parents, she embodies many of the characteristics associated with her generation. She likes to work hard and to do well—but to a point:

I'm definitely willing to work long hours during the week, but there's a limit. You need some time for yourself, for your family, for recreation. With people my age, there's more concern about quality of life. It's not really wanting the big, expensive vacation—it's just wanting to enjoy life. It's not just a matter of having more things.

It's related to the uncertainty of life. Life is just not the way it was in the 50s and 60s. There are so many nasty things that can happen along the way. There's disease, there's crime—I mean, you're bombarded so constantly with all these negative aspects, it makes you think you might as well enjoy some of life. Also, your family is just as important as your career. Many of my friends are considering staying at home to raise their kids even though they are really bright and have great careers.

Because of the yearning for life balance, this will be a more conflicted generation than its predecessors. For example, Gen X'ers value highly interesting work, which is often accompanied by longer hours and greater demands. At the same time, they want their weekends, and they want happy marriages.

This set of values may change as Generation X'ers move into mid-life, when career pressures soar, but for the present it appears to be a trademark. This generation will insist that organizations find more flexible ways to integrate time for family and private life into demanding careers.

MASTER OF MY DESTINY

Generation X'ers will prove to be far less willing to identify closely with any organization. They like to think of themselves as an independent lot who can move if they don't like where they are. They are continuing the independence trend begun with the boomers and taking it to its logical endpoint—little or no loyalty.

The attitudes of X'ers were in part shaped by an American president who preached self-sufficiency. As one 25-year-old manager commented to me:

One of the most influential individuals of our generation was Ronald Reagan. He basically said, 'Your destiny is in your own hands. You work hard, you can achieve. But it's up to you. You are the master of your ship. This is the land of opportunity. If you don't make it, it's your own fault.' Bill Clinton's recent dismantling of the national welfare system is only further reinforcing what has become a national mind-set.

In previous generations, you were obedient and made sacrifices in your personal life to demonstrate your loyalty to the company. The rewards were often promotions, lifetime employment, and the power to command others. This kind of contract means little to Generation X.

The erosion in Generation X's interest in loyalty was unleashed by the corporations themselves. Just as the X'ers were graduating from college, the wave of downsizing began, with companies unceremoniously dumping longtime employees on the sidewalk. Between 1979 and 1995, 43 million jobs disappeared due to downsizing.

Many of those downsized were the parents of Generation X'ers. On the covers of the business magazines sitting on their parents' coffee tables were such headlines as "Your Career Is in Your Own Hands" or "The New Employment Contract: Self-Sufficiency." The X'ers rightly sensed that company loyalty was definitely a thing of the past. The contract of lifetime employment, which began to deteriorate for the boomers, feels practically nonexistent for the X'ers.

These young managers make their attitude very clear when you ask them about their career expectations. Generation X'ers will tell you that they anticipate having—easily—three to five employers over their career. Ask them why so many and they'll say that, sooner or later, they expect to lose their jobs. A typical comment heard in my interviews, "You need to be prepared if there are adverse conditions in the industry you're in. I think a lot of our generation are prepared that they might at some point lose their job, so it's good to be ready and have a mix of skills."

Talk with them further and you'll encounter their belief that you get better opportunities, better salaries, better challenges, better locations not by waiting patiently to move up the ladder, but by moving to another company. The objective for each job is to use it to build skills that will create opportunities for the next job. Loyalty is only to yourself and your teammates, not to the boss or the company.

For this new generation, work is more than ever before a transaction. Their parents saw working hard and "following orders" as an investment likely to yield greater responsibility and rewards. Generation X'ers expect a more immediate payout from their employers. The words of a senior executive who works with this generation sum it all up:

The people who are my age [basically boomers] have been with the company for a while. There is an understanding that we are very committed to this organization and that we all truly want to work together to make this company a success. Over and over again, I've seen people put the organization ahead of their personal objectives.

But with the analysts, the associates, the junior managers [Generation X'ers], the commitment to this organization is not necessarily there. Instead, you have to continually show them what it is they're getting out of this organization. Continually, you have to make it a two-way street. That's the way you get their commitment. Commanding this generation won't do much to motivate them. They've got to be informed and convinced and involved.

From the other side, here's the perspective of a talented Gen X manager who observes the same phenomenon but has a different take on it:

We view employers with more cynicism than previous generations: You use me for a couple of years, and I will use you for a couple of years. As soon as you and I cease to be of use to the other, then farewell. Employers can expect long hours and travel from us, but we in turn expect to gain experience and training that we can take to the next job. With the death of lifetime employment, companies lost one of their most important tools for commitment. As a result, we are far more assertive and will walk away as soon as we feel our expectations and needs are not being met.

To illustrate this change, we will return to our senior banker in New York, who compares the way a restless, ambitious young employee would have been dealt with a generation ago, when he was beginning his career, with the way he would be dealt with today:

In the old days, the particularly assertive ones were pretty tame compared to how they are today. A restless junior employee would have gone to whomever he reported to and said, very politely, 'Jack, I'm not sure I'm cut out for this,' or whatever. Then Jack would have talked to his boss. That boss would have called the junior in and said, 'Now, I understand from Jack that you're a little bit restless. Let's talk about it.'

The discussion would have been very circumspect. There were certain unwritten codes of conduct about what the junior could and could not say. He could have said, 'Well, I'd like to move along a little faster.' That would have been perfectly acceptable.

The boss might have nodded sagely and said, 'Well, your day will come if you work hard.' He would have given the junior a 'be patient' lecture, mentioning all the good things that would come with time. Or he could have said, 'Well, now, Dave, you don't think you're moving along fast enough. Let me say that we think you're doing very well, and may I remind you of your high performance ratings and how highly the bank thinks of you?'

It was always sort of third person—the reference to how the bank thinks about you and how your seniors have a very high regard for you and all of that. There wouldn't have been much you could do about it. The boss held all the cards. The junior might have meekly said, 'Well, if it wouldn't be out of line, sir, I wonder if I could have a little more direct responsibility with clients.' And that might or might not have ended up being factored into some short-term plan for you.

Today's generation, however, comes on very differently and with an entirely different set of expectations. This afternoon, I have a meeting with a young man who is stewing over whether he should stay at the bank. He's a very bright, impatient fellow who doesn't think he's moving as fast as he should. He's going to tell me, in no uncertain terms and in a lot of detail, why he doesn't think he has enough responsibility. And why he thinks that he may go to Goldman Sachs because he's heard that in 1.8 years you can be at a certain position there, and you can be making this amount of money and so on. Thirty years ago, a boss just wouldn't have been exposed to that sort of challenge from a junior.

With great speed, this new attitude about loyalty is undermining the traditional models of managing.[11] To win this generation over, managers have to understand that Generation X'ers want experiences that fit their career aspirations and information that keeps them informed and growing.

The comments of one young product manager echoed throughout many of my interviews:

I have a very good supervisor. What I enjoy the most is that she shares information with me. It's really an issue of mutual respect. I like the person for whom I work to understand that I want information. I don't want to be excluded from things. Knowing what is happening makes your job more satisfying, makes you feel part of a team and that your opinion is valued. After all, why should information be selectively kept from you? It's absurd. It's just an artificial line when there should not be any. It should be based on how well you perform. If I were the CEO of a company, I would want everybody involved.

THE COMPUTER IS MY FRIEND

Boomers will remember the first computers showing up on their college campuses. They had special rooms all to themselves, and often their own building. These mainframes were a bit mystical, sitting in rows behind glass walls in special air-conditioned spaces while students typed madly away at terminals in nearby rooms.

For Generation X'ers, the computer story is quite different. They are truly the first generation raised on computers. As adolescents, they knew the computer at its most personal level—as a small box sitting on a desk.

In reality, the Computer Age began with the boomers. The first commercial computer, the Univac 1, made its appearance in the early 1950s. But for several decades, all that computing power remained relatively distant for most people. It was not until the creation of the microprocessor at Intel in 1970 that computing became truly accessible. This microprocessor, or "computer on a chip," proved to be the "big bang" for a new era, marked by the arrival of the personal computer.

By the time Generation X was entering high school, kids had begun playing simple computer games on machines made by Atari, Commodore, and Mattel—the forerunners to Nintendo and Sega. The first commercial personal computer was introduced in 1977 by Commodore. It was called the PET, after the popular pet rocks of the day. That same year, Apple Computer was born in a garage, destined to produce $500 million in revenues within five years from sales of its Apple I and II models. By 1981, IBM announced its own PC. The world would never be the same. Nor would the way kids learned and played.

Being computer savvy gives Generation X'ers two advantages. One is that they possess a facility at accessing and manipulating information that prior generations lack.

They are, in essence, the first true Information Age managers.

A suitable analogy is that older generations are using hammers to crack open sources of information while this generation is using pneumatic drills. This facility with the new "information tools" will give Gen X'ers both greater career portability and some measure of power. For example, computer skills are in universal demand—they can be transported easily from company to company. Witness the movement of programmers in Silicon Valley as they migrate to whatever company has the next best project.

Just as important, this facility will give Gen X'ers certain levels of control over the hierarchy of command—especially the senior levels, which are populated by those with less computer literacy. For hand in hand with the ability of Gen X'ers to access information goes the erosion of power and authority of executives who once controlled that data. Normally, when people begin losing power, they fight back. But with information technology, fighting back is likely, in the long run, to undermine an executive's credibility and ultimately his or her organization's competitiveness.

A very powerful example of this dynamic involves a young manager I studied, named Chris, who works for a billion-dollar company that distributes electronics parts. Chris monitors the creditworthiness of customers and the overall inventory, to see what is selling and what is not. He then forecasts sales to make sure the levels of inventory are appropriate. Along with 12 other asset managers, he reports directly to an operations vice president. Between Chris and his vice president, there are two key differences. One is age—Chris is 30 and his boss is 52. The other is computer literacy. Chris is literate, and the boss is not.

Once a month, the vice president hands Chris a 1,000-page computer printout to review. It takes Chris four to five days to examine it manually, searching for problems such as ballooning inventories of a certain part or credit difficulties. One day, Chris asked the vice president for a copy of the computer diskette that had produced the 1,000-page printout. With the diskette, he knew he could do his job a lot quicker. The vice president was reluctant, but after Chris pressed for several days, he handed it over.

Chris then performed in three hours what had previously taken him five days. As he went along searching the data base for credit problems, he took the opportunity to perform other analyses. He discovered some disturbing surprises. He learned, for example, that certain parts were being purchased for which there were either diminishing orders or none at all. In some cases, these errors were costing the company tens of thousands of dollars per part.

Chris brought his discoveries to the vice president. The vice president seemed uncomfortable, and the following month he denied Chris access to the diskette. Shocked by this response, Chris saw the implications of his simple request:

The vice president realized that it gave him information that he was totally unaware of. It would have taken him six weeks to do manually what I did in two hours. What he also realized is that I could replace him—because I knew what questions to ask of the computer. Imagine what I could do if I had total access. He wouldn't be needed anymore.

But this vice president is about to become the fall guy. The president is now saying, 'I can't understand what the problem is in operations. You keep hiring these high-priced asset managers, but the same problems have kept reappearing over the last two years. I'm going to hire a new director of asset managers, somebody who can get to the heart of this.'

The secret is out. The other VPs had access to my report. They've seen what the computer can do, and they know my results didn't take eight weeks to produce. They're coming to me, asking how to get the same information. One of these days, it's going to be revealed that the vice president is the one holding all the horsepower back. But by that time, it will be too late. A third of our asset managers have already left, and I figure the rest of us will be gone soon. Another asset manager and myself are leaving in a week.

The greatest power of information and information technology comes from its openness. To maintain control over it by restricting its use defeats its very purpose. What we have to understand is that a phenomenal skill gap is growing between the generations in computer literacy. In olden times, wisdom came with experience and age. Today, wisdom is increasingly tied to youth, thanks largely to very rapid rates of change in technology.

Older generations who feel threatened by this will simply be undermining themselves and the very advantages of technology. Instead, they must develop strong and trusting relationships, knowing that there will always be these gaps in wisdom between the generations. The key is to harness the knowledge and facility of Generation X, not to restrain it.

HOME, HOME ON THE CAMPUS

Looking over the last two decades at leading-edge companies that have sprung up on the West Coast— the Microsofts, the Nikes, the Sun Micro-systems—many are distinguished by a "campus culture."

In essence, their architecture and company services are designed to blur the distinction between the workplace, a college campus, and a hometown community. Company outings mirror fraternity life, with volleyball, barbecues, and dances. The companies house cafeterias that are open day and night. There are fitness centers just like at school. Refrigerators are always nearby, stacked with snacks and soft drinks like the one back home. There are convertible sofas or futons in the closets, so that offices can quickly and easily become dorm rooms. These places are in essence designed to create a sense that one never really left college.

The advantages of creating physical spaces reminiscent of university life are clear. At school, one often worked long hours without really noticing it. Exams and projects demanded intense work periods. But students accepted such demands. You knew that they would end when the exam ended. The sense of accomplishment made you forget that there were more ordeals ahead in the next semester— just as young software engineers and consultants always forget that there is a never-ending stream of projects down the road.

What made this all the more tolerable in college was the fact that your friends were working and playing alongside you. You were a community. You could escape your hardships with companions. The campus settings of corporations achieve similar outcomes—long, hard work but in a community.

What sets Generation X'ers apart from others is the redefining of what they consider their communities to be. Remember that their most intimate community, the family, was undergoing remarkable stress during their childhood—primarily caused by record divorce rates. At the same time, many of America's most important civic communities witnessed remarkable declines in membership. For example, participation in parent-teacher associations dropped to 5 million in 1982, from more than 12 million in 1964. Membership in the League of Women Voters has fallen 42 percent since 1969. The Boy Scouts are off by 26 percent since 1970; the Masons are down by 39 percent since 1959; the Jaycees by 44 percent since 1979.[12]

What Generation X'ers witnessed was a major decline in civic community. Even religion, which has traditionally played a more consistent role as a source of community, experienced a modest membership decline during their upbringing. While families from previous generations attended social events at churches and temples during the week and on weekends, attendance today is largely restricted to a one- or two-hour service on the weekend.

Robert Putnam, a professor of international affairs at Harvard, pointed out recently that while more Americans are bowling than ever before, bowling in leagues has dropped precipitously. From 1980 to 1993, the number of individuals who bowl increased by 10 percent, while bowling in leagues dropped by 40 percent. "Trends of the past quarter-century," Mr. Putnam concluded, "have apparently moved the United States significantly lower in the international rankings of social capital (networks, norms and social trust that facilitate coordination and cooperation for mutual benefit in a society). The recent deterioration...has been sufficiently great that another quarter-century of change at the same rate would bring the United States...to the midpoint of all these countries. Two generations' decline at the same rate would leave the United States at the level today of Chile, Portugal, and Slovenia."[13]

What this means is that Gen X'ers are the first generation to feel a significant absence of real community in their lives. Their communities, instead, tend to be small circles of friends. For this very reason, workplaces that are able to create a true sense of community become the preferred work environments for this generation. And teamwork is a favored way of creating momentary communities.

CONCLUSION

These are but a few of the trends that are shaping a new generation in workplaces across America. The message of this survey of Generation X has been to help managers and organizations recognize that each generation does indeed have a special character. To harness the potential of any generation, we must be sensitive to what motivates its members as individuals. Our tendency is often to see only the similarities, while a younger generation's tendency is to see only the differences. Neither perspective will do. To work effectively with these younger people, older generations will have to be far more perceptive. If you can provide the younger people with challenging projects, respect their needs for independence and create workplace communities for them, they will reward you with something quite rare—dedication.

ENDNOTES

[1] *Gallup Monthly Poll*, 1993.

[2] W. Fay, "Understanding Generation X," *Marketing Research, 5*, no. 2, (1993): 54–55.

[3] "The American Freshman," Higher Education Research Institute, University of California at Los Angeles, 1994.

[4] For more on the generations, see N. Howe, and W. Strauss, "The New Generation Gap," *The Atlantic Monthly*, December 1992; and C. Russell, *The Master Trend* (Plenum Publishing, 1993).

[5] C. Russell, 34–35.

[6] *Statistical Abstract of the United States*, Department of Commerce, 1993, 152–155.

[7] W. Kiechel, "The Workaholic Generation," *Fortune*, April 10. 1989.

[8] Statistical Abstract of the United States.

[9] N. Zill, and J. Robinson, "The Generation X," *American Demographics*, April 1995, 24–33.

[10] W. Fay.

[11] T. Stewart. "Managing in a Wired Company," *Fortune*, July 11, 1994, 50.

[12] R. Putnam, "Bowling Alone: America's Declining Social Capital," *The Journal of Democracy*, 1994.

[13] Ibid.

How to Earn Your Employees' Commitment*

Gary Dessler

MOTIVATING EMPLOYEES IN AN AGE OF EMPOWERMENT

Viacom recently reached an agreement to sell its Prentice Hall publishing operations to Pearson plc, for $4.6 billion. In announcing the sale, Prentice Hall's president thanked its employees for their past hard work and dedication, and reminded them that during the transition, "it is more important than ever to focus on our individual responsibilities to ensure that our company performs at the highest levels."[1] His message spotlights a dilemma all managers have today: maintaining employee commitment—an

---

*Reprinted from *Academy of Management Executive 13*, no. 2 (May 1999): 58–67.

employee's identification with and agreement to pursue the company's or the unit's mission in the face of downsizings, mergers, and turbulent change.[2]

Managers today have numerous motivation tools they can use, ranging from incentives to job enrichment to participative management. Why, then, go through the trouble of winning commitment at all? For several reasons.

First, today's focus on teamwork, empowerment, and flatter organizations puts a premium on self-control or organizational citizenship behavior, "discretionary contributions that are organizationally related, but are neither explicitly required nor contractually rewarded by the organization, yet nevertheless contribute to its effective functioning,"[3] and studies show commitment can encourage just such behavior. For example, one study concludes that "having a membership that shares the organization's goals and values can ensure that your individuals act instinctively to benefit the organization."[4] Commitment—both to the organization, and to one's team—was positively related to "willingness to help" in another study.[5] And another similarly concluded that organizational commitment was associated with the employees' and organization's ability to adapt to unforeseeable occurrences.[6] Commitment has other favorable outcomes, too. Committed employees tend to have better attendance records and longer job tenure than less committed employees.[7] Not surprisingly, they also tend to work harder at their jobs and perform better than do those with weak commitment.[8] In summary, there is considerable evidence that committed employees will be more valuable employees than those with weak commitment.[9] The question, then, is, "How can a manager foster employee commitment?"

In determining how companies win employee commitment, researchers have studied organizations ranging from Utopian communities to business organizations to law firms to labor unions in America, Europe, and Japan. Our examples of how managers can foster commitment is not exhaustive. Such possible precursors of commitment as money are not included, in part because of their obviousness or because of insufficient research evidence.[10] What follows, however, is a useful overview of the actions required to win commitment and how to implement them.

CLARIFY AND COMMUNICATE YOUR MISSION

A number of years ago, Rosabeth Moss Kanter conducted an investigation of commitment that focused not on businesses, but on Utopian communities such as the Shakers and the Oneida. Most of those communities were formed in the United States in the 1800s, usually with the aim of having people live together cooperatively, create their own governance, and operate according to a higher order of natural and spiritual laws. Communities like these, said Kanter, were held together not by coercion but by commitment. In Utopia, what people want to do is the same as what they have to do, and the interests of the individuals are congruent with those of the group.[11]

Life in these communities was organized to support what Kanter calls "core commitment building processes." Kanter called one of these core processes *transcendence*, a process whereby someone "attaches his decision making perspective to a power greater than himself, surrendering to the higher meaning contained by the group and submitting to something beyond himself." This permits the person "to find himself anew in something larger and greater."[12] The key to achieving this, said Kanter, is creating a strong linkage between the mission and ideology on the one hand, and the person's understanding of how his or her role in the commune fits with the transcendent mission on the other. The commitment in these communities derived, in other words, in part from the power of their mission and ideology and from their members' willingness to accept the community's aims, both as their own and as part of a greater mission. The members became crusaders.

Is it realistic for business organizations to try to achieve the same commitment to a mission? Not just realistic, but essential. For one thing, having goals without commitment is futile. "It's not just the presence of a goal that stimulates progress, [but] also the level of commitment to the goal," as James

Collins and Jerry Porras note in their book *Built to Last*.[13] Conversely, commitment without a cause is meaningless.

In practice, there are several things a firm can do to achieve this feeling among employees that they are part of something larger and greater than themselves: create a shared mission and an ideology that lays out a basic way of thinking and doing things; create institutional charisma by linking their missions and values to a higher calling; and promote the commitment of employees to the mission and ideology, for example through selective hiring and focused, value-based orientation.

CLARIFY THE MISSION AND IDEOLOGY

A clear mission and ideology provides a double benefit: the mission provides a focus to which employees can commit, while the values that make up the firm's ideology provide internalized guidelines for their behaviors.

Saturn Corporation provides a good illustration of how to clarify and communicate a mission and ideology. Each Saturn employee receives a pocket card listing Saturn's mission, philosophy, and values. The Saturn mission—"[to] market vehicles developed and manufactured in the United States that are world leaders in quality, cost and customer satisfaction"—is supported by the more detailed Saturn philosophy—showing how, for example, Saturn will meet its customers' and workers' needs. The pocket card then lists and explains Saturn's basic values, which focus on customer enthusiasm, excelling, teamwork, respect for the individual, and continuous improvement.

MAKE IT CHARISMATIC

While not all business firms would want to emulate the spiritual higher-callings of Kanter's early communes, it is possible to couch a mission so that it evokes a higher, charismatic calling that employees can espouse.[14] Like Medieval crusaders, employees then do their best for the firm, not just because they're paid to do so, but because it is a higher calling.

The mission of Ben & Jerry's Homemade symbolizes the founders' unique idea of what a business should be and provides the firm and its employees with an ideology that represents a higher, transcendent calling to which all can commit. The mission statement reads, in part:

> *Ben & Jerry's is dedicated to the creation and demonstration of a new corporate concept of linked prosperity...*
>
> *Social mission: To operate the company in a way that actively recognizes the central role that business plays in the structure of a society by initiating innovative ways to improve the quality of life of a broad community: local, national, and international...*[15]

The company's founders practice what they preach. Ben & Jerry's has "green teams" that are responsible for assessing the firm's environmental impact in all areas of operation. It still purchases many of its raw materials—often at above-market prices—from suppliers so as to benefit indigenous people in Maine or in the Brazilian rain forest.

However, formulating an ideology and a mission, even a charismatic one, isn't enough. Employees then need to be steeped in the ideology and to accept it as their own. In her study of Utopian communities, Kanter found that successful communities achieved this by requiring commitment to the ideology, by expecting recruits to take vows, by enforcing fairly exhaustive procedures for choosing members, and by emphasizing tradition. Modern-day equivalents to these practices in business firms include value-based hiring and orientation, and ceremonials that enhance tradition.

USE VALUE-BASED HIRING PRACTICES

In many firms the process of linking employees to ideology begins before the worker is even hired, with value-based hiring practices. These firms first clarify what their basic values are. Then they enforce procedures for screening new employees, require evidence of commitment to the firms' values by their candidates, and reject large numbers of prospective employees. The net effect is to select employees whose values and skills match the firm's ideology and who are thus well on the road to becoming believers before they are even hired. Value-based hiring screens out those who might not fit.

For example, using tests, interviews, and background checks, Ben & Jerry's screens out managers who don't share the firm's social goals, Toyota Manufacturing USA screens out non-team players, and Goldman Sachs emphasizes integrity. Toyota applicants traverse an extensive five-day testing and interviewing program focused on teamwork, quality orientation, and communications ability—the values Toyota covets.

STRESS VALUES-BASED ORIENTATION AND TRAINING

Steeping the new employees in the values and culture is also important.[16] For example, the orientation (or, as they call it, *assimilation*) program at Toyota covers traditional topics such as company benefits, but is intended mostly to convert new team members to the firm's ideology of quality, teamwork, personal development, open communication, and mutual respect. Combined with continuing team- and quality-oriented training, employees completing the four-day process are steeped in, and ideally converted to, Toyota's ideology, mission of quality, values of teamwork, unending incremental improvement, and problem solving.

BUILD THE TRADITION

Tradition-building symbols, stories, rites, and ceremonials can further enhance employees' conversion to cultural believers. One Saturn vice president commented, "Creating a value system that encourages the kind of behavior you want is not enough. The challenge is then to engage in those practices that symbolize those values, and tell people what it's really okay to do—and what not [to do]. Actions, in other words, speak much more loudly than words."[17]

Companies are doing this in a variety of ways. A company where having fun is both a basic value and an inalienable right, Ben & Jerry's has a "joy gang," a voluntary group that meets once or twice a week to create new ways to help employees enjoy their work. The joy gang is a concrete example of Ben & Jerry's ideology, which emphasizes charity, fun, and goodwill toward fellow workers. At the annual JCPenney "HCSC" inauguration meetings, new management associates solemnly swear allegiance to the JCPenney Idea and receive HCSC label pins, signifying the firm's basic values of honor, confidence, service, and cooperation.[18]

GUARANTEE ORGANIZATIONAL JUSTICE

Organizational justice—"the extent to which fair procedures and processes are in place and adhered to and the extent to which individuals see their leaders as being fair and sincere and having logic or rationale for what they do"[19]—also plays a role in fostering commitment. One study concluded that "Considerable evidence supports a link between the procedural justice associated with organizational policies and the affective commitment of employees."[20] Another found that satisfaction with the two-way communication in the organization contributed to organizational commitment.[21] Another study concluded that discretionary contributions above and beyond those specifically required by the organization increased with increases in perceived organizational justice.[22]

Fair procedures and processes embodied in formal grievance procedures are one obvious source of organizational justice. Involving employees in decisions by getting their input, and ensuring that they understand why decisions were made is another.[23]

HAVE COMPREHENSIVE GRIEVANCE PROCEDURES

Federal Express' Guaranteed Fair Treatment Procedure is a good example of the former. As its employee handbook says,

> *Perhaps the cornerstone of Federal Express' "people" philosophy is the Guaranteed Fair Treatment Procedure (GFTP). This policy affirms your right to appeal any eligible issue through this process of systematic review by progressively higher levels of management. Although the outcome is not assured to be in your favor, your right to participate within the guidelines of the procedure is guaranteed. At Federal Express, where we have a "people-first" philosophy, you have a right to discuss your complaints with management without fear of retaliation.[24]*

In brief, GFTP contains three steps. In step one, management review, a complainant submits a written complaint to a manager, who reviews all relevant information, holds a conference with the employee, and makes a decision either to uphold, modify, or overturn the original supervisor's actions.[25] In step two, officer review, the complainant can then submit a written complaint to a vice president or senior vice president, who reviews the case, conducts an additional investigation, and upholds, overturns, or modifies the manager's actions. In step three, executive appeals review, the complainant can then submit a written complaint to an appeals board comprising the CEO, president, chief personnel officer, and two senior vice presidents. The board reviews all relevant information and upholds or overturns the decision. When there is a question of fact, the appeals board may initiate a board of review.

PROVIDE EXTENSIVE TWO-WAY COMMUNICATIONS

Providing for plenty of opportunities for two-way communication is another way to cultivate the feeling that the work experience is a just one. Indeed, a Saturn assembly team, when asked, "What's the first thing you would tell a boss to do to get commitment?" responded, in unison, "Tell them to listen."[26]

Saturn's assemblers get information continuously via the plant's internal television network. FedEx's Survey Feedback Action program lets employees express feelings about the company and their managers. "Hotline" programs are another option. For example, Toyota's handbook states, "Don't spend time worrying about something. Speak up!" The company's "Hotline" gives team members a 24-hour channel for bringing questions or problems to management's attention. Employees can pick up any phone, dial the hotline extension, and leave messages on a recorder. All hotline messages are reviewed by the human resources manager and thoroughly investigated. If it is decided a particular question would be of interest to other Toyota team members, then the questions and Toyota's response is posted on plant bulletin boards. Employees wanting a personal response must leave their names, but no attempt is made to identify anonymous callers.[27]

CREATE A SENSE OF COMMUNITY

Kanter, in her study of Utopian communities, also observed that all the successful communities she studied shared a sense of community, one in which "connection, belonging, participation in a whole, mingling of the self and the group, and an equal opportunity to contribute and to benefit all are part."[28] This sense of community contributed to creating commitment among the communities' members, who developed a strong "we-feeling"—that they were like a family. The result was a "cohesive, emotionally involving, and effectively satisfying community."[29]

Kanter identified several practices through which the communities fostered this sense of community. There was usually some homogeneity of background among members, which made it easier for them to share common experiences and identify with one another and with the community. There was also some communal sharing of both property and work, as members shared to some extent the assets of the community and the output of its efforts. Communal work provided an opportunity for joint effort, with all members, as far as possible, performing all tasks for equal rewards. Finally, there was regularized group contact, continuing activities that brought the individual into periodic contact with the group as a whole. All these practices have their practical parallels in business organizations today.

BUILD VALUE-BASED HOMOGENEITY

Hiring a homogeneous workforce in these days of cultural diversity and equal employment opportunity requires focusing on values, skills, and interests rather than on discriminatory traits such as ethnic background. Many firms thus explicitly select employees based on those values that are desirable to the firm. At Goldman Sachs, these values include excellence, creativity, and imagination; the ability to assume responsibility rapidly; teamwork and dedication to the firm; intense effort in work; and integrity and honesty.[30] At Toyota, interpersonal skills, reasoning skills, flexibility, and willingness to be team members characterize successful employees (who are always referred to as *team members*). The point is that in firms like these, the people who are hired are already well on their way to fitting in. They are homogeneous, not in the sense of being all-white or all-male or all-Ivy league, but in their potential fit with the firm's values. They are people who by aspirations, values, and skills should fit right in.

SHARE AND SHARE ALIKE

Despite significant disparities between the salaries of executives and workers, it's also possible to foster a sense that everyone shares in a firm's fortunes. At FedEx, for instance, chairman Fred Smith has no assigned parking spot and there are no company cars. There is no executive lunchroom and the executives' offices are modest. "We do as much as we can to minimize differences between non-executive levels and ourselves," one top FedEx manager explained.

Profit sharing can play a role too. The legendary number of millionaires at Microsoft is one notable example. Increasingly, substantial bonuses, profit sharing, and pay-for-performance plans enable employees throughout industry to appreciate that not only top managers get a sizable share of the pie.

EMPHASIZE BARNRAISING, CROSS-UTILIZATION, AND TEAMWORK

Getting everyone to work cooperatively on a project and even to share work and jobs also fosters a sense of community. Even today in some Utopian communities, people still get together to build a house or a barn. Much the same applies in business: Delta Airlines airport work teams routinely rotate jobs; reservations clerks fill in at the check-in ramp or in baggage handling if the need arises. The Delta Policy Manual calls the practice *cross-utilization*.[31] Organizing around teams—especially self-managing teams—is another way to enhance the feeling that the work is shared. The members of self-managing teams at firms from Saturn to American Express often share each other's work and routinely rotate jobs.

GET TOGETHER

In many companies, frequent group meetings and other regularized contacts further enhance employees' sense of community. Ben & Jerry's has monthly staff meetings in the receiving bay of the Waterbury, Vermont plant. Production stops and all employees attend. The firm's joy gangs organize regular "joy events," including Cajun parties, table tennis contests, and manufacturing appreciation days, all aimed at getting employees together.

At Federal Express, daily teleconferenced meetings describe the previous day's accomplishments. Toyota has a TV system called Toyota Network News, and spends about $250,000 annually on a "perfect attendance" meeting to which all high-attendance employees are invited. At Mary Kay Cosmetics, weekly meetings of directors and their sales consultants similarly serve to reinforce the sense of communion and togetherness.

SUPPORT EMPLOYEE DEVELOPMENT

Studies also suggest employees are more committed to employers who are more committed to the employees' long-term career development.[32] For example, managers in eight large U.S. organizations were asked to evaluate whether their firms had fulfilled their promises and met the managers' expectations. Those who answered affirmatively were much more likely to be committed to the organization, results that underscore the role of career satisfaction and success in winning commitment.[33] "The best route to employee commitment," the study concluded, is "for the organization to take the time and the trouble to provide each manager with the experience he or she needs—even craves—at each stage of his or her career."[34]

An analysis of employee commitment among hospital administrators, nurses, service workers, and clerical employees and among scientists and engineers from a research lab concluded that the employer's ability to fulfill the employee's personal career aspirations had a marked effect on employee commitment. As this study summarized, individuals come to organizations with certain needs, desires, skills, and so forth and expect to find a work environment where they can utilize their abilities and satisfy many of their basic needs. When the organization provides such a vehicle, the likelihood of increasing commitment is apparently enhanced. When the organization is not dependable, however, or where it fails to provide employees with challenging and meaningful tasks, commitment levels tend to diminish.[35]

A study of employees of a manufacturing plant similarly found that internal mobility and promotion from within, company-sponsored training and development, and job security were all correlated with employee commitment. As these researchers concluded,

> *...commitment is higher among employees who believe they are being treated as resources to be developed rather than commodities to buy and sell. Even controlling for other known antecedents, employees are committed to the extent that they believe the company is providing a long-term developmental employment opportunity.*[36]

Anecdotal evidence from the author's studies at Saturn and Federal Express support this idea. In the words of one Saturn assembler,

> *I'm committed to Saturn in part for what they did for me; for the 300-plus hours of training in problem solving and leadership that helped me expand my personal horizons; for the firm's "Excel" program that helps me push myself to the limit; and because I know that at Saturn I can go as far as I can go. This company wants its people to be all that they can be...*[37]

Similarly, one Federal Express manager explained,

> *At Federal Express, the best I can be is what I can be here. I have been allowed to grow [at Federal Express]. People here are not turned on by money. The biggest benefit is that Federal Express made me a man. It gave me the confidence and self-esteem to become the person I had the potential to become.*

The net effect is that employees become committed to firms that are committed to them—to their development, to their well being, and to their desire to become the people they always hoped they could be. Employers can show such commitment in several ways.

COMMIT TO ACTUALIZING

What companies believe and commit to drives what they do. Employers seeking to actualize their employees must therefore start by committing to do so, and then memorialize that commitment in their literature and management training. A top executive at JCPenney described his company's policy on development this way:

> *We have an obligation to develop our people to the fullest. You never know how high is high…one of the best measures of a manager's effectiveness is the length of the list of names of those he helped to develop career wise. For me, one of the truest measures of a Penney manager's effectiveness is how many people would put you on the list of those who helped their careers here.*

PROVIDE FIRST-YEAR JOB CHALLENGE

Employees bring their needs, aspirations, and hopes to their jobs and become committed to employers that take concrete steps to help them develop their abilities and achieve their potential. Young graduates or new recruits often start their jobs expecting challenging assignments to help them test and prove their abilities. Providing such challenging first jobs is therefore a practice at many firms. Young professionals at Goldman Sachs are expected to contribute at once and immediately find themselves on teams involved in challenging projects. As one manager there explained,

> *Even our young people often start out handling millions of dollars of responsibility. And at a meeting with a client, the partner in charge will often not talk first at the meeting, but the youngest will. At Goldman Sachs, you take the responsibility and you're supported by the team. That's what attracts people to Goldman Sachs—ability to make decisions early.*

ENRICH AND EMPOWER

Behavioral scientists have long encouraged job enrichment—increasing the breadth of responsibility and self-management in the job—as a way to appeal to employees' higher level needs. The effect of such enrichment can, in fact, be almost intoxicating. Here's how one Saturn assembler described the experience of self-managing teams:

> *You don't have anyone here who is a supervisor. You don't experience supervision. We are supervised by ourselves. We become responsible to people we work with every day. What I do affects my people. In other firms you're treated like children and here we are treated like adults. We make up our own work schedule. We do our own budgeting and buying of tools. We decide and improve on the work process by consensus.*

PROMOTE FROM WITHIN

Promotion from within is not always feasible in today's business environment. But there are benefits to letting employees know a firm has fair promotional practices. Here it's important to distinguish between promotion from within programs and policies. Policies such as "open positions are filled, whenever possible, by qualified candidates from within the existing workforce" are one thing. The hard part is to breathe life into such policies by organizing your HR processes to support them.

Managers can do several things to create more meaningful promotion from within practices. Career-oriented appraisals are one component. Many employers don't just assess past performance, but link an employee's performance, career preferences, and developmental needs in a formal career plan. As Delta's HR manager explained:

Our annual evaluations are formal and include an interview. We touch on whether the employee is making progress or not, review his or her past experience, and discuss where that person is going with his or her career. The formal evaluation forces the supervisor and employee to communicate and talk about the person's career path.

An effective career-records/job-posting system can also bolster a firm's program of promotion from within by ensuring that an inside candidate's career goals and skills are matched openly, fairly, and effectively with promotional opportunities. For example, FedEx's electronic Job Change Applicant Tracking System announces new openings every Friday. All employees posting for a position are given numerical scores based on job performance and length of service and are advised whether they have been chosen as candidates.

PROVIDE DEVELOPMENTAL ACTIVITIES

Developmental activities such as career workshops enhance employees' opportunities for promotion from within, appeal to their desire to grow and to learn, provide more opportunities for lateral moves, and give them a chance to move on to another company. Saturn's career-growth workshop uses vocational guidance tools (including a skills-assessment disk) to help employees identify skills they need to develop. "You assess yourself and then your team assesses you," is how one Saturn employee put it. Tuition reimbursement, company-sponsored training and development, and other developmental activities are available to help Saturn employees develop those skills.

THE QUESTION OF EMPLOYEE SECURITY

While few firms promise lifetime employment, incurring the costs of value-based hiring, extensive training, empowering, and developing employees without some job security is somewhat self-defeating.

Some companies provide job security while making it clear that their commitment to job security is a commitment to do their best, but not a guarantee. A Federal Express executive emphasized that "No-layoff is a commitment, not a policy. There are no guarantees, but the firm is on record as having a strong commitment to make every effort not to lay off personnel except in the most extreme economic circumstances, as determined by the chief executive officer." Delta Airlines tries to minimize layoffs by keeping a small temporary workforce in airport operations and regional offices, that may ebb and flow with seasonal changes.

COMMIT TO PEOPLE-FIRST VALUES

The commitment-building processes—clarifying and communicating a mission, guaranteeing organizational justice, creating a sense of community, and supporting employee development—all rest on one foundation, and that is the employer's commitment to values that put people first.

Studies do suggest that treating employees as important and respected individuals contributes to their commitment.[38] The extent to which employees are made to feel that they are making important contributions to the organization is a "central theme" that emerges from the commitment research.[39] And, the research notwithstanding, it's hard to imagine being serious about organizational justice, creating a sense of community, or supporting employee development if you're not seriously committed to respecting your employees as individuals. Operationally, companies accomplish this in several ways.

Put It in Writing

A good first step is to replace talk with action and to codify and distribute the firm's people-first values. FedEx's Manager's Guide, for instance, states: "I have an inherent right to be treated with respect and dignity and that right should never be violated."[40]

Saturn employees carry pocket cards that list the firm's values, one of which says:

Trust and respect for the individual: we have nothing of greater value than our people. We believe that demonstrating respect for the uniqueness of every individual builds a team of confident, creative members possessing a high degree of initiative, self-respect, and self-discipline.

Hire "Right-Kind" Managers

Putting the company's people-first values into practice means that managers must have internalized these values and become committed to them. In many firms, this means hiring the right kind of people in the first place, and then carefully indoctrinating them in the gospel of respect. FedEx's program provides one good example. All FedEx supervisory candidates must enroll in a special leader identification program to prove they have the values and skills to be managers. About 20 percent of these candidates fall out after the first phase of the program—"Is Management for Me?"—a one-day session that familiarizes them with the manager's job. This session is followed by three months of self-evaluations and supervisory assessments of the candidates' values and skills, and a series of peer assessments and panel interviews with senior managers. Management training sessions in the firm's Leadership Institute then reinforce FedEx's values and indoctrinates the new managers in the principles and values of the firm.

Walk the Talk

Similarly, Saturn Corporation translates its people-first values into practice every day. Extensive two-way communication systems (frequent meetings, open-door policies, and so forth), job security, team-centered work groups, and an emphasis on employee self-actualization—giving each employee an opportunity to be all he or she can be through involvement in most job-related decisions, plus promotion from within and extensive career assessment, training, and development programs—all reflect Saturn's people-first values. As one Saturn vice president put it, Saturn's emphasis on igniting employee commitment stems from

…creating a value system that encourages the kind of behavior we knew we wanted. We knew we had to put in an actionable value system that changed how managers thought and how people built cars. If you start with the premise that you trust people and that they will do a good job, it takes you in a whole new direction. But if you really want to trust people, you have to show that you do and you start by eliminating all those things that say, "I don't trust you." That includes time clocks, gates, and hourly pay, for example.

SUMMING UP: HOW TO EARN YOUR EMPLOYEES' COMMITMENT

Managers today have a dilemma: maintaining employee commitment in the face of downsizings, mergers, and turbulent change. It is, in a very real sense, a paradoxical situation: on the one hand today's focus on teamwork, empowerment, and flatter organizations puts a premium on just the sort of self-motivation that one expects to get from committed employees; on the other hand, environmental forces are acting to diminish the foundations of employee commitment.

Over the past 30 years or so, we've learned quite a bit about how to win commitment. The evidence suggests that winning commitment requires a comprehensive, multifaceted management system, one consisting of an integrated and internally consistent package of concrete actions and policies. The main steps and substeps in implementing such a commitment-oriented management system would include the following:

- **Commit to people-first values**   Put it in writing; hire right-kind managers; walk the talk.
- **Clarify and communicate your mission**   Clarify the mission and ideology; make it charismatic; use value-based hiring practices; stress values-based orientation and training; build the tradition.
- **Guarantee organizational justice**   Have a comprehensive grievance procedure; provide for extensive two-way communications.
- **Create a sense of community**   Build value-based homogeneity; share and share alike; emphasize barnraising, cross-utilization, and teamwork; get together.
- **Support employee development**   Commit to actualizing; provide first year job challenge; enrich and empower; promote from within; provide developmental activities; provide employee security without guarantees.

ENDNOTES

[1] J. Newcomb, Letter to employees, May 17, 1998.

[2] A variety of definitions, generally focusing on different facets of commitment, have been proposed. Meyer and Allen, for instance, discuss affective commitment, which "refers to the employees' emotional attachment to, identification with, and involvement in the organization." Porter et al. defined organizational commitment as a strong belief in, and acceptance of, the organization's goals and values, a willingness to exert considerable effort on behalf of the organization, and a strong desire to remain in the organization. See J. P. Meyer and J. J. Allen, *Commitment in the Workplace: Theory, Research, and Application* (Thousand Oaks, CA: Sage Publications, Inc. 1997): 11, 12. For other definitions see, for instance, T. Becker, "The Multidimensional View of Commitment and the Theory of Reasoned Action: A Comparative Evaluation," *Journal of Management*, 21(4) (1995): 617–638; N. Allen, "Affective, Continuance, and Normative Commitment to the Organization: An Examination of Construct Validity," *Journal of Vocational Behavior*, 49(3) (December 1996): 252–276; D. Cooke, "Discriminant Validity of the Organizational Commitment Questionnaire." *Psychological Reports*, 8(2) (April 1997): 431–441; and P. M. Wright, et al. "On the Meaning and Measurement of Goal Commitment," *Journal of Applied Psychology*, 79(6) (1994): 795–803. Chris Argyris recently distinguished between two kinds of commitment, internal commitment and external commitment: see C. Argyris, "Empowerment: The Emperor's New Clothes," *Harvard Business Review* (May-June 1998): 99–100; Hollenback and Klein define goal commitment as the determination to try for a goal and the unwillingness to abandon or lower that goal: J. R. Hollenbeck and H. J. Klein, "Goal Commitment and the Goal Setting Process: Problems, Prospects, and Proposals for Future Research," *Journal of Applied Psychology*, 72, (1982): 212–220. L. W. Porter, R. Steers, R. T. Mowday, and P. V. Boulian, "Unit Performance, Situational Factors, and Employee Attitudes in Spatially Separated Work Units," *Organizational Behavior and Human Performance*, 15 (1974): 87–98.

[3] Meyer and Allen, 34.

[4] C. O'Reilly III and J. Chatman, "Organizational Commitment and Psychological Attachment: The Affective Compliance, Identification, and Internalization on Pro-Social Behavior," *Journal of Applied Psychology* (1986): 71, 493.

[5] J. W. Bishop and K. D. Scott, "How Commitment Affects Team Performance." *HRMagazine* (February 1997): 107–111.

[6] H. Angle and J. Perry, "An Empirical Assessment of Organizational Commitment and Organizational Effectiveness." *Administrative Science Quarterly* 26, (March 1981): 1–13.

[7] R. Mowday, L. Porter, and R. Steers, *Employee-Organization Linkages: The Psychology of Commitment, Absenteeism, and Turnover.* (New York: Academic Press 1982) 36–37; C. Kline and L. Peters, "Behavioral Commitment and Tenure of New Employees: A Replication and Extension," *The Academy of Management Journal*, 34(1), (March 1991): 194–204; M. J. Somers, "Organizational Commitment, Turnover and Absenteeism: An Examination of Direct and Interaction Affects," *Journal of Organizational Behavior 16*, (1995): 49–58; J. W. Bishop and K. D. Scott, "How Commitment Affects Team Performance." *HRMagazine* (February 1997): 107–111.

[8] Meyer and Allen, 28–29. Keep in mind, though, that the relations between commitment and performance are not always so predictable, and even in this particular case, according to the authors, "Many of these findings are based on employee reports of their own behavior." For further discussion see B. Benkhoff, "Ignoring Commitment Is Costly: New Approaches Establish the Missing Link Between Commitment and Performance," *Human Relations* 50(6) (June 1997): 701–726.

[9] Meyer and Allen, 38.

[10] Demographic variables, organizational factors (including organizational size), management style, and organizational climate are among the other antecedents of commitment that have been studied. See, for example, S. Sommer, S. H. Bae, and F. Luthans, "Organizational Commitment Across Cultures: The Impact of Antecedents on Korean Employees," *Human Relations* 49(7) (1996): 977–993; and J. Wallace, "Corporatist Control and Organizational Commitment Among Professionals: The Case of Lawyers Working in Law Firms," *Social Forces* 73(3) (March 1995): 811–839.

[11] R. M. Kanter, *Commitment and Community: Communes and Utopias in Sociological Perspective* (Cambridge, MA: Harvard University Press: 1972) 1. Copyright 1972 by the President and Fellows of Harvard College. Applying conclusions like hers—based, as they are, on a special type of organization—to a corporate setting is always risky. However, there are some corporate lessons to be learned in what she found.

[12] Kanter, 74.

[13] J. Collins and J. Porras, *Built to Last* (New York: Harper Business, 1997): 100.

[14] Based on G. Dessler, *Winning Commitment* (New York: McGraw-Hill: 1992).

[15] Ben & Jerry's 1990 Annual Report, 5.

[16] See, for example, D. Laker, "The Impact of Alternative Socialization Tactics on Self-Managing Behavior and Organizational Commitment." *Journal of Social Behavior and Personality 10*, no. 3 (September 1995): 645–660.

[17] Personal interview with Bob Boruff, vice president, Saturn, March 1992.

[18] Dessler, 86.

[19] For a discussion of definitions of organizational justice see, for example, D. Skarlicki and G. Latham, "Increasing Citizenship Behavior Within a Labor Union: A Test of Organizational Justice Theory," *Journal of Applied Psychology 81*(2) (1996): 161–169.

[20] Meyer and Allen, 47.

[21] F. Varona, "Communication Satisfaction and Organizational Commitment: A Study in Three Guatemalan Organizations," *Dissertation Abstracts International* 53(9-A) (March 1995): 3048.

[22] D. Skarlicki and G. Latham, *Increasing Citizenship Behavior.*

[23] W. C. Kim and R. Manborgne, "Fair Process: Managing in the Knowledge Economy," *Harvard Business Review*, (July/August 1997): 65–66.

[24] *The Federal Express Employee Handbook*, August 7, 1989, 89.

[25] Ibid.

[26] Dessler, 87.

[27] *Team Member Handbook*, Toyota Motor Manufacturing, USA, February 1988, 52–53.

[28] Kanter. You should note that the next line in her quote is "The principle is 'from each according to his abilities, to each according to his needs.'" Thus we have to be quite choosey about which practices might be applicable in a corporate setting.

[29] Ibid, 93.

[30] Except as noted, the discussion of "Creating a Sense of Community" is based on Dessler, 50–60.

[31] *Delta's Personnel Policy Manual*, 18.

[32] S. Wood and M. Albanese, "Can We Speak of High Commitment Management on the Shop Floor?" *Journal of Management Studies 32*(2) (March 1995): 215–247.

[33] B. Buchanan, "To Walk an Extra Mile: The Whats, Whens, and Whys of Organizational Commitment," *Organizational Dynamics* (Spring 1975): 75.

[34] Ibid.

[35] R. M. Steers, "Antecedents and Outcomes of Organizational Commitment," *Administrative Science Quarterly* 22, (March 1977): 53.

[36] K. Gaertner and S. Nollen, "Career Experiences, Perceptions of Employment Practices, and Psychological Commitment in the Organization," *Human Relations 42*(11) (1989): 987.

[37] Except as noted, the discussion on "Support Employee Development" is based on Dessler, 110–138.

[38] See, for example, Steers, 53.

[39] Meyer and Allen, 48.

[40] Except as noted, the discussion of "Commit to People-First Values" is based on Dessler, 28–33.

CHAPTER 2
THEORIES OF MANAGING PEOPLE

THE MANAGER'S JOB
  Henry Mintzberg

THE HUMAN SIDE OF MANAGEMENT
  Thomas Teal

MASTERING COMPETING VALUES: AN INTEGRATED APPROACH TO MANAGEMENT
  Robert E. Quinn

The second mental map we will examine has to do with theories of management. We all carry around models in our head about how managers should do their job or the best way to manage people. Sometimes these models are not made explicit or put into words until we run into managers who do not act like we think they should. Different people have different ideas about the role of managers.

Business scholars also have conflicting views on this topic. To settle this controversy, Henry Mintzberg carried out a classic, observational study of five chief executives at work, noting and timing everything they did. As a result, he was able to distinguish between the folklore and the facts surrounding managerial work. In an updated version of his original conclusions, "The Manager's Job," Mintzberg describes what managers actually do with their time as they manage action, people, and information.

In "The Human Side of Management," Thomas Teal tackles the issue of what constitutes a great manager based on what he learned working at the *Harvard Business Review*. From exposure to the personal stories of outstanding managers who faced serious challenges, he makes an argument for the importance of character. Teal describes in detail how some excellent managers struggled and succeeded in empowering cynical factory workers.

In addition to having character, successful management involves a careful balancing act and the ability to manage paradox. The final article in this chapter, Robert Quinn's "Mastering Competing Values: An Integrated Approach to Management," captures the balancing act that occurs when mental maps for managing are based on competing values. Quinn, a business professor, developed a framework that includes four of the classic theories of management and explained how master managers and organizations should adapt to changing situations in their organizations. This is a practical treatment of the real challenges managers face in complex organizations.

THE MANAGER'S JOB*

Henry Mintzberg

Tom Peters tells us that good managers are doers. (Wall Street says they "do deals.") Michael Porter suggests that they are thinkers. Not so, argue Abraham Zaleznik and Warren Bennis: good managers are really leaders. Yet, for the better part of this century, the classical writers—Henri Fayol and Lyndell Urwick, among others—keep telling us that good managers are essentially controllers.

It is a curiosity of the management literature that its best-known writers all seem to emphasize one particular part of the manager's job to the exclusion of the others. Together, perhaps, they cover all the parts, but even that does not describe the whole job of managing.

Moreover, the image left by all of this of the manager's job is that it is a highly systematic, carefully controlled job. That is the folklore. The facts are quite different.

We shall begin by reviewing some of the early research findings on the characteristics of the manager's job, comparing that folklore with the facts, as I observed them in my first study of managerial work (published in the 1970s), reinforced by other research. Then we shall present a new framework to think about the content of the job—what managers really do—based on some recent observations I have made of managers in very different situations.

SOME FOLKLORE AND FACTS ABOUT MANAGERIAL WORK

There are four myths about the manager's job that do not bear up under careful scrutiny of the facts.

Folklore: The manager is a reflective, systematic planner.

The evidence on this issue is overwhelming, but not a shred of it supports this statement.

Fact: Study after study has shown that managers work at an unrelenting pace, that their activities are characterized by brevity, variety, and discontinuity, and that they are strongly oriented to action and dislike reflective activities.

Consider this evidence:

- Half the activities engaged in by the five [American] chief executives [that I studied in my own research (Mintzberg, 1973a)] lasted less than nine minutes, and only 10 percent exceeded one hour. A study of 56 U.S. foremen found that they averaged 583 activities per eight-hour shift, an average of 1 every 48 seconds (Guest, 1956:478). The work pace for both chief executives and foremen was unrelenting. The chief executives met a steady stream of callers and mail from the moment they arrived in the morning until they left in the evening. Coffee breaks and lunches were inevitably work related, and ever-present subordinates seemed to usurp any free moment.
- A diary study of 160 British middle and top managers found that they worked for a half hour or more without interruption only about once every two days (Stewart, 1967).
- Of the verbal contacts of the chief executives in my study, 93 percent were arranged on an ad hoc basis. Only 1 percent of the executives' time was spent in open-ended observational tours. Only

*This paper combines excerpts from "The Manager's Job: Folklore and Fact," which appeared in the *Harvard Business Review* (July-August 1975) on the characteristics of the job, with the framework of the context of the job, which was published as "Rounding Out the Manager's Job" in the *Sloan Management Review* (Fall 1994). Reprinted with permission from H. Mintzberg and J. B. Quinn, *The Strategy Process: Concepts, Contexts, Cases* (Upper Saddle River, NJ: Prentice Hall, 1996) 19–34.

1 out of 368 verbal contacts was unrelated to a specific issue and could be called general planning. Another researcher finds that "in *not one single case* did a manager report the obtaining of important external information from a general conversation or other undirected personal communication" (Aguilar, 1967:102).

- No study has found important patterns in the way managers schedule their time. They seem to jump from issue to issue, continually responding to the needs of the moment.

Is this the planner that the classical view describes? Hardly. How, then, can we explain this behavior? The manager is simply responding to the pressures of the job. I found that my chief executives terminated many of their own activities, often leaving meetings before the end and interrupted their desk work to call in subordinates. One president not only placed his desk so that he could look down a long hallway but also left his door open when he was alone—an invitation for subordinates to come in and interrupt him.

Clearly, these managers wanted to encourage the flow of current information. But more significantly, they seemed to be conditioned by their own work loads. They appreciated the opportunity cost of their own time, and they were continually aware of their ever-present obligations—mail to be answered, callers to attend to, and so on. It seems that no matter what he or she is doing, the manager is plagued by the possibilities of what he or she might do and must do.

When the manager must plan, he or she seems to do so implicitly in the context of daily actions, not in some abstract process reserved for two weeks in the organization's mountain retreat. The plans of the chief executives I studied seemed to exist only in their heads—as flexible, but often specific, intentions. The traditional literature notwithstanding, the job of managing does not breed reflective planners; the manager is a real-time responder to stimuli, an individual who is conditioned by his or her job to prefer live to delayed action.

Folklore: The effective manager has no regular duties to perform.

Managers are constantly being told to spend more time planning and delegating, and less time on operating details. These are not, after all, the true tasks of the manager. To use the popular analogy, the good manager, like the good conductor, carefully orchestrates everything in advance, then sits back to enjoy the fruits of his or her labor, responding occasionally to an unforeseeable exception ...

Fact: In addition to handling exceptions, managerial work involves performing a number of regular duties, including ritual and ceremony, negotiations, and processing of soft information that links the organization with its environment.

Consider some evidence from the early research studies:

- A study of the work of the presidents of small companies found that they engaged in routine activities because their companies could not afford staff specialists and were so thin on operating personnel that a single absence often required the president to substitute (Choran in Mintzberg, 1973a).
- One study of field sales managers and another of chief executives suggest that it is a natural part of both jobs to see important customers, assuming the managers wish to keep those customers (Davis, 1957; Copeman, 1963).
- Someone, only half in jest, once described the manager as that person who sees visitors so that everyone else can get his or her work done. In my study, I found that certain ceremonial duties—meeting visiting dignitaries, giving out gold watches, presiding at Christmas dinners—were an intrinsic part of the chief executive's job.
- Studies of managers' information flow suggest that managers play a key role in securing "soft" external information (much of it available only to them because of their status) and in passing it along to their subordinates.

Folklore: The senior manager needs aggregated information, which a formal management information system best provides.

In keeping with the classical view of the manager as that individual perched on the apex of a regulated, hierarchical system, the literature's manager was to receive all important information from a giant, comprehensive MIS.

But this never proved true at all. A look at how managers actually process information makes the reason quite clear. Managers have five media at their command—documents, telephone calls, scheduled and unscheduled meetings, and observational tours.

Fact: Managers strongly favor the verbal media—namely, telephone calls and meetings.

The evidence comes from every one of the early studies of managerial work. Consider the following:

- In two British studies, managers spent an average of 66 percent and 80 percent of their time in verbal (oral) communication (Stewart, 1967; Burns, 1954). In my study of five American chief executives, the figure was 78 percent.
- These five chief executives treated mail processing as a burden to be dispensed with. One came in Saturday morning to process 142 pieces of mail in just over three hours, to "get rid of all the stuff." This same manager looked at the first piece of "hard" mail he had received all week, a standard cost report, and put it aside with the comment, "I never look at this."
- These same five chief executives responded immediately to 2 of the 40 routine reports they received during the five weeks of my study and to four items in the 104 periodicals. They skimmed most of the periodicals in seconds, almost ritualistically. In all, these chief executives of good-sized organizations initiated on their own—that is, not in response to something else—a grand total of 25 pieces of mail during the 25 days I observed them.

An analysis of the mail the executives received reveals an interesting picture—only 13 percent was of specific and immediate use. So now we have another piece of the puzzle: not much of the mail provides live, current information—the action of a competitor, the mood of a government legislator, or the rating of last night's television show. Yet this is the information that drove the managers, interrupting their meetings and rescheduling their workdays.

Consider another interesting finding. Managers seem to cherish "soft" information, especially gossip, hearsay, and speculation. Why? The reason is its timeliness; today's gossip may be tomorrow's fact. The manager who is not accessible for the telephone call informing him or her that the firm's biggest customer was seen golfing with its main competitor may read about a dramatic drop in sales in the next quarterly report. But then it's too late.

Consider the work of Richard Neustadt, who studied the information-collecting habits of Presidents Roosevelt, Truman, and Eisenhower.

It is not information of a general sort that helps a President see personal stakes; not summaries, not surveys, not the bland amalgams. Rather . . . it is the odds and ends of tangible detail that pieced together in his mind illuminate the underside of issues put before him. To help himself he must reach out as widely as he can for every scrap of fact, opinion, gossip, bearing on his interests and relationships as President. He must become his own director of his own central intelligence (1960:153–154).

The manager's emphasis on the verbal media raises two important points:

First, verbal information is stored in the brains of people. Only when people write this information down can it be stored in the files of the organization—whether in metal cabinets or computer memory—and managers apparently do not write down much of what they hear. Thus the strategic data bank of the organization is not in the memory of its computers but in the minds of its managers.

Second, the managers' extensive use of verbal media helps to explain why they are reluctant to delegate tasks. When we note that most of the managers' important information comes in verbal form and is stored in their heads, we can well appreciate their reluctance. It is not as if they can hand a dossier over to someone; they must take the time to "dump memory"—to tell that someone all they know about the subject. But this could take so long that the managers find it easier to do the task themselves. Thus the managers are damned by their own information systems to a "dilemma of delegation"—to do too much themselves or to delegate to their subordinates with inadequate briefing.

Folklore: Management is, or at least is quickly becoming, a science and a profession.

By almost any definitions of science and profession, this statement is false. Brief observation of any manager will quickly lay to rest the notion that managers practice a science. A science involves the enaction of systematic, analytically determined procedures or programs. If we do not even know what procedures managers use, how can we prescribe them by scientific analysis? And how can we call management a profession if we cannot specify what managers are to learn?

Fact: The managers' programs—to schedule time, process information, make decisions, and so on— remain locked deep inside their brains.

Thus, to describe these programs, we rely on words like judgment and intuition, seldom stopping to realize that they are merely labels for our ignorance.

I was struck during my study by the fact that the executives I was observing—all very competent by any standard—are fundamentally indistinguishable from their counterparts of a hundred years ago (or a thousand years ago, for that matter). The information they need differs, but they seek it in the same way—by word of mouth. Their decisions concern modern technology, but the procedures they use to make them are the same as the procedures of the nineteenth-century manager. In fact, the manager is in a kind of loop, with increasingly heavy work pressures but no aid forthcoming from management science.

Considering the facts about managerial work, we can see that the manager's job is enormously complicated and difficult. The manager is overburdened with obligations; yet he or she cannot easily delegate tasks. As a result, he or she is driven to overwork and is forced to do many tasks superficially. Brevity, fragmentation, and verbal communication characterize the work. Yet these are the very characteristics of managerial work that have impeded scientific attempts to improve it. As a result, the management scientists have concentrated their efforts on the specialized functions of the organization, where they could more easily analyze the procedure and quantify the relevant information. Thus the first step in providing managers with some help is to find out what their job really is.

TOWARD A BASIC DESCRIPTION OF MANAGERIAL WORK

Now let us try to put some of the pieces of this puzzle together. The manager can be defined as that person in charge of an organization or one of its units. Besides chief executive officers, this definition would include vice presidents, head nurses, hockey coaches, and prime ministers. Can all of these people have anything in common? Indeed, they can. Our description takes the form of a model, building the image of the manager's job from the inside out, beginning at the center with the person and his or her frame and working out from there, layer by layer.

THE PERSON IN THE JOB

We begin at the center, with the person who comes to the job. People are not neutral when they take on a new managerial job, mere putty to be molded into the required shape. Figure 1 shows that an individual comes to a managerial job with a set of *values*, by this stage in life probably rather firmly set,

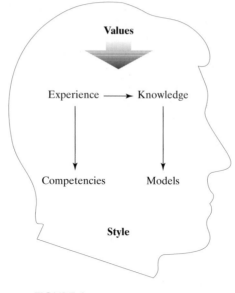

FIGURE 1   **The Person in the Job**

also a body of experience that, on the one hand, has forged a set of skills or *competencies*, perhaps honed by training, and, on the other, has provided a base of *knowledge*. That knowledge is, of course, used directly, but it is also converted into a set of *mental models*, key means by which managers interpret the world around them—for example, how the head nurse on a hospital ward perceives the behavior of the surgeons with whom she must work. Together, all these characteristics greatly determine how any manager approaches a given job—his or her *style* of managing. Style will come to life as we begin to see *how* a manager carries out *what* his or her job requires.

THE FRAME OF THE JOB

Embed the person depicted in a given managerial job and you get managerial work. At the core of it is some kind of *frame* for the job, the mental set the incumbent assumes to carry it out. Frame is strategy, to be sure, possibly even vision, but it is more than that. It is purpose, whether to create something in the first place, maintain something that has already been created or adapt it to changes, or else recreate something. Frame is also *perspective*—the broad view of the organization and its mission—and *positions*—concerning specific products, services, and markets.

Alain Noël, who studied the relationship between the frames and the work of the chief executives of three small companies, has said that managers have "occupations" and they have "preoccupations" (Noël, 1989). Frame describes the preoccupations, while roles (discussed later) describe the occupations. But frame does give rise to a first role in this model as well, which I call conceiving, namely thinking through the purpose, perspective, and positions of a particular unit to be managed over a particular period of time.

THE AGENDA OF THE WORK

Given a person in a particular managerial job with a particular frame, the question arises of how this is manifested in the form of specific activities. That happens through the *agenda* to carry out the work, and the associated role of **scheduling**, which has received considerable mention in the literature of management. Agenda is considered in two respects here. First, the frame gets manifested as a set of current issues, in effect, whatever is of concern to the manager, broken down into manageable units—what Tom Peters likes to call "chunks." Ask any manager about his or her work, and the almost inevitable first reply will be about the "issues" of central concern, those things "on the plate," as the saying goes. Or take a look at the agendas of meetings and you will likewise see a list of issues (rather than decisions). These, in effect, operationalize the frame (as well as change it, of course, by feeding in new concerns).

The sharper the frame, the more integrated the issues. The more realizable they may be as well, since it is a vague frame that gives rise to that all-too-common phenomenon of the unattainable "wish-list" in an organization. Sometimes a frame can be so sharp, and the issues therefore so tightly integrated, that they all reduce to what Noël has called one "magnificent obsession" (Noël, 1989). In effect, all the concerns of the manager revolve around one central issue, for example, making a new merger work.

Second, the frame and the issues get manifested in the more tangible *schedule*, the specific allocations of managerial time on a day-to-day basis. Also included here, however implicitly, is the setting of priorities among the issues. The scheduling of time and the prioritization of issues are obviously of great concern to all managers, and, in fact, are themselves significant consumers of managerial time. Accordingly, a great deal of attention has been devoted to these concerns, including numerous courses on "time management."

THE CORE IN CONTEXT

If we label the person in the job with a frame manifested by an agenda, the central *core* of the manager's job (shown by the concentric circles in Figure 2), then we turn next to the context in which this core is embedded, the milieu in which the work is practiced.

FIGURE 2   The Core in Context

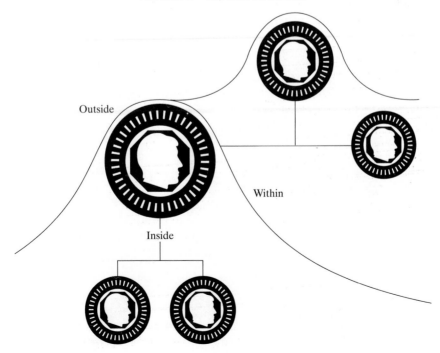

The context of the job is depicted in Figure 2 by the lines that surround the core. Context can be split into three areas, labeled inside, within, and outside on Figure 2.

Inside refers to the unit being managed, shown below the manager to represent his or her formal authority over its people and activities—the hospital ward in the case of the head nurse, for example. *Within*, shown to the right, refers to the rest of the organization—other members and other units with which the manager must work but over which he or she has no formal authority, for example, the doctors, the kitchen, the physiotherapists in the rest of the hospital, to continue with the same example. (Of course, in the case of the chief executive, there is no inside separate from within: that person has authority over the entire organization.) And outside refers to the rest of the context not formally part of the organization with which the manager must work—in this example, patients' relatives, long-term care institutions to which some of the unit's patients are discharged, nursing associations, and so on. The importance of this distinction (for convenience, we shall mostly refer to inside versus outside) is that much of managerial work is clearly directed either to the unit itself, for which the manager has official responsibility, or at its various boundary contexts, through which the manager must act without that responsibility.

MANAGING ON THREE LEVELS

We are now ready to address the actual behaviors that managers engage in to do their jobs. The essence of the model, designed to enable us to "see" managerial work comprehensively, in one figure, is that these roles are carried out on three successive levels, each inside and outside the unit. This is depicted by concentric circles of increasing specificity, shown in Figure 3.

FIGURE 3   **Three Levels of Evoking Action**

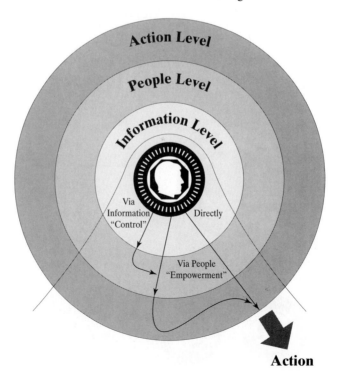

From the outside (or most tangible level) in, managers can manage *action* directly, they can manage *people* to encourage them to take the necessary actions, and they can manage *information* to influence the people in turn to take their necessary actions. In other words, the ultimate objective of managerial work, and of the functioning of any organizational unit, the taking of action, can be managed directly, indirectly through people, or even more indirectly by information through people. The manager can thus choose to intervene at any of the three levels, but once done, he or she must work through the remaining ones. Later we shall see that the level a given manager favors becomes an important determinant of his or her managerial style, especially distinguishing so-called "doers" who prefer direct action, "leaders" who prefer working through people, and "administrators" who prefer to work by information.

MANAGING BY INFORMATION

To manage by information is to sit two steps removed from the purpose of managerial work. The manager processes information to drive other people who, in turn, are supposed to ensure that necessary actions are taken. In other words, here the managers' own activities focus neither on people nor on actions per se, but rather on information as an indirect way to make things happen. Ironically, while this was the classic perception of managerial work for the first half of this century, in recent years it has also become a newly popular, in some quarters almost obsessional, view, epitomized by the so-called "bottom line" approach to management.

The manager's various informational behaviors may be grouped into two broad roles, here labeled communicating and controlling, shown in Figure 4.

Communicating refers to the collection and dissemination of information. In Figure 4, communicating is shown by double arrows to indicate that managers devote a great deal of effort to the two-way flow of information with the people all around them—employees inside their own units, others

FIGURE 4   The Information Roles

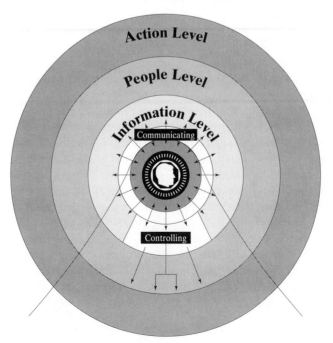

in the rest of the organization, and especially, as the empirical evidence makes abundantly clear, a great number of outsiders with whom they maintain regular contact. Thus the head of one regional division of the national police force spent a good part of the day I observed him passing information back and forth between the central headquarters and the people on his staff.

Managers "scan" their environments, they monitor their own units, and they share with and disseminate to others considerable amounts of the information they pick up. Managers can be described as "nerve centers" of their units, who use their status of office to gain access to a wide variety of informational sources. Inside the unit, everyone else is a specialist who generally knows more about his or her specialty than the manager. But, because the manager is connected to all those specialists, he or she should have the broadest base of knowledge about the unit in general. This should apply to the head of a huge health care system, with regard to broad policy issues, no less than to the clinical director of one of its hospital units, with regard to the service rendered there. And externally, by virtue of their status, managers have access to other managers who are themselves nerve centers of their own units. And so they tend to be exposed to powerful sources of external information and thus emerge as external nerve centers as well. The health care chief executive can thus talk to people running health care systems in other countries and so gain access to an array of information perhaps inaccessible even to his most influential reports.

The result of all this is that a considerable amount of the manager's information turns out to be privileged, especially when we consider how much of it is oral and nonverbal. Accordingly, to function effectively with the people around them, managers have to spend considerable time sharing their information, both with outsiders (in a kind of spokesperson role) and with insiders (in a kind of disseminator role).

I found in my initial study of chief executives that perhaps 40 percent of their time was devoted almost exclusively to the communicating role—just to gaining and sharing information—leaving aside the information processing aspects of all the other roles. In other words, the job of managing is fundamentally one of processing information, notably by talking and especially listening. Thus Figure 4 shows the inner core (the person in the job, conceiving and scheduling) connected to the outer rings (the more tangible roles of managing people and action) through what can be called the membrane of information processing all around the job.

What can be called the controlling role describes the managers' efforts, not just to gain and share information, but to use it in a directive way inside their units: to evoke or provoke general action by the people who report to them. They do this in three broad ways: they develop systems, they design structures, and they impose directives. Each of these seeks to control how other people work, especially with regard to the allocation of resources, and to what actions they are inclined to take.

First, developing systems is the most general of these three, and the closest to conceiving. It uses information to control peoples' behaviors. Managers often take charge of establishing and even running such systems in their units, including those of planning and performance control (such as budgeting). Robert Simons has noted how chief executives tend to select one such system and make it key to their exercise of control, in a manner he calls *interactive* (Simons, 1990, 1991).

Second, managers exercise control through designing the structures of their units. By establishing responsibilities and defining hierarchical authority, they again exercise control rather passively, through the processing of information. People are informed of their duties, which in turn is expected to drive them to carry out the appropriate actions.

Third is imposing directives, which is the most direct of the three, closest to the people and action, although still informational in nature. Managers pronounce: they make specific choices and give specific orders, usually in the process of "delegating" particular responsibilities and "authorizing" particular requests. In effect, managers manage by transmitting information to people so that they can act.

If a full decision-making process can be considered in the three stages of diagnosing, designing, and deciding—in other words, identifying issues, working out possible solutions, and selecting one—then here we are dealing with a restricted view of decision making. Delegating means mostly diagnosing ("Would you please handle this problem in this context"), while authorizing means mostly deciding ("OK, you can proceed"). Either way, the richest part of the process, the stage of designing possible solutions, resides with the person being controlled rather than with the manager him or herself, whose own behavior remains rather passive. Thus the manager as controller seems less an *actor* with sleeves rolled up, digging in, than a *reviewer* who sits back in the office and passes judgment. That is why this role is characterized as informational; I will describe a richer approach to decision making in the section on action roles.

The controlling role is shown in Figure 4 propelling down into the manager's own unit, since that is where formal authority is exercised. The single-headed arrows represent the imposed directives, while the pitchfork shape symbolizes both the design of structure and the development of systems. The proximity of the controlling role in Figure 4 to the manager's agenda reflects the fact that informational control is the most direct way to operationalize the agenda, for example, by using budgets to impose priorities or delegation to assign responsibilities. The controlling role is, of course, what people have in mind when they refer to the "administrative" aspect of managerial work.

MANAGING THROUGH PEOPLE

To manage through people, instead of by information, is to move one step closer to action, but still to remain removed from it. That is because here the focus of managerial attention becomes affect instead of effect. Other people become the means to get things done, not the manager him or herself, or even the substance of the manager's thoughts.

If the information roles (and controlling in particular) dominated our early thinking about managerial work, then after that, people entered the scene, or at least they entered the textbooks, as entities to be "motivated" and later "empowered." Influencing began to replace informing, and commitment began to vie with calculation for the attention of the manager. Indeed, in the 1960s and 1970s especially, the management of people, quite independent of content—of the strategies to be realized, the information to be processed, even the actions to be taken—became a virtual obsession of the literature, whether by the label of "human relations," "Theory Y," or "participative management" (and later "quality of work life," to be replaced by "total quality management").

For a long time, however, these people remained "subordinates" in more ways than one. "Participation" kept them subordinate, for this was always considered to be granted at the behest of the managers still fully in control. So does the currently popular term *empowerment*, which implies that power is being granted, thanks to the managers. (Hospital directors do not "empower" physicians!) People also remained subordinates because the whole focus was on those inside the unit, not outside it. Not until serious research on managerial work began did it become evident how important to managers were contacts with individuals outside their units. Virtually every single study of how all kinds of managers spent their time has indicated that outsiders, of an enormously wide variety, generally take as much of the managers' attention as so-called "subordinates." We shall thus describe two people roles here, shown in Figure 5, one internal, called *leading*, and one external, called *linking*.

The **leading** role has probably received more attention in the literature of management than all the other roles combined. And so we need not dwell on it here. But neither can we ignore it: managers certainly do much more than lead the people in their own units, and leading certainly infuses much else of what managers do (as, in fact, do all the roles, as we have already noted about communicating). But

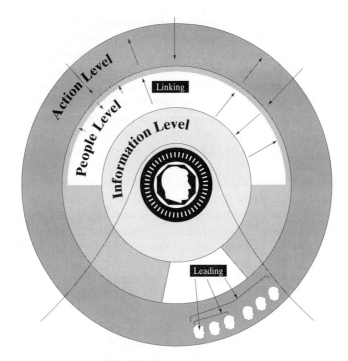

FIGURE 5   **The People Roles**

their work just as certainly cannot be understood without this dimension. We can describe the role of leading on three levels, as indicated in Figure 5.

First, managers lead on the *individual* level, "one on one," as the expression goes. They encourage and drive the people of their units—motivate them, inspire them, coach them, nurture them, push them, mentor them, and so on. All the managers I observed, from the chief executive of a major police force to the front-country manager in a mountain park, stopped to chat with their people informally during the day to encourage them in their work. Second, managers lead on the *group* level, especially by building and managing teams, an effort that has received considerable attention in recent years. Again, team meetings, including team building, figured in many of my observations; for example, the head of a London film company who brought film-making teams together for both effective and affective purposes. And third, they lead on the *unit* level, especially with regard to the creation and maintenance of culture, another subject of increasing attention in recent years (thanks especially to the Japanese). Managers, for example, engage in many acts of symbolic nature ("figurehead" duties) to sustain culture, as when the head of the national police force visited its officer training institute (as he did frequently) to imbue the force's norms and attitudes in its graduating class.

All managers seem to spend time on all three levels of leadership, although, again, styles do vary according to context and personality. If the communicating role describes the manager as the nerve center of the unit, then the leading role must characterize him or her as its "energy center," a concept perhaps best captured in Maeterlinck's wonderful description of the "spirit of the hive" (Maeterlinck, 1918). Given the right managerial "chemistry" (in the case of Maeterlinck's queen bee, quite literally!), it may be the manager's mere presence that somehow draws things together. By exuding that mystical substance, the leader unites his or her people, galvanizing them into action to accomplish the unit's mission and adapt it to a changing world.

The excess attention to the role of leading has probably been matched by the inadequate attention to the role of **linking**. For, in their sheer allocation of time, managers have been shown to be external linkers as much as they are internal leaders, in study after study. Yet, still the point seems hardly appreciated. Indeed, now more than ever, it must be understood, given the great growth of joint ventures and other collaborating and networking relationships between organizations, as well as the gradual reconception of the "captive" employee as an autonomous "agent" who supplies labor.

Figure 5 suggests a small model of the linking role. The arrows go in and out to indicate that the manager is both an advocate of its influence outside the unit and, in turn, a recipient of much of the influence exerted on it from the outside. In the middle are two parallel lines to represent the buffering aspect of this role—that managers must regulate the receipt of external influence to protect their units. To use a popular term, they are the *gate-keepers* of influence. Or, to add a metaphor, the manager acts as a kind of valve between the unit and its environment. Nowhere was this clearer than in my observation of three levels of management in a national park system—a regional director, the head of one mountain park, and the front-country manager of that park. They sit in an immensely complex array of forces—developers who want to enhance their business opportunities, environmentalists who want to preserve the natural habitat, tourists who want to enjoy the beauty, truckers who want to drive through the park unimpeded, politicians who want to avoid negative publicity, etc. It is a delicate balancing, or buffering, act indeed!

All managers appear to spend a great deal of time "networking"—building vast arrays of contacts and intricate coalitions of supporters beyond their own units, whether within the rest of the organization or outside, in the world at large. To all these contacts, the manager represents the unit externally, promotes its needs, and lobbies for its causes. In response, these people are expected to provide a steady inflow of information to the unit as well as various means of support and specific favors for it. This networking was most evident in the case of the film company managing director I observed, who exhibited an impressive network of contacts in order to negotiate her complex contracts with various media in different countries.

In turn, people intent on influencing the behavior of an organization or one of its sub-units will often exercise pressure directly on its manager, expecting that person to transmit the influence inside, as was most pointedly clear in the work of the parks manager. Here, then, the managerial job becomes one of delicate balance, a tricky act of mediation. Those managers who let external influence pass inside too freely—who act like sieves—are apt to drive their people crazy. (Of course, those who act like sponges and absorb all the influence personally are apt to drive themselves crazy!) And those who block out all influence—who act like lead to x-rays—are apt to detach their units from reality (and so dry up the sources of external support). Thus, what influence to pass on and how, bearing in mind the quid pro quo that influence exerted out is likely to be mirrored by influence coming back in, becomes another key aspect of managerial style, worthy of greatly increased attention in both the study of the job and the training of its occupants.

MANAGING ACTION

If managers manage passively by information and affectively through people, then they also manage actively and instrumentally by their own direct involvement in action. Indeed, this has been a long-established view of managerial work, although the excess attention in this century, first to controlling and then to leading, and more recently to conceiving (of planned strategy), has obscured its importance. Leonard Sayles, however, has long and steadily insisted on this, beginning with his 1964 book and culminating in *The Working Leader* (published in 1993), in which he makes his strongest statement yet, insisting that managers must be the focal points for action in and by their units (Sayles 1964, 1993). Their direct involvement must, in his view, take precedence over the pulling force of leadership and the pushing force of controllership.

I shall refer to this involvement as the **doing role**. But, in using this label—a popular one in the managerial vernacular ("Mary Ann's a doer")—it is necessary to point out that managers, in fact, hardly ever "do" anything. Many barely even dial their own telephones! Watch a manager and you will see someone whose work consists almost exclusively of talking and listening, alongside, of course, watching and "feeling." (That, incidentally, is why I show the manager at the core of the model as a head and not a full body!)

What "doing" presumably means, therefore, is getting closer to the action, ultimately being just one step removed from it. Managers as doers manage the carrying out of action directly, instead of indirectly through managing people or by processing information. In effect, a "doer" is really someone who gets it done (or, as the French put it with their expression *faire faire*, to "make" something "get made"). And the managerial vernacular is, in fact, full of expressions that reflect just this: "doing deals," "championing change," "fighting fires," "juggling projects." In the terms of decision making introduced earlier, here the manager diagnoses and designs as well as decides: he or she gets deeply and fully involved in the management of particular activities. Thus, in the day I spent with the head of the small retail chain, I saw a steady stream of all sorts of people coming and going, most involved with some aspect of store development or store operations, and there to get specific instructions on how to proceed next. He was not delegating or authorizing, but very clearly managing specific development projects step by step.

Just as they communicate all around the circle, so too do managers "do" all around it, as shown in Figure 6. *Doing inside* involves projects and problems. In other words, much "doing" has to do with changing the unit itself, both proactively and reactively. Managers champion change to exploit opportunities for their units, and they handle its problems and resolve its crises, often with "hands on" involvement. Indeed, the president I observed of a large French systems company spent part of his day in a meeting on a very specific customer contract. Asked why he attended, he said it was a leading-

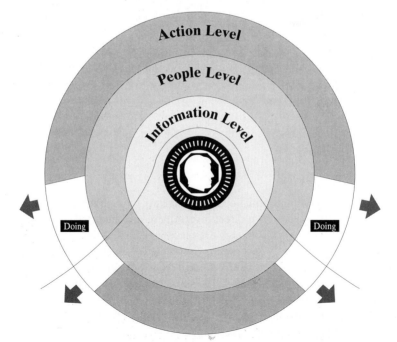

FIGURE 6   **The Action Roles**

edge project that could well change his company. He was being informed, to be sure, but also "doing" (more than controlling): he was an active member of the team. Here, then, the manager becomes a true designer (or, in the example above, a partner in the design), not of abstract strategies or of generalized structures, but of tangible projects of change. And the evidence, in fact, is that managers at all levels typically juggle many such projects concurrently, perhaps several dozen in the case of chief executives. Hence the popularity of the term "project management."

Some managers continue to do regular work after they have become managers as well. For example, a head nurse might see a patient, just as the Pope leads prayers, or a dean might teach a class. Done for its own sake, this might be considered separate from managerial work. But such things are often done for very managerial reasons as well. This may be an effective way of "keeping in touch" with the unit's work and finding out about its problems, in which case it falls under the role of communicating. Or it may be done to demonstrate involvement and commitment with others in the unit, in which case it falls under the role of culture building in the role of leading.

Doing outside takes place in terms of deals and negotiations. Again, there is no shortage of evidence on the importance of negotiating as well as dealing in managerial work. Most evident in my observations was the managing director of the film company, who was working on one intricate deal after another. This was a small company, and making deals was a key part of her job. But even in larger organizations, senior managers have to spend considerable time on negotiations themselves, especially when critical moments arise. After all, they are the ones who have the authority to commit the resources of their unit, and it is they who are the nerve centers of its information as well as the energy centers of its activity, not to mention the conceptual centers of its strategy. All around the circles, therefore, action connects to people who connect to information, which connects to the frame.

THE WELL-ROUNDED JOB OF MANAGING

I opened this article by noting that the best-known writers of management all seem to emphasize one aspect of the job—in the terms we now have, "doing" for Tom Peters, "conceiving" for Michael Porter, "leading" for Abraham Zaleznik and Warren Bennis, "controlling" for the classical writers. Now it can be appreciated why all may well be wrong: heeding the advice of any one of them must lead to the lopsided practice of managerial work. Like an unbalanced wheel at resonant frequency, the job risks flying out of control. That is why it is important to show all of the components of managerial work on a single integrated diagram, as in Figure 7, to remind people, at a glance, that these components form one job and cannot be separated.

Acceptance of Tom Peters' urgings—" 'Don't think, do' is the phrase I favor"—could lead to the centrifugal explosion of the job, as it flies off in all directions, free of a strong frame anchoring it at the core. But acceptance of the spirit of Michael Porter's opposite writings—that what matters most is conception of the frame, especially of strategic positions—could produce a result no better: centripetal implosion, as the job closes in on itself cerebrally, free of the tangible connection to its outer actions. Thinking is heavy and can wear down the incumbent, while acting is light and cannot keep him or her in place. Only together do they provide the balance that seems so characteristic of effective management.

Too much leading produces a job free of content—aimless, frameless, and actionless—while too much linking produces a job detached from its internal roots—public relations instead of public service. The manager who only communicates or only conceives never gets anything done, while the manager who only "does" ends up doing it all alone. And, of course, we all know that happens to managers who believe their job is merely to control. A bad pun may thus make for good practice: the manager must practice a well-rounded job.

In fact, while we may be able to separate the components of this job conceptually, I maintain that they cannot be separated behaviorally. In other words, it may be useful, even necessary, to delineate

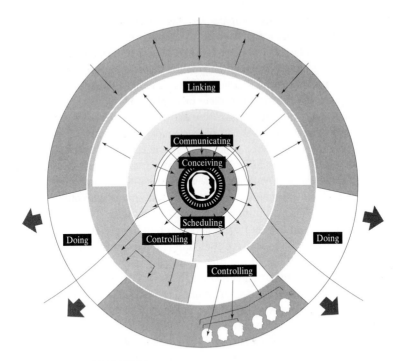

FIGURE 7   **Managerial Work Rounded Out**

the parts for purposes of design, selection, training, and support. But this job cannot be practiced as a set of independent parts. The core is a kind of magnet that holds the rest together, while the communication ring acts as a membrane that allows the flow of information between inner thinking and outer behaviors, which themselves tie people to action.

Indeed, the most interesting aspects of this job may well fall on the edges, between the component parts. For example, Andrew Grove, president of Intel, likes to describe what he does as "nudging," a perfect blend of controlling, leading, and doing (Grove, 1983). This can mean pushing people, tangibly but not aggressively, as might happen with pure doing, and not coldly, as with pure controlling, but with a sense of leading. There are similar edges between the inside and the outside, thinking and behaving, and communicating and controlling, as we shall see.

Managers who try to "do" outside without "doing" inside inevitably get themselves into trouble. Just consider all those chief executives who "did the deal," acquired the company or whatever, and then dropped it into the laps of others for execution. Likewise, it makes no more sense to conceive and then fail to lead and do (as has been the tendency in so-called "strategic planning," where controlling has often been considered sufficient for "implementation") than it makes sense to do or to lead without thinking through the frame in which to embed these activities. A single managerial job may be carried out by a small team, but only if its members are so tightly knitted together—especially by that ring of communication—that they act as a single entity. This is not to argue, of course, that different managers do not emphasize different roles or different aspects of the job. For example, we can distinguish a *conceptual* style of management, which focuses on the development of the frame, an *administrative* style, which concerns itself primarily with controlling, an *interpersonal* style, which favors leading on the inside or linking on the outside, and an *action* style, which is concerned mainly with tangible doing. And as we move out in this order, the overall style of managing can be described as less *opaque*, more *visible*.

A final aspect of managerial style has to do with the interrelationships among the various components of managerial work. For example, an important distinction can be made between *deductive* and *inductive* approaches to managerial work. The former proceeds from the core out, as the conceived frame is implemented through scheduling that uses information to drive people to get action done. We can call this a *cerebral* style of managing—highly deliberate. But there is an alternate, emergent view of the management process as well, which proceeds inductively, from the outer surface to the inner core. We might label it an *insightful* style. As Karl Weick puts it, managers act in order to think. They try things to gain experience, retain what works, and then, by interpreting the results, gradually evolve their frames (Weick, 1979).

Clearly, there is an infinity of possible contexts within which management can be practiced. But just as clearly, perhaps, a model such as the one presented here can help to order them and so come to grips with the difficult requirements of designing managerial jobs, selecting the right people to fill them, and training people accordingly.

THE HUMAN SIDE OF MANAGEMENT*

by Thomas Teal

Look closely at any company in trouble, and you'll probably find that the problem is management. Ask employees about their jobs, and they'll complain about management. Study large corporations, and you'll discover that the biggest barrier to change, innovation, and new ideas is very often management. Make an inventory of the things that have stifled your own creativity and held back your own career; summarize the critical factors that have stood in the way of your organization's success; name the individuals chiefly responsible for the missed opportunities and bungled projects you yourself have witnessed. Managers will top every list.

There is so much inferior management in the world that some people believe we'd be better off in completely flat organizations with no managers at all. Most of us spend the better part of our working lives convinced that we could do the boss's job better than the boss. Something about management looks so easy that we watch one anemic performance after another and never doubt that we could succeed where others repeatedly fail. Of course, a few of us would be terrific managers. But just as clearly, most of us would not. We know this is true because so many of us eventually get the chance to try.

As for the argument that management is unnecessary, think for a moment about what the world was like before the principles of scientific management rationalized production, democratized wealth, commercialized science, and effectively doubled life expectancy. Good management works miracles.

And still the troublesome fact is that mediocre management is the norm. This is not because some people are born without the management gene or because the wrong people get promoted or because the system can be manipulated—although all these things happen all the time. The overwhelmingly most common explanation is much simpler: capable management is so extraordinarily difficult that few people look good no matter how hard they try. Most of those lackluster managers we all complain about are doing their *best* to manage well.

In one form or another, managing has become one of the world's most common jobs, and yet we make demands on managers that are nearly impossible to meet. For starters, we ask them to acquire a long list of more or less traditional management skills in finance, cost control, resource allocation, product development, marketing, manufacturing, technology, and a dozen other areas. We also demand that they master the management arts—strategy, persuasion, negotiation, writing, speaking, listening. In addition, we ask them to assume responsibility for organizational success, make a great deal

---

*Reprinted with permission from *Harvard Business Review* (November-December, 1996): 35–44.

of money, and share it generously. We also require them to demonstrate the qualities that define leadership, integrity, and character—things like vision, fortitude, passion, sensitivity, commitment, insight, intelligence, ethical standards, charisma, luck, courage, tenacity, even from time to time humility. Finally, we insist that they should be our friends, mentors, or guardians, perpetually alert to our best interests. Practicing this common profession *adequately*, in other words, requires people to display on an everyday basis the combined skills of St. Peter, Peter the Great, and the Great Houdini. No wonder most managers seem to underperform.

And still not *all* of them do. Easy as it is to point out mediocre managers—and you can hardly swing a cat in the average workplace without hitting several—nearly everyone gets to see a few exemplary managers in the course of a career. These people fall into two categories: first, the good or very good managers, who are exceedingly rare because they actually meet the inhuman requirements for adequacy; second, the great managers, or rather the occasional bosses we don't hesitate to call great managers in spite of the fact that they lack a dozen of the skills and virtues that we would normally insist on (and that the job description probably requires). We need to take a closer look at this second category, great managers, because although their numbers are small, they tend to loom exceptionally large in the lives of the people around them.

One reason for the scarcity of managerial greatness is that in educating and training managers, we focus too much on technical proficiency and too little on character. The management sciences—statistics, data analysis, productivity, financial controls, service delivery—are things we can almost take for granted these days. They are subjects we know how to teach. But we're still in the Dark Ages when it comes to teaching people how to *behave* like great managers—somehow instilling in them capacities such as courage and integrity that can't be taught. Perhaps as a consequence, we've developed a tendency to downplay the importance of the human element in managing. Managers are not responsible for other people's happiness, we say. The workplace isn't a nursery school. We've got market share and growth and profits to worry about, and anyway, power is too useful and entertaining to dribble away on relationships—we've got our own nests to feather. But the only people who become great managers are the ones who understand in their guts that managing is not merely a series of mechanical tasks but a set of human interactions.

In the course of seven years at this magazine, I was lucky enough to come in contact with a surprising number of great managers. As editor of a department we called First Person, I was in a position to help several such people—many of them entrepreneurs or CEOs—tell their own stories about critical problems they had faced, analyzed, grappled with, and sometimes but not always resolved. Not all those stories ended happily, but all of them showed how extraordinarily difficult first-rate management can be. They all showed something else as well—that management is a supremely human activity, a fact that explains why, among all the preposterous demands that we make on managers, character means more to us than education. We may love and work hard for a manager who knows too little about computers or marketing but is a fine human being. We almost invariably dislike and thwart managers who are stingy or mean-spirited, however great their technical abilities. Look back three paragraphs to that long list of requirements. As it glides upward from acquirable skills to primal virtues, each item on the list grows less and less dispensable. Without courage and tenacity, for example, no manager can *hope* to achieve greatness. Consider a few of the other absolute prerequisites.

Great management requires imagination. If a company's vision and strategy are to differentiate its offerings and create competitive advantage, they must be original. Original has to mean unconventional, and it often means counterintuitive. Moreover, it takes ingenuity and wit to bring disparate people and elements together into a unified but uniquely original whole. There is even a name for this capacity. It's called esemplastic imagination, and although it's generally attributed only to poets, consider the Rosenbluth family.

When Hal Rosenbluth's great-grandfather Marcus opened a travel business in Philadelphia in 1892, he did not see himself as just another travel agent. Unlike his competitors, whose goals were limited to writing and selling tickets, he saw himself in the immigration business. For $50, he supplied poor Europeans with steamship tickets, assistance clearing the hurdles at Ellis Island, and transport to Philadelphia. And he didn't stop there. Since immigration was not usually an individual affair but involved entire families, Marcus Rosenbluth set himself up as a kind of banker for immigrants as well. When his immigrants were settled and had jobs, he collected their savings, $.05 and $.10 at a time, until there was enough money to bring over a second member of the family and a third and a fourth, until the whole clan was safely in America. From the day it was born, Rosenbluth Travel had the competitive advantage of imagination.

Years later, when immigration slowed (and when the company was forced to give up one of its licenses—travel or banking), Rosenbluth Travel moved into the business of leisure travel. Then in the late 1970s, nearly 90 years after the whole enterprise got off the ground, Hal Rosenbluth took over the business and reinvented it once again. Deregulation had just created turmoil out of order and stability. Between any two given cities, two or three standard airfares had suddenly mushroomed into a chaos of new airlines, schedules, and tariffs, all subject to change without notice. Customers were frustrated and angry trying to figure out what the fares really were, and travel agents, unable to cope or make sense of the confusion, were close to desperation. Hal saw it all as a grand opportunity, partly because he saw that the solution lay in another recent innovation—computers. He subscribed to every airline's electronic reservation network (in those days, the airlines charged for access), and he amalgamated all the fares on a computerized system of his own. He bought terminals for his agents and built a new spirit of teamwork using enthusiasm, incentives, and a determination to pay so much attention to his employees' interests that they would feel free to pay attention to the customers'. He guaranteed clients the lowest airfare on every route, and he set out to nail as many corporate accounts as he could find. But, as Hal put it, "I think our biggest competitive advantage was to understand that as deregulation changed the rules, we were no longer in the travel business as much as we were in the information business." The Rosenbluth imagination was still at work after four generations and nearly 100 years.

Another characteristic of great managers is integrity. All managers believe they behave with integrity, but in practice, many have trouble with the concept. Some think integrity is the same thing as secretiveness or blind loyalty. Others seem to believe it means consistency, even in a bad cause. Some confuse it with discretion and some with the opposite quality—bluntness—or with simply not telling lies. What integrity means in management is more ambitious and difficult than any of these. It means being responsible, of course, but it also means communicating clearly and consistently, being an honest broker, keeping promises, knowing oneself, and avoiding hidden agendas that hang other people out to dry. It comes very close to what we used to call *honor*, which in part means not telling lies to yourself.

Think of the way Johnson & Johnson dealt with the Tylenol poisoning crisis or how Procter & Gamble withdrew Rely Tampons, a newly launched product, because of an unproved but potentially serious health risk. Compare those cases with the way Johns-Manville handled the asbestos catastrophe. As a Manville manager for more than 30 years, Bill Sells witnessed what he calls "one of the most colossal corporate blunders of the twentieth century." This blunder was not the company's manufacture and sale of asbestos. Companies have been producing deadly chemicals and explosives for hundreds of years. According to Sells, the blunder that killed thousands of people and eliminated an industry was self-deception. Manville managers at every level were simply unwilling to acknowledge the evidence available in the 1940s, when so much of the damage was done, and their capacity for denial held steady through the following decades despite mounting evidence about old and newly identified hazards. The company developed a classic case of bunker mentality: refusing to accept facts; assuming that customers and employees were aware of the hazards and used asbestos at their own risk; denying the need for and the very possibility of change at a company that had successfully hidden its head in the sand for 100 years. Manville funded little medical research, made little effort to communicate what it already knew, and took little or no proactive responsibility for the damage asbestos might do. Captive to the notion that investments that make no product can make no contribution to success, the company pursued only haphazardly the few safety practices that were in place—with tragic consequences for workers' health and decidedly negative effects on maintenance costs, productivity, and profit. Once when he raised objections, Sells was told by his boss, "Bill, you're not loyal," to which he replied, "No, no, you've got it wrong. I'm the one who *is* loyal."

After eight years with the company, Sells was promoted in 1968 to manage a troubled asbestos facility in Illinois, where it was his job to juggle responsibilities that sometimes seemed to conflict— keeping the plant profitable, keeping it productive, and keeping it safe. Slowly and painfully over the next year and a half, he came to understand that labor relations, productivity, dust abatement, profitability, health, and safety were all aspects of the same issue—business integrity—and he launched a half-million-dollar program to replace or rebuild nearly all the safety equipment in the building. By the early 1970s, unfortunately, it was too late to save asbestos or its victims. But Sells did put his insight into practice in the 1980s, when he headed the company's fiberglass division. Among other things, the division funded arm's-length studies and practiced immediate total disclosure (by phone, fax, letter, news conference, videotape, live television, and printed warnings) of everything the company learned about the potential hazards and health risks of the product and made no disingenuous effort to put a procompany spin on the results.

Of course, business integrity means accepting the business consequences of a company's acts, but for great managers, it also means taking personal responsibility. The boss who accused Sells of disloyalty didn't want to hear uncomfortable facts or opposing points of view. But when Sells took over his own division, he opened himself to criticism and argument. This is stressful work for managers, partly because it means serving two masters—one organizational, one moral—and partly because they're not likely to get support for doing it, not even for doing it well. The rewards for great managers are more subtle.

In the early 1980s, William Peace was the general manager of the Synthetic Fuels Division at Westinghouse, a relatively small unit that faced liquidation as a result of declining oil prices unless he could make it attractive enough to sell. In an effort to pare costs, he decided to eliminate a number of the division's 130 jobs because he thought potential buyers would see them as inessential, and, under the circumstances, he had no choice but to lay off the people who held those jobs in spite of their sometimes excellent performance records. He and his department heads drew up the list of 15 positions in a long, emotional meeting, and when it was over and his senior managers were about to go off and convey the bad news, Peace stopped them. He felt this was news he had to communicate himself, in part because he didn't want the entire workforce to conclude that a wave of layoffs was in the making, in part because he felt he owed the individuals involved a face-to-face explanation.

The meeting with the 15 innocent victims the next morning was funereal. People wept openly or stared dejectedly at the floor. Peace walked through his reasoning, insisted that the layoffs were based on job descriptions, not individual performance, and begged the 15 victims to understand if not forgive the need to sacrifice some employees in order to save the division and all its other jobs. They argued, pleaded, and accused him of ingratitude and heartlessness. Peace commiserated, sympathized, accepted their criticism and disapproval, and did his best to give a frank, detailed answer to every question, taking all the heat they cared to give. Gradually the anger faded and the mood shifted from despondency to resignation and even to some grudging understanding and actual interest in the prospects for a sale. Peace recalls it as the most painful meeting he ever took part in. But by the time he shook their hands and wished them luck, he hoped and believed they had come to appreciate his motives if not his choice of sacrificial lambs.

It was months later that he learned how the confrontation had played to those 15 people. A buyer had been found for the division, Peace had been kept on as general manager, and the new owner was investing money in the enterprise. Suddenly Peace was in a position to rehire many of the people he'd laid off, and when he made them the offer, everyone, without exception, came back to work for him, even when it meant giving up good jobs found elsewhere. This is a story about moral and humanitarian compunctions. Equally to the point, however, it's about a manager drawing attention to his own responsibility in adversity, a piece of courage that in this case led to the eventual recapturing of loyal, experienced employees.

Great management has to involve the kind of respect Peace showed for his subordinates, and it must also involve empowerment. The managers people name with admiration are always the ones who delegate their authority, make subordinates feel powerful and capable, and draw from them so much creativity and such a feeling of responsibility that their behavior changes forever. In 1980, when Ricardo Semler took over Semco, his family's business in São Paulo, Brazil—five factories that manufactured, among other things, marine pumps, commercial dishwashers, and mixing equipment for everything from bubble gum to rocket fuel—productivity was low, new contracts were a rarity, and financial disaster loomed. Furthermore, the company was mired in regulations, hierarchy, and distrust. There were intricate rules for travel—strict ceilings on hotel expenses, calls home limited to a set number of minutes, and all the usual red tape about turning in receipts. Factory workers underwent daily theft-prevention security checks, needed permission to use the bathroom, and were generally treated like delinquents.

Semler swept this old world out the door. He reduced the hierarchy to three levels, threw out the rule book (putting in its place what he called the rule of common sense), initiated collegial decision making, and began submitting certain company decisions—such as a factory relocation and several critical acquisitions—to companywide democratic votes. He set up a profit-sharing plan, and, to make it work, he cut the size of the operating units to which it was tied and opened the company's books to everyone on the payroll. On the theory that he should not be sending people he didn't trust around the world to represent his company, he eliminated expense accounting and simply gave people whatever they claimed to have spent. On the theory that it was indecent to treat people like children who in private life were heads of families, civic leaders, and army reserve officers, he put hourly workers on monthly salaries, did away with time clocks and security checks, and let people on the factory floor set their own work goals, methods, and even work hours. He calculated that people whose bonuses depended on profits were neither going to waste the company's money on luxury hotels and cars nor sit around on their hands at work.

He was right. Sales doubled the first year, inventories fell, the company launched eight new products that had been lost in R&D for years, quality improved (for one product, the rejection rate dropped from more than 30 percent to less than 1 percent), costs declined, and productivity increased so dramatically that the company was able to reduce the workforce by 32 percent through attrition and incentives for workers to take early retirement. Semler had reversed the usual practice. Instead of choosing a few responsibilities he could delegate, he picked out a handful of responsibilities that had to remain his own—contracts, strategy, alliances, the authority to make changes in the style of company management—and gave away everything else. Perhaps, he says, some people take advantage of uncontrolled expense accounts or unlocked storage rooms—he would certainly prosecute anyone he found stealing—but his delegation of authority has been so radical and thorough (and effective) that he has no good way of finding out and no desire to know.

In some cases, however, urging people toward shared responsibility and authority is like pulling teeth, and when it means repressing your own instinct to control, like pulling your own teeth. The truth is, people often fail to embrace the opportunities they claim to want, and managers often fail to yield the authority they aim to delegate. Ralph Stayer of Johnsonville Sausage in Wisconsin is another CEO who, in the early 1980s, tried to empower and invigorate his workforce with large helpings of profit sharing and responsibility. But Stayer was his own worst enemy. He was still so deeply in love with his own control that he held onto it in ways that he was not even conscious of. By giving advice to every subordinate who asked him for help in addressing a problem, he continued to run the company and own the problems. By continuing to collect production data, he stayed in charge of production. By continuing to check the quality of the product, he effectively prevented successful delegation of quality control. His subordinates were simply afraid to make decisions unless they knew which decisions he wanted them to make. The only real difference was that now instead of telling them what he wanted, he was making them guess. Not surprisingly, they quickly became experts at correctly interpreting his tone of voice, deciphering his body language, inferring entire policies from a single offhand remark. Once he realized what he was doing and reminded himself that he really did want his employees to seize the company reins and own the problems that were wearing him down, he began teaching himself to suppress his own need for control. He fired the one or two direct reports he had trained so well they could hardly act on their own initiative, and he stopped attending the meetings in which production decisions were made or even discussed. Instead, he studied the arts of coaching, teaching, and facilitating, and he altered the job descriptions of managers in order to emphasize those skills even above technical expertise.

The payoff came several years later, when Johnsonville was offered a huge new contract that Stayer didn't believe the company was capable of handling. Rather than simply turn the contract down, however, as he would have done five years earlier, he presented it to his employees. For two weeks, in small groups and at larger team meetings (which Stayer did not attend), they studied the risks and challenges and developed plans to minimize the downside dangers. Ignoring his fears, they accepted and successfully carried out the contract despite the problems it could—and did—add to their lives.

As all these stories illustrate, great management is a continual exercise in learning, education, and persuasion. Getting people to do what's best—for customers, for the business, even for themselves—is often a struggle because it means getting people to understand and want to do what's best, and that requires integrity, the willingness to empower others, courage, tenacity, and great teaching skills. Sometimes it also requires managers to learn some difficult lessons of their own. Robert Frey, owner of Cin-Made, a small packaging plant in Cincinnati, falls into this category.

Frey had no desire to carry all his company's burdens by himself, so, like Ralph Stayer, he decided to share the responsibilities and rewards with his workforce. But his workforce said no thanks. Or rather, not even thanks, just no. They wanted nothing to do with power and self-government even if it really did mean profit sharing on a generous scale, which they very much doubted was the case.

With a partner, Frey had purchased the company in 1984, and at first his relations with employees had been adversarial and hostile. He had openly implied that they were morons, and he had declared their jobs to be easy. Even worse, he had refused them their annual wage hike. They went out on strike but eventually caved in when their war chest ran dry. Frey wouldn't take them back until they'd accepted reduced vacations and a pay *cut* of 12.5 percent. Beaten and humiliated, they hated him. He'd won a labor victory, but his prize was a factory full of sullen, angry workers determined to file grievances on every, tiny deviation from the contract he had made them sign.

Frey himself soon realized that even if his cost-cutting measures had been necessary, his manner had been arrogant, high-handed, and shortsighted. And he quickly tired of lying awake nights wondering if the company was going to survive. He wanted his employees to take on some of that worrying, and to achieve his end, he was prepared to do whatever it took. In fact, the strike had taught him that his contemptuous treatment of his workers had been a case of extremely poor judgment. The work they did was far from easy, as he'd discovered firsthand when he'd tried to do it himself, and he desperately needed their knowledge of equipment, products, and customers. Whatever his mistakes in the past, he was determined to turn his present predicament on its head and win the confidence and involvement of his workforce. He began consulting their expertise, and he started holding monthly state-of-the-business meetings to let them know exactly where the company stood financially. He also began to study profit-sharing plans. By the end of the contract's first year, the business was again making a profit, and he restored a big piece of the pay cut. Toward the end of its second and final year, he announced that he would restore the remainder and immediately begin a profit-sharing plan that would distribute 30 percent of pretax profits to employees, half of this to hourly workers. To give the plan teeth, he declared that he would open the company's books to union inspection and audit.

Many, perhaps most, of the hourly workers resisted. They didn't want more responsibility, they didn't want change—he could keep his profits. They wanted higher wages all right, but they wanted guarantees, not risks. Frey was relentless and relentlessly straightforward. He gave new responsibilities to his best people, with merit raises to match, and he found a factory manager who was good at coaxing people to study math and such techniques as statistical process control. He decreed that learning new skills would entitle people to raises. But he firmly refused to increase wages across the board beyond restoring the pay cut that had helped get the company back on its feet. Frey was sure that he and his workforce would continue to be adversaries until they all shared a common interest in the company's success. To that end, he wanted them to understand where wages came from and to grasp the trade offs between benefits and profits. He wanted them to earn more money than they had ever earned before, but only on the condition that extra money would come from profits: workers would have to share that portion of the risk and shoulder more responsibility.

He made two public announcements: "I do not choose to own a company that has an adversarial relationship with its employees" and "Employee participation will play an essential role in management." He began losing his temper every time someone refused to participate in decision making or said, "It's not my job." He started using the monthly meetings to share more and more complex information, look at profit projections, and examine numbers such as scrap rates and productivity—areas over which factory workers had direct control. He met with union leaders, told them exactly what he was trying to accomplish, and swore he was not out to break their shop. He ignored resentment, absorbed criticism as his due, delegated relentlessly, even did his best to listen and treat people with visible respect. Some of his workers began to like him. Many began to buy his ideas. Almost all came to believe they could trust what he told them. He explained, taught, learned, pressed nonstop for change, and refused to take no for an answer.

Gradually over the course of several years, the struggle began to pay off. Profits grew (individual profit shares over a four-year period averaged out to a 36 percent increment to wages), productivity rose 30 percent, absenteeism fell to nearly zero, and grievances declined to one or two per year. More important for Frey, workers began to make the connection between income and initiative, and today they carry out all the long-term planning and management of labor, materials, equipment, production runs, packing, and delivery. Perhaps best of all from Frey's point of view, some of them probably lie awake nights worrying about company performance.

Frey is an interesting case of a great manager who has great flaws that somehow just don't matter. Tact is not on the list of indispensable ingredients; neither is elegance. But there is one more indispensable capacity, and Frey possesses it, although in an unusually unpolished form: the capacity to create excitement. We generally call it the ability to motivate people, but that phrase is too bloodless to suggest the adrenaline that's needed to build great companies. Frey stirred people up, first to anger, it's true, but later to enterprise and creativity as well.

We want all our leaders—from politicians to movie stars—to stir our souls a little, and we want the same thing from our managers. They have become the most significant figures in our society, with as central a role to play as generals, lords, oracles, or politicians played in centuries past, and we look to them for more than guidance. These few stories can't possibly paint a comprehensive picture of great management in action, but they do give us a rough sketch of the objective, which is to magnify the social core of human nature, bring individual talents to fruition, create value, and combine those activities with enough passion to generate the greatest possible advantages for every player.

Which brings me to another observation about great managers, this one a little more extravagant. We've already noted that most of us demand something in a manager that is larger than life, and I suggest that in really great managers, we get it. Great managers are distinguished by something more than insight, integrity, leadership, and imagination, and that something more (part of it is tenacity; much of the rest is plain courage) bears a close resemblance to heroism.

Now, people whose concept of the heroic is inextricably tied to burning buildings and reckless self-sacrifice may find this suggestion offensive. *Heroism* certainly isn't a word we're comfortable using in the same breath with the word *self-interest*, and there's no escaping the fact that managers do what they do at least partially to serve themselves, even to make money, even to make a lot of money. Still and all, creating value where none existed; saving and creating jobs and careers and lifetime goals; doing what's right, productive, and beneficial; standing alone, often without support, often against formidable opposition; doing the hard intellectual work of conceiving a vision and the hard moral work of staying true to it—aren't these the kinds of acts we associate with heroism? Even if there *are* rewards? Even if the eventual rewards are great? For that matter, don't quite a few of our traditional story-book heroes—and our modern media heroes as well—reap lavish benefits? Half the kingdom, wealth, fame, a seat in the Senate, the presidency?

One of the most striking things about entrepreneurs, for example, is their sometimes awkward resemblance to Romantic heroes—their isolation, the fact that they are perpetually swimming against the current, against the wishes of one or more of their constituencies, against convention, against criticism, against heavy odds. Management at its finest has a heroic dimension because it deals with eternal human challenges and offers no excuse for failure and no escape from responsibility. Managers can be as thoughtless and selfish as any other human beings, but they can also be as idealistic and as noble.

Great managers also bring forth other great managers. William Peace, who confronted the employees he was about to lay off, tells a second story—one about a general manager named Gene Cattabiani, who had been his boss years earlier and who shaped the kind of manager Peace himself became. In the early 1970s, when the story took place, Cattabiani had just taken over the Westinghouse Steam Turbine Division in Philadelphia and faced serious problems. The division was not making money, and to save it, he needed to reduce costs and raise productivity. Yet the greatest room for improvement was on the factory floor, and the animosities between management and labor were intense. Union leaders had a reputation for intransigence, and several strikes had grown violent. On the other side, management saw labor as lazy and selfish, and it tended to treat workers with contempt. Cattabiani felt the time had come to break the impasse. Union cooperation was the key to the kind of change that could save the division, and he was determined to change attitudes and begin treating the workforce with respect and honesty. The method he chose was an unprecedented series of presentations to the entire labor force on the state of the business, with slides and a question-and-answer period. Against the better judgment of his immediate subordinates, he decided to make the presentations himself, and because the workforce numbered in the hundreds, he would have to repeat the talk several times.

The first presentation was a trial by fire. He wanted employees to see that the division was in trouble and that their very jobs depended on a new kind of management-labor relationship. But they saw Cattabiani as the enemy. They subjected him to catcalls, heckling, and open abuse, and it was not at all clear that they heard a word of his careful explanations. Peace and his colleagues were convinced he would see that the presentations were a mistake and cancel the rest of the series or ask someone else to do them. But with obvious dread, he persisted. Again and again, he exposed himself to the insults and epithets of people who didn't seem to believe a word he said. Afterward, he began to make regular visits to the shop floor, a thing none of his predecessors had ever done, and to banter and reason with the worst of his hecklers. As the weeks went by, the workers he spoke to began to nod to him when he appeared, to listen to what he had to say, and then to argue with him face to face. Gradually, in the midst of open animosity, the change that Cattabiani wanted began to take place. He ceased to be an ordinary useless manager and became a creature of flesh and blood. He acquired credibility, and a dialogue developed where before there had been nothing but grim silence or hostility.

The presentations and their aftermath were a watershed. Painful and lonely as the process was for Cattabiani, it gave him a human status that no manager had previously held. The workers wanted to confront the source of their problems. By giving them that opportunity, Cattabiani made himself difficult to demonize and impossible to dismiss, and from that moment forward, labor-management relations took a sharp turn for the better. Over the following months, he made big changes in the way the division was run. He introduced greater work flexibility, instituted higher standards for quality and productivity, and when necessary, laid people off. Each improvement was a new struggle, but Cattabiani continued to make himself a disarmingly open target for anger and argument, the necessary changes did take place, peace was maintained, and the division's performance improved more than enough to save its life and the hundreds of jobs it provided.

It is hard to read stories like this one and the one about Cattabiani's protégé, William Peace, and not get a sense that these two men and a great many men and women like them, at least brush the edges of something genuinely gallant, however industrial, however small the scale. Management is terrifically difficult. It takes exceptional, sometimes heroic people to do it well. But even doing it well *enough* is a much more honorable and arduous task than we commonly suppose.

NOTES

F. Aguilar, *Scanning the Business Environment* (New York: Macmillan, 1967).

G. Copeman, *The Role of the Managing Director* (London: Business Publications, 1963).

R. Davis, *Performance and Development of Field Sales Managers* (Boston: Harvard Business School, 1957).

A. Grove, *High Output Management* (New York: Random House, 1983).

R. Guest, "Of Time and the Foreman," *Personnel* (May 1956): 478–486.

M. Maeterlinck, *The Life of the Bee* (New York: Dodd, Mead, 1918).

H. Mintzberg, *The Nature of Managerial Work* (New York: Harper & Row, 1973).

R. Neustadt, *Presidential Power: The Politics of Leadership* (New York: John Wiley, 1960).

A. Noël, "Strategic Cores and Magnificent Obsessions: Discovering Strategy Formation through Daily Activities of CEOs," *Strategic Management Journal 10* (1989): 33–49.

L. Sayles, *Managerial Behavior: Administration in Complex Organizations* (New York: McGraw-Hill, 1964).

L. Sayles, *The Working Leader* (New York: Free Press, 1993).

R. Simons, "The Role of Management Control Systems in Creating Competitive Advantage: New Perspectives," *Accounting, Organizations, and Society 15* (1990): 127–143.

R. Simons, "Strategic Orientation and Top Management Attention to Control Systems," *Strategic Management Journal 12* (1991): 49–62.

R. Stewart, *Managers and Their Jobs* (London: Macmillan, 1967).

K. Weick, *The Social Psychology of Organizing* (Reading, MA: Addison-Wesley, 1979).

MASTERING COMPETING VALUES: AN INTEGRATED APPROACH TO MANAGEMENT*

Robert E. Quinn

It was awful. Everything was always changing and nothing ever seemed to happen. The people above me would sit around forever and talk about things. The technically right answer didn't matter. They were always making what I thought were wrong decisions, and when I insisted on doing what was right, they got pissed off and would ignore what I was saying. Everything was suddenly political. They would worry about what everyone was going to think about every issue. How you looked, attending cocktail parties—that stuff to me was unreal and unimportant.

I went through five and a half terrible years. I occasionally thought I had reached my level of incompetence, but I refused to give up. In the end, the frustration and pain turned out to be a positive thing because it forced me to consider some alternative perspectives. I eventually learned that there were other realities besides the technical reality.

I discovered perception and long time lines. At higher levels what matters is how people see the world, and everyone sees it a little differently. Technical facts are not as available or as important. Things are changing more rapidly at higher levels, you are no longer buffered from the outside world. Things are more complex, and it takes longer to get people on board. I decided I had to be a lot more receptive and a lot more patient. It was an enormous adjustment, but then things started to change. I think I became a heck of a lot better manager.

THE CONCEPT OF MASTERY

If there is such a thing as a master of management, what is it that differentiates the master from others? The answer has to do with how the master of management sees the world.

Most of us learn to think of the concept of organization in a very static way. Particularly at the lower levels, organizations seem to be characterized by relatively stable, predictable patterns of action. They appear to be, or at least we expect them to be, the product of rational-deductive thinking. We think of them as static mechanisms designed to accomplish some single purpose.

One of the most difficult things for most of us to understand is that organizations are dynamic. Particularly as one moves up the organizational ladder, matters become less tangible and less predictable. A primary characteristic of managing, particularly at higher levels, is the confrontation of change, ambiguity, and contradiction. Managers spend much of their time living in fields of perceived tensions. They are constantly forced to make tradeoffs, and they often find that there are no right answers. The higher one goes in an organization, the more exaggerated this phenomenon becomes. One-dimensional bromides (care for people, work harder, get control, be innovative) are simply half-truths representing single domains of action. What exists in reality are contradictory pressures, emanating from a variety of domains. This fact is important because much of the time the choice is not between good and bad, but between one good and another or between two unpleasant alternatives. In such cases the need is for complex, intuitive decisions, and many people fail to cope successfully with the resulting tension, stress, and uncertainty. This is well illustrated by the initial failure and frustration of the engineer who was quoted earlier.

The people who come to be masters of management do not see their work environment only in structured, analytic ways. Instead, they also have the capacity to see it as a complex, dynamic system

---

*Adapted from *Beyond Rational Management* (San Francisco: Jossey-Bass, Inc., 1988). With permission of author and publisher.

that is constantly evolving. In order to interact effectively with it, they employ a variety of different perspectives or frames. As one set of conditions arises, they focus on certain cues that lead them to apply a very analytic and structured approach. As these cues fade, they focus on new cues of emerging importance and apply another frame, perhaps this time an intuitive and flexible one. At another time they may emphasize the overall task, and at still another they may focus on the welfare of a single individual.

Because of these shifts, masters of management may appear to act in paradoxical ways. They engage the contradictions of organizational life by using paradoxical frames. Viewed from a single point in time, their behaviors may seem illogical and contradictory. Yet these seeming contradictions come together in a fluid whole. Things work out well for these people.

The ability to see the world in a dynamic fashion does not come naturally. It requires a dramatic change in outlook, a redefinition of one's world view. It means transcending the rules of mechanistic logic used for solving well-defined problems and adopting a more comprehensive and flexible kind of logic. It is a logic that comes from experience rather than from textbooks. It requires a change not unlike a religious conversion.

THE EVOLUTION OF MASTERY

Dreyfus, Dreyfus, and Athanasion (1986) provide a five-stage model that describes the evolution from novice to expert.

In the novice stage people learn facts and rules. The rules are learned as absolutes that are never to be violated. For example, in playing chess people learn the names of the pieces, how they are moved, and their value. They are told to exchange pieces of lower value for pieces of higher value. In management, this might be the equivalent of the classroom education of an M.B.A.

In the advanced beginner stage, experience becomes critical. Performance improves somewhat as real situations are encountered. Understanding begins to exceed the stated facts and rules. Observation of certain basic patterns leads to the recognition of factors that were not set forth in the rules. A chess player, for example, begins to recognize certain basic board positions that should be pursued. The M.B.A. discovers the basic norms, values, and culture of the workplace on the first job.

The third stage is competence. Here the individual has begun to appreciate the complexity of the task and now recognizes a much larger set of cues. The person develops the ability to select and concentrate on the most important cues. With this ability competence grows. Here the reliance on absolute rules begins to disappear. People take calculated risks and engage in complex trade-offs. A chess player may, for example, weaken board position in order to attack the opposing king. This plan may or may not follow any rules that the person was ever taught. The M.B.A. may go beyond the technical analysis taught in graduate school as he or she experiments with an innovation of some sort. Flow or excellence may even be experienced in certain specific domains or subareas of management, as in the case of the engineer at the beginning of the article who displayed technical brilliance.

In the proficiency stage, calculation and rational analysis seem to disappear and unconscious, fluid, and effortless performance begins to emerge. Here no one plan is held sacred. The person learns to unconsciously "read" the evolving situation. Cues are noticed and responded to, and attention shifts to new cues as the importance of the old ones recedes. New plans are triggered as emerging patterns call to mind plans that worked previously. Here there is a holistic and intuitive grasp of the situation. Here we are talking, for example, about the top 1 percent of all chess players, the people with the ability to intuitively recognize and respond to change in board positions. Here the M.B.A. has become an effective, upper-level manager, capable of meeting a wide variety of demands and contradictions.

Experts, those at the fifth stage, do what comes naturally. They do not apply rules but use holistic recognition in a way that allows them to deeply understand the situation. They have maps of the territory programmed into their heads that the rest of us are not aware of. They see and know things intuitively that the rest of us do not know or see (many dimensions). They frame and reframe strategies as they read changing cues (action inquiry). Here the manager has fully transcended personal style. The master manager seems to meet the contradictions of organizational life effortlessly.

THE NEED FOR MORE COMPLEX THEORY

In their popular book, *In Search of Excellence*, Peters and Waterman (1982) seek to discover what differentiates excellent companies from ordinary ones. Embedded in their work is an observation that is quite consistent with our observations. They conclude that managers in excellent companies have an unusual ability to resolve paradox, to translate conflicts and tensions into excitement, high commitment, and superior performance. In reviewing the book, Van de Ven (1983) applauds this insight and notes a grave inadequacy in the theories generated by administrative researchers. He argues that while the managers of excellent companies seem to have a capacity for dealing with paradox, administrative theories are not designed to take this phenomenon into account. In order to be internally consistent, theorists tend to eliminate contradiction. Hence, there is a need for a dynamic theory that can handle both stability and change, that can consider the tensions and conflicts inherent in human systems. Among other things, the theory would view people as complex actors in tension-filled social systems, constantly interacting with a "fast-paced, ever-changing array of forces" (Van de Ven, 1983, p. 624). The theory would center on transforming leadership that focuses on "the ethics and value judgments that are implied when leaders and followers raise one another to higher levels of motivation and morality" (Van de Ven, p. 624).

For most of us, discovering the contradictory nature of organizing is not easy. We have biases in how we process information, and we prefer to live in certain kinds of settings. Our biases are further influenced by our organizational experience at both the functional and cultural levels. At the functional level, for example, accountants and marketing people tend to develop very different assumptions about what is "good." At the cultural level, there is often a set of values that conveys "how we do things around here." Because these values tend to be so powerful, it is very difficult to see past them. It is difficult to recognize that there are weaknesses in our own perspective and advantages in opposing perspectives. It is particularly difficult to realize that these various perspectives must be understood, juxtaposed, and blended in a delicate, complex, and dynamic way. It is much more natural to see them as either/or positions in which one must triumph over the other.

A COMPETING VALUES MODEL

In the late seventies and early eighties, many of my colleagues and I became interested in the issue of organizational effectiveness. We were asking the question, What are the characteristics of effective organizations? Many studies were done in which people set out to measure the characteristics of organizations. These measures were then submitted to a technique called factor analysis. It produced lists of variables that characterized effective organizations. The problem was that these variables differed from one study to another. It seemed that the more we learned, the less we knew.

My colleague, John Rohrbaugh, and I therefore tried to reframe the question. Instead of asking what effective organizations looked like, we decided to ask how experts think about effective organizations. This would allow us to get to the assumptions behind the studies and perhaps make sense of what was causing the confusion. In a series of studies (Quinn and Rohrbaugh, 1983), we had organizational theorists and researchers make judgments regarding the similarity or dissimilarity between pairs of effectiveness criteria. The data were analyzed using a technique called multidimensional scaling. Results of the analyses suggested that organizational theorists and researchers share an implicit theoretical framework, or cognitive map (Figure 1).

Note that the two axes in the figure create four quadrants. The vertical axis ranges from flexibility to control, the horizontal axis ranges from an internal to an external focus. Each quadrant of the

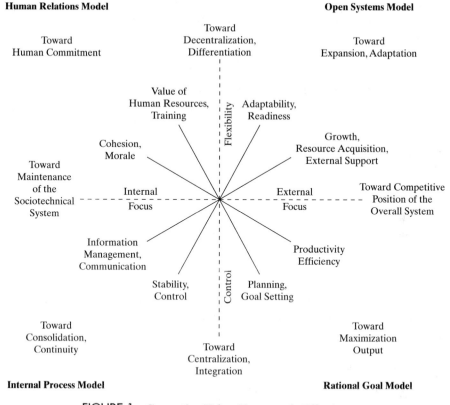

FIGURE 1   Competing Values Framework: Effectiveness

framework represents one of the four major models in organizational theory. The human relations model, for example, stresses criteria such as those in the upper-left quadrant: cohesion and morale, along with human resource development. The open systems model stresses criteria such as those in the upper-right quadrant. These include flexibility and readiness as well as growth, resource acquisition, and external support. The rational goal model stresses the kind of criteria found in the lower-right quadrant, including planning and goal setting and productivity and efficiency. The internal process model is represented in the lower-left quadrant. It stresses information management and communication, along with stability and control.

Each model has a polar opposite. The human relations model, which emphasizes flexibility and internal focus, stands in stark contrast to the rational goal model, which stresses control and external focus. The open systems model, which is characterized by flexibility and external focus, runs counter to the internal process model, which emphasizes control and internal focus. Parallels among the models are also important. The human relations and open systems models share an emphasis on flexibility. The open systems and rational goal models have an external focus (responding to outside change and producing in a competitive market). The rational goal and internal process models are rooted in the value of control. Finally, the internal process and human relations models share an internal focus (concern for the human and technical systems inside the organization).

Each model suggests a mode or type of organizing. The two sets of criteria in each quadrant also suggest an implicit means-ends theory that is associated with each mode. Thus, the rational goal model suggests that an organization is a rational economic firm. Here planning and goal setting are viewed as a means of achieving productivity and efficiency. In the open systems model we find the adhocracy, where adaptability and readiness are viewed as a means to growth, resource acquisition, and external support. In the internal process model is the hierarchy, where information management and communication are viewed as a means of arriving at stability and control. In the human relations quadrant we find the team. Here cohesion and morale are viewed as a means of increasing the value of human resources.

This scheme is called the competing values framework because the criteria seem to initially carry a conflictual message. We want our organizations to be adaptable and flexible, but we also want them to be stable and controlled. We want growth, resource acquisition, and external support, but we also want tight information management and formal communication. We want an emphasis on the value of human resources, but we also want an emphasis on planning and goal setting. The model does not suggest that these oppositions cannot mutually exist in a real system. It suggests, rather, that these criteria, values, and assumptions are oppositions in our minds. We tend to think that they are very different from one another, and we sometimes assume them to be mutually exclusive. In order to illustrate this point we will consider how values manifest themselves and, in so doing, consider some applied examples.

HOW VALUES MANIFEST THEMSELVES

In recent years much has been written about culture in organizations. When we think of the manifestation of values in organizations, it is their cultures that we are thinking of. Simply put, culture is the set of values and assumptions that underlie the statement, "This is how we do things around here." Culture at the organizational level, like information processing at the individual level, tends to take on moral overtones. While cultures tend to vary dramatically, they share the common characteristic of providing integration of effort in one direction while often sealing off the possibility of moving in another direction. An illustration may be helpful.

In October 1980 *Business Week* ran an article contrasting the cultures at JCPenney and PepsiCo. At Penney's the culture focuses on the values of fairness and long-term loyalty. Indeed, a manager was once chewed out by the president of the company for making too much money! To do so was unfair to the customers, and at Penney's one must never take advantage of the customer. Customers are free to return merchandise with which they are not satisfied. Suppliers know that they can establish stable, long-term relationships with Penney's. Employees know that if their ability to perform a given job begins to deteriorate, they will not find themselves out on the street; rather, an appropriate alternative position will be found for them.

The core of the company's culture is captured in "The Penney Idea." Although it was adopted in 1913, it is a very modern-sounding statement, consisting of seven points:

> *To serve the public, as nearly as we can, to its complete satisfaction; to expect for the service we render a fair remuneration and not all the profit the traffic will bear; to do all in our power to pack the customer's dollar full of value, quality, and satisfaction; to continue to train ourselves and our associates so that the service we give will be more and more intelligently performed; to improve constantly the human factor in our business; to reward men and women in our organization through participation in what the business produces; to test our every policy, method, and act in this wise: 'Does it square with what is right and just?'*

The culture at PepsiCo is in stark contrast to that at Penney's. After years as a sleepy company that took the back seat to Coca-Cola, PepsiCo underwent a major change by adopting a much more competitive culture. This new culture was manifest both externally and internally. On the outside PepsiCo directly confronted Coca-Cola. In bold ads customers were asked to taste and compare the products of the two companies. Internally, managers knew that their jobs were on the line and that they had to produce results. There was continuous pressure to show improvement in market share, product volume, and profits. Jobs were won or lost over a "tenth of a point" difference in these areas.

Staffs were kept small. Managers were constantly moved from job to job and expected to work long hours. The pressure never let up. During a blizzard, for example, the chief executive officer found a snowmobile and drove it to work. (This story is told regularly at PepsiCo.) Competitive team and individual sports are emphasized, and people are expected to stay in shape. The overall climate is reflected in the often repeated phrase, "We are the marines not the army."

The differences between these two companies could hardly be greater. Reading this account, you have probably concluded that one culture is more attractive than the other, and you would expect others to agree with your choice. But it is very likely that if you visited PepsiCo and spoke of "The Penney Idea," you would be laughed at. If you tried to press it upon PepsiCo employees, they would probably become incensed. Likewise, if you visited Penney's and described or tried to press upon them the values of PepsiCo, they would have the same reaction. You would be violating sacred assumptions.

Interestingly, the major problem at PepsiCo was seen as the absence of loyalty. Coca-Cola's response to the PepsiCo attack, for example, was to hire away some of PepsiCo's best "Tigers," and they were, because of the constant pressure, willing to go. (PepsiCo's rate of tenure is less than one-third of the rate at Penney's.) And what, according to *Business Week*, was the major problem at Penney's? Lack of competitiveness. Despite a reputation as one of the best places to work, and despite intense employee and customer loyalty, Penney's had been rapidly losing market share to K-Mart. Some critics expressed doubt that Penney's could respond to the challenge.

What is happening here? The surface conclusion is that two opposite cultures exist. Penney's reflects the human relations model in that the company seems to resemble a team, clan, or family. PepsiCo reflects the rational goal model in that it appears to be an instrumental firm. The strength of one is the weakness of the other. While this conclusion is true, there is a deeper insight to be gained. I will later return to this interesting contrast after considering the transformation of values.

INEFFECTIVENESS

The competing values framework consists of juxtaposed sets of organizational effectiveness criteria. Each of these "good" criteria can become overvalued by an individual and pursued in an unidimensional fashion. When this zealous pursuit of a single set of criteria takes place, a strange inversion can result. Good things can mysteriously become bad things. In Figure 2, I show how criteria of effectiveness, when pursued blindly, become criteria of ineffectiveness. These latter criteria are depicted in the negative zone on the outside of the diagram.

The structure of this model parallels the competing values framework of effectiveness. The axes, however, are negatively, rather than positively, labeled. Thus, the vertical dimension ranges from chaos (too much flexibility and spontaneity) to rigidity (too much order and predictability). The horizontal dimension ranges from belligerence and hostility (too much external focus and too much emphasis on competition and engagement) to apathy and indifference (too much internal focus and too much emphasis on maintenance and coordination within the system). Each quadrant represents a negative culture with negative effectiveness criteria. Embedded within these quadrants are eight criteria of ineffectiveness.

In the upper-left quadrant is the irresponsible country club. In this quadrant, human relations criteria are emphasized to the point of encouraging laxity and negligence. Discussion and participation, good in themselves, are carried to inappropriate lengths. Commitment, morale, and human development turn into extreme permissiveness and uncontrolled individualism. Here, administrators are concerned only with employees, to the exclusion of the task.

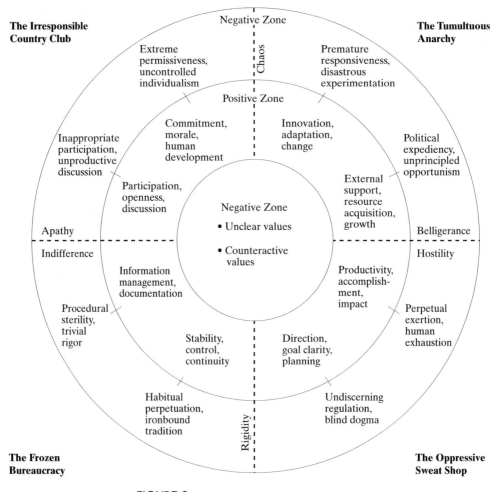

FIGURE 2   **The Positive and Negative Zones**

   In the upper-right quadrant is the tumultuous anarchy. In this quadrant, there is so much emphasis on the open systems criteria of effectiveness that disruption and discontinuity result. Emphasis on insight, innovation, and change turn into premature responsiveness and disastrous experimentation. Concern for external support, resource acquisition, and growth turn into political expediency and unprincipled opportunism. Here, administrators are concerned only with having a competitive advantage and show no interest in continuity and control of the work flow.

   In the lower-right quadrant is the oppressive sweatshop. In this quadrant, there is too much emphasis on the criteria of effectiveness associated with the rational goal model. Effort, productivity, and emphasis on profit or impact of service turn into perpetual exertion and human exhaustion. Here, we see symptoms of burnout. Concern for goal clarification, authority, and decisiveness turn into an emphasis on strict regulation and blind dogma. There is no room for individual differences; the boss has the final say.

   Finally, in the lower-left quadrant is the frozen bureaucracy. Here, there is too much concern with internal processes. The organization becomes atrophied as a result of excessive measurement and documentation; it becomes a system of red tape. Control measures, documentation, and computation turn into procedural sterility and trivial rigor. Everything is "by the book." The emphasis on stability, control, and continuity lead to the blind perpetuation of habits and traditions. Procedures are followed because "we've always done it this way"; there is no room for trying something new.

STRENGTH BECOMING WEAKNESS

Let us return to PepsiCo and JCPenney. Earlier I said that introducing the culture of one company into the other would be highly conflictual. Further, I pointed out that each culture had weaknesses. Now we can see that their very strengths put them at risk.

Because of the inability of the PepsiCo culture to tolerate the values in the human relations quadrant, the company is in danger of moving into the negative zone on the right side of Figure 2. Because of the inability of the JCPenney culture to more fully absorb the values on the right side of the figure, the company is in danger of moving into the negative zone on the left side of the figure. The more fully that each company pushes a particular set of positive values, without tending to the opposite positive values, the greater the danger to it.

The major point here is that everything in the two outer circles is related. The more that success is pursued around one set of positive values, the greater will be the pressure to take into account the opposite positive values. If these other values are ignored long enough, crisis and catastrophe will result.

STAYING IN THE POSITIVE ZONE: MASTERING PARADOX

Staying in the positive zone requires high levels of complex thought. Consider, for example, the stereotypical entrepreneur, like Steve Jobs of Apple Computer. Entrepreneurs are typically very creative and action oriented. They are usually not very sympathetic to the values in the hierarchy quadrant. When they build a new organization they often try to avoid hierarchy. Unfortunately, if their initial vision is successful, and their new company expands rapidly, the growth (an indicator of success) stimulates a need for hierarchical coordinating mechanisms (often seen as an indication of failure). This phenomenon is often called the formalization crisis. Many successful entrepreneurs are forced, like Steve Jobs at one point, to leave their company because they cannot comprehend the paradox or manage the competing values. For this reason, it is instructive to consider Bill Gates of Microsoft.

Microsoft is one of the largest software companies in the world. Run by Bill Gates, Microsoft has been best known for its widely used MS DOS system. But in 1987 Gates was successful in convincing IBM to adopt its newest product, called Windows, for use in IBM's new line of personal computers. Upon completion of the agreement analysts began to predict that within 12 months Microsoft would become the largest software company in the world.

In many ways, Gates is the stereotypical entrepreneur. He is a technical genius with a burning mission. He feels a drive to bring the power of computing to the masses. His company is marked by considerable flexibility and excitement. The median age of the workforce is 31. People work long days, with Gates himself setting the example with an early morning to midnight routine. There are frequent picnics, programmers set their own hours, dress is casual, and the turnover rate is less than 10 percent.

The company has grown rapidly. From 1980 to 1981, Gates watched his company go from 80 to 125 employees and saw profits double to $16 million. Given our earlier cases, all these indicators would lead us to worry about Gates and his ability to meet the demands for formalization.

In fact, however, Gates has already faced the formalization crisis and has come off well. What were the keys to this success? First, he made a very significant decision to bring in professional managers and to focus his own energies on technology. He seemed to grasp an important paradox that eludes most entrepreneurs: to have power means one must give up power. Maintaining a primary focus on technology, however, does not mean that he has abandoned the tasks of leadership. Instead, he has taken the time to learn the principles of law, marketing, distribution, and accounting and apply them to his work. He also has the paradoxical capacity of simultaneously caring and being tough. For example, dissatisfied with the performance of Microsoft's president, Gates removed him from office after only one year. But not long after, Gates was invited to be the best man at the wedding of the former president.

Perhaps the best summary of Gates and his abilities comes from one of his colleagues: "Bill Gates is very good at evaluating situations as they change." This, of course, is a key characteristic for staying in the positive zone.

Figure 2 has some important implications for management. It suggests that managers need to stay in the positive zone, that is, they need to pursue the seemingly "competing" positive values in the middle circle while also being careful to stay out of the external negative zone. They must maintain a dynamic, creative tension. Over time they must, like Bill Gates, be able to frame and reframe, that is, to move from one set of competing values to another.

SOME IMPLICATIONS FOR MANAGEMENT

The notions of mastery and competing values suggest a more complex and dynamic approach to management. The novice-like "rules" taught in the textbooks are misleading in that they usually represent only one of the competing perspectives or polarities embedded in organizational life. Theory X is not inherently better than theory Y. Change is not inherently better than the status quo. Productivity is not inherently better than cohesion and morale.

The challenge for experienced managers is threefold: the first is far more difficult than it sounds, to recognize and appreciate the positive (and the negative) aspects of all areas of the competing values framework; second, to assess and work on the roles and skills associated with each area; third, to analyze the present organizational moment, with all its dilemmas, and trust one's ability to integrate and employ the skills appropriate to that moment. Together these three steps are key points in the process of mastering management.

NOTES

H. Dreyfus, S. Dreyfus, and T. Athanasion, *Mind Over Machine: The Power of Human Intuition and Expertise in the Era of the Computer* (New York: Free Press, 1986).

R. Quinn and J. Rohrbaugh, "A Spatial Model of Effectiveness Criteria: Towards a Competing Values Approach to Organizational Analysis," *Management Science 39*, no. 3 (1983): 363–377.

T. Peters and R. Waterman Jr., *In Search of Excellence* (New York: Harper & Row, 1982).

A. Van de Ven, "In Search of Excellence: Lessons from America's Best Run Companies," *Administrative Science Quarterly 28*, no. 4 (1993): 621–624.

Chapter 3

Individual and Organizational Learning

LEARNING FROM EXPERIENCE THROUGH REFLECTION
Marilyn Wood Daudelin

THE LEADER'S NEW WORK: BUILDING LEARNING ORGANIZATIONS
Peter M. Senge

There are two links between the concept of mental maps and learning. One concerns different learning styles among individuals. According to David Kolb, the learning process consists of four stages: concrete experiences, reflective observation, abstract conceptualization, and active experimentation. People tend to emphasize certain stages, resulting in a typical approach toward learning.

Marilyn Wood Daudelin, a consultant and former Polaroid employee, focuses on the stage of the learning cycle that, historically, has been least emphasized in the business world. In "Learning from Experience Through Reflection," Daudelin describes the growing importance of reflection in corporations. She describes a process of reflection, similar to Kolb's learning cycle, and explains how it can be used effectively in the workplace.

The ability to learn from experience, both on the individual and the organizational level, is a key skill in a quickly changing business environment. The second article in this chapter, "The Leader's New Work: Building Learning Organizations" by Peter Senge, is a classic article on organizational learning. Senge, a former engineer who is the leading proponent of learning organizations, argues that companies have to surface and examine their mental maps—the assumptions on which decisions are based—in order to learn and survive. In addition to practical suggestions about the skills and tools needed in learning organizations, Senge provides us with yet another theory of management—the role of the leader in learning organizations.

LEARNING FROM EXPERIENCE THROUGH REFLECTION*

Marilyn Wood Daudelin

The forces affecting business environments change rapidly, frequently, and unpredictably. Gone are the days when managers could predict the future and prepare themselves to meet its demands with relatively stable, five-year plans. Instead, they find themselves imagining three or four possible future scenarios, then developing action plans that can be modified in response to impossible-to-predict technological or social changes.

How do managers prepare themselves to survive, let alone be successful, in such an environment?

---

* Excerpted with permission from *Organizational Dynamics 24*, no. 3 (Winter 1996): 36–48.

The more traditional avenues of development—MBA degrees, executive education programs, and management workshops and seminars—face the same turbulence. The designers of these educational experiences do their best to predict the kinds of knowledge, skills, and attitudes that will be most helpful. Yet there is an inherent game of "catch up" within this system. By the time these designers understand existing issues and trends, develop cases, write texts, and create workshop designs, a new wave of business challenges appears.

Without question, we need a more adaptable, responsive system of helping managers learn.

Recent studies have shown that the day-to-day experiences of managers as they confront challenges and problems on the job are rich sources of learning—perhaps more appropriate "classrooms" than the traditional venues described above. Consider, for example, recent research conducted by the Center for Creative Leadership in Greensboro, North Carolina. By studying 616 descriptions of experiences that 191 successful executives claimed made a lasting developmental difference, researchers were able to identify 16 types of experiences or "key events" that are critical to the development of specific managerial competencies.

UNCOVERING HIDDEN LEARNING POTENTIAL

The Center for Creative Leadership study recognizes the immense learning potential hidden in everyday experience. But such recognition is not enough. Managers need support in these efforts to make sense out of their developmental experiences. The word "experience" derives from the Latin word *experientia*, meaning trial, proof, or experiment. Thus challenging work experiences may be described as trial-and-error experiments that produce learning. Viewed this way, what is needed is a process of analysis that explores causes, develops and tests hypotheses, and eventually produces new knowledge.

Rather than creating a new system—with the danger of adding one more fad to those that surface repeatedly in management practice—we turn to a process that has roots as deep as the ancient Greek philosophers: the process of reflection.

Using Reflection to Learn from Experience

Reflection is a natural and familiar process. In school, we wrote papers, answered questions, engaged in classroom discussions, and analyzed cases, all as ways to develop new insights. In the business world, we analyze experiences and summarize our learning in reports, performance review sessions, and problem-solving processes. In our personal lives, we discuss troubling situations with friends, spouses, counselors, or support groups. Reflection occurs in less formal ways as well. We may have experienced breakthroughs while jogging, showering, or mowing the lawn.

Reflection as a way of learning has ancient roots. Socrates may have been one of the first to use this process as he tried to discover the nature of goodness by asking questions of others. He constantly challenged the statements and beliefs of his students, including Plato, whose work developed as a consequence of Socrates' training in how to reflect. Other early proponents of reflection as a way of learning include Sophocles, who declared that one learns by observing what one does time and time again, and John Locke, who believed that knowing is purely a function of thoughtful reaction to experience.

If the process of reflection is so natural and familiar, what keeps organizations from embracing formal reflective practices as a way to encourage learning? One explanation is that managers have always placed a higher value on action than reflection. Twenty years ago, Henry Mintzberg wrote in the *Harvard Business Review*, "Study after study has shown that managers work at an unrelenting pace, that their activities are characterized by brevity, variety, and discontinuity, and that they are strongly oriented to action and dislike reflective activities." More recently, Rosabeth Moss Kanter identified short-term managerial incentives and demands as forces working against managers' ability to pause and reflect.

RECOGNIZING EXISTING REFLECTION PRACTICES

In spite of these tendencies to resist reflection, evidence exists that it is becoming a part of the lifeblood of organizations today. Many of the tools taught and practiced in total quality management programs, for example, are actually processes of reflection. They allow individuals to call a halt, at least briefly, to the frantic pace of action and engage in processes that permit individuals to reflect upon important areas such as customer needs, root causes of problems, and dysfunctional work-flow patterns. In many companies, the improvements and innovations resulting from these processes have had a direct and powerful effect on both company profits and employee satisfaction.

Also, the trend toward greater employee involvement in corporate decision making has changed the relationship between leaders and followers in corporations. As the values of empowerment and participation increasingly appear in corporate vision and mission statements, the manager's role has shifted from that of charismatic leader (a person who has all the answers) to that of coach—a person who works with employees to help them discover the answers. This shift occurs when managers use reflective approaches to running the business: When they ask challenging questions from a position of mutual discovery; when they provide the time and the structure to reflect upon challenging work situations, both individually and collectively; and when they are open to and supportive of ideas that emerge from these processes.

Finally, the trend toward greater accountability to external shareholders, to boards of directors, and, most recently, to employee-owners for corporate performance has led to a new examination of the age-old method of planning and evaluating *individual* performance: the performance appraisal process.

This examination has, in turn, led to new techniques such as 360 degree feedback (soliciting data on strengths and weaknesses from immediate managers, peers, and direct reports) and customer input processes (collecting performance feedback from internal and external customers). These new practices place more emphasis on the need to reflect on prior performance over the course of a year, or longer. The skills applied in that reflection may then be used to plan for improvements in the following year's performance.

These two key elements of performance management—evaluation and planning—represent two important conditions for learning from experience: developing insights from past events and applying them to future actions.

Thus, as managers use quality improvement tools, as they empower others to participate in decision making, and as they develop procedures to measure performance, they have the opportunity to engage more actively in reflection. Taking the time to formally reflect during these processes is the key to whether the processes become mechanisms to unearth new and important meaning or simply the latest in a series of new management gimmicks.

THE NEED FOR MORE FORMAL REFLECTIVE PRACTICES

Even though reflection has been an important part of traditional educational experiences since ancient times, its power is just beginning to be harnessed as a deliberate tool of managerial learning. A recent *Fortune* article titled "Leaders Learn to Heed the Voice Within" reports that companies such as AT&T, PepsiCo, and Aetna are developing ways to introduce more introspection into their management development programs. In addition, Exxon, Motorola, General Motors, and Hewlett-Packard are just a few of the companies that are using a system called Action-Reflection Learning (ARL) to explore and find answers to important business problems.

These efforts signal an increased interest in using this powerful tool in corporate decision making. What is now needed is (a) an understanding of the core processes that make up reflection, (b) an understanding of which of these processes are most likely to promote learning from work experiences, and (c) a set of tools to help managers use reflection as a way of learning. The rest of this article addresses itself to these three needs.

THE NATURE OF REFLECTION

Reflection is a highly personal cognitive process. When a person engages in reflection, he or she takes an experience from the outside world, brings it inside the mind, turns it over, makes connections to other experiences, and filters it through personal biases. If this process results in learning, the individual then develops inferences to approach the external world in a way that is different from the approach that would have been used, had reflection not occurred. While the catalyst for the reflection is external, and while others may help in the process by listening, asking questions, or offering advice, the reflection occurs within the mental self.

Reflection and learning may therefore be defined in this context as follows: Reflection is the process of stepping back from an experience to ponder, carefully and persistently, its meaning to the self through the development of inferences; learning is the creation of meaning from past or current events that serves as a guide for future behavior.

Like many other cognitive activities, reflection is often spontaneous, and, at times, outside an individual's awareness. In fact, the "sorting through" nature of the reflection process is most efficient while we sleep. In his book *Sleep*, J. Allan Hobson, professor of psychiatry at Harvard Medical School and the director of the Laboratory of Neurophysiology at the Massachusetts Mental Health Center, explains that sleep reduces the level of incoming sensory data and allows for the reorganization and efficient storage of information already in the brain, thus better preparing us to handle the demands of our waking hours.

The same sort of spontaneous sorting through of existing information occurs during certain mindless, rhythmic physical activities like jogging, swimming laps, or mowing the lawn; or during habitual routines that no longer need the conscious brain's full attention, such as showering or commuting on the same route each day. Just as it does during sleep, this spontaneous process of reflection allows one to momentarily suspend the intense flow of new information to the brain. This enhances the processing of existing information, thereby better preparing the person to handle the demands of the rapidly changing environment.

THE STAGES IN THE REFLECTION PROCESS

Spontaneous reflection is often stimulated by the nagging, unresolved problems or challenges that are a normal part of any manager's job. Reflection then progresses through four distinct stages: (a) articulation of a problem, (b) analysis of that problem, (c) formulation and testing of a tentative theory to explain the problem, and (d) action (or deciding whether to act).

JOGGING FOR ANSWERS

- *Joe lifts his foot onto the concrete wall bordering the stairs leading from his office building. As he reties the lace on one of his new Nikes, he thinks again how glad he is that the renovation of this building included a shower and locker room in the basement. It was just the incentive he needed to introduce some much-needed exercise into the frantic pace of his work week.*

  He crosses the busy two-lane highway, turns left onto the jogging path he discovered along the river, and settles into a comfortable pace and rhythm. The first person he passes raises a hand in hello, and Joe thinks how much this fellow jogger looks like one of his employees, Hector. His mind turns to the performance review discussion he had with Hector earlier this week.

- *Although the review resulted in a fairly positive description of how Hector performed against the defined goals and objectives, it was an uncomfortable session. Joe has been perplexed*

---

about the source of the discomfort ever since. He resolves to get at the heart of this before his next three reviews—all with employees who have not been performing as well as Hector.

"What exactly is the problem here?" Joe wonders. It isn't the result: Joe completed the task in a timely manner, and the evaluation was fair, as evidenced by Hector's willingness to sign the acknowledgment at the bottom of the form.

- *Suddenly he remembers comments made at his own performance review last year. Joe's boss, Sally, was trying to express a concern she had regarding the way he managed his people. She felt he did not include them in the decisions that affected them. Maybe this is an example of what Sally meant.*

  As Joe thinks about what transpired from the time Hector entered his office to the time he signed the bottom of the form, he doesn't remember Hector saying very much. Joe suddenly realizes that his desire to do a good job led him to such a thorough and carefully presented analysis of Hector's strengths and weaknesses that there was little time or opportunity left for Hector's contribution.

- *Joe catches sight of the big steeple clock across the river, and realizes he must head back or he will be late for his project review meeting with Sally. While showering and changing, he resolves to take a few minutes of his upcoming meeting to tell Sally about this insight and enlist her help in working on the issue.*

Let's explore these four stages by considering the hypothetical example in the box, above.

The first stage of reflection, articulation of a problem, defines the issue that the mind will work on during the process of reflection. It is often preceded by what John Dewey calls "a state of doubt, hesitancy, perplexity, or mental difficulty." The clear articulation of a problem is often an insight in itself, and rewarding to the manager who has struggled to identify a vague sense of discomfort or dissatisfaction.

In our hypothetical example, Joe enters this first stage as he realizes what the problem is *not*. It is not the product of the review, which both he and Hector judged to be fair. It is not the completion of the task, which was timely. It is, in this case, some still-to-be-discovered element of the performance review process that caused a less-than-satisfactory feeling. Joe's process of problem articulation is a result of discarding possibilities and is based on what he defines as a negative situation. Others may find themselves in situations where they must discover what went right during a very positive experience, perhaps for the purpose of summarizing their learning in a report, coaching others, or relating past successes to similar but more challenging experiences. In either cases, clarifying the problem or challenge sets the stage for the next step in the process.

The second step, analysis of the problem, consists of a search for possibilities: in Joe's case, possible reasons for the problem as he has defined it. To quote Dewey once again, analysis is "an act of searching, hunting, or inquiring to find material that will resolve the doubt, and settle or dispose of the perplexity." It may involve asking and answering a series of questions about the situation, put forth by oneself or others. It may consist of searching the memory for similar situations or imagining how someone else might handle the same issue. It involves reviewing past behavior with intensity, as though under a microscope.

When Joe decided to review the hour-long performance discussion from the moment Hector entered the room, he was searching for important clues—ideas that were perhaps stored in the mind but still out of his conscious reach. During this stage, it is important to be ready to grasp elusive but potentially relevant thoughts that may enter the consciousness. In Joe's case, Sally's words from his own performance review came to mind. When he applied them to the current situation, he came up with a tentative hypothesis.

This generation of a hypothesis that addresses the problem is the first part of stage three of the re-flection process: formulation and testing of a tentative theory to solve the problem. The tentative the-ory that Joe developed in stage three is the following: his desire to do a good job led him to such a thorough and well-presented analysis of Hector's strengths and weaknesses that there was little time or opportunity left for Hector's contribution. After testing this possibility against the comments he had received from Sally in the past, it seemed to be a sound theory.

Stage four, action (or deciding whether to act) brings closure to the cycle and is the final "test" of the hypothesis. It is only through this last stage that true learning occurs. Learning, as defined earlier, is the creation of meaning from past or current events that serves as a guide for future behavior. Thus, this final stage involves the articulation of a new way of acting in the future. Even though Joe has been engaged in the process of reflection (stepping back from an experience to carefully and persistently ponder its meaning to the self through the development of inferences) since the beginning of his run, he has not yet truly learned.

We leave him at the end of stage three. Hopefully, as a result of his discussion with Sally, he will be able to develop an action plan that will guide his future behavior in performance reviews. This four-stage reflection process can be applied repeatedly to the many problems or challenges that arise in challenging work situations.

THE POWER OF QUESTIONS

One of the techniques for increasing the learning power of reflection is the posing and answering of questions. School systems have long recognized the power of questioning as a tool for reflection and learning. Questions form the basis of class discussions; they become topics for papers; they stimulate debates; they guide case analyses; and, when used in quizzes and tests, reinforce learning. Counselors and therapists use provocative questions to guide clients through the discovery process. And the best managers in corporations realize that posing thoughtful questions is often a better way to gain com-mitment than providing concise answers.

The types of questions that are most effective in enhancing reflection vary depending on the stage of reflection.

During problem articulation, "what" questions allow one to fully describe the situation: "What oc-curred?" "What did you see, think, feel?" "What was the most important thing?" These questions are use-ful in arriving at a thorough understanding of the problem to be solved or the challenge to be addressed.

In the problem analysis stage, "why" questions are most helpful: "Why was that important?" "Why do you think it happened?" "Why were you feeling that way?"

During hypothesis generation, "how" questions allow an individual to begin to formulate a tenta-tive theory to explain or address the problem: "How is this situation similar and different from other problems?" "How might you do things differently?"

Finally, during the action stage, "what" questions become important once again: "What are the im-plications of all this for future action?" "What should you do now?"

The most useful questions are rarely profound yet often produce powerful results. A simple "what else?" can open the mind to a myriad of possibilities previously untapped. The age-old one-word ques-tion "why?" has guided scientists and philosophers to discoveries and insights that have changed our world. Introducing an intervention with the question "may I?" performs the powerful functions of in-dicating respect, ascertaining readiness, and lowering defensive barriers.

Questions are thus one of the most basic and powerful elements of the reflection experience. They are used in the process of learning from challenging work situations in three ways: to open up possi-bilities, to clarify meaning, and to structure the progression through the four stages.

ALONE OR WITH OTHERS?

Individuals differ in the way they think about and make sense out of their challenges in life. One of these individual differences is whether one tends to reflect alone or with others. In the hypothetical case presented earlier, Joe is an introverted thinker who tends to work out problems by thinking about them on his own. He eventually recognized the need to get help from his boss, but it was not the first and most natural way for him to tackle a challenging situation. Others may do their best thinking out loud, bouncing ideas off trusted colleagues or friends. The box, below, lists a variety of examples of reflection in both categories.

In the case of reflecting alone, a major distinction is whether or not writing is involved. The ability to write out reflections (and the propensity to do so) varies greatly with individuals. In those cases where one is comfortable with the tool, writing can be a powerful vehicle to produce insights during the reflection process.

Reflection with others may be with one other person or in small groups. When only one other person is involved, that person often takes on a helper role. In the world of work, individuals often discuss challenging situations or problems with those who have greater experience (immediate managers, mentors) or with those who are helpful facilitators (career counselors, employee advocates, human resource professionals, organizational development consultants). Outside of work, people turn to clergy, therapists, astrologers, friends, parents, or spouses when they need to think through challenging situations.

When reflection takes place in a small group, ideas are generated by the sharing of different perspectives. For example, self-help support groups that unite people who face similar challenges assist participants in discovering important information about themselves. Although the total discussion time each individual has in these settings is less than in coaching discussions, the total reflection time is no less. While one person is sharing his or her experience, the others are relating the information to their own challenges. Thus, whether conducted alone or with others, reflection occurs and learning results if the four-stage process of problem articulation, problem analysis, theory formulation, and action planning takes place.[1]

EXAMPLES OF SOLITARY REFLECTION	**EXAMPLES OF REFLECTION WITH HELPER OR SMALL GROUP**
■ Spontaneous thinking during rhythmic, repetitive, mindless physical exercise (jogging, swimming laps, mowing the lawn) or routine habits (driving an established route, showering, shaving)	■ Performance appraisal discussions
■ Meditation	■ Counseling sessions
■ Prayer	■ Individual or group therapy
■ Journal writing	■ Problem-solving meetings
■ Business writing (project reports, professional papers, evaluations)	■ Project review sessions
■ Assessment instruments	■ Informal discussions with friends/colleagues
	■ Interviews
	■ Mentoring
	■ Feedback discussions

SUMMARY

Given the fast pace of change confronting managers today, it is critical that they develop capacities to learn from current work situations and adapt this learning to new situations. This need is driven by elaborate techniques and new processes that emerge regularly—initiatives that often require corporate-wide behavioral changes beginning at the top of the organization. In the midst of these time-consuming and expensive initiatives lies the simple and time-tested tool of reflection. To use it effectively, managers need only recognize that it has value, then create an amazingly small amount of time and structure for it to take place. With this process, managers take responsibility for their own learning—a responsibility that is, in some cases, too quickly turned over to workshop leaders, university professors, or consultants. No matter how qualified these educational providers may be, it is unlikely that any of them could create case studies with greater relevance or challenge than a manager's own work experiences.

NOTE

[1]An exploratory study compared the amount of learning that resulted from three ways of reflecting—alone, with a helper, or in a small group of peers—contrasted with a control group that did no reflection at all. Both the individual reflectors and helper pairs reported a greater number of learnings than the control group. There was no significant difference for the peer groups, however. Many of their interactions were limited to surfacing related experiences ("a similar thing happened to me") rather than plumbing the depth of a unique experience for lessons.

THE LEADER'S NEW WORK: BUILDING LEARNING ORGANIZATIONS*

Peter M. Senge

Human beings are designed for learning. No one has to teach an infant to walk, or talk, or master the spatial relationships needed to stack eight building blocks that don't topple. Children come fully equipped with an insatiable drive to explore and experiment. Unfortunately the primary institutions of our society are oriented predominately toward controlling rather than learning, rewarding individuals for performing for others rather than for cultivating their natural curiosity and impulse to learn. The young child entering school discovers quickly that the name of the game is getting the right answer and avoiding mistakes—a mandate no less compelling to the aspiring manager.

"Our prevailing system of management has destroyed our people," writes W. Edwards Deming, leader in the quality movement.[1] "People are born with intrinsic motivation, self-esteem, dignity, curiosity to learn, joy in learning. The forces of destruction begin with toddlers—a prize for the best Halloween costume, grades in school, gold stars, and up on through the university. On the job, people, teams, divisions are ranked—reward for the one at the top, punishment at the bottom. MBO, quotas, incentive pay, business plans, put together separately, division by division, cause further loss, unknown and unknowable."

Ironically, by focusing on performing for someone else's approval, corporations create the very conditions that predestine them to mediocre performance. Over the long run, superior performance depends on superior learning. A Shell study showed that, according to former planning director Arie de Geus, "a full one-third of the *Fortune* 500 industrials listed in 1970 have vanished by 1983."[2] Today, the average lifetime of the largest industrial enterprises is probably less than *half* the average lifetime of a person in an industrial society. On the other hand, de Geus and his colleagues at Shell also found a small number of companies that survived for seventy-five years or longer. Interestingly, the key to

---

* Reprinted from "The Leader's New Work," *Sloan Management Review* (Fall 1990), by permission of publisher. Copyright 1990 by the Sloan Management Review Association.

their survival was the ability to run "experiments in the margin," to continually explore new businesses and organizational opportunities that create potential new sources of growth.

If anything, the need for understanding how organizations learn and accelerating that learning is greater today than ever before. The old days when a Henry Ford, Alfred Sloan, or Tom Watson *learned for the organization* are gone. In an increasingly dynamic, interdependent, and unpredictable world, it is simply no longer possible for anyone to "figure it all out at the top." The old model, "the top thinks and the local acts," must now give way to integrating thinking and acting at all levels. While the challenge is great, so is the potential payoff. "The person who figures out how to harness the collective genius of the people in his or her organization," according to former Citibank CEO Walter Wriston, "is going to blow the competition away."

ADAPTIVE LEARNING AND GENERATIVE LEARNING

The prevailing view of learning organizations emphasizes increased adaptability. Given the accelerating pace of change, or so the standard view goes, "the most successful corporation of the 1990s," according to *Fortune*, "will be something called a learning organization, a consummately adaptive enterprise."[3] As the Shell study shows, examples of traditional authoritarian bureaucracies that responded too slowly to survive in changing business environments are legion.

But increasing adaptiveness is only the first stage in moving toward learning organizations. The impulse to learn in children goes deeper than desire to respond and adapt more effectively to environmental change. The impulse to learn, at its heart, is an impulse to be generative, to expand our capability. This is why leading corporations are focusing on *generative* learning, which is about creating, as well as *adaptive* learning, which is about coping.[4]

The total quality movement in Japan illustrates the evolution from adaptive to generative learning. With its emphasis on continuous experimentation and feedback, the total quality movement has been the first wave in building learning organizations. But Japanese firms' view of serving the customer has evolved. In the early years of total quality, the focus was on "fitness to standard," making a product reliably so that it would do what its designers intended it to do and what the firm told its customers it would do. Then came a focus on "fitness to need," understanding better what the customer wanted and then providing products that reliably *met* those needs. Today, leading edge firms seek to understand and meet the "latent need" of customers—what customers might truly value but have never experienced or would never think to ask for. As one Detroit executive commented recently, "You could never produce the Mazda Miata solely from market research. It required a leap of imagination to see what the customer *might* want."[5]

Generative learning, unlike adaptive learning, requires new ways of looking at the world, whether in understanding customers or in understanding how to better manage a business. For years, U.S. manufacturers sought competitive advantage in aggressive controls on inventories, incentive against overproduction, and rigid adherence to production forecasts. Despite these incentives, their performance was eventually eclipsed by Japanese firms who saw the challenges of manufacturing differently. They realized that eliminating delays in the production process was the key to reducing instability and improving cost, productivity, and service. They worked to build networks of relationships with trusted suppliers and to redesign physical production processes so as to reduce delays in materials procurement, production setup, and in-process inventory—a much higher-leverage approach to improving both cost and customer loyalty.

As Boston Consulting Group's George Stalk has observed, the Japanese saw the significance of delays because they see the process of order entry, production scheduling, materials procurement, production, and distribution *as an integrated system*. "What distorts the system so badly is time," observed Stalk—the multiple delays between events and responses. "These distortions reverberate throughout the system, producing disruptions, waste, and inefficiency."[6] Generative learning requires seeing the systems that control events. When we fail to grasp the systematic source of problems, we are left to "push on" symptoms rather than eliminate underlying causes. The best we can ever do is adaptive learning.

THE LEADERS' NEW WORK

"I talk with people all over the country about learning organizations, and the response is always very positive," says William O'Brien, CEO of the Hanover Insurance companies. "If this type of organization is so widely preferred, why don't people create such organizations? I think the answer is leadership. People have no real comprehension of the type of commitment it requires to build such an organization."[7]

Our traditional view of leaders—as special people who set the direction, make the key decisions, and energize the troops—is deeply rooted in an individualistic and nonsystemic worldview, especially in the West, leaders are *heroes*—great men (and occasionally women) who rise to the fore in times of crisis. So long as such myths prevail, they reinforce a focus on short-term events and charismatic heroes rather than on systematic forces and collective learning.

Leadership in learning organizations centers on subtler and ultimately more important work. In a learning organization, leaders' roles differ dramatically from that of the charismatic decision maker. Leaders are designers, teachers, stewards. These roles require new skills: the ability to build shared vision, to bring to the surface and challenge prevailing mental models, and to foster more systematic patterns of thinking. In short, leaders in learning organizations are responsible for *building organizations* where people are continually expanding their capabilities to shape their future—that is, leaders are responsible for learning.

CREATIVE TENSION: THE INTEGRATING PRINCIPLE

Leadership in a learning organization starts with the principle of creative tension.[8] Creative tension comes from seeing clearly where we want to be, our "vision," and telling the truth about where we are, our "current reality." The gap between the two generates a natural tension (see Figure 1).

Creative tension can be resolved in two basic ways: by raising current reality toward the vision, or by lowering the vision toward current reality. Individuals, groups, and organizations who learn how to work with creative tension learn how to use the energy it generates to move reality more reliably toward their visions.

The principle of creative tension has long been recognized by leaders. Martin Luther King, Jr., once said, "Just as Socrates felt that it was necessary to create a tension in the mind, so that individuals

FIGURE 1 **The Principle of Creative Tension**

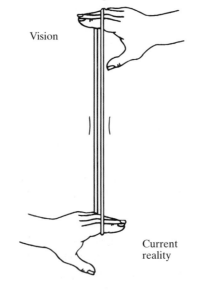

Vision

Current
reality

could rise from the bondage of myths and half truths . . . so must we . . . create the kind of tension in society that will help men rise from the dark depths of prejudice and racism."[9]

Without vision there is no creative tension. Creative tension cannot be generated from current reality alone. All the analysis in the world will never generate a vision. Many who are otherwise qualified to lead fail to do so because they try to substitute analysis for vision. They believe that, if only people understood current reality, they would surely feel the motivation to change. They are then disappointed to discover that people "resist" the personal and organizational changes that must be made to alter reality. What they never grasp is that the natural energy for changing reality comes from holding a picture of what might be that is more important to people than what is.

But creative tension cannot be generated from vision alone; it demands an accurate picture of current reality as well. Just as King had a dream, so too did he continually strive to "dramatize the shameful conditions" of racism and prejudice so that they could no longer be ignored. Vision without an understanding of current reality will more likely foster cynicism than creativity. The principle of creative tension teaches that *an accurate picture of current reality is just as important as a compelling picture of a desired future.*

Leading through creative tension is different than solving problems. In problem solving, the energy for change comes from attempting to get away from an aspect of current reality that is undesirable. With creative tension the energy for change comes from the vision, from what we want to create, juxtaposed with current reality. While the distinction may seem small, the consequences are not. Many people and organizations find themselves motivated to change only when their problems are bad enough to cause them to change. This works for a while, but the change process runs out of steam as soon as the problems driving the change become less pressing. With problem solving, the motivation for change is extrinsic. With creative tension, the motivation is intrinsic. This distinction mirrors the distinction between adaptive and generative learning.

NEW ROLES

The traditional authoritarian image of the leader as "the boss calling the shots" has been recognized as oversimplified and inadequate for some time. According to Edgar Schein, "Leadership is intertwined with culture formation." Building an organization's culture and shaping its evolution is the "unique and essential function" of leadership.[10] In a learning organization, the critical roles of leadership-designer, teacher, and steward have antecedents in the ways leaders have contributed to building organizations in the past. But each role takes on a new meaning in the learning organizations and, as will be seen in the following sections, demands new skills and tools.

LEADER AS DESIGNER

Imagine that your organization is an ocean liner and that you are "the leader." What is your role?

I have asked this question of groups of managers many times. The most common answer, not surprisingly, is "the captain." Others say, "The navigator, setting the direction." Still others say, "The helmsman, actually controlling the direction," or, "The engineer down there stroking the fire, providing energy," or, "The social director, making sure everybody's enrolled, involved, and communicating." While these are legitimate leadership roles, there is another which, in many ways, eclipses them all in importance. Yet rarely does anyone mention it.

The neglected leadership role is the *designer* of the ship. No one has a more sweeping influence than the designer. What good does it do for the captain to say, "Turn starboard 30 degrees," when the designer has built a rudder that will only turn to port, or which takes six hours to turn to starboard? It's fruitless to be the leader in an organization that is poorly designed.

The functions of design, or what some have called "social architecture," are rarely visible; they take place behind the scenes. The consequences that appear today are the result of work done long in the past, and work today will show its benefits far in the future. Those who aspire to lead out of a desire to control, or gain fame, or simply to be at the center of the action, will find little to attract them to the quiet design work of leadership.

But what, specifically, is involved in organizational design? "Organizational design is widely misconstrued as moving around boxes and lines," says Hanover's O'Brien. "The first task of organization design concerns designing the governing ideas of purpose, vision, and core values by which people will live." Few acts of leadership have a more enduring impact on an organization than building a foundation of purpose and core values.

In 1982, Johnson & Johnson found itself facing a corporate nightmare when bottles of its bestselling Tylenol were tampered with, resulting in several deaths. The corporation's immediate response was to pull all Tylenol off the shelves of retail outlets. Thirty-one million capsules were destroyed, even though they were tested and found safe. Although the immediate cost was significant, no other action was possible given the firm's credo. Authored almost 40 years earlier by president Robert Wood Johnson, Johnson & Johnson's credo states that permanent success is possible only when modern industry realizes that:

- service to its customers comes first;
- service to its employees and management comes second;
- service to the community comes third; and
- service to its stockholders, last.

Such statements might seem like motherhood and apple pie to those who have not seen the way a clear sense of purpose and values can affect key business decisions. Johnson & Johnson's crisis management in this case was based on that credo. It was simple, it was right, and it worked.

If governing ideas constitute the first design task of leadership, the second design task involves the policies, strategies, and structures that translate guiding ideas into business decisions. Leadership theorist Philip Selznick calls policy and structure the "institutional embodiment of purpose."[11] "Policy making (the rules that guide decisions) ought to be separated from decision making," says Jay Forrester.[12] "Otherwise, short-term pressures will usurp time from policy creation."

Traditionally, writers like Selznick and Forrester have tended to see policy making and implementation as the work of a small number of senior managers. But that view is changing. Both the dynamic business environment and the mandate of the learning organization to engage people at all levels now make it clear that this second design task is more subtle. Henry Mintzberg has argued that strategy is less a rational plan arrived at in the abstract and implemented throughout the organization than an "emergent phenomenon." Successful organizations "craft strategy" according to Mintzberg, as they continually learn about shifting business conditions and balance what is desired and what is possible.[13] The key is not getting the right strategy but fostering strategic thinking. "The choice of individual action is only part of the policymaker's need," according to Mason and Mitroff.[14] "More important is the need to achieve insight into the nature of the complexity and to formulate concepts and world views for coping with it."

Behind appropriate policies, strategies, and structures are effective learning processes; their creation is the third key design responsibility in learning organizations. This does not absolve senior managers of their strategic responsibilities. Now, they are not only responsible for ensuring that an organization have well-developed strategies and policies, but also for ensuring that processes exist whereby these are continually improved.

In the early 1970s, Shell was the weakest of the big seven oil companies. Today, Shell and Exxon are arguably the strongest, both in size and financial health. Shell's ascendence began with frustration. Around 1971 members of Shell's "Group Planning" in London began to foresee dramatic change and unpredictability in world oil markets. However, it proved impossible to persuade managers that the stable world of steady growth in oil demand and supply they had known for 20 years was about to change. Despite brilliant analysis and artful presentation, Shell's planners realized, in the words of Pierre Wack, that they "had failed to change behavior in much of the Shell organization."[15] Progress would probably have ended there, had the frustration not given way to a radically new view of corporate planning.

As they pondered this failure, the planner's view of their basic task shifted: "We no longer saw our task as producing a documented view of the future business environment 5 or 10 years ahead. Our real target was the microcosm (the 'mental model') of our decision makers." Only when the planners reconceptualized their basic task as fostering learning rather than devising plans did their insights begin to have an impact. The initial tool used was "scenario analysis," through which planners encouraged operating managers to think through how they would manage in the future under different possible scenarios. It mattered not that the managers believed the planners' scenarios absolutely, only that they became engaged in ferreting out the implications. In this way, Shell's planners conditioned managers to be mentally prepared for a shift from low prices to high prices and from stability to instability. The results were significant. When OPEC became a reality, Shell quickly responded by increasing local operating company control (to enhance maneuverability in the new political environment), building buffer stocks, and accelerating development of non-OPEC sources—actions that its competitors took much more slowly or not at all.

Somewhat inadvertently, Shell planners had discovered the leverage of designing institutional learning processes, whereby, in the words of former planning director de Geus, "Management teams change their shared mental models of their company, their markets, and their competitors."[16] Since then, "planning as learning" has become a byword at Shell, and Group Planning has continually sought out new learning tools that can be integrated into the planning process. Some of these are described later.

LEADER AS TEACHER

"The first responsibility of a leader," writes retired Herman Miller CEO Max de Pree, "is to define reality."[17] Much of the leverage leaders can actually exert lies in helping people achieve more accurate, more insightful, and more *empowering* views of reality.

Leader as teacher does *not* mean leader as authoritarian expert whose job it is to teach people the correct" view of reality. Rather, it is about helping everyone in the organization, oneself included, to gain more insightful views of current reality. This is in line with a popular emerging view of leaders as coaches, guides, or facilitators.[18] In learning organizations, this teaching role is developed further by virtue of explicit attention to people's mental models and by the influence of the system's perspective.

The role of leader as teacher starts with bringing to the surface people's mental models of important issues. No one carries an organization, a market, or a state of technology in his or her head. What we carry in our heads are assumptions. These mental pictures of how the world works have a significant influence on how we perceive problems and opportunities, identify courses of action, and make choices.

One reason that mental models are so deeply entrenched is that they are largely tacit. Ian Mitroff, in his study of General Motors, argues that an assumption that prevailed for years was that, in the United States, "Cars are status symbols. Styling is therefore more important than quality."[19] The Detroit automakers didn't say, "We have a mental model that all people care about is styling." Few actual managers would even say publicly that all people care about is styling. So long as the view remained unexpressed, there was little possibility of challenging its validity or forming more accurate assumptions.

But working with mental models goes beyond revealing hidden assumptions. "Reality," as perceived by most people in most organizations, means pressures that must be borne, crises that must be reacted to, and limitations that must be accepted. Leaders as teachers help people restructure their views of reality to see beyond the superficial conditions and events into the underlying causes of problems—and therefore to see new possibilities for shaping the future.

Specifically, leaders can influence people to view reality at three distinct levels: events, patterns of behavior, and systemic structure.

Systemic Structure
(Generative)
↓
Patterns of Behavior
(Responsive)
↓
Events
(Reactive)

The key question becomes *where do leaders predominantly focus their own and their organization's attention*?

Contemporary society focuses predominantly on events. The media reinforces this perspective, with almost exclusive attention to short-term, dramatic events. This focus leads naturally to explaining what happens in terms of those events: "The Dow Jones average went up 16 points because high fourth-quarter profits were announced yesterday."

Pattern-of-behavior explanations are rarer, in contemporary culture, than event explanations, but they do occur. "Trend analysis" is an example of seeing patterns of behavior. A good editorial that interprets a set of current events in the context of long-term historical changes is another example. Systemic, structural explanations go even further by addressing the questions, "What causes the patterns of behavior?"

In some sense, all three levels of explanation are equally true. But their usefulness is quite different. Event explanations—who did what to whom—doom their holders to a reactive stance toward change. Pattern-of-behavior explanations focus on identifying long-term trends and assessing their implications. They at least suggest how, over time, we can respond to shifting conditions. Structural explanations are the most powerful. Only they address the underlying causes of behavior at a level such that patterns of behavior can be changed.

By and large, leaders of our current institutions focus their attention on events and patterns of behavior, and, under their influence, their organizations do likewise. That is why contemporary organizations are predominantly reactive, or at best responsive—rarely generative. On the other hand, leaders in learning organizations pay attention to all three levels, but focus especially on systemic structure; largely by example, they teach people throughout the organization to do likewise.

LEADER AS STEWARD

This is the subtlest role of leadership. Unlike the roles of designer and teacher, it is almost solely a matter of attitude. It is an attitude critical to learning organizations.

While stewardship has long been recognized as an aspect of leadership, its source is still not widely understood. I believe Robert Greenleaf came closest to explaining real stewardship, in his seminal book *Servant Leadership*.[20] There, Greenleaf argues that "The servant leader is servant *first* ... It begins with the natural feeling that one wants to serve, to serve *first*. This conscious choice brings one to aspire to lead. That person is sharply different from one who is leader *first*, perhaps because of the need to assuage an unusual power drive or to acquire material possessions."

Leaders' sense of stewardship operates on two levels: stewardship for the people they lead and stewardship for the larger purpose or mission that underlies the enterprise. The first type arises from a keen appreciation of the impact one's leadership can have on others. People can suffer economically, emotionally, and spiritually under inept leadership. If anything, people in a learning organization are more vulnerable because of their commitment and sense of shared ownership. Appreciating this naturally instills a sense of responsibility in leaders. The second type of stewardship arises from a leader's sense of personal purpose and commitment to the organization's larger mission. People's natural impulse to learn is unleashed when they are engaged in an endeavor they consider worthy of their fullest commitment. Or, as Lawrence Miller puts it, "Achieving return on equity does not, as a goal, mobilize the most noble forces of our soul."[21]

Leaders engaged in building learning organizations naturally feel part of a larger purpose that goes beyond their organization. They are part of changing the way businesses operate, not from a vague philanthropic urge, but from a conviction that their efforts will produce more productive organizations, capable of achieving higher levels of organizational success and personal satisfaction than more traditional organizations. Their sense of stewardship was succinctly captured by George Bernard Shaw when he said,

> *This is the true joy in life, the being used for a purpose you consider a mighty one, the being a force of nature rather than a feverish, selfish clod of ailments and grievances complaining that the world will not devote itself to making you happy.*

NEW SKILLS

New leadership roles require new leadership skills. These skills can only be developed, in my judgment, through a lifetime commitment. It is not enough for one or two individuals to develop these skills. They must be distributed widely throughout the organization. This is one reason that understanding the disciplines of a learning organization is so important. These disciplines embody the principles and practices that can widely foster leadership development.

Three critical areas of skills (disciplines) are building shared vision, surfacing and challenging mental models, and engaging in systems thinking.[22]

BUILDING SHARED VISION

How do individual visions come together to create shared visions? A useful metaphor is the hologram, the three-dimensional image created by interacting light sources.

If you cut a photograph in half, each half shows only part of the whole image. But if you divide a hologram, each part, no matter how small, shows the whole image intact. Likewise, when a group of people come to share a vision for an organization, each person sees an individual picture of the organization at its best. Each shares responsibility for the whole, not just for one piece. But the component pieces of the hologram are not identical. Each represents the whole image from a different point of view. It's something like poking holes in a window shade; each hole offers a unique angle for viewing the whole image. So, too is each individual's vision unique.

When you add up the pieces of a hologram, something interesting happens. The image becomes more intense, more lifelike. When more people come to share a vision, the vision becomes more real in the sense of a mental reality that people can truly imagine achieving. They now have partners, co-creators; the vision no longer rests on their shoulders alone. Early on, when they are nurturing an individual vision, people may say it is "my vision." But, as the shared vision develops, it becomes both "my vision" and "our vision."

The skills involved in building shared vision include the following:

- **Encouraging Personal Vision** Shared visions emerge from personal visions. It is not that people only care about their own self-interest—in fact, people's values usually include dimensions that concern family, organization, community, and even the world. Rather, it is that people's capacity for caring is personal.
- **Communicating and Asking for Support** Leaders must be willing to continually share their own vision, rather than being the official representative of the corporate vision. They also must be prepared to ask, "Is this the vision worthy of your commitment?" This can be difficult for a person used to setting goals and presuming compliance.

- **Visioning as an Ongoing Process**   Building shared vision is a never-ending process. At any one point there will be a particular image of the future that is predominant, but that image will evolve. Today, too many managers want to dispense with the "vision business" by going off and writing the Official Vision Statement. Such statements almost always lack the vitality, freshness, and excitement of a genuine vision that comes from people asking, "What do we really want to achieve?"
- **Blending Extrinsic and Intrinsic Visions**   Many energizing visions are extrinsic—that is, they focus on achieving something relative to an outsider, such as a competitor. But a goal that is limited to defeating an opponent can, once the vision is achieved, easily become a defensive posture. In contrast, intrinsic goals like creating a new type of product, taking an established product to a new level, or setting a new standard for customer satisfaction can call forth a new level of creativity and innovation. Intrinsic and extrinsic visions need to coexist; a vision solely predicated on defeating an adversary will eventually weaken an organization.
- **Distinguishing Positive from Negative Visions**   Many organizations only truly pull together when their survival is threatened. Similarly, most social movements aim at eliminating what people don't want: for example, anti-drugs, anti-smoking, or anti-nuclear arms movements. Negative visions carry a subtle message of powerlessness: people will only pull together when there is sufficient threat. Negative visions also tend to be short term. Two fundamental sources of energy can motivate organizations: fear and aspiration. Fear, the energy source behind negative visions, can produce extraordinary changes in short periods, but aspiration endures as a continuing source of learning and growth.

SURFACING AND TESTING MENTAL MODELS

Many of the best ideas in organizations never get put into practice. One reason is that new insights and initiatives often conflict with established mental models. The leadership task of challenging assumptions without invoking defensiveness requires reflection and inquiry skills possessed by a few leaders in traditional controlling organizations.[23]

- **Seeing Leaps of Abstraction**   Our minds literally move at lightning speed. Ironically, this often slows our learning, because we leap to generalizations so quickly that we never think to test them. We then confuse our generalizations with the observable data upon which they are based, treating the generalizations as if they were data. The frustrated sales rep reports to the home office that "customers don't really care about quality, price is what matters," when what actually happened was that three consecutive large customers refused to place an order unless a larger discount was offered. The sales rep treats her generalization, "customers care only about price," as if it were absolute fact rather than an assumption (very likely an assumption reflecting her own views of customers and the market). This thwarts future learning because she starts to focus on how to offer attractive discounts rather than probing behind the customers' statements. For example, the customers may have been so disgruntled with the firm's delivery or customer service that they are unwilling to purchase again without larger discounts.
- **Balancing Inquiry and Advocacy**   Most managers are skilled at articulating their views and presenting them persuasively. While important, advocacy skills can become counterproductive as managers rise in responsibility and confront increasingly complex issues that require collaborative learning among different, equally knowledgeable people. Leaders in learning organizations need to have both inquiry and advocacy skills.[24]

   Specifically, when advocating a view, they need to be able to:
   - explain the reasoning and data that led to their view;
   - encourage others to test their view (e.g., Do you see gaps in my reasoning? Do you disagree with the data upon which my view is based?); and

- encourage others to provide different views (e.g., Do you have either different data, different conclusions, or both?).

When inquiring into another's views, they need to:

- actively seek to understand the other's view, rather than simply restating their own view and how it differs from the other's view; and
- make their attributions about the other and the other's view explicit (e.g., Based on your statement that ... ; I am assuming that you believe ... ; Am I representing your views fairly?).

If they reach an impasse (others no longer appear open to inquiry), they need to:

- ask what data or logic might unfreeze the impasse, or if an experiment (or some other inquiry) might be designed to provide new information.

- **Distinguishing Espoused Theory from Theory in Use**   We all like to think that we hold certain views, but often our actions reveal deeper views. For example, I may proclaim that people are trustworthy, but never lend friends money and jealously guard my possessions. Obviously, my deeper mental model (my theory in use) differs from my espoused theory. Recognizing gaps between espoused views and theories in use (which often requires the help of others) can be pivotal to deeper learning.

- **Recognizing and Defusing Defensive Routines**   As one CEO in our research program puts it, "Nobody ever talks about an issue at the 8:00 business meeting exactly the same way they talk about it at home that evening or over drinks at the end of the day." The reason is what Chris Argyris calls "defensive routines," entrenched habits used to protect ourselves from the embarrassment and threat that come with exposing our thinking. For most of us, such defenses began to build early in life in response to pressures to have the right answers in school or at home. Organizations add new levels of performance anxiety and thereby amplify and exacerbate this defensiveness. Ironically, this makes it even more difficult to expose hidden mental models, and thereby lessens learning.

The first challenge is to recognize defensive routines, then to inquire into their operation. Those who are best at revealing and defusing defensive routines operate with a high degree of self-disclosure regarding their own defensiveness (e.g., I notice that I am feeling uneasy about how this conversation is going. Perhaps I don't understand it or it is threatening to me in ways I don't yet see. Can you help me see this better?).

SYSTEMS THINKING

We all know that leaders should help people see the big picture. But the actual skills whereby leaders are supposed to achieve this are not well understood. In my experience, successful leaders often are "systems thinkers" to a considerable extent. They focus less on day-to-day events and more on underlying trends and forces of change. But they do this almost completely intuitively. The consequence is that they are often unable to explain their intuitions to others and feel frustrated that others cannot see the world the way they do.

One of the most significant developments in management science today is the gradual coalescence of managerial systems thinking as a field of study and practice. This field suggests some key skills for future leaders:

- **Seeing Interrelationships, Not Things, and Processes, Not Snapshots**   Most of us have been conditioned throughout our lives to focus on things and to see the world in static images. This leads us to linear explanations of systemic phenomenon. For instance, in an arms race each party is convinced that the other is the cause of problems. They react to each new move as an isolated event, not as part of a process. So long as they fail to see the interrelationships of these actions, they are trapped.
- **Moving Beyond Blame**   We tend to blame each other or outside circumstances for our problems. But it is poorly designed systems, not incompetent or unmotivated individuals, that cause most organizational problems. System thinking shows us that there is no outside—that you and the cause of your problems are part of a single system.

- **Distinguishing Detail Complexity from Dynamic Complexity**   Some types of complexity are more important strategically than others. Detail complexity arises when there are many variables. Dynamic complexity arises when cause and effect are distant in time and space, and when the consequences over time of interventions are subtle and not obvious to many participants in the system. The leverage in most management situations lies in understanding dynamic complexity, not detail complexity.
- **Focusing on Areas of Higher Leverage**   Some have called systems thinking the "new dismal science" because it teaches that most obvious solutions don't work—at best, they improve matters in the short run, only to make things worse in the long run. But there is another side to the story. Systems thinking also shows that small, well-focused actions can produce significant, enduring improvements, if they are in the right place. Systems thinkers refer to this idea as the principle of "leverage." Tackling a difficult problem is often a matter of seeing where the high leverage lies, where a change—with a minimum of effort—would lead to lasting, significant improvement.
- **Avoiding Symptomatic Solutions**   The pressures to intervene in management systems that are going awry can be overwhelming. Unfortunately, given the linear thinking that predominates in most organizations, interventions usually focus on symptomatic fixes, not underlying causes. This results in only temporary relief, and it tends to create still more pressures later and for further, low leverage intervention. If leaders acquiesce to these pressures, they can be sucked into an endless spiral of increasing intervention. Sometimes the most difficult leadership acts are to refrain from intervening though popular quick fixes and to keep the pressure on everyone to identify more enduring solutions.

While leaders who can articulate systemic explanations are rare, those who can will leave their stamps on an organization. One person who had this gift was Bill Gore, the founder and longtime CEO of W.L. Gore and Associates (makers of Gore Tex and other synthetic fiber products). Bill Gore was adept at telling stories that showed the organization's core values of freedom and individual responsibility required particular operating policies. He was proud of his egalitarian organization, in which there were (and still are) no "employees," only "associates," all of whom own shares in the company and participate in its management. At one talk, he explained the company's policy of controlled growth: "Our limitation is not financial resources. Our limitation is the rate at which we can bring in new associates. Our experience has been that if we try to bring in more than a 25 percent per year increase, we begin to bog down. Twenty-five percent per year growth is a real limitation; you can do much better than that with an authoritarian organization." As Gore tells the story, one of the associates, Esther Baum, went home after this talk and reported the limitation to her husband. As it happened, he was an astronomer and mathematician at Lowell Observatory. He said, "That's a very interesting figure." He took out his pencil and paper and calculated and said, "Do you realize that in only fifty-seven and a half years, everyone in the world will be working for Gore?"

Through the story, Gore explains the systemic rationale behind a key policy, limited growth rate—a policy that undoubtedly caused a lot of stress in the organization. He suggests that, at larger rates of growth, the adverse effects of attempting to integrate too many new people too rapidly would begin to dominate. (This is the "limits to growth" systems archetype explained later.) The story also reaffirms the organization's commitment to creating a unique environment for its associates and illustrates the types of sacrifices that the firm is prepared to make in order to remain true to its vision. The last part of the story shows that, despite the self-imposed limit, the company is still very much a growth company.

The consequences of leaders who lack systems thinking skills can be devastating. Many charismatic leaders manage almost exclusively at the level of events. They deal in visions and in crises, and little in between. Under the leadership, an organization hurtles from crisis to crisis. Eventually, the worldview of people in the organization becomes dominated by events and reactiveness. Many, especially those who are deeply committed, become burned out. Eventually, cynicism comes to pervade the organization. People have no control over their time, let alone their destiny.

Similar problems arise with the "visionary strategist," the leader with vision who sees both patterns of change and events. This leader is better prepared to manage change. She or he can explain strategies in terms of emerging trends, and thereby foster a climate that is less reactive. But such leaders still impart a responsive orientation rather than a generative one.

Many talented leaders have rich, highly systemic intuitions but cannot explain those intuitions to others. Ironically, they often end up being authoritarian leaders, even if they don't want to, because only they see the decisions that need to be made. They are unable to conceptualize their strategic insights so that these can become public knowledge, open to challenge and further improvement.

NEW TOOLS

Developing the skills described previously requires new tools—tools that will enhance leaders' conceptual abilities and foster communication and collaborative inquiry. What follows is a sampling of tools starting to find use in learning organizations.

SYSTEMS ARCHETYPES

One of the insights of the budding, managerial systems-thinking field is that certain types of systemic structures recur again and again. Countless systems grow for a period, then encounter problems and cease to grow (or even collapse) well before they have reached intrinsic limits to growth. Many other systems get locked in runaway vicious spirals where every actor has to run faster and faster to stay in the same place. Still others lure individual actors into doing what seems right locally, yet which eventually causes suffering for all.[25]

Some of the system archetypes that have the broadest relevance include:

- **Balancing Process with Delay** In this archetype, decision makers fail to appreciate the time delays involved as they move toward a goal. As a result, they overshoot the goal and may even produce recurring cycles. Classic example: Real estate developers who keep starting new projects until the market has gone soft, by which time an eventual glut is guaranteed by the properties still under construction.
- **Limits to Growth** A reinforcing cycle of growth grinds to a halt, and may even reverse itself, as limits are approached. The limits can be resource constraints, or external or internal responses to growth. Classic examples: Product life cycles that peak prematurely due to poor quality or service, the growth and decline of communication in a management team, and the spread of a new movement.
- **Shifting the Burden** A short-term "solution" is used to correct a problem, with seemingly happy immediate results. As this correction is used more and more, fundamental long-term corrective measures are used less. Over time, the mechanisms of the fundamental solution may atrophy or become disabled, leading to an even greater reliance on the symptomatic solution. Classic example: Using corporate human resource staff to solve local personnel problems, thereby keeping managers from developing their own interpersonal skills.
- **Eroding Goals** When all else fails, lower your standards. This is like "shifting the burden," except that the short-term solution involves letting a fundamental goal, such as quality standards or employee morale standards, atrophy. Classic example: A company that responds to delivery problems by continually upping its quoted delivery times.
- **Escalation** Two people or two organizations, who each see their welfare as depending on a relative advantage over the other, continually react to the other's advances. Whenever one side gets ahead, the other is threatened, leading it to act more aggressively to reestablish its advantage, which threatens the first, and so on. Classic examples: Arms race, gang warfare, price wars.
- **Tragedy of the Commons**[26] Individuals keep intensifying their use of a commonly available but limited resource until all individuals start to experience severely diminishing returns. Classic examples: Sheepherders who keep increasing their flocks until they overgraze the common pasture;

divisions in a firm that share a common salesforce and compete for the use of sales reps by upping their sales targets, until the salesforce bums out from overextension.

- **Growth and Underinvestment**   Rapid growth approaches a limit that could be eliminated or pushed into the future, but only by aggressive investment in physical and human capacity. Eroding goals or standards cause investment that is too weak, or too slow, and customers get increasingly unhappy, slowing demand growth and thereby making the needed investment (apparently) unnecessary or impossible. Classic example: Countless once-successful growth firms that allowed product or service quality to erode, and were unable to generate enough revenues to invest in remedies.

The Archetype Template is a specific tool that is helping managers identify archetypes operating in their own strategic areas (see Figure 2).[27] The template shows the basic structural form of the archetype but lets managers fill in the variables of their own situation. For example, the shifting the burden template involves two balancing processes ("B") that compete for control of a problem symptom. The upper, symptomatic solution provides a short-term fix that will make the problem symptom go away for a while. The lower, fundamental solution provides a more enduring solution. The side-effect feedback ("R") around the outside of the diagram identifies unintended exacerbating effects of the symptomatic solution, which, over time, make it more and more difficult to invoke the fundamental solution.

Several years ago, a team of managers from a leading consumer goods producer used the shifting the burden archetype in a revealing way. The problem they focused on was financial stress, which could be dealt with in two different ways: by running marketing promotions (the symptomatic solution) or by product innovation (the fundamental solution). Marketing promotions were fast. The company was expert in their design and implementation. The results were highly predictable. Product innovation was slow and much less predictable, and the company had a history over the past ten years of product-innovation mismanagement. Yet only through innovation could they retain a leadership position in their industry, which had slid over the past ten to twenty years. What the managers saw clearly was that the more skillful they became at promotions, the more they shifted the burden away from product innovation. But what really struck home was when one member identified the unintended side

FIGURE 2   **"Shifting the Burden" Archetype Template**   In the "shifting the burden" template, two balancing processes (B) compete for control of a problem symptom. Both solutions affect the symptom, but only the fundamental solution treats the cause. The symptomatic "solution" creates the additional side effect (R) of deferring the fundamental solution, making it harder and harder to achieve.

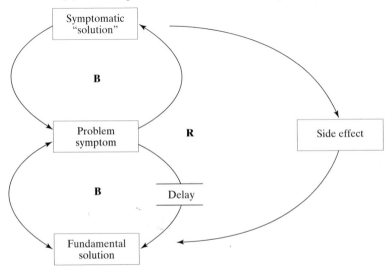

effect: the last three CEOs had all come from advertising, which had become the politically dominant function in the corporation, thereby institutionalizing the symptomatic solution. Unless the political values shifted back toward product and process innovation, the managers realized, the firm's decline would accelerate—which is just the shift that had happened over the past several years.

CHARTING STRATEGIC DILEMMAS

Management teams typically come unglued when confronted with core dilemmas. A classic example was the way U.S. manufacturers faced the low cost-high quality choice. For years, most assumed that it was necessary to choose between the two. Not surprisingly, given the short-term pressures perceived by most managements, the prevailing choice was low cost. Firms that chose high quality usually perceived themselves as aiming exclusively for high quality, high price market niche. The consequences of this perceived either-or choice have been disastrous, even fatal, as U.S. manufacturers have encountered increasing international competition from firms that have chosen to consistently improve quality and cost.

In a recent book, Charles Hampden-Turner presented a variety of tools for helping management teams confront strategic dilemmas creatively.[28] He summarizes the process in seven steps:

- **Eliciting the Dilemmas**   Identifying the opposed values that form the "horns" of the dilemma, for example, cost as opposed to quality, or local initiative as opposed to central coordination and control. Hampden-Turner suggests that humor can be a distinct asset in this process since "the admission that dilemmas even exist tends to be difficult for some companies."
- **Mapping**   Locating the opposing values as two axes and helping managers identify where they see themselves, or their organization, along the axes.
- **Processing**   Getting rid of nouns to describe the axes of the dilemma. Present participles formed by adding "ing" convert rigid nouns into processes that imply movement. For example, central control versus local control becomes "strengthening national office" and "growing local initiatives." This loosens the bond of implied opposition between the two values. For example, it becomes possible to think of "strengthening national services" from which local branches can benefit.
- **Framing/Contextualizing**   Further softening the adversarial structure among different values by letting "each side in turn be the frame or context for the other." This shifting of the "figure-ground" relationship undermines any implicit attempts to hold one value as intrinsically superior to the other, and thereby to become mentally closed to creative strategies for continuous improvement of both.
- **Sequencing**   Breaking the hold of static thinking. Very often, values like low cost and high quality appear to be in opposition because we think in terms of a point in time, not in terms of an ongoing process. For example, a strategy of investing in a new process technology and developing a new production-floor culture of worker responsibility may take time and money in the near term, yet reap significant long-term financial rewards.
- **Waving/Cycling**   Sometimes the strategic path toward improving both values involves cycles where both values will get "worse" for a time. Yet, at a deeper level, learning is occurring that will cause the next cycle to be at a higher plateau for both values.
- **Synergizing**   Achieving synergy where significant improvement is occurring along all axes of all relevant dilemmas. (This is the ultimate goal, of course.) Synergy, as Hampden-Turner points out, is a uniquely systemic notion, coming from the Greek *Syn-ergo* or "work together."

"THE LEFT-HAND COLUMN": SURFACING MENTAL MODELS

The ideas that the mental models can dominate business decisions and that these models are often tacit and even contradictory to what people espouse can be very threatening to managers who pride themselves on rationality and judicious decision making. It is important to have tools to help managers discover for themselves how their mental models operate to undermine their own intentions.

One tool that has worked consistently to help managers see their own mental models in action is the "left-hand column" exercise developed by Chris Argyris and his colleagues. This tool is especially helpful in showing how we leap from data to generalization without testing the validity of our generalizations.

When working with managers, I start this exercise by selecting a specific situation in which I am interacting with other people in a way that is not working, that is not producing the learning that is needed. I write out a sample of the exchange, with the script on the right-hand side of the page. On the left-hand side, I write what I am thinking but not saying at each stage in the exchange (see sidebar).

The left-hand column exercise not only brings hidden assumptions to the surface, it shows how they influence behavior. In the example, I make two key assumptions about Bill: he lacks confidence and he lacks initiative. Neither may be literally true, but both are evident in my internal dialogue, and both influence the way I handle the situation. Believing that he lacks confidence, I skirt the fact that I've heard the presentation was a bomb. I'm afraid that if I say it directly, he will lose what little confidence he has, or he will see me as unsupportive. So I bring up the subject of the presentation obliquely. When I ask Bill what we should do next, he gives no specific course of action. Believing he lacks initiative, I take this as evidence of his laziness; he is content to do nothing when action is definitely required. I conclude that I will have to manufacture some form of pressure to motivate him, or else I will simply have to take matters into my own hands.

THE LEFT-HAND COLUMN: AN EXERCISE

Imagine my exchange with a colleague, Bill, after he made a big presentation to our boss on a project we are doing together. I had to miss the presentation, but I've heard that it was poorly received.

Me: How did the presentation go?
Bill: Well, I don't know. It's really too early to say. Besides, we're breaking new ground here.
Me: Well, what do you think we should do? I believe that the issues you were raising were important.
Bill: I'm not so sure. Let's just wait and see what happens.
Me: You may be right, but I think we may need to do more than just wait.

Now, here is what the exchange looks like with my "left-hand column":

What I'm Thinking	**What Is Said**
Everyone says the presentation was a bomb.	**Me:** How did the presentation go?
Does he really not know how bad it was? Or is he not willing to face up to it?	**Bill:** Well, I don't know. It's too early to say. Besides we're breaking new ground here.
	Me: Well, what do you think we should do? I believe that the issues you were raising are important.
He really is afraid to see the truth. If he only had more confidence, he could probably learn from a situation like this.	**Bill:** I'm not so sure. Let's just wait and see what happens.
I can't believe he doesn't realize how disastrous that presentation was to our moving ahead.	**Me:** You may be right, but I think we may need to do more than just wait.
I've got to find some way to light a fire under the guy.	

The exercise reveals the elaborate webs of assumptions we weave, within which we become our own victims. Rather than dealing directly with my assumptions about Bill and the situation, we talk around the subject. The reasons for my avoidance are self-evident: I assume that if I raised my doubts, I would provoke a defensive reaction that would only make matters worse. But the price of avoiding the issue is high. Instead of determining how to move forward to resolve problems, we end our exchange with no clear course of action. My assumptions about Bill's limitations have been reinforced. I resort to a manipulative strategy to move things forward.

The exercise not only reveals the need for skills in surfacing assumptions, but that we are the ones most in need of help. There is no one right way to handle difficult situations like my exchange with Bill, but any productive strategy revolves around a high level of self-disclosure and willingness to have my views challenged. I need to recognize my own leaps of abstraction regarding Bill, share the events and reasoning that are leading to my concern over the project, and be open to Bill's views on both. The skills to carry on such conversations without invoking defensiveness take time to develop. But if both parties in a learning impasse start by doing their own left-hand column exercise and sharing them with each other, it is remarkable how quickly everyone recognizes their contribution to the impasse and progress starts to be made.

LEARNING LABORATORIES: PRACTICE FIELDS FOR MANAGEMENT TEAMS

One of the most promising new tools is the learning laboratory or "microworld": constructed microcosms of real-life settings in which management teams can learn how to learn together.

The rationale behind learning laboratories can be best explained by analogy. Although most management teams have great difficulty learning (enhancing their collective intelligence and capacity to create), in other domains team learning is the norm rather than the exception—team sports and the performing arts, for example. Great basketball teams do not start off great. They learn. But the process by which these teams learn is, by and large, absent from modern organizations. The process is a continual movement between practice and performance.

The vision guiding current research in management learning laboratories is to design and construct effective practice fields for management teams. Much remains to be done, but the broad outlines are emerging.

First, since team learning in organizations is an individual-to-individual and individual-to-system phenomenon, learning laboratories must combine meaningful business issues with meaningful interpersonal dynamics. Either alone is incomplete.

LEARNING AT HANOVER INSURANCE

Hanover Insurance has gone from the bottom of the property and liability industry to a position among the top 25 percent of U.S. insurance companies over the past 20 years, largely through the efforts of CEO William O'Brien and his predecessor, Jack Adam. The following comments are excerpted from series of interviews Senge conducted with O'Brien as background for his book.

Senge: Why do you think there is so much change occurring in management and organizations today? Is it primarily because of increased competitive pressures?

O'Brien: That's a factor, but not the most significant factor. The ferment in management will continue until we find models that are more congruent with human nature.

(continued)

One of the great insights of modern psychology is the hierarchy of human needs. As Maslow expressed this idea, the most basic needs are food and shelter. Then comes belonging. Once these three basic needs are satisfied, people begin to aspire toward self-respect and esteem, and toward self-actualization—the fourth—and fifth-order needs.

Our traditional hierarchical organizations are designed to provide for the first three levels, but not the fourth and fifth. These first three levels are now widely available to members of industrial society, but our organizations do not offer people sufficient opportunities for growth.

Senge: How would you assess Hanover's progress to date?

O'Brien: We have been on a long journey away from traditional hierarchical culture. The journey began with everyone understanding some guiding ideas about purpose, vision, and values as a basis for participative management. This is a better way to begin building a participative culture than by simply "letting people in on decision making." Before there can be meaningful participation, people must share certain values and pictures about where we are trying to go. We discovered that people have real need to feel that they're part of an ennobling mission. But developing shared visions and values is not the end, only the beginning.

Next we had to get beyond mechanical, linear thinking. The essence of our jobs as managers is to deal with "divergent" problems—problems that have no simple answer.

"Convergent" problems—problems that have a "right" answer-should be solved locally. Yet we are deeply conditioned to see the world in terms of convergent problems. Most managers try to force-fit simplistic solutions and undermine the potential for learning when divergent problems arise. Since everyone handles the linear issues fairly well, companies that learn how to handle divergent issues will have a great advantage.

The next basic stage in our progression was coming to understand inquiry and advocacy. We learned that real openness is rooted in people's ability to continually inquire into their own thinking. This requires exposing yourself to being wrong—not something that most managers are rewarded for. But learning is very difficult if you cannot look for errors or incompleteness in your own ideas.

What all this builds to is the capability throughout an organization to manage mental models. In a locally controlled organization, you have the fundamental challenge of learning how to help people make good decisions without coercing them into making particular decisions. By managing mental models, we create "self-concluding" decisions—decisions that people come to themselves—which will result in deeper conviction, better implementation, and the ability to make better adjustments when the situation changes.

Senge: What concrete steps can top managers take to begin moving toward learning organizations?

O'Brien: Look at the signals you send through the organization. For example, one critical signal is how you spend your time. It's hard to build a learning organization if people are unable to take the time to think through important matters. I rarely set up an appointment for less than one hour. If the subject is not worth an hour, it shouldn't be on my calendar.

Senge: Why is this so hard for so many managers?

O'Brien: It comes back to what you believe about the nature of your work. The authoritarian manager has a "chain gang" mental model: "The speed of the boss is the speed of the gang. I've got to keep things moving fast, because I've got to keep people working." In a learning organization, the manager shoulders an almost sacred responsibility: to create conditions that enable people to have happy and productive lives. If you understand the effects the ideas we are discussing can have on the lives of people in your organization, you will take the time.

Second, the factors that thwart learning about complex business issues must be eliminated in the learning lab. Chief among these is the inability to experience the long-term, systemic consequences of key strategic decisions. We all learn best from experience, but we are unable to experience the consequences of many important organizational decisions. Learning laboratories remove this constraint through system dynamics simulation games that compress time and space.

Third, new learning skills must be developed. One constraint on learning is the inability of managers to reflect insightfully on their assumptions, and to inquire effectively into each other's assumptions. Both skills can be enhanced in a learning laboratory, where people can practice surfacing assumptions in a low-risk setting. A note of caution: It is far easier to design an entertaining learning laboratory than it is to have an impact on real management practices and firm traditions outside the learning lab. Research on management simulations has shown that they often have greater entertainment value than the educational value. One of the reasons appears to be that many simulations do not offer deep insights into systemic structures causing business problems. Another reason is that they do not foster new learning skills. Also, there is no connection between experiments in the learning lab and real life experiments. These are significant problems that research on laboratory design is now addressing.

DEVELOPING LEADERS AND LEARNING ORGANIZATIONS

In a recently published retrospective on organization development in the 1980s, Marshall Sashkin and N. Warner Burke observe the return of an emphasis on developing leaders who can develop organizations.[29] They also note Schein's critique that most top executives are not qualified for the task of developing culture.[30] Learning organizations represent a potentially significant evolution of organizational culture. So it should come as no surprise that such organization will remain a distant vision until the leadership capabilities they demand are developed. "The 1990s may be the period," suggest Sashkin and Burke, "during which organization development and (a new sort) of management development are reconnected."

I believe that this new sort of management development will focus on the roles, skills, and tools for leadership in learning organizations. Undoubtedly, the ideas offered in this article are only a rough approximation of this new territory. The sooner we begin seriously exploring the territory, the sooner the initial map can be improved—and the sooner we will realize an age-old vision of leadership.

> *The wicked leader is he who the people despise.*
> *The good leader is he who the people revere.*
> *The great leader is he who the people say, "We did it ourselves."–Lao Tsu*

REFERENCES

[1] P. Senge, *The Fifth Discipline: The Art and Practice of the Learning Organization* (New York: Doubleday/Currency, 1990).

[2] A. P. de Geus, "Planning as Learning," *Harvard Business Review* (March-April 1988): 70–74.

[3] B. Domain, *Fortune*, July 3, 1989, 48–62.

[4] The distinction between adaptive and generative learning has its roots in the distinction between what Argyris and Schon have called their "single-loop" learning, in which individuals or groups adjust their behavior relative to fixed goals, norms, and assumptions, and "double-loop" learning, in which goals, norms, and assumptions, as well as behavior, are open to change (e.g., see C. Argyris and D. Schon, *Organizational Learning: A Theory-in-Action Perspective* [Reading, MA: Addison-Wesley, 1978]).

[5] All unattributed quotes are from personal communications with the author.

[6] G. Stalk, Jr., "Time: The Next Source of Competitive Advantage," *Harvard Business Review* (July-August 1988): 41–51.

[7] Senge (1990).

[8] The principle of creative tension comes from Robert Fritz' work on creativity. See R. Fritz, *The Path of Least Resistance* (New York: Ballantine, 1989) and *Creating* (New York: Ballantine, 1990).

[9] M. L. King, Jr., "Letter from Birmingham Jail," *American Visions*, January-February 1986, 52–59.

[10] E. Schein, *Organizational Culture and Leadership* (San Francisco: Jossey-Bass, 1985). Similar views have been expressed by many leadership theorists. For example, see: P. Selznick, *Leadership in Administration* (New York: Harper & Row, 1957); W. Bennis and B. Nanus, *Leaders* (New York: Harper & Row, 1985); and N. M. Tichy and M. A. Devanna, *The Transformational Leader* (New York: John Wiley & Sons, 1986).

[11] Selznick (1957).

[12] J. W. Forrester, "A New Corporate Design," *Sloan Management Review* (formerly *Industrial Management Review*) (Fall 1965): 5–17.

[13] See, for example, H. Mintzberg, "Crafting Strategy," *Harvard Business Review* (July-August 1987): 66–75.

[14] R. Mason and I. Mitroff, *Challenging Strategic Planning Assumptions* (New York: John Wiley & Sons, 1981) 16.

[15] P. Wack, "Scenarios: Uncharted Waters Ahead," *Harvard Business Review* (September-October 1985): 73–89.

[16] de Geus (1988).

[17] M. de Pree, *Leadership Is an Art* (New York: Doubleday, 1989) 9.

[18] For example, see T. Peters and N. Austin, *A Passion for Excellence* (New York: Random House, 1985); and J. M. Kouzes and B. Z. Posner, *The Leadership Challenge* (San Francisco: Jossey-Bass, 1987).

[19] I. Mitroff, *Break-Away Thinking* (New York: John Wiley & Sons, 1988) 66–67.

[20] R. K. Greenleaf, *Servant Leadership: A Journey into the Nature of Legitimate Power and Greatness* (New York: Paulist Press, 1977).

[21] L. Miller, *American Spirit: Visions of a New Corporate Culture* (New York: William Morrow, 1984) 15.

[22] These points are condensed from the practices of the five disciplines examined in Senge (1990).

[23] The ideas below are based to a considerable extent on the work of Chris Argyris, Donald Schon, and their Action Science colleagues: C. Argyris and D. Schon, *Organizational Learning: A Theory-in-Action Perspective* (Reading, MA: Addison-Wesley, 1978); C. Argyris, R. Putnam, and D. Smith, *Action Science* (San Francisco: Jossey-Bass, 1985); C. Argyris, *Strategy Change and Defensive Routines* (Boston: Pitman, 1985); and C. Argyris, *Overcoming Organizational Defenses* (Upper Saddle River, NJ: Prentice Hall, 1990).

[24] I am indebted to Diana Smith for the summary points that follow.

[25] The system archetypes are one of several systems diagramming and communication tools. See D. H. Kim, "Toward Learning Organizations: Integrating Total Quality Control and Systems Thinking" (Cambridge, MA: MIT Sloan School of Management, Working Paper No. 3037-89-BPS, June 1989).

[26] This archetype is closely associated with the work of ecologist Garrett Hardin, who coined its label: G. Hardin, "The Tragedy of the Commons," *Science*, December 13, 1968.

[27] These templates were originally developed by Jennifer Kemeny, Charles Kiefer, and Michael Goodman of Innovation Associates, Inc., Farmingham, Massachusetts.

[28] C. Hampden-Turner, *Charting the Corporate Mind* (New York: The Free Press, 1990).

[29] M. Sashkin and W. W. Burke, "Organization Development in the 1980s" and "An End-of-the-Eighties Retrospective," *Advances in Organization Development*, ed. F. Masarik (Norwood, NJ: Ablex, 1990).

[30] E. Schein (1985).

▲▲

CHAPTER 4

INDIVIDUAL AND ORGANIZATIONAL MOTIVATION

THAT URGE TO ACHIEVE
  David C. McClelland

MOTIVATION: A DIAGNOSTIC APPROACH
  David A. Nadler
  Edward E. Lawler III

RECOGNIZE CONTRIBUTIONS: LINKING REWARDS WITH PERFORMANCE
  James M. Kouzes
  Barry Z. Posner

Part of being a good manager is understanding what motivates employees and knowing how to design an organization that inspires people to work at their full potential. Once again, we find individual differences in motivation patterns, which can be viewed as yet another type of mental map.

There are many internal human needs that drive motivation. David McClelland devoted his academic career to studying three primary human needs—achievement, power, and affiliation. McClelland wrote the classic article, "That Urge to Achieve," and answered the question that often plagues managers—why some employees are hard workers and others are not.

Internal needs, however, are only one piece of the motivation puzzle. Employees make decisions about how hard to work based on their expectations about the results and rewards of their effort. Expectancy theory, developed by Victor Vroom, shows the effect of the environment, in particular the actions taken by managers, on employee motivation. David Nadler and Edward Lawler, two famous business scholars with a practical bent, describe expectancy theory in a classic article entitled, "Motivation: A Diagnostic Approach." Failure to understand this theory often results in demotivated employees (and students for that matter). Although managers cannot easily change the internal needs employees bring to work, they can place people in jobs that fit their needs, make sure they are capable of doing a good job and then reward them appropriately.

James Kouzes and Barry Posner spell out how to use rewards in "Recognize Contributions: Linking Rewards with Performance," a chapter from one of their best-selling books on leadership. Kouzes and Posner asked people who had been named by others as outstanding leaders to describe their "personal best" leadership experience, a time when they had accomplished something extraordinary in their organizations. By analyzing these experiences, Kouzes and Posner pinpointed five practices of effective leadership: challenging the process, inspiring a shared vision, enabling others to act, modeling the way, and encouraging the heart. The last practice highlighted the importance of linking rewards with performance as a means of recognizing individual contributions at work.

That Urge To Achieve*

David C. McClelland

Most people in this world, psychologically, can be divided into two broad groups. There is that minority which is challenged by opportunity and willing to work hard to achieve something, and the majority which really does not care all that much.

For nearly 20 years now, psychologists have tried to penetrate the mystery of this curious dichotomy. Is the need to achieve (or the absence of it) an accident, is it hereditary, or is it the result of environment? Is it a single, isolatable human motive, or a combination of motives—the desire to accumulate wealth, power, fame? Most important of all, is there some technique that could give this will to achieve to people, even whole societies, who do not now have it?

While we do not yet have complete answers for any of these questions, years of work have given us partial answers to most of them and insights into all of them. There is a distinct human motive, distinguishable from others. It can be found, in fact tested for, in any group.

Let me give you one example. Several years ago, a careful study was made of 450 workers who had been thrown out of work by a plant shutdown in Erie, Pennsylvania. Most of the unemployed workers stayed home for a while and then checked back with the U.S. Employment Service to see if their old jobs or similar ones were available. But a small minority among them behaved differently: the day they were laid off, they started job-hunting.

They checked both the United States and the Pennsylvania Employment Office: they studied the "Help Wanted" sections of the papers; they checked through their union, their church, and various fraternal organizations; they looked into training courses to learn a new skill; they even left town to look for work, while the majority when questioned said they would not under any circumstances move away from Erie to obtain a job. Obviously the members of that active minority were differently motivated. All the men were more or less in the same situation objectively: they needed work, money, food, shelter, job security. Yet only a minority showed initiative and enterprise in finding what they needed. Why? Psychologists, after years of research, now believe they can answer that question. They have demonstrated that these men possessed in greater degree a specific type of human motivation. For the moment let us refer to this personality characteristic as "Motive A" and review some of the other characteristics of the persons who have more of the motive than other persons.

Suppose they are confronted by a work situation in which they can set their own goals as to how difficult a task they will undertake. In the psychological laboratory, such a situation is very simply created by asking them to throw rings over a peg from any distance they may choose. Most persons throw more or less randomly, standing now close, now far away, but those with Motive A seem to calculate carefully where they are most likely to get a sense of mastery. They stand nearly always at moderate distances, not so close as to make the task ridiculously easy, nor so far away as to make it impossible. They set moderately difficult, but potentially achievable goals for themselves, where they objectively have only about a 1-in-3 chance of succeeding. In other words, they are always setting challenges for themselves, tasks to make them stretch themselves a little.

But they behave like this only if *they* can influence the outcome by performing the work themselves. They prefer not to gamble at all. Say they are given a choice between rolling dice with one in three chances of winning and working on a problem with a one-in-three chance of solving in the time

*Excerpted and reprinted by permission from *THINK Magazine*, published by IBM, © 1966 by International Business Machines Corporation, and from the author.

allotted, they choose to work on the problem even though rolling the dice is obviously less work and the odds of winning are the same. They prefer to work at a problem rather than leave the outcome to chance or to others.

Obviously they are concerned with personal achievement rather than with the rewards of success per se, since they stand just as much chance of getting those rewards by throwing the dice. This leads to another characteristic the Motive A persons show—namely, a strong preference for work situations in which they get concrete feedback on how well they are doing, as one does, say in playing golf, or in being a salesperson, but as one does not in teaching, or in personnel counseling. Golfers always know their score and can compare how well they are doing with par or with their own performance yesterday or last week. Teachers have no such concrete feedback on how well they are doing in "getting across" to their students.

THE *n*ACH PERSON

But why do certain persons behave like this? At one level the reply is simple: because they habitually spend their time thinking about doing things better. In fact, psychologists typically measure the strength of Motive A by taking samples of a person's spontaneous thoughts (such as making up a story about a picture they have been shown) and counting the frequency with which she mentions doing things better. The count is objective and can even be made these days with the help of a computer program for content analysis. It yields what is referred to technically as an individual's *n*Ach score (for "need for Achievement"). It is not difficult to understand why people who think constantly about "doing better" are more apt to do better at job-hunting, to set moderate achievable goals for themselves, to dislike gambling (because they get no achievement satisfaction from success), and to prefer work situations where they can tell easily whether they are improving or not. But why some people and not others come to think this way is another question. The evidence suggests it is not because they are born that way, but because of special training they get in the home from parents who set moderately high achievement goals but who are warm, encouraging, and nonauthoritarian in helping their children reach these goals.

Such detailed knowledge about one motive helps correct a lot of common sense ideas about human motivation. For example, much public policy (and much business policy) is based on the simpleminded notion that people will work harder "if they have to." As a first approximation, the idea isn't totally wrong, but it is only a half-truth. The majority of unemployed workers in Erie "had to" find work as much as those with higher *n*Ach, but they certainly didn't work as hard at it. Or again, it is frequently assumed that any strong motive will lead to doing things better. Wouldn't it be fair to say that most of the Erie workers were just "unmotivated?" But our detailed knowledge of various human motives shows that each one leads a person to behave in *different ways*. The contrast is not between being "motivated" or "unmotivated" but between being motivated toward A or toward B or C, etc.

A simple experiment makes the point nicely: subjects were told that they could choose as a working partner either a close friend or a stranger who was known to be an expert on the problem to be solved. Those with higher *n*Ach (more "need to achieve") chose the experts over their friends, whereas those with more *n*Aff (the "need to affiliate with others") chose friends over experts. The latter were not "unmotivated"; their desire to be with someone they liked was simply a stronger motive than their desire to excel at the task. Other such needs have been studied by psychologists. For instance, the need for Power is often confused with the need for Achievement because both may lead to "outstanding" activities. There is a distinct difference. People with a strong need for Power want to command attention, get recognition, and control others. They are more active in political life and tend to busy themselves primarily with controlling the channels of communication both up to the top and down to the people so that they are more "in charge." Those with high *n*Power are not as concerned with improving their work performance daily as those with high *n*Ach.

It follows, from what we have been able to learn, that not all "great achievers" score high in *n*Ach. Many generals, outstanding politicians, great research scientists do not, for instance, because their work requires other personality characteristics, other motives. A general or a politician must be more concerned with power relationships, a research scientist must be able to go for long periods without the immediate feedback the person with high *n*Ach requires, etc. On the other hand, business executives, particularly if they are in positions of real responsibility or if they are salespeople, tend to score high in *n*Ach. This is true even in a Communist country like Poland: apparently there, as well as in a private enterprise economy, a manager succeeds if he is concerned about improving all the time, setting moderate goals, keeping track of his or the company's performance, etc.

MOTIVATION AND HALF-TRUTHS

Since careful study has shown that common sense notions about motivation are at best half-truths, it also follows that you cannot trust what people tell you about their motives. After all, they often get their ideas about their own motives from common sense. Thus a general may say he is interested in achievement (because he has obviously achieved), or a businesswoman that is interested only in making money (because she has made money), or one of the majority of unemployed in Erie that he desperately wants a job (because he knows he needs one); but a careful check of what each one thinks about and how each one spends his or her time may show that each is concerned about quite different things. It requires special measurement techniques to identify the presence of *n*Ach and other such motives. Thus what people say and believe is not very closely related to these "hidden" motives which seem to affect people's "style of life" more than their political, religious or social attitudes. Thus *n*Ach produces enterprising women/men among labor leaders or managers, Republicans or Democrats, Catholics or Protestants, capitalists or communists.

Wherever people begin to think often in *n*Ach terms, things begin to move. People with higher *n*Ach get more raises and are promoted more rapidly, because they keep actively seeking ways to do a better job. Companies with many such people grow faster. In one comparison of two firms in Mexico, it was discovered that all but one of the top executives of a fast growing firm had higher *n*Ach scores than the highest scoring executive in an equally large but slow-growing firm. Countries with many such rapidly growing firms tend to show above-average rates of economic growth. This appears to be the reason why correlations have regularly been found between the *n*Ach content in popular literature (such as popular songs or stories in children's textbooks) and subsequent rates of national economic growth. A nation which is thinking about doing better all the time (as shown in its popular literature) actually does do better economically speaking. Careful quantitative studies have shown this to be true in Ancient Greece, in Spain in the Middle Ages, in England from 1400 to 1800, as well as among contemporary nations, whether capitalist or communist, developed or underdeveloped.

MOTIVATION: A DIAGNOSTIC APPROACH*

David A. Nadler
Edward E. Lawler III

- What makes some people work hard while others do as little as possible?
- How can I, as a manager, influence the performance of people who work for me?
- Why do people turn over, show up late to work, and miss work entirely?

* *Perspectives on Behavior in Organizations*, (New York: McGraw-Hill. 1977).

These important questions about employees' behavior can only be answered by managers who have a grasp of what motivates people. Specifically, a good understanding of motivation can serve as a valuable tool for understanding the causes of behavior in organizations, for predicting the effects of any managerial action, and for directing behavior so that organizational and individual goals can be achieved.

EXISTING APPROACHES

During the past 20 years, managers have been bombarded with a number of different approaches to motivation. The terms associated with these approaches are well known—*human relations*, *scientific management*, *job enrichment*, *need hierarchy*, *self-actualization*, etc. Each of these approaches has something to offer. On the other hand, each of these different approaches also has its problems in both theory and practice. Running through almost all of the approaches with which managers are familiar are a series of implicit but clearly erroneous assumptions.

Assumption 1: All employees are alike Different theories present different ways of looking at people, but each of them assumes that all employees are basically similar in their makeup. Employees all want economic gains, or all want a pleasant climate, or all aspire to be self-actualizing, etc.

Assumption 2: All situations are alike Most theories assume that all managerial situations are alike, and that the managerial course of action for motivation (for example, participation, job enlargement, etc.) is applicable in all situations.

Assumption 3: One best way Out of the other two assumptions there emerges a basic principle that there is "one best way" to motivate employees.

When these "one best way" approaches are tried in the "correct" situation they will work. However, all of them are bound to fail in some situations. They are therefore not adequate managerial tools.

A NEW APPROACH

During the past 10 years, a great deal of research has been done on a new approach to looking at motivation. This approach, frequently called *expectancy theory*, still needs further testing, refining, and extending. However, enough is known that many behavioral scientists have concluded that it represents the most comprehensive, valid, and useful approach to understanding motivation. Further, it is apparent that it is a very useful tool for understanding motivation in organizations.

The theory is based on a number of specific assumptions about the causes of behavior in organizations.

Assumption 1: Behavior is determined by a combination of forces in the individual and forces in the environment Neither the individual nor the environment alone determines behavior. Individuals come into organizations with certain "psychological baggage." They have past experiences and a developmental history, which has given them unique sets of needs, ways of looking at the world, and expectations about how organizations will treat them. These all influence how individuals respond to their work environment. The work environment provides structures (such as a pay system or a supervisor), which influence the behavior of people. Different environments tend to produce different behavior in similar people just as dissimilar people tend to behave differently in similar environments.

Assumption 2: People make decisions about their own behavior in organizations While there are many constraints on the behavior of individuals in organizations, most of the behavior that is observed is the result of individuals' conscious decisions. These decisions usually fall into two categories. First, individuals make decisions about *membership behavior*—coming to work, staying at work, and in other ways being a member of the organization. Second, individuals make decisions about the amount of *effort* they will direct towards performing their jobs. This includes decisions about how hard to work, how much to produce, at what quality, etc.

Assumption 3: Different people have different types of needs, desires, and goals Individuals differ on what kinds of outcomes (or rewards) they desire. These differences are not random; they can be examined systematically by an understanding of the differences in the strength of individuals' needs.

Assumption 4: People make decisions among alternative plans of behavior based on their perceptions (expectancies) of the degree to which a given behavior will lead to desired outcomes In simple terms, people tend to do those things which they see as leading to outcomes (which can also be called "rewards") they desire and avoid doing those things they see as leading to outcomes that are never desired.

In general, the approach used here views people as having their own needs and mental maps of what the world is like. They use these maps to make decisions about how they will behave, behaving in those ways which their mental maps indicate will lead to outcomes that will satisfy their needs. Therefore, they are inherently neither motivated nor unmotivated; motivation depends on the situation they are in, and how it fits their needs.

THE THEORY

Based on these general assumptions, expectancy theory states a number of propositions about the process by which people make decisions about their own behavior in organizational settings. While the theory is complex at first view, it is in fact made of a series of fairly straightforward observations about behavior. Three concepts serve as the key building blocks of the theory:

Performance-Outcome Expectancy   Every behavior has associated with it, in an individual's mind, certain outcomes (rewards or punishments). In other words, the individual believes or expects that if he or she behaves in a certain way, he or she will get certain things.

Examples of expectancies can easily be described. An individual may have an expectancy that if he produces 10 units he will receive his normal hourly rate while if he produces 15 units he will receive his hourly pay rate plus a bonus. Similarly an individual may believe that certain levels of performance will lead to approval or disapproval from members of her work group or from her supervisor. Each performance can be seen as leading to a number of different kinds of outcomes and outcomes can differ in their types.

Valence   Each outcome has a "valence" (value, worth, attractiveness) to a specific individual. Outcomes have different valences for different individuals. This comes about because valences result from individual needs and perceptions, which differ because they in turn reflect other factors in the individual's life.

For example, some individuals may value an opportunity for promotion or advancement because of their needs for achievement or power, while others may not want to be promoted and leave their current work group because of needs for affiliation with others. Similarly, a fringe benefit such as a pension plan may have great valence for an older worker but little valence for a young employee on his or her first job.

Effort-Performance Expectancy   Each behavior also has associated with it in the individual's mind a certain expectancy or probability of success. This expectancy represents the individual's perception of how hard it will be to achieve such behavior and the probability of his or her successful achievement of that behavior.

For example, you may have a strong expectancy that if you put forth the effort, you can produce 10 units an hour, but that you have only a fifty-fifty chance of producing 15 units an hour if you try.

Putting these concepts together, it is possible to make a basic statement about motivation. In general, the motivation to attempt to behave in a certain way is greatest when:

A. The individual believes that the behavior will lead to outcomes (performance outcome expectancy).

B. The individual believes that these outcomes have positive value for him or her (valence).

C. The individual believes that he or she is able to perform at the desired level (effort performance expectancy).

Given a number of alternative levels of behavior (10, 15, and 20 units of production per hour, for example) the individual will choose that level of performance which has the greatest motivational force associated with it, as indicated by the expectancies, outcomes, and valences.

In other words, when faced with choices about behavior, the individual goes through a process of considering questions such as, "Can I perform at that level if I try?" "If I perform at that level, what will happen?" "How do I feel about those things that will happen?" The individual then decides to behave in that way which seems to have the best chance of producing positive, desired outcomes.

A GENERAL MODEL

On the basis of these concepts, it is possible to construct a general model of behavior in organizational settings (see Figure 1). Working from left to right in the model, motivation is seen as the force on the individual to expend effort. Motivation leads to an observed level of effort by the individual. Effort, alone, however, is not enough. Performance results from a combination of the effort that an individual puts forth and the level of ability which he or she has (reflecting skills, training, information, etc.). Effort thus combines with ability to produce a given level of performance. As a result of performance, the individual attains certain outcomes. The model indicates this relationship in a dotted line, reflecting the fact that sometimes people perform but do not get desired outcomes. As this process of performance-reward occurs, time after time, the actual events serve to provide information which influences the individual's perceptions (particularly expectancies) and thus influences motivation in the future.

Outcomes, or rewards, fall into two major categories. First, the individual obtains outcomes from the environment. When an individual performs at a given level he or she can receive positive or negative outcomes from supervisors, coworkers, the organization's rewards systems, or other sources. These environmental rewards are thus one source of outcomes for the individual. A second source of outcomes is the individual. These include outcomes which occur purely from the performance of the task itself (feelings of accomplishment, personal worth, achievement, etc.). In a sense, the individual gives these rewards to himself or herself. The environment cannot give them or take them away directly; it can only make them possible.

FIGURE 1 **The Basic Motivation-Behavior Sequence**

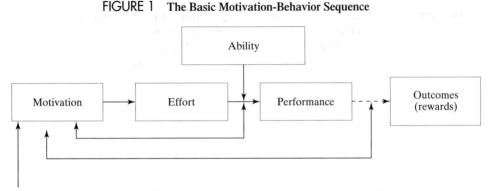

A person's motivation is a function of:

a. Effort-to-performance expectancies
b. Performance-to-outcome expectancies
c. Perceived valence of outcomes

Supporting Evidence

Over 50 studies have been done to test the validity of the expectancy-theory approach to predicting employee behavior.[1] Almost without exception, the studies have confirmed the predictions of the theory. As the theory predicts, the best performers in organizations tend to see a strong relationship between performing their jobs well and receiving rewards they value. In addition they have clear performance goals and feel they can perform well. Similarly, studies using the expectancy theory to predict how people choose jobs also show that individuals tend to interview for and actually take those jobs which they feel will provide the rewards they value. One study, for example, was able to correctly predict for 80 percent of the people studied which of several jobs they would take.[2] Finally, the theory correctly predicts that beliefs about the outcomes associated with performance (expectancies) will be better predictors of performance than will feelings of job satisfaction since expectancies are the critical causes of performance and satisfaction is not.

Questions about the Model

Although the results so far have been encouraging, they also indicate some problems with the model. These problems do not critically affect the managerial implications of the model, but they should be noted. The model is based on the assumption that individuals make very rational decisions after a thorough exploration of all the available alternatives and on weighing the possible outcomes of all these alternatives. When we talk to or observe individuals, however, we find that their decision processes are frequently less thorough. People often stop considering alternative behavior plans when they find one that is at least moderately satisfying, even though more rewarding plans remain to be examined.

People are also limited, in the amount of information they can handle at one time, and therefore the model may indicate a process that is much more complex than the one that actually takes place. On the other hand, the model does provide enough information and is consistent enough with reality to present some clear implications for managers who are concerned with the question of how to motivate the people who work for them.

Implications for Managers

The first set of implications is directed toward the individual manager who has a group of people working for him or her and is concerned with how to motivate good performance. Since behavior is a result of forces both in the person and in the environment, you as manager need to look at and diagnose both the person and the environment. Specifically, you need to do the following:

Figure out what outcomes each employee values As a first step, it is important to determine what kinds of outcomes or rewards have valence for your employees. For each employee you need to determine "what turns him or her on." There are various ways of finding this out, including a) finding out employees' desires through some structured method of data collection, such as a questionnaire, b) observing the employees' reactions to different situations or rewards, or c) the fairly simple act of asking them what kinds of rewards they want, what kind of career goals they have, or "what's in it for them." It is important to stress here that it is very difficult to change what people want, but fairly easy to find out what they want. Thus, the skillful manager emphasizes diagnosis of needs, not changing the individuals themselves.

Determine what kinds of behavior you desire Managers frequently talk about "good performance" without really defining what good performance is. An important step in motivating is for you yourself to figure out what kinds of performances are required and what are adequate measures or indicators of performance (quantity, quality, etc.). There is also a need to be able to define those performances in fairly specific terms so that observable and measurable behavior can be defined and subordinates can understand what is desired of them (e.g., produce 10 products of a certain quality standard-rather than only produce at a high rate).

Make sure desired levels of performance are reachable The model states that motivation is determined not only by the performance-to-outcome expectancy, but also by the effort-to-performance expectancy. The implication of this is that the levels of performance which are set as the points at which individuals receive desired outcomes must be reachable or attainable by these individuals. If the employees feel that the level of performance required to get a reward is higher than they can reasonably achieve, then their motivation to perform well will be relatively low.

Link desired outcomes to desired performances The next step is to directly, clearly, and explicitly link those outcomes desired by employees to the specific performances you desire. If your employee values external rewards, then the emphasis should be on the rewards systems concerned with promotion, pay, and approval. While the linking of these rewards can be initiated through your making statements to your employees, it is extremely important that employees see a clear example of the reward process working in a fairly short period of time if the motivating "expectancies" are to be created in the employees' minds. The linking must be done by some concrete public acts, in addition to statements of intent.

If your employee values internal rewards (e.g., achievement), then you should concentrate on changing the nature of the person's job, for he or she is likely to respond well to such things as increased autonomy, feedback, and challenge, because these things will lead to a situation where good job performance is inherently rewarding. The best way to check on the adequacy of the internal and external reward system is to ask people what their perceptions of the situation are. Remember it is the perceptions of people that determine their motivation, not reality. It doesn't matter for example whether you feel a subordinate's pay is related to his or her motivation. Motivation will be present only if the subordinate sees the relationship. Many managers are misled about the behavior of their subordinates because they rely on their own perceptions of the situation and forget to find out what their subordinates feel. There is only one way to do this: ask. Questionnaires can be used here, as can personal interviews.

Analyze the total situation for conflicting expectancies Having set up positive expectancies for employees, you then need to look at the entire situation to see if other factors (informal work groups, other managers, the organization's reward systems) have set up conflicting expectancies in the minds of the employees. Motivation will only be high when people see a number of rewards associated with good performance and few negative outcomes. Again, you can often gather this kind of information by asking your subordinates. If there are major conflicts, you need to make adjustments, either in your own performance and reward structure, or in the other sources of rewards or punishments in the environment.

Make sure changes in outcomes are large enough In examining the motivational system, it is important to make sure that changes in outcomes or rewards are large enough to motivate significant behavior. Trivial rewards will result in trivial amounts of effort and thus trivial improvements in performance. Rewards must be large enough to motivate individuals to put forth the effort required to bring about significant changes in performance.

Check the system for its equity The model is based on the idea that individuals are different and therefore different rewards will need to be used to motivate different individuals. On the other hand, for a motivational system to work it must be a fair one—one that has equity (not equality). Good performers should see that they get more desired rewards than do poor performers, and others in the system should see that also. Equity should not be confused with a system of equality where all are rewarded equally, with no regard to their performance. A system of equality is guaranteed to produce low motivation.

IMPLICATIONS FOR ORGANIZATIONS

Expectancy theory has some clear messages for those who run large organizations. It suggests how organizational structures can be designed so that they increase rather than decrease levels of motivation or organization members. While there are many different implications, a few of the major ones are as follows:

Implication 1: The design of pay and reward systems   Organizations usually get what they reward, not what they want. This can be seen in many situations, and pay systems are a good example.[3] Frequently, organizations reward people for membership (through pay tied to seniority, for example) rather than for performance. Little wonder that what the organization gets is behavior oriented towards "safe," secure employment rather than effort directed at performing well. In addition, even where organizations do pay for performance as a motivational device, they frequently negate the motivational value of the system by keeping pay secret, therefore preventing people from observing the pay-to-performance relationship that would serve to create positive, clear, and strong performance-to-reward expectancies. The implication is that organizations should put more effort into rewarding people (through pay, promotion, better job opportunities, etc.) for the performances which are desired, and that to keep these rewards secret is clearly self-defeating. In addition, it underscores the importance of the frequently ignored performance evaluation or appraisal process and the need to evaluate people based on how they perform clearly defined specific behaviors, rather than on how they score on ratings of general traits such as "honesty," "cleanliness," and other, similar terms which frequently appear as part of the performance appraisal form.

Implication 2: The design of tasks, jobs, and roles   One source of desired outcomes is the work itself. The expectancy-theory model supports much of the job enrichment literature, in saying that by designing jobs which enable people to get their needs fulfilled, organizations can bring about higher levels of motivation.[4] The major difference between the traditional approaches to job enlargement or enrichment and the expectancy-theory approach is the recognition by expectancy theory that different people have different needs and, therefore, some people may not want enlarged or enriched jobs. Thus, while the design of tasks that have more autonomy, variety, feedback, meaningfulness, etc., will lead to higher motivation in some, the organization needs to build in the opportunity for individuals to make choices about the kind of work they will do so that not everyone is forced to experience job enrichment.

Implication 3: The importance of group structures   Groups, both formal and informal, are powerful and potent sources of desired outcomes for individuals. Groups can provide or withhold acceptance, approval, affection, skill training, needed information, assistance, etc. They are a powerful force in the total motivational environment of individuals. Several implications emerge from the importance of groups. First, organizations should consider the structuring of at least a portion of rewards around group performance rather than individual performance. This is particularly important where group members have to cooperate with each other to produce a group product or service, and where the individual's contribution is often hard to determine. Second, the organization needs to train managers to be aware of how groups can influence individual behavior and to be sensitive to the kinds of expectancies which informal groups set up and their conflict or consistency with the expectancies that the organization attempts to create.

Implication 4: The supervisor's role   The immediate supervisor has an important role in creating, monitoring, and maintaining the expectancies and reward structures which will lead to good performance. The supervisor's role in the motivation process becomes one of defining clear goals, setting clear reward expectancies, and providing the right rewards for different people (which could include both organizational rewards and personal rewards such as recognition, approval, or support from the supervisor). Thus, organizations need to provide supervisors with an awareness of the nature of motivation as well as the tools (control over organizational rewards, skill in administering those rewards) to create positive motivation.

Implication 5: Measuring motivation If things like expectancies, the nature of the job, supervisor-controlled outcomes, satisfaction, etc., are important in understanding how well people are being motivated, then organizations need to monitor employee perceptions along these lines. One relatively cheap and reliable method of doing this is through standardized employee questionnaires. A number of organizations already use such techniques, surveying employees' perceptions and attitudes at regular intervals (ranging from once a month to once every year and-a-half) using either standardized surveys or surveys developed specifically for the organization. Such information is useful both to the individual manager and to top management in assessing the state of human resources and the effectiveness of the organization's motivational systems.[5]

Implication 6: Individualizing organizations Expectancy theory leads to a final general implication about a possible future direction for the design of organizations. Because different people have different needs and therefore have different valences, effective motivation must come through the recognition that not all employees are alike and that organizations need to be flexible in order to accommodate individual differences. This implies the "building in" of choice for employees in many areas, such as reward systems, fringe benefits, job assignments, etc., where employees previously have had little say. A successful example of the building in of such choice can be seen in the experiments at TRW and the Educational Testing Service with "cafeteria fringe-benefits plans" which allow employees to choose the fringe benefits they want, rather than taking the expensive and often unwanted benefits which the company frequently provides to everyone.[6]

SUMMARY

Expectancy theory provides a more complex model of humankind for managers to work with. At the same time, it is a model which holds promise for the more effective motivation of individuals and the more effective design of organizational systems. It implies, however, the need for more exacting and thorough diagnosis by the manager to determine (a) the relevant forces in the individual, and (b) the relevant forces in the environment, both of which combine to motivate different kinds of behavior. Following diagnosis, the model implies a need to act—to develop a system of pay, promotion, job assignments, group structures, supervision, etc.—to bring about effective motivation by providing different outcomes for different individuals.

Performance of individuals is a critical issue in making organizations work effectively. If a manager is to influence work behavior and performance, he or she must have an understanding of motivation and the factors which influence an individual's motivation to come to work, to work hard, and to work well. While simple models offer easy answers, it is the more complex models which seem to offer more promise. Managers can use models (like expectancy theory) to understand the nature of behavior and build more effective organizations.

REFERENCES

[1] For reviews of the expectancy theory research see T. R. Mitchell, "Expectancy Models of Job Satisfaction, Occupational Preference and Effort: A Theoretical, Methodological, and Empirical Appraisal," *Psychological Bulletin 81* (1974): 1053–1077. For a more general discussion of expectancy theory and other approaches to motivation see E. E. Lawler, *Motivation in Work Organizations* (Belmont CA: Brooks/Cole, 1973).

[2] E. E. Lawler, W. J. Kuleck, J. G. Rhode, and J. F. Sorenson, "Job Choice and Postdecision Dissonance," *Organizational Behavior and Human Performance 13* (1975): 133–145.

[3] For a detailed discussion of the implications of expectancy theory for pay and reward systems, see E. E. Lawler, *Pay and Organizational Effectiveness: A Psychological View* (New York: McGraw Hill, 1971).

[4] A good discussion of job design with an expectancy theory perspective is in J. R. Hackman, G. R. Oldham, R. Janson, and K. Purdy, "A New Strategy for Job Enrichment," *California Management Review* (Summer, 1975): 57.

[5] The use of questionnaires for understanding and changing organizational behavior is discussed in D. A. Nadler, *Feedback and Organizational Development: Using Data Based Methods* (Reading, MA: Addison-Wesley, 1977).

[6] The whole issue of individualizing organizations is examined in E. E. Lawler, "The Individualized Organization: Problems and Promise," *California Management Review 17* (2) (1974): 31–39.

[7] For a more detailed statement of the model see E. E. Lawler, "Job Attitudes and Employee Motivation: Theory, Research and Practice," *Personnel Psychology 23* (1970): 223–237.

RECOGNIZE CONTRIBUTIONS: LINKING REWARDS WITH PERFORMANCE*

James M. Kouzes
Barry Z. Posner

People value being appreciated for their contributions. Recognition does not have to be elaborate, just genuine.

—Alfonso Rivera, Engineering Consultant

"I was teaching math to sixth graders. We were working with students who had been 'low performers' and felt like they were already failures in math. Their attention spans seemed to be about two minutes long! The challenge was to increase their speed and accuracy in solving math problems." So begins Cheryl Breetwor's "Personal Best"—her story about a time when she accomplished something extraordinary as a leader. Breetwor, who went on to direct investor relations for Rolm Corporation before starting her own company (Share-Data), chose this experience as a sixth-grade teacher as one of her personal bests. Why?

"Because it's all about how you make work fun and rewarding. We wanted to show these kids they could win. If you can do that, you can get the best out of anybody," explains Breetwor. "And what's more, I knew we could do it!" Everyday, Breetwor handed out awards—awards primarily for "speed, skill, and accuracy," but also for persistence. Breetwor used these opportunities to recognize the small wins and milestones reached by the kids on their path toward mastering math fundamentals.

It's not unusual for people to work very intensely and for extraordinarily long hours during personal bests. To persist for months at such a pace, people need encouragement; they need the heart to continue with the journey. One important way that leaders give heart to others and keep them from giving up is by recognizing individual contributions. When participants in our workshops and seminars summarize the key leadership practices that make a difference in getting extraordinary things accomplished, recognizing people's contributions is on just about every list.

Likewise, when nonmanagers are polled regarding the skills their managers need in order to be more effective, at the top of the list is the ability to recognize and acknowledge the contributions of others.[1] Executives, too, need recognition, as indicated in a recent survey about why they leave their jobs: the number one reason given was limited praise and recognition.[2] To some people, praise and recognition may seem unimportant or inappropriate, even trivial. But assuming that constituents will know when their manager thinks they've done a good job doesn't work.

---

*Reprinted with permission from J. M. Kouzes and B. Z. Posner, *The Leadership Challenge* (San Francisco: Jossey-Bass, 1995): 269–291.

This assumption helped to account for the gap Paul Moran discovered between his perception of encouraging the heart and the views of his constituents (as measured by the Leadership Practices Inventory):

> *In the past, I usually neglected to celebrate my team's accomplishments (and my own accomplishments), because I never personally placed much importance on this aspect of the job for myself and I tended to forget about recognizing the accomplishments of others. Rather, I treated their accomplishments as part of their normal job, which required no unique recognition.*

To rectify this situation, when Moran was at Pacific Bell, he developed a specific outline of various recognition techniques to remind him of the importance of recognition and to make available a few simple techniques to recognize various types of accomplishments. When his team reached a key milestone in reengineering corporate accounting processes, he shook the hand of each member of the project team, took several key team members out to lunch, made telephone calls to all members thanking them personally for their efforts in the project, and invited them all to a small office party for cake and coffee. Upon further reflection, Moran felt that he should have done even more. The reason is found in an insight from Leonard (Swamp) Marsh, COO and executive vice president of Medical Coaches, Inc.: recognition "would have made folks more excited to get started on our next project," he noted, faulting his own personal-best leadership experience for inadequate recognition.

But there's much more at stake here than simply recognizing individuals for their contributions. Breetwor and the other leaders in our study practiced these *essentials* in their recognition of individuals:

- Building self-confidence through high expectations
- Connecting performance and rewards
- Using a variety of rewards
- Being positive and hopeful

By putting these four essentials into practice and recognizing contributions, leaders can stimulate and motivate the internal drives within each individual.

BUILDING SELF-CONFIDENCE THROUGH HIGH EXPECTATIONS

Successful leaders have high expectations, both of themselves and of their constituents. These expectations are powerful, because they're the frames into which people fit reality: we often wind up seeing what we expect rather than what's actually occurring. Social psychologists have referred to this as the self-fulfilling prophecy or the Pygmalion effect. In Greek mythology, the sculptor Pygmalion carved a statue of a beautiful woman, fell in love with the statue, and brought it to life by the strength of his perceptions. Leaders play Pygmalion-like roles in developing people. Research on the phenomenon of self-fulfilling prophecies provides ample evidence that other people act in ways that are consistent with our expectations of them.[3] If we expect others to fail, they probably will.

The self-fulfilling prophecy can be applied in a variety of situations. For example, Dov Eden, director of Israel's Institute of Business Research, Tel Aviv University, and his colleagues have shown that the rate of volunteering for special-forces military service can be increased by raising candidates' expectations about their ability to succeed. In a study he directed, the only difference between the experimental and control groups was that the recruiters stressed their own personal similarity to the experimental candidates (for example, "I've been where you are, and look where I am now").[4] In another study, the self-fulfilling prophecy was able to raise the productivity of an entire group, not just individuals (illustrating the fact that producing higher expectations for some doesn't require not raising expectations for others).[5]

Indeed, when we ask people to describe exemplary leaders, they consistently talk about people who have been able to bring out the best in them. This is one of the defining characteristics of a leader, one of the things that make constituents willing to be led: that person has our best interests at heart and wants us to be as successful as possible. Leading others requires that leaders have high expectations about what people can accomplish. Consequently, leaders treat people in ways that bolster their self-confidence, thereby making it possible for those people to achieve more than they may have initially believed possible. Leaders' belief in others creates a self-fulfilling prophecy: we do as we're expected to do. Leaders understand that feeling appreciated increases a person's sense of self-worth, which in turn precipitates success at school, home, and work.

It's also evident that the self-fulfilling prophecy is a reciprocal process; not only can leaders influence the expectations of others, but those expectations of constituents can influence the behaviors of their leaders. If constituents communicate high expectations of how good an individual could be as a leader, that potential leader may adjust his or her self-concept and self-expectation to be congruent with that of others. With this motivation for exemplary leadership behaviors, the constituents' prophecy is fulfilled.[6]

Nathaniel Branden, one of the pioneers in the field of self-esteem, has noted that "Of all the judgments we pass in life, none is more important than the judgment we pass on ourselves. That judgment impacts every moment and every aspect of our existence. Our self-evaluation is the basic context in which we act and react, choose our values, set our goals, meet the challenges that confront us. Our responses to events are shaped in part by whom and what we think we are."[7] Research and everyday experiences confirm that men and women with high self-esteem—regardless of their age, level of education, and socioeconomic background—"feel unique, competent, secure, empowered, and connected to the people around them."[8]

To illustrate this point, social psychologists Robert Wood and Albert Bandura had working professionals manage a simulated organization. Participants had to match employee attributes to job requirements and master a complex set of decision rules in how best to guide and motivate their employees. Half the subjects were told that decision-making skills are developed through practice (and hence are acquired skills); the others were informed that decision-making skills reflect the basic cognitive capabilities that people possess (and hence are stable skills).

Throughout the simulation, the subjects rated the strength of their perceived self-efficacy in getting the group they were managing to perform at various productivity levels. Initially subjects in both groups expressed a moderately strong sense of managerial effectiveness. However, as they tried to fulfill the difficult production standard, those in the stable-skill condition displayed a progressive decline in perceived self-efficacy, while those in the acquired-skill condition maintained their sense of managerial efficacy. Those in the stable-skill group were quite uncharitable in their views of their employees, regarding them as incapable of being motivated, unworthy of supervision, and deserving of termination. In contrast, those in the acquired-skill condition set more challenging goals in subsequent trials and made more efficient use of analytical strategies, because from their perspective errors didn't imply a basic cognitive deficiency.[9]

Nancy Tivol, executive director of Sunnyvale Community Services (SCS), believes strongly in her own ability and in the capacity of every staff member and volunteer at SCS to contribute something valuable. When Tivol first arrived, in 1991, volunteers were working at SCS in a very limited capacity. Certain staff members insisted, for example, that volunteers couldn't run the front office because they wouldn't be able to handle client and corporate contact adequately. Tivol refused to share that view, however, and today SCS has volunteers doing things that only staff members did previously. Indeed, every department at SCS is run by a volunteer over 70 years of age. And SCS is the county's only emergency assistance agency that doesn't turn people away, having increased its funding for preventing evictions, utility disconnections, and hunger by 421 percent and having increased the number of families served by its monthly food program by 365 percent—even while funding for operations was cut back significantly.

By recognizing the valuable contributions that others make, we can help bring about the achievement of extraordinary things. Tivol demonstrated this not only through her belief in the volunteer staff but through her faith in another unexpected group of volunteers. Tivol recognized how desperately the agency needed to become computerized. With some donated computers but no money for computer training, Tivol entrusted her 15-year-old son with that responsibility. For his Eagle Scout project, he wrote a 41-page manual and trained 10 Boy Scouts to teach agency staff and volunteers. Each Scout then "adopted" a staff member or volunteer and tutored that person in computer and software skills. Now everyone at SCS is computer-literate, and all office operations are computerized.

As Tivol demonstrated, leaders have a high degree of confidence in others and in themselves. To be sure, some people we surveyed were nervous or anxious on the eve of their personal bests, but each was also ready for the plunge. All were excited by and willing to accept the challenges they faced (either by circumstance or by choice). Without exception or hesitation, these people expressed confidence that they could work well with others and assemble a team to address whatever problems might lie ahead. The high expectations that leaders have of others are based in large part on their expectations of themselves. This is one reason why leaders model the way. What gives their expectations for others credibility is their own record of achievement and dedication, along with their daily demonstrations of what and how things need to be done.

Leaders' expectations have their strongest and most powerful influence in times of uncertainty and turbulence. When accepted ways of doing things aren't working well enough, leaders' strong expectations about the destination, the processes to follow, and the capabilities of the team serve to make dreams come true.

What's more, leaders tend not to give up on people, because doing so means giving up on themselves, their judgment, and their ability to get the best out of other people. Breetwor was convinced that she was a capable enough teacher to improve that group of sixth-graders' math skills. She never gave up on them; she never gave up on herself. Likewise, when Antonio Zárate turned Metalsa from a company with a 10 percent rejection rate and only a domestic market into an award-winning, world-class automotive metal stamping company with 40 percent exports, he did so using the same local Mexican workforce that had always staffed Metalsa. The difference was in what Zárate believed those workers could do. He believed that there are no poor-quality workers, only underled companies. He never gave up on his workers; he never gave up on himself.

CONNECTING PERFORMANCE AND REWARDS

The outcomes of our present actions play a major role in determining our future actions. People repeat behavior that's rewarded, avoid behavior that's punished, and drop or forget behavior that produces neither result.[10] If especially hard work and long hours on a project go unnoticed and unrewarded, people will soon minimize their efforts. That's why manufacturing support manager Russ Douglass used what he called "spot strokes" on his personal-best project—"instant payoffs like 'Have this lunch on me' or 'Take the afternoon off.'" As he said, "Sometimes we'd put on a party in the parking lot on a half-hour notice."

One of the oldest, most important, and strongest prescriptions for influencing motivation is to tie job-related outcomes (such as rewards and recognition) to job effort and/or performance.[11] If a concern for quality is desired, rewards should be given to those who consistently meet quality standards, and low-quality performers shouldn't be rewarded until they conform to this norm. Today we see performance-reward linkages everywhere.[12]

AT&T, General Mills, Continental Bank, and Nucor Steel, for example, have all instituted pay-for-performance systems or variable pay systems. Saloman Brothers, the New York investment firm, has found that linking performance and rewards works for brokers and traders with profit responsibility—and for staff and support groups as well. Under a system the organization calls Teamshare, as training and technology push costs down, back-office staffers (over 500 people in all) get to keep 10 percent of the savings.[13]

Another example of how specific performance-reward linkages affect behavior comes from U.S. Healthcare, a Pennsylvania-based health maintenance organization. U.S. Healthcare's quality-oriented compensation plan rewards primary-care providers for attaining certain quality-of-care standards as well as for controlling costs. Like most HMOs, U.S. Healthcare pays its physicians a monthly fee for each patient. However, unlike most HMOs, it also pays up to a 28 percent premium to physicians based upon a number of quality and customer service goals. Scheduling office hours at night, linking up with the HMO by computer, and attaining high immunization rates for children and mammography rates for women over age 40 are all rewarded, for example, as are accepting and retaining new U.S. Healthcare patients. And while doctors whose patients spend fewer days in the hospital or see fewer specialists are rewarded, those whose referral rate seems too low can be penalized. In evaluating physician performance, U.S. Healthcare audits medical records and surveys its members, whose views and satisfaction ratings further influence each physician's compensation. Healthcare physicians receive monthly reports on their quality and customer service performance.

The success of the program is evident. As a result of the organization's quality emphasis, all six U.S. Healthcare HMOs received full three-year accreditation, the best performance of any U.S. managed-care company. In addition, despite the bonus system (which can result in primary-care physicians receiving greater compensation for their U.S. Healthcare patients than for traditional fee-for-service patients), U.S. Healthcare has been able to keep its premiums competitive with other HMOs and well below traditional health insurance premiums, while providing a healthy return to investors. Since 1988, U.S. Healthcare's stock has risen twelvefold.[14]

When integrating performance with rewards, leaders must

- Make certain that people know what's expected of them.
- Provide feedback about contributors' performance.
- Reward only those who meet the standards.[15]

It's not always easy to meet these criteria, yet their significance shouldn't be underestimated. They've been shown across a wide variety of organizational settings to improve the job performance of such diverse workgroups as clerks in a small grocery store, mountain beaver trappers, engineers, telephone service crews, truck drivers, and salespeople.[16]

Consider how Nolan Dishongh linked performance and rewards—and achieved extraordinary results. During his first day as construction trades instructor and education coordinator for at-risk students at Alice Johnson Junior High School, he saw no order, no plan. When he asked students what they were supposed to be working on, they said it didn't matter: the instructor who had just quit had let them do anything they wanted, including doing nothing. Not surprisingly, most of them were failing not just construction trades but their other classes also.

Dishongh began planning projects and events to increase interest. To participate, however, his students had to do more than merely show up. Taking his role as education coordinator seriously, Dishongh required all construction trades students to give him a report from each of their academic instructors regarding their academic performance (class attendance and homework completion) before they could participate in class activities each week. And Dishongh graded each of these reports. Reports revealing unexcused absences or incomplete homework received a 0 and the student was "benched"; reports showing completed homework and perfect attendance were given a mark of 100. Each Monday morning, the reports were reviewed openly during a group discussion, with Dishongh giving praise and encouragement and eliciting group involvement when a member wasn't keeping up his commitments. Dishongh made it clear that each student's weekly average of what he called the "zero-zeros" reports counted for a full third of the grade in construction trades—and that no one with a class average below 70 would be allowed to attend the end-of-the-year field trip he was organizing to a wildly interesting and otherwise inaccessible location: the local heavy-metal radio station.

As the year progressed, the group's grades began to improve—in all academic classes as well as construction trades. Dishongh is still amazed by the dramatic change in Weldon Creech: he went from a depressing academic record of 47 Fs to an astounding record of all As and Bs within one year. And Creech wasn't alone: Dishongh made it possible for all of his students to accomplish something significant and was rewarded by seeing the growth of their self-respect. Kenton Miles reflected the deep feelings of many of his classmates when he handed Dishongh a plaque inscribed, "Thanks for being my friend and showing me even I can make a difference in the world."[17]

Like Dishongh, successful leaders strive skillfully and diligently to see that the system works. Two additional notes about the significance of linking performance and rewards. First, feedback is the loop that provides learning, both to the individuals involved and to the organizational system. Experience without feedback is unlikely to build or enhance competence. Put another way, learning results when people can see the relationship between what they're doing and how their needs are (or aren't) being met, as was certainly the case with Dishongh's students. This assessment is possible only when people are able to measure their performance, of course, whether through satisfaction surveys or units sold or words typed per minute. The most powerful measurements are those that offer timely feedback and can be monitored by the individuals doing the work. No one could imagine designing a measurement system for driving in which only the police could determine one's speed. Instead, each automobile is equipped with a speedometer, always visible to the driver. Why, then, do many organizations design feedback systems in which only the inspectors and managers (the police) have the tools to monitor performance?

Second, although compensation plans include rewards as a critical element, these are just one part of a total strategy—along with communication, employee involvement, feedback, and financial justifications. As a result, the size of rewards is important but not critical.[18]

USING A VARIETY OF REWARDS

Leaders use many types of rewards to recognize the efforts and contributions of their constituents. Indeed, the creative use of rewards is another defining characteristic of leaders. Leaders tend not to be dependent upon the organization's formal reward system (typically financial), which offers only a limited range of options. Breetwor, for example, relied on much more than grades to motivate students. In the business world, promotions and raises are scarce resources and can't be applied frequently. On the other hand, verbal or written praise, "spot strokes," buttons, and other informal and more personal rewards are almost unlimited resources.

Furthermore, relying upon an organization's formal reward system typically requires considerable effort and time. In one study, we found that the time lapse between performance and promotion is seldom less than six months. Similarly, most organizations' performance appraisal systems allow for raises or any other merit awards to be handed out only once per year.[19] Naturally enough, this delay limits people's ability to see the connection between their efforts, performance, and rewards and thereby diminishes motivation.

INTRINSIC REWARDS

Instead of relying only (or even primarily) on formal rewards, leaders make tremendous use of *intrinsic rewards*—rewards that are built into the work itself. Challenge is a powerful motivator. If work lacks challenge, no incentive system in the world can sustain long-term success. Other intrinsic rewards include a sense of accomplishment and the thrill of creation—rewards that are immediate outcomes of an individual's effort. Intrinsic rewards can also be as subtle as the leader's lending a helping hand and listening without interrupting. Other, more personal currencies include lunch with a key executive, a night out on the company, tickets for a ballgame or the theater, and the afternoon off.

Some people make the mistake of assuming that individuals respond only to money. Although salary increases and bonuses are certainly appreciated, individual needs for and appreciation of rewards extend much further. Verbal recognition of performance in front of one's peers and visible awards (such as certificates, plaques, and other tangible gifts), for example, are powerful rewards. Spontaneous and unexpected rewards are often more meaningful than the expected formal rewards. The motivational impact of Christmas bonuses, for example, is limited, because they're expected; the only unknown is what their amount will be. Many people consider these "entitlements" to be part of their annual salary expectations, not something extra for their efforts during a particular year. Thus annual bonuses are generally linked in workers' minds only to job level or even longevity, not performance.

Praise is a significant and underutilized form of recognition. Not enough people make adequate use of a very powerful and inexpensive two-word reward—"Thank you." Personal congratulations rank at the top of the most powerful nonfinancial motivators identified by employees.[20] There are few, if any, more basic needs than to be noticed, recognized, and appreciated for our efforts. That's as true for volunteers, teachers, doctors, priests, and politicians as it is for the maintenance staff and those in the executive suite. There's little wonder, then, that a greater volume of thank-you's is reported in highly innovative companies than in low-innovation firms.[21] Extraordinary achievements don't come easily and seldom bloom in barren and unappreciative settings.

Joan Carter discovered the powerful effect of publicly giving thanks when she was general manager and executive chef of the Faculty Club at Santa Clara University. Following her extremely successful (but difficult) first year at the club, in which revenues increased by 20 percent and costs decreased by 5 percent (ending a period of deficits that had threatened the club's continued existence), she sent a letter to all club members, club staff members, and university departments. In this "Open Letter of Thanks," she not only described in glowing detail the party the club had thrown to celebrate its dramatic turnaround but took the opportunity to describe the contributions of individuals, both on her staff and within the university community, who had made that night, and the past year, so successful. As she recalls,

> *So many people had come up to me during that party to thank me for the changes that had occurred at the club, and all I could think about was that it was my staff whose efforts and willingness to make changes had made us successful: they were the ones who needed to be thanked. So I wrote the letter. But as I wrote it, I realized that the list of people who needed to be thanked was endless, and I began feeling very humble. I needed to thank each staff member by name and contribution. I also needed to thank so many others on campus who helped every day—and our customers. I wanted them all to know that I knew we couldn't have done it without them.*

The response, she recalls, was totally unexpected:

> *I received dozens of phone calls and personal notes echoing the mutual admiration that had grown between the club and the university during that year. Those notes were posted on the bulletin board in the kitchen for the staff and further reinforced the staff's commitment to their customers.*

It was incredible. I never dreamed saying thank you would make me feel so good or be so good for our business.

Certainly, you can't buy people's commitment—to get them to care, to stay late, or come in early—with just thank-you notes, stickers, or plaques. What makes these effective is the leader's genuine concern and respect for those who are doing the work. Being at our personal best as leaders requires acknowledgment that we can't do it alone and recognition that unless constituents feel appreciated by their leaders, they're not likely to put forth great effort. Social scientist Daniel Yankelovich points out that overall organizational effectiveness and efficiency depend on employees' personal dedication and sense of responsibility. You get these intangibles, he says, "only when people are motivated to work hard, to give of themselves."[22] With this kind of motivation, leaders are able to help others get extraordinary things accomplished.

Consider the case of Albert "Smitty" Smith, room service captain for Marriott's Marquis in Atlanta. National Football League (NFL) teams playing in Atlanta had been staying with the Marriott for several years when a local competitor substantially reduced its rates. In response to that reduction, some of the teams began staying at that hotel instead. Smith was deeply disappointed. He loved football, and he wanted the NFL teams back at Marriott. Whenever a team was staying at the competing hotel, Smith would take the day off, contacting the coaches and team management to let them know that he was available to meet all of their special needs and reminding them that he understood those needs well after working with the teams for so many years. The teams were so impressed by Smith's one-person marketing effort that they all returned to the Atlanta Marriott the following year. At Marriott's International Marketing Meeting, Smith was featured as the guest speaker on salesmanship and received a special leadership trophy from J. Willard Marriott, Jr. Following his remarks, the group gave Smith the first standing ovation to be received at any of the organization's marketing meetings.[23]

Leaders are constantly on the lookout for ways to spread the psychological benefits of making people feel like winners, because winners contribute in important ways to the success of their projects. Leaders often serve as a mirror for the team, reflecting back to others what a job well done looks like and making certain not only that the members of the team know that they've done well but that others in the organization are aware of the group's effort and contributions.

Think about the impact of the "fabulous bragging sessions" held once per quarter at the corporate headquarters of Milliken & Company in Spartanburg, South Carolina. While attendance is voluntary, as many as 200 people participate in each Corporate Sharing Rally, as the sessions are called. Dozens of teams of workers from all areas of the company give crisp, five-minute reports in rapid-fire succession about improving product quality, describing their own programs and quantifying their impact. Everyone who attends receives an award signed by the president and framed on the spot. And everyone who attends is likely to go back to one of the company's 60 plants with a host of ideas—not demands that have been forced on them by top management but suggestions from their peers—about how all of them can be doing their jobs better and making the company more competitive and successful. These rallies are a wonderful example of providing recognition and celebrating people's accomplishments.

THE BLEND OF INTRINSIC AND EXTRINSIC REWARDS

What happens if people are given both intrinsic and extrinsic rewards? Unfortunately, while the idea of an additive effect is intuitively appealing, it doesn't always occur. There's some evidence that intrinsic and extrinsic rewards are negatively related and may actually work against one another. For example, in a situation that's already intrinsically rewarding, the addition of extrinsic rewards may reduce the effectiveness of the intrinsic rewards.[24] On the other hand, some studies show that while achievement-oriented people do find success rewarding in and of itself, money and fame are also important rewards, serving as symbols of that success.[25] One executive referred to this combination as the "fun being in playing the game down on the field, while the results are posted on the scoreboard." What we found among leaders wasn't so much an either/or mentality as a both/and type of thinking. Leaders are remarkably skillful in using these two types of rewards in complementary ways.

The Hampton Inn hotel group offers an example of creatively incorporating a variety of rewards. Winning the quarterly President's Award as an employee of the hotel group is a big deal, and everyone knows it. It starts with a personal phone call of thanks and congratulations from Ray Schultz, president and CEO. The phone call is followed by two plaques (one for the employee to take home and one for the hotel to display); a check for $500; publication of the winner's photo and profile in the company's quarterly magazine—a profile that features the winner's "extra mile" example and his or her personal guest service philosophy, as well as both a guest comment and a coworker comment about the recipient; and a trip to the company's annual conference for the Hampton Inn System Conference Awards Ceremony, where the current year's President's Award recipients take a prominent place in the ceremony's program.

Who wins these awards? Any employee—head housekeepers, guest service representatives, sales directors, maintenance workers, room attendants, and breakfast hostesses. The winners are the stars who "shine brightly in the Hampton Inn system" and who make its "100% Satisfaction Guarantee" a reality.

BEING POSITIVE AND HOPEFUL

By recognizing individual achievement, leaders give courage to their constituents. This courage enables people to maintain composure during anxiety-producing situations and to endure hardships. Courage to continue the quest and hope in a positive future were central elements of Don Quixote's legacy: "to dream the impossible dream."

Don Bennett's teenage daughter stayed by his side for over four hours during one particularly difficult stretch of his seemingly impossible dream of scaling Mount Rainier. With each new hop across the ice field, she told him, "You can do it, Dad. You're the best dad in the world. *You can do it, Dad.*" This spontaneous verbal encouragement kept Bennett going, strengthening his commitment to make it to the top. Bennett told us that there was no way he could have quit with his daughter voicing such words of love and encouragement.

Research points to the impact that positive feedback has on motivation and physical stamina. One study involved soldiers who had just finished several weeks of intensive training and were undergoing a forced march in competition for places in special units.[26] Motivation was extremely high among the recruits-failure to maintain the pace during the forced march meant losing the chance to join the special units. The soldiers were divided into four groups, which were unable to communicate with one another. All the men marched 20 kilometers (about $12\frac{1}{2}$ miles) over the same terrain on the same day. The first group was told how far the soldiers were expected to go and was kept informed of its progress along the way. The second group was told only that "this is the long march you hear about." These soldiers received no information about the total distance they were expected to travel or how far they had marched. The third group was told to march 15 kilometers, but when the soldiers had gone 14 kilometers, they were told that they had to go 6 kilometers farther. Members of the fourth group were told that they had to march 25 kilometers, but when they reached the 14-kilometer mark, they were told that they had only 6 more kilometers to go.

The groups were assessed as to which had the best performance and which endured the most stress. The results indicated that the soldiers in the first group—those who knew exactly how far they had to go and where they were during the march—were much better off than the soldiers who didn't get this information. The next-best group was the soldiers who thought that they were marching only 15 kilometers. Third-best was the group told to march a longer distance and then given the good news at the 14-kilometer mark. Those who performed worst were the soldiers who received neither information about the goal (total distance) nor feedback about the distance they had already traveled. Blood tests taken during the march and again 24 hours later showed similar patterns: blood levels of cortisol and prolactin (chemical substances whose levels rise as stress increases) were, as expected, highest for the group that knew the least about the march and lowest for those soldiers who knew exactly where they were and how much farther they were expected to go.

Even with highly motivated, achievement-oriented people, the type of leadership provided makes a definite difference in performance, in the levels of stress experienced, and in long-term health. Leaders provide people with a positive sense of direction that encourages them to reach inside and do their best. By having a positive outlook and being hopeful, leaders make the impossible a possibility and then motivate people in their drive to transform the possible into reality.

COMMITTING TO THE CHALLENGE: BUILDING CONFIDENCE AND COURAGE

Leaders have high expectations of themselves and of their constituents. They create self-fulfilling prophecies about how ordinary people can produce extraordinary actions and results. They provide people with clear directions, substantial encouragement, personal appreciation, and a positive outlook. Along the way, they offer feedback in response to small wins, stimulating, rekindling, and focusing people's energies and drive.

Leaders make people winners, and winning people like to up the ante, raise the standards, and conquer the next mountain. They want to serve more people, raise more money, enlarge market share, lower costs, increase production, reduce reject rates, experiment with technologies and processes, and explore uncharted territory. Leaders recognize and reward what individuals do to contribute to vision and values. And leaders express their appreciation far beyond the limits of the organization's formal performance appraisal system. Leaders enjoy being spontaneous and creative in saying thank you, whether they send personal notes, hand out stickers and buttons, listen without interrupting, or try one of the myriad other forms of recognition.

In this commitment, we provide a variety of strategies that you can adapt to any situation for help in using recognition as a leadership process.

Recognize Individual Contributions to the Success of Every Project

- Be creative about rewards and recognition and give them personally.
- Make recognition public.
- Design the reward and recognition system participatively.
- Provide feedback en route.
- Create Pygmalions.
- Find people who are doing things right.
- Coach.

Source: J. M. Kouzes and B. Z. Posner, *The Leadership Challenge*. Copyright © 1995.

- **Be creative about rewards and recognition and give them personally.**

People respond to all kinds of rewards other than promotions and raises. One of our university colleagues takes his highest-performing students each term out for lunch and bowling to show his appreciation for their hard work. A shop foreman we know presents employees who achieve their production objectives with a new chair for the workplace. The chairs are a good reward themselves, but a major part of the reward—the part that's even more pleasurable than comfortable seating to the employees—comes with the presentation. The employee being rewarded is called into the foreman's office, presented with the new chair, and then wheeled in the chair back to the work station by the foreman—amid the cheers of coworkers.

Make rewards and recognition tangible. By themselves, a meal, chair, check, or plaque won't significantly contribute to sustaining the value of the action rewarded. But tangibility does help sustain the memory and importance of the act and contributes positively to repetition of the behavior.

There's no limit—except your creativity—to creative rewards. Consider the following:

- "Super person of the month" awards
- Employee photographs with the president
- Verbal encouragement
- Spot strokes
- Pictures in annual reports and company newsletters
- Published thank-you's
- Contributions to employees' favorite charities
- Gift certificates and merchandise credits
- Embossed business cards
- Gifts for spouses and families
- Banners displayed in the cafeteria
- Symbolic stuffed animals
- Flextime

Place your emphasis on noticing and recognizing small wins—and do so personally. A sincere word of thanks from the right person at the right time can mean more to the recipient than fame, fortune, or a whole wall of certificates and plaques. It's well worth the effort.[27] Even movements in the right direction warrant your personal seal of appreciation and encouragement to continue the effort.

- **Make recognition public.**

You may be reluctant to recognize people in public, fearing that to do so might cause jealousy or resentment. But private rewards do little to set an example, and often the recipient, not wanting to brag or appear conceited, has no opportunity to share the story with others. So tell your workers and colleagues that they've done well as soon as you find out about it, and let other people know about the accomplishment too. When recognition is public, the individual's self-esteem is bolstered, the behavior being recognized serves as a model to others, and employees see that doing the right thing will be noticed and rewarded. While all recognition encourages others to continue their good work, public recognition portrays the recipient as a role model, conveying to all employees the message, "Here's someone just like you. You too can do this."

Recognition also helps to empower recipients by increasing their visibility. Military organizations, for example, make tremendous use of medals and insignias, which are almost always handed out at ceremonies. Awards serve the same purpose. Nolan Dishongh planned well in advance for a ceremony to reward and recognize his students. During the year, he entered his students' work in every contest he could find, collecting in a classroom display case the winning ribbons and trophies that would be awarded formally to their owners during the year-end banquet attended by parents and students. Public recognition also builds commitment, because it makes people's actions visible to their peers and therefore difficult to deny or revoke.

At Household Credit Services, extra effort by members of the young clerical staff is often rewarded with "casual dress" passes. For many staff members right out of high school, being able to wear their nice casual clothes (while their friends and coworkers have to wear business attire) provides public recognition. The passes are immediate (supervisors don't need higher-level approval to award them), inexpensive, and fun, and they're a very visible way to show appreciation for a job well done.

- **Design the reward and recognition system participatively.**

People are most excited about activities and events that they've had a hand in designing. In addition, when you involve others, you're more likely to design a system in which rewards are closely linked to performance norms. Because it's their system, people will feel more strongly that they can influence it directly through their efforts. For example, when the CEO of Alta Bates Hospital, in Berkeley, California, raved to food service staffers about the great job they were doing, expressing his pride in the creativity and conscientiousness of their attempt to make hospital food imaginative and tasty, they were pleased. But what they really wanted was to demonstrate just how good they were, to show that working in a hospital didn't mean that they were second-class restaurateurs and chefs.

After some discussion, food service personnel were given the chance to offer a Sunday buffet in the hospital cafeteria, open to the public and complemented by ice sculptures and a string quartet. During the buffet, crew members walked the line talking with customers (many of whom were on the hospital staff). The crew's pride in their food preparation and presentation created an atmosphere of sheer delight, increased their motivation, and generated more efficient operations overall.

- **Provide feedback en route.**

People produce best when they're given feedback about how they're progressing. Production may continue without feedback, but it will be less efficient and will exact a significant toll in the form of increased levels of stress and anxiety. Recognition signals successful accomplishment, reinforcing both the employee's "I can do it" attitude and the leader's expectations: "I knew you could do it."

A study of the winningest high school and college athletic coaches revealed that they pay great attention to providing real-time feedback on their players' performance and will, as appropriate, recognize and reward outstanding contributions. Players—regardless of fame or fortune—need to hear when they do well and when, they don't. As the coaches explained, ongoing feedback

> is a highly effective way to shape the behavior of the athletes so as to increase the team's ability to continue winning. Without immediate and precise feedback, the learning process ends and mediocrity is sure to emerge. Ongoing evaluation of the players' ability to play your game, to your expectations, is critical given the constant need to restock the team with younger athletes.[28]

What's true of athletes also applies to those on the factory floor, behind the counter, in city hall, and in the corner office.

By giving feedback, leaders enable people to persevere in moments of hardship and times of uncertainty and turbulence. In fact, studies show that learning is severely hampered without feedback and that people's motivation (and subsequent performance) diminishes over time unless they know how they're doing.[29] Leaders use feedback to make sure that people acquire the competence that should come with experience.

- **Create Pygmalions.**

Be more conscious about realizing that your behavior toward people is based upon your expectations about them. Treating people in a friendly, pleasant, and positive fashion and being attentive to their needs—behavior that reflects your high expectations of them—produces increased performance because that behavior has a favorable effect on their motivation. Likewise, when you have high expectations of others, you tend to give them more input—suggestions, helpful hints, and responsive answers to their questions—and more feedback about the results of their efforts. Both of these factors enhance people's learning and increase the likelihood that they'll achieve competence and mastery rather than repeat mistakes or let ineffective habits become ingrained.

Finally, the standards of performance (or "output levels") that you set communicate what your expectations of others are, and these in turn affect others' levels of aspiration. Therefore, make sure that these standards are high and that they're linked directly to what's important to the success of your organization. Make sure, too, that your performance standards include what's important to constituents as well as what's important to management, stockholders, or the larger organization.

Creating Pygmalions entails developing a winner's attitude, since only those who envision themselves as winners are likely to work hard, try new actions, and become leaders in their own fight. This means paying considerable attention to your constituents' successes and, should those people stumble or fall, discussing this result with them as only a temporary lack of success. If criticism is necessary, comments should be restricted to behavior rather than character. Similarly, feedback—preferably extensive—should stress continuous progress in terms of past performance rather than comparisons with other people.[30] Leaders also make certain that constituents understand that (and how) goal achievement is the result of their own efforts.

• **Find people who are doing things right.**

Rewards are most effective when they're highly specific and in close proximity to the appropriate behavior. In order to provide such timely and specific feedback, you have to go out and find the behavior you want to foster. One of the most important results of being out and about as a leader is that you can personally observe people doing things right and then reward them either on the spot or at the next public meeting.

Consider initiating a system for collecting information from constituents and customers about people who are observed doing things right. Weekly breakfast meetings are perfect opportunities to ask for such incidents. Add to your agenda the question, "Who have you seen doing something special this week that's really helped our organization?"

Once you've selected people for recognition, be sure to tell them—and everyone else—why they've been chosen. Make the recognition effective. Tell the story of why the person is being recognized, and make it specific. Stories that describe valued actions are very powerful ways to communicate what behaviors are expected and will be rewarded. Walk employees through the specific actions that contributed to goal attainment and explain why they were consistent with the shared values.

You might say something along these lines:

> *Sue was selected as the employee of the month because she called five different stores to locate an item that a customer requested but that we didn't have in stock. And because the store couldn't deliver the item until the next week, she picked it up on her way home from work so that the customer could have it in time for an important event. That's the kind of behavior that makes us so highly valued by our customers. Thank you, Sue. We make this award to you in appreciation of your contribution to our organization's goal of delighting every customer.*

This kind of positive example can be particularly useful to leaders trying to get people to understand the right things to do to achieve a high standard. It provides a behavioral map that people can store in their minds and rely on when a similar situation arises in the future.

To broaden the net for recognition, set up systems that make it possible for people to be recognized by their constituents—be they peers, customers, or suppliers—not just managers. This encourages everyone in the organization to be on the lookout for good behaviors—and to be mindful that others are observing their actions as well. The nursing home at St. Francis Hospital in Memphis, Tennessee, recognizes its staff with a simple pin that says, "Caught Caring." In an environment where the patients often can't say thank you, the pins mean a great deal to staff members: they announce that someone recognizes how much they give.[31]

- **Coach.**

Athletic coaches don't wait until the season is over to let their players know how they're doing, and neither should you. Coaching involves spending time with people on the job day by day, talking with them about game strategies, and providing them with feedback about their efforts and performance. Then, when the game is over, you need to get together with the players and analyze the results of your efforts. Where did we do well? Where do we need to improve our efforts? What will we have to do differently, better, or more of the next time? And then it's time for practice again and getting ready for the next game.

The best teams, whether in athletics, business, education, health care, government, or religion, always emphasize the fundamentals of their game. This means being clear about your vision and values, to which recognition and celebration should always be linked.

ENDNOTES

[1] T. E. Deal and W. A. Jenkins, *Managing the Hidden Organization: Strategies for Empowering Your Behind-the-Scenes Employees* (New York: Warner, 1994).

[2] Survey by Robert Hall International, Inc. (Menlo Park, CA), August 31, 1994.

[3] See, for example, E. C. Jones, "Interpreting Interpersonal Behavior: The Effects of Expectancies," *Science 234* (1986): 41–46; R. H. G. Field and D. A. Van Seters, "Management by Expectations (MBE): The Power of Positive Prophecy," *Journal of General Management 14* (2) (1988): 1–33; D. Eden, *Pygmalion in Management: Productivity as a Self-Fulfilling Prophecy* (New York: Lexington Books, 1990); and D. Eden, "Leadership and Expectations: Pygmalion Effects and Other Self-Fulfilling Prophecies in Organizations," *The Leadership Quarterly 3* (4) (1992): 271–305.

[4] D. Eden and J. Kinnar, "Modeling Galatea: Boosting Self-Efficacy to Increase Volunteering." *Journal of Applied Psychology 76* (6) (1991): 770–780.

[5] D. Eden, "Pygmalion Without Interpersonal Contrast Effects: Whole Groups Gain From Raising Manager Expectations," *Journal of Applied Psychology 75* (4) (1990): 394–398.

[6] D. Eden, "Pygmalion, Goal Setting, and Expectancy: Compatible Ways to Boost Productivity," *Academy of Management Executive 13* (4) (1988): 639–652.

[7] N. Branden, *The Six Pillars of Self-Esteem* (New York: Bantam, 1994).

[8] R. J. Blitzer, C. Peterson, and L. Rogers, "How to Build Self-Esteem," *Training and Development Journal* (February 1993): 59.

[9] R. Wood and A. Bandura, "Impact of Conceptions of Ability on Self-Regulatory Mechanisms and Complex Decision Making," *Journal of Personality and Social Psychology 56* (3) (1989): 407–415.

[10] A. R. Cohen, S. L. Fink, H. Gadon, and R. D. Willits, *Effective Behavior in Organizations*, 6th ed. (Homewood, IL: Irwin, 1994).

[11] Cohen, Fink, Gadon, and Willits, *Effective Behavior in Organizations*.

[12] J. L. McAdams and E. J. Hawke, *Executive Summary: Organizational Performance & Rewards* (Scottsdale, AZ: American Compensation Association, 1993) 35; see also C. Braddick, M. Pfefferle, and R. Gandossy, "How Malcolm Baldrige Winners Reward Employer Performance," *Journal of Compensation and Benefits 9* (3) (1993): 47–52.

[13] S. Tully, "Your Paycheck Gets Exciting," *Fortune*, November 1, 1993, 98.

[14] R. Winslow, "U.S. Healthcare Cuts Costs, Grows Rapidly, and Irks Some Doctors," *Wall Street Journal*, September 6, 1994, A1.

[15] C. C. Pinder, *Work Motivation: Theory, Issues, and Applications* (Glenview, IL: Scott, Foresman, 1984), 286–298; see also V. H. Vroom, *Work and Motivation* (San Francisco: Jossey-Bass, 1994).

[16] Pinder, *Work Motivation*, 226.

[17] K. Huber, "A Growing Desire to Learn," *Houston Chronicle*, July 14, 1994, Cl; and discussion with Nolan Dishongh, August 1994.

[18] McAdams and Hawke, *Executive Summary*, 12.

[19] J. L. Hall, B. Z. Posner, and J. W. Harder, "Performance Appraisal Systems: Matching Theory With Practice," *Group and Management Studies 14* (1) (1989): 51–69.

[20] G. Graham, "Going the Extra Mile: Motivating Your Workers Doesn't Always Involve Money," *San Jose Mercury News*, January 7, 1987, 4C.

[21] R. M. Kanter, "The Change Masters," Presentation to the Executive Seminar in Corporate Excellence, Santa Clara University, March 13, 1984.

[22] M. VerMeulen, "When Employees Give Something Extra," *Parade*, November 6, 1983, 11.

[23] R. J. Dow, "Keeping Employees Focused on Customer Service," Presentation to the Executive Seminar in Corporate Excellence, Santa Clara University, October 28, 1986.

[24] E. L. Deci, *Intrinsic Motivation* (New York: Plenum, 1975); E. L. Deci and R. M. Ryan, *Intrinsic Motivation and Self-Determination in Human Behavior* (New York: Plenum, 1985). For an intelligent critique of incentive systems and the potentially detrimental effect of reliance on rewards on long-term performance, see A. Kohn, *Punished by Rewards* (Boston: Houghton Mifflin, 1993).

[25] D. C. McClelland, *The Achieving Society* (New York: Van Nostrand Reinhold, 1961).

[26] S. Squires, "Clinging to Hope," *San Jose Mercury News*, February 25, 1984, 12C; see also S. Breznitz, "The Effect of Hope on Coping With Stress," *Dynamics of Stress: Physiological, Psychological, and Social Perspectives,* eds. M. H. Appley and R. Trumbell (New York: Plenum, 1986), 295–306; M. E. P. Seligman, *Learned Optimism* (New York: Knopf, 1990); and C. Peterson and L. M. Bossio, *Health and Optimism: New Research on the Relationship Between Positive Thinking and Physical Well-Being* (New York: Free Press, 1991).

[27] For more ideas, see B. Nelson, *1001 Ways to Reward Employees* (New York: Workman, 1994); and B. Basso and I. Klosek, *This Job Should Be Fun!* (Holbrook, MA: Bob Adams, 1991).

[28] A. E. Schnur and C. Butz, "The Best Finish First: Top Coaches Talk About Winning," *Towers Perrin* (San Francisco, 1994).

[29] A. Bandura and D. Cevone, "Self-Evaluative and Self-Efficacy Mechanisms Governing the Motivational Effects of Goal Systems," *Journal of Personality and Social Psychology 45* (1983): 1017–1028.

[30] Field and Van Seters, "Management by Expectations (MBE)."

[31] S. Shepard, "Quality Buy: St. Francis Avoids Reinventing Wheel," *Memphis Business Journal 15* (14) (1993): 3; and phone conversation on September 12, 1994 with the vice president of quality management, St. Francis Hospital.

CHAPTER 5
ETHICS AND VALUES

CHANGING UNETHICAL ORGANIZATIONAL BEHAVIOR
Richard P. Nielsen

WHEN ETHICS TRAVEL: THE PROMISE AND PERIL OF GLOBAL BUSINESS ETHICS
Thomas Donaldson
Thomas W. Dunfee

Ethics and values are yet another type of mental map and another source of individual differences in the workplace. Ethical conflicts often arise from incompatible ideas and assumptions about right and wrong. Another source of ethical conflict is determined by how different groups define the issue—where is the boundary that determines which stakeholders' needs have to be considered? For example, the WTO demonstrations indicate that for some people, globalization is not just an argument about the virtues of free trade and capital, but a question of cultural and political institutions and concern for environmental impact.

Richard Nielsen, a prolific scholarly writer and advocate for ethical behavior in business and government, has written one of the best practical guides for people confronted with unethical behavior in the workplace. As we know from the media, whistle blowing can be dangerous to one's career and should be undertaken only after careful consideration. Neilsen lists a variety of whistle blowing interventions, accompanied by examples and cautionary advice.

Whistle blowers often speak up when company actions go against their personal value system. Such value clashes are even more likely in cross-cultural interactions involving different sets of ethical customs. Thomas Donaldson and Thomas Dunfee, well-known business ethicists and consultants, portray some of the value differences that result in international ethics conflicts in "When Ethics Travel: The Promise and Peril of Global Business Ethics." They provide a model that managers can apply to such situations.

CHANGING UNETHICAL ORGANIZATIONAL BEHAVIOR*

Richard P. Nielsen

To be or not to be: that is the question:
Whether 'tis nobler in the mind to suffer
The slings and arrows of outrageous fortune,
Or to take arms against a sea of troubles,
And by opposing end them?
                    William Shakespeare, *Hamlet*

---

*"Changing Unethical Organizational Behavior," *The Academy of Management Executive 3*, no. 2 (1989): 123–130. Copyright © 1989. Reprinted by permission.

What are the implications of Hamlet's question in the context of organizational ethics? What does it mean to be ethical in an organizational context? Should one suffer the slings and arrows of unethical organizational behavior? Should one try to take arms against unethical behaviors and by opposing, end them?

The consequences of addressing organizational ethics issues can be unpleasant. One can be punished or fired, one's career can suffer, or one can be disliked, considered an outsider. It may take courage to oppose unethical and lead ethical organizational behavior.

How can one address organizational ethics issues? Paul Tillich, in his book, *The Courage To Be*, recognized, as Hamlet did, that dire consequences can result from standing up to and opposing unethical behavior. Tillich identified two approaches: being as an individual and being as a part of a group.[1]

In an organizational context, these two approaches can be interpreted as follows: (1) Being as an individual can mean intervening to end unethical organizational behaviors by working against others and the organizations performing the unethical behaviors, and (2) being as a part can mean leading an ethical organizational change by working with others and the organization. These approaches are not mutually exclusive; rather, depending on the individual, the organization, the relationships, and the situation, one or both of these approaches may be appropriate for addressing ethical issues.

BEING AS AN INDIVIDUAL

According to Tillich, the courage to be as an individual is the courage to follow one's conscience and defy unethical and/or unreasonable authority. It can even mean staging a revolutionary attack on that authority. Such an act can entail great risk and require great courage. As Tillich explains, "The anxiety conquered in the courage to be ... in the productive process is considerable, because the threat of being excluded from such a participation by unemployment or the loss of an economic basis is what, above all, fate means today."[2]

According to David Ewing, retired executive editor of the *Harvard Business Review*, this type of anxiety is not without foundation.

> *There is very little protection in industry for employees who object to carrying out immoral, unethical or illegal orders from their superiors. If the employee doesn't like what he or she is asked to do, the remedy is to pack up and leave. This remedy seems to presuppose an ideal economy, where there is another company down the street with openings for jobs just like the one the employee left.*[3]

How can one be as an individual, intervening against unethical organizational behavior? Intervention strategies an individual can use to change unethical behavior include: (1) secretly blowing the whistle within the organization, (2) quietly blowing the whistle, informing a responsible higher-level manager, (3) secretly threatening the offender with blowing the whistle, (4) secretly threatening a responsible manager with blowing the whistle outside the organization, (5) publicly threatening a responsible manager with blowing the whistle, (6) sabotaging the implementation of the unethical behavior, (7) quietly refraining from implementing an unethical order or policy, (8) publicly blowing the whistle within the organization, (9) conscientiously objecting to an unethical policy or refusing to implement the policy, (10) indicating uncertainty about or refusing to support a cover-up in the event that the individual and/or organization gets caught, (11) secretly blowing the whistle outside the organization, or (12) publicly blowing the whistle outside the organization. Cases of each are considered on the next few pages.

CASES

1. Secretly blowing the whistle within the organization A purchasing manager for General Electric secretly wrote a letter to an upper-level manager about his boss, who was soliciting and accepting bribes from subcontractors. The boss was investigated and eventually fired. He was also sentenced to six months' imprisonment for taking $100,000 in bribes, in exchange for which he granted favorable treatment on defense contracts.[4]

2. Quietly blowing the whistle to a responsible higher-level manager When Evelyn Grant was first hired by the company with which she is now a personnel manager, her job included administering a battery of tests that, in part, determined which employees were promoted to supervisory positions. Grant explained:

> *There have been cases where people will do something wrong because they think they have no choice. Their boss tells them to do it, and so they do it, knowing it's wrong. They don't realize there are ways around the boss ... When I went over his [the chief psychologist's] data and analysis, I found errors in assumptions as well as actual errors of computation ... I had two choices: I could do nothing or I could report my findings to my supervisor. If I did nothing, the only persons probably hurt were the ones who "failed" the test. To report my findings, on the other hand, could hurt several people, possibly myself.*

She spoke to her boss, who quietly arranged for a meeting to discuss the discrepancies with the chief psychologist. The chief psychologist did not show up for the meeting; however, the test battery was dropped.[5]

3. Secretly threatening the offender with blowing the whistle A salesman for a Boston-area insurance company attended a weekly sales meeting during which the sales manager instructed the salespeople, both verbally and in writing, to use a sales technique that the salesman considered unethical. The salesman anonymously wrote the sales manager a letter threatening to send a copy of the unethical sales instructions to the Massachusetts insurance commissioner and the *Boston Globe* newspaper unless the sales manager retracted his instructions at the next sales meeting. The sales manager did retract the instructions. The salesman still works for the insurance company.[6]

4. Secretly threatening a responsible manager with blowing the whistle outside the organization A recently hired manager with a San Francisco real estate development company found that the construction company his firm had contracted with was systematically not giving minorities opportunities to learn construction management. This new manager wrote an anonymous letter to a higher-level real estate manager threatening to blow the whistle to the press and local government about the contractor unless the company corrected the situation. The real estate manager intervened, and the contractor began to hire minorities for foremen-training positions.[7]

5. Publicly threatening a responsible manager with blowing the whistle A woman in the business office of a large Boston-area university observed that one middle-level male manager was sexually harassing several women in the office. She tried to reason with the office manager to do something about the offensive behavior, but the manager would not do anything. She then told the manager and several other people in the office that if the manager did not do something about the behavior, she would blow the whistle to the personnel office. The manager then told the offender that if he did not stop the harassment, the personnel office would be brought in. He did stop the behavior, but he and several other employees refused to talk to the woman who initiated the actions. She eventually left the university.[8]

6. Sabotaging the implementation of the unethical behavior   A program manager for a Boston-area local social welfare organization was told by her superior to replace a significant percentage of her clients who received disability benefits with refugee Soviet Jews. She wanted to help both the refugees and her current clients; however, she thought it was unethical to drop current clients, in part because she believed such an action could result in unnecessary deaths. Previously, a person who had lost benefits because of what the program manager considered unethical "bumping" had committed suicide: He had not wanted to force his family to sell their home in order to pay for the medical care he needed and qualify for poverty programs. After her attempts to reason with her boss failed, she instituted a paperwork chain with a partially funded federal agency that prevented her own agency from dropping clients for nine months, after which time they would be eligible for a different funding program. Her old clients received benefits and the new refugees also received benefits. In discussions with her boss, she blamed the federal agency for making it impossible to drop people quickly. Her boss, a political appointee who did not understand the system, also blames the federal agency office.[9]

7. Publicly blowing the whistle within the organization   John W. Young, the chief of NASA's astronaut office, wrote a 12-page internal memorandum to 97 people after the Challenger explosion that killed seven crew members. The memo listed a large number of safety-related problems that Young said had endangered crews since October 1984. According to Young, "If the management system is not big enough to stop the space shuttle program whenever necessary to make flight safety corrections, it will not survive and neither will our three space shuttles or their flight crews." The memo was instrumental in the decision to broaden safety investigations throughout the total NASA system.[10]

8. Quietly refraining from implementing an unethical order/policy   Frank Ladwig was a top salesman and branch manager with a large computer company for more than 40 years. At times, he had trouble balancing his responsibilities. For instance, he was trained to sell solutions to customer problems, yet he had order and revenue quotas that sometimes made it difficult for him to concentrate on solving problems. He was responsible for signing and keeping important customers with annual revenues of between $250,000 and $500,000 and for aggressively and conscientiously representing new products that had required large R&D investments. He was required to sell the full line of products and services, and sometimes he had sales quotas for products that he believed were not a good match for the customer or appeared to perform marginally. Ladwig would quietly not sell those products, concentrating on selling the products he believed in. He would quietly explain the characteristics of the questionable products to his knowledgeable customers and get their reactions, rather than making an all-out sales effort. When he was asked by his sales manager why a certain product was not moving, he explained what the customers objected to and why. However, Ladwig thought that a salesperson or manager with an average or poor performance record would have a difficult time getting away with this type of solution to an ethical dilemma.[11]

9. Conscientiously objecting to an unethical policy or refusing to implement it   Francis O'Brien was a research director for the pharmaceutical company Searle & Co. O'Brien conscientiously objected to what he believed were exaggerated claims for the Searle Copper 7 intrauterine contraceptive. When reasoning with upper-level management failed, O'Brien wrote them the following:

> *Their continued use, in my opinion, is both misleading and a thinly disguised attempt to make claims which are not FDA approved ... Because of personal reasons I do not consent to have my name used in any press release or in connection with any press release. In addition, I will not participate in any press conference.*

O'Brien left the company 10 years later. Currently, several lawsuits are pending against Searle, charging that its IUD caused infection and sterility.[12]

10. Indicating uncertainty about or refusing to support a cover-up in the event that the individual and/or organization gets caught   In the Boston office of Bear Stearns, four brokers informally worked together as a group. One of the brokers had been successfully trading on insider information, and he invited the other three to do the same. One of the three told the others that such trading was not worth the risk of getting caught, and if an investigation ever occurred, he was not sure he would be able to participate in a cover-up. The other two brokers decided not to trade on the insider information, and the first broker stopped at least that type of insider trading.[13]

11. Secretly blowing the whistle outside the corporations William Schwartzkopf of the Commonwealth Electric Company secretly and anonymously wrote a letter to the Justice Department alleging large-scale, long-time bid rigging among many of the largest U.S. electrical contractors. The secret letter accused the contractors of raising bids and conspiring to divide billions of dollars of contracts. Companies in the industry have already paid more than $20 million in fines to the government in part as a result of this letter, and they face millions of dollars more in losses when the victims sue.[14]

12. Publicly blowing the whistle outside the organization A. Earnest Fitzgerald, a former high-level manager in the U.S. Air Force and Lockheed CEO, revealed to Congress and the press that the Air Force and Lockheed systematically practiced a strategy of underbidding in order to gain Air Force contracts for Lockheed, which then billed the Air Force and received payments for cost overruns on the contracts. Fitzgerald was fired for his trouble, but eventually received his job back. The underbidding/cost overruns, on at least the C-5/A cargo plane, were stopped.[15]

LIMITATIONS OF INTERVENTION

The intervention strategies described above can be very effective, but they also have some important limitations.

1. The individual can be wrong about the organization's actions Lower-level employees commonly do not have as much or as good information about ethical situations and issues as higher-level managers. Similarly, they may not be as experienced as higher-level managers in dealing with specific ethical issues. The quality of experience and information an individual has can influence the quality of his or her ethical judgments. To the extent that this is true in any given situation, the use of intervention may or may not be warranted. In Case 8, for example, if Frank Ladwig had had limited computer experience, he could have been wrong about some of the products he thought would not produce the promised results.

2. Relationships can be damaged Suppose that instead of identifying with the individuals who want an organization to change its ethical behavior, we look at these situations from another perspective. How do we feel when we are forced to change our behavior? Further, how would we feel if we were forced by a subordinate to change, even though we thought that we had the position, quality of information, and/or quality of experience to make the correct decisions? Relationships would probably be, at the least, strained, particularly if we made an ethical decision and were nevertheless forced to change. If we are wrong, it may be that we do not recognize it at the time. If we know we are wrong, we still may not like being forced to change. However, it is possible that the individual forcing us to change may justify his or her behavior to us, and our relationship may actually be strengthened.

3. The organization can be hurt unnecessarily If an individual is wrong in believing that the organization is unethical, the organization can be hurt unnecessarily by his or her actions. Even if the individual is right, the organization can still be unnecessarily hurt by intervention strategies.

4. Intervention strategies can encourage "might makes right" climates If we want "wrong" people, who might be more powerful now or in the future than we are, to exercise self-restraint, then we may need to exercise self-restraint even when we are "right." A problem with using force is that the other side may use more powerful or effective force now or later. Many people have been punished for trying to act ethically both when they were right and when they were wrong. By using force, one may also contribute to the belief that the only way to get things done in a particular organization is through force. People who are wrong can and do use force, and win. Do we want to build an organizational culture in which force plays an important role? Gandhi's response to "an eye for an eye" was that if we all followed that principle, eventually everyone would be blind.

BEING AS A PART

While the intervention strategies discussed above can be very effective, they can also be destructive. Therefore, it may be appropriate to consider the advantages of leading an ethical change effort (being as a part) as well as intervening against unethical behaviors (being as an individual).

Tillich maintains that the courage to be as a part is the courage to affirm one's own being through participation with others. He writes,

> *The self affirms itself as participant in the power of a group, of a movement .... Self-affirmation within a group includes the courage to accept guilt and its consequences as public guilt, whether one is responsible or whether somebody else is. It is a problem of the group which has to be expiated for the sake of the group, and the methods of punishment and satisfaction ... are accepted by the individual ... In every human community, there are outstanding members, the bearers of the traditions and leaders of the future. They must distance in order to judge and to change. They must take responsibility and ask questions. This unavoidably produces individual doubt and personal guilt. Nevertheless, the predominant pattern is the courage to be a part in all members of the ... group ... The difference between the genuine Stoic and the neocollectivist is that the latter is bound in the first place to the collective and in the second place to the universe, while the Stoic was first of all related to the universal Logos and secondly to possible human groups .... The democratic-conformist type of the courage to be as a part was in an outspoken way tied up with the idea of progress. The courage to be as a part in the progress of the group to which one belongs ....*[16]

LEADING ETHICAL CHANGE

A good cross-cultural conceptualization of leadership is offered by Yoshino and Lifson: "The essence of leadership is the influential increment over and above mechanical compliance with routine directives of the organization."[17] This definition permits comparisons between and facilitates an understanding of different leadership styles through its use of a single variable: created incremental performance. Of course, different types of leadership may be more or less effective in different types of situations; yet, it is helpful to understand the "essence" of leadership in its many different cultural forms as the creation of incremental change beyond the routine.

For example, Yoshino and Lifson compare generalizations (actually overgeneralizations) about Japanese and American leadership styles:

> *In the United States, a leader is often thought of as one who blazes new trails, a virtuoso whose example inspires awe, respect, and emulation. If any individual characterizes this pattern, it is surely John Wayne, whose image reached epic proportions in his own lifetime as an embodiment of something uniquely American. A Japanese leader rather than being an authority, is more of a communications channel, a mediator, a facilitator and most of all, a symbol and embodiment of group unity. Consensus building is necessary in decision making, and this requires patience and an ability to use carefully cultivated relationships to get all to agree for the good of the unit. A John Wayne in this situation might succeed temporarily by virtue of charisma, but eventually the inability to build strong emotion-laden relationships and use these as a tool of motivation and consensus building would prove fatal.*[18]

A charismatic, "John Wayne type" leader can inspire and/or frighten people into diverting from the routine. A consensus-building, Japanese-style leader can get people to agree to divert from the routine. In both cases, the leader creates incremental behavior change beyond the routine. How does leadership (being as a part) in its various cultural forms differ from the various intervention (being as an individual) strategies and cases discussed above? Some case data may be revealing.

CASES

1. Roger Boisjoly and the Challenger Launch[19] In January 1985, after the postflight hardware inspection of Flight 52C, Roger Boisjoly strongly suspected that unusually low temperatures had compromised the performance effectiveness of the O-ring seals on two field joints. Such a performance compromise could cause an explosion. In March 1985, laboratory tests confirmed that low temperature did negatively affect the ability of the O-rings to perform this sealing function. In June 1985, the postflight inspection of Flight 51B revealed serious erosion of both primary and backup seals that, had it continued, could have caused an explosion.

These events convinced Boisjoly that a serious and very dangerous problem existed with the O-rings. Instead of acting as an individual against his supervisors and the organization, for example, by blowing the whistle to the press, he tried to lead a change to stop the launching of flights with unsafe O-rings. He worked with his immediate supervisor, the director of engineering, and the organization in leading this change. He wrote a draft of a memo to Bob Lund, vice-president of engineering, which he first showed and discussed with his immediate supervisor to "maintain good relationships." Boisjoly and others developed potential win-win solutions, such as investigating remedies to fix the O-rings and refraining from launching flights at too-low temperatures. He effectively established a team to study the matter and participated in a teleconference with 130 technical experts.

On the day before the *Challenger* launch, Boisjoly and other team members were successful in leading company executives to reverse their tentative recommendation to launch because the overnight temperatures were predicted to be too low. The company recommendation was to launch only when temperatures were above 53 degrees. To this point, Boisjoly was very effective in leading a change toward what he and other engineering and management people believed was a safe and ethical decision.

However, according to testimony from Boisjoly and others to Congress, the top managers of Morton Thiokol, under pressure from NASA, reversed their earlier recommendation not to launch. The next day, *Challenger* was launched and exploded, causing the deaths of all the crew members. While Boisjoly was very effective in leading a change within his own organization, he was not able to counteract subsequent pressure from the customer, NASA.

2. Dan Phillips and Genco, Inc[20] Dan Phillips was a paper products group division manager for Genco, whose upper-level management adopted a strategy whereby several mills, including the Elkhorn Mill, would either have to reduce costs or close down. Phillips was concerned that cost cutting at Elkhorn would prevent the mill from meeting government pollution-control requirements, and that closing the mill could seriously hurt the local community. If he reduced costs, he would not meet pollution-control requirements; if he did not reduce costs, the mill would close and the community would suffer.

Phillips did not secretly or publicly blow the whistle, nor did he sabotage, conscientiously object, quietly refrain from implementing the plan, or quit; however, he did lead a change in the organization's ethical behavior. He asked research and development people in his division to investigate how the plant could both become more cost efficient and create less pollution. He then asked operations people in his division to estimate how long it would take to put such a new plant design on line, and how much it would cost. He asked cost accounting and financial people within his division to estimate when such a new operation would achieve a break even payback. Once he found a plan that would work, he negotiated a win-win solution with upper-level management: in exchange for not closing the plant and increasing its investment in his division, the organization would over time benefit from lower costs and higher profitability. Phillips thus worked with others and the organization to lead an inquiry and adopt an alternative ethical and cost-effective plan.

3. Lotus and Brazilian Software Importing[21] Lotus, a software manufacturer, found that in spite of restrictions on the importing of much of its software to Brazil, many people there were buying and using Lotus software. On further investigation, the company discovered that Brazilian businessmen, in alliance with a Brazilian general, were violating the law by buying Lotus software in Cambridge, Massachusetts, and bringing it into Brazil.

Instead of blowing the whistle on the illegal behavior, sabotaging it, or leaving Brazil, Lotus negotiated a solution: In exchange for the Brazilians' agreement to stop illegal importing, Lotus helped set them up as legitimate licensed manufacturers and distributors of Lotus products in Brazil. Instead of working against them and the Lotus salespeople supplying them, the Lotus managers worked with these people to develop an ethical, legal, and economically sound solution to the importing problem.

And in at least a limited sense, the importers may have been transformed into ethical managers and business people. This case may remind you of the legendary "old West," where government officials sometimes negotiated win-win solutions with "outlaw gunfighters," who agreed to become somewhat more ethical as appointed sheriffs. The gunfighters needed to make a living, and many were not interested in or qualified for such other professions as farming or shop-keeping. In some cases, ethical behavior may take place before ethical beliefs are assumed.

4. Insurance company office/sales manager and discrimination[22] The sales/office manager of a very large Boston-area insurance company tried to hire female salespeople several times, but his boss refused to permit the hires. The manager could have acted against his boss and the organization by secretly threatening to blow the whistle or actually blowing the whistle, publicly or secretly. Instead he decided to try to lead a change in the implicit hiring policy of the organization.

The manager asked his boss why he was not permitted to hire a woman. He learned that his boss did not believe women made good salespeople and had never worked with a female salesperson. He found that reasoning with his boss about the capabilities of women and the ethics and legality of refusing to hire women was ineffective.

He inquired within the company about whether being a woman could be an advantage in any insurance sales areas. He negotiated with his boss a six-month experiment whereby he hired on a trial basis one woman to sell life insurance to married women who contributed large portions of their salaries to their home mortgages. The woman he hired was not only very successful in selling this type of life insurance, but became one of the office's top salespeople. After this experience, the boss reversed his policy of not hiring female salespeople.

LIMITATIONS TO LEADING ETHICAL ORGANIZATIONAL CHANGE

In the four cases described above, the individuals did not attack the organization or people within the organization, nor did they intervene against individuals and/or the organization to stop an unethical practice. Instead, they worked with people in the organization to build a more ethical organization. As a result of their leadership, the organizations used more ethical behaviors. The strategy of leading an organization toward more ethical behavior, however, does have some limitations. These are described below.

1. In some organizational situations, ethical win-win solutions or compromises may not be possible. For example, in 1975 a pharmaceutical company in Raritan, New Jersey decided to enter a new market with a new product.[23] Grace Pierce, who was then in charge of medical testing of new products, refused to test a new diarrhea drug product on infants and elderly consumers because it contained high levels of saccharin, which was feared by many at the time to be a carcinogen. When Pierce was transferred, she resigned. The drug was tested on infant and elderly consumers. In this case,

Pierce may have been faced with an either-or situation that left her little room to lead a change in organizational behavior.

Similarly, Errol Marshall, with Hydraulic Parts and Components, Inc.,[24] helped negotiate the sale of a sub-contract to sell heavy equipment to the U.S. Navy while giving $70,000 in kickbacks to two materials managers of Brown & Root, Inc., the project's prime contractor. According to Marshall, the prime contractor "demanded the kickbacks … It was cut and dried. We would not get the business otherwise." While Marshall was not charged with any crime, one of the upper-level Brown & Root managers, William Callan, was convicted in 1985 of extorting kickbacks, and another manager, Frank DiDomenico, pleaded guilty to extorting kickbacks from Hydraulic Parts & Components, Inc. Marshall has left the company. In this case, it seems that Marshall had no win-win alternative to paying the bribe. In some situations it may not be possible to lead a win-win ethical change.

2. Some people do not understand how leadership can be applied to situations that involve organizational-ethics issues. Also, some people—particularly those in analytical or technical professions, which may not offer much opportunity for gaining leadership experience—may not know how to lead very well in any situation. Some people may be good leaders in the course of their normal work lives, but do not try to lead or do not lead very well when ethical issues are involved. Some people avoid discussing ethical, religious, and political issues at work.

For example, John Geary was a salesperson for U.S. Steel when the company decided to enter a new market with what he and others considered an unsafe new product.[25] As a leading salesperson for U.S. Steel, Geary normally was very good at leading the way toward changes that satisfied customer and organizational needs. A good salesperson frequently needs to coordinate and spearhead modification in operations, engineering, logistics, product design, financing, and billing/payment that are necessary for a company to maintain good customer relationships and sales. Apparently, however, he did not try to lead the organization in developing a win-win solution, such as soliciting current orders for a later delivery of a corrected product. He tried only reasoning against selling the unsafe product and protested its sale to several groups of upper-level engineers and managers. He noted that he believed the product had a failure rate of 3.6 percent and was therefore both unsafe and potentially damaging to U.S. Steel's longer-term strategy of entering higher technology/profit margin businesses. According to Geary, even though many upper-level managers, engineers, and salespeople understood and believed him, "the only desire of everyone associated with the project was to satisfy the instructions of Henry Wallace (the sales vice president). No one was about to buck this man for fear of his job."[26] The sales vice president fired Geary, apparently because he continued to protest against sale of the product.

Similarly, William Schwartzkopf of Commonwealth Electric Co.[27] did not think he could either ethically reason against or lead an end to the large-scale, long-time bid rigging between his own company and many of the largest U.S. electrical contractors. Even though he was an attorney and had extensive experience in leading organizational changes, he did not try to lead his company toward an ethical solution. He waited until he retired from the company, then wrote a secret letter to the Justice Department accusing the contractors of raising bids and conspiring to divide billions of dollars of contracts among themselves.

Many people—both experienced and inexperienced in leadership—do not try to lead their companies toward developing solutions to ethical problems. Often, they do not understand that it is possible to lead such a change; therefore, they do not try to do so—even though as the cases here show, many succeed when they do try.

3. Some organizational environments—in both consensus-building and authoritarian types of cultures—discourage leadership that is noncomforming. For example as Robert E. Wood, former CEO of the giant international retailer Sears, Roebuck, has observed, "We stress the advantages of the free enterprise system, we complain about the totalitarian state, but in our individual organizations we have created more or less a totalitarian system in industry, particularly in large industry."[28] Similarly, Charles

W. Summers, in a *Harvard Business Review* article, observes, "Corporate executives may argue that . . . they recognize and protect . . . against arbitrary termination through their own internal procedures. The simple fact is that most companies have not recognized and protected that right."[29]

David Ewing concludes that "It [the pressure to obey unethical and illegal orders] is probably most dangerous however, as a low-level infection. When it slowly bleeds the individual conscience dry and metastasizes insidiously, it is most difficult to defend against. There are no spectacular firings or purges in the ranks. There are no epic blunders. Under constant and insistent pressure, employees simply give in and conform. They become good 'organization people.'"[30]

Similar pressures can exist in participative, consensus-building types of cultures. For example, as mentioned above, Yoshino and Lifson write, "A Japanese leader, rather than being an authority, is more of a communications channel, a mediator, a facilitator, and most of all, a symbol and embodiment of group unity. Consensus building is necessary to decision making, and this requires patience and an ability to use carefully cultivated relationships to get all to agree for the good of the unit."[31]

The importance of the group and the position of the group leaders as a symbol of the group are revealed in the very popular true story, "Tale of the Forty-Seven Ronin." The tale is about 47 warriors whose lord is unjustly killed. The Ronin spend years sacrificing everything, including their families, in order to kill the person responsible for their leader's death. Then all those who survive the assault killed themselves.

Just as authoritarian top-down organizational cultures can produce unethical behaviors, so can participative, consensus-building cultures. The Japanese novelist Shusaku Endo, in his *The Sea and Poison*, describes the true story of such a problem.[32] It concerns an experiment cooperatively performed by the Japanese Army, a medical hospital, and a consensus-building team of doctors on American prisoners of war. The purpose of the experiment was to determine scientifically how much blood people can lose before they die.

Endo describes the reasoning and feelings of one of the doctors as he looked back at this behavior:

> *At the time nothing could be done . . . If I were caught in the same way, I might, I might just do the same thing again . . . We feel that getting on good terms ourselves with the Western Command medical people, with whom Second [section] is so cozy, wouldn't be a bad idea at all. Therefore we feel there's no need to ill-temperedly refuse their friendly proposal and hurt their feelings . . . Five doctors from Kando's section most likely will be glad to get the chance . . . For me the pangs of conscience . . . were from childhood equivalent to the fear of disapproval in the eyes of others—fear of the punishment which society would bring to bear.*
>
> *. . . To put it quite bluntly, I am able to remain quite undisturbed in the face of someone else's terrible suffering and death . . . I am not writing about these experiences as one driven to do so by his conscience . . . all these memories are distasteful to me. But looking upon them as distasteful and suffering because of them are two different matters. Then why do I bother writing? Because I'm strangely ill at ease. I, who fear only the eyes of others and the punishment of society, and whose fears disappear when I am secure from these, am now disturbed . . . I have no conscience, I suppose. Not just me, though. None of them feel anything at all about what they did here.*

The only emotion in his heart was a sense of having fallen as low as one can fall.[33]

WHAT TO DO AND HOW TO BE

In light of the discussion of the two approaches to addressing organization ethics issues and their limitations, what should we do as individuals and members of organizations? To some extent that depends on the circumstances and our own abilities. If we know how to lead, if there's time for it, if the key people in authority are reasonable, and if a win-win solution is possible, one should probably try leading an organizational change.

If, on the other hand, one does not know how to lead, time is limited, the authority figures are unreasonable, a culture of strong conformity exists, and the situation is not likely to produce a win-win outcome, then the chances of success with a leadership approach are much lower. This may leave one with only the choice of using one of the intervention strategies discussed above. If an individual wishes to remain an effective member of the organization, then one of the more secretive strategies may be safer.

But what about the more common, middle range of problems? Here there is no easy prescription. The more win-win potential the situation has, the more time there is, the more leadership skills one has, and the more reasonable the authority figures and organizational cultures are, the more likely a leadership approach is to succeed. If the opposite conditions exist, then forcing change in the organization is the likely alternative.

To a large extent, the choice depends on an individual's courage. In my opinion, in all but the most extreme and unusual circumstances, one should first try to lead a change toward ethical behavior. If that does not succeed, then mustering the courage to act against others and the organization may be necessary. For example, the course of action that might have saved the Challenger crew was for Boisjoly or someone else to act against Morton Thiokol, its top managers, and NASA by blowing the whistle to the press.

If there is an implicitly characteristic American ontology, perhaps it is some version of William James' 1907 Pragmatism, which, for better or worse, sees through a lens of interactions the ontologies of being as an individual and being as a part. James explains our situation as follows:

> *What we were discussing was the idea of a world growing not integrally but piecemeal by the contributions of its several parts. Take the hypothesis seriously and as a live one. Suppose that the world's author put the case to you before creation, saying: "If I am going to make a world not certain to be saved, a world the perfection of which shall be conditional merely, the condition being that each agent does its own 'level best,' I offer you the chance of taking part in such a world. Its safety, you see, is unwarranted. It is a real adventure, with real danger yet it may win through. It is a social scheme of cooperative work genuinely to be done. Will you join the procession? Will you trust yourself and trust the other agents enough to face the risk? ... Then it is perfectly possible to accept sincerely a drastic kind of universe from which the element of "seriousness" is not to be expelled. Who so does so, it seems to me, a genuine pragmatist. He is willing to live on a scheme of uncertified possibilities which he trusts; willing to pay with his own person, if need be, for the realization of the ideals which he frames. What now actually are the other forces which he trusts to co-operate with him, in a universe of such a type? They are at least his fellow men, in the stage of being which our actual universe has reached.*[34]

In conclusion, there are realistic ethics leadership and intervention action strategies. We can act effectively concerning organizational ethics issues. Depending upon the circumstances including our own courage, we can choose to act and be ethical both as individuals and as leaders. Being as a part and leading ethical change is the more constructive approach generally. However, being as an individual intervening against others and organizations can sometimes be the only short- or medium-term effective approach.

ENDNOTES

[1] P. Tillich, *The Courage To Be* (New Haven, CT: Yale University Press, 1950).
[2] Ibid, 159.

[3] D. Ewing, *Freedom Inside the Organization* (New York: McGraw-Hill, 1977).

[4] The person blowing the whistle in this case wishes to remain anonymous. See also Elizabeth Neuffer, "GE Managers Sentenced for Bribery," *The Boston Globe*, July 26, 1988, 67.

[5] B. L. Toffler, *Tough Choices: Managers Talk Ethics* (New York: John Wiley, 1986) 153–169.

[6] R. P. Nielsen, "What Can Managers Do About Unethical Management?" *Journal of Business Ethics 6* (1987): 153–161. See also Nielsen's "Limitations of Ethical Reasoning as an Action Strategy," *Journal of Business Ethics 7* (1988): 625–733, and "Arendt's Action Philosophy and the Manager as Eichmann, Richard III, Faust or Institution Citizen," *California Management Review 26*, no. 3 (Spring 1984) 191–201.

[7] The person involved wishes to remain anonymous.

[8] The person involved wishes to remain anonymous.

[9] Nielsen, "What Can Managers Do About Unethical Management?"

[10] R. Reinhold, "Astronauts' Chief Says NASA Risked Life for Schedule," *New York Times*, 1986, 1.

[11] Personal conversation and letter with Frank Ladwig, 1986. See also Frank Ladwig and Associates' Advanced Consultative Selling for Professionals. Stonington, CT.

[12] W. G. Glaberson, "Did Searle Lose Its Eyes to a Health Hazard?" *Business Week*, October 14, 1985, 120–122.

[13] The person involved wishes to remain anonymous.

[14] A. Pasztor, "Electrical Contractors Reel under Charges That They Rigged Bids," *Wall Street Journal*, November 29, 1985, 1, 14.

[15] A. E. Fitzgerald, *The High Priests of Waste* (New York: McGraw-Hill, 1977).

[16] Tillich, 89, 93.

[17] M. Y. Yoshino and T. B. Lifson, *The Invisible Link: Japan's Saga Shosha and the Organization of Trade* (Cambridge, MA: MIT Press, 1986).

[18] Ibid. 178.

[19] Roger Boisjoly, address given at Massachusetts Institute of Technology on January 7, 1987. Reprinted in *Books and Religion* (March/April 1987):3–4, 12–13. See also C. Whitbeck, "Moral Responsibility and the Working Engineer," *Books and Religion 3* (March/April 1987): 22–23.

[20] Personal conversation with Ray Bauer, Harvard Business School, 1975. See also R. Ackerman and R. Bauer, *Corporate Social Responsiveness* (Reston, VA: Reston Publishing, 1976).

[21] The person involved wishes to remain anonymous.

[22] The person involved wishes to remain anonymous.

[23] David Ewing, *Do It My Way or You're Fired* (New York: John Wiley, 1983).

[24] E. T. Pound, "Investigators Detect Pattern of Kickbacks for Defense Business," *Wall Street Journal*, November 14, 1985, 1, 25.

[25] Ewing. See also *Geary vs. U.S. Steel Corporation*, 319 A. 2nd 174, Supreme Court of PA.

[26] Ewing, 86.

[27] A. Pasztor.

[28] Ewing, 21.

[29] C. W. Summers, "Protecting All Employees against Unjust Dismissal," *Harvard Business Review 58* (1980): 132–139.

[30] D. Ewing, 216–217.

[31] Yoshino's Lifson, 187.

[32] S. Endo, *The Sea and Poison* (New York: Taplinger Publishing Company, 1972). See also Y. Yasuda, *Old Tales of Japan* (Tokyo: Charles Tuttle Company, 1947).

[33] S. Endo and Y. Yasuda.

[34] W. James, *Pragmatism: A New Name for Some Old Ways of Thinking* (New York: Longmans, Green and Co., 1907) 290, 297–298.

WHEN ETHICS TRAVEL: THE PROMISE AND PERIL OF GLOBAL BUSINESS ETHICS*

Thomas Donaldson
Thomas W. Dunfee

Global managers often must navigate the perplexing gray zone that arises when two cultures—and two sets of ethics—meet. Suppose:

> *You are a manager of Ben & Jerry's in Russia. One day you discover that the most senior officer of your company's Russian joint venture has been 'borrowing' equipment from the company and using it in his other business ventures. When you confront him, the Russian partner defends his actions. After all, as a part owner of both companies, isn't he entitled to share in the equipment?*[1]
>
> *Or, competing for a bid in a foreign country, you are introduced to a 'consultant' who offers to help you in your client contacts. A brief conversation makes it clear that this person is well connected in local government and business circles and knows your customer extremely well. The consultant will help you prepare and submit your bid and negotiate with the customer ...for a substantial fee. Your peers tell you that such arrangements are normal in this country—and that a large part of the consulting fee will go directly to staff people working for your customer. Those who have rejected such help in the past have seen contracts go to their less-fussy competitors.*[2]

What should you do in such cases? Should you straighten out your Russian partner? How should you deal with the problem of bribery? Bribery is just like tipping, some people say. Whether you tip for service at dinner or bribe for the benefit of getting goods through customs, you pay for a service rendered. But while many of us balk at a conclusion that puts bribery on a par with tipping, we have difficulty articulating why.

Most Western companies' codes of ethics never dreamed of cross-cultural challenges like these. How can managers successfully maneuver the disturbing gray zones that lie at the intersections of different cultures? Issues such as these have tended to bedazzle many modern multinational corporations. Companies are finding—and stumbling over—ethics issues abroad as never before. Corporate ethics and values programs are in vogue; and many companies are asking whether they should take their ethics and values programs global. But confusion abounds.

Some companies, recognizing cultural differences, simply accept whatever prevails in the host country. This is a mistake because it exposes the company (and its brand names) to corruption and public affairs disasters, and because it misses the opportunity to find the glue that cements morale and cooperative strategy. It neglects the important role for hypernorms.** It substitutes unmitigated relativism for good sense. Years ago, foreign companies operating in South Africa broke the South African apartheid law that required segregated washrooms for employees. Not to break that South African law, and to leave the washrooms segregated, would have been unethical. Consider a more recent example:

**Hypernorms are principles so fundamental that, by definition, they serve to evaluate lower-order norms, reaching to the root of what is ethical for humanity. They represent norms by which all others are to be judged.

The SS United States, *arguably the most luxurious ocean liner during the 1950s, was loaded with asbestos and would have cost about $100 million to be refurbished for luxury cruising. In 1992 it was towed to Turkey, where the cost of removing the asbestos was only S2 million. Turkish officials refused to allow the removal because of the danger of cancer. In October 1993 it was towed to the Black Sea port of Sebastopol where laws are lax. It will have more than one-half million square feet of carcinogenic asbestos removed for even less than $2 million, and in the context we can predict that the safety standards will be even lower.*[3]

Few would argue that exposing workers to hazardous asbestos is the ethically correct policy. A company must sometimes refuse to adopt host-country standards even when there is no law requiring it. Yet it is all too possible to make exactly the opposite mistake. Some companies attempt to export all home-country values to the host country. Wanting to duplicate successful ethics and values programs, these companies "photocopy" home-country ethics initiatives. Photocopying values is a mistake because it is disrespectful of other cultures. It neglects the important role of moral free space.

To create and succeed with a clear, consistent overseas policy, any company must face up to home-/host-country conflicts in ethics. It must develop responses and craft relevant policies. It must anticipate that sometimes the policies it discovers in other countries will appear to fall below its own standards. The Gordian knot of international business ethics is formed around the vexing question, how should a company behave when the standards followed in the host country are lower than those followed in the home country?

This article will show ways in which Integrative Social Contracts Theory (ISCT)* can provide a practical guide for corporations operating globally. In particular, it will demonstrate how cutting the Gordian knot of international business ethics means utilizing two key aspects of ISCT: hypernorms and microsocial contracts. First, it is important to make use of hypernorms, especially the structural hypernorm of necessary social efficiency.** Second, many problems dissolve when relevant microsocial contracts are carefully identified and the proper priority is established among them. In order to illustrate the application of these and other concepts in ISCT, we will look once again at the issue of corruption. As we will see here, ISCT is capable of unraveling such problems, and it has obvious application to many other problems in international business, including those of intellectual property, host government relations, sourcing, and environmental policy.

MAPPING INTERNATIONAL BUSINESS ETHICS: IS THERE EVIDENCE OF MICROSOCIAL CONTRACTS AND MORAL FREE SPACE?

No one denies that cultural differences abound in global business activities. That much is indisputable. The real question is whether these differences add up to different microsocial contracts with different authentic, legitimate norms being affirmed by different cultures: in other words, attitudes and behaviors operating in true moral free space. Might it be the case, instead, that in every instance of cultural

---

*ISCT (an approach developed by the authors in their book) is "pluralism," not "relativism." It allows for tolerance without amoralism by combining two previously unconnected traditions of social contract thinking—the hypothetical or "macro" contract and the extant or "micro" contract. Under ISCT, business communities cannot claim that their set of ethical norms is necessarily universal: they must exercise tolerance of some approaches from different communities.

**The hypernorm of "necessary social efficiency," or "efficiency" hypernorm, speaks to the need for institutions and coexistent duties designed to enable people to achieve basic or "necessary" social goods. These are goods desired by all rational people, such as health, education, housing, food, clothing, and social justice.

difference, one side is invariably more "right" than the other is? If so, the task of an international manager turns out to be simply one of discovering what the "right" norms are, and acting accordingly. ISCT's notion of the microsocial contract provides a tool for interpreting the significance of ethical differences, a tool we will use here.

Kluckhorn,[4] Hofstede,[5] Turner and Trompenaars,[6] and many other management theorists have shown the importance of cultural differences to business-but the further issue of the ethical implications of many of these differences remains unexplored. For example, researchers have documented the importance of understanding the time sensitivity of the Swiss in contrast to the time laxity of South Americans, or the group orientation of the Japanese in contrast to the individualism of the Americans. Not understanding such differences, most business managers now recognize, can trigger missteps and financial losses. But the importance of understanding ethical differences among cultures is much less well understood; this is a puzzling oversight, since ethical differences often take a volatile, sensitive form.

On a positive note, a clearer picture of the significance of cultural differences has slowly been emerging in the last decade, and a few of these have shed light on implicit ethical differences. In one study,[7] for example, thousands of international managers around the world responded to the following question:

> *While you are talking and sharing a bottle of beer with a friend who was officially on duty as a safety inspector in the company you both work for, an accident occurs, injuring a shift worker. The national safety commission launches an investigation and you are asked for your evidence. There are other witnesses. What right has your friend to expect you to protect him?*
>
> *The choices offered as answers to the question were these:*
>
> *1. A definite right?*
> *2. Some right?*
> *3. No right?*

Here the explicit ethical notion of a "right" and the implicit notion of the duties of friendship come into play. The results of the questionnaire were striking, with cultural patterns perspicuous. To cite only one set of comparisons, approximately 94 percent of U.S. managers and 91 percent of Austrian managers answered "3" (i.e., "no right") whereas only 53 percent of French and 59 percent of Singaporean managers did.

Surveys of international managers also show striking differences among cultural attitudes towards profit. When asked whether they affirmed the view that "the only real goal of a company is making profit," 40 percent of U.S. managers, 33 percent of British managers, and 35 percent of Austrian managers affirmed the proposition, in contrast to only 11 percent of Singaporean managers, and only 8 percent of Japanese managers selected.[8]

Or, consider studies that show striking differences among ethical attitudes toward everyday business problems. One study revealed that Hong Kong managers rank taking credit for another's work at the top of a list of unethical activities, and, in contrast to their Western counterparts, they consider it more unethical than bribery or the gaining of competitor information. The same study showed that among Hong Kong respondents, 82 percent indicated that additional government regulation would improve ethical conduct in business, whereas only 27 percent of U.S. respondents believed it would.[9]

Not only individual, but group ethical attitudes vary. This clearly holds for corporations; different corporations can have strikingly different cultures and sets of beliefs. ISCT implies that companies as well as cultures vary in microsocial contract norms. But what is it that stamps a company's culture as unique from the vantage point of ethics? Theorists have recently begun distinguishing global companies in terms of their distinctive styles of ethical approach. George Enderle, for example, has identified four types of approach, each of which is analogous to a posture taken historically by nation-states.[10] These are:

- Foreign Country Type
- Empire Type
- Interconnection Type
- Global Type

The first, or Foreign Country, type does not apply its own, home-country concepts to host countries abroad. Instead, as the Swiss have historically done in Nigeria, it conforms to local customs, assuming that what prevails as morality in the host climate is an adequate guide. The second, or Empire type, resembles Great Britain in India and elsewhere before 1947. This type of company applies domestic concepts and theories without making any serious modifications. Empire-type companies export their values in a wholesale fashion—and often do so regardless of the consequences. Next, the Interconnection type of company is analogous to states engaging in commercial relations in the European Union, or NAFTA. Such companies regard the international sphere as differing significantly from the domestic sphere, and one in which the interconnectedness of companies transcends national identities. In this model, the entire notion of national interest is blurred. Companies don't see themselves as projecting or defending a national identity.

Finally, the Global type abstracts from all regional differences. Just as the phenomenon of global warming exhibits the dominance of the international sphere over that of the domestic, so the Global type views the domestic sphere as irrelevant. From this vantage point the citizens of all nations, whether they are corporate or individual citizens, must become more cosmopolitan. The nation-state is vanishing, and in turn, only global citizenry makes sense.

It is helpful to analyze these basic types of corporate approaches from the standpoint of ISCT's two key concepts (i.e., moral free space and hypernorms). Each type may be seen to have strengths and weaknesses explainable through these concepts. What is ethically dangerous about the Foreign Country type is that nothing limits the moral free space of the host-country culture. If a given culture accepts government corruption and environmental degradation, then so much the worse for honest people and environmental integrity. From the vantage point of the Foreign Country type, no rules of thumb restrain granting an automatic preference to host-country norms—whatever they are.

Both the Global and the Empire types succeed in avoiding the vicious relativism that characterizes the Foreign Country type, but manage to fall prey to exactly the opposite problem. Since each type acts from a fixed blueprint of right and wrong, each suffocates the host country's moral free space and leaves no room for legitimate local norms. The Empire type displays a version of moral imperialism. It is bedazzled, as it were, by its own larger-than-life goodness. Just as the nations of Western Europe have so often in the past colonized others in a smug, self-righteous manner, so too a company adopting the Empire posture sees itself as the bearer of moral truth. The Global type, too, suffocates the host country's moral free space, but for a different reason. Instead of imposing its home morality on a host culture, it imposes its interpretation of a global morality on a host culture. Because only global citizenry makes sense, the company can be numb to the moral differences that mark a culture's distinctiveness. The opportunity for host cultures to define their moral and economic identity is lost; it is dissolved by the powerful solvent of global Truth, administered by the all-knowing multinational.

The Interactive type alone satisfies ISCT by acknowledging both universal moral limits and the ability of communities to set moral standards of their own. It balances better than the other types a need to retain local identity with the acknowledgment of values that transcend individual communities. Its drawbacks are practical rather than moral. As noted earlier, the entire notion of national interest is blurred in this model, an ambiguity that may make it difficult to integrate the interests of any nation-state in the corporation's deliberations. Even so, it manages to balance moral principles with moral free space in a way that makes it more convincing than its three counterparts.

As intriguing as the differences in global ethical attitudes in business are, they leave nagging questions in their wake. Granted, differences in global ethical attitudes abound, and granted also that it may be possible to map and identify those differences. As Enderle suggests, even global companies may be seen to vary along ethical dimensions, and these differences, too, can be mapped. So far so good. But does it follow that those differences entail the existence of moral free space? It did not turn out to be true, as noted earlier, that in every instance of cultural difference, one side is simply more "right" than the other is. If such an explanation were true, then the task of an international manager would be simply to discover what the "right" norms were, and to act accordingly. Moral free space, and in turn, the need for corporations to attend to subtle differences among cultures, would vanish.

Evidence does exist to confirm the existence of different, legitimate norms in domestic contexts. For example, in the area of employee drug testing, Strong and Ringer have shown that microsocial contracts differ among employee and non-employee populations, with non-employees affirming significantly different norms for privacy in such testing than employees, even when the views of both populations appear authentic and legitimate.[11]

New evidence suggests global ethical differences exist that are not only quite subtle, but that represent beliefs treated as both legitimate and authentic by ISCT. They are beliefs, in other words, residing in what we have called "moral free space." Bigoness and Blakely used measures drawn from Milton Rokeach's Value Scale to investigate cross-national differences in managerial values.[12] A total of 567 managers from twelve nations participated. Their data indicated that different values not only existed, but also converged neatly in most instances on a national basis. The Rokeach value matrix contains values such as "responsible," "honest," "clean," and "broad-minded," none of which are likely to be over-turned by hypernorms. And yet groups differed significantly by national type. For example, analysis by means of Duncan multiple range tests showed that Japanese managers assigned a significantly higher priority than did managers from other nations to the value dimension that included the characteristics "clean, obedient, polite, responsible, and self-controlled."[13] The three other available value groupings were:

- Forgiving, helpful, loving, and cheerful
- Broad-minded, capable, and courageous
- Imaginative, independent, and intellectual

Swedish and Brazilian managers, for their part, assigned much higher significance than their global peers did to the category of "broad-minded, capable, and courageous."

DIFFERING ADVICE FROM ACADEMICS

Having seen evidence that business ethics vary from country to country, and that at least some of these constitute authentic, legitimate norms, the obvious question for a multinational manager is: "What should I do?" How does a manager navigate these moving, complex currents of international values?

Many business writers lack clear solutions and give sharply differing advice. Some seem hopelessly callous, and others idealistically impractical. At one extreme, Boddewyn and Brewer have defended the view that managers should consider the host-country government on a par with any other competitive factor.[14] The government is seen merely as another factor of production, or set of "agents" that international firms can use in the management of their chain of economic value-adding activities in cross-border activity.[15] For his own part, Boddewyn has even argued that when companies seek competitive advantages, bribery, smuggling, and buying absolute market monopolies are not necessarily ruled out.[16]

At the other extreme, DeGeorge has postulated ten guidelines for multinational corporations.[17] The second of these 10 guidelines specifies that every company must "produce more good than harm for the host country." This claim seems innocent enough until one realizes that it entails information and decision-making requirements possessed by few if any large multinational corporations. How is a company to know with confidence that on balance it is doing more good than harm? This is an enormously challenging requirement involving an all-things-considered assessment of, for example, pollution effects, wage labor effects, hypothetical alternatives (what would have happened if the MNC had not done business in the country), host-country government effects, and so on. It would at a minimum require a separate moral "accounting" process. That DeGeorge means for the evaluation to be intentionally undertaken is obvious, for in explaining the guideline he remarks, "If an American chemical company builds a chemical plant in a less developed country, it must ensure that its plant brings more good than harm to the country.[18] While the requirement is reasonable as a general principle, it imposes accounting requirements that may divert corporate resources in an inefficient manner. It exists in stark contrast to Boddewyn's blunt, self-seeking prescriptions, and reflects well-wishing idealism.

THE ISCT GLOBAL VALUES MAP

In the face of such conflicting and confusing advice, the application of ISCT categories to global problems is helpful. The broadest categories for sorting authentic global norms through ISCT may be displayed in a diagram (see Figure 1).

The concentric circles represent core norms held by particular corporations, industries, or economic cultures. Particular values of a corporation, as expressed through its actions and policies, may be plotted as points within the circles.

- **Hypernorms** These include, for example, fundamental human rights or basic prescriptions common to most major religions. The values they represent are by definition acceptable to all cultures and all organizations.
- **Consistent Norms** These values are more culturally specific than those at the center, but are consistent both with hypernorms and other legitimate norms, including those of other economic cultures. Most corporations' ethical codes and vision-value statements would fall within this circle. Johnson & Johnson's famous "Credo" and AT&T's "Our Common Bond" are examples.

FIGURE 1   Categories of Authentic Global Norms under ISCT

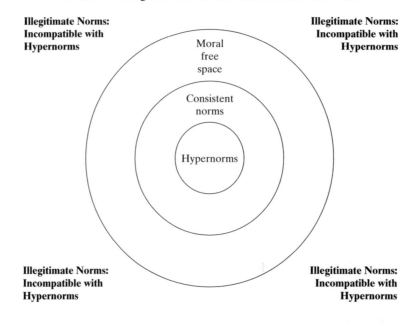

- **Moral Free Space**   As one moves away from the center of the circle to the circle signifying moral free space, one finds norms that are inconsistent with at least some other legitimate norms existing in other economic cultures. Such norms can be in mild tension with hypernorms, even as they are compatible with them. They often express unique, but strongly held, cultural beliefs.
- **Illegitimate Norms**   These are norms that are incompatible with hypernorms. When values or practices reach a point where they transgress permissible limits (as specified, say, by fundamental human rights), they fall outside the circle and into the "incompatible" zone. Exposing workers to unreasonable levels of carcinogens (asbestos), for example, is an expression of a value falling outside the circle.

NAVIGATING USING THE ISCT MAP: THE CASE OF BRIBERY AND SENSITIVE PAYMENTS

To gain an understanding of the implications of ISCT for international business, it helps to apply it to a single, concrete instance. Accordingly, we shall probe the issue of corruption—in particular, the question of bribery or "sensitive payments." Although a single example, it is one with ringing significance for contemporary global business. It is widely known that sensitive payments flourish in many parts of the globe. Once this illustrative application is complete, we will draw—later in the article—implications of ISCT for a much broader array of international cases.

Consider two typical instances of sensitive payments. First, there is the practice of low-level bribery of public officials in some developing nations. In some developing countries, for example, it is difficult for any company, foreign or national, to move goods through customs without paying low-level officials a few dollars. The payments are relatively small, uniformly assessed, and accepted as standard practice. But the salaries of such officials are sufficiently low that the officials require the additional income. One suspects the salary levels are set with the prevalence of bribery in mind.

Or consider a second kind of instance where a company is competing for a bid in a foreign country, and where in order to win the competition a payment must be made not to a government official, but to the employee of a private company. Nonetheless, it is clear that the employee, instead of passing on the money to the company, will pocket the payment. In a modified version of this scenario, the bribe may even appear one level deeper. For example, a company competing for a bid may be introduced to a "consultant" who offers to help to facilitate client contacts. (See the example that begins this article.)

It is not obvious where the norms and issues that arise from such cases should be situated on the ISCT map, if indeed they belong there at all. Are practices involving such payments examples of authentic norms, thus qualifying them to be located on the map? Are payments invariably direct violations of hypernorms and hence located outside the circles in the "illegitimate" arena? Or, instead, do some practices tolerating payments qualify as expressions of moral free space?

Ethical views about business vary around the globe. Bribery is no exception. Not only does the incidence of bribery vary, so does its perception as being unethical. In one study, for example, Greeks perceived the actions in some bribery scenarios as being less unethical than Americans.[19] In another, Hong Kong managers were shown to be somewhat less critical of bribery than their American counterparts.[20] Tsalikis showed that ethical reactions to bribery vary, with Nigerians perceiving some scenarios being less unethical than they seemed to Americans.[21]

From the vantage point of ISCT, then, are there ethical problems with bribery? The answer is *yes*, as the following list clarifies:

1. From the standpoint of the bribe recipient, the acceptance usually violates a microsocial contract specifying the duties of the agent (i.e., the bribe recipient, to the principal or the employing body, such as the government, a private company, etc.).

Perhaps the most obvious problem with bribery is that it typically involves the violation of a duty by the person accepting the bribe to the principal for whom he acts as an agent. Note that in both the illustrative cases above, the bribe recipient performs an action at odds with the policies established by his employer. In the case of the customs official, he accepts money for a service that he was supposed to provide anyway. In the case of the company competing for a bid, the employee pockets money in violation of company policy, and the company is shortchanged. In other words, if the money belongs to anyone, it belongs to the customer's company, not the individual employee. Such policies may or may not be written down. Often they are explicit, but even where they are not, they usually reflect well-understood, implicit agreements binding the employee as agent to the interests of his employer (the principal). In short, even when not formally specified, such duties flow from well-understood microsocial contracts existing within the relevant economic community.

But while this rationale shows one ethical problem with bribery, it is inconclusive. To begin with, it shows an ethical objection to accepting a bribe, but says nothing about offering a bribe. Has the person making the payment also committed an ethical error? Second, although violating a duty to an employer is one reason for considering an act unethical, it remains uncertain whether this reason could not be overridden by other, more pressing reasons. Perhaps other microsocial contracts in the culture firmly endorse the ethical correctness of bribe giving and bribe taking. Perhaps these microsocial contracts, along with an employee's legitimate interest in supporting his family, etc., override the prima facie obligation of the employee to follow the policies of his employer. It makes sense to explore the further implications of ISCT.

2.   Bribery is typically not an authentic norm.

The mythology is that bribery is accepted wherever it flourishes. This image is badly distorted. Despite the data mentioned earlier that shows variance in the degree to which various people regard bribery as unethical in comparison with other unethical activity, there is a surprising amount of fundamental agreement that bribery is unethical.

All countries have laws against the practice. This is a striking fact often overlooked by individuals who have something to gain by the practice. "There is not a country in the world," writes Fritz Heimann, "where bribery is either legally or morally acceptable." That bribes have to be paid secretly everywhere, and that officials have to resign in disgrace if the bribe is disclosed, makes it clear that bribery violates the moral standards of the South and the East, just as it does in the West.[22]

Some countries, even ones where the practice has flourished, not only outlaw it, but prescribe draconian penalties. "In Malaysia, which is significantly influenced by the Moslem prescriptions against bribery, execution of executives for the offense of bribery is legal."[23] In China in 1994, the President of the Great Wall Machinery and Electronics High-Technology Industrial Group Corp., Mr. Shen Haifu, was executed by a bullet to the back of his neck for bribery and embezzlement offenses.

Many broad efforts are currently being made against bribery. The OECD is among the leading organizations mounting such efforts, in part due to U.S. pressure resulting from a provision in the amendment of the Foreign Corrupt Practices Act, which requires the President to take steps to bring about a level playing field of global competition. At a symposium held in Paris, France, in March 1994, the OECD launched a campaign aimed at reducing the incidence of bribery in trade transactions, especially in international contracts.[24] And in 1996 an OECD committee, with support from an international nongovernmental organization (NGO) dedicated to eradicating bribery, Transparency International, passed a resolution requiring that all member countries pass laws prohibiting the tax-deductibility of bribery in foreign transactions undertaken by their domestic firms. The outcome of this last effort is unclear at the time of this writing; but the OECD is clearly ramping up its battle against bribery. Reflecting this same spirit, some academics have suggested the implementation of a worldwide code against bribery and the use of ethical impact statements by corporations.[25] Many leading accounting firms, among them Arthur Andersen, KPMG, and Coopers & Lybrand, now offer services that enhance the ability of internal auditing functions to control the payment of bribes.

When one of the authors of this article (Donaldson) interviewed CEOs in India in 1993, he discovered that they were willing to acknowledge that their companies constantly engaged in bribery and payoffs. (They justify their actions on grounds of extortion—the practice began with the Indian government, and they were forced to bribe.) More surprising, however, was their disgust for the practice. They had no illusions about the propriety of bribery, and were aware that its most pernicious aspect was its effect on efficiency. Under ISCT this implies that even among a community of bribe payers, bribery cannot necessarily be established as an authentic norm.

Philip Nichols cites specific references from each of the world's major religions condemning bribery. "Corruption is condemned and proscribed," he writes, "by each of the major religious and moral schools of thought. Buddhism, Christianity, Confucianism, Hinduism, Islam, Judaism, Sikhism, and Taoism each proscribe corruption. Adam Smith and David Ricardo condemned corruption, as did Karl Marx and Mao Tse Tung."[26]

In short, in many if not most instances, the necessary condition imposed by ISCT that the norm be authentic (i.e., that it is both acted upon and believed to be ethically correct by a substantial majority of the members of a community) cannot be met. To the extent that this is true, most instances of bribery would fail the ISCT test.

3. Bribery may violate the hypernorm supporting political participation as well as the efficiency hypernorm.

Even this last consideration, however, leaves a nagging doubt behind. In particular, is bribery only wrong because most people dislike it? Is there nothing more fundamentally wrong with bribery? Suppose, hypothetically, that the world came to change its mind about bribery over the next 30 years. Suppose that in some future state, a majority of people finds bribery morally acceptable. If so, would bribery be ethically correct? In such a world, would reformers who spoke out against bribery be speaking illogical nonsense?

The answer to this question turns on the further question of whether a hypernorm disallowing bribery exists. For if such a hypernorm existed, then no legitimate microsocial norm could support bribery, and, in turn, it would deserve moral condemnation even in a world whose majority opinion endorsed it.

At least two hypernorms may be invoked in seeking a more fundamental condemnation of bribery. The first is rather obvious. To the extent that one places a positive, transnational value on the right to political participation, large bribes of publicly elected officials damage that value. For example, when Prime Minister Tanaka of Japan bought planes from the American aircraft manufacturer Lockheed in the 1970s, after accepting tens of millions of dollars in bribes, people questioned whether he was discharging his duties as a public official correctly. In addition to the fact that his actions violated the law, the Japanese citizenry was justified in wondering whether their interests, or Tanaka's personal political interest, drove the decision. Implicit in much of the political philosophy written in the Western world in the last 300 years—in the writings of Rousseau, Mill, Locke, Jefferson, Kant, and Rawls—is the notion that some transcultural norm supports a public claim for the citizenry of a nation-state to participate in some way in the direction of political affairs. Many have discussed and articulated the implications of this right in current contexts.[27] If such a right exists, then it entails obligations on the part of politicians and prospective bribe givers to not violate it. In turn, large-scale bribery of high government officials of the sort that the Lockheed Corporation engaged in during the 1970s would be enjoined through the application of a hypernorm. It would thus be wrong regardless of whether a majority of the members of an economic community, or even the majority of the world's citizens, endorsed it.

This, then, is the first hypernorm that may affect an ISCT interpretation of bribery. But notice that it, too, leaves nagging questions unanswered. Suppose it is true that large-scale payoffs to public officials in democratic or quasi-democratic countries are proscribed by considerations of people's right to political participation. In such countries, bribery may defeat meaningful political rights. But many countries in which bribery is prevalent are not democratic. Bribery in countries such as Zaire, Nigeria, and China may not have a noticeable effect on political participation by ordinary citizens, since that participation is directly repressed by authoritarian governments.

Many other troubling questions may be raised. What about much smaller payoffs to public officials? And what about bribes not to public officials, but to employees of corporations? It seems difficult to argue that small, uniformly structured bribes to customs officials, or that bribes to purchasing agents of companies in host countries, seriously undermine people's right to political participation. These questions prompt the search for yet another hypernorm relevant to the issue of bribery.

The second hypernorm that appears relevant to the present context is the efficiency hypernorm, which requires that economic agents efficiently utilize resources in which their society has a stake. This hypernorm arises because all societies have an interest in husbanding public resources, developing strategies to promote aggregate economic welfare (Efficiency Strategies), and, in turn, developing economizing parameters to do so. Indeed, nations and NGOs that oppose bribery most commonly couch their opposition in terms of the damage bribery does to the economic efficiency of the nation-state.

Is bribery inefficient? It certainly appears to be. As the economist Kenneth Arrow noted years ago, "a great deal of economic life depends for its viability on a certain limited degree of ethical commitment."[28] To the extent that market participants bribe, they interfere with the market mechanism's rational allocation of resources, and their actions impose significant social costs. When people buy or sell on the basis of price and quality, with reasonable knowledge about all relevant factors, the market allocates resources efficiently. The best products relative to price, and, in turn, the best production mechanisms, are encouraged to develop. But when people buy or sell not on the basis of price and quality, but on the basis of how much money goes into their own pockets, the entire market mechanism is distorted. By misallocating resources, bribery damages economic efficiency. As economists Bliss and Di Tella note, "Corrupt agents exact money from firms."[29] Corruption affects, they observe, the number of firms in a free-entry equilibrium, and in turn increases costs relative to profits. In contrast, "the degree of deep competition in the economy increases with lower overhead costs relative to profits; and with a tendency towards similar cost structures."[30] Corruption can even be shown to take a toll on social efforts to improve economic welfare, including industrial policy initiatives,[31] and on predictability in economic arrangements.

A striking example of the effect of corruption on predictability occurred recently in Brazil. When a large U.S. company's crates were unloaded on the docks of Rio de Janeiro, handlers regularly pilfered them. The handlers would take about 10 percent of the contents of the crates. Not only did the company lose this portion of the contents, it also never knew which 10 percent would be taken. Finally, in desperation, the company began sending two crates for every one sent in the past. The first crate contained 90 percent of the merchandise normally sent; the second contained 10 percent. The handlers learned to take the second crate and to leave the first untouched. The company viewed this as an improvement. It still suffered a 10 percent loss—but it now knew which 10 percent it would lose![32]

Interviews with Indian CEOs in 1993 revealed that they were well aware that inefficiency metastasizes as decisions are made not on the basis of price and quality, but on the basis of how much money people are getting under the table. This they acknowledged as their principal reason for concern about the widespread phenomenon of Indian bribery. Again, the market is a remarkably efficient tool for allocating resources, but it only works if people buy based on price and quality—not clandestine payoffs. A trip to the streets of Calcutta in 1993 would have brought home the bitter fruits of corruption. The Indian economy in 1993 was one so inefficient that even dramatic redistribution of wealth would leave most of its inhabitants in dire poverty. The poverty is so stark that social activists have given up their attempt to enforce child labor laws, and have turned instead to advocating better working conditions for children—better conditions, for example, for eight-year-old children in match factories. Most of the Indian executives interviewed believed that a great deal of India's economic inefficiency was driven by the presence of massive corruption.

NGOs and government bodies usually cite the negative impact of bribery on efficiency as their principal rationale for attempting to eliminate it. From 1993 to 1997, the OECD targeted bribery as one of its key concerns. Its rationale has focused almost exclusively on the way corrupt practices hamper development of international trade by "distorting competition, raising the cost of transactions and restricting the operation of free markets."[33]

As David Vogel notes, the conviction that bribery harms efficiency is especially pronounced in the United States, the only country to pass a comprehensive act against bribery that prohibits bribes to officials of non-U.S. countries (i.e., the Foreign Corrupt Practices Act). He writes, "The U.S. view that not only bribery but other forms of corruption are regarded as inefficient ... [helps] account for the fact that during the 15-year period from 1977 to 1992, the United States fined or imprisoned more corporate officers and prominent businessmen than all other capitalist countries combined."[34]

The rejection of bribery through ISCT using an appeal to hypernorms, refutes the claim often heard that bribery is inevitably the product of primitive, non-universalistic perspectives. For example, the philosopher David Fisher once commented:

> *Bribery, as a practice, belongs to a pre-modern world in which inequality of persons is assumed, and in which moral obligation is based on (1) birth into gender and class, (2) birth order, and (3) personal relationships that define duties. The theoretical perspectives of modern ethics, such as those of Kant or Mill, have little to offer those who inhabit such worlds, because they construe moral identity in ways that deny the universalism implied by all forms of modern ethics.*[35]

This seems wrong-headed. Developing countries possess at least as many universalistic conceptions as developed ones. To think otherwise is to indulge in the kind of moral imperialism that brought well-educated scientists in the nineteenth century to regard all primitive people as "savages." Recent studies of the moral development of people in Belize, for example, found that they scored higher on Kohlberg-style moral development tests than did people in the United States. A comparative field study evaluated the moral reasoning used by U.S. and Belize business students in resolving business-related moral dilemmas. The Belize business students, inhabitants of a less-developed country, though with a Western heritage, resolved the dilemmas using higher stages of moral judgment than did the U.S. business students.[36]

Nonetheless, at the level most individual managers confront it, bribery has no satisfactory solution. Refusing to bribe is very often tantamount to losing business. Often sales and profits are lost to more unscrupulous companies, with the consequence that both the ethical company and the ethical individual are penalized. (Of course, companies help employees caught in the bribery trap by having clear policies, and giving support to employees who follow them.) The answer, then, lies not at the level where individuals face bribery, but at the level of the host country's background institutions. A solution involves a broadly based combination of business pressure, legal enforcement, and political will. Companies, in turn, should make a point not only of speaking out against bribery, but of doing so in cooperation with other companies.

PRACTICAL IMPLICATIONS OF ISCT FOR GLOBAL COMPANIES

The principles of moral free space and adherence to hypernorms imply a balanced approach for companies attempting to navigate global international waters. The presence of hypernorms means that companies must never simply adopt a "do in Rome as the Romans do" philosophy. They must be alert to the transcultural value implications of their actions. Moral free space, in turn, implies the need to precede judgment with an attempt to understand.

HYPERNORMS

Hypernorms are more than abstractions. The research over the last 15 years shows that in business ethics we're more alike than we think. Practically speaking, hypernorms mean that sometimes there is no compromising in business ethics. In 1992 Levi-Strauss cited its "Business Partners Terms of Engagement" when it broke off business with the Tan family in the Mariana Islands, a U.S. Territory. The Tan family reportedly "held twelve hundred Chinese and Philippine women in guarded compounds, working them seventy-four hours a week."[37] Strauss's "Business Partners Terms of Engagement" deals with the selection of contractors and requires practices compatible with the company's values on issues such as working hours, child labor, prison labor, discrimination, and disciplinary practices. Yet hypernorms should be applied carefully in the international arena and without rigidity. Even when it comes to ethics, facts make a difference. Consider the issue of price gouging in controlled economies. Price gouging is more unethical in a closed market than an open one because free markets automatically restrain arbitrary pricing (if one seller gouges, then another will grab his customers). In a controlled market, however, sellers can exploit customers by manipulating prices. When polled, Soviet Enterprise Executives in the former Soviet Union once ranked price gouging as the worst ethical problem they confronted in business.[38] This is not because the Soviet executives were confused; rather, it was because the rules of the Soviet game were different. When the rules of the game are different, so are the ethics of playing it.

Complying with hypernorms often demands considerable managerial creativity. Consider another situation confronted by Levi-Strauss, this time involving the hypernorms connected with child labor. The company discovered in the early 1990s that two of its suppliers in Bangladesh were employing children under the age of 14—a practice that violated the company's principles but was tolerated in Bangladesh. Forcing the suppliers to fire the children would not have insured that the children received an education, and it would have caused serious hardship for the families depending on the children's wages. In a creative arrangement, the suppliers agreed to pay the children's regular wages while they attended school and to offer each child a job at age 14. Levi-Strauss, in turn, agreed to pay the children's tuition and provide books and uniforms. This approach allowed Levi-Strauss to uphold its principles and provide long-term benefits to its host country.[39]

MORAL FREE SPACE

Despite the importance of hypernorms, it is well to remember that ISCT implies the need for moral free space in global transactions. Here too, managerial creativity is often required. The most tempting and popular answer available for global companies is the "photocopy approach." Its simple advice is, "Do the same thing abroad you do at home." Falling into this trap, CEOs are often heard boasting that their companies act the same way ethically around the globe. Such claims are well-meaning, but eventually subvert the very ethics they intend to support. Saying "we pride ourselves on doing the same thing around the globe" is a bit like saying "I pride myself on saying the same thing to every one of my friends." Friends are different; cultures are different. And the demonstration of a company's ethics must be different as it recognizes cultural differences abroad.

Being true to one's own ethics often means not only sticking by one's own sense of right and wrong, but respecting the right of other cultures to shape their own cultural and economic values. Forgetting this can be a disaster. Consider the mess one well-intentioned effort created. In 1993, a large U.S. computer-products company insisted on using exactly the same sexual harassment exercises and lessons with Muslim managers halfway around the globe that they used with American employees in

California. It did so in the name of "ethical consistency." The result was ludicrous. The managers were baffled by the instructors' presentation, and the instructors were oblivious of the intricate connections between Muslim religion and sexual manners.

The U.S. trainers needed to know that Muslim ethics are especially strict about male/female social interaction. By explaining sexual harassment in the same way to Muslims as to Westerners, the trainers offended the Muslim managers. To the Muslim managers, their remarks seemed odd and disrespectful. In turn, the underlying ethical message about avoiding coercion and sexual discrimination was lost. Clearly sexual discrimination does occur in Muslim countries. But helping to eliminate it there means respecting—and understanding—Muslim differences.

Such cultural conflicts suggest that we should revise a common litmus test for ethics, the one that asks, "How would you react if your action were described on the front page of the *Wall Street Journal?*" Instead we should sometimes ask the additional question: "How would you react if your action were described on the front page of Bangkok's *Daily News*, Rome's *Corriere Della Sera*, or the *Buenos Aires Herald?*" For example, in Africa, a businessperson may be invited to a family banquet following business dealings—and in order to attend he is expected to pay. This invitation is likely not to be a bribe, but a genuine sign of friendship and a commitment to good-faith business dealings in the future.

Companies in India sometimes promise employees a job for one of their children when the child reaches the age of majority. Yet while such a policy may be in tension with Western notions of egalitarianism and antinepotism, it is clearly more in step with India's traditional values of clan and extended family. The ISCT framework we propose acknowledges that the Indian company's policy is in tension with the norms of other economic communities around the globe (hence placing it in the "moral free space" ring of the ISCT circle) while stopping short of declaring it ethically impermissible (a conclusion that would place it outside the circle). This third ring of the circle of the ISCT framework depicts an inevitable tension in values that any global manager must confront, and accept.

In short, ISCT suggests that international business ethics seldom come in black and white. On the one hand, managers must respect moral free space and cultural diversity. On the other, they must reject any form of relativism. Common humanity and market efficiency are part of the equation, but so too is a certain amount of moral tension. The lesson? Any manager unprepared to live with moral tension abroad should pack her bags and come home. Because ISCT is designed to help managers navigate the gray zones between ethical worlds, it pictures reality in more than black and white.

ENDNOTES

[1] S. Puffer and D. J. McCarthy, "Finding the Common Ground in Russian and American Business Ethics," *California Management Review*, 37/2 (Winter 1995): 29–46.

[2] Anonymous case study.

[3] M. J. Satchell, "Deadly Trade in Toxics," *U.S. News and World Report*, March 7, 1994, 64.

[4] C. Kluckhom, "Ethical Relativity: Sic et Non," *Journal of Philosophy 52* (1955): 663–677.

[5] G. Hofstede, *Culture's Consequences* (Beverly Hills, CA: Sage, 1980).

[6] C. H. Turner and A. Trompenaars, *The Seven Cultures of Capitalism* (New York, NY: Doubleday, 1993).

[7] Ibid.

[8] Ibid.

[9] G. M. MacDonald, "Ethical Perceptions of Hong Kong/Chinese Business Managers," *Journal of Business Ethics 7* (1988): 835–845.

[10] G. Enderle, "What Is International? A Topology of International Spheres and Its Relevance for Business Ethics," paper presented at the annual meeting of the International Association of Business and Society, Vienna, Austria, 1995.

[11] K. C. Strong and R. C. Ringer, "An Empirical Test of Integrative Social Contracts Theory: Social Hypernorms and Authentic Community Norms in Corporate Drug Testing Programs," Proceedings of the International Association for Business and Society Annual Meeting, 1997.

[12] W. J. Bigoness and G. L. Blakely, "A Cross-National Study of Managerial Values," *Journal of International Business Studies*, 27/4 (1996): 739–752.

[13] Ibid., 747.

[14] J. J. Boddewyn and T. L. Brewer, "International-Business Political Behavior: New Theoretical Directions," *Academy of Management Review*, 19/1 (1994): 119–143.

[15] Ibid., 126

[16] J. J. Boddewyn, "International Political Strategy: A Fourth 'Generic' Strategy," paper presented at the Annual Meeting of the American Academy of Management and at the Annual Meeting of the International Academy of Business, 1986.

[17] R. T. DeGeorge, *Competing with Integrity in International Business* (Oxford: Oxford University Press, 1993).

[18] Ibid.

[19] J. Tsalikis and M. S. LaTour, "Bribery and Extortion in International Business: Ethical Perceptions of Greeks Compared to Americans," *Journal of Business Ethics 4* (1995): 249–265.

[20] MacDonald, op. cit.

[21] J. Tsalikis and O. Wachukwu, "A Comparison of Nigerian to American Views of Bribery and Extortion in International Commerce," *Journal of Business Ethics*, 10/2 (1991): 85–98.

[22] F. F. Heimann, 1994. "Should Foreign Bribery Be a Crime?" cited in P. M. Nichols, "Outlawing Transnational Bribery through the World Trade Organization," *Law and Policy in International Business*, 28/2 (1997): 305–386, footnote 73.

[23] S. J. Carroll and M. J. Gannon, *Ethical Dimensions of International Management* (Thousand Oaks, CA: Sage, 1997).

[24] C. Yannaca-Small, "Battling International Bribery: The Globalization of the Economy," *OECD Observer* (1995): 16–18.

[25] G. R. Laczniak, "International Marketing Ethics," *Bridges* (1990), 155–177.

[26] P. M. Nichols, "Outlawing Transnational Bribery through the World Trade Organization," *Law and Policy in International Business*, 28/2 (1997): 321–322.

[27] See, for example, H. Shue, *Basic Rights: Subsistence, Affluence, and U.S. Foreign Policy* (Princeton, NJ: Princeton University Press, 1980); T. Donaldson, *The Ethics of International Business* (New York, NY: Oxford University Press, 1989); *Universal Declaration of Human Rights*, 1948, reprinted in T. Donaldson and P. Werhane, eds., *Ethical Issues in Business* (Upper Saddle River, NJ: Prentice Hall, 1979), 252–255.

[28] K. J. Arrow, "Social Responsibility and Economic Efficiency," *Public Policy*, 3/21 (1973): 300–317, 313.

[29] C. Bliss and R. Di Tella, "Does Competition Kill Corruption?" paper presented at the University of Pennsylvania, Philadelphia, 1997.

[30] Ibid., 1.

[31] A. Ades and A. Di Tella, "National Champions and Corruption: Some Unpleasant Interventionist Arithmetic," paper presented at the University of Pennsylvania, Philadelphia, 1997.

[32] T. Donaldson, "Values in Tension: Ethics Away from Home," *Harvard Business Review*, 74/5 (1996): 48–56.

[33] Yannaca-Small, op. cit.

[34] D. Vogel, "The Globalization of Business Ethics: Why America Remains Distinctive." *California Management Review*, 35/1 (Fall 1992): 30–49.

[35] D. Fisher, "A Comment on Bribery," e-mail communication, in LABS Listserver, April 16, 1996.

[36] D. Worrell, B. Walters, and T. Coalter, "Moral Judgment and Values in a Developed and a Developing Nation: A Comparative Analysis," *Academy of Management Best Paper Proceedings*, 1995, 401–405.

[37] Franklin Research and Development Corporation, "Human Rights: Investing for a Better World," Boston, MA, 1992.

[38] J. M. Ivancevich, R. S. DeFrank, and P. R. Gregory "The Soviet Enterprise Director: An Important Resource Before and After the Coup," *Academy of Management Executive*, 6/1 (1992): 42–55.

[39] J. Kline, "Corporate Social Responsibility and Transnational Corporations," *World Investment Report 1994: Transnational Corporations, Employment and the Workplace* (New York and Geneva: United Nations, 1994) 313–324.

CHAPTER 6
PERSONAL GROWTH AND WORK STRESS

ON THE REALIZATION OF HUMAN POTENTIAL: A PATH WITH A HEART
  Herbert A. Shepard

THE NEW PROTEAN CAREER CONTRACT: HELPING ORGANIZATIONS
AND EMPLOYEES ADAPT
  Douglas T. Hall
  Jonathan E. Moss

THE GROWING EPIDEMIC OF STRESS
  Susan Cartwright
  Cary L. Cooper

Given the job insecurity engendered by downsizing, restructuring, and mergers and acquisitions, employees are taking on more responsibility for managing their own careers. The burden lies on employees to continuously learn skills that are in demand to maintain their employability. Nevertheless, companies that want to develop and retain a workforce capable of implementing their strategic goals are well aware that training and career development are crucial issues. Both employees and employers therefore can profit from educating themselves on career issues and developing career management skills.

Career development begins with self-awareness, which facilitates the all-important fit between the job and the person. Herb Shepard, one of the earliest writers and practitioners of organization behavior and development, wrote a classic essay entitled, "On the Realization of Human Potential: A Path With a Heart." Shepard criticizes the societal institutions that prevent people from seeking their own road to fulfillment, a phenomenon that still occurs. We've included this article to encourage you to consider whether your own path is the right one for you.

The second selection in this chapter spells out the new relationship between employers and employees, "The New Protean Career Contract: Helping Organizations and Employees Adapt." Douglas Hall, who has been tracking changes in careers throughout his academic and consulting career, and Jonathan Moss, an organization development consultant, emphasize the continuous learning required by a turbulent environment and provide practical advice for managers who want to facilitate their employees' career development. Their findings are based on interviews with 49 employees about the psychological contract they have with their employers.

Stress is an unavoidable topic when we look at current career issues. "The Growing Epidemic of Stress," by Susan Cartwright and Cary Cooper, two well-respected British scholars, delineates the nature of stress and its effects, based on an overview of the stress literature. They provide a comprehensive treatment of the factors that cause workplace stress, as well as a questionnaire you can use to measure your own level of stress symptoms. Unlike the previous articles, which were all written by U.S. scholars, the primary audience and frame of reference for Cartwright and Cooper is British.

On the Realization of Human Potential: A Path with a Heart*

Herbert A. Shepard

A VISION UNFULFILLED

The central issue is a life fully worth living. The test is how you feel each day as you anticipate that day's experience. The same test is the best predictor of health and longevity. It is simple.

If it's simple, why doesn't everyone know it? The answer to that question is simple, too. We have been brought up to live by rules that mostly have nothing to do with making our lives worth living; some of them in fact are guaranteed not to. Many of our institutions and traditions introduce cultural distortions into our vision, provide us with beliefs and definitions that don't work, distract us from the task of building lives that are fully worth living, and persuade us that other things are more important.

The human infant is a life-loving bundle of energy with a marvelous array of potentialities, and many vulnerabilities. It is readily molded. If it is given a supportive environment, it will flourish and continue to love its own life and the lives of others. It will grow to express its own gifts and uniqueness, and to find joy in the opportunity for doing so. It will extend these talents to the world and feel gratified from the genuine appreciation of others. In turn, it will appreciate the talents of others and encourage them, too, to realize their own potential and to express their separate uniqueness.

But if a child is starved of a supportive environment, it will spend the rest of its life trying to compensate for that starvation. It becomes hungry for what it has been denied, and compulsively seeks to satisfy perceived deficiencies. In turn, these perceived deficiencies become the basis for measuring and relating to others. As Maslow pointed out, such deficiency motivation does not end with childhood (Maslow, 1962; Maslow and Chang, 1969). Rather, the struggle makes a person continually dependent on and controllable by any source that promises to remove the deficiencies.

DEFICIENCY MOTIVATION IN OPERATION

Frequently we refer to deficiency motivation in terms of needs: needs for approval, recognition, power, control, status; needs to prove one's masculinity, or smartness, or successfulness in other's eyes—and in one's own eyes, which have been programmed to see the world in terms of one's deficiencies. An emphasis on such needs can lead to a denial of individual uniqueness and may make us vulnerable to exploitation. In either case, the outcome for the individual can be devastating, and the rich promise of human potential remains unfulfilled.

Denial of Uniqueness   The way this process takes place can be illustrated by a fable, "The School for Animals":

> *Once upon a time the animals got together and decided to found a school. There would be a core curriculum of six subjects: swimming, crawling, running, jumping, climbing and flying. At first the duck was the best swimmer, but it wore out the webs of its feet in running class, and then couldn't swim as well as before. And at first the dog was the best runner, but it crash landed twice in flying class and injured a leg. The rabbit started out as the best jumper, but it fell in climbing class and hurt its back. At the end of the school year, the class valedictorian was an eel, who could do a little bit of everything, but nothing very well.*

---

* *Working with Careers* by Michael B. Arthur, Lotte Barilyn, Daniel J. Levinson, and Herbert A. Shepard. Columbia University School of Business, 1984.

The school for animals, of course, is much like our schools for people. And the notion of a common, unindividualized curriculum has permeated the whole fabric of our society, bringing with it associated judgments about our worth as human beings. It is all too easy for uniqueness to go unrecognized, and to spend a lifetime trying to become an eel.

Exploitation of Uniqueness   A second, perhaps subtler way that deficiency motivation can operate is illustrated by the story of the cormorant. Dr. Ralph Siu, when asked what wisdom the ancient oriental philosophers could contribute to modern men in modern organizations on how to preserve their mental health, developed a list of "advices." One of them was as follows:

> *Observe the cormorant in the fishing fleet. You know how cormorants are used for fishing. The technique involves a man in a rowboat with about half a dozen or so cormorants, each with a ring around the neck. As the bird spots a fish, it will dive into the water and unerringly come up with it. Because of the ring, the larger fish are not swallowed but held in the throat. The fisherman picks up the bird and squeezes out the fish through the mouth. The bird then dives for another, and the cycle repeats itself.*
>
> *Observe the cormorant ... Why is it that of all the different vertebrates the cormorant has been chosen to slave away day and night for the fisherman? Were the bird not greedy for fish, or not efficient in catching it, or not readily trained, would society have created an industry to exploit the bird? Would the ingenious device of a ring around its neck, and the simple procedure of squeezing the bird's neck to force it to regurgitate the fish have been devised? Of course not (Siu, 1971).*

The neo-Taoist alerts us to how the cormorant's uniqueness is exploited by the fisherman for his own selfish use. Similarly, human motives can get directed to making others prosper, but not always in a way that benefits the person providing the talent. Human life can too easily parallel that of the captive cormorant.

INSTITUTIONS AND DEFICIENCY MOTIVATION

Let us stay with Dr. Siu's cormorant story a little longer. His advice continues:

> *Greed, talent, and capacity for learning, then, are the basis of exploitation. The more you are able to moderate and/or hide them from society, the greater will be your chances of escaping the fate of the cormorant ... It is necessary to remember that the institutions of society are geared to making society prosper, not necessarily to minimize suffering on your part. It is for this reason, among others, that the schools tend to drum into your mind the high desirability of those characteristics that tend to make society prosper—namely, ambition, progress, and success. These in turn are valued in terms of society's objectives. All of them gradually but surely increase your greed and make a cormorant out of you (Siu, 1971).*

The further point here is even more far-reaching: that the institutions and organizations in which we spend our lives collude with one another in causing denials, deflections, or distortions of human potential. In particular, three sets of institutions—parents, schools, and organizations—demand consideration.

Parents   First, parents, sincerely concerned for their children's ability to survive in the world, unwittingly ignore their individuality and measure their offspring's progress by a simple set of common standards. What parents are not delighted to be able to say that their children are ambitious, talented, and have a great capacity for learning? It is something to boast about, rather than something to hide. Outside confirmation of achievement earns love and recognition, its absence draws disapproval. Any evidence of "A" student behavior is immediately rewarded. Lesser performance calls for added effort so that deficiencies can be corrected. Much of this parental energy is targeted toward helping children qualify for an occupational future that will in no way reflect their true interests and abilities. The expression or suppression of talent is externally defined, and parents stand as the most immediate custodians of society's standards and its dogma.

Schools   In our schools, the ideal is the "Straight A" student. It is this student who is most sought after, either at the next stage of institutional learning, or by employers from the world of work. What "Straight A" means is that the student has learned to do a number of things at a marketable level of performance, regardless of whether the student has any interest in or innate talent for the activity, and regardless of whether it brings pain, joy, or boredom. The reward is in the grade, not the activity. On the one hand, schools collaborate with parents to reinforce this concern over grades as ends in themselves. On the other, as Dr. Siu points out, the school's objectives are to serve the needs of society, not necessarily those of the student. Once more, a person's uniqueness is not valued for its own sake. Schools are selective about the talents they identify, and represent outside interests in the talents that they choose to develop.

Organizations   Lastly, in organizations, the continued external denial or manipulation of talent has its direct career consequences. Organizations have implicit ways of teaching about careers, regardless of whether they have explicit career planning and development programs. Reward systems are geared to common deficiencies—needs for status, approval, power—and a career consists of doing the right things to move up the ladder. A vice president of one company counselled his subordinates: "The work day is for doing your job; your overtime is for your promotion."

In many companies the message about careers is very clear: not only is your career more important than the rest of your life, it is more important than your life. In one large corporation, great emphasis was placed on moving young professionals and managers through many company functions as their preparation for general management responsibility. The career plan was well understood: "When you're rotated, don't ask if it's up, down or sideways; the time to worry is when you stop rotating." In such companies, successful careers are based on working hard at any job you are given whether you like it or not, and on conforming to the organization's unwritten rules and to the expectations of your superiors in such matters as office manners, dress, presentation style, language, and prejudices.

Do these paths have "heart"? Do they provide for the expression of human potential and facilitate individual growth? For some, as much through good luck as good management, they do. But perhaps a greater number ultimately lose their way, and get labeled as suffering from "burnout" or "retiring on the job."

In one company that recruits only top graduates, that devotes a great deal of managerial time to tracking their performance, that moves each one along at what is judged to be an appropriate pace into jobs that are judged to be suited to his or her talents and potentials, the amount of burnout observed in mid-career management ranks became a matter of concern. As a result, the company offered career planning workshops to mid-career managers, the main objective of which was, according to one executive: "... to revitalize them by reminding them that in an ultimate sense each of them is in business for themself!"

For deficiency-motivated people, moving up the hierarchy of management is likely to be such a compelling need that they may desert careers that did have some heart for them. In an informal survey of industrial research scientists conducted by the author some years ago, it was possible to identify the ones for whom their career path had a heart, by their response to the question: "What is your main goal over the next two or three years?" Some responded in such terms as: "Some equipment I've tried to get for three years has finally made it into this year's budget. With it, I can pursue some very promising leads." Others responded in such terms as: "I hope to become a department head." But the second group seemed to have lost its zest. Many of them enjoyed their work and had no real desire to leave it in order to direct the work of others. They were just singing the preferred organizational song.

Don Juan, in teaching Carlos Castaneda about careers, asserted that to have a path of knowledge, a path with a *heart*, made for a joyful journey and was the only conceivable way to live. But he emphasized the importance of thinking carefully about our paths before we set out on them. For by the time people discover that their path "has no heart," the path is ready to kill then. At that point, he cautions, very few people stop to deliberate, and leave that path (Castaneda, 1968). For example, in a life/career planning workshop for the staff of a mid-west military research laboratory, a 29-year-old engineer confessed that he was bored to death with the laboratory work, but his eyes lit up at the prospect of teaching physical education and coaching athletic teams at the high school level. He emerged with a career plan to do just that, and to do it in his favorite part of the country, northern New England. He resolved to do it immediately upon retirement from his civil service job as an engineer—at age 65, a mere 36 years away!

Thus, all these institutions—parents, schools, and organizations—are suspect when they attempt to give career guidance. Suspect if, like the school for animals, they discourage uniqueness and enforce conformity. Suspect if, like the fisherman with his cormorant, they harness talent only to serve their vested interests. Suspect if they address only the development of a career, so that the rest of life becomes an unanticipated consequence of the career choice. Suspect if they stress only the how-to's of a career and not its meaning in your life. And suspect, too, if they describe a career as a way to make a living, and fail to point out that the wrong career choice may be fatal. In sum, suspect because they are not concerned with whether a life is fully worth living.

A FRAMEWORK FOR UNDERSTANDING HUMAN POTENTIAL

An outcome of people's experience with society and its institutions is that many adults cannot remember, if they ever knew, what their unique talents and interests were. They cannot remember what areas of learning and doing were fulfilling for them, what paths had heart. These have to be discovered and rediscovered.

For many, the relationship between formal schooling and subsequent occupation needs to be reexamined. In adult life/career planning workshops, the author has found that of the things participants actually enjoy doing, less than 5 percent are things they learned in school as part of formal classroom work. A related outcome is that adults distinguish between work and play. Work is something you have to be "compensated" for, because it robs you of living. Play is something you usually have to pay for, because your play is often someone else's work. Children have to be taught these distinctions carefully, for they make no sense to anyone whose life is fully worth living. As one philosopher put it:

> *A master in the art of living draws no sharp distinction between his work and his play, his labor and his leisure, his mind and his body, his education and his recreation. He scarcely knows which is which.* He simply pursues his vision of excellence *through whatever he is doing and leaves others to determine whether he is working or playing. To himself he always seems to be doing both.*

But pursuing a vision of excellence is not always simple. What does "vision of excellence" mean? How do you acquire your own? We can be reasonably sure that it has little to do with getting A's, excelling against others in competition, or living up to someone else's standards. It is one's own unique vision. It will not emerge in school, if each person must be comparable to every other person so that grades and rank can be assigned. Such a system defines individuality as differences in degree, not in kind. Consider, too, the word "genius." To most of us it means a person with a high IQ. But differences in IQ are differences of degree, whereas the notion of "unique" makes it impossible to rank and compare.

In the search for your own unique vision, you need a different definition of *genius*, one closer to the dictionary definition as "the unique and identifying spirit of a person or place." By this definition, your genius consists of those of your talents that you love to develop and use. These are the things that you can now or potentially could do with excellence, which are fulfilling in the doing of them; so fulfilling that if you also get paid to do them, it feels not like compensation, but like a gift.

Discovering Genius and Developing Autonomy

Discovering your genius may be easy or difficult. At some level of your being you already know it; you are fortunate if it is in your conscious awareness. If not, there are several routes to discovery, and many sources of pertinent information.

The first source is *play*. Make a list of the things you enjoy doing and find the common themes. Observe what you do when you are not obliged to do anything. What activities are you likely to engage in? What catches your eye when you thumb through a magazine? When you are in an unfamiliar environment, what interests you, what catches your attention? What are the contents of your fantasies and daydreams? What do you wish you were doing? Your sleep-dreams are also important. Record them, for some of them contain important wishes that you may want to turn into plans.

The second source is your own *life history*. Record in some detail the times in your past when you were doing something very well and enjoying it very much. What themes or patterns of strength, skill, and activity pervade most of those times? What were the sources of satisfaction in them?

The third source is *feedback* from others. What do those who know you have to say about your strengths and talents? As they see it, what seems to excite you, give you pleasure, engage you? And if you can find people who knew you when you were a child, can they recall what used to capture your attention and curiosity, what activities you enjoyed, what special promise and talents you displayed?

The fourth source is *psychological instruments*, which provide a variety of ways of helping you to organize and interpret your experience. There are many such instruments that can provide you with clues to your interests, strengths, and sources of satisfaction. Perhaps the most valuable is the Myers-Briggs Type Indicator, which is based on the insights of the psychologist Carl Jung. A recent book, based on these ideas, identifies four basic temperaments, four quite different ways of approaching life (Keirsey and Bats, 1978). One of these is oriented to tradition and stability in the world, and devoted to making systems work and to the maintenance of order. The second type loves action, freedom, excitement, and the mastery of skills. The third type is oriented to the future and to mastery of the unknown. The fourth loves to work in the service of humanity and bring about a better world. One can learn to perform competently in activities that do not fit one's temperament, and to some extent one must, but it always feels like "work." In contrast, if the activities are in accord with one's temperament, it feels more like "play." It follows that your temperament is one of the important components of your genius.

As you take these four routes, you may find the same messages about yourself over and over again—and you may also find a few surprises and contradictions. In general, the truth strategy you employ is the one enunciated in *Alice in Wonderland*: "What I tell you three times is true." You may emerge from the search with some hunches to explore further; you may emerge with certainty about a new direction to take; or you may simply affirm what you already knew—confirming or disconfirming the life and career choices you have already made. This discovery or affirmation of your genius is a first step, but it needs also to be nourished and developed, and you need to learn how to create the conditions that will support you in practicing it. The second step then, is to acquire the resources you need in order to build a world for yourself that supports you in the pursuit and practice of your genius. The process of acquiring these resources can be called the *development of autonomy*—learning the skills needed to build that world.

Consider the following case:

Jerome Kirk, a well-known sculptor, discovered his genius through play, though not until his late twenties. Alone on an island off the Maine coast for a week, he amused himself by fashioning sculptures out of driftwood. It was a dazzling experience. But his education had prepared him for work in the field of personnel administration. For the following 20 years he developed his skill as a sculptor, "while earning a living" as a personnel administrator—and he was quite successful in this profession. After 20 years, his sculptures matched his own vision of excellence, he was a recognized artist, and the income from his art was sufficient to enable him to devote all his time to it. It was the realization of a dream. His comment: "I was good in the personnel field, but I never really enjoyed it. It wasn't me. And now I'm utterly convinced that if a person really loves something, and focuses his energy there, there's just no way he can fail to fulfill his 'vision of excellence.'"

The point of this story is not to idealize the creative arts. For others, discovery of genius would take them in a different direction, perhaps toward greater interaction with people rather than away from it. But the story does illustrate the qualities that get released when a person discovers his or her genius. Passion, energy, and focus all came as a natural by-product of Kirk's discovery. These were the qualities needed to develop the autonomy that ultimately allowed Kirk to realize his dream. They were inspired by the knowledge of his genius that he carried within him. The same qualities will be evident in any person who has discovered his or her genius, whether it is in sculpture or in the leadership of organizations (Vaill, 1982).

Living Out Your Potential

You began your life as a bundle of life-loving energy with a marvelous array of potentialities. As you grew up you learned to do many things and not to do other things. Some of these things were good for you, some bad for you, some good for others, some bad for others. Out of the things you learned, you fashioned an identity, a self-image. Thus, your self-image is a cultural product, and the distortion it contains may prevent you from recognizing yourself anymore as a bundle of life-loving energy with a marvelous array of potentialities. Acquiring a renewed identity, an identification with what is truly wonderful about yourself and therefore worth nourishing and loving, is not an easy task. It requires a lot of unlearning and letting go, as well as new learning and risk-taking.

How can you tell when you have achieved this goal? What can you feel from communion with others that confirms your own life as fully worth living? What should living out your potential mean in relationship to the outer world? Three qualities are critical indications that you have achieved a life fully worth living. They can be called tone, resonance, and perspective. Tone refers to feeling good about yourself, resonance to feeling good about your relationships, and perspective to feeling good about the choices in your life. To experience these qualities consistently is to know that you are living life well. Once again, though, our society interferes with and disguises the messages that we receive. Therefore, it is necessary not only to grasp the essence of these qualities, but also to recognize and to separate oneself from the distortions of them that our culture imposes.

Tone   Tone refers to your aliveness as an organism. When you think of good muscle tone, you think of a relaxed alertness, a readiness to respond. As used here, the term tone refers to your entire being, your mental and emotional life as well as your muscle and organ life. Hence anxiety is as much the enemy of tone as drugs or being overweight. Lowen expressed this idea as follows:

A person experiences the reality of the world only through his body .... If the body is relatively unalive, a person's impressions and responses are diminished. The more alive the body is, the more vividly does he perceive reality and the more actively does he respond to it. We have all experienced the fact that when we feel particularly good and alive, we perceive the world more sharply .... The aliveness of the body denotes its capacity for feeling. In the absence of feeling, the body goes "dead" insofar as its ability to be impressed by or respond to situations is concerned .... It is the body that melts with love, freezes with fear, trembles in anger, and reaches for warmth and contact. Apart from the body these words are poetic images. Experienced in the body, they have a reality that gives meaning to existence (Lowen, 1967).

But the self-images we forge on our journey through society's institutions often deprive us of our ability to maintain tone. We are no longer in touch with our bodies or with our genuine feelings, and our self-images have been distorted.

One of the most common distortions is to comprise your self-image out of some role or roles you play in society. Great actors and actresses use their capacity for total identification with another human being as a basis for a great performance, but their self-image is not that of a person portrayed. That costume is removed at the end of each performance. Comelia Otis Skinner declared that the first law of the theater is to love your audience. She meant, of course, that the actor or actress, rather than the character portrayed, must love the audience. You cannot love the audience unless you love yourself, and yourself is not a role. Thus, it is vitally important to recognize your roles as costumes you wear for particular purposes, and not to let them get stuck to you. Your prospects at retirement from your profession or organization will otherwise be for a very short life.

A second common distortion is to make your head (your brain) your self-image, and the rest of you part of your environment. Cutting your body into two segments places enormous stress on it, and your tone will suffer severely. "You don't exist within your body. Your body is a person" (Lowen, 1967). A third distortion is to make your gender your self-image. The sexual-reproductive aspects of people are among their most wonderful potentialities, but to identify with your gender leads you to spend the first years of your life learning some bad habits that you spend the rest of your life trying to liberate yourself from.

Other common distortions include being the public relations representative of your family (often forced on boys and girls), being an underdog, a clown, or a representative of superior values. All such distortions will exact their price by robbing you of tone: by causing you to eat too much or drink too much or worry too much or keep your body in continuous stress, and miss the joy of being alive.

Resonance   The second quality for living out your genius is your capacity for resonance. This involves an enhanced, stimulated, and yet relaxed vitality that you can experience in interaction with particular others and particular environments. Discovering those others and those environments that are able to provide resonance can be one of the most fulfilling aspects of the journey through a life fully worth living. The word *resonance* is chosen rather than the word *love*, with which it has much in common, because the very meaning of love has become distorted in our society. It has become a commodity in short supply, a marketable item, a weapon used to control others; it is difficult to distinguish love from exploitation or imprisonment.

The term *resonance* is chosen for other reasons as well. It conveys the notion of being "in tune" with other people and environments; it suggests the synergy and expansion of tone when your energy has joined with the energy of others. It also implies harmony. Harmony is a beautiful arrangement of different sounds, in contrast to mere noise, which is an ugly arrangement. Resonance, as used here, implies people's capacity to use their differences in ways that are beautiful rather than ugly.

The world you build that supports you in the pursuit of your genius is not worth living in if it lacks resonance. But once again, your capacity to build and maintain resonant relationships, and to transform dead or noisy relationships into resonant ones, may have been damaged. To regain that capacity first requires that you become aware of the cultural forces that have damaged it, and robbed you of the potential resonance in your life.

Perhaps the greatest distortion to resonance that we face comes from our intensely adversarial society. Almost everything is perceived in competitive, win-lose, success-failure terms. "Winning isn't everything. It's the *only* thing!" We have been encouraged to believe that the world is our enemy. One must be either on the defensive or offensive, or both at once. One must conquer, control, exploit, or be conquered, controlled, exploited. One must fight or run away. As a result one experiences others and is experienced by them either as hostile, aggressive, aloof, or as frightened, shy, withdrawn. Under these circumstances, resonance is hard to come by and short-lived. For many people, win-lose competitiveness does not dominate all aspects of their lives, but is induced by particular kinds of situations—and destroys the potential resonance and synergy of those situations.

For example, many seminars and staff meetings bring in thoughts of winning or losing, succeeding or failing, proving oneself or making points. These displace the potential resonance and synergy that can evolve when a group works creatively together, building on one another's thoughts, stimulating each other's ideas, and mixing work and laughter.

Three further cultural themes that can cripple the capacity for resonance are materialism, sexism, and violence. Materialism is defined as the tendency to measure one's self-worth by the number and kinds of possessions one has, and the tendency to turn experiences into things so that they can be possessions. Collectibles are a way of "life." Sexism is defined as the tendency to turn sexual relationships and partners into materials, and to use sexual labels to sum oneself and others up—gay, macho, or liberated. Morality and fidelity have lost all but their sexual meanings. Lastly, "Violence is as American as apple pie." We have more guns than people. Our folk heroes were violent men.

Various combinations of adversarial, materialistic, sexist, and violent themes are commonly destructive of resonance in intimate relationships, such as marriage. Jealousy, possessiveness, and feelings of being exploited can dominate the relationship and the partners become each other's prisoners and jailers. But if they are able to free themselves of these distortions, the relationship can be transformed and resonance restored. If you think of any intimate relationships as consisting of three creatures: yourself, the other person, and the couple, you can see that the phrase "a life fully worth living" applies to each. It follows that you would reserve for the couple only those things that are growthful and fulfilling for it. In pursuing the other aspects of your life, your partner can be a resource to you, and you a resource to your partner. Rather than being each other's jailers, you become the supporters of each other's freedom—and this will enhance your resonance. An application of this principle is not difficult for most parents to grasp: your delight in seeing your child leading a fulfilling life as a result of the support you provided. Cultural distortions make it more difficult to understand that the principle applies equally to intimate relationships among adults.

Perspective The third important quality of a worthwhile life is the perspective necessary to guide choices and to inform experience. If you have only one way of looking at the situation you are in, you have no freedom of choice about what to do. And if you have only one framework for understanding your experience, all of your experiences will reinforce that framework. If your outlook is adversarial, you will interpret whatever happens as evidence that the world is hostile, and your choices will be limited to fighting or running away. If you fight, it will confirm your belief that the world is hostile. If you run away, you will know that you were wise to do so. If your perspective is differentiated—if you can see, for example, the potential of a new relationship to be either collaborative or adversarial—you enlarge your range of choices. Thus, if you are aware of "the multiple potential of the moment," you will usually be able to make a choice that will make the next moment better for you and for the others in the situation.

The cultural distortions that lock you into a limited undifferentiated perspective, which lead you to make self-destructive choices, are the same ones that interfere with your tone and self-image, or your capacity for resonance. The messages of adversarialism, materialism, and sexism seek to dictate to you how you should see the world. And your life roles, as defined by other people, are an all too convenient set of prescriptions for your behavior. Take heed of your own feelings, ask what may be causing them, and whether cultural forces are at work. That such distortions are blocking your access to a useful perspective is evidenced whenever you find yourself humorless. The essence of humor is a sudden shift in point of view. To be without humor is to be dying, and laughter is one of the most valuable sources of health and well-being on the journey called a life fully worth living (Cousins, 1979).

Thus tone, resonance, and perspective are the signs that you have discovered your genius and have developed the autonomy to live by it, rather than by society's dictates.

PROSPECTS FOR CHANGE

The foregoing pages have offered a framework for understanding human potential, parts of which may be familiar, parts of which may be new. In some ways the categories of genius, autonomy, tone, resonance, and perspective are arbitrary, and they should only be used when they fit your purposes. And, clearly, these aspects of life are not separable. The expression of genius needs autonomy. Poor tone, low resonance, and limited perspective almost always have a confirming effect upon one another, and serve to limit autonomy. The essential point is to work in a direction that will begin to free human potential, and to rid it of its cultural fetters.

A ROLE FOR INSTITUTIONS

The view presented here is critical of the way society's institutions impose cultural distortions on people, and prevent them from finding a path with a heart. Does this mean that, for the well-being of all of us, our institutions should refrain from showing any interest in careers? Does it mean that there can be no institution with a vested interest in people having a life that is fully worth living?

I believe the answer to both questions is no. Two concurrent forces are operating to change the culture quite rapidly. One of these is the dawning realization in many American organizations that the theories of management and organization on which our society has operated in the past have failed us, and will not serve us in the future. They have failed because they have regarded human beings as part of a social machine and have treated as irrelevant individual spirit and well-being. Nor have these theories capitalized on individuals' needs and capacities to work harmoniously with each other. This realization of past failure is bringing about a transformation in industrial organizations, and non-industrial organizations will eventually catch up. The second force for change is technological progress, especially the rapid development of electronic communications and computers. The more that routine operations are performed by machines, the more demand there is that the non-routine operations be performed with excellence. This kind of excellence in human performance can only be attained by persons who are fully alive and operating in the area of their genius. Only if the path has a heart will it sustain excellence.

When the aerospace industry was in its infancy, the technical challenge, and hence the need for creativity and teamwork, was immense. One of the most successful companies recognized this fully in its organizational structure and culture. It invented new organizational forms that were suited to its mission and the capacities of its members to work together creatively. In the process, it created most of the principles and processes that are in use today in what has come to be called organization development. Among other things, it offered its members Life and Career Planning workshops, to help them identify their talents and interests. The approach was somewhat different from the one outlined in this paper, but its intent was the same. The spirit of these workshops was summed up in the way the company introduced them: "What you do with your life and career is your responsibility. But because you are a member of this company, the company shares some of that responsibility with you. Perhaps it's 80 percent yours, 20 percent the company's. This workshop is the company's effort to contribute towards its 20 percent." In a similar spirit, another company offers workshops based on their version of Dalton and Thompson's career-stages model, to help employees identify their position on the path, understand their potential more clearly, and find ways of fulfilling it (Dalton, Thompson, and Price, 1977).

These companies have a vested interest in having their members rediscover their genius. Our hope for changing the order of things is that more and more organizations will follow their example. But we must insist that their interventions be explicitly on their members' behalf. And their processes must seek to liberate people from their cultural surroundings—including organizational cultures—rather than to reaffirm their dependencies. Then their example can be picked up by the schools, who can help others much earlier in their lives. Parents, in turn, will come to appreciate the freedom of spirit that they can encourage in their own children. The path with a heart is also the path to improving our institutions. Let our teaching about careers stand for nothing less.

THE NEW PROTEAN CAREER CONTRACT: HELPING ORGANIZATIONS AND EMPLOYEES ADAPT*

Douglas T. Hall
Jonathan E. Moss

We're brutalizing the workforce right now during this transitional period. If we're going to get what we need, the brutalization has to stop.

James Champy,
co-author of *Reengineering the Corporation*,
in the *Wall Street Journal*, January 17, 1995.

The headlines scream from the covers of our major publications: "What Ever Happened to the Great American Job?", "The Pain of Downsizing," "Downsizing Government," "The End of Jobs."

The message is relentless: The deal has changed. The career contract is dead. Organizations are in constant flux. The job is a thing of the past. America's largest employer is now a temporary agency, Manpower, Inc. All bets are off. Even the champion of reengineering, James Champy, sees the corrosive effect of restructuring on employee commitment.

It's clear that organizational transformation is taking place on a global scale. To be competitive, firms have to be smaller, smarter, and swifter in their response to changing market conditions. And it's clear that the workplace has been similarly transformed for everyone. Employees must be equally flexible and adaptive.

It's unclear, however, just how an organization and its employees can adapt in a satisfying and productive way to these new dynamics. We will address this question by sharing the "observations from the trenches" of 49 people we interviewed about changes in what can be called the "psychological contract" in their organizations. To gain a more balanced picture, we interviewed individuals in organizations selected to represent a range of adjustment periods (i.e., length of time elapsed since a major business crisis or environmental shock to the present). AT&T, for example, had navigated through divestitures in 1984 and again in the mid-1990s, and we wanted to see how that organization had adjusted to its new competitive situation. Other firms, such as IBM and Apple Computer, hit their crises much later, and we wanted to see what the differences were in the state of the psychological contract there, compared with the earlier-crisis firms.

---

*Reprinted with permission from *Organizational Dynamics* (Winter 1998): 22–37.

THE NATURE OF A PSYCHOLOGICAL CONTRACT

The idea of the psychological contract gained currency in the early 1960s when writers such as Chris Argyris, Harry Levinson, and Edgar Schein used the term to describe the employer-employee relationship. Schein saw the contract as the foundation for the employment arrangement, in that the continuation of the relationship (including the employee's contributions to the company and subsequent rewards) depended on the degree to which mutual expectations were met. Around the same time, David E. Berlew and Douglas Hall, in a longitudinal study conducted at AT&T, found that if, in a given year, the contract was not met for either party, the employee was likely to leave the organization in the following year.

Later, Ian MacNeil discussed two forms of what he called the "social contract." The first, which he called *relational*, was based on assumptions of a long-term, mutually satisfying relationship. In contrast, the *transactional* contract was based on a shorter term exchange of benefits and contributions. Although MacNeil's discussion focused on the role of an individual in a larger society, his concepts seem applicable to organizations as well.

In fact, his distinction proved useful in analyzing our interview data. The participants frequently mentioned the relational aspects of the old contract, often using the metaphor of the family—representing perhaps the ultimate unconditional relationship. At Hewlett-Packard, one manager reported that a variety of "parental" benefits (lifetime employment, generous pension plans) led to a high level of financial security: "A trust was built, leading to employees' not thinking much about change or the future."

Identification with the organization formed another aspect of the relational contract. This was expressed as a sense of pride in being associated with the company, a feeling often confirmed by the reactions of other people. Kevin Parker (a pseudonym, like all other names used here), formerly in charge of management development at Digital Equipment Corporation, used what he called the "cocktail party test" to monitor the status of the contract. "The cocktail party test told all," he explained. "If you said you worked for Digital, and the response was, 'Gee, isn't that great,' then the contract was doing well. Later, as the contract began to change under crisis, responses were more varied."

But Was It All Just a Myth?

If we pause and take a deeper look at what the old contract was and where it existed, a different picture emerges. We would argue that to a great extent the old contract was a myth. The long-term, relationship-based employment we have just described was not the norm in United States business organizations. Nor, we suspect, was it common in other countries. In much the same way as employment security in Japan has existed only in certain large corporations during the post-World War II period, this old contract was operative in only those U.S. organizations with strong internal labor markets and human resource policies favoring long-term employment security.

However, it was precisely these large firms that, through their prominence and visibility, seemed to symbolize U.S. business, thus giving the appearance that their mode of managing people was the norm. The companies with these long-term career cultures, such as AT&T, IBM, Sears, Exxon, Digital Equipment Corporation, Polaroid, and Procter & Gamble, were hugely successful firms that tended to be relatively stable during fluctuations in the economic cycle. Many other equally successful companies, such as General Motors or General Electric, were more strongly affected by swings in the economy, so that periodic layoffs were understood to be part of doing business. And of course, smaller firms had even less of the financial resource base that would permit them to carry employees through an economic downturn.

While no precise figures exist on the number of firms or employees that operated under the so-called "old contract," we would estimate that in 1975—to pick a year well in advance of the turbulent

1980s—fewer than five percent of Americans worked under any implicit agreement regarding long-term security.

Let us explain how we arrived at this estimate. Only about 30 generally larger companies, such as AT&T, IBM, and Procter & Gamble, had full-employment practices that guaranteed workers a certain number of paid weeks each year. (Our colleague, Fred Foulkes, identified 30 such firms in an earlier study, and we are assuming there were others that were simply less visible.) Consider that the total employment of the *Fortune* 500 in 1975 represented only about 17 percent of the total U.S. workforce. So, even if these 50 full-employment firms represented as much as 20 percent of the total workforce of the *Fortune* 500, it would mean that only 3.4 percent of the U.S. workforce had lifetime employment guarantees. (And, in fact, these were never stated as "guarantees" or "policies." They were referred to by ambiguous, nonbinding terms like "traditions," "practices," "philosophies," or "intentions.")

Thus, despite current analyses that tout the "old contract" as part of the work arrangements for the U.S. workforce overall, only those privileged workers in the "Fortunate 50" experienced the kind of employment security implied by the contract. And, even in these firms, it was rarely stated as a guarantee.

THE NATURE OF THE NEW CONTRACT

Denise Rousseau, in her book, *Psychological Contracts in Organizations: Written and Unwritten Agreements*, explores MacNeil's theory in order to examine contemporary changes in the psychological employment contract. She argues that employment contracts have moved in recent years from a longer term relational basis to a shorter term transactional one. As we heard in our interviews, some employees react by wanting the transaction to be a more explicit contract now, in contrast to the more implicit old contract. As Sarah Lorey, vice president, Boston University Medical Center (now part of the merged entity known as Boston Medical Center), put it: "People are literally looking for a contract. They want to know what they will be doing for the next 12 months. They would like to know a little bit about what to expect."

Another way to frame this career contract change, from the perspective of the individual, is to say that we are seeing a shift from the organizational career to what can be called the "protean career." The characteristics of this career can be described as follows:

> The protean career is a process which the person, not the organization, is managing. It consists of all of the person's varied experiences in education, training, work in several organizations, changes in occupational field, etc. The protean person's own personal career choices and search for self-fulfillment are the unifying or integrative elements in his or her life. The criterion of success is internal (psychological success), not external.

Exhibit 1 summarizes the terms of the new contract based on the protean career and raises a number of issues we will discuss throughout this article.

If the old contract was with the organization, the protean contract is with the self and one's work. Evidence of this shift comes from various sources. In a study comparing data collected in 1978 with similar data from 1989, Linda Stroh and her colleagues found that satisfaction with the company decreased from 1978 to 1989, but job involvement and job satisfaction increased.

In addition, the popular media continue to provide accounts of the new contract that support this move from an organization-focus to a self-focus. A *Fortune* cover story by Kenneth Labich, "Kissing Off Corporate America: Why Big Companies Can't Hire the Best and the Brightest" (February 20, 1995), cited an Opinion Research Corporation study in which only one percent of the 1,000 adult respondents said they would choose to be corporate managers. Far more popular were work opportunities that provided the autonomy of a protean career, such as law and medicine.

1. The career is managed by the person, not the organization.
2. The career is a lifelong series of experiences, skills, learnings, transitions, and identity changes. ("Career age" counts, not chronological age.)
3. Development is
   - continuous learning,
   - self-directed,
   - relational, and
   - found in work challenges.
4. Development is not (necessarily)
   - formal training,
   - retraining, or
   - upward mobility.
5. The ingredients for success change
   - from know-how to learn-how,
   - from job security to employability,
   - from organizational careers to protean careers, and
   - from "work self" to "whole self."
6. The organization provides
   - challenging assignments,
   - developmental relationships,
   - information and other developmental resources.
7. The goal: psychological success.

EXHIBIT 1   The New "Protean" Career Contract

In 1990, a quarter of Columbia University's graduating MBAs went to work for large manufacturers; in 1994 only 13 percent chose this route. Similarly, at Stanford in 1989 almost 70 percent of the MBA class went with bigger companies (e.g., those with over 1,000 employees); only about half did so in 1994. As John Martin, president of the Kellogg Graduate School of Management's 1995 MBA class, put it, "I don't know anyone who wants to be like Jack Welch or Jack Smith."

IS THERE A ROLE FOR THE ORGANIZATION IN THE NEW CONTRACT?

If the new contract is with the self and not with the organization, what then is the role of the organization? Unfortunately, many employers are interpreting the new contract to mean that the employee should be completely responsible for his or her career, that the employer bears no responsibility at all. This line of thinking views employees, even core employees, as being in sort of a "free agent" role, similar to contract workers.

Other employers, however, still see a responsibility for providing the resources and opportunities for core employees to grow and develop in their careers. In this group of forward-thinking companies, the employer's responsibility is seen as providing opportunities for continuous learning, which will result in the creation of employability (and thus a degree of security) for the employee. And, at the same time, the organization values the ongoing relationship it has with the employee and takes the long view in its employment practices.

To explore in more depth the role of the organization in the new contract, let's turn to our company interviews and look at how different employers and their employees are dealing with the contract changes.

Current Trauma: Lost in the Trees	Trauma Survivors: Sees the Forest	Continuous Learning: Comfortable in Woods
Apple Computer	DuPont	Beth Israel Hospital
Digital Equipment Corp.	First Chicago	Hannaford Brothers
Kodak	Ingersoll-Rand	Hewlett-Packard
Philip Morris	Reader's Digest	Polaroid
Texaco	AT&T	Xerox
Nynex	IBM	

EXHIBIT 2   Status of the Psychological Contract in Three Types of Organizations

STAGES OF ADAPTATION: THREE TYPES OF COMPANIES

As we listened to people talk, we could hear three quite distinct types of company experiences, based on what stage of adaptation the firms and their employees were in. To help explain their experiences, many people used variations of a "wilderness metaphor" (i.e., references to getting lost in the woods and finding one's way out).

One type of firm was experiencing current trauma (still "Lost in the Trees"). A second group was either "Out of the Woods" (for the time being) or was at least able to "See the Forest for the Trees." Companies and employees in this latter group could see the larger picture and were accepting the new contract.

A third, very intriguing group never experienced one single traumatic event that marked an end of the old contract or the start of a new one. This type of company was characterized by a continuous learning process. To continue the wilderness metaphor, this type of firm learned to adapt to continuously changing terrain and is now "Comfortable in the Forest." (Exhibit 2 shows the three groups of companies.)

CURRENT TRAUMA: "LOST IN THE TREES"

One group of companies is currently undergoing radical instability from economic trauma—their employees cannot yet see the forest (the contract required by the new competitive environment) for the trees (the latest business downturn or layoff announcement). They are still grieving the loss of the old contract.

Comments from Janet Lancaster of Apple Computer typify the "Lost in the Trees" experience.

There was a significant lay-off. There had been other lay-offs but this one hit the hardest. People who were doing a good job were laid off, too. It was a stiff psychological blow. There was a significant impact on people ... on loyalty.

Major turmoil for many of these companies (e.g., Digital, Philip Morris, Kodak, Nynex, Apple, Texaco) occurred in the early 1990s. These firms have been working for several years to evolve a different company-employee relationship. Most have not yet totally resolved how the company will survive, but have made distinct strides in the direction of adapting to the new situation.

LIVING THE NEW CONTRACT: "SEES THE FOREST"

For some companies, the people we interviewed described the drastic change as occurring "a long time ago"—they had gained sufficient psychological distance to see the forest from the trees and become clear on the nature of the new contract. In fact, many employees now embrace the new arrangement, with its greater freedom, responsibility, and opportunities for psychological success.

One factor separating the "Lost in the Trees" companies from the "Sees the Forest" group is timing. The peak of the latter group's turmoil often occurred in the early 1980s. Since that time, people in these companies have had about a dozen years to learn about and react to the changes in the environment, and they have implemented a new psychological contract that allows them to stay competitive and adaptable in the new business era.

A manager at Ingersoll-Rand, a company that "hit the wall" in the early 1980s in the wake of the energy crisis and a world-wide recession, provided a typical description of this experience:

> *We're trying to accommodate the change in the economy. We like loyalty, though, and don't want to jeopardize the loyal relationships .... We went through downsizing in '82-'83 and have returned. We're years ahead of many. Our people are more dedicated and educated than ever before .... People wonder about how it felt to go through a period where 20,000 people lost their jobs here, but I look at it differently: we saved the jobs of 35,000 people.*

AT&T also experienced the contract change a long time ago (divestiture of the old "Bell System" by Judge Greene on January 1, 1984) and then went through a second divestiture (actually a trivestiture) in the 1990s. Although the stress level is high, employees there seem to have an understanding of the new contract. Other companies that experienced these changes long ago, such as First National Bank of Chicago, DuPont, and Reader's Digest, now appear to be functioning under the new contract.

Continuous Learning: "Comfortable in Woods"

In other companies, the contract changed gradually; employees never felt that the old contract was "broken." Organizations in this group included Hewlett-Packard, Beth Israel Hospital, Hannaford Brothers, Polaroid, and Xerox. Although these firms faced financial difficulties, they were generally successful in staying competitive, in part because of exceptional leadership and high employee involvement. In the process of competitive adaptation, they managed to maintain their core values about people through difficult economic and environmental changes.

We would argue that as organizations learn how to learn, this mode will become more common—as a consequence of a natural selection process. That is, continuous learners will survive (and some will thrive) while nonlearners and slower learners will not.

Companies in the continuous learning group have a fundamental respect for the individual—both the employee and the customer—and this value provides continuity between the old and new contracts. To illustrate, Helen Johnson of Beth Israel Hospital offered this description of how the changes at her workplace have evolved:

> *Dr. Rabkin came in as president in 1966. He was keen on the subject of personalized care and established it as a clear philosophy. He felt that the patient and employees are on an equal footing. Both people ought to be treated with respect and dignity by Beth Israel .... The underlying commitment to the employee was evident several years ago as the private doctors' cafeteria was discarded back in the 1960s .... Even during rapid growth, the diverse workforce was taken into account. The culture and the philosophy of the hospital have a very narrow gap between them.*

The case of Beth Israel Hospital also illustrates the emergence of a new form of loyalty in continuous learning firms. Here, respect for the individual manifests itself as loyalty to employees, but not blind loyalty based on length of experience. No employee is guaranteed a job after they have been with the hospital for a certain period of time. It is loyalty based on performance and development, and employee performance is rewarded. (More detail on the continuous learning process at Beth Israel Hospital is provided in the box on page 161.)

CONTINUOUS LEARNING:
A VIEW OF BETH ISRAEL HOSPITAL (BOSTON)

Over 30 years ago, Dr. Mitchell Rabkin was hired as the president of Beth Israel Hospital. By most accounts, this change in leadership was a remarkable event in BI's history. One of Dr. Rabkin's first official acts was to shut down the physician dining area. All employees would share a single dining area. This change, among many others, communicated a sense of solidarity, emphasizing the idea that all employees are an integral part of the institution and will make it great or break it together.

This same attitude has pervaded the institution since. Twenty-two years ago, Joyce Clifford was brought in to lead the nurses (one-quarter of the hospital staff) toward a new era. She was instrumental in instituting the concept of primary nursing, a philosophy that brings more decision making and greater accountability to the profession. Her work influenced the national healthcare environment to rethink the entire nursing profession.

In the mid-1980s, BI initiated a plan called PREPARE/21. Modeled after the Scanlon Plan, PREPARE/21 was designed by a committee of 75 staff from throughout the hospital and formalized the mutual commitments between the hospital and its employees.

The PREPARE acronym stands for Participation, Responsibility, Education, Productivity, Accountability, Recognition, and Excellence in the 21st century. It means that each person is to be held more accountable for the success of the enterprise. We heard staff comments such as. "We are taking advantage of the collective wisdom in the hospital" and "The employees are partners in this." Gainsharing takes place as a result of some of the activities arising from PREPARE.

The advantages of the program are two-fold. First, it is educational, in that it helps employees understand the organization. It keeps them abreast of what is working and what is not. Secondly, it is symbolic. The program supports the message that participation and contribution are highly valued. And the sharing of the financial gains with employees clearly strengthens the collaborative climate.

In the past 20 years, BI has quadrupled the size of its staff and the physical plant has also expanded to a 510-bed facility. BI is a frequent recipient of grants from the National Institutes of Health, a fact that testifies to its status. The facility is viewed as the leader among teaching hospitals and as a healthcare innovator.

Responding to the needs of its highly diverse workforce, BI introduced an array of flexible benefits. These include on-site daycare and a health club, a cafeteria, subsidies for monthly subway passes, flexible work-hours, and earned-time-off (a set number of days-off employees can use for any personal reason, including sick days, holidays, and vacations). The hospital realized that the costs of this flexibility are almost insignificant compared to the value given to the employees. Consequently, BI has been listed among the top 10 employers in the United States by *Working Mother* and in Levering and Moskowitz's *The 100 Best Companies to Work for in America.*

The healthcare industry is clearly in a state of disarray. Beth Israel Hospital, now going through a major merger, is aware that the relationship they have with their employees is just as important as the one they have with their patients. "We certainly have our challenges before us," said one BI interviewee.

This new kind of loyalty is described by Fred Reichheld in his book, *The Loyalty Effect.* As the head of what is called the "loyalty practice" at Bain Consulting, Reichheld finds empirical evidence for the benefits of loyalty based on performance, mutual value added, and satisfaction. Data from

Bain's research show that the longer a company's relationships are with its employees and customers, the more profitable the firm is. There are several reasons for this. For one, it is much more expensive to attract a new customer, through special discounts, premiums, and extra advertising, than it is to maintain an old customer. (This is why, if you are a magazine subscriber, you get a better deal if you let your subscription expire and then be won back, through lower rates, free issues, special videotapes, and other free gifts.) And similarly, it is more costly to recruit and train new employees than it is to train and develop experienced personnel. And in producing customer satisfaction, much greater value is created by experienced employees than by new employees. The key to the new loyalty, however, is that it has to be based on high performance and ability to learn continuously.

And in a fascinating discussion, Reicheld also finds financial benefits resulting from stakeholder retention. Companies whose stock is held primarily by "high churn" investors tend to be poorer performers than those companies that are owned by investors who are known for forming partnering relationships with companies in which they invest. These results show, then, that a firm can have an effect on its economic environment by actively cultivating relationships with long-term investors and by not encouraging the high-churn pension fund or mutual fund.

RECYCLING

These three contract states are not as clear or as simple as the above description may make them appear. When we went back to some of our original interviewees to ask how these categories fit with their experiences, they pointed out some additional considerations. They stressed, for example, how fluid these categories are. Even though a firm may have survived an earlier trauma and people felt out of the woods for a while, a new force (e.g., a new CEO) could raise the uncertainty level again. Thus, a firm might cycle back through a previous state.

AT&T's experience provides one example of this phenomenon. Employees were thrown back into a state of trauma over the uncertainties of the second divestiture in 1995, and again in 1997 with talk of a merger with SBC, one of the former Baby Bell telephone companies. However, our sense is that when this recycling happens, it tends to happen at a higher level of awareness, with a higher degree of knowing how to learn, and with a somewhat higher level of comfort. Thus, it appears to us that AT&T is now back in the middle stage, "Sees the Forest." In other words, organizations may learn from prior experience, which may make future forays into rough terrain more hopeful.

CONTINUOUS LEARNING VIA PSYCHOLOGICAL SUCCESS

While the continuous learning culture has obvious benefits for the companies in our third group ("Comfortable in Woods"), we might well ask what employees have to gain. Perhaps the most important driver of learning for employees is the fact that the new career contract is not with the organization; it is with the self and one's work. The path to the top has been replaced by what Herb Shepard called the "path with a heart."

Shepard used this term to describe success in terms of one's unique vision and central values in life—in short, what we call psychological success. Shepard also pointed out that the path with a heart encompasses one's most-loved talents, so that being paid in pursuit of one's work feels not like compensation, but like a gift.

Unfortunately, it is too easy for a person to become successful in an organizational sense and even in a psychological sense (i.e., in terms of job satisfaction) and still lose sight of living out one's most deeply held values. For example, Karen Camp, an account manager with responsibilities that spanned eight states, told us about her experience as an absentee parent. She was on a business trip just after her son Webb's first birthday. She called home and learned from the sitter that Webb had just taken his first steps. Her reaction: "I realized that his first year had gone by so quickly, I had been like a visitor in his life."

One of the reasons a person loses sight of the path with a heart relates to the internal navigation system. He or she may start off in the right direction and then keep going in the same direction, through thick and thin, even though her or his "internal compass" has changed. Early career and life choices may not necessarily be the best fit for a person in mid-career. As one shocked 42-year-old manager exclaimed in the middle of a self-reflective career planning exercise, "Oh, no! I just realized I let a 20-year-old choose my wife and my career!"

CAREER META-COMPETENCIES: SELF-KNOWLEDGE AND ADAPTABILITY

Pursuing the protean career, then, entails a high level of self-awareness and personal responsibility. There is both good news and bad news here. Many people cherish the autonomy of the protean career, but many others find this freedom terrifying, experiencing it as a lack of external support. There is a developmental or learning process here, as people need time to adapt to this new freedom. As psychologist Robert Kegan reports in his book, *In Over Our Heads: The Mental Demands of Modern Life*, fewer than half of the adults in his samples had reached the level of psychological development at which they were comfortable operating independently in today's complex organizational environment.

To realize the potential of the new career, the individual must develop new competencies related to the management of self and career. The new career has become a continuous learning process. In particular, the person must learn how to develop self-knowledge (identity awareness) and adaptability. We call these "meta-competencies," since they are the skills required for learning how to learn. The need for adaptability is perhaps self-evident. It enables the person to be self-correcting in response to new demands from the environment, without waiting for formal training and development from the organization. However, without self-awareness, this adaptability could be a blind, reactive process, and the person could risk changing in ways that are not consistent with his or her own values and goals. Adaptability alone might produce what Chris Argyris calls "Model 1" reactive change, while adaptability plus self-knowledge promotes "Model 2" generative change.

IMPLICATIONS FOR ORGANIZATIONAL CAREER MANAGEMENT

In the future, the most effective organizations will take a relational approach to the development of employees' careers and thus promote continuous learning. By this we mean that firms will not "manage" employees' careers, as they did in the past. Rather, the employer will provide opportunities and resources—particularly people resources—to enable the employee to develop identity and adaptability and thus be in charge of his or her own career. The entrepreneurial coffee company, Starbucks, provides one example of how an organization develops many of these relational ingredients for psychological success. (See the box on page 164.)

Douglas Hall and Associates discuss this relational approach in their book, *The Career is Dead—Long Live the Career: A Relational Approach to Careers*. (The meaning of the title is that the organizational career is dead, while the protean career is thriving.) In this new environment, the major sources of learning available to the employee will be new work challenges and relationships. The best way to promote adaptability in employees is to provide varied experience through a series of new assignments. A person should not be left to stagnate in one kind of work. (In fact, the good news in today's turbulent corporate environment is that restructuring has eliminated stagnation!) The cheapest, simplest way to provide continuous stimulation and challenge is to keep moving the person through different assignments that demand different skills. We call this the "Mae West rule": She was quoted as saying, "When choosing between two evils, I prefer the one I haven't tried yet."

Like variety, relationships are also in generous supply in the work environment, and they represent a key source of continuous learning. Coworkers, especially if they come from diverse backgrounds (in terms of race, ethnicity, nationality, age, gender, functional training, education, ability, etc.), represent a variety of skills, attitudes, and world views that can stretch a person, especially an older employee. In team-based systems especially, bosses and subordinates, as well as people from different parts of the organization, provide excellent sources for learning. In quality-oriented organizations, customers provide excellent inputs for learning. And, of course, mentoring, networking, team structures, and coaching are also important in promoting growth.

TEN STEPS TO MORE RAPID ADAPTATION

One of the most sobering thoughts in our interviews related to adaptation time: it appears that it takes on average about seven years for an organization and its members to arrive at an understanding of the new relationship. This figure seemed to make sense to people in our feedback discussions as they thought back over how long and difficult the change process had been (that is, for those in companies that had reached the "Sees the Forest" stage).

STARBUCKS: THE NEW LOYALTY

Employees can develop a high degree of loyalty to an organization that is committed to them and with whose purpose they can identify. And these loyal employees will, in turn, produce loyal customers.

Consider the fast-growing Starbucks Coffee organization, run by entrepreneur Howard Schultz, who launched the company in 1987 by purchasing a local Seattle business that sold coffee beans. He envisioned an empire of stores "based on the notion that even though the term 'coffee break' is part of the vernacular, there's traditionally been no place to enjoy one." He sees his coffee houses as "an extension of people's front porch." The firm is now the largest coffee-bar chain in the United States, with a very loyal clientele.

To implement his strategy of having Starbucks stores become "an extension of people's front porch," Schultz takes care of employees first, so that they will in turn take care of customers. "The customer does not come first the employee does. It's sort of the corporate version of 'I'm O.K., You're O.K.'." Starbucks was the first company in the United States to grant full health-care benefits and stock options to its part-time workers (who make up 65 percent of its workforce). As Schultz described his mission,

> *I always saw myself wanting to be deemed successful and good at the same time .... Service is a lost art in America. I think people want to do a good job, but if they are treated poorly they get beaten down .... We want to provide our people with dignity and self-esteem, and we can't do that with lip service. So we offer tangible benefits. The attrition rate in retail fast food is between 200 and 400 percent a year. At Starbucks, it's 60 percent.*

Interviews with the manager and employees at a recently opened store in Cambridge MA, confirmed that this philosophy is working. Serving coffee can be difficult work, but the workers were clearly satisfied with their positions. With medical benefits and the option of a free pound of coffee every week, the employees feel well compensated. And then there is the issue of upward mobility: The manager of the store had worked for Starbucks for only 10 months and had come aboard with no previous experience in the food service industry. A fairly new employee we talked to was inspired by the manager, commenting, "I hope to be managing my own store in not too many months."

Schultz describes the origin of his management philosophy in very personal terms:

My father didn't finish high school, and what I remember most was the way he was treated in his adult life, which beat him down. He didn't have the self-esteem to feel worthy of a good job. So, I try to give people hope and self-esteem through a company that respects them. Dad never had that opportunity .... Every one of our actions have to be compatible with the quality of our coffee. It never lets you down.

When asked about the secret of his success, Schultz looked a bit embarrassed and reflected, "Maybe I wasn't jaded. I always wanted to do something to make a difference. Maybe people gravitated to that." Starbucks' performance seems to be an example of the notion that in business "you can do well by doing good."

Although it seemed to take about seven years for natural processes to produce an adaptation to the new contract, we would argue that with intervention the process could be accelerated. Consider that, in most firms, the contract changes were "nondiscussable." If there were to be conscious attempts to create dialogue with employees regarding these career contract changes, they could more quickly understand the environmental forces involved and embrace the degree of autonomy and self-responsibility available to them.

What specific actions should an organization or a manager take to facilitate the career development of employees in this new environment? The ten steps summarized in Exhibit 3 provide one answer to this question. The following discussion examines each step.

1 Start with the Recognition that the Individual "Owns" the Career

Employers, even if they wanted to, cannot do meaningful planning for an employee's career, not even for managers and key executives. Like other business processes, development now takes place "closer to the customer," in the form of coaching, 360-degree feedback, mentoring, challenging assignments, and other relational activities. Many of these are spontaneous, everyday activities that are better integrated by the employee, through personal reflection and planning, rather than by the organization.

2 Create Information and Support for the Individual's Own Efforts at Development

Although the organization cannot do much directly to develop a person's career, it can provide the necessary empowering resources for career development, the most important of which are

EXHIBIT 3   Ten Steps To Promoting Successful Protean Careers

1. Start with the recognition that the individual "owns" the career.
2. Create information and support for the individual's own development efforts.
3. Recognize that career development is a relational process; the organization and career practitioner play a broker role.
4. Integrate career information, assessment technology, career coaching, and consulting.
5. Provide excellent career communication.
6. Promote work planning; discourage career planning.
7. Focus on relationships and work challenges for development.
8. Provide career interventions aimed at work challenge and relationships.
9. Favor the learner identity over job mastery.
10. Develop the mind-set of using "natural resources for development."

information about opportunities throughout the organization and support in obtaining that information and in taking developmental action.

Information technology makes it possible for employees to learn about the strategic direction of the business, about work opportunities in different areas, about specific position openings, and about upcoming training and development programs. Internet career information and self-assessment sites, company web pages, electronic resumes, career software (e.g., Career Architect, CareerSearch, PeopleSoft, SIGI), and the like assist employees in self-assessment and in gathering company opportunity information. Many corporate and university career centers now have rich offerings available on-line. For example, the Talent Alliance, a multicompany partnership, provides career information on the Internet for companies seeking employees and for individuals seeking employment.

In addition, there is a vast array of career self-help resources (books, mentoring programs, seminars, etc.). Professional organizations are becoming increasingly active in providing career services for members. Increasingly, the practice of organizational career development is shifting from being a direct provider to being a career resource and referral agent. Which leads us to our next point.

3 Recognize that Career Development Is a Relational Process in which the Organization and Career Practitioner Play a "Broker" Role

Being a career broker can mean many things. It can mean linking people and assignments in a way that gives more importance to developmental benefits. It can mean facilitating mentoring and other developmental relationships. It can mean creating various kinds of dialogue groups for employees to voice career concerns and interests and to share ideas for action. Or it could mean helping work teams and individuals find ways to create settings for reflection and "time out" to work on their own development.

4 Provide Expertise on Career Information and Assessment Technology, Integrated with Career Coaching and Consulting

In the past, organizations often provided specialized career information and assessment assistance, and often this function was performed by someone other than the human resource generalists who created career development programs. Now, with fewer human resource staff, career practitioners must be both specialists and generalists. This means being certified on the latest assessment and development instruments, becoming familiar with the most recent computer software, and knowing how to work with line management to create experience-based career development processes. To accomplish this, personal networking, developing alliances and partnerships, participating regularly in professional conferences, keeping current on the professional literature, and the like are all "must do's."

THE TALENT ALLIANCE

To illustrate the use of information technology for career growth, consider the Talent Alliance, a U.S. and Internet-based collaborative coalition of companies, industry and trade associations, professional service firms, academic organizations, and government officials whose mission is to establish best-in-class practices for skill development and employability of the American workforce. The founding companies include AT&T, DuPont, GTE, Johnson & Johnson, Lucent Technologies, NCR, TRW, Unisys, and UPS. These firms contribute time, talent, and financial support to the Alliance, which is organized as a membership-based organization. Activities of the Alliance will focus on research, career growth and development, FuturesForum programs, training and education, job/talent matches, industry trends, high-tech careers, displaced employees, and recruitment and academic relationships.

A sample of "Frequently Asked Questions" from the Alliance's web page give an idea of how the Alliance will operate.

HOW WILL THE TALENT ALLIANCE ACCOMPLISH ITS GOALS?

- FuturesForum will support research conferences and the development of position papers on emerging workforce issues and workplace trends. The Talent Alliance FuturesForum will seek to influence United States workforce and workplace policy, set new industry standards, and provide a forum to debate alternative scenarios for the workplace of the future.
- Career Growth Centers will provide on-line and onsite career planning tools and professional counseling that provide direction and enhance employability.
- Education and Training programs will enhance skills and employability of member company employees by providing ready access to the best-in-class training and education. Most of these programs will be delivered on-line.
- The Job/Talent Matching System will provide member companies with access to the nation's richest job bank and most qualified talent pool.

WHO IS ELIGIBLE TO PARTICIPATE IN THE TALENT ALLIANCE?

Currently, member companies determine eligibility criteria for their employees. In the future, the Talent Alliance plans to provide fee-based services to individuals and unaffiliated member companies.

WHO PAYS FOR TALENT ALLIANCE SERVICES?

At present member companies pay for services.

HOW CAN INTERESTED COMPANIES OR INDIVIDUALS JOIN?

Two ways: by accessing the How To Participate section on the Talent Alliance Web Site (www.talentalliance.org) or by calling 1-888-WorkWays.

5 Provide Excellent Communication with Employees About Career Services and the New Career Contract   All of the above steps are of little value if their existence is not communicated to the employee who is now required to be more proactive and autonomous. Career professionals, both internal and independent, now publish career newsletters. Company web pages are an excellent vehicle for communicating career resources to employees. And external communication (e.g., through the careers column in the *Wall Street Journal*) can also be an excellent way to communicate with your own employees.

6 Promote Work Planning, Not Career Planning   The key task for the individual in a complex, changing environment is finding a good fit with work that is needed in the world. This means that employees should be encouraged to think in terms of areas of work and projects that they would like to pursue over a time period of, say, three to five years. This is not as easy as it sounds. It means providing resources to help employees assess their own identities and values so they can be clear on their own sense of direction, to pursue their own "path with a heart." And it means being organizationally flexible to enable employees to make changes in their work activities based on their personal interests.

7 Promote Learning Through Relationships and Work   The silver lining in the world of corporate turbulence is that the two key resources for learning—relationships and challenging work—are widely available. In the restructured firm, the jobs for the people who remain are more challenging and more team based than were the jobs in the old organization. Successful organizations are becoming learning organizations by encouraging employees to help each other learn the new skills and competencies needed in these more demanding jobs. Although some of this learning comes from formal training programs, we would argue that most real training comes from peer-assisted, self-directed learning through such vehicles as project teams, task forces, electronic communication, personal networks, support groups, customer relationships, and boss or subordinate relationships.

8 Provide Career-Enhancing Work and Relational Interventions   To truly help people learn through relationships and work, managers and career practitioners must be able to influence the kind of work they do and the kinds of people they encounter. This means playing an active role in organizational practices, such as how job and other work assignments (task forces, projects) are made.

9 Favor the "Learner Identity" Over Job Mastery   If major sources of career learning are challenging work and helpful coworkers, this implies that continuous learning should be promoted by continuous mobility. The criterion of success in a selection decision should not be limited to mastery of a position; rather, success should be defined as the person's ability to move easily from job to job. We need to promote a culture in which it is just as highly valued to be a learner as to be a peak performer. After all, it is good learners who provide an organization with that ultimate competitive advantage: flexibility.

10 Develop the Mind-Set of Using "Natural Resources for Development"   Organizations today are seeing that several naturally occurring resources use the everyday work environment as a development tool. The role of the organization, manager, and career practitioner is to help the individual recognize such resources and to find ways to utilize them. Elements in the natural work environment that can be used to aid career development include assignments (jobs, teams, task forces, committees); feedback (360-degree performance review); developmental relationships (such as mentoring); and coaching (skill-building, not just remedial). Increasingly, it will be the manager's responsibility to manage the work environment not only to maximize effective performance but also to promote continuous learning and development.

CONCLUSION

This, then, is the new protean career contract in practice. Instead of mourning the passing of the old contract, many firms are now in the implementation period of the new contract. For firms that have made this transition from mourning the old to practicing the new, the old contract looks like paternalism, and the new one is described with words that emphasize growth, responsibility, empowerment, performance, and hard work. Reaching the point where the new contract is "on stream" is a difficult developmental process for employee and employer alike. It takes on the order of seven years.

Those organizations that have had the most success with the new contract are those that have consciously confronted its existence. They have made explicit efforts to identify the new contract. And they have clearly communicated their central business purpose, strategy, and values, from which they have derived clear management development philosophies. In organizations as diverse as Beth Israel Hospital and Starbucks, employees know what the mission of the organization is and how they fit into the larger enterprise. And they derive personal identity and pride from working toward a "good" purpose.

It is also becoming clear that consciously attending to issues of diversity in career and management development provides the organization with a clear competitive advantage in responding to new, diverse markets and rapidly changing technologies. The more diverse and complex the workforce, and the more effective the firm is in utilizing and providing career learning opportunities for all members of that workforce, the more successful it will be in meeting the demands of a complex and turbulent environment.

Finally, organizations that have succeeded in creating a new contract for the new business environment have recognized that the career of the future is a continuous learning process. And continuously learning employees are what the organization needs to be a continuously improving business.

As James Champy, the "father of reengineering," points out, the success of restructuring depends on the firm's success in developing and enabling its employees. One final anecdote suggests how this activity can strengthen a company and benefit all stake-holders. After hearing Starbucks President Howard Shultz speak in 1991, Terry Diamond of Talon Asset Management, an investment company, decided to buy Starbucks stock if the company ever went public. "Shultz didn't even mention one financial number. Instead, he talked about how all employees, even temporary employees, got health insurance," recalls Diamond. "After the conference, I walked up to him and told him how much he had impressed me." In July 1997, the stock was selling in the mid $30 range, versus $8\frac{1}{2}$, adjusted for a 2-for-1 split, when it went public in June 1992. Diamond compared the relationship between a firm's top management and its employees to a marriage: "You get out of it what you put into it. If [a leader] cares about his employees, he also cares about customers."

In those organizations where it has worked the best, the new career contract does not represent a discontinuous corporate trauma. Rather, it is simply an intelligent response to a turbulent and unforgiving economic environment. In this environment, "success" comes disguised as an ongoing and difficult struggle, but one with a clear sense of values and vision, an appreciation of the crucial role of employees in achieving that vision, and a lifelong process of continuous learning.

THE GROWING EPIDEMIC OF STRESS*

Susan Cartwright
Cary L. Cooper

THE NEXT MILLENNIUM

During the 1980s, we had "The Enterprise Culture," which helped to transform economies in Western Europe and North America, as well as British industry at home and abroad. But as we were to discover by the end of the decade, there was a substantial personal cost for many individual employees, both managers and shop floor workers. This cost was captured by a single word, *stress*. Indeed, stress has found as firm a place in our modern lexicon as *fast foods*, *junk bonds*, and *software packages*. We toss the term about casually to describe a wide range of "aches and pains" resulting from our hectic pace

---

*Reprinted with permission from *Managing Workplace Stress* (Thousand Oaks, CA: Sage, 1997) 1–24.

of work and domestic life. "I really feel stressed," someone says to describe a vague yet often acute sense of disquiet. "She's under a lot of stress," we say when trying to understand a colleague's irritability or forgetfulness. "It's a high-stress job," someone says, awarding an odd sort of prestige to his or her occupation. But to those whose ability to cope with day-to-day matters is at crisis point, the concept of stress is no longer a casual one; for them, stress can be translated into a four-letter word—*pain* (see Cooper, Cooper, & Eaker, 1988).

Excessive pressure in the workplace was costly to business in the 1980s. For example, the collective cost of stress to U.S. organizations for absenteeism, reduced productivity, compensation claims, health insurance, and direct medical expenses has been estimated at approximately $150 billion per year (Karasek & Theorell, 1990). In the United Kingdom, stress-related absences were 10 times more costly than all other industrial relations disputes put together. In terms of sickness, absence, and premature death or retirement due to alcoholism, stress costs the U.K. economy a staggering 2 billion per annum. Heart disease in industry, the single biggest killer, is estimated by the British Heart Foundation to cost an average U.K. company of 10,000 employees 73,000 lost working days each year; additional costs include the annual death of 42 employees between 35 and 64 years of age and lost value in products or services of more than 2.5 million. Of all absence for sickness in the United Kingdom, 21 percent was due to stress-related heart disease. Similarly, in Norway, the economic costs of work-related sickness and accidents amount to more than 10 percent of the gross national product (GNP) (Lunde-Jensen, 1994), a high proportion of which is considered stress related.

For the next millennium, it is likely to get worse. Stress is primarily caused by the fundamentals of change, lack of control, and high workload. The buildup and aftermath of the recession, the development of the European Union/North American Free Trade Association (EU/NAFTA), increasing cross-national mergers, increasing international competition, and joint ventures between organizations across national boundaries will lead inevitably to a variety of corporate "re's": reorganizations, relocations of personnel, redesign of jobs, and reallocations of roles and responsibilities. *Change* will be the byword of the next millennium, with its accompanying job insecurities, corporate culture clashes, and significantly different styles of managerial leadership—in other words, massive organizational change and inevitable stress. In addition, change will bring with it an increased workload as companies try to create "lean fighting machines" to compete in the European, Far East, and other international economic arenas. This will mean fewer people performing more work, putting enormous pressure on them.

Finally, as we move away from our own internal markets and enter larger economic systems (i.e., the EU/NAFTA, etc.), individual organizations will have less control over business life. Rules and regulations will begin to be imposed in terms of labor laws; health and safety at work; methods of production, distribution, and remuneration; and so on—all laudable issues of concern in their own right but, nevertheless, workplace constraints that will inhibit individual control and autonomy. Without being too gloomy, it is safe to say that we have in the next millennium all the ingredients of corporate stress: an ever-increasing workload with a decreasing workforce in a climate of rapid change and with control over the means of production increasingly being taken over by free-trade institutions and their bureaucracies, whether the EU/NAFTA or some larger unit in the longer term. It appears, therefore, that stress is here to stay and is not just a bygone remnant of the entrepreneurial 1980s. The purpose of this book is to highlight those aspects of people's working lives likely to be problematic in the future and what individuals might do to overcome them. Although a great deal has been written in recent years about the sources of stress, less attention has been focused on what people can do about them. In this book, an attempt will be made to redress this balance, while at the same time highlighting stressful work situations that we can begin to *de-stress*.

DEFINING STRESS

Stress is derived from the Latin word *stringere*, meaning to draw tight, and was used in the 17th century to describe hardships or affliction. During the late 18th century, stress denoted "force, pressure, strain or strong effort," referring primarily to an individual or to an individual's organs or mental powers (Hinkle, 1973).

Early definitions of strain and load used in physics and engineering eventually came to influence one concept of how stress affects individuals. Under the meaning of this concept, external forces (load) are seen as exerting pressure on an individual, producing strain. Proponents of this view claim that we can measure the stress to which an individual is subjected in the same way we can measure physical strain on a machine or bridge or any physical object.

Although this first concept looked at stress as an outside stimulus, a second concept defines stress as a person's response to a disturbance. In 1910, Sir William Osler explored the idea of stress and strain causing disease when he saw a relationship between angina pectoris and a hectic pace of life. The idea that environmental forces could actually cause disease rather than just short-term ill effects, and that people have a natural tendency to resist such forces, was seen in the work of Walter B. Cannon in the 1930s (see Hinkle, 1973). Cannon studied the effects of stress on animals and people and, in particular, studied the "fight-or-flight" reaction. Because of this reaction, people and animals will choose to stay and fight or attempt to escape when confronted by extreme danger. Cannon observed that when his subjects experienced situations of cold, lack of oxygen, or excitement, he could detect physiological changes such as emergency adrenaline secretions. He described these individuals as being "under stress."

One of the first scientific attempts to explain the process of stress-related illness was made by Hans Selye in 1946, who described three stages an individual experiences in stressful situations:

1. **Alarm reaction**, in which an initial phase of lowered resistance is followed by countershock, during which the individual's defense mechanisms become active.
2. **Resistance**, the stage of maximum adaptation and, ideally, successful return to equilibrium for the individual. If, however, the stress continues or the defense mechanism does not work, one will move on to a third stage.
3. **Exhaustion**, when adaptive mechanisms collapse.

Critics of Selye's work say it ignores both the psychological impact of stress on an individual and the individual's ability to recognize stress and act in various ways to change his or her situation.

Newer and more comprehensive theories of stress emphasize the interaction between a person and his or her environment. Stress was described by researchers in the 1950s as a "response to internal or external processes which reach those threshold levels that strain its physical and psychological integrative capacities to, or beyond, their limit" (Basowitz, Persky, Karchin, & Grinker, 1955).

In the 1970s, Lazarus (1976) suggested that an individual's stress reaction "depends on how the person interprets or appraises (consciously or unconsciously) the significance of a harmful, threatening or challenging event." Lazarus's work disagrees with that of others who see stress simply as environmental pressure. Instead, "the intensity of the stress experience is determined significantly by how well a person feels he or she can cope with an identified threat. If a person is unsure of his/her coping abilities, they are likely to feel helpless and overwhelmed."

Similarly, Cox (1978) rejected the idea of looking at stress as simply either environmental pressures or as physiological responses. He and his fellow researchers suggested that stress can best be understood as "part of a complex and dynamic system of transaction between the person and his [or her] environment." Cox further criticized the mechanical model of stress: "Men and their organizations are not machines . . . . Stress has to be perceived or recognized by man. A machine, however, does not have to recognize the load or stress placed upon it."

By looking at stress as resulting from a misfit between an individual and his or her particular environment, we can begin to understand why one person seems to flourish in a certain setting, whereas another suffers. Cummings and Cooper (1979) have designed a way of understanding the stress process that can be simply explained:

- Individuals, for the most part, try to keep their thoughts, emotions, and relationships with the world in a "steady state."
- Each factor of a person's emotional and physical state has a "range of stability," in which that person feels comfortable. On the other hand, when forces disrupt one of these factors beyond the range of stability, the individual must act or cope to restore a feeling of comfort.
- An individual's behavior aimed at maintaining a steady state makes up his or her "adjustment process" or coping strategies.

Included in the preceding description of the stress process are the ideas described next.

A stress is any force that puts a psychological or physical function beyond its range of stability, producing a strain within the individual. Knowledge that a stress is likely to occur constitutes a threat to the individual. A threat can cause a strain because of what it signifies to the person (Cummings & Cooper, 1979).

As can be seen, the idea of stress and its effects on people has evolved from different research perspectives. Figure 1 summarizes these different approaches into a general overview of the concept of stress.

FIGURE 1   **The Copper-Cummings Framework**

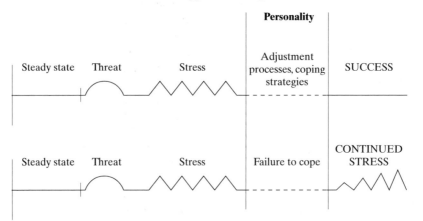

THE BIOLOGICAL MECHANISMS OF STRESS

Stress is clearly part of the human condition. Because of its universal occurrence, stress is not looked at in terms of its presence or absence but, rather, according to its intensity and the effect it has on individuals. Many of us seem to cope well with the pressures of work and family life that we encounter daily. But when and why is stress harmful to us? Consider what happens to the human body when it is subjected to a strain or pressure of some kind.

As Melhuish (1978), a physician specializing in stress-related illnesses, has suggested, stress is the product of many thousands of years of evolution, and human survival in a hostile environment required a quick physical response to dangers. In other words, the body "developed the ability to rev-up" for a short time. This mobilization of forces is the well-known fight-or-flight reaction mentioned earlier. "Primitive man expended this burst of energy and strength in physical activity, such as a life and death struggle with a predator."

Modern humans have retained their hormonal and chemical defense mechanisms through the millennia. But for the most part, today's lifestyles do not permit physical reaction to the stress agents we face. Attacking the boss, hitting the biology teacher who has refused to accept overdue homework, or smashing an empty automatic teller machine are not solutions allowed by today's society. Today, even the nonaggressive "flight" reaction would hardly be judged appropriate in most situations. The student who walks out in the middle of a difficult exam, the teacher who flees from a rowdy class, or the assembly worker who dashes out in the middle of a shift will likely suffer adverse consequences for their actions. Our long-evolved defense mechanisms prepare us for dramatic and rapid action but find little outlet otherwise. The body's strong chemical and hormonal responses, then, are like frustrated politicians: all dressed up with nowhere to go.

This waste of our natural response to stress may harm us. Although scientists do not fully understand this process, many believe that our thought patterns regarding ourselves and the situations we are in trigger events within the two branches of our autonomic nervous system, the *sympathetic* and the *parasympathetic*. To paraphrase Albrecht (1979), in a situation of challenge, tension, or pressure, the sympathetic nervous system comes into play and activates a virtual orchestra of hormone secretions. Through this activation, the hypothalamus, recognizing a danger, triggers the pituitary gland. The pituitary releases hormones, causing the adrenal glands to intensify their secretion of adrenaline into the bloodstream. Adrenaline, along with corticosteroid hormones released through the same process, enhances one's arousal level. All these stress chemicals stimulate the brain, nerves, heart, and muscles to action.

These physiological changes combine to improve individual performance: Blood supply to the brain is increased, initially improving judgment and decision-making ability; the heart speeds up, increasing blood supply to the muscles; lung function improves; and glucose and fats are released into the bloodstream to provide additional energy. As part of these physiochemical changes, blood pressure rises (due to increased cardiac output), and blood is redeployed to voluntary muscles from the stomach and intestines as well as from the skin, resulting in the cold hands and feet often associated with a nervous disposition (Albrecht, 1979).

Although these changes result from actions of the sympathetic nerves, parasympathetic nerves can induce an opposing state of relaxation and tranquillity. As Albrecht notes, "People who have spent much of their time in an over-anxious or tense state have difficulty in bringing into action the parasympathetic branch" and its helpful capabilities.

All of the body's "rev-up" activity is designed to improve performance. But if the stress that launches this activity continues unabated, researchers believe the human body will weaken from the bombardment of overstimulation and stress-related chemicals. Many long-term effects of pressure are described by Melhuish (1978) in Table 1.

TABLE 1   Effects of Stress on Bodily Functions

	Normal (relaxed)	Under Pressure	Acute Pressure	Chronic Pressure (stress)
Brain	Blood supply normal	Blood supply up	Thinks more clearly	Headaches and migraines, tremors and nervous tics
Mood	Happy	Serious	Increased concentration	Anxiety, loss of sense of humor
Saliva	Normal	Reduced	Reduced	Dry mouth, lump in throat
Muscles	Blood supply normal	Blood supply up	Improved performance	Muscular tension and pain
Heart	Normal heart rate and blood pressure	Increased heart rate and blood pressure	Improved performance	Hypertension and chest pain
Lungs	Normal respiration	Increase respiration rate	Improved performance	Coughs and asthma
Stomach	Normal blood supply and acid secretion	Reduced blood supply Increased acid secretion	Reduced blood supply reduces digestion	Ulcers due to heartburn and indigestion
Bowels	Normal	Reduced blood supply Increased bowel activity	Reduced blood supply reduces digestion	Abdominal pain and diarrhea
Bladder	Normal	Frequent urination	Frequent urination due to increased nervous stimulation	Frequent urination, prostatic symptoms
Sexual organs	(M) Normal (F) Normal periods, etc.	(M) Impotence (decreased blood supply) (F) Irregular periods	Decreased blood supply	(M) Impotence (F) Menstrual disorders
Skin	Healthy	Decreased blood supply, dry skin	Decreased blood supply	Dryness and rashes
Biochemistry	Normal: oxygen consumed, glucose and fats liberated	Oxygen consumption up, glucose and fat consumption up	Decreased blood supply	Dryness and rashes

STRESS AND HEART DISEASE

Stress is also seen to play a part in diseases related to lifestyle, where the degree to which a person eats, smokes, drinks alcohol, and exercises plays a role. High blood pressure (hypertension) and heart disease are accepted now as having a proven link to stress. Hypertension has in most cases no obvious organic basis—it simply sets in. A majority of patients are diagnosed with "essential hypertension," meaning that the condition does not arise from any medically detectable abnormality.

Although other factors, such as diet, obesity, and smoking, surely play a role, many researchers now believe that stress is the primary cause of hypertension. The connection, as Melhuish (1978) indicates, is that hypertension is believed to result partially from changes in the resistance of blood vessels. The diameter of the arterial vessels, which carry blood to the tissues, is partly controlled by the sympathetic nervous system and its release of chemicals through the vessels. Continual activation of the sympathetic nervous system's chemical response is believed to result in reduced elasticity of the arteries and raised blood pressure. This resulting hypertension can lead to heart disease because of the increased workload on the heart as it pushes blood out against a high arterial back pressure. Also, high blood pressure increases the likelihood of a possibly fatal ruptured artery; the rupture of a vessel in the brain can cause stroke. Chronic stress, and its resulting release of fats into the blood stream during the fight-or-flight response, is also believed to increase the risk of coronary heart disease by fatty deposition in the lining of coronary arteries, which carry oxygen to the heart muscle. Carruthers (1976) highlights the combination of factors that can result in a life-threatening crisis (see Figure 2).

STRESS COSTS

The cost of stress for a nation and for particular organizations is currently extremely high. For example, if we explore costs to the U.K. economy, the British Heart Foundation Coronary Prevention Group has calculated that 180,000 people die each year from coronary heart disease, almost 500 people a

FIGURE 2   **Flight Path to a Heart Attack**

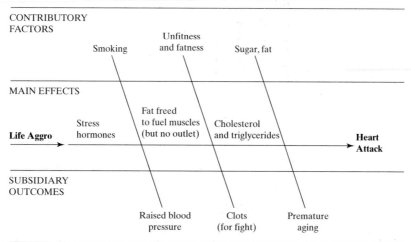

Note: LIFE AGGRO refers to life "aggravation": stress agents at work, in the home, and elsewhere.
Source: Adapted from Malcolm Carruthers, Maudsley Hospital.

day, and heart disease accounts each year for 70 million lost working days to industry and commerce. In addition, MIND, the mental health charity, estimates that between 30 percent to 40 percent of all sickness absence from work is attributable to mental and emotional disturbance, with another 40 million working days lost to the nation's economy. The country has also suffered increased rates of suicide, particularly among younger workers, rising 30 percent from the late 1970s to the early 1990s. Instability and life stress have led to divorce rates rising from 27,000 in 1961 to 155,000 by 1988; they are still rising. Indeed, RELATE, the U.K. marriage guidance organization, estimates that by the year 2000 there will be 4 divorces in every 10 marriages. Finally, Alcohol Concern suggests that alcohol misuse costs society more than 2 billion per annum, with an annual cost to industry from this cause alone of nearly 1 billion. The latter group estimates that 1 in 4 men in the United Kingdom drink more than the medically recommended units per week and that between 8 and 14 million days are lost each year from alcohol-related problems, with 25 percent of accidents at work involving intoxicated workers. To assess your own stress levels, you may find it useful to complete the following questionaire (see Table 2).

WHO PAYS THE COSTS?

Let's start at the beginning. Why is it that some countries (e.g., the United States or Finland) seem to be showing declines in their levels of stress-related illnesses, such as heart disease and alcoholism, while the levels of these illnesses are still rising in other countries? Is it that American employers, for example, are becoming more altruistic and caring for their employees, less concerned about the bottom line? Unfortunately, the answer is "No." Two trends in the United States are forcing American firms to take action. First, industry there is facing an enormous and ever-spiraling bill for employee health care costs. Individual insurance costs rose by 50 percent over the past two decades, but employers' contribution rose by over 140 percent. Estimates are that more than $700 million a year is spent by American employers to replace the 200,000 men aged 45 to 65 who die or are incapacitated by coronary artery disease alone. Management officials at Xerox Corporation estimated the cost of losing just one executive to stress-related illness at $600,000. In Europe, however, employers can create intolerable levels of stress for their employees, and it is the taxpayer who picks up the bill through the various national health systems. There is no direct accountability or incentive for firms to maintain the health of their employees. Of course, the indirect costs are enormous, but rarely does a firm actually attempt to estimate this cost; absenteeism, labor turnover, and even low productivity are treated as intrinsic parts of running a business (Dale and Cooper, 1992).

There is another source of growing costs. More and more employees, in American companies at least, are litigating against their employers through worker compensation regulations and laws concerning job-related stress, or what is being lately termed *cumulative stress disorder*. For example, in California, the number of stress-related compensation claims for psychiatric injury now total over 3,000 a year, since the California Supreme Court upheld its first stress disability case in the early 1970s. The California labor code now states specifically that worker compensation is allowable for disability or illness caused by "repetitive mentally or physically traumatic activities extending over a period of time, the combined effect of which causes any disability or need for medical treatment." California may be first in this regard, but what happens there has a habit of reaching other places after a longer or shorter time lapse (Ivancevich, Matteson, and Richards, 1985).

In Europe, however, we are just beginning to see a move toward increasing litigation by workers about their conditions of work. Several unions are supporting cases by individual workers, and the

TABLE 2   Behavioral and Physical Symptoms of Stress

To assess your own level of stress symptoms, indicate how often you have been troubled by the following behavioral and physical symptoms.

0 = Never or rarely
1 = Occasionally
2 = Frequently
3 = Always or nearly always

Behavioral symptoms of stress

Constant irritability with people	0	1	2	3
Difficulty in making decisions	0	1	2	3
Loss of sense of humor	0	1	2	3
Suppressed anger	0	1	2	3
Difficulty concentrating	0	1	2	3
Inability to finish one task before rushing into another	0	1	2	3
Feeling the target of other people's animosity	0	1	2	3
Feeling unable to cope	0	1	2	3
Wanting to cry at the smallest problem	0	1	2	3
Lack of interest in doing things after returning home from work	0	1	2	3
Waking up in the morning and feeling tired after an early night	0	1	2	3
Constant tiredness	0	1	2	3

Physical symptoms of stress

Lack of appetite	0	1	2	3
Craving for food when under pressure	0	1	2	3
Frequent indigestion or heartburn	0	1	2	3
Constipation or diarrhea	0	1	2	3
Insomnia	0	1	2	3
Tendency to sweat for no good reason	0	1	2	3
Nervous twitches, nail biting, etc.	0	1	2	3
Headaches	0	1	2	3
Cramps and muscle spasms	0	1	2	3
Nausea	0	1	2	3
Breathlessness without exertion	0	1	2	3
Fainting spells	0	1	2	3
Impotency or frigidity	0	1	2	3
Eczema	0	1	2	3

Note: Scoring: It is not the total score in each section that is important, but the number of either behavioral or physical symptoms on which you score 2 or 3. If in either category you are showing more than 3 symptoms with scores of 2 or 3, then it is indicative potentially of some current stress-related problem.

trend is certainly in the direction of future disability claims and general damages being awarded on the basis of work stress in the United Kingdom, as Earnshaw and Cooper (1996) highlight in their report on worker compensation and stress-related claims.

THE MAJOR STRESSES OF WORK

During the 1980s, much research in the field of workplace stress suggested six major sources of pressure at work (Cooper, Cooper, and Eaker, 1988). Although we can find each of these six implicated in an individual's stress profile or, indeed, in an organization's profile, these factors vary in the degree to which they are found to be causally linked to stress in a particular job or organization (see Figure 3).

FACTORS INTRINSIC TO THE JOB

As a starting point to understanding work stress, researchers have studied those factors that may be intrinsic to the job itself, such as poor working conditions, shift work, long hours, travel, risk and danger, new technology, work overload, and work underload.

Working Conditions   Our physical surroundings—noise, lighting, smells, and all the stimuli that bombard our senses—can affect mood and overall mental state, whether or not we find them consciously objectionable (Cooper and Smith, 1985).

Each occupation has its own potential environmental sources of stress. For example, in jobs that require close detail work, poor fighting can create eye strain. Conversely, extremely bright lighting or glare can present problems for money market dealers.

The design or physical setting of the workplace may be another source of stress. If an office is poorly designed, with relevant personnel spread throughout a building, poor communication networking can arise, resulting in role ambiguity and poor functional relationships. This problem is not restricted to

FIGURE 3   **Dynamics of Work Stress**

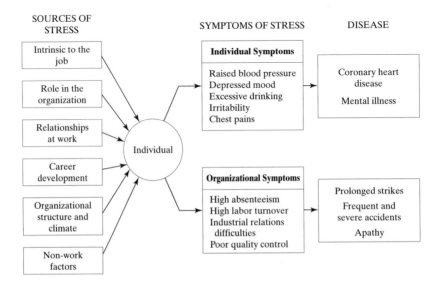

offices. For example, one company had high turnover and absenteeism among its assembly line workers, most of whom were female. When researchers looked into the problem, they discovered that the women were isolated from each other due to the layout of conveyor belts used in their work. They felt bored and lonely working without human interaction. Once the assembly line was reorganized to put them into groups, absenteeism dropped substantially.

Shift Work   Many workers today have jobs requiring them to work in shifts, some of which go around the clock. Studies have found that shift work is a common occupational stressor that affects blood temperature, metabolic rate, blood sugar levels, mental efficiency, and work motivation; shift work also influences sleep patterns and family and social life. In one study of air traffic controllers (Cobb and Rose, 1973), shift work was isolated as a major problem, although other major job stressors were also present. These workers had four times the prevalence of hypertension, and also more mild diabetes and peptic ulcers than did a control group of second-class airmen.

Long Hours   The long working hours required by many jobs appear to take a toll on employee health. Studies have established a link between extended shifts and deaths due to coronary heart disease. In one investigation of light-industry workers in the United States, Breslow and Buell (1960) found that individuals under 45 years of age who worked more than 48 hours a week had twice the risk of death of coronary heart disease as did similar individuals working a maximum of 40 hours a week. Another study (Russek and Zohman, 1958) of 100 young coronary patients revealed that 25 percent of them had been working at two jobs, and an additional 40 percent worked for more than 60 hours a week. Many individuals, such as executives working long hours and medical residents who might have no sleep for 36 hours or more, may experience health problems and lowered efficiency at work. It is now commonly recognized that working beyond 40 to 50 hours a week results in time spent that is increasingly unproductive. Indeed, the European Community's Social Charter has specifically attempted to limit community countries to a 48-hour working week.

Travel   Although travel opportunities are appealing to many senior managers, travel itself can also be a source of stress: Traffic jams on the roads or at airports, delayed flights or trains, people, and the logistics of unknown places can present stressful challenges. Marriages and families can suffer if one member spends significant time away. In addition, a traveling manager spends less time with fellow workers and may miss out on opportunities or feel out of step with "office politics."

New Technology   The introduction of new technology into the work environment has required management and workers alike to continually adapt to new equipment, systems, and ways of working. Having a boss trained in the "old ways" may be an extra burden for the new employee trained in the latest methods, raising questions about the adequacy of supervision and employee doubts about those in senior positions.

In a study investigating sources of stress among executives in 10 countries (Cooper, 1984), Japanese executives suffered particularly from pressure to "keep up with new technology"—that is, to maintain their technological superiority. Managers in developing countries felt pressure due to the increasing emphasis on new technology, the need to deal with an inadequately trained workforce, and the imposition of deadlines. Also, in Britain, a high percentage of executives (second only to Japan) found that keeping up with new technology was a great source of pressure at work. This is not surprising in a country that privitized in the 1980s and underwent massive technological change.

Work Overload   Two different types of work overload have been described by researchers. Quantitative overload refers simply to having too much work to do. Qualitative overload refers to work that is too difficult for an individual. Quantitative overload often leads to working long hours, with the attendant problems described above. A too-heavy work burden has also been associated with increased cigarette smoking, alcohol consumption, and other stress indicators (French and Caplan, 1972).

ROLE IN THE ORGANIZATION

When a person's role in an organization is clearly defined and understood and when expectations placed on the individual are also clear and nonconflicting, stress can be kept to a minimum. But researchers have clearly seen that this is not the case in many work sites. Three critical factors—role ambiguity, role conflict, and the degree of responsibility for others—are seen as major sources of stress (Ivancevich and Matteson, 1980).

Role Ambiguity   Role ambiguity arises when an individual does not have a clear picture of work objectives, coworkers' expectations, and the scope and responsibilities of his or her job. Often, this ambiguity results simply because a senior executive does not lay out for this person exactly what his or her role is. The stress indicators found to relate to role ambiguity are depressed mood, lowered self-esteem, life dissatisfaction, low motivation to work, and the intention to leave a job.

Role Conflict   Role conflict exists when an individual is torn by conflicting job demands: doing things he or she really does not want to do or things not considered to be part of the job. Managers may often feel torn between two groups of people who demand different types of behavior or who believe the job entails different functions. As might be expected, studies have shown that people with high anxiety levels suffer more from role conflicts than do people who are more flexible in their approach to life (Quick and Quick, 1984).

Responsibility   Responsibility is another organizational role stressor. In an organization, there are basically two types of responsibility: that for people and that for things-budgets, equipment, buildings, and so on. Responsibility for people has been found to be especially stressful. Studies in the 1960s revealed that responsibility for people was far more likely to lead to coronary heart disease than was responsibility for things. Being accountable for people usually requires spending more time interacting with others, attending meetings, and attempting to meet deadlines. An early investigation of 1,200 managers sent by their companies for annual medical examinations linked physical stress to age and level of responsibility (Pincherle, 1972). The older the executive and the more responsibility held by this person, the greater the probability of detecting coronary heart disease risk factors.

The stressful nature of having responsibility for others has grown in the economic climate of the 1990s, with so many industries facing cost-cutting constraints. As they implement needed cutbacks in production and sales, managers are caught between the two goals of "keeping personnel costs to a minimum," while also looking after the "welfare of subordinates" in terms of job security and stability.

RELATIONSHIPS AT WORK

Other people—in our varied encounters with them at work—can be major sources of both stress and support. This is especially so in dealings with bosses, peers, and subordinates, which can dramatically influence the way we feel at the end of the day. Hans Selye (1946) suggested that learning to live with other people is one of the most stressful aspects of life: "Good relationships between members of a group," he observed, "are a key factor in individual and organizational health." There are three critical relationships at work: those with superiors, those with subordinates, and those with colleagues or coworkers.

Relationships with Boss   Physicians and clinical psychologists support the idea that problems with emotional stability often result when the relationship between a subordinate and a boss is psychologically unhealthy for one reason or another. A U.S. study that focused on the relationship of workers to an immediate boss found that when the boss was perceived as "considerate," there was "friendship, mutual trust, respect and a certain warmth between boss and subordinate." Workers who said their bosses were low on consideration reported feeling more job pressure. Workers who were under pressure reported that their bosses did not give them criticism in a helpful way, played favorites, and "pulled rank and took advantage of them whenever they had got a chance" (Buck, 1972).

Relationships with Subordinates   The way in which a manager supervises the work of others has always been considered a critical feature of any job. For instance, "inability to delegate" has been a common criticism leveled against some managers. Managerial stress may be particularly high for those individuals with technical and scientific backgrounds, which may be more "things oriented." For these managers, personal relationships may appear more "trivial" and "time-consuming" than for managers who are more people oriented. This is particularly true of individuals promoted to management positions on the basis of their technical skills without management training; they often encounter serious relationship problems at work.

Relationships with Colleagues   Stress among coworkers can arise from the competition and personality conflicts usually described as "office politics." Adequate social support can be critical to the health and well-being of an individual and to the atmosphere and success of an organization. Because most people spend so much time at work, relationships between coworkers can provide valuable support or, conversely, can be a significant source of stress.

People with a particular personality—that of the abrasive, hard-driving individual—will create stress for those around them. Levinson (1973) suggests that these abrasive people cause stress for others because they ignore the interpersonal aspects of feelings and sensibilities of social interaction. Such a highly technical, achievement-oriented, hard-driving individual finds no time to cultivate amiable working relationships and so may be an important source of interpersonal stress for others.

CAREER DEVELOPMENT

A host of issues can act as potential stressors throughout one's working life. Lack of job security; fear of job loss, obsolescence, or retirement; and numerous performance appraisals—all can create pressure and strain. In addition, the frustration of having reached a career ceiling, or having been over-promoted, can induce extreme stress.

Job Security   For many workers, career progression is of overriding importance. By promotion, people not only earn more money but gain increased status and experience new challenges. In the early years at a job, striving and ability required to deal with a rapidly changing environment are usually rewarded by monetary and promotional rewards. At middle age, however, many people find their career progress slowed or stopped. Job opportunities may become fewer, available jobs can require longer to master, old knowledge may be obsolete, and energy levels can flag while younger competition is threatening. Fear of demotion or obsolescence can be overpowering for those who believe they will suffer some erosion of status before retirement.

Job Performance   The process of being evaluated and appraised can be a stressful experience for all of us. It must be recognized that performance appraisals are anxiety provoking, for both that individual being examined and the person doing the judging and appraising. The supervisor making performance judgments faces the threat of union grievance procedures in some cases, as well as interpersonal strains and the responsibility of making decisions affecting a subordinate's livelihood.

How an evaluation is carried out can affect the degree of anxiety experienced. For example, taking a written examination can be a short-term stressor, although continuous and confidential appraisals by supervisors may exert a more long-term effect, depending on the structure and climate of the organization.

ORGANIZATIONAL STRUCTURE AND CLIMATE

Just being part of an organization can present threats to a person's sense of freedom and autonomy. Organizational workers sometimes complain that they do not have a sense of belonging and that they lack adequate opportunities to participate; they may feel that their behavior is unduly restricted and that they are not included in office communications and consultations.

As early as the 1940s, researchers began reporting that workers who were allowed more participation in decision making produced more and had higher job satisfaction (Coch and French, 1948). Later researchers found that nonparticipation at work was a significant predictor of strain and job-related stress. It was seen to be related to overall poor health, escapist drinking, depression, low self-esteem, absenteeism, and plans to leave work (Margolis, Kroes, and Quinn, 1974). Participation in the decision-making process by workers may help increase feelings of investment in the company's success, create a sense of belonging, and improve communication channels within the organization. The resulting control, or sense of control, that participation provides seems vital for the well-being of all employees (Sauter, Hurrell, and Cooper, 1989).

HOME: WORK PRESSURES

Another danger of current economic stringencies is the effect that work pressures—fear of job loss, thwarted ambition, work overload, and so on—have on the families of employees. For instance, in the very best of times, young managers face the inevitable conflict between organizational and family demands during the early development of their careers. But during a crisis of the sort we are currently experiencing, problems increase in geometrical proportion as individuals strive to cope with basic economic and security needs. Under normal circumstances, individuals find home a refuge from the competitive and demanding environment at work, a place where they get support and comfort. But when there is a career crisis (or stress from job insecurity, as many employees now face), tensions of the job are not left behind and soon affect the family and home environment in ways that may imperil this last "sanctuary." It may be very difficult, then, for a spouse to provide the supportive domestic scene that a worker requires when the spouse is feeling insecure or is worried about the family's economic, educational, and social future.

Not only is it difficult for a housebound wife to support her breadwinning husband and at the same time cope with family demands, but increasingly, women are seeking full-time careers themselves. According to the U.S. Department of Labor, a "typical American family" with a working husband, a homemaker wife, and two children now makes up only 7 percent of the nation's families. In the United Kingdom, nearly 65% of all women now work, mostly full-time. Many psychologists and sociologists claim that dual-career family development is the primary culprit in the very large increase in the divorce rate over the past 10 years in the United States and countries in Western Europe.

This dual-career culture creates problems especially for women, because they are expected by men to work the "double shift," pursue a job, and manage the home (Cooper and Lewis, 1994). Women, and society at large, are discovering the myth of the New Man, who seems to exist only in the wishful thinking of women's magazine journalists! The dual-career family model also creates problems for men as well. For example, many managers and executives are expected, as part of their job, to be mobile, to be readily available for job transfers both within and between countries. Indeed, a man's promotional prospects might depend wholly on availability and willingness to accept geographic career moves. In the late 1980s and 1990s when women themselves began to pursue full-time careers, as opposed to part-time work, the prospects of professional men being available for rapid redeployment decreased substantially. In the past, these men had, with few exceptions, accepted promotional moves almost without family discussion. Now, however, such decisions will create major obstacles for both breadwinners in the family. We are already seeing this happen throughout Europe and the United States, and it is particularly exacerbated by the fact that corporations have not adapted to this changing social phenomenon. Currently, few organizations have facilities to help dual-career members of family units, particularly by career-break schemes or flexible working years.

The stressors have been highlighted in research throughout the present and past decades. Organizations have introduced global changes to deal with some of these issues, such as improving career development, redesigning jobs, or providing counseling for interpersonal problems (Murphy, Hurrell, Sauter, and Keita, 1995). Research evidence as to the effectiveness of these interventions is encouraging, at least in the short term, and a growing number of stress reduction programs have demonstrated considerable economic savings to organizations in reduced rates of sickness and absenteeism as well as reduced health care costs (Cooper, Liukkonen, and Cartwright, 1996; Cooper and Sadri, 1991).

Most books in this field aimed at helping the individual to cope with stress have focused on health-promoting activities—for example, improved dietary habits, exercise programs, and relaxation techniques. Although their health message is important, and one we would strongly reinforce, comparatively little attention is devoted to more specific issues and situations that trouble managers and others at work and to pragmatic ways for handling them. Virtually ignored are issues such as dealing with interruptions, coping with everyday hassles in using new technology, managing the stresses of work travel, finessing bad relationships with a boss or colleague, making presentations, tolerating ineffective or debilitating meetings, and so on. These everyday hassles accumulate into real stress outcomes, or as Americans put it, "cumulative stress disorder." Completion of the scale in Table 3 may help you to identify aspects of your daily work life which cause you the most stress.

TABLE 3 Daily Hassles at Work Scale

Please circle the number that best reflects the degree to which the particular statement is a source of stress for you at work.

	No Stress at All		Stress		A Great Deal of Stress	
Trouble with client/customer	0	1	2	3	4	5
Having to work late	0	1	2	3	4	5
Constant people interruptions	0	1	2	3	4	5
Trouble with boss	0	1	2	3	4	5
Deadlines and time pressures	0	1	2	3	4	5
Decision making	0	1	2	3	4	5
Dealing with the bureaucracy at work	0	1	2	3	4	5
Technological breakdowns (e.g., computer)	0	1	2	3	4	5
Trouble with work colleagues	0	1	2	3	4	5
Tasks associated with job not stimulating	0	1	2	3	4	5
Too much responsibility	0	1	2	3	4	5
Too many jobs to do at once	0	1	2	3	4	5
Telephone interruptions	0	1	2	3	4	5
Traveling to and from work	0	1	2	3	4	5
Traveling associated with job	0	1	2	3	4	5
Making mistakes	0	1	2	3	4	5
Conflict with organization goals	0	1	2	3	4	5
Job interfering with home/family life	0	1	2	3	4	5
Can't cope with "in" box	0	1	2	3	4	5
Can't say "no" when I should work	0	1	2	3	4	5
Not enough stimulating things to do	0	1	2	3	4	5
Too many meetings	0	1	2	3	4	5
Don't know where career is going	0	1	2	3	4	5
Worried about job security	0	1	2	3	4	5
Spouse or partner not supportive about work	0	1	2	3	4	5
Family life adversely affecting work	0	1	2	3	4	5
Having to tell subordinates unpleasant things (e.g., firing)	0	1	2	3	4	5

CHAPTER 7
INTERPERSONAL COMMUNICATION

ACTIVE LISTENING
  Carl R. Rogers
  Richard E. Farson

DEFENSIVE COMMUNICATION
  Jack R. Gibb

THE POWER OF TALK: WHO GETS HEARD AND WHY
  Deborah Tannen

Communication is one of the most important and frequently used workplace skills. Good communication skills range from the basic ability to transmit and decode messages accurately and effectively to running meetings well, to figuring out how best to disseminate information in a large company and understanding the symbolic meaning of one's actions as a manager. Communication is much more than the actual words that are said.

Carl Rogers, a noted psychologist, is famous for his work on active listening. Rogers and Richard Farson wrote "Active Listening," the classic description of this crucial skill. They wrote this article long before the advent of gender-neutral language, so be prepared for a raft of masculine pronouns and see whether this type of writing has any effect on you personally.

In another classic communication article, "Defensive Communication," Jack Gibb expanded on Rogers' work. Gibb explains why it's important to avoid making other people defensive when you communicate with them and distinguishes between behaviors that result in defensive versus supportive communication climates.

Deborah Tannen used her training as a linguist to pinpoint U.S. differences in male and female conversation. Her research broke new ground and taps into our ongoing curiosity about male-female relations at work. "The Power of Talk: Who Gets Heard and Why" is based on Tannen's research into workplace communication patterns and explains the misunderstandings and misinterpretations that result from different male and female styles.

❧

ACTIVE LISTENING*

  Carl R. Rogers
  Richard E. Farson

THE MEANING OF ACTIVE LISTENING

One basic responsibility of the supervisor or manager is the development, adjustment, and integration of individual employees. He tries to develop employee potential, delegate responsibility, and achieve

---

*Reprinted by special permission of the Industrial Relations Center of the University of Chicago and the authors.

cooperation. To do so, he must have, among other abilities, the ability to listen intelligently and carefully to those with whom he works.

There are, however, many kinds of listening skills. The lawyer, for example, when questioning a witness, listens for contradictions, irrelevancies, errors, and weaknesses. But this is not the kind of listening skill we are concerned with. The lawyer usually is not listening in order to help the witness adjust, cooperate, or produce. Our emphasis will be on listening skills of the supervisor or manager that will help employees gain a clearer understanding of their situations, take responsibility, and cooperate with each other.

TWO EXAMPLES

The kind of listening we have in mind is called "active listening." It is called "active" because the listener has a very definite responsibility. He does not passively absorb words which are spoken to him. He actively tries to grasp the facts and the feelings in what he hears, and he tries, by his listening, to help the speaker work out his own problems.

To get a clearer picture of what active listening means, let us consider two different approaches to the same work problem. The example is set in the printing industry, but the behavior of the men could surface in any organization.

Example no. 1

Foreman: Hey, Al, I don't get this rush order. We can't handle any 50,000 run today. What do they think we are?
Supervisor: But that's the order. So get it out as soon as you can. We're under terrific pressure this week.
F: Don't they know we're behind schedule already because of that press breakdown?
S: Look, Kelly, I don't decide what goes on upstairs. I just have to see that the work gets out and that's what I'm gonna do.
F: The guys aren't gonna like this.
S: That's something you'll have to work out with them, not me.

Example no. 2

F: Hey, Ross, I don't get this rush order. We can't handle any run of 50,000 today. What do they think we are?
S: They're pushing you pretty hard, aren't they Kelly?
F: They sure are and I'm getting sore. We were just about back to schedule after the press breakdown. Now this comes along.
S: As if you didn't have enough work to do, huh?
F: Yeah. I don't know how I'm going to tell the pressman about this.
S: Hate to face him with a rush order now, is that it?
F: I really do. Joe is under a real strain today. Seems like everything we do around here is rush, rush, rush!
S: I guess you feel it's unfair to load anything more on him today.
F: Well, yeah. I know there must be plenty of pressure on everybody to get the work out, but—well, Joe doesn't deserve all the rush orders. But, if that's the way it is—I guess I'd better get the word to him and see how I can rearrange the work flow.

There are obviously many differences between these two examples. The main one, however, is that Ross, the supervisor in the second example, is using the active listening approach. He is listening and responding in a way that makes it clear that he appreciates both the meaning and the feeling behind what Kelly is saying.

Active listening does not necessarily mean long sessions spent listening to grievances, personal or otherwise. It is simply a way of approaching those problems which arise out of the usual day-to-day events of any job.

To be effective, active listening must be firmly grounded in the basic attitudes of the user. We cannot employ it as a technique if our fundamental attitudes are in conflict with its basic concepts. If we try, our behavior will be empty and sterile, and our associates will be quick to recognize such behavior. Until we can demonstrate a spirit which genuinely respects the potential worth of the individual, which considers his rights and trusts his capacity for self-direction, we cannot begin to be effective listeners.

WHAT WE ACHIEVE BY LISTENING

Active listening is an important way to bring about changes in people. Despite the popular notion that listening is a passive approach, clinical and research evidence clearly shows that sensitive listening is a most effective agent for individual personality change and group development. Listening brings about changes in people's attitudes toward themselves and others, and also brings about changes in their basic values and personal philosophy. People who have been listened to in this new and special way become more emotionally mature, more open to their experiences, less defensive, more democratic, and less authoritarian.

When people are listened to sensitively, they tend to listen to themselves with more care and make clear exactly what they are feeling and thinking. Group members tend to listen more to each other, become less argumentative, more ready to incorporate other points of view. Because listening reduces the threat of having one's ideas criticized, the person is better able to see them for what they are and is more likely to feel that his contributions are worthwhile.

Not the least important result of listening is the change that takes place within the listener himself. Besides the fact that listening provides more information about people than any other activity, it builds deep, positive relationships and tends to alter constructively the attitudes of the listener. Listening is a growth experience.

HOW TO LISTEN

The goal of active listening is to bring about changes in people. To achieve this end, it relies upon definite techniques—things to do and things to avoid doing. Before discussing these techniques, however, we should first understand why they are effective. To do so, we must understand how the individual personality develops.

THE GROWTH OF THE INDIVIDUAL

Through all of our lives, from early childhood on, we have learned to think of ourselves in certain, very definite ways. We have built up pictures of ourselves. Sometimes these self-pictures are pretty realistic but at other times they are not. For example, an average, overweight lady may fancy herself a youthful, ravishing siren, or an awkward teenager regard himself as a star athlete.

All of us have experiences which fit the way we need to think about ourselves. These we accept. But it is much harder to accept experiences which don't fit. And sometimes, if it is very important for us to hang on to this self-picture, we don't accept or admit these experiences at all.

These self-pictures are not necessarily attractive. A man, for example, may regard himself as incompetent and worthless. He may feel that he is doing his job poorly in spite of favorable appraisals by the organization. As long as he has these feelings about himself he must deny any experiences which would seem not to fit this self-picture, in this case any that might indicate to him that he is competent. It is so necessary for him to maintain this self-picture that he is threatened by anything which would tend to change it. Thus, when the organization raises his salary, it may seem to him only additional proof that he is a fraud. He must hold onto this self-picture, because, bad or good, it's the only thing he has by which he can identify himself.

This is why direct attempts to change this individual or change his self-picture are particularly threatening. He is forced to defend himself or to completely deny the experience. This denial of experience and defense of the self-picture tends to bring on rigidity of behavior and create difficulties in personal adjustment.

The active-listening approach, on the other hand, does not present a threat to the individual's self-picture. He does not have to defend it. He is able to explore it, see it for what it is, and make his own decision as to how realistic it is. He is then in a position to change.

If I want to help a man or woman reduce defensiveness and become more adaptive, I must try to remove the threat of myself as a potential changer. As long as the atmosphere is threatening, there can be no effective communication. So I must create a climate which is neither critical, evaluative, nor moralizing. The climate must foster equality and freedom, trust and understanding, acceptance and warmth. In this climate and in this climate only does the individual feel safe enough to incorporate new experiences and new values into his concept of himself. Active listening helps to create this climate.

WHAT TO AVOID

When we encounter a person with a problem, our usual response is to try to change his way of looking at things—to get him to see his situation the way we see it, or would like him to see it. We plead, reason, scold, encourage, insult, prod—anything to bring about a change in the desired direction, that is, in the direction we want him to travel. What we seldom realize, however, is that under these circumstances we are usually responding to *our own* needs to see the world in certain ways. It is always difficult for us to tolerate and understand actions which are different from the ways in which *we* believe *we* should act. If, however, we can free ourselves from the need to influence and direct others in our own paths, we enable ourselves to listen with understanding, and thereby employ the most potent available agent of change.

One problem the listener faces is that of responding to demands for decisions, judgments, and evaluations. He is constantly called upon to agree or disagree with someone or something. Yet, as he well knows, the question or challenge frequently is a masked expression of feelings or needs which the speaker is far more anxious to communicate than he is to have the surface questions answered. Because he cannot speak these feelings openly, the speaker must disguise them to himself and to others in an acceptable form. To illustrate, let us examine some typical questions and the type of answers that might best elicit the feeling beneath them.

These responses recognize the questions but leave the way open for the employee to say what is really bothering him. They allow the listener to participate in the problem or situation without shouldering all responsibility for decision-making or actions. This is a process of thinking *with* people instead of *for* or *about* them.

Passing judgment, whether critical or favorable, makes free expression difficult. Similarly, advice and information are almost always seen as efforts to change a person and thus serve as barriers to his self-expression and the development of a creative relationship. Moreover, advice is seldom taken and information hardly ever utilized. The eager young trainee probably will not become patient just because he is advised that, "The road to success is a long, difficult one, and you must be patient." And it is no more helpful for him to learn that "only one out of a hundred trainees reach top management positions."

Employee's Question	Listener's Answer
Just who is responsible for getting this job done?	Do you feel that you don't have enough authority?
Don't you think talent should count more than seniority in promotions?	What do you think are the reasons for your opinion?
What does the boss expect us to do about those broken-down machines?	You're tired of working with worn-out equipment, aren't you?
Don't you think my performance has improved since the last review?	Sounds as if you feel your work has picked up over these last few months.

Interestingly, it is a difficult lesson to learn that *positive evaluations* are sometimes as blocking as negative ones. It is almost as destructive to the freedom of a relationship to tell a person that he is good or capable or right, as to tell him otherwise. To evaluate him positively may make it more difficult for him to tell of the faults that distress him or the ways in which he believes he is not competent.

Encouragement also may be seen as an attempt to motivate the speaker in certain directions or hold him off rather than as support. "I'm sure everything will work out O.K." is not a helpful response to the person who is deeply discouraged about a problem.

In other words, most of the techniques and devices common to human relationships are found to be of little use in establishing the type of relationship we are seeking here.

WHAT TO DO

Just what does active listening entail, then? Basically, it requires that we get inside the speaker, that we grasp, from his point of view, just what it is he is communicating to us. More than that, we must convey to the speaker that we are seeing things *from his point of view*. To listen actively, then, means that there are several things we must do.

Listen for Total Meaning   Any message a person tries to get across usually has two components: the content of the message and the *feeling* or attitude underlying this content. Both are important, both give the message *meaning*. It is this total *meaning* of the message that we must try to understand. For example, a secretary comes to her boss and says, "I've finished that report." This message has obvious factual content and perhaps calls upon the boss for another work assignment. Suppose, on the other hand, that the secretary says, "Well! I'm finally finished with your damn report!" The factual content is the same, but the total meaning of the message has changed—and changed in an important way for both supervisor and worker. Here sensitive listening can facilitate the work relationship in this office. If the boss were to respond by simply giving his secretary some letters to type, would the secretary feel that she had gotten her total message across? Would she feel free to talk to her boss about the difficulty of her work? Would she feel better about the job, more anxious to do good work on her next assignment?

Now, on the other hand, suppose the supervisor were to respond, "Glad to get that over with, huh?" or "That was a rough one, wasn't it?" or "Guess you don't want another one like that again," or anything that tells the worker that he heard and understands. It doesn't necessarily mean that her next work assignment need be changed or that he must spend an hour listening to the worker complain about the problems she encountered. He may do a number of things differently in the light of the new information he has from the worker—but not necessarily. It's just that extra sensitivity on the part of the supervisor that can transform an average working climate into a good one.

Respond to Feelings   In some instances the content is far less important than the feeling which underlies it. To catch the full flavor or meaning of the message one must respond particularly to the feeling component. If, for instance, our secretary had said, "I'd like to pile up all those carbons and make a bonfire out of them!" responding to content would be obviously absurd. But to respond to her disgust or anger in trying to work with the report recognizes the meaning of this message. There are various shadings of these components in the meaning of any message. Each time the listener must try to remain sensitive to the total meaning the message has to the speaker. What is she trying to tell me? What does this mean to her? How does she see this situation?

Note All Cues   Not all communication is verbal. The speaker's words alone don't tell us everything he is communicating. And hence, truly sensitive listening requires that we become aware of several kinds of communication besides verbal. The way in which a speaker hesitates in his speech can tell us much about his feelings. So too can the inflection of his voice. He may stress certain points loud-ly and clearly, and he may mumble others. We should also note such things as the person's facial ex-pressions, body posture, hand movements, eye movements, and breathing. All of these help to convey his total message.

WHAT WE COMMUNICATE BY LISTENING

The first reaction of most people when they consider listening as a possible method for dealing with human beings is that listening cannot be sufficient in itself. Because it is passive, they feel, listening does not communicate anything to the speaker. Actually, nothing could be farther from the truth.

By consistently listening to a speaker you are conveying the idea that:

I'm interested in you as a person, and I think that what you feel is important. I respect your thoughts, and even if I don't agree with them, I know that they are valid for you. I feel sure that you have a contribution to make. I'm not trying to change you or evaluate you. I just want to un-derstand you. I think you're worth listening to, and I want you to know that I'm the kind of per-son you can talk to.

The subtle but most important aspect of this is that it is the *demonstration* of the message that works. Although it is most difficult to convince someone that you respect him by *telling* him so, you are much more likely to get this message across by really *behaving* that way—by actually *having* and *demon-strating* respect for this person. Listening does this most effectively.

Like other behavior, listening behavior is contagious. This has implications for all communications problems, whether between two people, or within a large organization. To insure good communication between associates up and down the line, one must first take the responsibility for setting a pattern of listening. Just as one learns that anger is usually met with anger, argument with argument, and de-ception with deception, one can learn that listening can be met with listening. Every person who feels responsibility in a situation can set the tone of the interaction, and the important lesson in this is that any behavior exhibited by one person will eventually be responded to with similar behavior in the other person.

It is far more difficult to stimulate constructive behavior in another person but far more valuable. Listening is one of these constructive behaviors, but if one's attitude is to "wait out" the speaker rather than really listen to him, it will fail. The one who consistently listens with understanding, however, is the one who eventually is most likely to be listened to. If you really want to be heard and understood by another, you can develop him as a potential listener, ready for new ideas, provided you can first de-velop yourself in these ways and sincerely listen with understanding and respect.

TESTING FOR UNDERSTANDING

Because understanding another person is actually far more difficult than it at first seems, it is impor-tant to test constantly your ability to see the world in the way the speaker sees it. You can do this by reflecting in your own words what the speaker seems to mean by his words and actions. His response to this will tell you whether or not he feels understood. A good rule of thumb is to assume that one never really understands until he can communicate this understanding to the other's satisfaction.

Here is an experiment to test your skill in listening. The next time you become involved in a live-ly or controversial discussion with another person, stop for a moment and suggest that you adopt this ground rule for continued discussion. Before either participant in the discussion can make a point or express an opinion of his own, he must first restate aloud the previous point or position of the other person. This restatement must be in his own words (merely parroting the words of another does not prove that one has understood, but only that he has heard the words). The restatement must be accurate enough to satisfy the speaker before the listener can be allowed to speak for himself.

You might find this procedure useful in a meeting where feelings run high and people express themselves on topics of emotional concern to the group. Before another member of the group expresses his own feelings and thought, he must rephrase the *meaning* expressed by the previous speaker to that person's satisfaction. All the members in the group should be alert to the changes in the emotional climate and the quality of the discussion when this approach is used.

PROBLEMS IN ACTIVE LISTENING

Active listening is not an easy skill to acquire, it demands practice. Perhaps more important, it may require changes in our own basic attitudes. These changes come slowly and sometimes with considerable difficulty. Let us look at some of the major problems in active listening and what can be done to overcome them.

THE PERSONAL RISK

To be effective in active listening, one must have a sincere interest in the speaker. We all live in glass houses as far as our attitudes are concerned. They always show through. And if we are only making a pretense of interest in the speaker, he will quickly pick this up, either consciously or subconsciously. And once he does, he will no longer express himself freely.

Active listening carries a strong element of personal risk. If we manage to accomplish what we are describing here—to sense the feelings of another person, to understand the meaning his experiences have for him, to see the world as he sees it, we risk being changed ourselves. For example, if we permit ourselves to listen our way into the life of a person we do not know or approve of—to get the meaning that life has for him, we risk coming to see the world as he sees it. We are threatened when we give up, even momentarily, what we believe and start thinking in someone else's terms. It takes a great deal of inner security and courage to be able to risk one's self in understanding another.

For the manager, the courage to take another's point of view generally means that he must see *himself* through another's eyes—he must be able to see himself as others see him. To do this may sometimes be unpleasant, but it is far more difficult than *unpleasant*. We are so accustomed to viewing ourselves in certain ways—to seeing and hearing only what we want to see and hear—that it is extremely difficult for a person to free himself from the need to see things his way.

Developing an attitude of sincere interest in the speaker is thus no easy task. It can be developed only by being willing to risk seeing the world from the speaker's point of view. If we have a number of such experiences, however, they will shape an attitude which will allow us to be truly genuine in our interest in the speaker.

HOSTILE EXPRESSIONS

The listener will often hear negative, hostile expressions directed at himself. Such expressions are always hard to listen to. No one likes to hear hostile words or experience hostility which is directed against them. And it is not easy to get to the point where one is strong enough to permit these attacks without finding it necessary to defend himself or retaliate.

Because we all fear that people will crumble under the attack of genuine negative feelings, we tend to perpetuate an attitude of pseudo-peace. It is as if we cannot tolerate conflict at all for fear of the damage it could do to us, to the situation, to the others involved. But of course the real damage is done by the denial and suppression of negative feelings.

Out-of-Place Expressions

Expressions dealing with behavior that are not usually acceptable in our society also pose problems for the listener. These out-of-place expressions can take the extreme forms that psychotherapists hear—such as homicidal fantasies or expressions of sexual perversity. The listener often blocks out such expressions because of their obvious threatening quality. At less extreme levels, we all find unnatural or inappropriate behavior difficult to handle. Behavior that brings on a problem situation may be anything from telling an "off-color" story in mixed company to seeing a man cry.

In any face-to-face situation, we will find instances of this type which will momentarily, if not permanently, block any communication. In any organization, expressions of weakness or incompetency will generally be regarded as unacceptable and therefore will block good two-way communication. For example, it is difficult to listen to a manager tell of his feelings of failure in being able to "take charge" of a situation in his department because all administrators are supposed to be able to "take charge."

Accepting Positive Feelings

It is both interesting and perplexing to note that negative or hostile feelings or expressions are much easier to deal with in any face-to-face relationship than are positive feelings. This is especially true for the manager because the culture expects him to be independent, bold, clever, and aggressive and manifest no feelings of warmth, gentleness, and intimacy. He therefore comes to regard these feelings as soft and inappropriate. But no matter how they are regarded, they remain a human need. The denial of these feelings in himself and his associates does not get the manager out of a problem of dealing with them. The feelings simply become veiled and confused. If recognized they would work for the total effort; unrecognized, they work against it.

Emotional Danger Signals

The listener's own emotions are sometimes a barrier to active listening. When emotions are at their height, when listening is most necessary, it is most difficult to set aside one's own concerns and be understanding. Our emotions are often our own worst enemies when we try to become listeners. The more involved and invested we are in a particular situation or problem, the less we are likely to be willing or able to listen to the feelings and attitudes of others. That is, the more we find it necessary to respond to our own needs, the less we are able to respond to the needs of another. Let us look at some of the main danger signals that warn us that our emotions may be interfering with our listening.

Defensiveness   The points about which one is most vocal and dogmatic, the points which one is most anxious to impose on others—these are always the points one is trying to talk oneself into believing. So one danger signal becomes apparent when you find yourself stressing a point or trying to convince another. It is at these times that you are likely to be less secure and consequently less able to listen.

Resentment of Opposition   It is always easier to listen to an idea which is similar to one of your own than to an opposing view. Sometimes, in order to clear the air, it is helpful to pause for a moment when you feel your ideas and position being challenged, reflect on the situation, and express your concern to the speaker.

Clash of Personalities   Here again, our experience has consistently shown us that the genuine expression of feelings on the part of the listener will be more helpful in developing a sound relationship than the suppression of them. This is so whether the feelings be resentment, hostility, threat, or admiration. A basically honest relationship, whatever the nature of it, is the most productive of all. The other party becomes secure when he learns that the listener can express his feelings honestly and openly to him. We should keep this in mind when we begin to fear a clash of personalities in the listening relationship. Otherwise, fear of our own emotions will choke off full expression of feelings.

LISTENING TO OURSELVES

To listen to oneself is a prerequisite to listening to others. And it is often an effective means of dealing with the problems we have outlined above. When we are most aroused, excited, and demanding, we are least able to understand our own feelings and attitudes. Yet, in dealing with the problems of others, it becomes most important to be sure of one's own position, values, and needs.

The ability to recognize and understand the meaning which a particular episode has for you, with all the feelings which it stimulates in you, and the ability to express this meaning when you find it getting in the way of active listening, will clear the air and enable you once again to be free to listen. That is, if some person or situation touches off feelings within you which tend to block your attempts to listen with understanding, begin listening to yourself. It is much more helpful in developing effective relationships to avoid suppressing these feelings. Speak them out as clearly as you can, and try to enlist the other person as a listener to your feelings. A person's listening ability is limited by his ability to listen to himself.

ACTIVE LISTENING AND ORGANIZATION GOALS

"How can listening improve productivity?"

"We're in business, and it is a rugged, fast, competitive affair. How are we going to find time to counsel our employees?"

"We have to concern ourselves with organizational problems first."

"We can't afford to spend all day listening when there is work to do."

"What's morale got to do with service to the public?"

"Sometimes we have to sacrifice an individual for the good of the rest of the people in the organization."

Those of us who are trying to advance the listening approach in organizations hear these comments frequently. And because they are so honest and legitimate, they pose a real problem. Unfortunately, the answers are not so clear-cut as the questions.

INDIVIDUAL IMPORTANCE

One answer is based on an assumption that is central to the listening approach. That assumption is: The kind of behavior which helps the individual will eventually be the best thing that could be done for the work group. Or saying it another way: The things that are best for the individual are best for the organization. This is a conviction of ours, based on our experience in psychology and education. The research evidence from organizations is still coming in. We find that putting the group first, at the expense of the individual, besides being an uncomfortable individual experience, does not unify the group. In fact, it tends to make the group less a group. The members become anxious and suspicious.

We are not at all sure in just what ways the group does benefit from a concern demonstrated for an individual, but we have several strong leads. One is that the group feels more secure when an individual member is being listened to and provided for with concern and sensitivity. And we assume that a secure group will ultimately be a better group. When each individual feels that he need not fear exposing himself to the group, he is likely to contribute more freely and spontaneously. When the leader of a group responds to the individual, puts the individual first, the other members of the group will follow suit, and the group comes to act as a unit in recognizing and responding to the needs of a particular member. This positive, constructive action seems to be a much more satisfying experience for a group than the experience of dispensing with a member.

LISTENING AND PRODUCTIVITY

As to whether or not listening or any other activity designed to better human relations in an organization actually makes the organization more productive—whether morale has a definite relationship to performance is not known for sure. There are some who frankly hold that there is no relationship to be expected between morale and productivity—that productivity often depends upon the social misfit, the eccentric, or the isolate. And there are some who simply choose to work in a climate of cooperation and harmony, in a high-morale group, quite aside from the question of achievement or productivity.

A report from the Survey Research Center at the University of Michigan on research conducted at the Prudential Life Insurance Company lists seven findings related to production and morale. First-line supervisors in high-production work groups were found to differ from those in low-production groups in that they:

1. Are under less close supervision from their own supervisors.
2. Place less direct emphasis upon production as the goal.
3. Encourage employee participation in the making of decisions.
4. Are more employee-centered.
5. Spend more of their time in supervision and less in straight production work.
6. Have a greater feeling of confidence in their supervisory roles.
7. Feel that they know where they stand with the company.

After mentioning that other dimensions of morale, such as identification with the company, intrinsic job satisfaction, and satisfaction with job status, were not found significantly related to productivity, the report goes on to suggest the following psychological interpretation:

> *People are more effectively motivated when they are given some degree of freedom in the way in which they do their work than when every action is prescribed in advance. They do better when some degree of decision-making about their jobs is possible than when all decisions are made for them. They respond more adequately when they are treated as personalities than as cogs in a machine. In short if the ego motivation of self-determination, of self-expression, of a sense of personal worth can be tapped, the individual can be more effectively energized. The use of external sanctions, or pressuring for production may work to some degree, but not to the extent that the more internalized motives do. When the individual comes to identify himself with his job and with the work of his group, human resources are much more fully utilized in the production process.*

The Survey Research Center has also conducted studies among workers in other industries. In discussing the results of these studies, Robert L. Kahn writes:

> *In the studies of clerical workers, railroad workers, and workers in heavy industry, the supervisors with the better production records gave a larger proportion of their time to supervisory functions, especially to the interpersonal aspects of their jobs. The supervisors of the lower-producing sections were more likely to spend their time in tasks which the men themselves were performing, or in the paper-work aspects of their jobs.*

MAXIMUM CREATIVENESS

There may never be enough research evidence to satisfy everyone on this question. But speaking from an organizational point of view, in terms of the problem of developing resources for productivity, the maximum creativeness and productive effort of the human beings in the organization are the richest untapped source of power available. The difference between the maximum productive capacity of people and that output which the organization is now realizing is immense. We simply suggest that this maximum capacity might be closer to realization if we sought to release the motivation that already exists within people rather than try to stimulate them externally.

This releasing of the individual is made possible first of all by listening, with respect and understanding. Listening is a beginning toward making the individual feel himself worthy of making contributions, and this could result in a very dynamic and productive organization. Profit making organizations are never too rugged or too busy to take time to procure the most efficient technological advances or to develop rich sources of raw materials. But technology and materials are but paltry resources in comparison with the resources that are already within the people in the organization.

G. L. Clements, of Jewel Tea Co., Inc., in talking about the collaborative approach to management says:

> We feel that this type of approach recognizes that there is a secret ballot going on at all times among the people in any business. They vote for or against their supervisors. A favorable vote for the supervisor shows up in the cooperation, teamwork, understanding, and production of the group. To win this secret ballot, each supervisor must share the problems of his group and work for them.

The decision to spend time listening to employees is a decision each supervisor or manager has to make for himself. Managers increasingly must deal with people and their relationships rather than turning out goods and services. The minute we take a man from work and make him a supervisor he is removed from the basic production of goods or services and now must begin relating to men and women instead of nuts and bolts. People are different from things and our supervisor is called upon for a different line of skills completely. These new tasks call for a special kind of person. The development of the supervisor as a listener is a first step in becoming this special person.

DEFENSIVE COMMUNICATION*

Jack R. Gibb

One way to understand communication is to view it as a people process rather than as a language process. If one is to make fundamental improvement in communication, he must make changes in interpersonal relationships. One possible type of alteration—and the one with which this paper is concerned—is that of reducing the degree of defensiveness.

DEFINITION AND SIGNIFICANCE

"Defensive behavior" is behavior which occurs when an individual perceives threat or anticipates threat in the group. The person who behaves defensively, even though he also gives some attention to the common task, devotes an appreciable portion of his energy to defending himself. Besides talking about the topic, he thinks about how he appears to others, how he may be seen more favorably, how

---

*Reprinted from the *Journal of Communication 11*, no. 3 (September 1961), 141–48, by permission of the author and the publisher.

he may win, dominate, impress or escape punishment, and/or how he may avoid or mitigate a perceived or anticipated attack.

Such inner feelings and outward acts tend to create similarly defensive postures in others; and, if unchecked, the ensuing circular response becomes increasingly destructive. Defensive behavior, in short, engenders defensive listening, and this in turn produces postural, facial, and verbal cues which raise the defense level of the original communicator.

Defensive arousal prevents the listener from concentrating upon the message. Not only do defensive communicators send off multiple value, motive, and affect cues, but also defensive recipients distort what they receive. As a person becomes more and more defensive, he becomes less and less able to perceive accurately the motives, the values, and the emotions of the sender. The writer's analysis of tape recorded discussions revealed that increases in defensive behavior were correlated positively with losses in efficiency in communication.[1] Specifically, distortions became greater when defensive states existed in the groups.

The converse also is true. The more "supportive" or defense reductive the climate the less the receiver reads into the communication distorted loadings which arise from projections of his own anxieties, motives, and concerns. As defenses are reduced, the receivers become better able to concentrate upon the structure, the content, and the cognitive meanings of the message.

CATEGORIES OF DEFENSIVE AND SUPPORTIVE COMMUNICATION

In working over an eight-year period with recordings of discussions occurring in varied settings, the writer developed the six pairs of defensive and supportive categories presented in Table 1. Behavior which listeners perceive as possessing any of the characteristics listed in the left-hand column arouses defensiveness, whereas that which they interpret as having any of the qualities designated as supportive reduces defensive feelings. The degree to which these reactions occur depend upon the personal level of defensiveness and upon the general climate in the group at the time.[2]

EVALUATION AND DESCRIPTION

Speech or other behavior which appears evaluative increases defensiveness. If by expression, manner of speech, tone of voice, or verbal content the sender seems to be evaluating or judging the listener, then the receiver goes on guard. Of course, other factors may inhibit the reaction. If the listener thinks that the speaker regards him as an equal and is being open and spontaneous, for example, the evaluativeness in a message will be neutralized and perhaps not even perceived. This same principle applies equally to the other five categories of potentially defense-producing climates. The six sets are interactive.

Because our attitudes toward other persons are frequently, and often necessarily, evaluative, expressions which the defensive person will regard as nonjudgmental are hard to frame. Even the simplest

TABLE 1   Categories of Behavior Characteristic of Supportive and Defensive Climates in Small Groups

Defensive Climates	Supportive Climates
1. Evaluation	1. Description
2. Control	2. Problem orientation
3. Strategy	3. Spontaneity
4. Neutrality	4. Empathy
5. Superiority	5. Equality
6. Certainty	6. Provisionalism

question usually conveys the answer that the sender wishes or implies the response that would fit into his value system. A mother, for example, immediately following an earth tremor that shook the house, sought for her small son with the question: "Bobby, where are you?" The timid and plaintive "Mommy, I didn't do it" indicated how Bobby's chronic mild defensiveness predisposed him to react with a projection of his own guilt and in the context of his chronic assumption that questions are full of accusation.

Anyone who has attempted to train professionals to use information-seeking speech with neutral affect appreciates how difficult it is to teach a person to say even the simple "Who did that?" without being seen as accusing. Speech is so frequently judgmental that there is a reality base for the defensive interpretations which are so common.

When insecure, group members are particularly likely to place blame, to see others as fitting into categories of good or bad, to make moral judgments of their colleagues, and to question the value, motive, and affect loadings of the speech which they hear. Since value loadings imply a judgment of others, a belief that the standards of the speaker differ from his own causes the listener to become defensive.

Descriptive speech, in contrast to that which is evaluative, tends to arouse a minimum of uneasiness. Speech acts which the listener perceives as genuine requests for information or as material with neutral loadings is descriptive. Specifically, presentations of feelings, events, perceptions, or processes which do not ask or imply that the receiver change behavior or attitude are minimally defense-producing. The difficulty in avoiding overtone is illustrated by the problems of news reporters in writing stories about unions, Communists, Negroes, and religious activities without tipping off the "party" line of the newspaper. One can often tell from the opening words in a news article which side the newspaper's editorial policy favors.

CONTROL AND PROBLEM ORIENTATION

Speech which is used to control the listener evokes resistance. In most of our social intercourse someone is trying to do something to someone else—to change an attitude, to influence behavior, or to restrict the field of activity. The degree to which attempts to control produce defensiveness depends upon the openness of the effort, for a suspicion that hidden motives exist heightens resistance. For this reason attempts of non-directive therapists and progressive educators to refrain from imposing a set of values, a point of view, or a problem solution upon the receivers meet with many barriers. Since the norm is control, non-controllers must earn the perceptions that their efforts have no hidden motives. A bombardment of persuasive "messages" in the fields of politics, education, special causes, advertising, religion, medicine, industrial relations, and guidance has bred cynical and paranoidal responses in listeners.

Implicit in all attempts to alter another person is the assumption by the change agent that the person to be altered is inadequate. That the speaker secretly views the listener as ignorant, unable to make his own decisions, uninformed, immature, unwise, or possessed of wrong or inadequate attitudes is a subconscious perception which gives the latter a valid base for defensive reactions.

Methods of control are many and varied. Legalistic insistence on detail, restrictive regulations and policies, conformity norms, and all laws are among the methods. Gestures, facial expressions, other forms of non-verbal communication, and even such simple acts as holding a door open in a particular manner are means of imposing one's will upon another and hence are potential sources of resistance.

Problem orientation, on the other hand, is the antithesis of persuasion. When the sender communicates a desire to collaborate in defining a mutual problem and in seeking its solution, she tends to create the same problem orientation in the listener; and, of greater importance, she implies that she has no predetermined solution, attitude, or method to impose. Such behavior is permissive in that it allows the receiver to set his own goals, make his own decisions, and evaluate his own progress—or to share with the sender in doing so. The exact methods of attaining permissiveness are not known, but they must involve a constellation of cues, and they certainly go beyond mere verbal assurances that the communicator has no hidden desires to exercise control.

STRATEGY AND SPONTANEITY

When the sender is perceived as engaged in a stratagem involving ambiguous and multiple motivations, the receiver becomes defensive. No one wishes to be a guinea pig, a role player, or an impressed actor, and no one likes to be the victim of some hidden motivation. That which is concealed, also, may appear larger than it really is, with the degree of defensiveness of the listener determining the perceived size of the suppressed element. The intense reaction of the reading audience to the material in the *Hidden Persuaders* indicates the prevalence of defensive reactions to multiple motivations behind strategy. Group members who are seen as "taking a role, " as feigning emotion, as toying with their colleagues, as withholding information, or as having special sources of data are especially resented. One participant once complained that another was "using a listening technique" on him!

A large part of the adverse reaction to much of the so-called human relations training is a feeling against what are perceived as gimmicks and tricks to fool or to "involve" people, to make a person think he is making his own decision, or to make the listener feel that the sender is genuinely interested in him as a person. Particularly violent reactions occur when it appears that someone is trying to make a stratagem appear spontaneous. One person has reported a boss who incurred resentment by habitually using the gimmick of "spontaneously" looking at his watch and saying. "My gosh, look at the time—I must run to an appointment." The belief was that the boss would create less irritation by honestly asking to be excused.

Similarly, the deliberate assumption of guilelessness and natural simplicity is especially resented. Monitoring the tapes of feedback and evaluation sessions in training groups indicates the surprising extent to which members perceive the strategies of their colleagues. This perceptual clarity may be quite shocking to the strategist, who usually feels that he has cleverly hidden the motivational aura around the "gimmick."

This aversion to deceit may account for one's resistance to politicians who are suspected of behind-the-scenes planning to get his vote; to psychologists whose listening apparently is motivated by more than the manifest or content-level interest in his behavior, or to the sophisticated, smooth, or clever person whose "one-upmanship" is marked with guile. In training groups the role-flexible person frequently is resented because his changes in behavior are perceived as strategic maneuvers.

Conversely, behavior which appears to be spontaneous and free of deception is defense reductive. If the communicator is seen as having a clean id, as having uncomplicated motivations, as being straightforward and honest, and as behaving spontaneously in response to the situation, he is likely to arouse minimal defense.

NEUTRALITY AND EMPATHY

When neutrality in speech appears to the listener to indicate a lack of concern for his welfare, he becomes defensive. Group members usually desire to be perceived as valued persons, as individuals of special worth, and as objects of concern and affection. The clinical, detached, person-is-an-object-of-study attitude on the part of many psychologist-trainers is resented by group members. Speech with low affect that communicates little warmth or caring is in such contrast with the affect-laden speech in social situations that it sometimes communicates rejection.

Communication that conveys empathy for the feelings and respect for the worth of the listener, is particularly supportive and defense reductive. Reassurance results when a message indicates that the speaker identifies himself with the listener's problems, shares his feelings, and accepts his emotional reactions at face value. Abortive efforts to deny the legitimacy of the receiver's emotions by assuring the receiver that he need not feel bad, that he should not feel rejected, or that he is overly anxious, though often intended as support giving, may impress the listener as lack of acceptance. The combination of understanding and empathizing with the other person's emotions with no accompanying effort to change him apparently is supportive at a high level.

The importance of gestural behavior cues in communicating empathy should be mentioned. Apparently spontaneous facial and bodily evidences of concern are often interpreted as especially valid evidence of deep-level acceptance.

SUPERIORITY AND EQUALITY

When a person communicates to another that he feels superior in position, power, wealth, intellectual ability, physical characteristics, or other ways, he arouses defensiveness. Here, as with the other sources of disturbance, whatever arouses feelings of inadequacy causes the listener to center upon the affect loading of the statement rather than upon the cognitive elements. The receiver then reacts by not hearing the message, by forgetting it, by competing with the sender, or by becoming jealous of him.

The person who is perceived as feeling superior communicates that he is not willing to enter into a shared problem-solving relationship, that he probably does not desire feedback, that he does not require help, and/or that he will be likely to try to reduce the power, the status, or the worth of the receiver.

Many ways exist for creating the atmosphere that the sender feels himself equal to the listener. Defenses are reduced when one perceives the sender as being willing to enter into participative planning with mutual trust and respect. Differences in talent, ability, worth, appearance, status, and power often exist, but the low defense communicator seems to attach little importance to these distinctions.

CERTAINTY AND PROVISIONALISM

The effects of dogmatism in producing defensiveness are well known. Those who seem to know the answers, to require no additional data, and to regard themselves as teachers rather than as co-workers tend to put others on guard. Moreover, in the writer's experiment, listeners often perceived manifest expressions of certainty as connoting inward feelings of inferiority. They saw the dogmatic individual as needing to be right, as wanting to win an argument rather than solve a problem, and as seeing his ideas as truths to be defended. This kind of behavior often was associated with acts which others regarded as attempts to exercise control. People who were right seemed to have low tolerance for members who were "wrong" (i.e., who did not agree with the sender).

One reduces the defensiveness of the listener when he communicates that he is willing to experiment with his own behavior, attitudes, and ideas. The person who appears to be taking provisional attitudes, to be investigating issues rather than taking sides on them, to be problem solving rather than debating, and to be willing to experiment and explore tends to communicate that the listener may have some control over the shared quest or the investigation of the ideas. If a person is genuinely searching for information and data, he does not resent help or company along the way.

CONCLUSION

The implications of the above material for the parent, the teacher, the manager, the administrator, or the therapist are fairly obvious. Arousing defensiveness interferes with communication and thus makes it difficult—and sometimes impossible—for anyone to convey ideas clearly and to move effectively toward the solution of therapeutic, educational, or managerial problems.

ENDNOTES

[1] J. R. Gibb, "Defense Level and Influence in Small Groups," *Leadership and Interpersonal Behavior*, eds. L. Petrullo and B. M. Bass (New York: Holt, Rinehart & Winston, 1961) 66–81.
[2] J. R. Gibb, "Sociopsychological Processes of Group Instruction," *The Dynamics of Instructional Groups*, ed. N. B. Henry (Fifty-Ninth Yearbook of the National Society for the Study of Education, Part 11, 1960) 115–35.

THE POWER OF TALK: WHO GETS HEARD AND WHY*

Deborah Tannen

The head of a large division of a multinational corporation was running a meeting devoted to performance assessment. Each senior manager stood up, reviewed the individuals in his group, and evaluated them for promotion. Although there were women in every group, not one of them made the cut. One after another, each manager declared, in effect, that every woman in his group didn't have the self-confidence needed to be promoted. The division head began to doubt his ears. How could it be that all the talented women in the division suffered from a lack of self-confidence?

In all likelihood, they didn't. Consider the many women who have left large corporations to start their own businesses, obviously exhibiting enough confidence to succeed on their own. Judgments about confidence can be inferred only from the way people present themselves, and much of that presentation is in the form of talk.

The CEO of a major corporation told me that he often has to make decisions in five minutes about matters on which others may have worked five months. He said he uses this rule: If the person making the proposal seems confident, the CEO approves it. If not, he says no. This might seem like a reasonable approach. But my field of research, socio-linguistics, suggests otherwise. The CEO obviously thinks he knows what a confident person sounds like. But his judgment, which may be dead right for some people, may be dead wrong for others.

Communication isn't as simple as saying what you mean. How you say what you mean is crucial, and differs from one person to the next, because using language is learned social behavior: How we talk and listen are deeply influenced by cultural experience. Although we might think that our ways of saying what we mean are natural, we can run into trouble if we interpret and evaluate others as if they necessarily felt the same way we'd feel if we spoke the way they did.

Since 1974, I have been researching the influence of linguistic style on conversations and human relationships. In the past four years, I have extended that research to the workplace, where I have observed how ways of speaking learned in childhood affect judgments of competence and confidence, as well as who gets heard, who gets credit, and what gets done.

The division head who was dumbfounded to hear that all the talented women in his organization lacked confidence was probably right to be skeptical. The senior managers were judging the women in their groups by their own linguistic norms, but women—like people who have grown up in a different culture—have often learned different styles of speaking than men, which can make them seem less competent and self-assured than they are.

WHAT IS LINGUISTIC STYLE?

Everything that is said must be said in a certain way—in a certain tone of voice, at a certain rate of speed, and with a certain degree of loudness. Whereas often we consciously consider what to say before speaking, we rarely think about how to say it, unless the situation is obviously loaded—for example, a job interview or a tricky performance review. Linguistic style refers to a person's characteristic

---

*Reprinted with permission from *Harvard Business Review* (September-October, 1995): 138–148.

speaking pattern. It includes such features as directness or indirectness, pacing and pausing, word choice, and the use of such elements as jokes, figures of speech, stories, questions, and apologies. In other words, linguistic style is a set of culturally learned signals by which we not only communicate what we mean but also interpret others' meaning and evaluate one another as people.

Consider turn taking, one element of linguistic style. Conversation is an enterprise in which people take turns: One person speaks, then the other responds. However, this apparently simple exchange requires a subtle negotiation of signals so that you know when the other person is finished and it's your turn to begin. Cultural factors such as country or region of origin and ethnic background influence how long a pause seems natural. When Bob, who is from Detroit, has a conversation with his colleague Joe, from New York City, it's hard for him to get a word in edgewise because he expects a slightly longer pause between turns than Joe does. A pause of that length never comes because, before it has a chance to, Joe senses an uncomfortable silence, which he fills with more talk of his own. Both men fail to realize that differences in conversational style are getting in their way. Bob thinks that Joe is pushy and uninterested in what he has to say, and Joe thinks that Bob doesn't have much to contribute. Similarly, when Sally relocated from Texas to Washington, D.C., she kept searching for the right time to break in during staff meetings—and never found it. Although in Texas she was considered outgoing and confident, in Washington she was perceived as shy and retiring. Her boss even suggested she take an assertiveness training course. Thus slight differences in conversational style—in these cases, a few seconds of pause—can have a surprising impact on who gets heard and on the judgments, including psychological ones, that are made about people and their abilities.

Every utterance functions on two levels. We're all familiar with the first one: Language communicates ideas. The second level is mostly invisible to us, but it plays a powerful role in communication. As a form of social behavior, language also negotiates relationships. Through ways of speaking, we signal—and create—the relative status of speakers and their level of rapport. If you say, "Sit down!" you are signaling that you have higher status than the person you are addressing, that you are so close to each other that you can drop all pleasantries, or that you are angry. If you say, "I would be honored if you would sit down," you are signaling great respect—or great sarcasm, depending on your tone of voice, the situation, and what you both know about how close you really are. If you say, "You must be so tired—why don't you sit down," you are communicating either closeness and concern or condescension. Each of these ways of saying "the same thing"—telling someone to sit down—can have a vastly different meaning.

In every community known to linguists, the patterns that constitute linguistic style are relatively different for men and women. What's "natural" for most men speaking a given language is, in some cases, different from what's "natural" for most women. That is because we learn ways of speaking as children growing up, especially from peers, and children tend to play with other children of the same sex. The research of sociologists, anthropologists, and psychologists observing American children at play has shown that, although both girls and boys find ways of creating rapport and negotiating status, girls tend to learn conversational rituals that focus on the rapport dimension of relationships whereas boys tend to learn rituals that focus on the status dimension.

Girls tend to play with a single best friend or in small groups, and they spend a lot of time talking. They use language to negotiate how close they are; for example, the girl you tell your secrets to becomes your best friend. Girls learn to downplay ways in which one is better than the others and to emphasize ways in which they are all the same. From childhood, most girls learn that sounding too sure of themselves will make them unpopular with their peers—although nobody really takes such modesty literally. A group of girls will ostracize a girl who calls attention to her own superiority and criticize her by saying, "She thinks she's something"; and a girl who tells others what to do is called "bossy." Thus girls learn to talk in ways that balance their own needs with those of others—to save face for one another in the broadest sense of the term.

Boys tend to play very differently. They usually play in larger groups in which more boys can be included, but not everyone is treated as an equal. Boys with high status in their group are expected to emphasize rather than downplay their status, and usually one or several boys will be seen as the leader or leaders. Boys generally don't accuse one another of being bossy, because the leader is expected to tell lower-status boys what to do. Boys learn to use language to negotiate their status in the group by displaying their abilities and knowledge, and by challenging others and resisting challenges. Giving orders is one way of getting and keeping the high-status role. Another is taking center stage by telling stories or jokes.

This is not to say that all boys and girls grow up this way or feel comfortable in these groups or are equally successful at negotiating within these norms. But, for the most part, these childhood play groups are where boys and girls learn their conversational styles. In this sense, they grow up in different worlds. The result is that women and men tend to have different habitual ways of saying what they mean, and conversations between them can be like cross-cultural communication: You can't assume that the other person means what you would mean if you said the same thing in the same way.

My research in companies across the United States shows that the lessons learned in childhood carry over into the workplace. Consider the following example: A focus group was organized at a major multinational company to evaluate a recently implemented flextime policy. The participants sat in a circle and discussed the new system. The group concluded that it was excellent, but they also agreed on ways to improve it. The meeting went well and was deemed a success by all, according to my own observations and everyone's comments to me. But the next day, I was in for a surprise.

I had left the meeting with the impression that Phil had been responsible for most of the suggestions adopted by the group. But as I typed up my notes, I noticed that Cheryl had made almost all those suggestions. I had thought that the key ideas came from Phil because he had picked up Cheryl's points and supported them, speaking at greater length in doing so than she had in raising them.

It would be easy to regard Phil as having stolen Cheryl's ideas—and her thunder. But that would be inaccurate. Phil never claimed Cheryl's ideas as his own. Cheryl herself told me later that she left the meeting confident that she had contributed significantly, and that she appreciated Phil's support. She volunteered, with a laugh, "It was not one of those times when a woman says something and it's ignored, then a man says it and it's picked up." In other words, Cheryl and Phil worked well as a team, the group fulfilled its charge, and the company got what it needed. So what was the problem?

I went back and asked all the participants who they thought had been the most influential group member, the one most responsible for the ideas that had been adopted. The pattern of answers was revealing. The two other women in the group named Cheryl. Two of the three men named Phil. Of the men, only Phil named Cheryl. In other words, in this instance, the women evaluated the contribution of another woman more accurately than the men did.

Meetings like this take place daily in companies around the country. Unless managers are unusually good at listening closely to how people say what they mean, the talents of someone like Cheryl may well be undervalued and underutilized.

ONE UP, ONE DOWN

Individual speakers vary in how sensitive they are to the social dynamics of language—in other words, to the subtle nuances of what others say to them. Men tend to be sensitive to the power dynamics of interaction, speaking in ways that position themselves as one up and resisting being put in a one-down position by others. Women tend to react more strongly to the rapport dynamic, speaking in ways that save face for others and buffering statements that could be seen as putting others in a one-down position. These linguistic patterns are pervasive; you can hear them in hundreds of exchanges in the workplace every day. And, as in the case of Cheryl and Phil, they affect who gets heard and who gets credit.

GETTING CREDIT

Even so small a linguistic strategy as the choice of pronoun can affect who gets credit. In my research in the workplace, I heard men say "I" in situations where I heard women say "we." For example, one publishing company executive said, "I'm hiring a new manager. I'm going to put him in charge of my marketing division," as if he owned the corporation. In stark contrast, I recorded women saying "we" when referring to work they alone had done. One woman explained that it would sound too self-promoting to claim credit in an obvious way by saying, "I did this." Yet she expected—sometimes vainly—that others would know it was her work and would give her the credit she did not claim for herself.

Managers might leap to the conclusion that women who do not take credit for what they've done should be taught to do so. But that solution is problematic because we associate ways of speaking with moral qualities: The way we speak is who we are and who we want to be.

Veronica, a senior researcher in a high-tech company, had an observant boss. He noticed that many of the ideas coming out of the group were hers but that often someone else trumpeted them around the office and got credit for them. He advised her to "own" her ideas and make sure she got the credit. But Veronica found she simply didn't enjoy her work if she had to approach it as what seemed to her an unattractive and unappealing "grabbing game." It was her dislike of such behavior that had led her to avoid it in the first place.

Whatever the motivation, women are less likely than men to have learned to blow their own horn. And they are more likely than men to believe that if they do so, they won't be liked.

Many have argued that the growing trend of assigning work to teams may be especially congenial to women, but it may also create complications for performance evaluation. When ideas are generated and work is accomplished in the privacy of the team, the outcome of the team's effort may become associated with the person most vocal about reporting results. There are many women and men—but probably relatively more women—who are reluctant to put themselves forward in this way and who consequently risk not getting credit for their contributions.

CONFIDENCE AND BOASTING

The CEO who based his decisions on the confidence level of speakers was articulating a value that is widely shared in U.S. businesses: One way to judge confidence is by an individual's behavior, especially verbal behavior. Here again, many women are at a disadvantage.

Studies show that women are more likely to downplay their certainty and men are more likely to minimize their doubts. Psychologist Laurie Heatherington and her colleagues devised an ingenious experiment, which they reported in the journal *Sex Roles* (Volume 29, 1993). They asked hundreds of incoming college students to predict what grades they would get in their first year. Some subjects were asked to make their predictions privately by writing them down and placing them in an envelope; others were asked to make their predictions publicly, in the presence of a researcher. The results showed that more women than men predicted lower grades for themselves if they made their predictions publicly. If they made their predictions privately, the predictions were the same as those of the men—and the same as their actual grades. This study provides evidence that what comes across as lack of confidence—predicting lower grades for one-self—may reflect not one's actual level of confidence but the desire not to seem boastful.

These habits with regard to appearing humble or confident result from the socialization of boys and girls by their peers in childhood play. As adults, both women and men find these behaviors reinforced by the positive responses they get from friends and relatives who share the same norms. But the norms of behavior in the U.S. business world are based on the style of interaction that is more common among men—at least, among American men.

ASKING QUESTIONS

Although asking the right questions is one of the hallmarks of a good manager, how and when questions are asked can send unintended signals about competence and power. In a group, if only one person asks questions, he or she risks being seen as the only ignorant one. Furthermore, we judge others not only by how they speak but also by how they are spoken to. The person who asks questions may end up being lectured to and looking like a novice under a schoolmaster's tutelage. The way boys are socialized makes them more likely to be aware of the underlying power dynamic by which a question asker can be seen in a one-down position.

One practicing physician learned the hard way that any exchange of information can become the basis for judgments—or misjudgments—about competence. During her training, she received a negative evaluation that she thought was unfair, so she asked her supervising physician for an explanation. He said that she knew less than her peers. Amazed at his answer, she asked how he had reached that conclusion. He said, "You ask more questions."

Along with cultural influences and individual personality, gender seems to play a role in whether and when people ask questions. For example, of all the observations I've made in lectures and books, the one that sparks the most enthusiastic flash of recognition is that men are less likely than women to stop and ask for directions when they are lost. I explain that men often resist asking for directions because they are aware that it puts them in a one-down position and because they value the independence that comes with finding their way by themselves. Asking for directions while driving is only one instance—along with many others that researchers have examined—in which men seem less likely than women to ask questions. I believe this is because they are more attuned than women to the potential face-losing aspect of asking questions. And men who believe that asking questions might reflect negatively on them may, in turn, be likely to form a negative opinion of others who ask questions in situations where they would not.

CONVERSATIONAL RITUALS

Conversation is fundamentally ritual in the sense that we speak in ways our culture has conventionalized and expect certain types of responses. Take greetings, for example. I have heard visitors to the United States complain that Americans are hypocritical because they ask how you are but aren't interested in the answer. To Americans, "How are you?" is obviously a ritualized way to start a conversation rather than a literal request for information. In other parts of the world, including the Philippines, people ask each other, "Where are you going?" when they meet. The question seems intrusive to Americans, who do not realize that it, too, is a ritual query to which the only expected reply is a vague "Over there."

It's easy and entertaining to observe different rituals in foreign countries. But we don't expect differences, and are far less likely to recognize the ritualized nature of our conversations, when we are with our compatriots at work. Our differing rituals can be even more problematic when we think we're all speaking the same language.

APOLOGIES

Consider the simple phrase *I'm sorry.*

> Catherine: *How did that big presentation go?*
> Bob: *Oh, not very well. I got a lot of flak from the VP for finance, and I didn't have the numbers at my fingertips.*
> Catherine: *Oh,* I'm sorry. *I know how hard you worked on that.*

In this case, I'm sorry probably means "I'm sorry that happened," not "I apologize," unless it was Catherine's responsibility to supply Bob with the numbers for the presentation. Women tend to say I'm sorry more frequently than men, and often they intend it in this way—as a ritualized means of expressing concern. It's one of many learned elements of conversational style that girls often use to establish rapport. Ritual apologies—like other conversational rituals—work well when both parties share the same assumptions about their use. But people who utter frequent ritual apologies may end up appearing weaker, less confident, and literally more blameworthy than people who don't.

Apologies tend to be regarded differently by men, who are more likely to focus on the status implications of exchanges. Many men avoid apologies because they see them as putting the speaker in a one-down position. I observed with some amazement an encounter among several lawyers engaged in a negotiation over a speakerphone. At one point, the lawyer in whose office I was sitting accidentally elbowed the telephone and cut off the call. When his secretary got the parties back on again, I expected him to say what I would have said: "Sorry about that. I knocked the phone with my elbow." Instead, he said, "Hey, what happened? One minute you were there; the next minute you were gone!" This lawyer seemed to have an automatic impulse not to admit fault if he didn't have to. For me, it was one of those pivotal moments when you realize that the world you live in is not the one everyone lives in and that the way you assume is the way to talk is really only one of many.

Those who caution managers not to undermine their authority by apologizing are approaching interaction from the perspective of the power dynamic. In many cases, this strategy is effective. On the other hand, when I asked people what frustrated them in their jobs, one frequently voiced complaint was working with or for someone who refuses to apologize or admit fault. In other words, accepting responsibility for errors and admitting mistakes may be an equally effective or superior strategy in some settings.

FEEDBACK

Styles of giving feedback contain a ritual element that often is the cause for misunderstanding. Consider the following exchange: A manager had to tell her marketing director to rewrite a report. She began this potentially awkward task by citing the report's strengths and then moved to the main point: the weaknesses that needed to be remedied. The marketing director seemed to understand and accept his supervisor's comments, but his revision contained only minor changes and failed to address the major weaknesses. When the manager told him of her dissatisfaction, he accused her of misleading him: "You told me it was fine."

The impasse resulted from different linguistic styles. To the manager, it was natural to buffer the criticism by beginning with praise. Telling her subordinate that his report is inadequate and has to be rewritten puts him in a one-down position. Praising him for the parts that are good is a ritualized way of saving face for him. But the marketing director did not share his supervisor's assumption about how feedback should be given. Instead, he assumed that what she mentioned first was the main point and that what she brought up later was an afterthought.

Those who expect feedback to come in the way the manager presented it would appreciate her tact and would regard a more blunt approach as unnecessarily callous. But those who share the marketing director's assumptions would regard the blunt approach as honest and no-nonsense, and the manager's as obfuscating. Because each one's assumptions seemed self-evident, each blamed the other: The manager thought the marketing director was not listening, and he thought she had not communicated clearly or had changed her mind. This is significant because it illustrates that incidents labeled vaguely as "poor communication" may be the result of differing linguistic styles.

COMPLIMENTS

Exchanging compliments is a common ritual, especially among women. A mismatch in expectations about this ritual left Susan, a manager in the human resources field, in a one-down position. She and her colleague Bill had both given presentations at a national conference. On the airplane home, Susan told Bill, "That was a great talk!" "Thank you," he said. Then she asked, "What did you think of mine?" He responded with a lengthy and detailed critique, as she listened uncomfortably. An unpleasant feeling of having been put down came over her. Somehow she had been positioned as the novice in need of his expert advice. Even worse, she had only herself to blame, since she had, after all, asked Bill what he thought of her talk.

But had Susan asked for the response she received? When she asked Bill what he thought about her talk, she expected to hear not a critique but a compliment. In fact, her question had been an attempt to repair a ritual gone awry. Susan's initial compliment to Bill was the kind of automatic recognition she felt was more or less required after a colleague gives a presentation, and she expected Bill to respond with a matching compliment. She was just talking automatically, but he either sincerely misunderstood the ritual or simply took the opportunity to bask in the one-up position of critic. Whatever his motivation, it was Susan's attempt to spark an exchange of compliments that gave him the opening.

Although this exchange could have occurred between two men, it does not seem coincidental that it happened between a man and a woman. Linguist Janet Holmes discovered that women pay more compliments than men (*Anthropological Linguistics*, Volume 28, 1986). And, as I have observed, fewer men are likely to ask, "What did you think of my talk?" precisely because the question might invite an unwanted critique.

In the social structure of the peer groups in which they grow up, boys are indeed looking for opportunities to put others down and take the one-up position for themselves. In contrast, one of the rituals girls learn is taking the one-down position but assuming that the other person will recognize the ritual nature of the self-denigration and pull them back up.

The exchange between Susan and Bill also suggests how women's and men's characteristic styles may put women at a disadvantage in the workplace. If one person is trying to minimize status differences, maintain an appearance that everyone is equal, and save face for the other, while another person is trying to maintain the one-up position and avoid being positioned as one down, the person seeking the one-up position is likely to get it. At the same time, the person who has not been expending any effort to avoid the one-down position is likely to end up in it. Because women are more likely to take (or accept) the role of advice seeker, men are more inclined to interpret a ritual question from a woman as a request for advice.

RITUAL OPPOSITION

Apologizing, mitigating criticism with praise, and exchanging compliments are rituals common among women that men often take literally. A ritual common among men that women often take literally is ritual opposition.

A woman in communications told me she watched with distaste and distress as her office mate argued heatedly with another colleague about whose division should suffer budget cuts. She was even more surprised, however, that a short time later they were as friendly as ever. "How can you pretend that fight never happened?" she asked. "Who's pretending it never happened?" he responded, as puzzled by her question as she had been by his behavior. "It happened," he said, "and it's over." What she took as literal fighting to him was a routine part of daily negotiation: a ritual fight.

Many Americans expect the discussion of ideas to be a ritual fight—that is, an exploration through verbal opposition. They present their own ideas in the most certain and absolute form they can, and wait to see if they are challenged. Being forced to defend an idea provides an opportunity to test it. In the same spirit, they may play devil's advocate in challenging their colleagues' ideas—trying to poke holes and find weaknesses—as a way of helping them explore and test their ideas.

This style can work well if everyone shares it, but those unaccustomed to it are likely to miss its ritual nature. They may give up an idea that is challenged, taking the objections as an indication that the idea was a poor one. Worse, they may take the opposition as a personal attack and may find it impossible to do their best in a contentious environment. People unaccustomed to this style may hedge when stating their ideas in order to fend off potential attacks. Ironically, this posture makes their arguments appear weak and is more likely to invite attack from pugnacious colleagues than to fend it off.

Ritual opposition can even play a role in who gets hired. Some consulting firms that recruit graduates from the top business schools use a confrontational interviewing technique. They challenge the candidate to "crack a case" in real time. A partner at one firm told me, "Women tend to do less well in this kind of interaction, and it certainly affects who gets hired. But, in fact, many women who don't 'test well' turn out to be good consultants. They're often smarter than some of the men who looked like analytic powerhouses under pressure."

The level of verbal opposition varies from one company's culture to the next, but I saw instances of it in all the organizations I studied. Anyone who is uncomfortable with this linguistic style—and that includes some men as well as many women—risks appearing insecure about his or her ideas.

NEGOTIATING AUTHORITY

In organizations, formal authority comes from the position one holds. But actual authority has to be negotiated day to day. The effectiveness of individual managers depends in part on their skill in negotiating authority and on whether others reinforce or undercut their efforts. The way linguistic style reflects status plays a subtle role in placing individuals within a hierarchy.

MANAGING UP AND DOWN

In all the companies I researched, I heard from women who knew they were doing a superior job and knew that their coworkers (and sometimes their immediate bosses) knew it as well, but believed that the higher-ups did not. They frequently told me that something outside themselves was holding them back and found it frustrating because they thought that all that should be necessary for success was to do a great job, that superior performance should be recognized and rewarded. In contrast, men often told me that if women weren't promoted, it was because they simply weren't up to snuff. Looking around, however, I saw evidence that men more often than women behaved in ways likely to get them recognized by those with the power to determine their advancement.

In all the companies I visited, I observed what happened at lunch time. I saw young men who regularly ate lunch with their boss, and senior men who ate with the big boss. I noticed far fewer women who sought out the highest-level person they could eat with. But one is more likely to get recognition for work done if one talks about it to those higher up, and it is easier to do so if the lines of communication are already open. Furthermore, given the opportunity for a conversation with superiors, men and women are likely to have different ways of talking about their accomplishments because of the different ways in which they were socialized as children. Boys are rewarded by their peers if they talk up their achievements, whereas girls are rewarded if they play theirs down. Linguistic styles common among men may tend to give them some advantages when it comes to managing up.

All speakers are aware of the status of the person they are talking to and adjust accordingly. Everyone speaks differently when talking to a boss than when talking to a subordinate. But, surprisingly, the ways in which they adjust their talk may be different and thus may project different images of themselves.

Communications researchers Karen Tracy and Eric Eisenberg studied how relative status affects the way people give criticism. They devised a business letter that contained some errors and asked 13 male and 11 female college students to role-play delivering criticism under two scenarios. In the first, the speaker was a boss talking to a subordinate; in the second, the speaker was a subordinate talking to his or her boss. The researchers measured how hard the speakers tried to avoid hurting the feelings of the person they were criticizing.

One might expect people to be more careful about how they deliver criticism when they are in a subordinate position. Tracy and Eisenberg found that hypothesis to be true for the men in their study but not for the women. As they reported in *Research on Language and Social Interaction* (Volume 24, 1990/1991), the women showed more concern about the other person's feelings when they were playing the role of superior. In other words, the women were more careful to save face for the other person when they were managing down than when they were managing up. This pattern recalls the way girls are socialized: Those who are in some way superior are expected to downplay rather than flaunt their superiority.

In my own recordings of workplace communication, I observed women talking in similar ways. For example, when a manager had to correct a mistake made by her secretary, she did so by acknowledging that there were mitigating circumstances. She said, laughing, "You know, it's hard to do things around here, isn't it, with all these people coming in!" The manager was saving face for her subordinate, just like the female students role-playing in the Tracy and Eisenberg study.

Is this an effective way to communicate? One must ask, effective for what? The manager in question established a positive environment in her group, and the work was done effectively. On the other hand, numerous women in many different fields told me that their bosses say they don't project the proper authority.

INDIRECTNESS

Another linguistic signal that varies with power and status is indirectness—the tendency to say what we mean without spelling it out in so many words. Despite the widespread belief in the United States that it's always best to say exactly what we mean, indirectness is a fundamental and pervasive element in human communication. It also is one of the elements that vary most from one culture to another, and it can cause enormous misunderstanding when speakers have different habits and expectations about how it is used. It's often said that American women are more indirect than American men, but in fact everyone tends to be indirect in some situations and in different ways. Allowing for cultural, ethnic, regional, and individual differences, women are especially likely to be indirect when it comes to telling others what to do, which is not surprising, considering girls' readiness to brand other girls as bossy. On the other hand, men are especially likely to be indirect when it comes to admitting fault or weakness, which also is not surprising, considering boys' readiness to push around boys who assume the one-down position.

At first glance, it would seem that only the powerful can get away with bald commands such as, "Have that report on my desk by noon." But power in an organization also can lead to requests so indirect that they don't sound like requests at all. A boss who says, "Do we have the sales data by product line for each region?" would be surprised and frustrated if a subordinate responded, "We probably do" rather than "I'll get it for you."

Examples such as these notwithstanding, many researchers have claimed that those in subordinate positions are more likely to speak indirectly, and that is surely accurate in some situations. For example, linguist Charlotte Linde, in a study published in *Language in Society* (Volume 17, 1988), examined the black-box conversations that took place between pilots and copilots before airplane crashes. In one particularly tragic instance, an Air Florida plane crashed into the Potomac River immediately after attempting take-off from National Airport in Washington, D.C., killing all but 5 of the 74 people on board. The pilot, it turned out, had little experience flying in icy weather. The copilot had a bit more, and it became heartbreakingly clear on analysis that he had tried to warn the pilot but had done so indirectly. Alerted by Linde's observation, I examined the transcript of the conversations and found evidence of her hypothesis. The copilot repeatedly called attention to the bad weather and to ice buildup on other planes:

> Copilot: *Look how the ice is just hanging on his, ah, back, back there, see that? See all those icicles on the back there and everything?*
> Pilot: *Yeah.*
> *[The copilot also expressed concern about the long waiting time since deicing.]*
> Copilot: *Boy, this is a, this is a losing battle here on trying to deice those things; it [gives] you a false feeling of security, that's all that does.*
> *[Just before they took off, the copilot expressed another concern—about abnormal instrument readings—but again he didn't press the matter when it wasn't picked up by the pilot.]*
> Copilot: *That don't seem right, does it? [3-second pause]. Ah, that's not right. Well—*
> Pilot: *Yes it is, there's 80.*
> Copilot: *Naw, I don't think that's right. [7-second pause] Ah, maybe it is.*

Shortly thereafter, the plane took off, with tragic results. In other instances as well as this one, Linde observed that copilots, who are second in command, are more likely to express themselves indirectly or otherwise mitigate, or soften, their communication when they are suggesting courses of action to the pilot. In an effort to avert similar disasters, some airlines now offer training for copilots to express themselves in more assertive ways.

This solution seems self-evidently appropriate to most Americans. But when I assigned Linde's article in a graduate seminar I taught, a Japanese student pointed out that it would be just as effective to train pilots to pick up on hints. This approach reflects assumptions about communication that typify Japanese culture, which places great value on the ability of people to understand one another without putting everything into words. Either directness or indirectness can be a successful means of communication as long as the linguistic style is understood by the participants.

In the world of work, however, there is more at stake than whether the communication is understood. People in powerful positions are likely to reward styles similar to their own, because we all tend to take as self-evident the logic of our own styles. Accordingly, there is evidence that in the U.S. workplace, where instructions from a superior are expected to be voiced in a relatively direct manner, those who tend to be indirect when telling subordinates what to do may be perceived as lacking in confidence.

Consider the case of the manager at a national magazine who was responsible for giving assignments to reporters. She tended to phrase her assignments as questions. For example, she asked, "How would you like to do the X project with Y? " or said, "I was thinking of putting you on the X project. Is that okay?" This worked extremely well with her staff; they liked working for her, and the work got done in an efficient and orderly manner. But when she had her midyear evaluation with her own boss, he criticized her for not assuming the proper demeanor with her staff.

In any work environment, the higher-ranking person has the power to enforce his or her view of appropriate demeanor, created in part by linguistic style. In most U.S. contexts, that view is likely to assume that the person in authority has the right to be relatively direct rather than to mitigate orders. There also are cases, however, in which the higher-ranking person assumes a more indirect style. The owner of a retail operation told her subordinate, a store manager, to do something. He said he would do it, but a week later he still hadn't. They were able to trace the difficulty to the following conversation: She had said, "The bookkeeper needs help with the billing. How would you feel about helping her out?" He had said, "Fine." This conversation had seemed to be clear and flawless at the time, but it turned out that they had interpreted this simple exchange in very different ways. She thought he meant, "Fine, I'll help the bookkeeper out." He thought he meant, "Fine, I'll think about how I would feel about helping the bookkeeper out." He did think about it and came to the conclusion that he had more important things to do and couldn't spare the time.

To the owner, "How would you feel about helping the bookkeeper out?" was an obviously appropriate way to give the order "Help the bookkeeper out with the billing." Those who expect orders to be given as bald imperatives may find such locutions annoying or even misleading. But those for whom this style is natural do not think they are being indirect. They believe they are being clear in a polite or respectful way.

What is atypical in this example is that the person with the more indirect style was the boss, so the store manager was motivated to adapt to her style. She still gives orders the same way, but the store manager now understands how she means what she says. It's more common in U.S. business contexts for the highest-ranking people to take a more direct style, with the result that many women in authority risk being judged by their superiors as lacking the appropriate demeanor—and, consequently, lacking confidence.

WHAT TO DO?

I am often asked, What is the best way to give criticism? or What is the best way to give orders?—in other words, What is the best way to communicate? The answer is that there is no one best way. The results of a given way of speaking will vary depending on the situation, the culture of the company, the relative rank of speakers, their linguistic styles, and how those styles interact with one another. Because of all those influences, any way of speaking could be perfect for communicating with one person in one situation and disastrous with someone else in another. The critical skill for managers is to become aware of the workings and power of linguistic style, to make sure that people with something valuable to contribute get heard.

It may seem, for example, that running a meeting in an unstructured way gives equal opportunity to all. But awareness of the differences in conversational style makes it easy to see the potential for unequal access. Those who are comfortable speaking up in groups, who need little or no silence before raising their hands, or who speak out easily without waiting to be recognized are far more likely to get heard at meetings. Those who refrain from talking until it's clear that the previous speaker is finished, who wait to be recognized, and who are inclined to link their comments to those of others will do fine at a meeting where everyone else is following the same rules but will have a hard time getting heard in a meeting with people whose styles are more like the first pattern. Given the socialization typical of boys and girls, men are more likely to have learned the first style and women the second, making meetings more congenial for men than for women. It's common to observe women who participate actively in one-on-one discussions or in all-female groups but who are seldom heard in meetings with a large proportion of men. On the other hand, there are women who share the style more common among men, and they run a different risk—of being seen as too aggressive.

A manager aware of those dynamics might devise any number of ways of ensuring that everyone's ideas are heard and credited. Although no single solution will fit all contexts, managers who understand the dynamics of linguistic style can develop more adaptive and flexible approaches to running or participating in meetings, mentoring or advancing the careers of others, evaluating performance, and so on. Talk is the lifeblood of managerial work, and understanding that different people have different ways of saying what they mean will make it possible to take advantage of the talents of people with a broad range of linguistic styles. As the workplace becomes more culturally diverse and business becomes more global, managers will need to become even better at reading interactions and more flexible in adjusting their own styles to the people with whom they interact.

CHAPTER 8
PERCEPTION AND ATTRIBUTION

COMMUNICATING ACROSS CULTURES
  Nancy J. Adler

WHERE BIAS BEGINS: THE TRUTH ABOUT STEREOTYPES
  Annie Murphy Paul

In the preceding selection, Deborah Tannen noted in "The Power of Talk" that men observed the way women communicate in the workplace and made interpretations about their behavior based on those perceptions. Such interpretations, however, are not always accurate. This chapter deals with perception, the process by which we select, organize, and evaluate the stimuli in our environment to make it meaningful for ourselves. The potential for inaccurate perceptions and mistaken attributions are very obvious in cross-cultural interactions. Attributions refer to the process of assigning a cause to a behavior.

Nancy Adler, a well-known international scholar and consultant, describes the primary difficulties of "Communicating Across Cultures," an excerpt from her textbook on international organizational behavior. She analyzes cultural misperceptions and provides numerous examples from around the world. Adler contends that stereotypes can be both helpful and harmful.

Stereotyping occurs when we attribute behavior or attitudes to people on the basis of the group or category to which they belong. Annie Murphy Paul, senior editor at *Psychology Today*, argues that everyone uses stereotypes—not just bigots—in "Where Bias Begins: The Truth About Stereotypes." She reviews the research on the unconscious biases and automatic stereotyping of people who are different from us and discusses how to reduce the negative aspect of stereotyping.

⤳

COMMUNICATING ACROSS CULTURES*

  Nancy J. Adler

If we seek to understand a people, we have to try to put ourselves, as far as we can, in that particular historical and cultural background . . . It is not easy for a person of one country to enter into the background of another country. So there is great irritation, because one fact that seems obvious to us is not immediately accepted by the other party or does not seem obvious to him at all . . . . But that extreme irritation will go when we think . . . that he is just differently conditioned and simply can't get out of that condition. One has to recognize that whatever the future may hold, countries and people differ . . . in their approach to life and their ways of living and thinking. In order to understand them, we have to understand their way of life and approach. If we wish to convince

---

*Excerpted and reprinted with permission from *International Dimensions of Organizational Behavior* (Cincinnati, OH: South-Western, 1997): 67–94.

them, we have to use their language as far as we can, not language in the narrow sense of the word,
but the language of the mind. That is one necessity. Something that goes even further than that is
not the appeal to logic and reason, but some kind of emotional awareness of other people.

Jawaharlan Nehru, *Visit to America*

All business activity involves communication. Within the global business environment, activities such as leading, motivating, negotiating, decision making, and exchanging information and ideas are all based on the ability of managers and employees from one culture to communicate successfully with colleagues, clients, and suppliers from other cultures. Communicating effectively challenges managers worldwide even when the work force is culturally homogeneous, but when employees speak a variety of languages and come from an array of cultural backgrounds, effective communication becomes considerably more difficult (10:3–5, 121–128; 16:1).

CROSS-CULTURAL COMMUNICATION

Communication is the exchange of meaning: it is my attempt to let you know what I mean. Communication includes any behavior that another person perceives and interprets: it is your understanding of what I mean. Communication includes sending both verbal messages (words) and nonverbal messages (tone of voice, facial expression, behavior, and physical setting). It includes consciously sent messages as well as messages that the sender is totally unaware of having sent. Whatever I say and do, I cannot *not* communicate. Communication therefore involves a complex multilayered, dynamic process through which we exchange meaning.

Every communication has a message sender and a message receiver. As shown in Figure 1, the sent message is never identical to the received message. Why? Communication is not direct, but rather indirect; it is a symbolic behavior. I cannot communicate my ideas, feelings, or information directly; rather, I must externalize or symbolize them before they can be communicated. *Encoding* describes the producing of a symbol message. *Decoding* describes the receiving of a meaning from a symbol message. Message senders must encode their meaning into a form that the receiver will recognize—that is, into words and behavior. Receivers must then decode the words and behavior—the symbols—back into messages that have meaning for them.

FIGURE 1   **Cross-Cultural Communication Model**

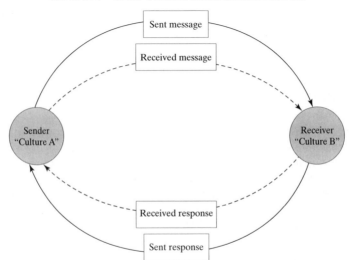

For example, because the Cantonese word for *eight* sounds like *faat*, which means prosperity, a Hong Kong textile manufacturer Mr. Lau Ting-Pong paid 85 million in 1988 for car registration number 8. A year later, a European millionaire paid $4.8 million at Hong Kong's Lunar New Year auction for vehicle registration number 7, a decision that mystified the Chinese, since the number 7 has little significance in the Chinese calculation of fortune (20).

Similarly, the members of Hong Kong's prestigious Legislative Council refrained from using numbers ending in 4 to identify their newly installed lockers. Some Chinese consider numbers ending with the digit 4 to be jinxed, because the sound of the Cantonese word *sei* is the same for *four* and *death*. The number 24, for instance, sounds like *yee sei*, or *death-prone* in Cantonese (9).

The process of translating meanings into words and behaviors—that is, into symbols—and back again into meanings is based on a person's cultural background and differs accordingly for each person. The greater the difference in background between senders and receivers, the greater the difference in meanings attached to particular words and behaviors. For example:

> *A British boss asked a new, young American employee if he would like to have an early lunch at 11 A.M. each day. The employee answered, "Yeah, that would be great!" The boss, hearing, the word yeah instead of the word yes, assumed that the employee was rude, ill-mannered, and disrespectful. The boss responded curtly, "With that kind of attitude, you may as well forget about lunch!" The employee was bewildered. What had gone wrong? In the process of encoding agreement (his meaning into yeah- a word symbol) and decoding the yeah spoken by a new employee to the boss (a word, behavior, and content symbol), the boss received an entirely different message than the employee had meant to send. Unfortunately, as is the case in most miscommunication, neither the sender nor the receiver was fully aware of what had gone wrong and why.*

Cross-cultural communication occurs when a person from one culture sends a message to a person from another culture. Cross- cultural miscommunication occurs when the person from the second culture does not receive the sender's intended message. The greater the difference between the sender's and the receiver's cultures, the greater the chance for cross-cultural miscommunication. For example:

> *A Japanese businessman wants to tell his Norwegian client that he is uninterested in a particular sale. To be polite, the Japanese says, "That will be very difficult." The Norwegian interprets the statement to mean that there are still unresolved problems, not that the deal is off. The Norwegian responds by asking how her company can help solve the problems. The Japanese, believing he has sent the message that there will be no sale, is mystified by the Norwegian's response.*

CULTURALLY "BIZARRE" BEHAVIOR

ONLY IN THE EYES OF THE BEHOLDER

While in Thailand, a Canadian expatriate's car was hit by a Thai motorist who had crossed over the double line while passing another vehicle. After failing to establish that the fault lay with the Thai driver, the Canadian flagged down a policeman. After several minutes of seemingly futile discussion, the Canadian pointed out the double line in the middle of the road and asked the policeman directly, "What do these lines signify?" The policeman replied, "They indicate the center of the road and are there so I can establish just how far the accident is from that point." The startled Canadian become silent. It had never occurred to him that the double line might not mean "no passing allowed."

(continued)

Unwritten rules reflect a culture's interpretation of its surroundings. A foreign columnist for the English-language *Bangkok Post* once proclaimed that the unwritten traffic rule in Thailand is: "When there are more than three cars in front of you at a stop sign or intersection, start your own line!" This contravenes the Western stay-in-line ethic, of course, but it effectively portrays, albeit in slightly exaggerated fashion, a fairly consistent form of behavior at intersections in Thailand. And it drives non-Thais crazy! (14)

Communication does not necessarily result in understanding. Cross-cultural communication continually involves misunderstanding caused by misperception, misinterpretation, and misevaluation. When the sender of a message comes from one culture and the receiver from another, the chances of accurately transmitting a message are low. People from different countries see, interpret, and evaluate things differently, and consequently act upon them differently. In approaching cross-cultural situations, effective businesspeople therefore *assume difference until similarity is proven*. They recognize that all behavior makes sense through the eyes of the person behaving and that logic and rationale are culturally relative. In cross-cultural business situations, labeling behavior as bizarre usually reflects culturally based misperception, misinterpretation, and misevaluation; rarely does it reflect intentional malice or pathologically motivated behavior.

CROSS-CULTURAL MISPERCEPTION

Do the French and the Chinese see the world in the same way? No. Do Venezuelans and Ghanaians see the world in the same way? Again, no. No two national groups see the world in exactly the same way. Perception is the process by which individuals select, organize, and evaluate stimuli from the external environment to provide meaningful experiences for themselves (2; 12; 16; 18). For example, when Mexican children simultaneously view tachistoscopic pictures of a bullfight and a baseball game, they only remember seeing the bullfight. Looking through the same tachistoscope, American children only remembered seeing the baseball game (3). Similarly, adult card players, when shown cards by researchers, fail to see black hearts and diamonds, or red clubs and spades.

Why didn't the children see both pictures? Why did the adults fail to see the unexpected playing card colors? The answer lies in the nature of perception. Perceptual patterns are neither innate nor absolute. They are selective, learned, culturally determined, consistent, and inaccurate.

- **Perception is *selective*** At any one time there are too many stimuli in the environment for us to observe. Therefore, we screen out most of what we see, hear, taste, and feel. We screen out the overload and allow only selected information through our perceptual screen to our conscious mind (5).
- **Perceptual patterns are *learned*** We are not born seeing the world in one particular way. Our experience teaches us to perceive the world in certain ways.
- **Perception is culturally *determined*** We learn to see the world in a certain way based on our cultural background.
- **Perception tends to remain *consistent*** Once we see something in a particular way, we continue to see it that way.
- **Perception is *inaccurate*** We see things that do not exist and do not see things that do exist. Our background, values, interests, and culture act as filters and lead us to distort, block, and even create what we choose to see and to hear. We perceive what we expect to perceive. We perceive things according to what we have been trained to see, according to our cultural map.

For example read the following sentence:

> # FINISHED FILES ARE THE RESULT OF YEARS OF SCIENTIFIC STUDY COMBINED WITH THE EXPERIENCE OF YEARS.

Now, quickly count the number of *F*'s in the sentence. Most non-native English speakers see all six *F*'s. Many native English speakers only see three *F*'s, they do not see the *F*'s in the word *of* because *of* is not an important word in understanding the sentence's meaning. We selectively see those words that are important according to our cultural conditioning (in this case, our linguistic conditioning). Once we see a phenomenon in a particular way, we usually continue to see it in that way. Once we stop seeing *of*'s, we do not see them again (even when we look for them); we do not see things that do exist. One particularly astute manager at Canadian National Railways makes daily use of perceptual filters to her firm's advantage. She gives reports written in English to bilingual Francophones to proofread and those written in French to bilingual Anglophones. She uses the fact that the English secretaries can "see" more errors—specially small errors—in French and that the French secretaries can "see" more errors in English.

The distorting impact of perceptual filters, which are based on our personal experiences, causes us to see things that do not exist. This phenomenon has been powerfully demonstrated for years in training sessions for executives as well as for other groups.[1] For example, in one session, American executives were asked to study the picture shown in Figure 2 and then to describe it to a colleague who had not seen the picture. The first colleague then attempted to describe it to a second colleague who had not seen the picture, and so on. Finally, the fifth colleague described his perception of the picture to the group of executives and compared it with the original picture. Among the numerous distortions, the executives, as with other groups, consistently described the black and the white man as fighting; the knife as being in the hand of the black man; and the white man as wearing a business suit and the black man as wearing laborer's overalls. Clearly the inaccurate stereotypes of blacks (as poorer, working class, and more likely to commit crimes) and of whites (as richer, upper class, and less likely to be

FIGURE 2   Impact of Perceptual Filters

Source: Rumor Clinic. Anti-Defamation League. Reprinted with permission.

involved in violent crime) radically altered or shifted the observers' perceptions and totally changed the meaning of the picture (1). The executives' personal experiences, and therefore their perceptual filters, allowed them to see things that did not exist and to miss seeing things that did exist.

CROSS-CULTURAL MISINTERPRETATION

Interpretation occurs when an individual gives meaning to observations and their relationships; it is the process of making sense out of perceptions. Interpretation organizes our experience to guide our behavior. Based on our experience, we make assumptions about our perceptions so we will not have to rediscover meanings each time we encounter similar situations. For example, we make assumptions about how doors work, based on our experience of entering and leaving rooms; thus we do not have to relearn how to open a door each time we encounter a new door. Similarly, when we smell smoke, we generally assume there is a fire. We do not have to stop and wonder if the smoke indicates a fire or a flood. Our consistent patterns of interpretation help us to act appropriately and quickly within our day-to-day world.

CATEGORIES

Since we are constantly bombarded with more stimuli than we can absorb and more perceptions than we can keep distinct or interpret,we only perceive those images that may be meaningful to us. We group perceived images into familiar categories that help us to simplify our environment, become the basis for our interpretations, and allow us to function in an otherwise overly complex world. For example, as a driver approaching an intersection, I may or may not notice the number of children in the back seat of the car next to me, but I will notice whether the traffic light is red or green (selective perception). If the light is red, I automatically place it in the category of all red traffic signals (categorization). This time, like prior times, I stop (behavior based on interpretation). Although people are capable of distinguishing thousands of different colors, I do not take the time to notice if the red light in Istanbul is brighter or duller than the one in Singapore or more orange or purple than the one in Nairobi; I just stop. Categorization helps me to distinguish what is most important in my environment and to behave accordingly.

Categories of perceived images become ineffective when we place people and things in the wrong groups. Cross-cultural miscategorization occurs when I use my home country categories to make sense out of situations abroad. For example, a Korean businessman entered a client's office in Stockholm and encountered a woman sitting behind the desk. Assuming that she was a secretary, he announced that he wanted to see Mr. Silferbrand. The woman responded by saying that the secretary would be happy to help him. The Korean became confused. In assuming that most women are secretaries rather than managers, he had misinterpreted the situation and acted inappropriately. His categorization made sense because most women in Korean offices are secretaries, but it proved inaccurate and counterproductive here, since this particular Swedish woman was not a secretary.

STEREOTYPES

Stereotyping involves a form of categorization that organizes our experience and guides our behavior toward ethnic and national groups. Stereotypes never describe individual behavior; rather, they describe the behavioral norm for members of a particular group. For example, stereotypes of English and French businesspeople, as analyzed by Intercultural Management Associates in Paris, are described as follows:

> We have found that to every set of negative stereotypes distinguishing the British and French there corresponds a particular values divergence that, when recognized, can prove an extraordinary resource. To illustrate: The French, in describing the British as "perfidious," "hypocritical," and "vague," are in fact describing English ... [managers'] typical lack of a general model or theory and ... their preference for a more pragmatic, evolutionary approach. This fact is hard for the

French ... to believe, let alone accept as a viable alternative, until, working alongside one anoth-er, the French ... come to see that there is usually no ulterior motive behind ... English ... [man-agers'] vagueness but rather a capacity to think aloud and adapt to circumstances. For [their] part, the English ... come to see that, far from being "distant," "superior," or "out of touch with reali-ty," the ... concern [of French managers] for a general model or theory is what lends vision, focus, and cohesion to an enterprise or project, as well as leadership and much needed authority (7).

Stereotypes, like other forms of categories, can be helpful or harmful depending on how we use them. Effective stereotyping allows people to understand and act appropriately in new situations. A stereotype becomes helpful when it is:

- **Consciously held**   People should be aware that they are describing a group norm rather than the characteristics of a specific individual.
- **Descriptive rather than evaluative**   The stereotype should describe what people from this group will probably be like and not evaluate those people as good or bad.
- **Accurate**   The stereotype should accurately describe the norm for the group to which the per-son belongs.
- **The first best guess** about a group prior to having direct information about the specific person or persons involved.
- **Modified** based on further observation and experience with the actual people and situations.

A subconsciously held stereotype is difficult to modify or discard even after we collect real infor-mation about a person, because it is often thought to reflect reality. If a subconscious stereotype also in-accurately evaluates a person or situation, we are likely to maintain an inappropriate, ineffective, and frequently harmful guide to reality. For example, assume that I subconsciously hold the stereotype that Anglophone Québecois[2] refuse to learn French and that therefore they should have no rights within the province (an inaccurate, evaluative stereotype). I then meet a monolingual Anglophone and say, "See, I told you that Anglophones aren't willing to speak French! They don't deserve to have rights here." I next meet a bilingual Anglophone and conclude, "He must be an American because Canadian Anglophones always refuse to learn french." Instead of questioning, modifying, or discarding my stereotype ("Some Anglophone Canadians speak French"), I alter reality to fit the stereotype ("He must be American"). Stereotypes increase effectiveness only when used as a first best guess about a person or situation prior to having direct information. They never help when adhered to rigidly. Indrei Ratiu (17), in his work with INSEAD, a leading international business school in France, and the London Business School, found that managers identified as "most internationally effective" by their colleagues altered their stereotypes to fit the actual people involved, whereas managers identified as "least internationally effective" contin-ued to maintain their stereotypes even in the face of contradictory information. For example, interna-tionally effective managers, prior to their first visit to Germany, might stereotype Germans as being extremely task oriented. Upon arriving and meeting a very friendly and lazy Herr Schmidt, they would alter their description to say that most Germans appear extremely task oriented, but Herr Schmidt seems friendly and lazy. Months later, the most internationally effective managers would only be able to say that some Germans appear very task oriented, whereas others seem quite relationship oriented (friendly); it all depends on the person and the situation. In this instance, the highly effective managers use the stereo-type as a first best guess about the group's behavior prior to meeting any individuals from the group. As time goes on, they modify or discard the stereotype entirely; information about each individual supersedes the group stereotype. By contrast, the least internationally effective managers maintain their stereotypes. They assume that the contradictory evidence in Herr Schmidt's case represents an exception, and they con-tinue to believe that all Germans are highly task oriented. In drawing conclusions too quickly on the basis of insufficient information—premature closure (12)—their stereotypes become self-fulfilling (19).

Canadian psychologist Donald Taylor (4; 5; 21) found that most people maintain their stereotypes even in the face of contradictory evidence. Taylor asked English and French Canadians to listen to one of three tape recordings of a French Canadian describing himself. In the first version, the French Canadian used the Francophone stereotype and described himself as religious, proud, sensitive, and expressive. In the second version, he used neutral terms to describe himself. In the third version, he used terms to describe himself that contradicted the stereotype, such as not religious, humble, unexpressive, and conservative. After having listened to one of the three versions, each person was asked to describe the Francophone on the tape (not Francophones in general). Surprisingly, people who listened to each of the three versions used the same stereotypic terms—religious, proud, sensitive, and expressive—even when the voice on the tape had conveyed the opposite information. People evidently maintain stereotypes even in the face of contradictory information.

To be effective, global managers therefore become aware of their cultural stereotypes and learn to set them aside when faced with contradictory evidence. They do not *pretend* not to stereotype.

If stereotyping is so useful as an initial guide to reality, why do people malign it? Why do parents and teachers constantly admonish children not to stereotype? Why do sophisticated managers rarely admit to stereotyping, even though each of us stereotypes every day? The answer is that we have failed to accept stereotyping as a natural process and have consequently failed to learn to use it to our advantage. For years we have viewed stereotyping as a form of primitive thinking, as an unnecessary simplification of reality. We have also viewed stereotyping as unethical: stereotypes can be inappropriate judgments of individuals based on inaccurate descriptions of groups. It is true that labeling people from a certain ethnic group as "bad" is not ethical, but grouping individuals into categories is neither good nor bad—it simply reduces a complex reality to manageable dimensions. Negative views of stereotyping simply cloud our ability to understand people's actual behavior and impair our awareness of our own stereotypes. *Everyone* stereotypes.

In conclusion, some people stereotype effectively and others do not. Stereotypes become counterproductive when we place people in the wrong group, when we incorrectly describe group norms, when we inappropriately evaluate the group or category, when we confuse the stereotype with the description of a particular individual, and when we fail to modify the stereotype based on our actual observations and experience.

SOURCES OF MISINTERPRETATION

Misinterpretation can be caused by inaccurate perceptions of a person or situation that arise when what actually exists is not seen. It can be caused by an inaccurate interpretation of what is seen; that is, by using my meanings to make sense out of your reality. An example of this type of misinterpretation (or misattribution) comes from an encounter between an Austrian businessman and a North American.

> *I meet my Austrian client for the sixth time in as many months. He greets me as Herr Smith. Categorizing him as a businessman, I interpret his very formal behavior to mean that he does not like me or is uninterested in developing a closer relationship with me. (North American attribution: people who maintain formal behavior after the first few meetings do so because they dislike or distrust the associates so treated.) In fact, I have misinterpreted his behavior. I have used the norms for North American business behavior, which are more informal and demonstrative (I would say "Good morning, Fritz," not "Good morning, Herr Ranschburg"), to interpret the Austrian's more formal behavior ("Good morning, Herr Smith").*

Culture strongly influences, and in many situations determines, our interpretations. Both the categories and the meanings we attach to them are based on our cultural background. Sources of cross-cultural misinterpretation include subconscious cultural "blinders," a lack of cultural self-awareness, projected similarity, and parochialism.

Subconscious Cultural Blinders

Because most interpretation goes on at a subconscious level, we lack awareness of the assumptions we make and their cultural basis. Our home culture reality never forces us to examine our assumptions or the extent to which they are culturally based, because we share our cultural assumptions with most other citizens from our country. All we know is that things do not work as smoothly or logically when we work outside our own culture as when we work with people more similar to ourselves. For example:

Canadians conducting business in Kuwait became surprised when their meeting with a high-ranking official was not held in a closed office and was constantly interrupted. Using the Canadian-based cultural assumptions that important people have large private offices with secretaries to monitor the flow of people into the office, and that important business takes precedence over less important business and is therefore not interrupted, the Canadians interpreted the Kuwaiti's open office and constant interruptions to mean that the official was neither as high ranking nor as interested in conducting the business at hand as they had previously thought. The Canadians' interpretation of the office environment led them to lose interest in working with the Kuwaiti.

The problem is that the Canadians' interpretation derives from their own North American norms, not from Middle Eastern cultural norms. The Kuwaiti may well have been a high-ranking official who was very interested in doing business. The Canadians will never know.

Cases of subconscious cross-cultural misinterpretation occur frequently. For example, in the 1980s a Soviet Russian poet, after lecturing at American universities for two months, said, "Attempts to please an American audience are doomed in advance, because out of twenty listeners five may hold one point of view, seven another, and eight may have none at all" (10). The Soviet poet confused Americans' freedom of thought and speech with his ability to please them. He assumed that one can only please an audience if all members hold the same opinion. Another example of well-meant misinterpretation comes from the United States Office of Education's advice to American teachers working with newly arrived Vietnamese refugee students (22):

Students' participation was discouraged in Vietnamese schools by liberal doses of corporal punishment, and students were conditioned to sit rigidly and speak out only when spoken to. This background . . . makes speaking freely in class hard for a Vietnamese student. Therefore, don't mistake shyness for apathy.

Perhaps the extent to which this is a culturally based interpretation becomes clearer if we imagine the opposite advice that the Vietnamese Ministry of Education might have given to Vietnamese teachers planning to receive American children for the first time.

Students' proper respect for teachers was discouraged by a loose order and students were conditioned to chat all the time and to behave in other disorderly ways. This background makes proper and respectful behavior in class hard for an American student. Therefore, do not mistake rudeness for lack of reverence.

LACK OF CULTURAL SELF-AWARENESS

Although we may think that a major obstacle in conducting business around the world is in understanding foreigners, the greater difficulty involves becoming aware of our own cultural conditioning. As anthropologist Edward Hall explains, "What is known least well, and is therefore in the poorest position to be studied, is what is closest to oneself" (8:45). We are generally least aware of our own cultural characteristics and are quite surprised when we hear foreigners describe us. For example, many Americans are surprised to discover that foreigners see them as hurried, overly law-abiding, very hard working, extremely explicit, and overly inquisitive (see the box "Cross-Cultural Awareness: Americans as Others

TABLE 1   How Others See Americans

Characteristics Most Commonly Associated with Americans*

France	Japan	Western Germany	Great Britain	Brazil	Mexico
Industrious	Nationalistic	Energetic	Friendly	Intelligent	Industrious
Energetic	Friendly	Inventive	Self-indulgent	Inventive	Intelligent
Inventive	Decisive	Friendly	Energetic	Energetic	Inventive
Decisive	Rude	Sophisticated	Industrious	Industrious	Decisive
Friendly	Self-indulgent	Intelligent	Nationalistic	Nationalistic	Greedy

Characteristics Least Commonly Associated with Americans*

France	Japan	Western Germany	Great Britain	Brazil	Mexico
Lazy	Industrious	Lazy	Lazy	Lazy	Lazy
Rude	Lazy	Sexy	Sophisticated	Self-indulgent	Honest
Honest	Honest	Greedy	Sexy	Sexy	Rude
Sophisticated	Sexy	Rude	Decisive	Sophisticated	Sexy

*From a list of fourteen characteristics.

Source: Newsweek (July 11,1983), p. 50, Copyright 1981 by Newsweek, Inc. All rights reserved, reprinted by permission.

See Them"). Many American businesspeople were equally surprised by a *Newsweek* survey reporting the characteristics most and least frequently associated with Americans (see Table 1). Asking a foreign national to describe businesspeople from your country is a powerful way to see yourself as others see you.

CROSS-CULTURAL AWARENESS:
AMERICANS AS OTHERS SEE THEM

People from other countries often become puzzled and intrigued by the intricacies and enigmas of American culture. Below is a selection of actual observations by people from around the world visiting the United States. As you read them, ask yourself in each case if the observer is accurate and how you would explain the trait in question.

India: *"Americans seem to be in a perpetual hurry. Just watch the way they walk down the street. They never allow themselves the leisure to enjoy life; there are too many things to do."*
Kenya: *"Americans appear to us rather distant. They are not really as close to other people—even fellow Americans—as Americans overseas tend to portray. It's almost as if an American says, 'I won't let you get too close to me.' It's like building a wall."*
Turkey: *"Once we were out in a rural area in the middle of nowhere and saw an American come to a stop sign. Though he could see in both directions for miles and no traffic was coming, he still stopped!"*
Colombia: *"The tendency in the United States to think that life is only work hits you in the face. Work seems to be the one type of motivation."*
Indonesia: *"In the United States, everything has to be talked about and analyzed. Even the littlest thing has to be "Why, Why, Why? I get a headache from such persistent questions."*
Ethiopia: *"Americans are very explicit; ... [they] want a 'yes' or 'no.' If someone tries to speak figuratively, the American is confused."*

> ***Iran:*** *"The first time … my [American] professor told me, 'I don't know the answer; I will have to look it up,' I was shocked. I asked myself, 'Why is he teaching me?' In my country a professor would give the wrong answer rather than admit ignorance."*[3]

Another very revealing way to understand the norms and values of a culture is to listen to common sayings and proverbs. What does a society recommend, and what does it prohibit? The box "North American Values: Proverbs" lists some common North American proverbs and the values each teaches.

To the extent that we can begin to see ourselves clearly through the eyes of people from other cultures, we can begin to modify our behavior, emphasizing our most appropriate and effective characteristics and minimizing those least helpful. To the extent that we are culturally self- aware, we can begin to predict the effect our behavior will have on others.

NORTH AMERICAN VALUES: PROVERBS

It is evidently much more potent in teaching practicality, for example, to say, "Don't cry over spilt milk" than "You'd better learn to be practical." North Americans have heard this axiom hundreds of times, and it has made its point. Listed below are North American proverbs on the left and the values they seem to be teaching on the right.[4]

Proverb	Value
Cleanliness is next to godliness.	Cleanliness
A penny saved is a penny earned.	Thriftiness
Time is money.	Time thriftiness
Don't cry over spilt milk.	Practicality
Waste not; want not.	Frugality
Early to bed, early to rise, makes one healthy, wealthy, and wise.	Diligence; Work ethic
God helps those who help themselves.	Initiative
It's not whether you win or lose, but how you play the game.	Good sportsmanship
A person's home is his castle.	Privacy; Value of personal property
No rest for the wicked.	Guilt; Work ethic
You've made your bed, now sleep in it.	Responsibility
Don't count your chickens before they're hatched.	Practicality
A bird in the hand is worth two in the bush.	Practicality
The squeaky wheel gets the grease.	Aggressiveness
Might makes right.	Superiority of physical power
There's more than one way to skin a cat.	Originality; Determination
A stitch in time saves nine.	Timeliness of action
All that glitters is not gold.	Wariness
Clothes make the man.	Concern for physical appearance
If at first you don't succeed, try, try again.	Persistence; Work ethic
Take care of today, and tomorrow will take care of itself.	Preparation for future
Laugh, and the world laughs with you; weep and you weep alone.	Pleasant outward appearance

PROJECTED SIMILARITY

Projected similarity refers to the assumption that people are more similar to you than they actually are or that another person's situation is more similar to your own situation than it in fact is. Projecting similarity reflects both a natural and a common process. American professors asked managers from 14 countries to describe the work and life goals of a colleague in their work team from another country (6). As shown in Figure 3, in every case the managers assumed that their foreign colleagues were more like themselves than they actually were. Projected similarity involves assuming, imagining, and actually perceiving similarity when differences exist. Projected similarity particularly handicaps people in cross-cultural situations. As a South African, I assume that my Greek colleague is more South African than he actually is. As an Egyptian, I assume that my Chilean colleague is more similar to me than she actually is. When I act based on this assumed similarity, I often find that I have acted inappropriately and thus ineffectively.

At the base of projected similarity is a subconscious parochialism. I assume that there is only one way to be: my way. I assume that there is only one way to see the world: my way. I therefore view other people in reference to me and to my way of viewing the world. People may fall into an

> *illusion of understanding while being unaware of ... [their] misunderstandings. "I understand you perfectly but you don't understand me" is an expression typical of such a situation. Or all communicating parties may fall into a collective illusion of mutual understanding. In such a situation, each party may wonder later why other parties do not live up to the "agreement" they had reached.*

Most global managers do not see themselves as parochial. They believe that as world travelers they are able to see the foreigner's point of view. This is not always true. The following are examples of projected similarity and consequent cultural misinterpretation:

> *When Danish managers work with a Saudi and the Saudi states that the plant will be completed on time, "En shah allah" ("If God is willing"), the Danes rarely believe that God's will is really going to influence the progress of construction. They continue to see the world from their parochial Danish perspective and assume that "En shah allah" is just an excuse for not getting the work done, or is meaningless altogether.*
>
> *Similarly, when Balinese workers' families refuse to use birth control methods, explaining that it will break the cycle of reincarnation, few Western managers really consider that there is a possibility that they too will be reborn a number of times. Instead, they assume that the Balinese either are superstitious, or that they simply do not understand, or are afraid of, Western medicine.*

While it is important to understand and respect the other culture's point of view, it is not necessary to either accept or adopt it. Understanding and respect do not imply acceptance. However, a rigid adherence to our own belief system expresses a form of parochialism, and parochialism underlies projected similarity.

FIGURE 3 **Projected Similarity**

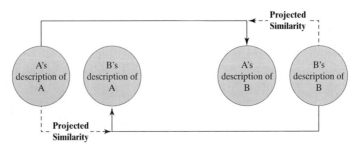

CROSS-CULTURAL MISEVALUATION

Even more than perception and interpretation, cultural conditioning strongly affects evaluation. Evaluation involves judging whether someone or something is good or bad. Cross-culturally, we use our own culture as a standard of measurement, judging that which is like our own culture as normal and good and that which is different as abnormal and bad. Our own culture becomes a self-reference criterion: since no other culture is identical to our own, we tend to judge all other cultures as inferior. Evaluation rarely helps in trying to understand, communicate with, or do business with people from another culture. The following example highlights the consequences of misevaluation:

A Swiss executive waits more than an hour past the appointed time for his Spanish colleague to arrive and to sign a supply contract. In his impatience he concludes that Spaniards must be lazy and totally unconcerned about business. The Swiss executive has misevaluated his colleague by negatively comparing him to his own cultural standards for business punctuality. Implicitly, he has labeled his own culture's behavior as good ("The Swiss arrive on time and that is good") and the other culture's behavior as bad ("The Spanish do not arrive on time and that is bad").

COMMUNICATION: GETTING THEIR MEANING, NOT JUST THEIR WORDS

Effective cross-cultural communication is possible; however, global managers cannot approach communication in the same way as do domestic managers. First, effective global managers "*know that they don't know.*" They assume difference until similarity is proven rather than assuming similarity until difference is proven.

Second, in attempting to understand their colleagues from other cultures, effective global managers emphasize description, by observing what is actually said and done, rather than interpreting or evaluating it. Describing a situation is the most accurate way to gather information about it. Interpretation and evaluation, unlike description, are based more on the observer's own culture and background than on the observed situation. My interpretations and evaluations therefore tell me more about myself than about the actual situation. Although managers, as decision makers, must evaluate people (e.g., performance appraisal) and situations (e.g., project assessment) in terms of organizational standards and objectives, effective global managers delay judgment until they have had sufficient time to observe and interpret the situation from the perspective of all cultures involved.

Third, when attempting to understand or interpret an international situation, effective global managers try to see it through the eyes of their international colleagues. This role reversal limits the myopia of viewing situations strictly from one's own perspective.

Fourth, once effective global managers develop an explanation for a situation, they treat the explanation as a guess (as a hypothesis to be tested) and not as a certainty. They systematically check with colleagues both from home and abroad to make certain that their guesses—their initial interpretations—are plausible. This checking process allows them to converge meanings—to delay accepting their interpretations of the situation until they have confirmed them with others.

UNDERSTANDING: CONVERGING MEANINGS

There are many ways to increase the chances for accurately understanding businesspeople from other cultures. Each technique is based on presenting the message through multiple channels (for example, stating your position and showing a graph to summarize the same position), paraphrasing to check that colleagues from other cultures have understood your meaning (and not just your words), and converging meanings (always double-checking with the other person to verify that you have communicated what you had intended to communicate).

STANDING BACK FROM YOURSELF

Perhaps the most difficult skill in cross-cultural communication involves standing back from yourself; being aware that you do not know everything, that a situation may not make sense, that your guesses may be wrong, and that the ambiguity in the situation may continue. In this sense the ancient Roman dictum "knowledge is power" becomes true. In knowing yourself, you gain power over your perceptions and reactions; you can control your own behavior and your reactions to others' behavior. Cross-cultural awareness complements in-depth self-awareness. A lack of self-awareness negates the usefulness of cross-cultural awareness.

One of the most poignant examples of the powerful interplay between description, interpretation, evaluation, and empathy involved a Scottish businessman's relationship with a Japanese colleague. The box "Cross-Cultural Communication: Japanese Pickles and Mattresses, Incorporated" recounts the Scottish businessman's experience.

CROSS-CULTURAL COMMUNICATION

JAPANESE PICKLES AND MATTRESSES, INCORPORATED

It was my first visit to Japan. As a gastronomic adventurer, and because I believe cuisine is one route that is freely available and highly effective as a first step towards a closer understanding of another country, I was disappointed on my first evening when the Japanese offered me a Western meal.

As tactfully as possible, I suggested that sometime during my stay I would like to try a Japanese menu, if that could be arranged without inconvenience. There was some small reluctance evident on the part of my hosts (due of course to their thought that I was being very polite asking for Japanese food which I didn't really like, so to be good hosts they had to politely find a way of not having me eat it!). But eventually, by an elegantly progressive route starting with Western food with a slightly Japanese bias through to genuine Japanese food, my hosts were convinced that I really wanted to eat Japanese style and was not "posing."

From then on they became progressively more enthusiastic in suggesting the more exotic Japanese dishes, and I guess I graduated when, after an excellent meal one night (apart from the Japanese pickles) on which I had lavished praise, they said, "Do you like Japanese pickles?" To this, without preamble, I said, "No!" To this reply, with great laughter all around, they responded, "Nor do we!"

During this gastronomic getting-together week, I had also been trying to persuade them that I really did wish to stay in traditional Japanese hotels rather than the very Westernized ones my hosts had selected because they thought I would prefer my "normal" lifestyle. (I should add that, at this time, traditional Japanese hotels were still available and often cheaper than, say, the Osaka Hilton.)

Anyway, after the pickles joke, it was suddenly announced that Japanese hotels could be arranged. For the remaining two weeks of my stay, as I toured the major cities, on most occasions a traditional Japanese hotel was substituted for the Western one on my original schedule.

Many of you will know that a traditional Japanese room has no furniture except a low table and a flower arrangement. The "bed" is a mattress produced just before you retire from a concealed cupboard, accompanied by a cereal-packed pillow.

One memorable evening my host and I had finished our meal together in "my" room. I was expecting him to shortly make his "goodnight" and retire, as he had been doing all week, to his own room.

However, he stayed unusually long and was, to me, obviously in some sort of emotional crisis. Finally, he blurted out, with great embarrassment, "Can I sleep with you?!"

As they say in the novels, at this point I went very still! My mind was racing through all the sexual taboos and prejudices my own upbringing had instilled, and I can still very clearly recall how I analyzed: "I'm bigger that he is so I can fight him off, but then he's probably an expert in the martial arts, but on the other hand he has shown no signs of being gay up until now and he is my host and there is a lot of business at risk and there's no such thing as rape, et cetera . . . !"

It seemed a hundred years, though it was only a few seconds, before I said, feeling as if I was pulling the trigger in Russian roulette, "Yes, sure."

Who said that the Orientals are inscrutable? The look of relief that followed my reply was obvious. Then he looked worried and concerned again, and said, "Are you sure?"

I reassured him and he called in the maid, who fetched his mattress from his room and laid it on the floor alongside mine. We both went to bed and slept all night without any physical interaction.

Later I learned that for the traditional Japanese one of the greatest compliments you can be paid is for the host to ask, "Can I sleep with you?" This goes back to the ancient feudal times, when life was cheap, and what the invitation really said was, "I trust you with my life. I do not think that you will kill me while I sleep. You are my true friend."

To have said "No" to the invitation would have been an insult—"I don't trust you not to kill me while I sleep"—or, at the very least, my host would have been acutely embarrassed because he had taken the initiative. If I refused because I had failed to perceive the invitation as a compliment, he would have been out of countenance on two grounds: the insult to him in the traditional context and the embarrassment he would have caused me by "forcing" a negative, uncomprehending response from me.

As it turned out, the outcome was superb. He and I were now "blood brothers," as it were. His assessment of me as being "ready for Japanization" had been correct and his obligations under ancient Japanese custom had been fulfilled. I had totally misinterpreted his intentions through my own cultural conditioning. It was sheer luck, or luck plus a gut feeling that I'd gotten it wrong, that caused me to make the correct response to his extremely complimentary and committed invitation.[6]

SUMMARY

Cross-cultural communication confronts us with limits to our perceptions, our interpretations, and our evaluations. Our cultural perspectives tend to render everything relative and slightly uncertain. Entering a culture that is foreign to us is tantamount to knowing the words without knowing the music, or knowing the music without knowing the beat. Our natural tendencies lead us back to our prior experience: our default option becomes the familiarity of our own culture, thus precluding our accurate understanding of others' cultures.

Strategies to overcome our natural parochial tendencies exist. With care, we can avoid our ethnocentric default options. We can learn to see, understand, and control our own cultural conditioning. When working in other cultures, we can emphasize description rather than interpretation or evaluation, and thus minimize self-fulfilling stereotypes and premature judgments. We can recognize and use our stereotypes as guides rather than rejecting them as unsophisticated simplifications. Effective cross-cultural communication presupposes the interplay of alternative realities. It rejects the actual or potential domination of one reality over another.

ENDNOTES

[1] The Anti-Defamation League Rumor Clinic designed the sessions to show how rumors operate and how to distinguish rumors from gossip.

[2] Anglophone Québecois are native English speakers living in the predominantly French-speaking province of Quebec, Canada.

[3] Individual country quotes taken from J. P. Feig and G. Blair, *There Is a Difference*, 2nd ed. (Washington, D.C.: Meridian House International, 1980).

[4] List of proverbs and associated values from L. R. Kohls, *Survival Kit for Overseas Living* (Yarmouth, ME: Intercultural Press, 1979), 30–31.

[5] Based on N. J. Adler and M. N. Kiggundu, "Awarenessat the Crossroad: Designing Translator-Based Training Programs," in D. Landis and R. Brislin, *Handbook of Intercultural Training: Issues in Training Methodology, Vol. II* (New York: Pergamon Press, 1983), 124–150.

[6] This is the true experience of a Scottish executive as described to his colleagues after participating in the Managerial Skills for International Business executive seminar at INSEAD, in Fontainebleau, France.

REFERENCES

1. Anti-Defamation League Rumor Clinic.

2. Asch, S. "Forming Impressions of Persons," *Journal of Abnormal and Social Psychology 40* (1946), 258–290.

3. Bagby, J. W. "Dominance in Binocular Rivalry in Mexico and the United States," in I. Al-Issa and W. Dennis, eds., *Cross-Cultural Studies of Behavior* (New York: Holt, Rinehart and Winston, 1970), 49–56. Originally in *Journal of Abnormal and Social Psychology 54* (1957), 331–334.

4. Berry, J.; Kalin, R.; and Taylor, D. "Multiculturalism and Ethnic Attitudes in Canada," *Multiculturalism as State Policy* (Ottawa: Government of Canada, 1976).

5. Berry, J.; Kalin, R.; and Taylor, D. *Multiculturalism and Ethnic Attitudes in Canada* (Ottawa: Minister of Supply and Services, 1977).

6. Burger, P., and Bass, B. M. *Assessment of Managers: An International Comparison* (New York: Free Press, 1979).

7. Gancel, C., and Ratiu, I. Internal document, Inter Cultural Management Associates, Paris, France, 1984.

8. Hall, E. T. *Beyond Culture* (Garden City, NY: AnchorPress/Doubleday, 1976). Also see E. T. Hall's *The Silent Language* (Doubleday, 1959, and Anchor Books, 1973) and *The Hidden Dimension* (Doubleday, 1966, and Anchor Books, 1969).

9. Ho, A. "Unlucky Numbers Are Locked out of the Chamber," South China Morning Post (December 26, 1988), 1.

10. Kanungo, R. N. *Biculturalism and Management* (Ontario: Butterworth, 1980).

11. Korotich, V. "Taming of a Desert of the Mind," *Atlas* (June 1977).

12. Lau, J. B., and Jelinek, M. "Perception and Management," *Behavior in Organizations: An Experiential Approach* (Homewood, IL: Irwin, 1984), 213–220.

13. Maruyama, M. "Paradigms and Communication," *Technological Forecasting and Social Change, 6* (1974), 3–32.

14. Miles, M. *Adaptation to a Foreign Environment* (Hull, Quebec: Canadian International Development Agency, Briefing Centre, (1986).

15. Miller, J. G. "Adjusting to Overloads of Information," *The Association for Research in Nervous and Mental Disease, Disorders of Communication, 42* (Research Publications, A.R.N.M.D., 1964).

16. Prekel, T. "Multi-Cultural Communication: A Challenge to Managers," paper delivered at the International Convention of the American Business Communication Association, New York, November 21, 1983.

17. Ratui, I. "Thinking Internationally: A Comparison of How International Executives Learn" *International Studies of Management and Organization, 13*, no. 1–2 (1983), 139–150. Reprinted by permission of publisher, M. E. Sharpe, Inc., Armonk, N.Y.

18. Singer, M. "Culture: A Perceptual Approach," L. A. Samovar and R. E. Porter, eds., *Intercultural Communication: A Reader* (Belmont, Calif.: Wadsworth, 1976), 110–119.

19. Snyder, M. "Self-Fulfilling Stereotypes," *Psychology Today* (July 1982), 60–68.

20. *South China Morning Post*, "Mystery Man Gives a Fortune for Lucky '7'" (January 22, 1989), p. 3; and "Lucky '7' to Go on Sale" (January 4, 1989), 4.

21. Taylor, D. "American Tradition," R. G. Gardner and R. Kalin, eds., *A Canadian Social Psychology of Ethnic Relations* (Toronto: Methuen Press, 1980).

22. U.S. Office of Education, *On Teaching the Vietnamese* (Washington, D.C.: General Printing Office, 1976).

WHERE BIAS BEGINS:
THE TRUTH ABOUT STEREOTYPES*

Annie Murphy Paul

Psychologists once believed that only bigoted people used stereotypes. Now the study of unconscious bias is revealing the unsettling truth: We all use stereotypes, all the time, without knowing it. We have met the enemy of equality, and the enemy is us.

Mahzarin Banaji doesn't fit anybody's idea of a racist. A psychology professor at Yale University, she studies stereotypes for a living. And as a woman and a member of a minority ethnic group, she has felt firsthand the sting of discrimination. Yet when she took one of her own tests of unconscious bias, "I showed very strong prejudices," she says. "It was truly a disconcerting experience." And an illuminating one. When Banaji was in graduate school in the early 1980s, theories about stereotypes were concerned only with their explicit expression: outright and unabashed racism, sexism, anti-Semitism. But in the years since, a new approach to stereotypes has shattered that simple notion. The bias Banaji and her colleagues are studying is something far more subtle, and more insidious: what's known as automatic or implicit stereotyping, which, they find, we do all the time without knowing it. Though out-and-out bigotry may be on the decline, says Banaji, "if anything, stereotyping is a bigger problem than we ever imagined."

Previously, researchers who studied stereotyping had simply asked people to record their feelings about minority groups and had used their answers as an index of their attitudes. Psychologists now understand that these conscious replies are only half the story. How progressive a person seems to be on the surface bears little or no relation to how prejudiced he or she is on an unconscious level—so that a bleeding-heart liberal might harbor just as many biases as a neo-Nazi skinhead.

As surprising as these findings are, they confirmed the hunches of many students of human behavior. "Twenty years ago, we hypothesized that there were people who said they were not prejudiced but who really did have unconscious negative stereotypes and beliefs," says psychologist Jack Dovidio, Ph.D., of Colgate University. "It was like theorizing about the existence of a virus, and then one day seeing it under a microscope."

The test that exposed Banaji's hidden biases—and that this writer took as well, with equally dismaying results—is typical of the ones used by automatic stereotype researchers. It presents the subject with a series of positive or negative adjectives, each paired with a characteristically "white" or "black" name. As the name and word appear together on a computer screen, the person taking the test presses a key, indicating whether the word is good or bad. Meanwhile, the computer records the speed of each response.

A glance at subjects' response times reveals a startling phenomenon: Most people who participate in the experiment—even some African-Americans—respond more quickly when a positive word is paired with a white name or a negative word with a black name. Because our minds are more accustomed to making these associations, says Banaji, they process them more rapidly. Though the words and names aren't subliminal, they are presented so quickly that a subject's ability to make deliberate choices is diminished—allowing his or her underlying, assumptions to show through. The same technique can be used to measure stereotypes about many different social groups, such as homosexuals, women, and the elderly.

THE UNCONSCIOUS COMES INTO FOCUS

From these tiny differences in reaction speed—a matter of a few hundred milliseconds—the study of automatic stereotyping was born. Its immediate ancestor was the cognitive revolution of the 1970s, an explosion of psychological research into the way people think. After decades dominated by the study

---

*Reprinted with permission from *Psychology Today 31*, no. 3 (May-June 1998): 52–56.

of observable behavior, scientists wanted a closer look at the more mysterious operation of the human brain. And the development of computers—which enabled scientists to display information very quickly and to measure minute discrepancies in reaction time—permitted a peek into the unconscious.

At the same time, the study of cognition was also illuminating the nature of stereotypes themselves. Research done after World War II—mostly by European emigrés struggling to understand how the Holocaust had happened—concluded that stereotypes were used only by a particular type of person: rigid, repressed, authoritarian. Borrowing from the psychoanalytic perspective then in vogue, these theorists suggested that biased behavior emerged out of internal conflicts caused by inadequate parenting.

The cognitive approach refused to let the rest of us off the hook. It made the simple but profound point that we all use categories—of people, places, things—to make sense of the world around us. "Our ability to categorize and evaluate is an important part of human intelligence," says Banaji. "Without it, we couldn't survive." But stereotypes are too much of a good thing. In the course of stereotyping, a useful category—say, woman—becomes freighted with additional associations, usually negative. "Stereotypes are categories that have gone too far," says John Bargh, Ph.D., of New York University. "When we use stereotypes, we take in the gender, the age, the color of the skin of the person before us, and our minds respond with messages that say hostile, stupid, slow, weak. Those qualities aren't out there in the environment. They don't reflect reality."

Bargh thinks that stereotypes may emerge from what social psychologists call in-group/out-group dynamics. Humans, like other species, need to feel that they are part of a group, and as villages, clans, and other traditional groupings have broken down, our identities have attached themselves to more ambiguous classifications, such as race and class. We want to feel good about the group we belong to—and one way of doing so is to denigrate all those who aren't in it. And while we tend to see members of our own group as individuals, we view those in out-groups as an undifferentiated—stereotyped—mass. The categories we use have changed, but it seems that stereotyping itself is bred in the bone.

Though a small minority of scientists argue that stereotypes are usually accurate and can be relied upon without reservations, most disagree—and vehemently. "Even if there is a kernel of truth in the stereotype, you're still applying a generalization about a group to an individual, which is always incorrect," says Bargh. Accuracy aside, some believe that the use of stereotypes is simply unjust. "In a democratic society, people should be judged as individuals and not as members of a group," Banaji argues. "Stereotyping flies in the face of that ideal."

PREDISPOSED TO PREJUDICE

The problem, as Banaji's own research shows, is that people can't seem to help it. A recent experiment provides a good illustration. Banaji and her colleague, Anthony Greenwald, Ph.D., showed people a list of names—some famous, some not. The next day, the subjects returned to the lab and were shown a second list, which mixed names from the first list with new ones. Asked to identify which were famous, they picked out the Margaret Meads and the Miles Davises—but they also chose some of the names on the first list, which retained a lingering familiarity that they mistook for fame. (Psychologists call this the "famous overnight-effect.") By a margin of two-to-one, these suddenly "famous" people were male.

Participants weren't aware that they were preferring male names to female names, Banaji stresses. They were simply drawing, on an unconscious stereotype of men as more important and influential than women. Something similar happened when she showed subjects a list of people who might be criminals: without knowing they were doing so, participants picked out an overwhelming number of African-American names. Banaji calls this kind of stereotyping implicit, because people know they are making a judgment—but just aren't aware of the basis upon which they are making it.

Even further below awareness is something that psychologists call *automatic processing*, in which stereotypes are triggered by the slightest interaction or encounter. An experiment conducted by Bargh required a group of white participants to perform a tedious computer task. While performing the task, some of the participants were subliminally exposed to pictures of African-Americans with neutral expressions. When the subjects were then asked to do the task over again, the ones who had been exposed to the faces reacted with more hostility to the request—because, Bargh believes, they were responding in kind to the hostility which is part of the African-American stereotype. Bargh calls this the "immediate hostile reaction," which he believes can have a real effect on race relations. When African-Americans accurately perceive the hostile expressions that their white counterparts are unaware of, they may respond with hostility of their own—thereby perpetuating the stereotype.

Of course, we aren't completely under the sway of our unconscious. Scientists think that the automatic activation of a stereotype is immediately followed by a conscious check on unacceptable thoughts—at least in people who think that they are not prejudiced. This internal censor successfully restrains overtly biased responses. But there's still the danger of leakage, which often shows up in non-verbal behavior: our expressions, our stance, how far away we stand, how much eye contact we make.

The gap between what we say and what we do can lead African-Americans and whites to come away with very different impressions of the same encounter, says Jack Dovidio. "If I'm a white person talking to an African-American, I'm probably monitoring my conscious beliefs very carefully and making sure everything I say agrees with all the positive things I want to express," he says. "And I usually believe I'm pretty successful because I hear the right words coming out of my mouth." The listener who is paying attention to non-verbal behavior, however, may be getting quite the opposite message. An African-American student of Dovidio's recently told him that when she was growing up, her mother had taught her to observe how white people moved to gauge their true feelings toward blacks. "Her mother was a very astute amateur psychologist—and about 20 years ahead of me," he remarks.

WHERE DOES BIAS BEGIN?

So where exactly do these stealth stereotypes come from? Though automatic-stereotype researchers often refer to the unconscious they don't mean the Freudian notion of a seething mass of thoughts and desires, only some of which are deemed presentable enough to be admitted to the conscious mind. In fact, the cognitive model holds that information flows in exactly the opposite direction: connections made often enough in the conscious mind eventually become unconscious. Says Bargh: "If conscious choice and decision making are not needed, they go away. Ideas recede from consciousness into the unconscious over time."

Much of what enters our consciousness, of course, comes from the culture around us. And like the culture, it seems that our minds are split on the subjects of race, gender, class, sexual orientation. "We not only mirror the ambivalence we see in society, but also mirror it in precisely the same way," says Dovidio. Our society talks out loud about justice, equality, and egalitarianism, and most Americans accept these values as their own. At the same time, such equality exists only as an ideal, and that fact is not lost on our unconscious. Images of women as sex objects, footage of African-American criminals on the six o'clock news—"this is knowledge we cannot escape," explains Banaji. "We didn't choose to know it, but it still affects our behavior."

We learn the subtext of our culture's messages early. By five years of age, says Margo Monteith, Ph.D., many children have definite and entrenched stereotypes about blacks, women, and other social groups. Adds Monteith, professor of psychology at the University of Kentucky: "Children don't have a choice about accepting or rejecting these conceptions, since they're acquired well before they have the cognitive abilities or experiences to form their own beliefs." And no matter how progressive the parents, they must compete with all the forces that would promote and perpetuate these stereotypes: peer pressure, mass media, the actual balance of power in society. In fact, prejudice may be as much a result as a cause of this imbalance. We create stereotypes—African-Americans are lazy, women are emotional—to explain why things are the way they are. As Dovidio notes, "Stereotypes don't have to be true to serve a purpose."

WHY CAN'T WE ALL GET ALONG?

The idea of unconscious bias does clear up some nettlesome contradictions. "It accounts for a lot of people's ambivalence toward others who are different, a lot of their inconsistencies in behavior," says Dovidio. "It helps explain how good people can do bad things." But it also prompts some uncomfortable realizations. Because our conscious and unconscious beliefs may be very different—and because behavior often follows the lead of the latter—"good intentions aren't enough," as John Bargh puts it. In fact, he believes that they count for very little. "I don't think free will exists," he says, bluntly—because what feels like the exercise of free will may be only the application of unconscious assumptions.

Not only may we be unable to control our biased responses, we may not even be aware that we have them. "We have to rely on our memories and our awareness of what we're doing to have a connection to reality," says Bargh. "But when it comes to automatic processing, those cues can be deceptive." Likewise, we can't always be sure how biased others are. "We all have this belief that the important thing about prejudice is the external expression of it," says Banaji. "That's going to be hard to give up."

One thing is certain: We can't claim that we've eradicated prejudice just because its outright expression has waned. What's more, the strategies that were so effective in reducing that sort of bias won't work on unconscious beliefs. "What this research is saying is that we are going to have to change dramatically the way we think can influence people's behaviors," says Banaji. "It would be naive to think that exhortation is enough." Exhortation, education, political protest—all of these hammer away at our conscious beliefs while leaving the bedrock below untouched. Banaji notes, however, that one traditional remedy for discrimination—affirmative action—may still be effective since it bypasses our unconsciously compromised judgment.

But some stereotype researchers think that the solution to automatic stereotyping lies in the process itself. Through practice, they say, people can weaken the mental links that connect minorities to negative stereotypes and strengthen the ones that connect them to positive conscious beliefs. Margo Monteith explains how it might work. "Suppose you're at a party and someone tells a racist joke—and you laugh," she says. "Then you realize that you shouldn't have laughed at the joke. You feel guilty and become focused on your thought processes. Also, all sorts of cues become associated with laughing at the racist joke: the person who told the joke, the act of telling jokes, being at a party, drinking." The next time you encounter these cues, "a warning signal of sorts should go off—'wait, didn't you mess up in this situation before?'—and your responses will be slowed and executed with greater restraint."

That slight pause in the processing of a stereotype gives conscious, unprejudiced beliefs a chance to take over. With time, the tendency to prevent automatic stereotyping may itself become automatic. Monteith's research suggests that, given enough motivation, people may be able to teach themselves to inhibit prejudice so well that even their tests of implicit bias come clean.

The success of this process of "de-automatization" comes with a few caveats, however. First, even its proponents concede that it works only for people disturbed by the discrepancy between their conscious and unconscious beliefs, since unapologetic racists or sexists have no motivation to change. Second, some studies have shown that attempts to suppress stereotypes may actually cause them to return later, stronger than ever. And finally, the results that Monteith and other researchers have achieved in the laboratory may not stick in the real world, where people must struggle to maintain their commitment to equality under less-than-ideal conditions.

Challenging though that task might be, it is not as daunting as the alternative researchers suggest: changing society itself. Bargh, who likens de-automatization to closing the barn door once the horses have escaped, says that "it's clear that the way to get rid of stereotypes is by the roots, by where they come from in the first place." The study of culture may someday tell us where the seeds of prejudice originated; for now, the study of the unconscious shows us just how deeply they're planted.

▲▲

CHAPTER 9
GROUP DYNAMICS AND WORK TEAMS

CRITICAL SUCCESS FACTORS FOR CREATING SUPERB SELF-MANAGING TEAMS
Ruth Wageman

VIRTUAL TEAMS: THE NEW WAY TO WORK
Jessica Lipnack
Jeffrey Stamps

Understanding group dynamics has always been an important skill; the proliferation of teams in the workplace, however, has focused even more attention on this area. More and more companies are relying on self-managed work teams. This trend has empowered employees and thinned the ranks of middle managers, whose tasks, in many cases, are now carried out by teams.

Ruth Wageman, business professor and consultant, lists many good arguments in "Critical Success Factors for Creating Superb Self-Managing Teams" for using teams while acknowledging that the reality is not always quite so rosy. Wageman and her research colleagues asked managers to identify Xerox teams that were either superb or ineffective. She describes the seven critical success factors that were present in the superb teams and absent in the ineffective teams. Wageman makes yet another contribution to our mental maps about the role of managers by outlining the leader's role in the life of the team.

One of the hottest topics in business is virtual teams. Thanks to technology, it is no longer necessary for team members to share the same physical space. Team members and companies have been feeling their way with this recent organizational animal. Much of the "first to market" knowledge in this area is coming from the consulting field. Jessica Lipnack and Jeffrey Stamps, husband and wife co-chief executive officers of a consulting company, are the authors of "Virtual Teams: The New Way To Work." They present a model for virtual teams and examples from their work with businesses. They refer to the double bottom line in teams—the task and social capital. This is similar to the task and process aspects traditionally found in discussions of group dynamics.

At the end of the Lipnack and Stamps article, you'll find a list of "Tips For Virtual Teams" that we compiled from recent books on virtual teams.

≈

CRITICAL SUCCESS FACTORS
FOR CREATING SUPERB SELF–MANAGING TEAMS*

Ruth Wageman

Self-managing teams are fast becoming the management practice of choice for organizations that wish to become more flexible, push decision making to the front lines, and fully use employees' intellectual

---

*Reprinted with permission from *Organizational Dynamics* (Summer 1997): 49–61.

and creative capacities. Indeed, claims for the astounding potential of teamwork in general and self-managing teams in particular are abundant and increasing. Partisans of teamwork claim that organizations need teams to compete; and the proliferation of manufacturing teams, cross-functional teams, quality teams, and the like suggest that managers are listening.

The central principle behind self-managing teams is that the teams themselves, rather than managers, take responsibility for their work, monitor their own performance, and alter their performance strategies as needed to solve problems and adapt to changing conditions. This way of running an organization's day-to-day activities is said to:

- enhance the company's performance, because those closest to the customer and best able to respond to customer demands have the authority to meet those demands;
- enhance organizational learning and adaptability, because members of self-managing teams have the latitude to experiment with their work and to develop strategies that are uniquely suited to tasks; and
- enhance employees' commitment to the organization, because self-managing teams offer wider participation in and ownership of important organizational decisions.

Clearly, self-managing teams have the potential to make a multifaceted contribution to an organization's competitiveness.

WHY, THEN, MIXED RESULTS?

What sounds straightforward in principle—a change in authority—turns out to be troublesome in practice. While numerous examples of the gains to performance, learning, and commitment attributed to self-managing teams are offered in evidence of their value, an increasing number of organizations are becoming disenchanted with the idea. Managers observe slow and sometimes nonexistent progress in team members' efforts to take on responsibility for decisions that previously belonged to managers. They note that many teams continue to operate much as they always have: Members divide their work and do it independently, showing little inclination to join in a collective effort to improve their work strategies, take responsibility for difficult decisions, or solve problems.

These dysfunctions are not surprising when one considers that, in many U.S. companies, teamwork is an "unnatural act." These organizations have long histories of hierarchical decision making cemented with a work ethic based on individual achievement. Given this culture and context, team members will balk at the idea of relying on one another to get work done.

For all their claimed promise, then, many self-managing teams never contribute to organization performance and adaptability because they never operate as intended. This raises a critical question for many organizations: How can managers get teams to take on self-management and ensure that those teams will perform superbly—especially if this means bucking a long history of manager-directed, individualistic work?

CASE IN POINT: CUSTOMER SERVICE TEAMS AT XEROX

This is precisely the question that faced the Xerox Corporation's Customer Service organization. "Working solo" was part of this unit's culture. In fact, the customer service engineers (CSEs) were hired, in part, because of their ability to work alone, independently, and without supervision.

For many years, each individual CSE handled specific territories and customer accounts. This changed when the unit's senior management created interdependent self-managing teams, each composed of multiple CSEs who would share responsibility for the team's collective customers. Moreover, the groups would be responsible for more than simply fixing equipment—they would design maintenance procedures for their many kinds of machines, analyze and monitor the machines' performance levels, manage the costs of their work, and solve the problems created by unpredictable customer needs.

In many cases, management intended the groups to go even further in the decisions they made: Teams would select their own members, provide peer feedback, and assist in the design of support systems. The Xerox teams provide the main point of contact between the company and its customers—and their effectiveness is critical to the company's ultimate success.

How well do these self-managed service teams actually function? In general, the results are quite positive. But a closer look shows that the teams vary in the degree to which they have embraced self-management and matured into the proactive problem-solving units they were intended to be. Consider two examples, selected from our observations of the Xerox teams.

One team of veteran CSEs approached their machine maintenance responsibilities in a way that was distinctively different from the other groups. When our researchers asked what was going on, a team member explained that they were running an experiment. The team was attempting to increase the time certain copier parts lasted by cleaning related machine areas more frequently. Each team member was trying this process on several machines and recording the length of time that the parts lasted. If the experiment proved successful, they could make substantial savings in parts expenses.

This same team conducted a team meeting after work hours, giving our researchers an opportunity to see its problem-solving dynamics in action. A team member who had been absent earlier in the day explained that he was actually on vacation and had come in just for the meeting. We asked if this happened often. "When we need to," he replied. "We're in charge of our own schedules, so we have to make our vacation plans work with no decrease in care for our customers. All of us have come in on vacation days at some time or another when the call rate got too high for the rest of the team to handle."

We observed a second team, also composed of veteran CSEs, as it reviewed performance data at a group meeting. This team's leader (first-line manager) presented graphical data indicating problems with machine reliability—customers often had to call back to fix repeated problems. What was the team going to do about it? He put this question on the table, then left the meeting, expecting that the group would analyze and solve the problem.

Once the leader had gone, however, the conversation took a different tack. Some team members focused on problems with the data: "It's more than a month old. Who knows if that's even accurate anymore?" Others laid the problem at the feet of their customers: "Some of these call-backs are for trivial problems, and at least one of those machines was abused." Still others chose not to participate in the conversation: "Those aren't my customers."

While these critiques of the data and the customers may have been accurate, the conversation avoided any focus on what could be done—even on how to get better data or how to manage their customers better to prevent machine abuse.

While both teams had responsibility for managing their own work, the degree to which real self-management was expressed in their actual behavior varied dramatically. Members of teams that are genuinely managing themselves show three basic characteristics in the way they approach their work:

- They take personal responsibility for the outcomes of their team's work.
- They monitor their own work performance, actively seeking data about how well they are performing.
- They alter their performance strategies as needed, creating suitable solutions to work problems.

All these signs were visible in the first team discussed above, and all were absent in the second.

A QUESTION OF LEVERAGE: DESIGN OR COACHING?

How can leaders help their teams become more like the first team? Where should they concentrate their resources and energy to help guide their teams toward effective, proactive self-management? A fast-growing body of advice centers on two basic influences: (1) how the team is set up and supported and (2) how the team's leader (or coach) behaves in his or her day-to-day interactions with the team.

Although some research addresses team design features such as team composition and organizational reward systems, a much larger body of writings focuses on the second influence—leader behavior vis-à-vis the team. Many consulting practices, skill-assessment instruments, and training courses address how the role of the manager/leader needs to change, from directing and controlling the work to coaching the team as it decides how best to get its work done.

Just how important is high-quality coaching relative to high-quality team design? To find out, we conducted an in-depth examination of 43 self-managing teams in the Xerox service organization. The researchers looked at both the basic design features of the teams and the day-to-day actions of team leaders to see which of these had the greater impact on effective team self-management. The study sought to answer the following question: "If we have limited resources (such as time and money), what critical few factors should we focus on to increase the chances our self-managing teams will be superb?"

A CLOSE LOOK AT THE DIFFERENCES

To launch the research, we first asked Xerox managers to identify teams that were either superb or ineffective. Superb teams (a) consistently met the needs of their customers, (b) appeared to be operating with increasing effectiveness over time, and (c) were made up of members who were engaged in and satisfied with their work. Ineffective teams (a) frequently failed to meet customer needs, (b) appeared to be operating increasingly poorly over time, and (c) were made up of members who were alienated from or dissatisfied with their work.

The researchers then assessed a wide variety of team features to determine which most strongly differentiated between the superb and the ineffective. Each self-managing team participated in a two-hour interview, describing their history, their work, and the context in which they operated. Their first-line managers provided extensive descriptions of how these teams were set up and supported. Finally, each team member completed an extensive survey describing the team, its interactions, and its environment.

Team self-management was measured by assessing such behaviors as the degree to which the team monitored its own performance and acted to improve its work strategies without waiting for direction.

Researchers also measured a range of coaching behaviors, some of which were expected to promote self-management, others to undermine it. Appropriate coaching included sending cues that the team was responsible for its own performance, providing timely feedback and information, and helping the team develop problem-solving strategies. Ineffective coaching included intervening in the team's day-to-day work and providing solutions to team problems.

Design factors covered a wide range of features, including team composition, team size, the design of the task, the design of the reward system, and many others (see Exhibit 1 for a list of the full range of potential influences assessed).

These measures allowed a direct test of the question, Which makes a bigger difference in team self-management and performance: how well leaders coach their teams, or how well the teams are designed and supported?

Design Features
1. Clear, engaging direction
2. Task interdependence
3. Authority to manage the work
4. Performance goals
5. Skill diversity of team members
6. Demographic diversity of team members
7. Team size
8. Length of time the team has had stable membership
9. Group rewards
10. Information resources
11. Availability of training
12. Basic material resources

Coaching Behaviors
Potential positive influences:
1. Providing reinforcers and other cues that the group is responsible for managing itself
2. Appropriate problem-solving consultation
3. Dealing with interpersonal problems in the team through team-process consultation
4. Attending team meetings*
5. Providing organization-related data*

Potential negative influences:
1. Signaling that individuals (or the leader/manager) were responsible for the team's work
2. Intervening in the task
3. Identifying the team's problems
4. Overriding group decisions**

---

*Because all leaders engaged in this behavior, it was impossible to determine whether it influenced team behavior.
**Because very few leaders engaged in this behavior, it was impossible to determine whether it influenced team effectiveness.

EXHIBIT 1   Potential Influences on Team Self-Management Measured in the Research

CRITICAL INGREDIENTS FOR TEAM SELF-MANAGEMENT

We asked 43 team leaders (the first-line managers) to draw on their considerable experience and predict how our research would answer this question. Almost without exception, they chose coaching as the critical differentiating factor—and they were wrong.

The quality of a team's design, our data showed, actually had a larger effect on its level of self-management than coaching—by a wide margin. Well-designed teams show far stronger signs of self-managing than poorly designed teams. While high-quality coaching does influence how well a team manages itself, it does so to a much smaller degree.

For team leaders, a most important finding to note is the joint effect of design and coaching. Exhibit 2 shows how quality of design and coaching work together to influence team self-management. The first diagram shows the influence of high-quality coaching on well-designed vs. poorly designed teams. Note that good coaching had a far more powerful effect on well-designed teams than on poorly designed ones. The implication is that teams whose leaders are good coaches are better self-managers only when the team structures are well designed.

Teams that had many of the critical design features in place became even more self-managing when their leaders provided effective coaching—for example, helping the team build its problem-solving repertoire. Poorly designed teams hardly responded at all to good coaching. Leaders who tried to help a poorly designed team had almost no impact on the team's ability to self-manage, despite the fact that the leaders followed the principles of effective coaching.

Moreover, ineffective coaching had a much more detrimental effect on poorly designed teams than on well-designed teams. At the same time, coaching errors (such as intervening in the team's

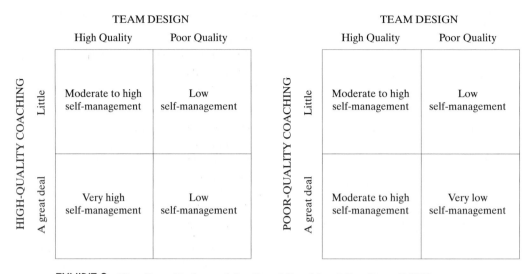

EXHIBIT 2   **How Team Design and Quality of Coaching Affect Team Self-Management**

work and overriding decisions) had very little negative impact on well-designed teams. These teams were robust enough to remain highly self-managing in spite of a leader's blunders—whereas poorly designed teams were hindered by such errors. (The second panel in Exhibit 2 shows the influence of poor coaching on well-designed vs. poorly designed teams.)

These findings suggest that the first step in creating effective self-managing teams is to get the team designed right. Only then does it make sense to tackle the hands-on coaching and counseling that are part of a leader's day-to-day interactions with the team. To have the greatest possible influence, then, a team leader needs:

1. knowledge of the design factors that most strongly influence the effectiveness of self-managing teams;
2. the diagnostic skills to tell which factors are present and which are absent; and
3. the ability to act—to put the missing factors in place.

The following discussion addresses each of these three issues. We first focus on the seven critical success factors that the study revealed had the most impact. To address the second issue, we present a set of diagnostic questions to help assess whether a particular factor is in place for a team. To address the third area, the discussion of critical factors includes examples of actions leaders took to put high quality design factors in place.

CRITICAL SUCCESS FACTORS

Seven features emerged as the ones most likely to be seen in superb teams and not in ineffective teams. Collectively, they were strongly related to a wide range of performance measures such as customer satisfaction, speed of response to customer calls, and expense management.

Moreover, each factor is something that team leaders can influence. That is, first-line managers can determine whether or not their teams have each supportive feature and can take action to get the missing ingredients in place. The seven success factors are discussed in descending order of importance.

FACTOR 1: CLEAR, ENGAGING DIRECTION

Superb teams, far more than ineffective ones, have a clear and engaging direction—a sense of why the group exists and what it is trying to accomplish. One team, for example, stated its mission as follows: "This team exists to keep customers so pleased with Xerox that they will remain with Xerox; and the team aims to do so in a way that uses Xerox resources as efficiently as possible." This statement of direction is exemplary for the following reasons:

1. It is clear and simple. That is, it contains only a few objectives. But those objectives can orient the team and allow its members to make intelligent trade-offs. Faced with a decision regarding whether a course of action is sensible, the statement invites the team to ask "Would this action please the customer, and would it do so without excessive cost to Xerox?"
2. It specifies the ends, but not the means. That is, it is clear about the team's purpose but does not say how the team should get there. Research has shown that this is the best way to enhance team motivation—a leader should be clear about where the team is going and let the team choose the path.

Two common errors in setting direction emerged from the study: (1) failing to set any direction at all and (2) setting a direction that is all about means—the how—but doesn't specify ends—the why. The first error occurs when leaders assume "we all know what we're here for" and launch the team without a discussion of its basic purpose. The second error occurs when there is excessive specification of how a team should operate. This undermines members' motivation to manage themselves.

FACTOR 2: A REAL TEAM TASK

A self-managing team requires work that is designed to be done by a team. That is, basic elements of the work should require members to work *together* to complete significant tasks. Spending time together as a whole team is critical—especially in organizations where members have little experience with teamwork.

In the Xerox customer service teams, the basic task elements included sharing responsibility for all its customers (vs. having customers assigned to specific individuals), managing expenses, designing basic work practices, and solving problems. Groups with real team tasks do all these things collectively. That is, they have no individual territories—rather, members respond to calls from any of the team's customers (often consulting about which member should handle a particular call). They design their work practices collectively and monitor members' compliance with those practices; they meet every week or two; they are fully cross-trained and are thus able to help each other at any time; and they are given a group budget, with only group-level information about expenses—that is, they manage the parts budget as a group.

Two common task design errors are (1) creating a "team-in-name-only"; or worse, (2) designing a task that only occasionally requires a real team. The first error involves designating some group of individuals a team without changing the nature of the work. Previous research has shown that such teams perform relatively well, but only because they continue to operate precisely as they had before—as a loose collection of individuals. They learn little from each other, cooperate infrequently, and make few decisions collectively.

The second design error—creating a task that sometimes requires significant team activity, sometimes significant individual activity—results in what can be called a "hybrid" task. In this study, a typical hybrid task design asked the team to handle one set of activities as a team (for example, members designed their work practices as a collective, met occasionally, and managed expenses for the group as a whole) and another set of tasks individually (for example, members had specific customers and product specialties).

Hybrid task designs create difficulties for teams because they send mixed signals to the group about whether or not this really is a team. The pull in both directions—to operate alone and to operate as a team—leaves these groups floundering, as some members attend more to their solo tasks than to collective activities. Moreover, hybrid designs prevent a group from investing significant time in learning how to operate effectively as a team. And when members work together only periodically, they discover that much of their "together" time is more difficult and less effective than their "solo" time. In the end, both team members and their leaders may be convinced that teamwork is not such a good idea after all.

This issue is a particular problem for organizations in which members are relatively inexperienced at teamwork—as many U.S. companies are. Self-managing teams need a task that is defined as a team task, that is measured as a team task, and that requires the members to spend a great deal of time accomplishing something together. A task designed this way creates the opportunity—indeed, the necessity—of learning how to operate effectively as a unit.

FACTOR 3: REWARDS FOR TEAM EXCELLENCE

This study, as well as previous research, shows that team rewards (not individual or mixed rewards) are strongly associated with superior team self-management. In our study, teams were considered to have team rewards if at least 80 percent of the available rewards were distributed equally among team members. The exceptions to this were (1) small rewards from the leader that are given to individual team members for actions that supported the team and (2) rewards given to the team as a whole but distributed differentially by team members themselves.

The use of mixed rewards—about half provided to individuals and half to the team—emerged as the most common error in reward system design. Leaders tend to provide mixed rewards for the same reason they create "hybrid" tasks—they assume that it is best to introduce team members gradually to the idea of being fully dependent on each other. Like hybrid tasks, mixed rewards send mixed signals to the team and undermine its ability to operate as an effective unit.

This success factor is often a major challenge for front-line managers interested in getting the design right for their teams. It often requires exercising upward influence in the organization to redesign established reward systems. This has been an uncomfortable process in many organizations, especially in cases where employees have participated in designing the former individual merit system. In these cases, getting group rewards in place means a leader must exercise authority over the teams themselves and create an appropriate team-based reward structure. Some lingering discomfort remains in many companies—among managers and employees alike—about "group-only" rewards. But, contrary to what many managers believe, rewards that are about 50/50 individual/group are associated with the lowest team performance.

FACTOR 4: BASIC MATERIAL RESOURCES

These are the physical materials the team needs: the tools, appropriate meeting space, access to computing services, and other resources that make it possible for the team to work in a timely, proactive, and effective fashion. Teams that had such resources readily available strongly outperformed teams that did not. My observations suggest that leaders are sometimes reluctant to provide resources to struggling teams, under the premise that "they haven't learned to manage them yet." But this very lack of resources may be among the factors demoralizing the team and preventing it from embracing self-management.

Some leaders dealt with their reluctance to hand over resources to struggling teams by engaging the teams in a discussion of resources they really needed to perform well. They then negotiated an agreement in which the teams committed to tackling particular performance problems in exchange for additional resources. Such practices helped the teams see more clearly what they needed to do—and assured them that they would have the basic materials necessary to solve their work problems.

FACTOR 5: AUTHORITY TO MANAGE THE WORK

Authority to manage the work means that the team—and not the leader—has decision rights over basic work strategies. We asked teams and their leaders to tell us who—the leader, the team, or some combination—made decisions about basic day-to-day tasks. In this study, such tasks might include deciding which customer call to take next, how to allocate tasks to team members, how to schedule their time when members were away at training, and how to solve customer problems. These are decisions about the work itself—how the basic tasks are accomplished. Teams with the prerogative to make these decisions themselves, without interference from their leader, strongly outperformed those that did not.

While many of these decisions might "officially" belong to the team, some leaders frequently intervened—for example, by monitoring call rates during the day or asking a team member to take a particular call. These interventions compromise a team's sense of ownership for the work. Moreover, when things go wrong, they can easily attribute the cause to their leaders rather than to themselves. Leaders' ambivalence about the teams' authority erodes the very purpose of having self-managed teams.

By contrast, the leaders of the more effective teams explicitly addressed the teams' authority and the boundaries around it. And they made it clear that they were available for consultation—but that the ultimate decision-making authority for solving work problems belonged to the team.

What about decisions regarding distribution of rewards, team involvement in performance appraisal, and changes in team membership? Should the team decide these issues as well? Actually, these are decisions about the context in which the team operates—different from decisions about managing the work itself. The study discovered that leaders tend to empower teams with this kind of decision making once they have matured into high-performance units capable of making solid decisions about the work itself.

FACTOR 6: TEAM GOALS

This critical success factor refers to whether the team has performance goals that are congruent with the organization's objectives. Unlike the team's statement of its overall purpose, goals are specific (often quantified) descriptions of work the team is to accomplish within a specific time frame. In this study, we classified a team as having such goals if members could articulate what they wanted to accomplish as a team by some clear deadline: "maintaining 100 percent customer satisfaction this year," or "improving our customer satisfaction performance by 2.5 percent and our parts expense performance by 5 percent this year."

In some cases, the leader set these goals, and in some cases, the team itself did. For a goal to enhance performance, it had to be congruent with the team's overall direction, challenging, and completed by a specified deadline. For example, one team said that its goal was to become the best-performing team in the district by the end of the year; another identified "over-achieving the performance targets of the district by the end of the second quarter" as its goal.

FACTOR 7: TEAM NORMS THAT PROMOTE STRATEGIC THINKING

Norms are the informal rules that guide team members' behavior. Our findings showed that norms which promote strategic thinking about work issues were related to team effectiveness. Self-managing teams, unlike manager-led teams, require an outward focus on the part of team members—they must be aware of their environment, able to detect problems, and accustomed to developing novel ways of working.

This kind of forward thinking may not come naturally to teams, especially if members shoulder greater responsibility than they ever had before. But group norms that promote proactive strategic thinking are very important for effective team self-management.

Superb teams encourage members to (1) experiment with new ways to work more effectively, (2) seek best practices from other teams and other parts of the organization, (3) take action to solve problems without waiting for direction, and (4) discuss differences in what each member has to contribute to the work. These are all ways in which the team encourages a proactive stance toward problems and increases its responsiveness to changing demands.

Norms emerge naturally in teams, regardless of whether a leader attempts to guide their development. However, norms that are left to emerge on their own often do not support strategic planning. Leaders can—and should—help appropriate norms develop. One way to do this, as demonstrated by the Xerox managers, is to recognize and reinforce strategic thinking early in the team's life. If, for example, a team notes a trend in customers' needs and brainstorms approaches to that opportunity, the leader can reinforce that behavior through praise and rewards. Modeling long-term planning and rewarding teams that think strategically about their work increased the chances that the members themselves would support and encourage such behavior within the group.

Another distinction of note emerges from the comparison of well-designed and poorly designed teams. In the former, such norms were more likely to emerge naturally, and they were even more likely to take root when a leader explicitly encouraged them. The implication is that when a leader gets the other six critical success factors in place, norms that supported active problem-solving and strategic thinking tend to take hold more quickly and to be more carefully maintained by team members. Tackling the other six factors first greatly increased the chances that a leader was successful in building appropriate team norms.

ON COACHING WELL

For many team leaders, the struggle to learn how to coach effectively has been a difficult one. It requires new behaviors that differ widely from their old habits of directing and coordinating work. Such habits are difficult to unlearn. For these leaders, the study findings on team design should come as good news: Once their teams are designed well, leaders have the latitude to experiment with their own behavior and learn how to coach effectively. If their teams are set up right, a leader's coaching errors will not harm the teams much. And as leaders develop their coaching skills, they will see much more evidence of their effectiveness.

We collected behavioral descriptions from teams and their leaders regarding how the leader spent his or her time in day-to-day interactions with the team. We used these data to assess which kinds of common coaching behaviors were positively or negatively related to effective team self-management. Among the leader behaviors that helped a team were:

- providing rewards and other signals that the team is responsible for managing itself (e.g., rewarding the team for solving a problem; spending more time in interaction with the group as a whole, rather than with individuals); and
- broadening the team's repertoire of problem-solving skills (e.g., teaching the team how to use a problem-solving process; facilitating problem-solving discussions without imposing one's own view of a solution).

These behaviors underscored the team's responsibility for its own outcomes, motivated the team to tackle problems as a group, and enhanced members' basic self-management skills.

Among the coaching behaviors that undermined a team were:

- signaling that individuals (or the manager/leader) were responsible for managing the team (e.g., by spending more time with individuals than with the team; by running team meetings rather than coaching the team on how to run its own meetings effectively); and
- intervening in the task in ways that undermined the team's authority (e.g., monitoring team actions and assigning a team member a particular responsibility; dealing directly with a team's customer without involving the team; and overriding a team decision—even if it seemed to be a poor one).

Coaching behaviors do influence whether the team takes responsibility for its work and monitors and manages its own performance. The most critical thing to remember about coaching is that, as we saw above, high-quality coaching had much more positive influence on teams that already had the majority of the critical success factors in place.

THE ROLE OF THE LEADER

Why were leaders so convinced that their day-to-day coaching was the key to effective self-management? Perhaps it is because their ongoing interactions with teams are highly visible. By contrast, team design is invisible—part of the background. But, as we have seen, those background elements are of critical importance.

Do leaders matter? The findings of this study might be taken to imply that leaders don't matter much. A better interpretation is that our emphasis on a leader's day-to-day coaching is misplaced. After all, setting up a team right in the first place and ensuring that it has the needed resources are critical leadership functions. The elements of team design discussed here are all features that a leader or first-line manager can and should influence.

Exhibit 3 presents a guide to help leaders determine where their leadership is most needed to get their teams set up right. The guide can serve as a diagnostic tool to determine which of the critical success factors need most attention.

EXHIBIT 3   Critical Success Factors: Diagnostic Questions for Team Leaders

1. **Clear direction**
   Can team members articulate a clear direction, shared by all members, of the basic purpose that the team exists to achieve?

2. **A real team task**
   Is the team assigned collective responsibility for all the team's customers and major outputs?
   Is the team required to make collective decisions about work strategies (rather than leaving it to individuals)?
   Are members cross-trained, able to help each other?
   Does the team get team-level data and feedback about its performance?
   Is the team required to meet frequently, and does it do so?

3. **Team rewards**
   Counting all reward dollars available, are more than 80 percent available to teams only, and not to individuals?

4. **Basic material resources**
   Does the team have its own meeting space?
   Can the team easily get basic materials needed for the work?

5. **Authority to manage the work**
   Does the team have the authority to decide the following (without first receiving special authorization)?
   ■ How to meet client demands
   ■ Which actions to take, and when
   ■ Whether to change their work strategies when they deem necessary

6. **Team goals**
   Can the team articulate specific goals?
   Do these goals stretch their performance?
   Have they specified a time by which they intend to accomplish these goals?

7. **Strategy norms**
   Do team members encourage each other to detect problems without the leader's intervention?
   Do members openly discuss differences in what members have to contribute to the team?
   Do members encourage experimentation with new ways of operating?
   Does the team actively seek to learn from other teams?

ON LEADERSHIP AND TIMING

Leaders do have an important role in the life of teams—but that role differs at various stages in the team's life. It is useful to look back at the critical success factors to see how the leader's role changes as he or she takes action to get all the pieces in place.

Role 1: Designer (critical success factors one through five)   This role is most critical when the team is first launched. The leader's action at this stage is to set a direction for the performing unit, design a team task and a team reward system, make sure the team has the basic material resources it needs to do the work, and establish the team's authority over and its responsibility for its performance strategies. These actions serve to get a team started in the right direction and with the right supports for high-quality performance.

Role 2: Midwife (critical success factors six and seven)   This role becomes important after the team is launched; it is best played at natural break-points in the team's work. In this role, the leader works with the team to establish appropriate performance goals. Goals represent measurable aims that specify how a team will take on its work in ways that fulfill its overall direction. Consequently, the critical factors related to task and direction must be firmly in place.

The leader also helps establish norms about strategic thinking, thus influencing how the team uses its resources and authority. In shaping these norms, the leader is helping the team develop work strategies that use the team's decision-making power over how it operates. This keeps the team moving in an upward direction—toward growth and excellence.

Role 3: Coach   Finally, the coaching role takes over and continues throughout the life of the team. With the critical success factors in place, the team is now positioned to take full advantage of high-quality coaching. This means that the time and energy a leader invests in day-to-day coaching will be resources well used, not wasted effort. Moreover, because well-designed teams are robust enough to bounce back from inappropriate leader actions, the leader now has the latitude to unlearn old managerial habits and take the time that is needed to learn effective team coaching skills.

CONCLUSION

The seven critical success factors matter for anyone leading a team—from front-line managers leading shop-floor teams to senior managers launching problem-solving groups. Indeed, the messages here may be especially critical for senior managers. Putting the success factors in place may require organization-wide changes—in reward systems, in work design, in resources available to teams. Because it is middle and senior managers who have the most opportunity and authority to change these design features, it is particularly critical that they be aware of what teams require throughout the organization. Putting these factors in place gives the organization the greatest possible chance of getting the creativity, flexibility, and responsiveness that are the whole point of building self-managing teams.

VIRTUAL TEAMS: THE NEW WAY TO WORK*

Jessica Lipnack
Jeffrey Stamps

Twenty-first century problems require 21st century organizations. The bureaucratic-hierarchical pattern that characterizes almost all organizations today was developed in the industrial age of 19th

---

*Reprinted with permission from *Strategy and Leadership* 27, no. 1 (January-February 1999): 14–19.

century. Then people had to be in the same place if they were to work together. As we move into the 21st century, the broad array of communication options permits the refiguring of our organizations in order to meet the rapidly changing demands of the business environment.

THE AGE OF THE NETWORK

The 21st century organization is made up of virtual teams and networks of teams. The network—rather than the pyramid—becomes the conceptual model for how people work together to accomplish the goals of the enterprise. A physical model of a networked organization would look like one of Buckminster Fuller's geodesic domes—many tetrahedrons joined together at key intersections. One of the interesting things about the geodesic dome is that it's the only built structure in the universe that gets stronger as it gets larger. A networked organization can increase in effectiveness as it grows. In team-based organizations, networks can help teams avoid a sense of fragmentation and isolation. Networks can even extend beyond the boundaries of a single organization. There are networks of organizations, networks of companies, and networks of nations.

Virtual teams and networked organizations are the latest stage in the evolution of organization. In the nomadic era, the small group was the first organization people invented. Hierarchy evolved rapidly in the agricultural era, as towns of 10,000 or more developed. The industrial era required a more robust form of organization—so bureaucracies emerged.[1] And finally, as we moved into the information era, another form of organization began to appear. This new form has been called by many names, but in essence it is a networked organization.

The networked organization will not wipe out all the old forms. Rather, it includes them and adds new capabilities. When hierarchies formed, we didn't lose the ability to work in small groups. A complex, networked organization will, in fact, involve hierarchy, bureaucracy, and small groups, as well as distinctly networked relationships. The key is to select the best form of organization for a particular kind of work.

Hierarchy is a fundamental principle of organization in the universe. Our cells, organs, organisms, and communities are all based on hierarchies. We don't want to lose the structure, but we need to change the one-way paths of information, which create bottlenecks.

A hierarchy alone is a tall structure without much of a horizontal base. Bureaucracies are formed as organizations spread out and work is divided into specialized departments. This lateral extension helps to create a stronger structure, which is able to grow larger and handle more complexity. But this organization is still quite vulnerable to change. In particular, any pressure on the top of the structure could cause the whole thing to collapse.

The easiest way to transition from hierarchy/bureaucracy to a networked organization is to add links to connect the various functions. The result is a strong but flexible geodesic structure based on connected tetrahedrons—a structure better able to resist the impact of change. Bureaucratic specialization is not going away, but the new links allow communication to flow horizontally as well as vertically, and precious time is saved. Gradually, a new form of organization will emerge.

All four of these ways of organizing coexist in many organizations. Exhibit 1 shows the organization chart of Eastman Chemical Company. It's not a metaphor for the organization chart—it's the actual way the company's chief executive, Earnest Deavenport, drew it.

The hierarchy is in the hub-and-spoke design. It has the same logic as a tree diagram, but putting it in a wheel gives it a very different sense. The bureaucracy is there in that each of the circles has a different name and focuses on a specific purpose, The thick outer line defines the boundary of the organization. The white space in the chart is where all the connections are, and that's what makes it a networked organization. Communication goes directly between the people who need the information and the people who have it.

Eastman uses self-managed teams at all levels. For example, the presidents of each of the manufacturing facilities have formed a Presidents' Council, and the role of executive vice president for

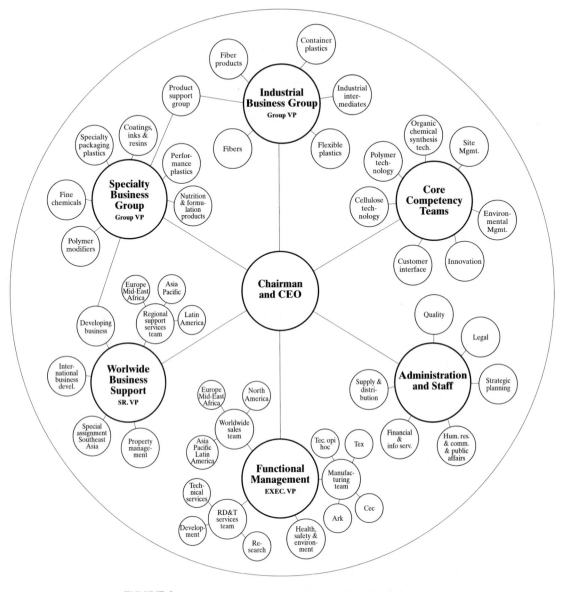

EXHIBIT 1   **Organization Chart of Eastman Chemical Company**

manufacturing rotates every quarter. They have assembled an information system that keeps everyone up to date as the responsibility passes from one person to the next.

One of the earliest companies to move in this direction where information flows quickly is Buckman Labs, a specialty chemical company located in Memphis. While he was confined to bed after back surgery, Bob Buckman, then the company's chief executive, realized that their traditional way of solving problems was not very cost effective.

At that time, if a customer had a problem, Buckman Labs typically would send its most experienced person out to the customer's site to work on it. For a company that does business all over the world, this became very costly. The solution was to put all 1,200 people at Buckman Labs on-line. That was 10 years ago, and the technology they used was CompuServe—not Lotus Notes, not web pages, not even live chats on CompuServe, but CompuServe forums. The discussions went on 24 hours a day, and problems were solved quickly. Even with what we would today consider primitive technology for this purpose, Buckman Labs was able to become an around-the-clock, global organization.

THE EMERGENCE OF VIRTUAL TEAMS

In today's business environment, teams have been accepted as the smart way to organize for flexible and cost-effective operations. With recent advances in technology, however, team members no longer must be housed in one location in order to work together. They can become virtual teams—teams with a common purpose that use technology to cross time zones, distance, and the boundaries of organizations.

A practical example from the publishing world demonstrates the potential of virtual teams. *Esquire*, *Men's Health*, and *Rolling Stone* are three of the four largest men's magazines with a combined circulation of about 3 million. Together they equal the circulation of the fourth magazine in this category—*Sports Illustrated*. Several years ago, the three magazines were asked to work together on a joint proposal for a major advertising project for Haggar, the men's clothing manufacturer. Their combined bid would be pitched against a *Sports Illustrated* proposal.

Until this project, the three magazines were fierce competitors who barely even spoke with one another. But within a day's time, thanks to the efforts of Goodby Silverstein, a San Francisco advertising agency representing Haggar, they were meeting in each other's offices. Within a month, they had put together a bid that defeated their joint competitor. They learned to put their competitive instincts aside and cooperate for their mutual benefit. They used virtual teams to cross their physical and corporate boundaries to put this highly lucrative deal together.

Telecommunications in the global economy has brought new partners and ways of working to millions of people. Colleagues can sleep in different time zones and still be members of the same team. This is true, but it's not easy. The explosion of links across every conceivable boundary is staggering in its complexity as languages, cultures, governments, distances, and the mysterious nuances of human behavior all play their parts.

When NCR was spun off by AT&T, it used virtual teams to achieve its turnaround. In 1996, NCR brought out its WorldMark enterprise computer server, machines so massive that they may weigh 10 or 12 tons. Involving over 1,000 people in 17 primary locations, the WorldMark project housed internal groups situated in five U.S. states, Ireland, India, and China. Outside partners were in six other locations. Unbelievably, given the number of players and their diverse locations, the project was completed on budget and ahead of schedule.

Three things made the WorldMark project successful. First, everyone involved understood what the project was about—there was a clear mission, and it was well communicated. Second, they had common work processes. Everyone knew how to set goals, describe the tasks and the ultimate results, and create schedules to work toward those results. And finally, they had superb communications.

The virtual team worked together on a daily basis even though they were a continent apart. The engineers were connected by a high-speed, full-bandwidth, continuously available, audio, video, and data link that they affectionately nicknamed "the Worm Hole." (A worm hole is an intergalactic phenomenon found in science fiction—a portal of instant transport from one place in the universe to another.) NCR's Worm Hole is made possible by a switched T1 line, a very high speed telecommunications link that connects three videoconferencing rooms separated by thousands of miles.

In the Worm Hole, each screen serves a different purpose. One shows the people at the other location, a second serves as an overhead projector to display materials being used, and a third allows a standard PC to facilitate information sharing and distribution. At their frequent meetings, team members discuss strategy, argue points, solve problems, make presentations, exchange documents, use flip charts, and share files. They work not only with each other, but also with colleagues in many other locations. Using this technology, it took the team 11 months to develop NCR's next generation computer system.

When Sun Microsystems had some quality problems a few years ago, Scott McNeely, Sun's chief executive, invited the CEOs of Federal Express, Motorola, and Xerox to offer suggestions. In every case, the CEOs said that what made a difference in their companies was teams.

At that time, Sun was the archetype of the cowboy/cowgirl mentality—the brilliant engineer working alone, never in teams. To address its problems, employees were invited to form teams to investigate the 32 top "customer dissatisfiers." Seventy boundary-crossing virtual teams were formed, and they were highly effective in solving the problems. Each team had an executive sponsor, clear guidelines about what needed to done to be successful, and a fantastic technology infrastructure.

Virtual teams are a type of small group. They differ from other small groups in forms of communication, number of relationships, and in the ability to create in a global context. The technology is here today that allows people to work together at a distance just as though they were next door to one another in an office setting. Successful virtual teams, however, depend more on people than they do on technology. "It's 90 percent people and 10 percent technology," Bob Buckman says. The technology won't work unless the people issues are addressed first. Working in a virtual environment requires a new kind of organization, a new kind of management, and a new kind of leadership.

A MODEL FOR VIRTUAL TEAMS

The basic principles that underlie all of our case examples have three facets: purpose, people, and links (see Exhibit 2). The virtual team model also applies to networks, as the "people" node of the model can represent members, organizations, companies, or countries. But to understand it as a model for virtual teams, it must be rooted in people.

Purpose   Purpose is very important to any form of organization. But it is critical to virtual organizations and teams because purpose is the glue that holds them together. Hierarchy has the power to hire and fire. Bureaucracy has rules, regulations, constitutions, and laws. But truly networked organizations and virtual teams often have only purpose. For example, a team that's pulled together because several companies are in an alliance together has no common reporting structure. They will stay together only if their shared purpose is robust and agreed upon by all the members of the team.

In a virtual team, purpose goes beyond a mission statement that is put on the wall and forgotten. Purpose must be translated into action steps that become the basis for the work people will do together. It requires cooperative goals, interdependent tasks, and concrete results. Teams exist to produce results. Without cooperative goals, the project will never get started. And if the tasks are all independent, then a team is unnecessary. Virtual teams are usually created because one person or one organization can't get the desired results alone.

EXHIBIT 2   **Virtual Team Model**

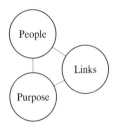

	Inputs	**Processes**	**Outputs**
PEOPLE	Independent members	Shared leadership	Integrated levels
PURPOSE	Cooperative goals	Interdependent tasks	Concrete results
LINKS	Multiple media	Boundary-crossing interactions	Trusting relationships

Source: © 1998 NetAge, Inc.

EXHIBIT 3   Virtual Team Principles

People   People are the core of virtual teams. But there are key factors that must be considered. The first is independence. Everyone in the virtual team must be autonomous and self-reliant but still able to be interdependent. They must know how to be "me," while simultaneously holding on to being "we."

The second aspect is shared leadership. At some point, each member of the virtual team will play a leadership role, depending on where the team is in the process. Leadership will shift, depending on the task at hand. Each person brings a particular set of skills and expertise that will be called upon in the process.

The third aspect is integrated levels. Virtual teams are not only horizontally articulated teams; they must connect up and down in the organization.

Links   Links are connections not just technology. These connections may be through face-to-face conversation or through communication technologies. But the connections themselves are totally passive. Results require interaction of some kind. Over time, those interactions will produce relationships, and if they are trusting relationships they will endure. Relationships make the organization. What makes the information age different is not the relationships or the interactions, it's the digital technologies.

Digital technologies offer a fantastic cornucopia of interactive capabilities. we are now beginning to explore how these technologies might affect the way we organize ourselves. We won't lose other forms of communication; we'll just add to them. There are things you can do face-to-face that you can't do at a distance, such as build trust quickly. Once you determine the purpose and the people you can decide which linkages are most useful for tying those people together to accomplish the work they've agreed upon.

Exhibit 3 shows the nine principles of virtual teams as an input-output systems model. Virtual teams are small systems, while networks tend to be much larger systems. But all of these characteristics will be present in all successful, distributed organizations.

SOCIAL CAPITAL: THE OTHER BOTTOM LINE

There is a double bottom line in the work of any team. There's a task result or outcome that is usually visible and obvious, and there is a social outcome, based on the team's interactions. The social effect may not be apparent in the quality of the task outcome. In one team, there may have been really unpleasant interactions, a lot of loud talk, banging of heads, and long nights. In another team, the same result may have been achieved through cooperation, collaboration, and mutual assistance, making the entire experience a very positive one. The next time a teaming opportunity arises, those who went through a bad experience may decide they never want to be part of another team, while those who had a good experience are apt to participate and, in fact, will be more effective because they have built relationships and learned how to work as a team.

These contrasting team experiences have either increased or decreased the organization's social capital. Increased social capital means there is increased capability to do work. In the reverse situation, capacity has been taken away. It is impossible not to have some impact. The team experience will either add to or deplete the organization's existing stock of "relationship resources." James Coleman first developed the concept of social capital in the early 80s.[2] Today social capital is recognized as a valuable addition to an organization's total resources, which include physical property, financial capital, and human capital.

According to Harvard History Professor Robert Putnam, three things are necessary to develop social capital: trust, reciprocity, and dense social networks.[3]

- **Trust is No. 1**   All else flows from it. Often, seemingly irrelevant, unrelated-to-work conversations among employees build trust that will make their working relationships more effective in the future.
- **Reciprocity means give and take**   It is not necessary in the immediate moment; rather, people need the sense that giving will eventually result in receiving.
- **Research shows that in communities where people are well-connected in dense social networks, they tend to be healthier and more economically stable**   The same holds true for organizations.

Companies like Eastman Chemical are deliberately working to increase their levels of trust. In the early 1980s, Eastman conducted a survey to determine the level of trust within the company, and its leaders were shocked to find that trust was very low. According to the survey, the No. 1 item that accounted for that low level of trust was the company's use of the Hay compensation system that used the normal, bell-shaped curve to determine pay and reward. Here was a company that hired the best and the brightest and then immediately told half of them that they were underperformers and would be paid accordingly. The pay system was radically reformed.

Eastman also had a suggestion box program through which an individual could win up to $25,000 for a successful idea, but it created competition among employees instead of collaboration. So the individual-suggestion box was discontinued. Teams were asked to work together on suggestions and were rewarded accordingly.

There are also hazards in giving team rewards. First, the teams themselves can become unproductively competitive. Second, who's to say who exactly contributed to a given team's success? There's an apocryphal story about Hewlett-Packard, in which the leader of a team that had a tremendous success was purported to have sent an e-mail inviting everyone who contributed to the team's success to come to dinner. They were expecting about 50 responses, and instead they got 1,500. They had to rent a football field. Teams have porous boundaries, and many people throughout the organization may consider themselves to be a part.

Social capital is built in small groups and internal organizations, but it doesn't stop there. AnnaLee Saxenian has compared Silicon Valley with the Route 128 area in Boston.[4] Both of these regions have had to respond to threats to their dominance: The PC challenge to minicomputers in Boston and the Japanese semiconductor challenge to the chip industry in the Valley. The Valley not only came back, it became the unquestioned world leader in this industry, while the economy around Route 128 has never regained its 1980's level of prominence. It is recovering today, thanks to a burgeoning telecommunications industry.

What made the difference? Saxenian says the difference was social capital writ large. In the Valley, organizations were more open—people could move easily from Sun to Apple to Silicon Graphics. They competed very vigorously, but they also traded ideas. In the East, companies are more insular and vertically oriented. In the heyday of the Digital Equipment Corporation, an employee who left the company was considered a traitor—an outcast. This attitude closed doors and prevented the formation of social capital.

We are only at the beginning of our understanding of virtual teams and their impact on organizations of the future. We believe that, in time, virtual teams will become the accepted way to work. Virtual teams and networks—effective, value-based, swiftly reconfiguring, high-performance, cost-sensitive, and decentralized—will profoundly reshape our world.

NOTES

[1] Very recent archaelogical discoveries indicate that agriculture may well have been developed by nomadic tribes and that cities were settled without being supported by agriculture. Even so, hierarchies developed quickly in large agriculturally based cities.

[2] J. S. Coleman, "Social Capital in the Creation of Human Capital," *American Journal of Sociology* (1988 Supplement), S98.

[3] R. D. Putnam, *Making Democracy Work: Civic Traditions in Modern Italy* (Princeton, NJ: Princeton University Press, 1993).

[4] A. Saxenian, *Regional Advantage: Culture and Competition in Silicon Valley and Route 128* (Cambridge: Harvard University Press, 1994).

TIPS FOR VIRTUAL TEAMS

1. Identify the team sponsors, stakeholders, and champions who serve as liaisons between the team and the organization's power brokers.
2. With management and key stakeholders, the team leader should develop a team charter that spells out the team's purpose, mission, and goals.
3. Make sure the team has the necessary tools to communicate and interact (compatible computers, etc.).
4. Carefully select team members and which category they will fit. The three categories are: core members who work regularly on the team project, extended members who provide support and counsel, and ancillary members who review and approve work. In addition to having the required competencies to help the team, core team members should be self-motivated individuals who do not require close supervision.
5. Bring the team together for an initial, face-to-face meeting that will involve team building exercises and an opportunity to form relationships and begin building trust. It is easier to deal with problems that may develop later if team members can put a face to a name and have a relationship with each other.
6. In this first meeting, establish team norms such as telephone, audio and video-conferencing etiquette, guidelines for sending and replying to e-mails and phone calls, determining which meetings have to be physically attended and by whom, and establish how meetings will be scheduled.
7. The leader should develop a team process that specifies how the work will be managed and reviewed and how information will be stored, etc.
8. Virtual teams require multiple leadership, which emerges naturally as the team confronts issues related to the expertise of various team members. The official team leader will not be successful with a controlling style of leadership, given the autonomous nature of a virtual team, but he or she is still responsible for making some decisions.

These tips compiled by J. Osland are based on D. Duarte and N. Tennant Snyder, *Mastering Virtual Teams: Strategies, Tools, and Techniques That Succeed* (San Francisco, CA: Jossey Bass, 1999) and J. Lipnack and J. Stamps, *Virtual Teams: Reaching Across Space, Time, and Organizations with Technology* (New York: John Wiley & Sons, 1997).

CHAPTER 10
PROBLEM SOLVING AND CREATIVITY

PUTTING YOUR COMPANY'S WHOLE BRAIN TO WORK
Dorothy Leonard
Susaan Straus

OF BOXES, BUBBLES, AND EFFECTIVE MANAGEMENT
David K. Hurst

CREATIVITY AS INVESTMENT
Robert J. Sternberg
Linda A. O'Hara
Todd I. Lubart

A talent for problem solving has always been essential for running a business or any type of organization. In recent years, however, problem solving has received more attention as a key element of programs designed to improve organizational effectiveness, such as employee involvement groups, total quality efforts, continuous improvement, reengineering, and organizational learning. Individual and organizational creativity influences both problem solving and an organization's survival chances. One of the basic tenets of both creativity and problem solving is drawing on diverse perspectives.

Dorothy Leonard, business professor, and Susaan Straus, consultant, provide advice on "Putting Your Company's Whole Brain To Work." Individuals do not approach problem solving in the same way, which can be a source of conflict in today's highly integrated ways of working. They underscore the importance of understanding, appreciating, and working effectively with people who have different cognitive preferences and communication styles.

The necessity of balancing both right-and left-brain ways of thinking and approaching problems is nowhere more visible than in the creative problem solving shown by one Canadian company in severe crisis. The second article, "Of Boxes, Bubbles, and Effective Management" is a classic management article by businessman and writer David Hurst. He describes how his management team was forced to revise their ideas about the role of managers and create new ways to organize the company and work together.

In "Creativity as Investment" the authors argue that it takes more than a creativity training session to make creative employees. They identify six resources that both individuals and companies should support and develop. Their approach includes lessons from the research on creativity as well as practical examples from business. Robert Sternberg is a psychology professor at Yale where Linda O'Hara is a research associate; Todd Lubart is a professor in Paris, France.

PUTTING YOUR COMPANY'S WHOLE BRAIN TO WORK*

Dorothy Leonard
Susaan Straus

Innovate or fall behind: the competitive imperative for virtually all businesses today is that simple. Achieving it is hard, however, because innovation takes place when different ideas, perceptions, and ways of processing and judging information collide. That, in turn, often requires collaboration among various players who see the world in inherently different ways. As a result, the conflict that should take place constructively among ideas all too often ends up taking place unproductively among people who do not innately understand one another. Disputes become personal, and the creative process breaks down.

Stakes are high enough. That said, we all tend to have one or two preferred habits of thought that influence our decision-making styles and our interactions with others—for good or for ill.

The most widely recognized cognitive distinction is between left-brained and right-brained ways of thinking. This categorization is more powerful metaphorically than it is accurate physiologically; not all the functions commonly associated with the left brain are located on the left side of the cortex and not all so-called right-brained functions are located on the right. Still, the simple description does usefully capture radically different ways of thinking. An analytical, logical, and sequential approach to problem framing and solving (left-brained thinking) clearly differs from an intuitive, values-based, and nonlinear one (right-brained thinking).

Cognitive preferences also reveal themselves in work styles and decision-making activities. Take collaboration as opposed to independence. Some people prefer to work together on solving problems, whereas others prefer to gather, absorb, and process information by themselves. Each type does its best work under different conditions. Or consider thinking as opposed to feeling. Some people evaluate evidence and make decisions through a structured, logical process, whereas others rely on their values and emotions to guide them to the appropriate action.

The list goes on. Abstract thinkers, for instance, assimilate information from a variety of sources, such as books, reports, videos, and conversations. They prefer learning about something rather than experiencing it directly. Experiential people, in contrast, get information from interacting directly with people and things. Some people demand quick decisions no matter the issue, whereas others prefer to generate a lot of options no matter the urgency. One type focuses on details, whereas the other looks for the big picture: the relationships and patterns that the data form.

Not surprisingly, people tend to choose professions that reward their own combination of preferences. Their work experience, in turn, reinforces the original preferences and deepens the associated skills. Therefore, one sees very different problem-solving approaches among accountants, entrepreneurs, social workers, and artists. Proof to an engineer, for example, resides in the numbers. But show a page of numerical data to a playwright, and, more persuaded by his intuition, he may well toss it aside. Of course, assessing people's likely approaches to problem solving only by their discipline can be as misleading as using gender or ethnicity as a guide. Within any profession, there are always people whose thinking styles are at odds with the dominant approach.

The best way for managers to assess the thinking styles of the people they are responsible for is to use an established diagnostic instrument as an assessment tool. A well-tested tool is both more objective and more thorough than the impressions of even the most sensitive and observant of managers. Dozens of diagnostic tools and descriptive analyses of human personality have been developed to

---

*Reprinted with permission from *Harvard Business Review* (July-August 1997): 112–121.

identify categories of cognitive approaches to problem solving and communication. All the instruments agree on the following basic points:

- Preferences are neither inherently good nor inherently bad. They are assets or liabilities depending on the situation. For example, politicians or CEOs who prefer to think out loud in public create expectations that they sometimes cannot meet; but the person who requires quiet reflection before acting can be a liability in a crisis.
- Distinguishing preferences emerge early in our lives, and strongly held ones tend to remain relatively stable through the years. Thus, for example, those of us who crave certainty are unlikely ever to have an equal love of ambiguity and paradox.
- We can learn to expand our repertoire of behaviors, to act outside our preferred styles. But that is difficult—like writing with the opposite hand.
- Understanding others' preferences helps people communicate and collaborate.

Managers who use instruments with the credibility of the Myers-Briggs Type Indicator (MBTI®) or the Herrmann Brain Dominance Instrument (HBDI) find that their employees accept the outcomes of the tests and use them to improve their processes and behaviors. (See the box "Identifying How We Think: The Myers-Briggs Type Indicator® and the Herrmann Brain Dominance Instrument.")

IDENTIFYING HOW WE THINK: THE MYERS-BRIGGS TYPE INDICATOR® AND THE HERRMANN BRAIN DOMINANCE INSTRUMENT

The Myers-Briggs Type Indicator (MBTI®) is the most widely used personality-assessment instrument in the world. Designed by a mother-and-daughter team, Isabel Myers and her mother Katherine Cook Briggs, the MBTI® is based on the work of Carl Jung. Myers and Briggs developed the instrument during World War II on the hypothesis that an understanding of personality preferences might aid those civilians who were entering the workforce for the first time to find the right job for the war effort. The instrument conforms to standard testing conventions and, at last count in 1994, had been taken by more than two and a half million people around the world. The MBTI® is widely used in business, psychology, and education, as well as in career counseling.

The MBTI® uses four different pairs of attributes to create a matrix of 16 personality types:

- **Introversion Versus Extraversion**[1]   The first pair measures the degree to which one is an introvert (I) or an extravert (E). These I/E descriptors focus on the source of someone's mental energy: extraverts draw energy from other people; introverts draw energy from themselves. Each finds the other's preferred operating conditions enervating.
- **Sensing Versus "INtuiting"**   The second pair identifies how one absorbs information. "Sensors" (S) gather data through their five senses, whereas "iNtuitives" (N) rely on less direct perceptions, such as patterns, relationships, and hunches. For example, when asked to describe the same painting, a group of S's might comment on the brush strokes or the scar on the subject's left cheek, whereas a group of N's might imagine from the troubled look in the subject's eyes that he lived in difficult times or suffered from depression.
- **Thinking Versus Feeling**   The third pair measures how one makes decisions once information is gathered. Feeling types (F) use their emotional intelligence to make decisions based on values—their internal sense of right and wrong. Thinking types (T) tend to make decisions based on logic and "objective" criteria—their assessment of truth and falsehood.
- **Judging Versus Perceiving**   The fourth pair reflects how slowly or rapidly one comes to a decision. Judging types (J) have a high need for closure. They reach conclusions quickly

The MBTI®			
Sensing Types (S)		**Intuitive Types (N)**	
Thinking (T)	**Feeling (F)**	**Feeling (F)**	**Thinking (T)**

		Sensing Types (S) Thinking (T)	Sensing Types (S) Feeling (F)	Intuitive Types (N) Feeling (F)	Intuitive Types (N) Thinking (T)
Introverts (I)	**Judging (J)**	**ISTJ** Serious, quiet, earn success by concentration and throughness. Practical, orderly, matter-of-fact, logical, realistic, and dependable. Take responsibility.	**ISFJ** Quiet, friendly, responsible and conscientious. Work devotedly to meet their obligations. Thorough painstaking, accurate. Loyal, considerate.	**INFJ** Succeed by perseverance, originality, and desire to do whatever is needed or wanted. Quietly forceful, conscientious, concerned for others. Respected for their firm principles.	**INTJ** Usually have original minds and great drive for their own ideas and purposes. Skeptical, critical, independent, determined often stubborn.
Introverts (I)	**Perceiving (P)**	**ISTP** Cool onlookers-quiet, reserved, and analytical. Usually interested in impersonal principles, how and why mechanical things work. Flashes of original humor.	**ISFP** Retiring, quietly friendly, sensitive, kind, modest about their abilities. Shun disagreements. Loyal followers. Often relaxed about getting things done.	**INFP** Care about learning, ideas, language and independent projects of their own. Tend to undertake too much, then somehow get it done. Friendly, but often too absorbed.	**INTP** Quiet, reserved, impersonal. Enjoy theoretical or scientific subjects. Usually interested mainly in ideas, little liking for parties or small talk Sharply defined interests.
Extraverts (E)	**Perceiving (P)**	**ESTP** Matter-of-fact, do not worry or hurry, enjoy whatever comes along. May be a bit blunt or insensitive. Best with real things that can be taken apart or put together.	**ESFP** Outgoing, easygoing, accepting, friendly, make things fun for others by their enjoyment. Like sports and making things. Find remembering facts easier than mastering theories.	**ENFP** Warmly enthusiastic, high-spirited, ingenious, imaginative. Able to do almost anything that interests them. Quick with a solution and to help with a problem.	**ENTP** Quick, ingenious, good at many things. May argue either side of a question for fun. Resourceful in solving challenging problems, but may neglect routine assignments.
Extraverts (E)	**Judging (J)**	**ESTJ** Practical, realistic, matter-of-fact, with a natural head for business or mechanics. Not interested in subject they see no use for. Like to organize and run activities.	**ESFJ** Warm-hearted, talkative, popular, conscientious, born cooperators. Need harmony. Work best with encouragement. Little interest in abstract thinking or technical subjects.	**ENFJ** Responsive and responsible. Generally feel real concern for what others think or want. Sociable, popular. Sensitive to praise and criticism.	**ENTJ** Hearty, frank, decisive, leaders. Usually good at anything that requires reasoning and intelligent talk. May sometimes be more positive than their experience in an area warrants.

Source: Modified and reproduced by special permission of the Publisher, Consulting Psychologists Press, Palo Alto, CA 94303 from *Report Form from the Myers-Briggs Type Indicator* by Isabel Briggs Myers. Copyright 1991 by Peter B. Myers and Katharine D. Myers. All rights reserved. Further reproduction is prohibited without the publisher's written consent.

based on available data and move on. Perceiving types (P) prefer to keep their options open. They wait until they have gathered what they consider to be enough information to decide. J's crave certainty, and P's love ambiguity.

To read descriptions of the personality types identified in the MBTI®, see the matrix above. Ned Herrmann created and developed the Herrmann Brain Dominance Instrument (HBDI) while he was a manager at General Electric. Starting his research with large groups within GE,

(continued)

he expanded it over 20 years through tens of thousands of surveys and has validated the data with prominent psychometric research institutions, including the Educational Testing Service.

The HBDI measures a person's preference both for right-brained or left-brained thinking and for conceptual or experiential thinking. These preferences often correspond to specific professions. Engineers, for example, consistently describe themselves as analytical, mathematical, and logical, placing them on the left end of the continuum. Artists, in contrast, describe themselves as emotional, spatial, and aesthetic, placing them on the right end of the continuum.

The charts below show how the different preferences combine into four distinct quadrants and how one can use the chart to analyze teams with different cognitive preferences:

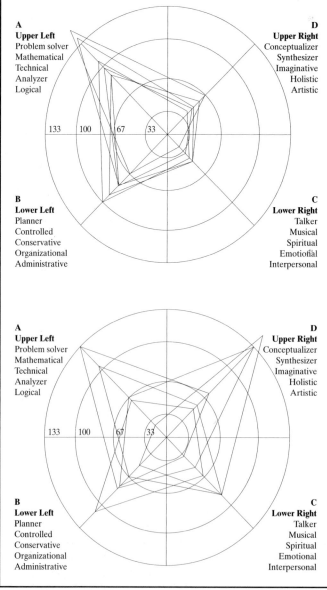

Composite One:
The Homogeneous Team

The chart on the left shows that everyone in the group approaches problems and challenges with the same emphasis on correctness. As engineers, the members of the team know how to do things correctly. Although the quality of their work is excellent, the members are difficult to work with. They have their own ways of doing things, and they reject variations from set standards. As a corporate function, the team has long enjoyed a captive audience in the company. Recently, members found themselves in trouble when the company restructured and other functions in the organization were allowed to outsource engineering.

Composite Two:
The Heterogeneous Team

The Management Services Group includes managers from information technology, the mail room, and the cafeteria. Although members share such goals as an orientation toward quality, they encounter a wide range of business problems. The manager's dominant thinking style is in the lower right quadrant: a natural facilitator, she develops people, listens empathetically, and fosters a spirit of respect among her reports. Her leadership unified what had been a fragmented, inefficient collection of functions. Members regard one another as resources, enjoy the group's diversity, and take great pride in their work.

HOW WE ACT

All the assessment in the world means nothing unless new understanding brings different actions. Instruments such as the MBTI® and the HBDI will help you understand yourself and will help others understand themselves. The managerial challenge is to use the insights that these instruments offer to create new processes and encourage new behaviors that will help innovation efforts succeed.

Understand Yourself   Start with yourself. When you identify your own style, you gain insight into the ways your preferences unconsciously shape your style of leadership and patterns of communication. You may be surprised to discover that your style can stifle the very creativity you seek from your employees. Consider the experiences of two managers of highly creative organizations. Each was at odds with his direct reports—but for very different reasons.

Jim Shaw, executive vice president of MTV Networks, is a left-brained guy in a right-brained organization. Said Shaw:

> *I have always characterized the creative, right-brained, visionary-type people here as dreamers. What I've realized is that when a dreamer expressed a vision, my gut reaction was to say, 'Well, if you want to do that, what you've got to do is A, then B, then you have to work out C, and because you've got no people and you've got no satellite up-link, you'll have to do D and E.' I've learned that saying that to a creative type is like throwing up on the dream. When I say that stuff too soon, the dreamer personalizes it as an attack. I've learned not to put all of the things that need to be done on the table initially. I can't just blurt it all out—it makes me look like a naysayer. What I've learned to do is to leak the information gradually, then the dreamer knows that I am meeting him halfway.*

Jerry Hirshberg, president of Nissan Design International, ran into precisely the opposite problem. Hirshberg discovered that some of his employees craved the very kind of structure that he personally abhorred. Before this epiphany, he inundated them with information and expected creativity in return. In short, he tried to manage his employees the way *he* would have wanted to be managed. Hirshberg found, however, that a few individuals reacted to every suggestion with a "yes, but ..." Initially, he interpreted such hesitancy as an anti-innovation bias. But he eventually realized that some of his employees preferred to have more time both to digest problems and to construct logical approaches to his intuitively derived ideas. Given a bit of extra time, they would return to the project with solid, helpful, and insightful plans for implementation. Ironically, it was their commitment to the success of the initiative that caused the employees to hesitate: they wanted the best possible result. Hirshberg recognized that their contributions were as critical as his own or those of any of the other "right-brainers" in the company.

Both Shaw and Hirshberg came to realize that their own cognitive preferences unconsciously shaped their leadership styles and communication patterns. In fact, their automatic reactions initially stifled the very creativity they sought from their employees. And note that it was just as important for the predominantly right-brained manager to recognize the contributions of the logicians as it was for the left-brained manager to acknowledge the organic approach of the visionaries. Except in theoretical models, creativity is not the exclusive province of one side or the other.

If you want an innovative organization, you need to hire, work with, and promote people who make you uncomfortable. You need to understand your own preferences so that you can complement your weaknesses and exploit your strengths. The biggest barrier to recognizing the contributions of people who are unlike you is your own ego. Suppose you are stalled on a difficult problem. To whom do you go for help? Usually to someone who is on the same wavelength or to someone whose opinion you respect. These people may give you soothing strokes, but they are unlikely to help spark a new idea. Suppose you were to take the problem instead to someone with whom you often find yourself at odds, someone who rarely validates your ideas or perspectives. It may take courage and tact to get constructive feedback, and the process may not be exactly pleasant. But that feedback will likely improve the quality of your solution. And when your adversary recovers from his amazement at your request, he may even get along with you better because the disagreement was clearly intellectual, not personal.

Forget the Golden Rule Don't treat people the way you want to be treated. Tailor communications to the receiver instead of the sender. In a cognitively diverse environment, a message sent is not necessarily a message received. Some people respond well to facts, figures, and statistics. Others prefer anecdotes. Still others digest graphic presentations most easily. Information must be delivered in the preferred "language" of the recipient if it is to be received at all.

For example, say you want to persuade an organization to adopt an open office layout. Arguments appealing to the analytical mind would rely on statistics from well-documented research conducted by objective experts that prove that open architecture enhances the effectiveness of communication. Arguments geared toward the action-oriented type would answer specific questions about implementation: How long will the office conversion take?

Exactly what kind of furniture is needed? What are the implications for acoustics? Arguments aimed at people-oriented individuals would focus on such questions as, How does an open office affect relationships? How would this setup affect morale? and Are people happy in this sort of setup? Arguments crafted for people with a future-oriented perspective would include graphics as well as artists' renderings of the proposed environment. In short, regardless of how you personally would prefer to deliver the message, you will be more persuasive and better understood if you formulate messages to appeal to the particular thinking style of your listener.

Create "Whole-Brained" Teams Either over time or by initial design, company or group cultures can become dominated by one particular cognitive style. IBM, in the days when it was known as "Big Blue," presented a uniform face to the world; Digital Equipment prided itself on its engineering culture. Such homogeneity makes for efficient functioning—and limited approaches to problems or opportunities. Companies with strong cultures can indeed be very creative, but within predictable boundaries: say, clever marketing or imaginative engineering. When the market demands that such companies innovate in different ways, they have to learn new responses. Doing so requires adopting a variety of approaches to solving a problem—using not just the right brain or the left brain but the *whole* brain.

Consider the all-too-common error made by John, a rising star in a large, diversified instrument company: he forfeited an important career opportunity because he failed to see the need for a whole-brained team. Appointed manager of a new-product development group, John had a charter to bring in radically innovative ideas for products and services for launch in three to six years. "Surprise me," the CEO said.

Given a free hand in hiring, John lured in three of the brightest M.B.A.'s he could find. They immediately went to work conducting industry analyses and sorting through existing product possibilities, applying their recently acquired skills in financial analysis. To complete the team, John turned to the pile of résumés on his desk sent to him by human resources. All the applicants had especially strong quantitative skills, and a couple were engineers. John was pleased. Surely a group of such intelligent, well-trained, rigorous thinkers would be able to come up with some radical innovations for the company. Ignoring advice to hire some right-brained people to stimulate different ideas, he continued to populate his group with left-brained wizards. After 18 months, the team had rejected all the proposed new projects in the pipeline on the basis of well-argued and impressively documented financial and technical risk analysis. But the team's members had not come up with a single new idea. The CEO was neither surprised nor pleased, and the group was disbanded just short of its second anniversary.

In contrast, Bob, a successful entrepreneur embarking on his latest venture, resisted the strong temptation to tolerate only like-minded people. He knew from his prior ventures that his highly analytical style alienated some of his most creative people. Despite his unusual degree of self-aware-ness, Bob came within a hair's breadth of firing a strong and experienced manager: Wally, his direc-tor of human resources. According to Bob, after several months on board, Wally appeared to be "a quart and a half low." Why? Because he was inattentive in budget meetings and focused on what Bob perceived as trivia—day care, flextime, and benefits. Before taking action, however, Bob decided to look at the management team through the lens of thinking styles. He soon realized that Wally was ex-actly the kind of person he needed to help him grow his small company. Wally contributed a key ele-ment that was otherwise missing in the management team: a sensitivity to human needs that helped the company foresee and forestall problems with employees. So Bob learned to meet Wally halfway. De-scribing his success in learning to work with Wally, he told us, "You would have been proud of me. I started our meetings with five minutes of dogs, kids, and station wagons." Although the concern Wally demonstrated for the workers in the company did not eliminate union issues completely, it did mini-mize antagonism toward management and made disputes easier to resolve.

The list of whole-brained teams that continue to innovate successfully is long. At Xerox PARC, social scientists work alongside computer scientists. For instance, computer scientist Pavel Curtis, who is creating a virtual world in which people will meet and mingle, is working with an anthropol-ogist who understands how communities form. As a result, Curtis's cyberspace meeting places have more human touches and are more welcoming than they would have been had they been designed only by scientists. Another example is the PARC PAIR (PARC Artist In Residence) program, which links computer scientists with artists so that each may influence the other's perceptions and representations of the world. At Interval Research, a California think tank dedicated to multimedia technologies, Di-rector David Liddle invites leaders from various disciplines to visit for short "sabbaticals." The pur-pose is to stimulate a cross-fertilization of ideas and approaches to solving problems. The resulting exchanges have helped Interval Research create and spin off several highly innovative start-ups. And Jerry Hirshberg applies the whole-brain principle to hiring practices at Nissan Design by bringing de-signers into his organization in virtual pairs. That is, when he hires a designer who glories in the free-dom of pure color and rhythm, he will next hire a very rational, Bauhaus-trained designer who favors analysis and focuses on function.

Complete homogeneity in an organization's cognitive approach can be very efficient. But as man-agers at Xerox PARC, Interval Research, and Nissan Design have learned, no matter how brilliant the group of individuals, their contributions to innovative problem solving are enhanced by coming up against totally different perspectives.

Look for the Ugly Duckling   Suppose you don't have the luxury of hiring new people yet find your organization mired in a swamp of stale thinking patterns. Consider the experience of the CEO of the U.S. subsidiary of a tightly controlled and conservative European chemical company. Even though the company's business strategy had never worked well in the United States, headquarters pushed the CEO to do more of the same. He knew he needed to figure out a fresh approach because the U.S. company was struggling to compete in a rapidly changing marketplace. But his direct reports were as uniformly left-brained as his superiors in Europe and were disinclined to work with him to figure out new solutions.

Rather than give up, the CEO tested thinking preferences further down in the organization. He found the cognitive disparity that he needed in managers one layer below his direct reports—a small but dy-namic set of individuals whose countercultural thinking patterns had constrained their advancement. In this company, people with right-brained preferences were seen as helpful but were not considered top management material. They were never promoted above a certain level.

The CEO changed that. He elevated three managers with right-brained proclivities to the roles of senior vice president and division head-lofty positions occupied until then exclusively by left-brained individuals. The new executives were strong supporters of the CEO's intentions to innovate and worked with him to develop new approaches to the business. They understood that their communication strategy with headquarters would be critical to their success. They deliberately packaged their new ideas in a way that appealed to the cognitive framework of their European owner. Instead of lecturing about the need to change and try new ideas as they had in the past, the Americans presented their ideas as ways of solving problems. They supported their positions with well-researched quantitative data and with calculated anticipated cost savings and ROI—and described how similar approaches had succeeded elsewhere. They detailed the specific steps they would follow to succeed. Within two years, the U.S. subsidiary embarked on a major organizational redesign effort that included such radical notions as permitting outside competition for internal services. The quality of internal services soared—as did the number of innovations generated by the company in the United States.

Manage the Creative Process   Abrasion is not creative unless managers make it so. Members of whole-brained teams don't naturally understand one another, and they can easily come to dislike one another. Successful managers of richly diverse groups spend time from the outset getting members to acknowledge their differences—often through a joint exploration of the results of a diagnostic analysis—and devise guidelines for working together before attempting to act on the problem at hand. Managers who find it awkward or difficult to lead their groups in identifying cognitive styles or in establishing guidelines can usually enlist the aid of someone who is trained in facilitation.

People often feel a bit foolish creating rules about how they will work together. Surely, the thinking goes, we are all adults and have years of experience in dealing with group dynamics. That, of course, is the problem. Everyone has practiced dysfunctional behavior for years. We learn to value politeness over truth at our mothers' knees. (Who hasn't mastered the art of the white lie by age 16?) We often discount an argument if it has an element of emotion or passion. We opt out if we feel ignored—people with unappreciated thinking styles learn to sit against the wall during meetings (the organizational back-of-the-bus). And we usually don't even notice those behaviors because they are so routine.

But the cost of allowing such behaviors to overtake a group is too high. Bob Meyers, senior vice president of interactive media at NBC, uses a sports analogy to make the point: "On a football team, for example, you have to use all kinds of people. Like the little, skinny guy who can only kick the ball. He may not even look as if he belongs on the team. This guy can't stand up to the refrigerator types that play in other positions. But as long as he does his job, he doesn't need to be big. He can just do what he does best. The catch is that the team needs to recognize what the little skinny guy can do—or they lose the benefit of his talent."

Managing the process of creative abrasion means making sure that everyone is at the front of the bus and talking, Some simple but powerful techniques can be helpful. First, clarify why you are working together by keeping the common goal in front of the group at all times. "If the goal is a real-world one with shared accountability and timetables attached," one manager observed, "then everyone understands the relevance of honoring one another's differences."

Second, make your operating guidelines explicit. Effective guidelines are always simple, clear, and concise. For example, one group set up the following principles about handling disagreements: "Anyone can disagree about anything with anyone, but no one can disagree without stating the reason" and "When someone states an objection, everyone else should listen to it, try to understand it, treat it as legitimate, and counter with their reasons if they don't agree with it." Some principles are as simple as "discuss taboo subjects," "verify assumptions," and "arrive on time with your homework done."

Third, set up an agenda ahead of time that explicitly provides enough time for both divergent discussion to uncover imaginative alternatives and convergent discussion to select an option and plan its implementation. Innovation requires both types of discussion, but people who excel at different types can, as one manager observed, "drive each other nuts." Another manager said, "If you ask people comfortable with ambiguity whether they prefer A or B, they will ask, 'How about C?'" Meanwhile, the people who crave closure will be squirming in their seats at the seemingly pointless discussion. Moreover, if one approach dominates, the unbalanced group process can risk producing an unacceptable or unfeasible new product, service, or change. Clearly allocating time to the two different types of discussion will contain the frustrations of both the decisive types, who are constantly looking at their watches wanting the decision to be made now, and the ambiguous types, who want to be sure that all possible avenues for creativity have been explored. Otherwise, the decisive members generally will pound the others into silence by invoking time pressures and scheduling. They will grab the first viable option rather than the best one. Or if the less decisive dominate, the group may never reach a conclusion. Innovation requires both divergent and convergent thinking, both brainstorming and action plans.

Depersonalize Conflict Diverse cognitive preferences can cause tremendous tensions in any group, yet innovation requires the cross-fertilization of ideas. And because many new products are systems rather than stand-alone pieces, many business projects cannot proceed without the cooperation of people who receive different messages from the same words and make different observations about the same incidents. The single most valuable contribution that understanding different thinking and communication styles brings to the process of innovation is taking the sting out of intellectual disagreements that turn personal.

Consider the experience of the product manager of a radically new product for a medical supplies company. Facing a strict deadline of just 14 months to design and deliver a new surgical instrument, the manager's team needed to pull together fast. Design felt misled by marketing, however, and manufacturing couldn't understand design's delay in choosing between two mechanical hinges. The disagreements turned personal, starting with "you always . . ." and ending with "irresponsible ignorance." Two months into the project, the manager began to wonder whether he should disband the team and start over again. But he knew that his boss, the vice president of marketing, would not agree to extend the deadline. "I was desperate," he recalled. "I decided to make one last attempt at getting them to work together."

The manager decided to experiment with an offsite gathering of his staff, including sessions diagnosing cognitive preferences. When they returned to work, the team members used the new language they had learned to label their differences in opinion and style. "At first, using the terms was kind of a joke," the manager recalled. "They'd say things like, 'Well, of course I want the schedule right now. I'm a J!' Yet you could tell that people were really seeing one another in a different light, and they weren't getting angry." The team made its deadline; perhaps even more important, several members voluntarily joined forces to work on the next iteration of the product. This willingness to work together generated more value for the company than just "warm fuzzies." Critical technical knowledge was preserved in one small, colocated group—knowledge that would have been scattered had project members dispersed to different product lines. Moreover, keeping part of the team together resulted in a rapid development time for the derivative product.

People who do not understand cognitive preferences tend to personalize conflict or avoid it—or both. The realization that another person's approach is not wrongheaded and stubborn, but merely predictably different, diffuses anger. For example, at Viacom, a planning session involving two managers had ground to a halt. One manager simply wouldn't buy into the idea that the other was presenting.

Suddenly, the presenter slapped his head and said, "Oooohhh! I get it! You're left-brained! Give me half an hour to switch gears, and I'll be right back. Let me try this one more time." The left-brained manager laughingly agreed—he understood the paradigm—and the meeting resumed with the presenter armed with quantitative data and a much more cohesive and logical presentation. Establishing that kind of effective two-way communication led to a common understanding of the issues at hand and, ultimately, a solution.

Understanding that someone views a problem differently does not mean you will agree. But an important element in understanding thinking styles is recognizing that no one style is inherently better than another. Each style brings a uniquely valuable perspective to the process of innovation, just as each style has some negatives associated with it. Stereotypes of the cold-hearted logician, the absentminded, creative scientist, and the bleeding-heart liberal have some basis in reality. If people even partially internalize the inherent value of different perspectives, they will take disagreements less personally and will be better able to argue and reach a compromise or a consensus with less animosity. They will be open to the possibility that an alien view of the world might actually enhance their own. They will be better equipped to listen for the "a-ha" that occurs at the intersection of different planes of thought.

CAVEAT EMPTOR

Personality analysis of the type we describe is no more than a helpful tool, and it has many limitations. The diagnostic instruments measure only one aspect of personality: preferences in thinking styles and communication. They do not measure ability or intelligence, and they do not predict performance. Neither the MBTI® nor the HBDI measure other qualities that are critical to successful innovation such as courage, curiosity, integrity, empathy, or drive.

Preferences tend to be relatively stable, but life experiences can affect them. For example, repeated application of the MBTI® over a period of years has revealed a tendency for people to drift from a thinking style toward a feeling style when they have children. For the most part, however, studies done with both the MBTI® and the HBDI suggest that people retain their dominant preferences throughout a variety of work and social circumstances.

One critical warning label should be attached to any of these diagnostic instruments: only trained individuals should administer them. Not only can results be incorrectly interpreted (for instance, what are intended to be neutral descriptions of preferences might be labeled "right" or "wrong" behavior), but they can also be misused to invade people's privacy or to stereotype them. Of course, it is a human tendency to simplify in order to comprehend complexities; we stereotype people all the time on the basis of their language, dress, and behavior. Because these diagnostics have the weight of considerable psychological research behind them, however, they can be dangerous when misused. Without structured, reliable diagnoses, judgments are likely to be superficial and flawed. And without a substantial investment of time and resources, managers can't expect abrasion to be creative.

One of the paradoxes of modern management is that, in the midst of technical and social change so pervasive and rapid that it seems out of pace with the rhythms of nature, human personality has not altered throughout recorded history. People have always had distinct preferences in their approaches to problem solving. Why then is it only now becoming so necessary for managers to understand those differences? Because today's complex products demand integrating the expertise of individuals who do not innately understand one another. Today's pace of change demands that these individuals quickly develop the ability to work together. If abrasion is not managed into creativity, it will constrict the constructive impulses of individuals and organizations alike. Rightly harnessed, the energy released by the intersection of different thought processes will propel innovation.

OF BOXES, BUBBLES, AND EFFECTIVE MANAGEMENT*

David K. Hurst

Harvard Business Review
Soldiers Field Road
Boston, Massachusetts 02163

Dear Editors:

We are writing to tell you how events from 1979 on have forced us, a team of four general managers indistinguishable from thousands of others, to change our view of what managers should do. In 1979 we were working for Hugh Russel, Inc., the fiftieth largest public company in Canada. Hugh Russel was an industrial distributor with some $535 million in sales and a net income of $14 million. The organization structure was conventional: 16 divisions in four groups, each with a group president reporting to the corporate office. Three volumes of corporate policy manuals spelled out detailed aspects of corporate life, including our corporate philosophy. In short, in 1979 our corporation was like thousands of other businesses in North America.

During 1980, however, through a series of unlikely runs, that situation changed drastically. Hugh Russel found itself acquired in a 100 percent leveraged buyout and then merged with a large, unprofitable (that's being kind!) steel fabricator, York Steel Construction, Ltd. The resulting entity was York Russel, Inc., a privately held company except for the existence of some publicly owned preferred stock which obliged us to report to the public.

As members of the acquired company's corporate office, we waited nervously for the ax to fall. Nothing happened. Finally, after about six weeks, Wayne (now our president) asked the new owner if we could do anything to help the deal along. The new chairman was delighted and gave us complete access to information about the acquirer.

It soon became apparent that the acquiring organization had little management strength. The business had been run in an entrepreneurial style with hundreds of people reporting to a single autocrat. The business had, therefore, no comprehensive plan and, worse still, no money. The deal had been desperately conceived to shelter our profits from taxes and use the resulting cash flow to fund the excessive debt of the steel fabrication business.

Our first job was to hastily assemble a task force to put together a $300 million bank loan application and a credible turnaround plan. Our four-member management team (plus six others who formed a task force) did it in only six weeks. The merged business, York Russel, ended up with $10 million of equity and $275 million of debt on the eve of a recession that turned out to be the worst Canada had experienced since the Great Depression. It was our job then to save the new company, somehow.

Conceptual frameworks are important roads to managers' perceptions, and every team should have a member who can build them. Before the acquisition, the framework implicit in our organization was a "hard," rational model rather like those Thomas Peters and Robert Waterman describe.[1] Jay Galbraith's elaborate model is one of the purest examples of the structure-follows-strategy school.[2] The model clearly defines all elements and their relationships to each other, presumably so that they can be measured (see the Exhibit).

Because circumstances changed after the acquisition, our framework fell apart almost immediately. Overnight we went from working for a growth company to working for one whose only objective was survival. Our old decentralized organization was cumbersome and expensive; our new organization

---

*Reprinted with permission from *Harvard Business Review* (May-June 1984).

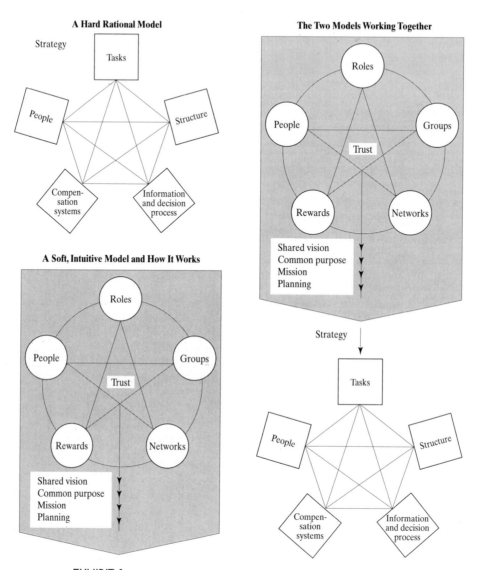

EXHIBIT 1 The Hard and Soft Model and How They Work Together

needed cash, not profits. Bankers and suppliers swarmed all over us, and the quiet life of a management-controlled public company was gone.

Compounding our difficulties, the recession quickly revealed all sorts of problems in businesses that up to that time had given us no trouble. Even the core nuggets offered up only meager profits, while merest rates of up to 25 percent quickly destroyed what was left of the balance sheet.

In the heat of the crisis, the management team jelled quickly. At first each member muddled in his own way, but as time went by, we started to plan a new understanding of how to be effective. Even now we do not completely understand the conceptual framework that has evolved, and maybe we never will. What follows is our best attempt to describe to you and your readers what guides us today.

Yours truly,

The management team

TWO MODELS ARE BETTER THAN ONE

The hard, rational model isn't wrong; it just isn't enough. There is something more. As it turns out, there is a great deal more.

At York Russel we have had to develop a "soft," intuitive framework that offers a counterpart to every element in the hard, rational framework. As the exhibit shows and the following sections discuss, in the soft model, roles are the counterparts of tasks, groups replace structure, networks operate instead of information systems, the rewards are soft as opposed to hard, and people are viewed as social animals rather than as rational beings.

That may not sound very new. But we found that the key to effective management of not only our crisis but also the routine is to know whether we are in a hard "box" or a soft "bubble" context. By recognizing the dichotomy between the two, we can choose the appropriate framework.

TASKS	... & ...	ROLES
☐ Static		○ Fluid
☐ Clarity		○ Ambiguity
☐ Content		○ Process
☐ Fact		○ Perception
☐ Science		○ Art

These are some of our favorite words for contrasting these two aspects of management. Here's how we discovered them.

The merger changed our agenda completely. We had new shareholders, a new bank, a new business (the steel fabrication operations consisted of nine divisions), and a new relationship with the managers of our subsidiaries, who were used to being left alone to grow. The recession and high interest rates rendered the corporation insolvent. Bankruptcy loomed large. Further, our previously static way of operating became very fluid.

In general, few of us had clear tasks, and for the most part we saw the future as ambiguous and fearful. We found ourselves describing what we had to do as roles rather than as tasks. At first our descriptions were crude. We talked of having an "inside man" who deals with administration, lawyers, and bankers versus an "outside man" who deals with operations, customers, and suppliers. Some of us were "readers," others "writers," some "talkers," and others "listeners." As the readers studied the work of behavioral science researchers and talked to the listeners, we found more useful classifications. Henry Mintzberg's description of managers' work in terms of three roles—interpersonal (figurehead, leaders, liaison), informational (monitor, disseminator, spokesperson), and decisional—helped us see the variety of the job.[3] Edgar Schein's analysis of group roles helped us concentrate on the process of communication as well as on what was communicated.[4]

The most useful framework we used was the one Ichak Adize developed for decision-making roles.[5] In his view, a successful management team needs to play four distinct parts. The first is that of producer of results. A *producer* is action oriented and knowledgeable in his or her field; he or she helps compile plans with an eye to their implementability. The *administrator* supervises the system and manages the detail. The *entrepreneur* is a creative risk taker who initiates action, comes up with new ideas, and challenges existing policies. And the *integrator* brings people together socially and their ideas intellectually, and interprets the significance of events. The integrator gives the team a sense of direction and shared experience.

According to Adize, each member must have some appreciation of the others' roles (by having some facility in those areas), and it is essential that they get along socially. At York Russel the producers (who typically come out of operations) and administrators (usually accountants) tend to be hard box players, while the entrepreneurs tend to live in the soft bubble. Integrators (friendly, unusually humble

MBAs) move between the hard and the soft, and we've found a sense of humor is essential to being able to do that well.

The key to a functioning harmonious group, however, has been for members to understand that they might disagree with each other because they are in two different contexts. Different conceptual frameworks may lead people to different conclusions based on the same facts. Of the words describing tasks and roles, our favorite pair is *fact* versus *perception*. People in different boxes will argue with each other over facts, for facts in boxes are compelling—they seem so tangible. Only from the bubble can one see them for what they are: abstractions based on the logical frameworks, or boxes, being used.

STRUCTURE   ... & ...   GROUPS

☐ Cool	○ Warm
☐ Formal	○ Informal
☐ Closed	○ Open
☐ Obedience	○ Trust
☐ Independence	○ Autonomy

Our premerger corporation was a pretty cold place to work. Senior management kept control in a tight inner circle and then played hardball (in a hard box, of course) with the group presidents. Managers negotiated budgets and plans on a win-lose basis; action plans almost exclusively controlled what was done in the organization. Top managers kept a lot of information to themselves. People didn't trust each other very much.

The crises that struck the corporation in 1980 were so serious that we could not have concealed them even if we had wanted to. We were forced to put together a multitude of task forces consisting of people from all parts of the organization to address these urgent issues, and in the process, we had to reveal everything we knew, whether it was confidential or not.

We were amazed at the task forces' responses: instead of resigning en masse (the hard box players had said that people would leave the company when they found out that it was insolvent), the teams tackled their projects with passion. Warmth, a sense of belonging, and trust characterized the groups; the more we let them know what was going on, the more we received from them. Confidentiality is the enemy of trust. In the old days strategic plans were stamped "confidential." Now we know that paper plans mean nothing if they are not in the minds of the managers.

Division managers at first resented our intrusion into their formal, closed world. "What happened to independence?" they demanded. We described the soft counterpart—autonomy—to them. Unlike independence, autonomy cannot be granted once and for all. In our earlier life, division personnel told the corporate office what they thought it wanted to hear. "You've got to keep those guys at arm's length" was a typical division belief. An autonomous relationship depends on trust for its nourishment. "The more you level with us," we said, "the more we'll leave you alone." That took some getting used to.

But in the end autonomy worked. We gave division managers confidential information, shared our hopes and fears, and incorporated their views in our bubble. They needed to be helped out of their boxes, not to abandon them altogether but to gain a deeper appreciation of and insight into how they were running their businesses. Few could resist when we walked around showing a genuine interest in their views. Because easy access to each other and opportunities for communication determine how groups form and work together, we encouraged managers to keep their doors open. We called this creation of opportunities for communication by making senior management accessible "management by walking around." Chance encounters should not be left to chance.

Although the primary objective of all this communication is to produce trust among group members, an important by-product is that the integrators among us have started to "see" the communication process.[6] In other words, they are beginning to understand why people say what they say. This ability to "see" communication is elusive at times, but when it is present, it enables us to "jump out of the box"—that is, to talk about the frameworks supporting conclusions rather than the conclusions themselves. We have defused many potential confrontations and struck many deals by changing the context of the debate rather than the debate itself.[7]

Perhaps the best example of this process was our changing relationship with our lead banker. As the corporation's financial position deteriorated, our relationship with the bank became increasingly adversarial. The responsibility for our account rose steadily up the bank's hierarchy (we had eight different account managers in 18 months), and we received tougher and tougher "banker's speeches" from successively more senior executives. Although we worried a great deal that the bank might call the loan, the real risk was that our good businesses would be choked by overzealous efforts on the part of individual bankers to "hold the line."

Key to our ability to change the relationship was to understand why individuals were taking the position they were. To achieve that understanding we had to rely on a network of contacts both inside and outside the bank. We found that the bank had as many views as there were people we talked to. Fortunately, the severity of the recession and the proliferation of corporate loan problems had already blown everyone out of the old policy "boxes." It remained for us to gain the confidence of our contacts, exchange candid views of our positions, and present options that addressed the corporation's problems in the bank's context and dealt with the bank's interests.

The "hard" vehicle for this was the renegotiation of our main financing agreements. During the more than six-month negotiating process, our relationship with the bank swung 180 degrees from confrontation to collaboration. The corporation's problem became a joint bank-corporation problem. We had used the bubble to find a new box in which both the corporation and the bank could live.

INFORMATIONAL PROCESSES … & …	**NETWORKS**
☐ Hard	○ Soft
☐ Written	○ Oral
☐ Know	○ Feel
☐ Control	○ Influence
☐ Decision	○ Implementation

Over the years our corporation has developed some excellent information systems. Our EDP facility is second to none in our industry. Before the acquisition and merger, when people talked about or requested information, they meant hard, quantitative data and written reports that would be used for control and decision making. The crisis required that we make significant changes to these systems. Because, for example, we became more interested in cash flow than earnings per share, data had to be aggregated and presented in a new way.

The pivotal change, however, was our need to communicate with a slew of new audiences over which we had little control. For instance, although we still have preferred stock quoted in the public market, our principal new shareholders were family members with little experience in professional management of public companies. Our new bankers were in organizational turmoil themselves and took 18 months to realize the horror of what they had financed. Our suppliers, hitherto benign, faced a stream of bad financial news about us and other members of the industry. The rumor mill had us in receivership on a weekly basis.

Our plant closures and cutbacks across North America brought us into a new relationship with government, unions, and the press. And we had a new internal audience: our employees, who were understandably nervous about the "imminent" bankruptcy.

We had always had some relationship with these audiences, but now we saw what important sources of information they were and expanded these networks vastly.[8] Just as we had informed the division managers at the outset, we decided not to conceal from these other groups the fact that the corporation was insolvent but worthy of support. We made oral presentations supported by formal written material to cover the most important bases.

To our surprise, this candid approach totally disarmed potential antagonists. For instance, major suppliers could not understand why we had told them we were in trouble before the numbers revealed the fact. By the time the entire war story was news, there was no doubt that our suppliers' top managers, who tended not to live in the hard accounting box, were on our side. When their financial specialists concluded that we were insolvent, top management blithely responded, "We've known that for six months."

Sharing our view of the world with constituencies external to the corporation led to other unexpected benefits, such as working in each other's interests. Our reassurance to customers that we would be around to deliver on contracts strengthened the relationship. Adversity truly is opportunity!

Management by walking around was the key to communicating with employees in all parts of the company. As a result of the continual open communication, all employees appreciated the corporation's position. Their support has been most gratifying. One of our best talker-listeners (our president) tells of a meeting with a very nervous group of employees at one facility. After he had spent several hours explaining the company's situation, one blue-collar worker who had been with the company for years took him aside and told him that a group of employees would be prepared to take heavy pay cuts if it would save the business. It turns out that when others hear this story it reinforces *their* belief in the organization.

We have found that sharing our views and incorporating the views of others as appropriate has a curious effect on the making and the implementing of decisions. As we've said, in our previous existence the decisions we made were always backed up by hard information; management was decisive, and that was good. Unfortunately, too few of these "good" decisions ever got implemented. The simple process of making the decision the way we did often set up resistance down the line. As the decision was handed down to consecutive organizational levels, it lost impetus until eventually it was unclear whether the decision was right in the first place.

Now we worry a good deal less about making decisions; they arise as fairly obvious conclusions drawn from a mass of shared assumptions. It's the assumptions that we spend our time working on. One of our "producers" (an executive vice president) calls it "conditioning" and indeed it is. Of course, making decisions this way requires that senior management build networks with people many layers down in the organization. This kind of communication is directly at odds with the communication policy laid down in the premerger corporation, which emphasized direct-line reporting.

A consequence of this network information process is that we often have to wait for the right time to make a decision. We call the wait a "creative stall." In the old organization it would have been called procrastination, but what we're doing is waiting for some important players to come "on-side" before making an announcement.[9] In our terms, you "prepare in the box and wait in the bubble."

Once the time is right, however, implementation is rapid. Everyone is totally involved and has given thought to what has to be done. Not only is the time it takes for the decision to be made and implemented shorter than in the past but also the whole process strengthens the organization rather than weakening it through bitterness about how the decision was made.

PEOPLE	...&...	PEOPLE
☐ Rational		○ Social
☐ Produce		○ Create
☐ Think		○ Imagine
☐ Tell		○ Inspire
☐ Work		○ Play

In the old, premerger days, it was convenient to regard employees as rational, welfare-maximizing beings; it made motivating them so much easier and planning less messy.

But because the crisis made it necessary to close many operations and terminate thousands of employees, we had to deal with people's social nature. We could prepare people intellectually by sharing our opinions and, to some extent, protect them physically with severance packages, but we struggled with how to handle the emotional aspects. Especially for long service employees, severing the bond with the company was the emotional equivalent of death.

Humor is what rescued us. Laughter allows people to jump out of their emotional boxes or rigid belief structures. None of us can remember having laughed as much as we have over the past three years. Although much of the humor has inevitably been of the gallows variety, it has been an important ingredient in releasing tension and building trust.

Now everyone knows that people are social as well as rational animals. Indeed, we knew it back in the premerger days, but somehow back then we never came to grips with the social aspect, maybe because the rational view of people has an appealing simplicity and clarity. Lombard's Law applied to us—routine, structured tasks drove out nonroutine, unstructured activities.[10]

COMPENSATION SYSTEMS	...&...	REWARDS
☐ Direct		○ Indirect
☐ Objective		○ Subjective
☐ Profit		○ Fun
☐ Failure		○ Mistake
☐ Hygiene		○ Motivator
☐ Managing		○ Caring

In our premerger organization, the "total compensation policy" meant you could take your money any way you liked—salary, loans, fringes, and so forth. Management thought this policy catered to individual needs and was, therefore, motivating. Similarly, the "Personnel Development Program" required managers to make formal annual reviews of their employees' performances. For some reason, management thought that this also had something to do with motivation. The annual reviews, however, had become a meaningless routine, with managers constrained to be nice to the review subject because they had to work with him or her the next day.

The 1981 recession put a stop to all this by spurring us to freeze all direct compensation. Profit-based compensation disappeared; morale went up.

The management team discussed this decision for hours. As the savings from the freeze would pay for a few weeks' interest only, the numbers made no sense at all. Some of us prophesied doom. "We will lose the best people," we argued. Instead, the symbolic freeze brought the crisis home to everyone. We had all made a sacrifice, a contribution that senior management could recognize at a future time.

Even though the academics say they aren't scientifically valid, we still like Frederick Herzberg's definition of motivations (our interpretations of them are in parentheses):[11]

Achievement (what you believe you did).
Recognition (what others think you did).
Work itself (what you really do).
Responsibility (what you help others do).
Advancement (what you think you can do).
Growth (what you believe you might do).

THE NEW FRAMEWORK AT WORK

The diagram of the soft model in the exhibit shows our view of how our management process seems to work. When the motivating rewards are applied to people playing the necessary roles and working together in groups that are characterized by open communication and are linked to networks throughout the organization, the immediate product is a high degree of mutual trust. This trust allows groups to develop a shared vision that in turn enhances a sense of common purpose. From this process people develop a feeling of having a mission of their own. The mission is spiritual in the sense of being an important effort much larger than oneself. This kind of involvement is highly motivating. Mission is the soft counterpart of strategy.

STRATEGY	... & ...	**MISSION**
☐ Objectives		○ Values
☐ Policies		○ Norms
☐ Forecasts		○ Vision
☐ Clockworks		○ Frameworks
☐ Right		○ Useful
☐ Target		○ Direction
☐ Precise		○ Vague
☐ Necessary		○ Sufficient

Listed are some of our favorite words for contrasting these two polarities. We find them useful for understanding why clear definition of objectives is not essential for motivating people. Hard box planners advocate the hard box elements and tend to be overinvested in using their various models, or "clockworks" as we call them. Whether it's a Boston Consulting Group matrix or an Arthur D. Little life-cycle curve, too often planners wind them up and managers act according to what they dictate without looking at the assumptions, many of which may be invalid, implicit in the frameworks.

We use the models only as take-off points for discussion. They do not have to be right, only useful. If they don't yield genuine insights we put them aside. The hard box cannot be dispensed with. On the contrary, it is essential—but not sufficient.

The key element in developing a shared purpose is mutual trust. Without trust, people will engage in all kinds of self-centered behavior to assert their own identities and influence coworkers to their own ends. Under these circumstances, they just won't hear others, and efforts to develop a shared vision are doomed. Nothing destroys trust faster than hard box attitudes toward problems that don't require such treatment.

Trust is self-reproductive. When trust is present in a situation, chain reactions occur as people share frameworks and exchange unshielded views. The closer and more tightly knit the group is, the more likely it is that these reactions will spread, generating a shared vision and common purpose.

Once the sense of common purpose and mission is established, the managing group is ready to enter the hard box of strategy (see the right-hand side of the exhibit). Now the specifics of task, structure, information, and decision processes are no longer likely to be controversial or threatening. Implementation becomes astonishingly simple. Action plans are necessary to control hard box implementation, but once the participants in the soft bubble share the picture, things seem to happen by themselves as team members play their roles and fill the gaps as they see them. Since efforts to seize control of bubble activity are likely to prove disastrous, it is most fortunate that people act spontaneously without being "organized." Paradoxically, one can achieve control in the bubble only by letting go—which gets right back to trust.

In the hard box, the leadership model is that of the general who gives crisp, precise instructions as to who is to do what and when. In the soft bubble, the leadership model is that of the shepherd, who follows his flock watchfully as it meanders along the natural contours of the land. He carries the weak and collects the strays, for they all have a contribution to make. This style may be inefficient, but it is effective. The whole flock reaches its destination at more or less the same time.[12]

BOXES	... & ...	BUBBLES
☐ Solve		○ Values
☐ Sequential		○ Norms
☐ Left Brain		○ Vision
☐ Serious		○ Frameworks
☐ Explain		○ Useful
☐ Rational		○ Direction
☐ Conscious		○ Unconscious
☐ Learn		○ Remember
☐ Knowledge		○ Wisdom
☐ Lens		○ Mirror
☐ Full		○ Empty
☐ Words		○ Pictures
☐ Objects		○ Symbols
☐ Description		○ Parable

Thought and language are keys to changing perceptions. Boxes and bubbles describe the hard and soft thought structures, respectively. Boxes have rigid, opaque sides; walls have to be broken down to join boxes, although if the lid is off one can jump out. Bubbles have flexible, transparent sides that can easily expand and join with other bubbles. Bubbles float but can easily burst. In boxes problems are to be solved; in bubbles they are dissolved. The trick is to change the context of the problem, that is, to jump out of the box. This technique has many applications.

We have noticed a number of articles in your publication that concern values and ethics in business, and some people have suggested that business students be required to attend classes in ethics. From our view of the world, sending students to specific courses is a hard box solution and would be ineffective. Ethical behavior is absent from some businesses not because the managers have no ethics (or have the wrong ones) but because the hard "strategy box" does not emphasize them as being valuable. The hard box deals in objectives, and anyone who raises value issues in that context will not survive long.

In contrast, in the "mission bubble" people feel free to talk about values and ethics because there is trust. The problem of the lack of ethical behavior is dissolved.

We have found bubble thinking to be the intellectual equivalent of judo; a person does not resist an attacker but goes with the flow, thereby adding his strength to the other's momentum. Thus, when suppliers demanded that their financial exposure to our lack of creditworthiness be reduced, we agreed and suggested that they protect themselves by supplying goods to us on consignment. After all, their own financial analysis showed we couldn't pay them any money! In some cases we actually got consignment deals, and where we didn't the scheme failed because of nervous lawyers (also hard box players) rather than reluctance on the part of the supplier.

Bubble thought structures are characterized by what Edward de Bono calls *lateral thinking*.[13] The sequential or vertical thought structure is logical and rational; it proceeds through logical stages and depends on a yes-no test at each step. De Bono suggests that in lateral thinking the yes-no test must be suspended, for the purpose is to explore not explain, to test assumptions not conclusions.

We do the same kind of questioning when we do what we call "humming a lot." When confronted with what initially appears to be an unpalatable idea, an effective manager will say "hmm" and wait until the idea has been developed and its implications considered. Quite often, even when an initial idea is out of the question, the fact that we have considered it seriously will lead to a different, innovative solution.

We have found it useful to think of the action opposite to the one we intend taking. When selling businesses we found it helpful to think about acquiring purchasers. This led to deeper research into purchasers' backgrounds and motives and to a more effective packaging and presentation of the businesses to be sold. This approach encourages novel ideas and makes the people who generate them (the entrepreneurs) feel that their ideas, however "dumb," will not be rejected out of hand.

In hard box thought structures, one tends to use conceptual frameworks as lenses, to sit on one side and examine an object on the other. In bubble structures, the frameworks are mirrors reflecting one's own nature and its effect on one's perceptions; object and subject are on the same side. In the hard box, knowledge is facts, from learning; in the bubble knowledge is wisdom, from experience.

Bubble thought structures are not easily described in words. Language itself is a box reflecting our cultural heritage and emphasizing some features of reality at the expense of others. Part of our struggle during the past three years has been to unlearn many scientific management concepts and develop a new vocabulary. We have come up with some new phrases and words: *management by walking around, creative stall, asking dumb questions, jumping out of the box, creating a crisis, humming a lot,* and *muddling*. We have also attached new meanings to old words such as *fact* and *perception, independence* and *autonomy, hard* and *soft, solve* and *dissolve,* and so forth.

THREE YEARS LATER

What we have told you about works in a crisis. And we can well understand your asking whether this approach can work when the business is stable and people lapse back into boxes. We have developed two methods of preventing this lapse.

1. IF THERE ISN'T A CRISIS, WE CREATE ONE

One way to stir things up is familiar to anyone who has ever worked in a hard box organization. Intimidation, terror, and the use of raw power will produce all the stress you need. But eventually people run out of adrenaline and the organization is drained, not invigorated.

In a bubble organization, managers dig for opportunities in a much more relaxed manner. During the last three years, for instance, many of our divisions that were profitable and liquid were still in need of strategic overhaul. During the course of walking around, we unearthed many important issues by asking dumb questions.

The more important of the issues that surface this way offer an opportunity to put a champion (someone who believes in the importance of the issue) in charge of a team of people who can play all the roles required to handle the issue. The champion then sets out with his or her group to go through the incremental development process—developing trust, building both a hard box picture and a shared vision, and, finally, establishing strategy. By the time the strategy is arrived at, the task force disciples have such zeal and sense of mission that they are ready to take the issue to larger groups, using the same process.

Two by-products of asking dumb questions deserve mention. First, when senior management talks to people at all levels, people at all levels start talking to each other. Second, things tend to get fixed before they break. In answering a senior manager's casual question, a welder on the shop floor of a steel fabrication plant revealed that some critical welds had failed quality tests and the customer's inspector was threatening to reject an entire bridge. A small ad hoc task force, which included the inspector (with the customer's permission), got everyone off the hook and alerted top management to a potential weakness in the quality control function.

Applying the principles in other areas takes years to bear fruit. We are now using the process to listen to customers and suppliers. We never knew how to do this before. Now it is clear that it is necessary to create an excuse (crisis) for going to see them, share "secrets," build trust, share a vision, and capture them in your bubble. It's very simple, and early results have been excellent. We call it a soft revolution.

2. INFUSE ACTIVITIES THAT SOME MIGHT THINK PROSAIC WITH REAL SIGNIFICANCE

The focus should be on people first, and always on caring rather than managing. The following approach works in good times as well as bad:

Use a graphic vocabulary that describes what you do.

Share confidential information, personal hopes, and fears to create a common vision and promote trust.

Seize every opportunity (open doors, management by walking around, networks) to make a point, emphasize a value, disseminate information, share an experience, express interest, and show you care.

Recognize performance and contribution of as many people as possible. Rituals and ceremonies—retirements, promotions, birthdays—present great opportunities.

Use incentive programs whose main objective is not compensation but recognition.

We have tried to approach things this way, and for us the results have been significant. Now, we are a very different organization. Of our 25 divisions, we have closed 7 and sold 16. Five of the latter were bought by Federal Industries, Ltd. of Winnipeg. Some 860 employees including us, the four members of the management team, have gone to Federal. These divisions are healthy and raring to go. Two divisions remain at York Russel, which has changed its name to YRI-YORK, Ltd.

Now we face new questions, such as how one recruits into a management team. We know that we have to help people grow into the team, and fortunately we find that they flourish in our warm climate. But trust takes time to develop, and the bubble is fragile. The risk is greatest when we have to transplant a senior person from outside, because time pressures may not allow us to be sure we are compatible. The danger is not only to the team itself but also to the person joining it.

Our new framework has given us a much deeper appreciation of the management process and the roles effective general managers play. For example, it is clear that while managers can delegate tasks in the hard box rather easily—perhaps because they can define them—it's impossible to delegate soft bubble activities. The latter are difficult to isolate from each other because their integration takes place in one brain.

Similarly, the hard box general management roles of producer and administrator can be formally taught, and business schools do a fine job of it. The soft roles of entrepreneur and integrator can probably not be taught formally. Instead, managers must learn from mentors. Over time they will adopt behavior patterns that allow them to play the required roles. It would seem, however, that natural ability and an individual's upbringing probably play a much larger part in determining effectiveness in the soft roles than in the hard roles; it is easier to teach a soft bubble player the hard box roles than it is to teach the soft roles to a hard box player.

In the three-year period when we had to do things so differently, we created our own culture, with its own language, symbols, norms, and customs. As with other groups, the acculturation process began when people got together in groups and trusted and cared about each other.[14]

In contrast with our premerger culture, the new culture is much more sympathetic toward and supportive of the use of teams and consensus decision making. In this respect, it would seem to be similar to oriental ways of thinking that place a premium on the same processes. Taoists, for instance, would have no trouble recognizing the polarities of the hard box and the soft bubble and the need to keep a balance between the two.[15]

HEAVEN ... & ... **EARTH**

□ Yang	○ Yin
□ Father	○ Mother
□ Man	○ Woman

These symbols are instructive. After all, most of us grew up with two bosses: father usually played the hard box parts, while mother played the soft, intuitive, and entrepreneurial roles. The family is the original team, formed to handle the most complex management task ever faced. Of late, we seem to have fired too many of its members—a mistake we can learn from.

TOWARD A MANAGERIAL THEORY OF RELATIVITY

The traditional hard box view of management, like the traditional orientation of physics, is valid (and very useful) only within a narrow range of phenomena. Once one gets outside the range, one needs new principles. In physics, cosmologists at the macro level as well as students of subatomic particles at the micro level use Einstein's theory of relativity as an explanatory principle and set Newton's physics aside.[16] For us, the theory in the bubble is our managerial theory of relativity. At the macro level it reminds us that how management phenomena appear depends on one's perspective and biases. At the micro level we remember that all jobs have both hard and soft components.

This latter point is of particular importance to people like us in the service industry. The steel we distribute is indistinguishable from anyone else's. We insist on rigid standards regarding how steel is handled, what reporting systems are used, and so forth. But hard box standards alone wouldn't be enough to set us apart from our competitors. That takes service, a soft concept. And everyone has to be involved. Switchboard operators are in the front line; every contact is an opportunity to share the bubble. Truck drivers and warehouse workers make their own special contribution—by taking pride in the cleanliness of their equipment or by keeping the inventory neat and accessible.

With the box and bubble concept, managers can unlock many of the paradoxes of management and handle the inherent ambiguities. You don't do one or the other absolutely; you do what is appropriate. For instance, the other day in one of our operations the biweekly payroll run deducted what appeared to be random amounts from the sales representatives' pay packets. The branch affected was in an uproar. After taking some hard box steps to remedy the situation, our vice president of human resources seized the opportunity to go out to the branch and talk to the sales team. He was delighted with the response. The sales force saw that he understood the situation and cared about them, and he got to meet them all, which will make future contacts easier. But neither the hard box nor soft bubble approach on its own would have been appropriate. We need both. As one team member put it, "You have to find the bubble in the box and put the box in the bubble." Exactly.

The amazing thing is that the process works so well. The spirit of cooperation among senior managers is intense, and we seem to be getting "luckier" as we go along. When a "magic" event takes place it means that somehow we got the timing just right.[17] And there is great joy in that.

REFERENCES

[1] T. I. Peters and R. H. Waterman, *In Search of Excellence* (New York: Harper and Row, 1981), 29.

[2] For the best of the hard box models we have come across, see J. R. Galbraith, *Organization Design* (Reading, MA: Addison-Wesley, 1977).

[3] H. Mintzberg, "The Manager's Job: Folklore and Fact," *Harvard Business Review* (July-August 1975): 49.

[4] E. H. Schein, *Process Consultation: Its Role in Organization Development* (Reading, MA: Addison-Wesley, 1969).

[5] I. Adize, *How to Solve the Mismanagement Crisis* (Los Angeles, MDOR Institute, 1979).

[6] E. H. Schein's *Process Consultation*, page 10, was very helpful in showing us how the process differs from the content.

[7] Getting consensus among a group of managers poses the same challenge as negotiating a deal. *Getting to Yes* by Robert Fisher and William Ury (Boston: Houghton Mifflin, 1981) is a most helpful book for understanding the process.

[8] For discussion of the importance of networks, see J. Kotter, "What Effective General Managers Really Do," *Harvard Business Review* (November-December 1982): 156.

[9] For discussion of a "creative stall" being applied in practice, see S. Sherman, "Muddling to Victory at Geico," *Fortune*, September 5, 1983, 66.

[10] L. B. Bames, "Managing the Paradox of Organizational Trust," *Harvard Business Review* (March-April 1981): 107.

[11] In "One More Time: How Do You Motivate Employees?" *Harvard Business Review* (January-February 1968): 53.

[12] For another view of the shepherd role, see the poem by N. Esposito, "The Good Shepherd," *Harvard Business Review* (July-August 1983): 121.

[13] See E. de Bono, *The Use of Lateral Thinking* (London: Jonathan Cape, 1967) and *Beyond Yes and No* (New York: Simon and Schuster, 1972).

[14] To explore the current concern with creating strong organizational cultures in North American corporations, see T. E. Deal and A. A. Kennedy, *Corporate Cultures* (Reading, MA: Addison-Wesley, 1982).

[15] For discussion of Tao and some applications, we highly recommend B. Hoff, *The Tao of Pooh* (New York: E. Dutton, 1982) 67; also A. Watts, *Tao: The Watercourse Way* (New York: Pantheon Books, 1975).

[16] Frity of Capra, *The Tao of Physics* (London: Fontana Paperbacks, 1963).

[17] Carl Jung developed the concept of synchronicity to explain such events. See, for example, I. Progoff, *Jung Synchronicity and Human Destiny—Non-Causal Dimensions of Human Experience* (New York: Julian Press, 1973). For an excellent discussion of Jung's work and its relevance to our times, see L. van de Post, *Jung and the Story of Our Time* (New York: Random House, 1975).

CREATIVITY AS INVESTMENT*

Robert J. Sternberg
Linda A. O'Hara
Todd I. Lubart

Almost every company wants more highly creative employees. Millions of dollars are spent each year on creativity training programs or creativity consultants, often with very disappointing results from the standpoint of management as well as the consultant. Robert Burnside from the Center for Creative Leadership complained about generating ideas that come to nothing and making "feel-good-in-the-moment and soon-forgotten presentations" that lead to no real impact.[1] Another very successful creativity consultant admitted that many of the people who went through his company's training program quit

*Reprinted with permission from the *California Management Review 40*, no. 1 (Fall 1997): 8–21.

their jobs after it, presumably wanting to try out some of their bright ideas someplace else. It doesn't take long before management wises up and drops such a program. In some cases, employees come back energized and excited for a few weeks but eventually end up back in the doldrums. In other cases, people just feel silly and childish in the exercises and never really go along with them.

The purpose here is not to criticize creativity training. Some of the companies like Synectics, The Center for Creative Leadership, and The Creative Education Foundation and consultants like Roger von Oech and Edward de Bono and others have impressive stories to tell, although careful quantitative validations of such programs are rare. If there are disappointing results, one reason may be that the training often focuses on creative thinking, which is only one of the six resources needed for creative enterprise. These six resources include knowledge, intellectual abilities, thinking styles, motivation, personality, and the environment. What brings them together is an investment stance creative people take toward life, a stance any of us can adopt but rarely do (and may not want to, given the risks and sacrifices involved).[2]

Creative people practice in the realm of ideas what financial investors do in the stock market. They defy the crowd to "buy low and sell high."[3] Buying low means pursuing ideas that are unknown, or at least slightly out of favor, but with growth potential. Just as not every stock with a low price-earnings ratio is a good financial investment, neither is every new idea a good creativity investment. Buying low is inherently risky. Selling high means finding buyers for one's work, convincing them of its worth, and moving on to new projects when it becomes valued and yields a significant return. Analogous to stock market investment success, sometimes creativity fails to occur because a person puts forth ("sells") an idea prematurely or holds an idea so long that it becomes common or obsolete. The six resources noted above need to be invested in the idea market to earn a creative return, just as money is invested in the stock market for a financial return.

KNOWLEDGE

To do original work, one needs the basic knowledge of the field so as to go beyond the status quo. To go beyond, one has to know where the status quo is. A poignant example is the Indian mathematician Srinivasa Ramanujan, considered one of the most brilliant mathematical thinkers ever.[4] Because of his lack of contact with the outside world, he unwittingly spent part of his lifetime single-handedly "rediscovering" much of what was already known in Western mathematics. Mathematicians have been wondering for half a century how their field could have been advanced had Ramanujan been brought up in different circumstances with better access to the existing mathematical knowledge base of his day.

Knowledge is also necessary because creativity has been shown to be fairly domain specific, meaning that people are not generally creative in every field but rather in specific areas. In one of our studies, adults had to produce two creative products in each of four domains: writing, art, advertising, and science.[5] The materials for each task consisted of a list of topics, from which two were to be selected, and an array of supplies (e.g., pens, paper, pastels). Writing topics included a list of titles such as "Beyond the Edge" and "A Fifth Chance," to be expanded into very short stories. Some topics for drawing were "hope," "rage," and "earth from an insect's point of view." Advertising commercials were requested for things such as bow-ties, Brussels sprouts, and the IRS. An example of a science problem was "How could we detect extraterrestrial aliens hiding among us?" Three to ten topics were provided for each domain.

Our creativity rating procedure was modeled on Teresa Amabile's consensual assessment technique,[6] with the exception that peer judges were used. Peers, rather than experts, were chosen to be raters because peers are the most likely audience for lay persons' work, and peers typically evaluate each others' work. Fifteen raters judged the creativity of the products people produced. We analyzed the creativity ratings across the four domains and found at best weak to moderate relationships. For example, a person who did well in advertising did not necessarily do well in the creative writing or drawing task. One reason for this domain specificity is the considerable amount of time needed to acquire extensive knowledge of a field. Dean Simonton has estimated that substantial creative achievements occur on average after at least 10 years of involvement in a field.[7] The stock tip from the famous investor Peter Lynch, "Invest in things you understand," is good advice as well for the creativity investor.[8]

While knowledge is important, there can be too much. Often creative ideas involve combining seemingly unrelated things. If a person is so knowledgeable about a specific area, as the joke about some academics goes, he knows more and more about less and less until he knows everything about nothing. His mind is closed to making these "unrelated" connections. He thinks he "knows" that a given idea won't work. Lewis Platt, the chairman of Hewlett-Packard, told a story about how HP's product divisions had to be forced into taking on the hand-held calculator developed by their Research and Development lab.[9] The product divisions were selling desk-top calculators and "knew" there was no market for the smaller ones. In their heyday, IBM knew what their computer customers wanted, Sears knew what their retail customers wanted, and the Detroit auto makers knew what car buyers wanted. Maybe they knew too much. Their extensive knowledge of their fields—of their customers and competitors and of how things worked—blinded them to the changes occurring and could have been one of the factors which led to their losses in market share. Creative people and companies don't get locked in by what they know; they are able to move on to the next idea. When a successful software company releases a new product, it's already old to the engineers. They're on to the next release, or better, to a new product.

An impressive example of not knowing too much is what the Eastman School of Music is doing to combat the decline in the classical music business.[10] Eastman is part of the University of Rochester and one of the most prestigious music schools in the country. It has always seen itself as a training ground for students studying 18th and 19th century composers, such as Mozart and Brahms, who want to prepare for careers with major orchestras. But the shrinking and graying audiences for traditional concert-hall performances and the decline in classical music's share of the recorded-sound market have necessitated a change in Eastman's philosophy. Professors at the school are preparing their students to be musical entrepreneurs, given the financial troubles of many symphony orchestras. They have undertaken an extensive effort to bring the school's curriculum more in tune with the music world of today, expanding the curriculum to include the study of rock, folk, and even contemporary religious music. Eastman is redefining what music education is about.

INTELLECTUAL ABILITIES

As mentioned earlier, creativity often involves making new connections—seeing things in new ways and redefining problems. The wife of a high-level executive in one of the "Big-Three" automobile companies in Detroit told one of us a story that is a superb example of redefining problems. Her husband loved his job, but hated his boss. After years of putting up with the tyrant, he finally decided he had had enough, and so he went to see a headhunter. The headhunter assured the executive that a new job was easily within reach. That night, the executive told his wife what had happened during his day; she, in turn, described the main event of her day—teaching her college students how to redefine the problems they faced in school and in life. The executive, seeing the relevance of her lesson for his own situation, took her message to heart. He returned to the headhunter, and gave the headhunter his boss's name. The surprised boss soon received a job offer and took it. The executive had redefined his problem, and found his boss rather than himself a new job. A fringe benefit also emerged: the opening up of his boss's job, a job, that the executive soon got.

The first intellectual ability that applies to creativity is this synthetic ability to see connections and redefine problems. While individuals vary in this capacity, everyone can improve it. It is the resource many creativity training programs concentrate on. Many of the games and imagination exercises in such programs are designed to get people to think outside the box, make connections, or look at a problem from a different viewpoint. Roger von Oech has his Creative Whack Pack. Synectics has its excursions. Edward de Bono has his six hats. Everybody seems to have some variation on "Pretend you're a vacuum cleaner." Sometimes they're silly; sometimes, they're brilliant. But they're never enough.

The second intellectual ability is analytic. One needs to be able to judge the value or potential in an idea. Depending on the task, it is sometimes better to postpone using this ability until you've practiced the synthetic ability for a time so that you can generate more options to evaluate. Eventually, though, you have to analyze the ideas for their potential return, just as you have to decide which stocks to invest in.

The third intellectual ability is practical. Sometimes, idea-people like to think they are above the dirty details of selling their ideas. They think the value of each of their ideas is obvious and ought to be celebrated upon introduction. Well, unfortunately, life doesn't work that way. If you can't figure out a way to present your ideas so that your audience sees the same value you do, nothing creative happens. If you can't figure out (or get somebody to help you figure out) all the steps necessary to implement the idea, nothing happens.

Our research shows that these three intellectual abilities—the synthetic, analytic, and practical abilities—are relatively independent.[11] One can be adept in any one of these three abilities without being adept in any of the others. Unfortunately, conventional tests of abilities assess only the analytical abilities, not the synthetic and practical ones, thereby failing to spot a great deal of talent.

THINKING STYLE PREFERENCES

People vary in the way they prefer to use their intellectual abilities. They have a certain style or characteristic way of acting. Some like to do things their own way. We call that an inventing style. Others who like to follow established ways of doing things could be said to have an implementing style. They prefer to implement the ideas of others rather than invent their own. Another group of people who prefer to sit back and observe others and analyze or criticize what those others do could be said to have an evaluating style. They typically act as critics or judges, rather than performers. Everyone possesses every style to some degree. What differs across individuals is the strength of preferences and the kinds of tasks and situations that evoke various preferences.

To be creative, a person has to like using the inventing thinking style and have a preference for thinking in novel ways of his own choosing. We have seen people who have the ability to forge their own paths but simply prefer not to. Although they are wired for creativity, they never turn on the juice. On the other hand, there are some people who want to come up with new ideas—who have the inventing style preference—but who don't have the synthetic intellectual ability to do so effectively. Although their switches are turned on, the wiring is incomplete. It may help to understand this point by imagining somebody who loves to sing but can't carry a tune. They have the style preference but not the ability. Or imagine somebody who is great at detail work but hates it and always delegates it. The person has the ability but not the style preference. Style, then, is not ability—it is whether and how one uses that ability. It is how characteristic the demonstration of a particular ability is for one. And style is a key ingredient in creativity, as it is needed to help complete the circuit—to "switch on" abilities that otherwise might lie dormant.

Style preferences can also be understood as habits or practice with a particular intellectual ability. If a person habitually criticizes the ideas of others without practicing the generation of his own ideas, his analytical ability may become sharp and precise, but his synthetic, inventing ability will become dull from lack of use.

MOTIVATION

A person can have all the knowledge, ability, and style in the world, but he still has to be motivated to make something happen. Motivation in this case means making an investment. Buying low in the realm of ideas is an action, not a thought or a daydream. Too often, managers think they need more ideas. But as Theodore Levitt said. "Ideas are useless unless used .... A powerful new idea can kick around unused in a company for years, not because its merits are not recognized, but because nobody has assumed the responsibility for converting it from words into action." [12] As buying is an action, there needs to be an actor responsible for converting the idea into an action. The "champion" that Tom Peters and Bob Waterman described in *In Search of Excellence.*

The amount of motivation needed to buy low can be minuscule compared with the motivation and persistence needed to get to the point where one can sell high. The years that it takes to build up the necessary knowledge to make a major creative contribution in a field is not spent in passive learning, but rather in constant experimentation, revising, discarding, playing, and pulling one's hair out. Edison learned 1,800 ways not to build a light bulb before he got it right. Clarence Birdseye had his flash of insight 40 years before all the pieces were in place for the frozen food industry he started. [13] It took Bill Bowerman and Philip Knight of Nike more than 20 years to gather the resources and technical skills to synthesize them into one shoe. [14] 3M Chairman Lewis Lehr told the story about how 3M got into the business of making roofing granules for asphalt shingles because one worker persisted in trying to find a way to use rejected sandpaper minerals. He was actually fired because of the time and effort he spent on this problem. But he kept coming to work anyway. The 3M roofing granules division subsequently earned substantial revenue and the man who wouldn't quit playing with the rejected sandpaper eventually retired as vice president of the division. [15] Twenty or forty years is a long time to wait for a reward; clearly, creative people are focused more on the task or problem than on immediate rewards.

PERSONALITY

Creativity requires a risk-taking personality, someone who can take a stand and be a contrarian. Neil Aronson, a lawyer who helps companies prepare to go public, says the price in an initial public offering might be reasonable, but the after-market involves "people [who] get caught up in the buying craziness .... Everyone wants to follow the crowd." [16] Buying low means defying the crowd and going on your own. It means that people you admire and respect may say you are crazy. Market surveys for 3M's Post-It note pads, for example, were negative and major office-supply distributors told the creator of the pads that they were silly. [17] Someone easily dismayed by criticism will have a tough time being creative. Buying low is not easy to do. Standing on one's own is obviously risky, but the risks are minimized by the other creative capital resources invested: knowledge, intellectual abilities, thinking styles, motivation/persistence, and the environment.

ENVIRONMENT

It is the environment that determines how large the risks appear to the creative person. Daniel Kahneman and Amos Tversky, two well-known psychologists, found that people are risk-averse when choosing between potential gains and risk-seeking only when choosing between potential losses. [18] For example, suppose your company has 600 important targeted customers and you are trying to decide between two trade shows. Your hot-shot marketing director tells you that 200 customers will be at Show 1 for sure but that there is a one-third probability that all 600 customers will be at Show 2 and a two-thirds probability that no one will be there. Which show should you choose? If you're like most people, you will choose Show 1, figuring that a bird in the hand is better than two in the bush. In other words, the certainty of seeing 200 customers is preferable to the risky prospect of just a one-in-three chance of seeing all of them. You are risk averse when selecting between possible gains. But wait: The even-hotter-shot assistant to the marketing director rushes into your office to say that, at Show 1, you're sure to miss 400 customers but at Show 2, although there is a two-in-three probability that you'll miss all 600, there is a one-in-three probability that you won't miss any. Now which show will you choose? This time, it may seem like Show 2 would be better. If you're going to miss that many customers with a sure bet, it might be worth taking the gamble on the one-third chance of not missing any. In both scenarios, the benefits of the two shows are statistically equal. In fact, the two scenarios yield exactly the same results. They differ in the way they are worded: one in terms of gains—customers seen in the first scenario; the other in terms of losses—customers missed in the second scenario. Thus, whether one selects the riskier bet is likely to depend on whether gains or losses are involved.

To relate this research on risk preferences to the obstacles encountered by a creative person, consider the difference in the views of a young scientist and an older scientist in a large R&D department trying to decide whether or not to present a risky idea to senior managment. From the young scientist's point of view, she's deciding between maintaining a sure negative (her status as an unknown) and a possible gain (her potential status as a rising star if her idea is accepted), which leads her to take the risk. From the older scientist's point of view, he's deciding between maintaining a sure positive (his established good reputation) and a possible loss (his potential involuntary early retirement if senior management hates the idea), which leads him to be risk averse. Over the life of your career, your early need to succeed can be replaced by a need to avoid failure. Couple this risk avoidance that accompanies experience with the extensive knowledge developed over the years that can cause blindness to change and it is no wonder that it is often hard to find creativity in large, established companies. These companies are like people who have been in their jobs for a long time. Creative ideas may involve risks that can seem too great and/or contradict what is "known" to be true.

People fear change. Despite the fact that many people claim to value novel ideas, there is strong evidence that they don't like them. One of the most solid findings in psychology is the "mere-exposure effect": People like most what is familiar to them.[19] The more they hear rap music or study cubist art, the more comfortable they become with it, and the more they like it. Thus, research indicates that although people may value creativity because it will bring progress, they are often uncomfortable with it and hence may initially react negatively to creative work.

One example of the sort of entrenchment that occurs due to the mere exposure effect is the QWERTY keyboard, which was originally designed to slow people down in their typing so that the keys would not jam. There are no keys to jam with word processors, but no matter how much better a different keyboard is, it will be a long time before people will give up the QWERTY. They know how to type and have no intention of learning how to type all over again—experts, be damned. Anybody who has ever had to change software systems knows what a challenge it is to get people to give up the familiar. Any company trying to compete with Gold Medal flour or Eveready batteries or a dozen other name brands that have been market leaders for over 60 years knows the same challenge.[20]

Another normal reaction that dampens creativity, particularly in meeting or other group situations, is our negativity bias[21] in evaluating others' intellectual work and our tendency to perceive critics as more intelligent than praise-givers.[22] Teresa Amabile gave people edited excerpts from actual negative and positive book reviews written by the same reviewer for the Sunday *New York Times* and asked them to make assessments of the reviewer's intelligence and other characteristics. The negative reviews were perceived to be written by someone more intelligent, competent, and expert than the positive reviews, even when the content of the positive review was independently judged as being of higher quality and greater forcefulness.

We see these unfortunate negative patterns in students in classrooms, in professors in academic colloquia, and in managers in business meetings. It can happen anywhere people care about impressing higher-status others with their intelligence. If you want to look smart in front of your boss, there's nothing like a good dig about a rival's idea. What can result is a double whammy for creativity—everybody in the meeting looks for flaws and the decision maker over-weights the comments of the critics because the critics seem smarter than the idea generators.

Brainstorming sessions, which allow only idea generation and not criticism, were an attempt to overcome this critical environment. Much research has shown that people in face-to-face brainstorming meetings are less efficient at generating ideas than when working alone.[23] But at IDEO, the largest product design consulting company in the United States, brainstorming is a way of life. In their analysis of brainstorming's effectiveness at IDEO, Sutton and Hargadon found that

> *IDEO brainstorms may not be the most efficient means for generating ideas or for doing any other single task, but they are efficient for accomplishing a variety of important tasks at once. In addition to generating possible design solutions, brain storms support the organization's memory of technical solutions, provide skill variety, support an attitude of wisdom in and outside the session, create a status auction that maintains a focus on designing products, and they impress clients and generate income.[24]*

Some years ago we did a study investigating conceptions of creativity, wisdom, and intelligence in different groups, including experts in philosophy, physics, art, and business, as well as lay people.[25] There was one particularly striking finding with respect to the experts in business. In most fields there was little or no relation between the behaviors believed to characterize the creative person and the behaviors believed to characterize the wise person. But in the business group, the relation was actually negative: Business people tended to believe that it was unwise to be creative. In fact, our experience suggests that creative people in an organization are often viewed as oddballs and are likely to become outcasts. If this attitude exists in an organizational environment, creativity will surely be stifled.

WHAT CAN A COMPANY DO TO ENCOURAGE CREATIVITY?

To be creative, a company has to invest in the same six resources as the individual: knowledge, intellectual abilities, thinking styles, motivation, personality, and environment.

KNOWLEDGE

If it takes 10 years for a person to acquire expertise in a field, the company has to adopt a long-term perspective and give a person that time to develop. The typical obsession with the next quarter's earnings does not help develop creative talent. It is also important to be careful about not over-weighting the criticisms of the most senior people in the organization when evaluating the merits of a creative proposal, because too much knowledge can sometimes lead to rigidity in thinking and intolerance of change. Your senior people cannot help but remind you of the investment the company has in an existing structure, product, or method. They were probably the original champions of those structures or products or methods when they were instituted. Their criticisms will sound very intelligent and confident. In contrast, the new idea will sound more tentative and undeveloped.

INTELLECTUAL ABILITIES

Although synthetic, analytical, and practical talents are necessary for any creative enterprise, the mix and weight of the talents needed change over the life cycle of an idea or product. In the idea-generation phase, synthetic ability is the most important. During this phase, a manager would do well to include in the team some people with high synthetic ability and encourage all team members to use that particular ability. Having someone with superior analytical abilities in an idea-generation meeting can be quite damaging if the person cannot turn off the criticism. Only after many ideas have been generated, choosing which ideas to pursue requires more analytical ability. At this stage, a manager could replace or supplement some of the idea generators with team members with high analytical ability, or specifically instruct the existing team to bring this ability to the forefront. After a selection of the most promising ideas has been made and execution of those ideas is the task at hand, the manager could introduce new members to the team who have the high practical ability that is required during this stage.

THINKING STYLE PREFERENCES

Our research shows that creative people tend to prefer an inventing style. However, most schools and businesses encourage an implementing style. Teachers and managers often want students and employees to do just what they are told. As a result, the best students and the employees selected for promotion are often those with the style that the school or company has encouraged, that is, the implementing style. They are very good at following directions but may not be so good at inventing new ways to do things. In entry level jobs and lower levels of management, following directions may be directions. At higher levels, it is an inventing style that is necessary. Unfortunately, the people with a natural inventing style were long ago derailed for not fitting in and not doing what they were told.

To some extent, our thinking-style preferences follow the reward structure of our environment. We prefer the styles that get rewarded. We also try to adapt to the organizational culture and fit in. If we can't fit in, we leave.[26] If a manager continually rewards an employee for following instructions to the letter or finding flaws in other people's work, she is encouraging that employee to use the implementing or the evaluating thinking style. Letting someone do a job his own way (especially when that way is not the manager's way) encourages him to use the creative inventing style. Seeing a colleague get rewarded for using the inventing style encourages a person to try it himself. The best thing a manager can do to encourage an inventing style is to serve as a role model and use that style herself.

MOTIVATION

People are generally creative only in pursuits they enjoy. If you don't enjoy an activity, you won't invest the often incredible amounts of time and energy necessary to succeed in it. Probably the single most important thing a manager can do to encourage creativity on a project is to make it fun to work on that project. Anita Roddick, of The Body Shop, gives these three recommendations: "First, you have to have fun. Second, you have to put love where your labour is. Third, you have to go in the opposite direction to everyone else."[27] Talking about Southwest Airlines being "consistently profitable in an industry stuck in intensive care." Tom Peters said, "Southwest's secret to success: making sure its workers have fun."[28] Joline Godfrey, the founder of Odysseum, an international learning-game design company she spun off from Polaroid and sold in 1990, believes, "All work and no play doesn't just make Jill and Jack dull, it kills the potential of discovery, mastery, and openness to change and flexibility and it hinders innovation and invention."[29] She recruited her colleagues at Polaroid to help her on their own time by making it "look like working on an 'illicit,' 'underground' project was an adventure." Data General had "pinball ... You win one game, you get to play another. You win with this machine, you get to build the next."[30] Kodak has a humor room for people to unwind in, play games, or watch funny videos.[31] IDEO designers describe their brainstorms as one of the most fun things they do.[32]

Morris Stein reminds us: "This playfulness is not such as to make the person whimsical and lacking in seriousness with regard to work. Rather it is a playfulness which enables the individual to play with ideas and mix things which they see before him/her so that new combinations form."[33] If creativity is a goal, all of these pieces of advice make clear the importance of designing work to be more intrinsically satisfying,[34] that is, more fun. As Matt Weinstein, author of *Managing to Have Fun* and founder of Playfair, Inc., said, "The company that plays together stays together."[35]

If all this fun and games sounds too unprofessional or too similar to previous failed attempts to link job satisfaction and productivity, be comforted by some serious research by Barry Staw and Sigal Barsade, who found that happier people were more effective at both managerial decision-making tasks and interpersonal negotiations than their so-called sadder-but-wiser colleagues.[36]

PERSONALITY

People who have their own way of thinking and doing things often appear strange to people who are more conventional. As mentioned earlier, they often become outcasts. We need these outcasts because they are tuned in to a reality many of us do not see. Organizations need to be concerned with keeping sufficient diversity inside the organization to sense accurately the variety outside it because any individual has only limited experiences from which to make the connections that may suggest an innovation.[37] It is as if we all have a unique antenna that picks up a few channels of reality. If we have only people similar to ourselves in a company (and most senior management teams comprise members who are similar to each other), we will all be tuned to the same channels and miss the rest of the world. We need the outcasts to provide those other channels we are missing.

Executives at the Walt Disney Company know good movie ideas can come from anybody, not just those with the appropriate business card. Three times a year, they host a "Gong Show," in which everyone in the company—including secretaries, janitors, and mailroom staff—gets to pitch ideas to the top executives.[38] Putting the need-for-outcasts idea more bluntly, Jeffrey Beir, a former vice president at Lotus (now CEO of Instinctive Technology), said, "You have to put your corporation's destiny into the hands of someone you wouldn't want your daughter dating."[39]

ENVIRONMENT

Because we cannot predict the future with much accuracy, both the company and the creative individual need to manage the risk involved in playing with creative ideas. Not all low P/E or out-of-favor stocks are good buys; many are out-of-favor because they are junk. You cannot always tell in advance. A company supporting an odd bunch of creative people doing their own things needs to spread the risk, just as a wise stock-market investor does. A company might act as a venture capitalist does. Venture capitalists invest in a portfolio of high-risk investments. They don't invest their entire fund in one project and they don't promise their investors that every investment will be a winner. In most cases, the majority of investments are losers that are offset with a few huge winners.

A mistake sometimes made in trying to manage the uncertainty associated with creative projects is to try to control them or somehow establish some order. As uncomfortable as it is, it's important to let the messiness exist. IDEO has no organization charts, no titles, not even permanent offices.[40] Employees' file cabinets and bookcases are on wheels so they can easily move to another office more convenient for the project team. Rosabeth Moss Kanter described one innovative company's organization charts as resembling "plates of spaghetti more than a conventional set of boxes."[41] She said, "Creativity does not derive from order but from the attempt to impose order where it does not exist, to make new connections."[42] In her studies, she found that innovating companies provide the freedom to act, which arouses the desire to act.

> *The way innovating companies are designed leaves ambiguities, overlaps, decisions, conflicts, or decision vacuums in some parts of the organization. People rail at this, curse it—and invent innovative ways to overcome it. People wait for the decision makers to do what they "ought to do," and then, in frustration perhaps conclude, "Darn it, I'll have to do it myself."*[43]

What Kanter points out is that some kinds of uncertainty create opportunities. These somewhat chaotic environments are not easy to manage and may not work for all companies but they can enhance creativity and lead to successful products.

SUMMARY

In summary, creativity requires investing in six distinct but interrelated resources, all of which must be present to get a positive result when they are combined:

- knowledge—knowing what is new, not just reinvented;
- intellectual abilities—generating, evaluating, and executing ideas:
- thinking styles—a preference for thinking in novel ways of one's own choosing:
- motivation—making a move, having fun;
- personality—determination and persistence in overcoming obstacles; and
- environment—one that supports the investment game and spreads the risk.

In other words, creativity is buying low and selling high.

ENDNOTES

[1] R. M. Burnside, "Ideas Dancing in the Human Being," *Creative Action in Organizations: Ivory Tower Visions and Real World Voices,* eds. C. M. Ford and D. A. Gioia (Thousand Oaks, CA: Sage Publications, 1995) 302–307.

[2] B. M. Staw, "Why No One Really Wants Creativity," *Creative Action in Organizations: Ivory Tower Visions and Real World Voices* eds. C. M. Ford and D. A. Gioia (Thousand Oaks, CA: Sage Publications, 1995) 161–166.

[3] R. J. Sternberg and T. I. Lubart, *Defying the Crowd. Cultivating Creativity in a Culture of Conformity* (New York, NY: Free Press, 1995).

[4] G. Golata, "Remembering a 'Magical Genius,'" *Science 236*, June 19, 1987, 1519–1521.

[5] T. I. Lubart and R. J. Sternberg, "An Investment Approach to Creativity: Theory and Data," *The Creative Cognition Approach*, eds. S. M. Smith, T. B. Ward, and R. A. Finke (Cambridge, MA: MIT Press, 1995).

[6] T. M. Amabile, *The Social Psychology of Creativity* (New York, NY: Springer-Verlag, 1983).

[7] D. K. Simonton, "Foresight in Insight? A Darwinian Answer," *The Nature of Insight,* eds. R. J. Sternberg and J. E. Davidson (Cambridge, MA: MIT Press, 1995), 479.

[8] J. Hyatt, "Going Public—Show Time," *Inc.* (May 1996): 34.

[9] L. E. Platt, "Managing Innovation: An Oxymoron?" speech at Yale University, February 28, 1997.

[10] R. Wilson, "To Help Its Students Find Jobs, Eastman School Expands Its Musical Repertoire Beyond the Classical," *The Chronicle of Higher Education*, March 14. 1997, A 10–11.

[11] R. J. Sternberg, "What Does It Mean To Be Smart?" *Educational Leadership 54* (1997): 20–24. R. J. Sternberg. *Successful Intelligence* (New York: Plume, 1997).

[12] T. J. Peters and R. H. Waterman, Jr., *In Search of Excellence: Lessons from America's Best-Run Companies* (New York: Harper & Row, 1982).

[13] T. Peters and N. Austin, *A Passion for Excellence: The Leadership Difference* (New York: Random House, 1985).

[14] P. R. Nayak and J. M. Ketteringham, *Break-Throughs!* (New York: Rawson Associates, 1986).

[15] Peters and Waterman.

[16] Hyatt.

[17] Peters and Austin.

[18] D. Kahneman and A. Tversky, "The Psychology of Preferences," *Scientific American 246*/1 (1982): 160–173.

[19] R. B. Zajonc, "Attitudinal Effects of Mere Exposure," *Journal of Personality and Social Psychology Monograph Supplement* 9 (1968): 1–27.

[20] "Old Standbys Hold Their Own," *Advertising Age*, September 19, 1983, 32.

[21] T. M. Amabile and A. H. Glazebrook, "A Negativity Bias in Interpersonal Evaluation," *Journal of Experimental Social Psychology 18* (January 1982): 1–22.

[22] T. M. Amabile, "Brilliant But Cruel: Perceptions of Negative Evaluators," *Journal of Experimental Social Psychology 19* (March 1983): 146–156

[23] R. J. Sutton and A. Hargadon, "Brainstorming Groups In Context: Effectiveness in a Product Design Firm," *Administrative Science Quarterly 41* (1996): 685–718.

[24] Ibid., 710.

[25] R. J. Sternberg, "Implict Theories of Intelligence. Creativity, and Wisdom," *Journal of Personality and Social Psychology 49* (1985): 607–627.

[26] B. Schneider, "Organizational Behavior," *Annual Review of Psychology 36* (1985): 573–611. R. J. Sternberg, *Thinking Styles* (New York: Cambridge, 1997).

[27] A. Roddick, *Body and Soul: Profits with Principles—The Amazing Success Story of Anita Roddick and the Body Shop* (New York: Crown Publishers, 1991).

[28] T. Peters, "Tom Peters on Excellence," *San Jose Mercury News*, September 19, 1994, 3D.

[29] J. Godfrey, *Our Wildest Dreams: Women Entrepreneurs Making Money, Having Fun, Doing Good* (New York: Harper Business, 1992).

[30] T. Kidder, *The Soul of a New Machine* (Boston, MA: Atlantic-Little, Brown Books, 1981), 228.

[31] S. Caudron, "Humor is Healthy in the Workplace," *Personnel Journal 71* (June 1992): 66.

[32] Sutton and Hargadon, 700.

[33] M. I. Stein, "Creativity Is People," *Leadership and Organization Development Journal* [Special Issue: *Leadership and Personal Creativity*], 12/6 (1991): 6.

[34] T. M. Amabile, *Social Psychology of Creativity* (New York: Springer-Verlag, 1983).

[35] M. Weinstein. *Managing to Have Fun* (New York: Simon & Schuster, 1996), 204.

[36] B. M. Staw and S. G. Barsade, "Affect and Managerial Performance: A Test of the Sadder-but-Wiser vs. Happier-and-Smarter Hypothesis," *Administrative Science Quarterly 38* (1993): 304–331.

[37] K. E. Weick, *The Social Psychology of Organizing*, 2nd ed. (New York: Random House, 1979).

[38] J. McGowan, "How Disney Keeps Ideas Coming. Disney Feature Animation President Peter Schneider (Interview)." *Fortune*. April 1, 1996, 131–134.

[39] J. R. Beir, "Managing Creatives: Our Creative Workers Will Excel—If We Let Them," *Vital Speeches of the Day*, June 1, 1995, 501–506.

[40] T. S. Perry, "How Small Firms Innovate: Designing a Culture for Creativity." *Research Technology Management 38*: (1995): 14–17.

[41] R. M. Kanter, *The Change Masters: Innovation and Entrepreneurship in the American Corporation* (New York: Simon & Schuster, 1983) 133.

[42] Ibid., 138.

[43] Ibid., 142–143.

▲▲

CHAPTER 11
CONFLICT AND NEGOTIATION

HOW MANAGEMENT TEAMS CAN HAVE A GOOD FIGHT
Kathleen M. Eisenhardt
Jean L. Kahwajy
L. J. Bourgeois III

WORLD-CLASS NEGOTIATING STRATEGIES
Frank L. Acuff

Learning to manage conflict, an essential skill for both managers and employees, can be a challenging, sometimes uncomfortable process. The negative results of poorly managed conflict are readily observed in many organizations. When there is too much conflict, we find people consumed by negative feelings, who fail to perceive common goals they may share with their adversaries. Valuable time, energy, and resources are devoted to competitive actions and counteractions that simply escalate the hostilities. The absence of conflict, however, is not the answer. A recurring theme in organizational behavior, as evidenced in this book, is the benefit of surfacing and listening to diverse opinions. Fighting for ideas in a constructive manner creates a healthy, moderate level of conflict that is far preferable to either too much or too little conflict.

One characteristic of effective teams is the ability to challenge ideas and disagree constructively. In the first article, Kathleen Eisenhardt, Jean Kahwajy, and L. J. Bourgeois, III, business professors, focus on constructive conflict in teams. Their decade-long research program on the relationship among conflict, politics and speed in strategic decision making in top management teams made it possible for them to follow and observe several teams in action. In "How Management Teams Can Have a Good Fight," they contrast teams in which conflict produced healthy disagreement with teams in which conflict ended up in interpersonal hostility. The outcome is six tactics teams can use for managing interpersonal conflict.

The second article also includes lessons that can be learned from contrasting effective and ineffective practice. In "World-Class Negotiating Strategies," Frank Acuff explains how highly skilled negotiators differ from average negotiators. This chapter from Acuff's book, *How to Negotiate with Anyone from Anywhere*, draws primarily on his extensive experience and observations as an international businessman and negotiator. Acuff relates anecdotes from all over the world and spells out numerous practical tips on negotiating and getting along with people from other cultures.

HOW MANAGEMENT TEAMS CAN HAVE A GOOD FIGHT*

Kathleen M. Eisenhardt
Jean L. Kahwajy
L. J. Bourgeois III

Top managers are often stymied by the difficulties of managing conflict. They know that conflict over issues is natural and even necessary. Reasonable people, making decisions under conditions of uncertainty, are likely to have honest disagreements over the best path for their company's future. Management teams whose members challenge one another's thinking develop a more complete understanding of the choices, create a richer range of options, and ultimately make the kinds of effective decisions necessary in today's competitive environments.

But, unfortunately, healthy conflict can quickly turn unproductive. A comment meant as a substantive remark can be interpreted as a personal attack. Anxiety and frustration over difficult choices can evolve into anger directed at colleagues. Personalities frequently become intertwined with issues. Because most executives pride themselves on being rational decision makers, they find it difficult even to acknowledge—let alone manage—this emotional, irrational dimension of their behavior.

The challenge—familiar to anyone who has ever been part of a management team—is to keep constructive conflict over issues from degenerating into dysfunctional interpersonal conflict, to encourage managers to argue without destroying their ability to work as a team.

We have been researching the interplay of conflict, politics, and speed in strategic decision making by top-management teams for the past 10 years. In one study, we had the opportunity to observe closely the work of a dozen top-management teams in technology-based companies. All the companies competed in fast changing, competitive global markets. Thus all the teams had to make high-stakes decisions in the face of considerable uncertainty and under pressure to move quickly. Each team consisted of between five and nine executives; we were allowed to question them individually and also to observe their interactions firsthand as we tracked specific strategic decisions in the making. The study's design gives us a window on conflict as top-management teams actually experience it and highlights the role of emotion in business decision making.

In 4 of the 12 companies, there was little or no substantive disagreement over major issues and therefore little conflict to observe. But the other 8 companies experienced considerable conflict. In 4 of them, the top-management teams handled conflict in a way that avoided interpersonal hostility or discord. We've called those companies Bravo Microsystems, Premier Technologies, Star Electronics, and Triumph Computers. Executives in those companies referred to their colleagues as *smart, team player*, and *best in the business*. They described the way they work as a team as *open, fun*, and *productive*. The executives vigorously debated the issues, but they wasted little time on politicking and posturing. As one put it, "I really don't have time." Another said, "We don't gloss over the issues; we hit them straight on. But we're not political." Still another observed of her company's management team, "We scream a lot, then laugh, and then resolve the issue."

The other four companies in which issues were contested were less successful at avoiding interpersonal conflict. We've called those companies Andromeda Processing, Mega Software, Mercury Microdevices, and Solo Systems. Their top teams were plagued by intense animosity. Executives often failed to cooperate, rarely talking with one another, tending to fragment into cliques, and openly

---

*Reprinted with permission from *Harvard Business Review* (July-August, 1997): 77–85.

displaying their frustration and anger. When executives described their colleagues to us, they used words such as *manipulative, secretive, burned out,* and *political.*

The teams with minimal interpersonal conflict were able to separate substantive issues from those based on personalities. They managed to disagree over questions of strategic significance and still get along with one another. How did they do that? After analyzing our observations of the teams' behavior, we found that their companies used the same six tactics for managing interpersonal conflict. Team members:

- worked with more, rather than less, information and debated on the basis of facts;
- developed multiple alternatives to enrich the level of debate;
- shared commonly agreed-upon goals;
- injected humor into the decision process;
- maintained a balanced power structure; and
- resolved issues without forcing consensus.

Those tactics were usually more implicit than explicit in the decision-making work of the management teams, and if the tactics were given names, the names varied from one organization to the next. Nonetheless, the consistency with which all four companies employed all six tactics is testimony to their effectiveness. Perhaps most surprising was the fact that the tactics did not delay—and often accelerated—the pace at which the teams were able to make decisions.

FOCUS ON THE FACTS

Some managers believe that working with too much data will increase interpersonal conflict by expanding the range of issues for debate. We found that more information is better—if the data are objective and up-to-date—because it encourages people to focus on issues, not personalities. At Star Electronics, for example, the members of the top-management team typically examined a wide variety of operating measures on a monthly, weekly, and even daily basis. They claimed to "measure everything." In particular, every week they fixed their attention on indicators such as bookings, backlogs, margins, engineering milestones, cash, scrap, and work-in-process. Every month, they reviewed an even more comprehensive set of measures that gave them extensive knowledge of what was actually happening in the corporation. As one executive noted, "We have very strong controls."

Star's team also relied on facts about the external environment. One senior executive was charged with tracking such moves by competitors as product introductions, price changes, and ad campaigns. A second followed the latest technical developments through his network of contacts in universities and other companies. "We over-M.B.A. it," said the CEO, characterizing Star's zealous pursuit of data. Armed with the facts, Star's executives had an extraordinary grasp of the details of their business, allowing them to focus debate on critical issues and avoid useless arguments rooted in ignorance.

At Triumph Computer, we found a similar dedication to current facts. The first person the new CEO hired was an individual to track the progress of engineering-development projects, the new-product lifeblood of the company. Such knowledge allowed the top-management team to work from a common base of facts.

In the absence of good data, executives waste time in pointless debate over opinions. Some resort to self-aggrandizement and ill-formed guesses about how the world might be. People—and not issues—become the focus of disagreement. The result is interpersonal conflict. In such companies, top managers are often poorly informed both about internal operations, such as bookings and engineering milestones, and about external issues, such as competing products. They collect data narrowly and infrequently. In these companies, the vice presidents of finance, who oversee internal data collection, are usually weak. They were often described by people in the companies we studied as "inexperienced" or "detached." In contrast, the vice president of finance at Premier Technologies, a company with little interpersonal conflict, was described as being central to taking "the constant pulse of how the firm is doing."

Management teams troubled by interpersonal conflict rely more on hunches and guesses than on current data. When they consider facts, they are more likely to examine a past measure, such as profitability, which is both historical and highly refined. These teams favor planning based on extrapolation and intuitive attempts to predict the future, neither of which yields current or factual results. Their conversations are more subjective. The CEO of one of the four high-conflict teams told us his interest in operating numbers was "minimal," and he described his goals as "subjective." At another such company, senior managers saw the CEO as "visionary" and "a little detached from the day-to-day operations." Compare those executives with the CEO of Bravo Microsystems, who had a reputation for being a "pragmatic numbers guy."

There is a direct link between reliance on facts and low levels of interpersonal conflict. Facts let people move quickly to the central issues surrounding a strategic choice. Decision makers don't become bogged down in arguments over what the facts *might* be. More important, reliance on current data grounds strategic discussions in reality. Facts (such as current sales, market share, R&D expenses, competitors' behavior, and manufacturing yields) depersonalize the discussion because they are not someone's fantasies, guesses, or self-serving desires. In the absence of facts, individuals' motives are likely to become suspect. Building decisions on facts creates a culture that emphasizes issues instead of personalities.

MULTIPLY THE ALTERNATIVES

Some managers believe that they can reduce conflict by focusing on only one or two alternatives, thus minimizing the dimensions over which people can disagree. But, in fact, teams with low incidences of interpersonal conflict do just the opposite. They deliberately develop multiple alternatives, often considering four or five options at once. To promote debate, managers will even introduce options they do not support.

For example, Triumph's new CEO was determined to improve the company's lackluster performance. When he arrived, new products were stuck in development, and investors were getting anxious. He launched a fact-gathering exercise and asked senior executives to develop alternatives. In less than two months, they developed four. The first was to sell some of the company's technology. The second was to undertake a major strategic redirection, using the base technology to enter a new market. The third was to redeploy engineering resources and adjust the marketing approach. The final option was to sell the company.

Working together to shape those options enhanced the group's sense of teamwork while promoting a more creative view of Triumph's competitive situation and its technical competencies. As a result, the team ended up combining elements of several options in a way that was more robust than any of the options were individually.

The other teams we observed with low levels of interpersonal conflict also tended to develop multiple options to make major decisions. Star, for example, faced a cash flow crisis caused by explosive growth. Its executives considered, among other choices, arranging for lines of credit from banks, selling additional stock, and forming strategic alliances with several partners. At Bravo, managers explicitly relied on three kinds of alternatives: sincere proposals that the proponent actually backed; support for someone else's proposal, even if only for the sake of argument; and insincere alternatives proposed just to expand the number of options.

There are several reasons why considering multiple alternatives may lower interpersonal conflict. For one, it diffuses conflict: choices become less black and white, and individuals gain more room to vary the degree of their support over a range of choices. Managers can more easily shift positions without losing face.

Generating options is also a way to bring managers together in a common and inherently stimulating task. It concentrates their energy on solving problems, and it increases the likelihood of obtaining integrative solutions—alternatives that incorporate the views of a greater number of the decision makers. In generating multiple alternatives, managers do not stop at obvious solutions; rather, they continue generating further—usually more original—options. The process in itself is creative and fun, setting a positive tone for substantive, instead of interpersonal, conflict.

By contrast, in teams that vigorously debate just one or two options, conflict often does turn personal. At Solo Systems, for instance, the top-management team considered entering a new business area as a way to boost the company's performance. They debated this alternative versus the status quo but failed to consider other options. Individual executives became increasingly entrenched on one side of the debate or the other. As positions hardened, the conflict became more pointed and personal. The animosity grew so great that a major proponent of change quit the company in disgust while the rest of the team either disengaged or slipped into intense and dysfunctional politicking.

CREATE COMMON GOALS

A third tactic for minimizing destructive conflict involves framing strategic choices as collaborative, rather than competitive, exercises. Elements of collaboration and competition coexist within any management team: executives share a stake in the company's performance, yet their personal ambitions may make them rivals for power. The successful groups we studied consistently framed their decisions as collaborations in which it was in everyone's interest to achieve the best possible solution for the collective.

They did so by creating a common goal around which the team could rally. Such goals do not imply homogeneous thinking, but they do require everyone to share a vision. As Steve Jobs, who is associated with three high-profile Silicon Valley companies—Apple, NeXT, and Pixar—has advised, "It's okay to spend a lot of time arguing about which route to take to San Francisco when everyone wants to end up there, but a lot of time gets wasted in such arguments if one person wants to go to San Francisco and another secretly wants to go to San Diego."

Teams hobbled by conflict lack common goals. Team members perceive themselves to be in competition with one another and, surprisingly, tend to frame decisions negatively, as reactions to threats. At Andromeda Processing, for instance, the team focused on responding to a particular instance of poor performance, and team members tried to pin the blame on one another. That negative framing contrasts with the positive approach taken by Star Electronics executives, who, sharing a common goal, viewed a cash crisis not as a threat but as an opportunity to "build the biggest war chest" for an impending competitive battle. At a broad level, Star's executives shared the goal of creating "the computer firm of the decade." As one Star executive told us, "We take a corporate, not a functional, viewpoint most of the time."

Likewise, all the management team members we interviewed at Premier Technologies agreed that their common goal—their rallying cry—was to build "the best damn machine on the market." Thus in their debates they could disagree about critical technical alternatives—in-house versus offshore manufacturing options, for example, or alternative distribution channels—without letting the conflict turn personal.

Many studies of group decision making and intergroup conflict demonstrate that common goals build team cohesion by stressing the shared interest of all team members in the outcome of the debate. When team members are working toward a common goal, they are less likely to see themselves as individual winners and losers and are far more likely to perceive the opinions of others correctly and to learn from them. We observed that when executives lacked common goals, they tended to be closed-minded and more likely to misinterpret and blame one another.

USE HUMOR

Teams that handle conflict well make explicit—and often even contrived—attempts to relieve tension and at the same time promote a collaborative esprit by making their business fun. They emphasize the excitement of fast-paced competition, not the stress of competing in brutally tough and uncertain markets.

All the teams with low interpersonal conflict described ways in which they used humor on the job. Executives at Bravo Microsystems enjoyed playing gags around the office. For example, pink plastic flamingos—souvenirs from a customer—graced Bravo's otherwise impeccably decorated headquarters. Similarly, Triumph Computers' top managers held a monthly "dessert pig-out," followed by group weight watching. Those seemingly trivial activities were part of the CEO's deliberate plan to make work more fun, despite the pressures of the industry. At Star Electronics, making the company "a fun place" was an explicit goal for the top-management team. Laughter was common during management meetings. Practical jokes were popular at Star, where executives—along with other employees—always celebrated Halloween and April Fools' Day.

At each of these companies, executives acknowledged that at least some of the attempts at humor were contrived—even forced. Even so, they helped to release tension and promote collaboration.

Humor was strikingly absent in the teams marked by high interpersonal conflict. Although pairs of individuals were sometimes friends, team members shared no group social activities beyond a standard holiday party or two, and there were no conscious attempts to create humor. Indeed, the climate in which decisions were made was often just the opposite—hostile and stressful.

Humor works as a defense mechanism to protect people from the stressful and threatening situations that commonly arise in the course of making strategic decisions. It helps people distance themselves psychologically by putting those situations into a broader life context, often through the use of irony. Humor—with its ambiguity—can also blunt the threatening edge of negative information. Speakers can say in jest things that might otherwise give offense because the message is simultaneously serious and not serious. The recipient is allowed to save face by receiving the serious message while appearing not to do so. The result is communication of difficult information in a more tactful and less personally threatening way.

Humor can also move decision making into a collaborative rather than competitive frame through its powerful effect on mood. According to a large body of research, people in a positive mood tend to be not only more optimistic but also more forgiving of others and creative in seeking solutions. A positive mood triggers a more accurate perception of others' arguments because people in a good mood tend to relax their defensive barriers and so can listen more effectively.

How Teams Argue but Still Get Along

Tactic ➝	Strategy
Base discussion on current, factual information. Develop multiple alternative to enrich the debate.	Focus on issues, not personalities.
Rally around goals. Inject humor into the decision-making process.	Frame decisions as collaborations aimed at achieving the best possible solution for the company.
Maintain balanced power structure. Resolve issues without forcing consensus.	Establish a sense of fairness and equity in the process.

BALANCE THE POWER STRUCTURE

We found that managers who believe that their team's decision-making process is fair are more likely to accept decisions without resentment, even when they do not agree with them. But when they believe the process is unfair, ill will easily grows into interpersonal conflict. A fifth tactic for taming interpersonal conflict, then, is to create a sense of fairness by balancing power within the management team.

Our research suggests that autocratic leaders who manage through highly centralized power structures often generate high levels of interpersonal friction. At the other extreme, weak leaders also engender interpersonal conflict because the power vacuum at the top encourages managers to jockey for position. Interpersonal conflict is lowest in what we call *balanced power structures*, those in which the CEO is more powerful than the other members of the top-management team, but the members do wield substantial power, especially in their own well-defined areas of responsibility. In balanced power structures, all executives participate in strategic decisions.

At Premier Technologies, for example, the CEO—described by others as a "team player"—was definitely the most powerful figure. But each executive was the most powerful decision maker in some clearly defined area. In addition, the entire team participated in all significant decisions. The CEO, one executive observed, "depends on picking good people and letting them operate."

The CEO of Bravo Microsystems, another company with a balanced power structure, summarized his philosophy as "making quick decisions involving as many people as possible." We watched the Bravo team over several months as it grappled with a major strategic redirection. After many group discussions, the final decision was made at a multiday retreat involving the whole team.

In contrast, the leaders of the teams marked by extensive interpersonal conflict were either highly autocratic or weak. The CEO at Mercury Microdevices, for example, was the principal decision maker. There was a substantial gap in power between him and the rest of the team. In the decision we tracked, the CEO dominated the process from start to finish, identifying the problem, defining the analysis, and making the choice. Team members described the CEO as "strong" and "dogmatic." As one of them put it, "When Bruce makes a decision, it's like God!"

At Andromeda, the CEO exercised only modest power, and areas of responsibility were blurred within the top-management team, where power was diffuse and ambiguous. Senior executives had to politick amongst themselves to get anything accomplished, and they reported intense frustration with the confusion that existed at the top.

Most executives expected to control some significant aspect of their business but not the entirety. When they lacked power—because of either an autocrat or a power vacuum—they became frustrated by their inability to make significant decisions. Instead of team members, they became politicians. As one executive explained, "We're all jockeying for our spot in the pecking order." Another described "maneuvering for the CEO's ear."

The situations we observed are consistent with classic social-psychology studies of leadership. For example, in a study from the 1960s, Ralph White and Ronald Lippitt examined the effects of different leadership styles on boys in social clubs. They found that boys with democratic leaders—the situation closest to our balanced power structure—showed spontaneous interest in their activities. The boys were highly satisfied, and within their groups there were many friendly remarks, much praise, and significant collaboration. Under weak leaders, the boys were disorganized, inefficient, and dissatisfied. But the worst case was autocratic rule, under which the boys were hostile and aggressive, occasionally directing physical violence against innocent scapegoats. In imbalanced power situations, we observed adult displays of verbal aggression that colleagues described as violent. One executive talked about being "caught in the cross fire." Another described a colleague as "a gun about to go off." A third spoke about "being beat up" by the CEO.

SEEK CONSENSUS WITH QUALIFICATION

Balancing power is one tactic for building a sense of fairness. Finding an appropriate way to resolve conflict over issues is another—and, perhaps, the more crucial. In our research, the teams that managed conflict effectively all used the same approach to resolving substantive conflict. It is a two-step process that some executives call *consensus with qualification*. It works like this: executives talk over an issue and try to reach consensus. If they can, the decision is made. If they can't, the most relevant senior manager makes the decision, guided by input from the rest of the group.

When a competitor launched a new product attacking Premier Technologies in its biggest market, for example, there was sharp disagreement about how to respond. Some executives wanted to shift R&D resources to counter this competitive move, even at the risk of diverting engineering talent from a more innovative product then in design. Others argued that Premier should simply repackage an existing product, adding a few novel features. A third group felt that the threat was not serious enough to warrant a major response.

After a series of meetings over several weeks, the group failed to reach consensus. So the CEO and his marketing vice president made the decision. As the CEO explained, "The functional heads do the talking. I pull the trigger." Premier's executives were comfortable with this arrangement—even those who did not agree with the outcome—because everyone had had a voice in the process.

People usually associate consensus with harmony, but we found the opposite: teams that insisted on resolving substantive conflict by forcing consensus tended to display the most interpersonal conflict. Executives sometimes have the unrealistic view that consensus is always possible, but such a naive insistence on consensus can lead to endless haggling. As the vice president of engineering at Mega Software put it, "Consensus means that everyone has veto power. Our products were too late, and they were too expensive." At Andromeda, the CEO wanted his executives to reach consensus, but persistent differences of opinion remained. The debate dragged on for months, and the frustration mounted until some top managers simply gave up. They just wanted a decision, any decision. One was finally made when several executives who favored one point of view left the company. The price of consensus was a decimated team.

In a team that insists on consensus, deadlines can cause executives to sacrifice fairness and thus weaken the team's support for the final decision. At Andromeda, executives spent months analyzing their industry and developing a shared perspective on important trends for the future, but they could never focus on making the decision. The decision-making process dragged on. Finally, as the deadline of a board meeting drew imminent, the CEO formulated and announced a choice—one that had never even been mentioned in the earlier discussions. Not surprisingly, his team was angry and upset. Had he been less insistent on reaching a consensus, the CEO would not have felt forced by the deadline to act so arbitrarily.

BUILDING A FIGHTING TEAM

How can managers encourage the kind of substantive debate over issues that leads to better decision making? We found five approaches that help generate constructive disagreement within a team:

1. **Assemble a heterogeneous team, including diverse ages, genders, functional backgrounds, and industry experience** If everyone in the executive meetings looks alike and sounds alike, then the chances are excellent that they probably think alike, too.
2. **Meet together as a team regularly and often** Team members that don't know one another well don't know one another's positions on issues, impairing their ability to argue effectively.

(continued)

Frequent interaction builds the mutual confidence and familiarity team members require to express dissent.

3. **Encourage team members to assume roles beyond their obvious product, geographic, or functional responsibilities** Devil's advocates, sky-gazing visionaries, and action-oriented executives can work together to ensure that all sides of an issue are considered.

4. **Apply multiple mind-sets to any issue** Try role-playing, putting yourself in your competitors' shoes or conducting war games. Such techniques create fresh perspectives and engage team members, spurring interest in problem solving.

5. **Actively manage conflict** Don't let the team acquiesce too soon or too easily. Identify and treat apathy early, and don't confuse a lack of conflict with agreement. Often, what passes for consensus is really disengagement.

How does consensus with qualification create a sense of fairness? A body of research on procedural justice shows that process fairness, which involves significant participation and influence by all concerned, is enormously important to most people. Individuals are willing to accept outcomes they dislike if they believe that the process by which those results came about was fair. Most people want their opinions to be considered seriously but are willing to accept that those opinions cannot always prevail. That is precisely what occurs in consensus with qualification. As one executive at Star said, "I'm happy just to bring up my opinions."

Apart from fairness, there are several other reasons why consensus with qualification is an important deterrent to interpersonal conflict. It assumes that conflict is natural and not a sign of interpersonal dysfunction. It gives managers added influence when the decision affects their part of the organization in particular, thus balancing managers' desires to be heard with the need to make a choice. It is an equitable and egalitarian process of decision making that encourages everyone to bring ideas to the table but clearly delineates how the decision will be made.

Finally, consensus with qualification is fast. Processes that require consensus tend to drag on endlessly, frustrating managers with what they see as time-consuming and useless debate. It's not surprising that the managers end up blaming their frustration on the shortcomings of their colleagues and not on the poor conflict-resolution process.

LINKING CONFLICT, SPEED, AND PERFORMANCE

A considerable body of academic research has demonstrated that conflict over issues is not only likely within top-management teams but also valuable. Such conflict provides executives with a more inclusive range of information, a deeper understanding of the issues, and a richer set of possible solutions. That was certainly the case in the companies we studied. The evidence also overwhelmingly indicates that where there is little conflict over issues, there is also likely to be poor decision making. "Groupthink" has been a primary cause of major corporate—and public-policy debacles. And although it may seem counterintuitive, we found that the teams that engaged in healthy conflict over issues not only made better decisions but moved more quickly as well.

Without conflict, groups lose their effectiveness. Managers often become withdrawn and only superficially harmonious. Indeed, we found that the alternative to conflict is usually not agreement but apathy and disengagement. Teams unable to foster substantive conflict ultimately achieve, on average, lower performance. Among the companies that we observed, low-conflict teams tended to forget to consider key issues or were simply unaware of important aspects of their strategic situation. They missed opportunities to question falsely limiting assumptions or to generate significantly different alternatives. Not surprisingly, their actions were often easy for competitors to anticipate.

In fast-paced markets, successful strategic decisions are most likely to be made by teams that promote active and broad conflict over issues without sacrificing speed. The key to doing so is to mitigate interpersonal conflict.

WORLD-CLASS NEGOTIATING STRATEGIES*

Frank L. Acuff

If I listen, I have the advantage; if I speak, others have it.

From the Arabic

There are many negotiating strategies that tend to work very well in one culture but are ineffective in other cultures. A case in point is the Miami-based project manager who put together a very detailed, thorough, research-oriented proposal and presentation for his Brazilian client. "I felt good that we had done our homework," he later noted. "I was very disappointed, however, to find that the Brazilian representatives were flatly uninterested in the details I was prepared to explain. A similar approach worked extremely well in Germany only four months earlier."

In spite of the many different negotiating approaches required among cultures, there are 10 strategies that tend to be effective anywhere in the world. While there may be local variations in how these strategies are applied, their basic premises remain viable.

TEN NEGOTIATING STRATEGIES THAT WILL WORK ANYWHERE

The 10 strategies that tend to be effective in negotiations throughout the world are as follows:

1. Plan the negotiation.
2. Adopt a win-win approach.
3. Maintain high aspirations.
4. Use language that is simple and accessible.
5. Ask lots of questions, then listen with your eyes and ears.
6. Build solid relationships.
7. Maintain personal integrity.
8. Conserve concessions.
9. Make patience an obsession.
10. Be culturally literate and adapt negotiating strategies to the host country environment.

STRATEGY 1: PLAN THE NEGOTIATION

Everybody wants to get a good deal, to get a sizable share of the pie, and to feel good about the negotiation. Everybody wants to be a winner. Yet not everyone is willing to do the homework necessary to achieve these ends. The essential steps necessary to plan your negotiation are as follows: (1) identify all the issues (2) prioritize the issues (3) establish a settlement range and (4) develop strategies and tactics. Make this preparation a habit and you will set the stage for getting what you want.

There are other factors to consider prior to global negotiations. You can use the Tune-Up Checklist to ensure that you put yourself in the strongest possible position before the negotiation.

**Reprinted with permission from *How To Negotiate Anything with Anyone Anywhere Around the World* (New York: Amacom, 1997): 68–94.*

The Tune-Up Checklist: Prior to the Negotiation   This is the data-gathering stage where you should get background information related to The Other Side (TOS), to his or her culture and its effects on the negotiating process, to TOS's organization and other potential players in the negotiation, and to the history of any past negotiations. What do you know about:

TOS

- Family status (e.g., married, single, children)?
- Leisure or recreational activities?
- Work habits (e.g., long hours, early to work)?
- Behavior style (e.g., perfectionist, "big picture"-oriented, task-oriented, people-oriented)?
- Number of years with current organization?
- Stability in current position?
- Overall reputation as a negotiator?
- What special-interest groups might affect the negotiator?

TOS's Culture and Its Effects on Negotiations

- Are meetings likely to be punctual?
- What can you expect the pace of the negotiations to be?
- How important is "saving face" likely to be?
- Are differences of opinion likely to be emotional or argumentative?
- Will TOS bring a large team?
- Will you need an agent or interpreter?
- Should you prepare a formal agenda?

TOS's Organization

- What is the organization's main product or service?
- What is its past, present, and projected financial status?
- What organizational problems exist (e.g., downsizing, tough competition)?
- Who is TOS's boss, and what do you know about him or her?
- Is the organization under any time pressures?

Past Negotiations

- What were the subjects of past negotiations?
- What were the main obstacles and outcomes of the negotiations?
- What objections were raised?
- What strategies and tactics were used by TOS?
- How high were the initial offers compared with the eventual settlement?
- How was the outcome achieved, and over what period of time?

There are many ways to plan negotiations. One study identified five approaches skilled negotiators share when planning their negotiations:

1. They consider twice as wide a range of action options and outcomes as do less skilled negotiators.
2. They spend over three times as much attention on trying to find common ground with TOS.
3. They spend more than twice as much time on long-term issues.
4. They set range objectives (such as a target price of $50 to $60 per unit), rather than single-point objectives (e.g., $55). Ranges give negotiators flexibility.
5. They use "issue planning" rather than "sequence planning." That is, skilled negotiators discuss each issue independently rather than in a predetermined sequence or order of issues.[1]

STRATEGY 2: ADOPT A WIN-WIN APPROACH

We don't adopt the win-win approach simply because we are wonderful human beings. It helps us get what we want. There is a difference between how skilled and unskilled negotiators prepare for the win-win approach. Skilled negotiators, for example, tend to spend less time on defense/attack behavior and in disagreement. They also tend to give more information about their feelings and have fewer arguments to back up their position.[2] This last point may seem odd. It might seem that the more arguments one has for one's position, the better. Skilled negotiators know, however, that having only a few strong arguments is more effective than having too many arguments. With too many arguments, weak arguments tend to dilute strong arguments, and TOS often feels pressured or manipulated into settlement.

To achieve a win-win situation, you must tune in to the frequency with which TOS can identify: WIIFT ("What's In It For Them"). This means different things in different cultures. For example, in Saudi Arabia a certain amount of haggling back and forth on terms may indicate your sincerity about striking a deal. To refuse a somewhat expressive give-and-take would be an insult to many Saudi negotiators. A Dallas-based commercial building contractor now experienced in Saudi Arabia discovered this on his first trip there. "I really got off-base in our early discussions in Riyadh. I felt we were being extremely polite as we patiently explained the reasonableness of our proposal. We fell flat on our faces. The Saudis felt we were inflexible and not serious about doing business. The next project we bid had a lot of fat built into it. We haggled back and forth for four meetings, and they ended up loving us. That's what they wanted—someone to bargain with back and forth. It showed them we cared." This negotiator adds, "I still get a knot in my stomach sometimes when I go through a Saudi negotiation, but at least I know what works now."

Fortunately for this negotiator, he quickly learned the win-win approach for his Saudi client. Yet the very idea of haggling would be a sure win-lose proposition in many parts of the world. In England, for example, it would be hard to come up with a worse idea than to engage TOS in an emotional afternoon of haggling back and forth. The British idea of win-win is a somewhat formal, procedural, and detailed discussion of the facts.

Achieving a win-win result also requires careful scrutiny of both parties' overall goals. You may be seeking short-term profit and cash flow, while your Japanese counterparts may be more interested in long-term viability. In many cases, different goals can lead to overall win-win results. Consider the company president negotiating a joint venture in Hungary in order to take advantage of a skilled, inexpensive workforce, while her TOS is motivated to find business linkages outside Eastern Europe.

Wherever you negotiate, focusing on win-win results sharply increases your chances for success, particularly in the long term.

STRATEGY 3: MAINTAIN HIGH ASPIRATIONS

In the spring of 1978, the International Air Transport Association (IATA) discontinued its policy of airline ticket price compliance. IATA had been for many years a powerful enforcer that had maintained a firm grip on the airline ticket prices of the world's domestic and international airlines. Immediately after this announcement was made, Leroy Black, my boss, suggested I contact the airlines to determine what, if any, ticket price concessions we might extract as a result of this policy change. The Middle East Division where we worked was located in Dubai, United Arab Emirates, a small oil sheikdom adjoining Saudi Arabia. Our 3,500 workers and many of their family members collectively logged millions of air miles per year.

"That's a good idea," I remember telling Leroy. Shaving 5 or 10 percent—perhaps even 15 percent—would amount to substantial savings on our $4 million annual airline expenses. I was stunned, though, when Leroy suggested we ask for a 50 percent price decrease in ticket costs.

"Are you kidding?" I asked, quite shocked.

"I think that 50 percent is about right," Leroy said serenely.

Our first appointment was with representatives from British Airways. They told us, in a reserved, nice kind of way, to take a hike.

Then KLM, in a not particularly nice kind of way, suggested the same recourse as British Airways. The same with Lufthansa. "We really are being a bit chintzy on this thing," I thought to myself.

"Leroy, let's try asking for a little less and see what happens," I suggested.

"I don't know. Let's hang in there awhile longer," Leroy insisted.

Next was Alitalia. As in our appointments with the other airlines, I went through a short prologue explaining the company's position, and assertively put forth that we would like to see a 50 percent reduction in future fares. This caused quite a commotion with the Alitalia representatives, who waved their arms and with great conviction gave us several reasons why this was not possible.

"This is really a little embarrassing," I thought.

They then asked if they could privately telephone their regional headquarters staff. They returned in about 10 minutes in a solemn mood.

"Mr. Acuff," one of the representatives said with a grave look on his face. "What you ask is quite impossible. The very most we can offer you is a 40 percent reduction," he said apologetically.

"Excuse me?" I asked. He repeated his offer.

"Unbelievable," I thought to myself. "Give us some time to think about it," I replied.

As soon as they were out of earshot, Leroy and I almost jumped for joy. As it turned out, this was the first of several key concessions we received from the various airlines, ranging from 15 to 45 percent discounts. British Airways, KLM, Sabena, and Lufthansa all soon after reduced their rates well beyond my initial expectations.

This situation was a valuable lesson with regard to aspiration levels in negotiations. What at first seemed like a brash, overbearing approach to business turned out to be very positive. But was it win-win?, you ask. Didn't you just bleed the airlines at a time when they were vulnerable? Not at all. We later found out that the airlines were quite pleased with the new arrangements. They thought discounts might be greater than they were, and, of course, some of the airlines were delighted that they had negotiated better terms than their competitors.

We have all kinds of negative fantasies about high initial demands (HIDs):

"They won't like me anymore. I'll make them really mad and it will hurt the relationship."

"I'll price myself out of the market."

"Maybe we aren't being reasonable."

"This is embarrassing."

In spite of these concerns, there are compelling reasons to go for it, which are summarized in the following World-Class Tips.

WORLD-CLASS TIPS:

Seven Reasons Why You Should Have High Initial Demands

1. Don't take away your own power. TOS may do it to you, but don't do it to yourself.
2. HIDs teach people how to treat you.
3. They lower the expectations of TOS.
4. HIDs demonstrate your persistence and conviction.
5. You can always reduce your asking offer or demand. HIDs give you room to make concessions.
6. Remember that time is on your side. Making HIDs gives you more time to learn about your counterpart, and time heals many wounds.

7. There is an emotional imperative for TOS to beat you down. It's important for TOS to feel that they've "won."[3]

World-Class Tip 7 is especially important. Many negotiators find it hard to accept that there is an emotional imperative for TOS to beat you down. To illustrate this point, let's get in the other person's shoes to see how the TOS might feel. You are in Germany to negotiate the purchase of the Drillenzebit, a precision tool-making machine from a Munich-based firm. You say to yourself, "This time won't be like the other times. This time I'm going to do my homework—I will read appropriate industry periodicals and talk to consultants, clients, suppliers, and others who know a lot about the Germans, the German business environment, and the competitive market for precision tool-making machines." So you do your homework and begin to negotiate with the Germans for the Drillenzebit machine. When the subject of price arises, you are ready. You've got the facts, figures, and some savoir-faire about German negotiating practices. So you say, "Mr. Dietrich, today I'm going to offer you one price and one price only for this fine Drillenzebit machine. That final price is $74,000—that's U.S. dollars."

Dietrich looks at you for a moment and says, "Let me see if I have this right. That's $74,000—in US. dollars?"

"That's right," you repeat, proud that you're sticking by your guns.

"Seventy-four thousand dollars. You've got it. The machine is yours!" he beams.

How would you feel in this situation? Wonderful? Exuberant? If you are like most people, you would have a morbid, sinking feeling that you had just been taken. Your first thought would probably be, "Damn. I should have offered less." Is this reaction logical? No. You did, after all, get what you asked for. You reacted as you did because only part of your needs were met—the logical part—while the emotional part was not.

There are cultural differences as to how high our aspiration level should be with our foreign counterparts, but as a rule of thumb, go for it! If you really want $30,000 for your widget machine, don't ask for $30,500. Ask for $60,000. Put TOS in the position of saying to his or her boss, "You know, this woman came in asking $60,000. This price was completely off-the-wall. Excellent negotiator that I am, I got her down to $38,000. I saved us $22,000." And if you are in a competitive bidding situation, stress the quality, service, and other aspects that make your price an excellent value.

STRATEGY 4: USE LANGUAGE THAT IS SIMPLE AND ACCESSIBLE

American English is filled with thousands of clichés and colloquialisms that make it very hard for others to understand. Phrases such as "getting down to brass tacks," "getting down to the nitty-gritty," wanting to "zero in on problems," or "finding out where the rubber meets the road" only clog communication channels.

Don't assume that because your foreign counterpart speaks English, he or she fully understands it. This individual may know English as it was taught in school but may not be able to speak it or understand it in conversation with an American. An American executive who regularly travels to Taiwan makes this point. "When I first asked my Taiwanese client if he spoke English, he told me yes. I found out the hard way that his understanding was very elementary and that I used way too many slang expressions. We still do business together, but now I speak more slowly and simply, and I'm learning some Chinese."

This doesn't apply only to slang. Make sure you use the simplest, most basic words possible. Exhibit 1 provides examples of simplified words and terms you should use, even if you're speaking English.

This reliance on slang makes it very difficult for TOS to grasp our meaning, even if TOS speaks English. By using simple, straightforward language, we can help ourselves by helping others understand us.

Don't use this ...	when this will do.	
annual premium	annual payment	
accrued interest	unpaid interest	
maturity date	final payment date	
commence	start	
utilize	use	
acquaint	tell	
demonstrate	show	
endeavor	try	
modification	change	
proceed	go	
per diem	daily	

Phrases	Typical Meanings	Sport
"What's your game plan?"	"What's your approach to this negotiation?"	American football, basketball, etc.
"We're not going to throw in the towel."	"We're not going to give up."	Boxing, American football, etc.
"They're trying an end run."	"They are going around normal organizational channels."	American football
"You threw us a curve."	"We didn't do well in this situation."	Baseball
"You're batting a thousand."	"You've had all your demands met."	Baseball
"Have we covered all the bases?"	"Have we considered all the options?"	Baseball
"That's the way the ball bounces."	"It was unpredictable but it is over now and there is no use to worrying about it."	American football, basketball, etc.

EXHIBIT 1   Simplifying English words and terms.

TEENAGE WHAT?

The session had been interesting, with a good exchange of ideas. About thirty top Russian managers were learning about "How to Negotiate With Americans." Each of the participants was wired so that we could communicate with each other through an interpreter. I would say a few words and wait four or five seconds for the translation from English to Russian to be completed, listening through my earphones to the translator's crisp, confident tone.

All this was working fine until we began discussing Americans' need for achievement and how this affected the competitive approach of many American negotiators. One of the participants asked about what heroes represented this achievement orientation, and whether this achievement orientation impacted American children. I made a few observations about various American heroes and then made my big mistake. I noted that, yes, American children have their achievement-oriented heroes too, and I mentioned the Teenage Mutant Ninja Turtles as an example. Suddenly there was silence from the translator. I looked to the back of the room where he was sitting in a booth. The participants looked around nervously at him. He had a blank look on his face. Finally, after about 15 seconds, some tentative, awkward sounds came forth.

Then I realized how impossible a job I had given him. What would his translation possibly be ... something like, "Turtles in their teenage years ... who have physical deformities ... and practice Far Eastern martial arts?"

STRATEGY 5: ASK LOTS OF QUESTIONS, THEN LISTEN WITH YOUR EYES AND EARS

Asking good questions is vital throughout the negotiation, but particularly in the early stages. Your main goal is receiving information. Making a brilliant speech to TOS about your proposal may make you feel good, but it does far less in helping you achieve your ends than asking questions that give you data about content and the emotional needs of TOS.

Exhibit 2 illustrates the importance of asking questions. Skilled negotiators ask more than twice the number of questions as unskilled negotiators. They also engage in much more active listening than those who are less skilled.

There is one important consideration when asking questions: Don't do anything that would embarrass your international counterpart. Questions can be much more direct and open in cultures such as the United States, Canada, Australia, Switzerland, Sweden, and Germany than in Japan, Taiwan, Brazil, or Colombia, where indirectness is prized.

Judge a man by his questions rather than by his answers.

Voltaire

Effective listening is especially challenging when different cultures are involved. This can be the case even when English is the first language of TOS. Mike Apple, an American engineering and construction executive, found this to be the case in England and Scotland. Apple notes that even though English is spoken, one must listen very carefully to English and Scottish negotiators because of their dialects. "When I first got to Scotland, I wondered if some kind of challenge was in the making when a union negotiator told me he was going to 'mark my card.' I asked a colleague about it. As it turned out, the term is one used by Scottish golfers to explain the best approach to the course for those who

EXHIBIT 2   Questioning and listening in skilled and average negotiators.

Negotiating Behavior	Skilled Negotiators	Average Negotiators
Questions, as a percentage of all negotiating behavior	21.3%	9.6%
Active listening ■ Testing for understanding ■ Summarizing	9.7 7.5	4.1 4.2

Source: Neil Rackham, "The Behavior of Successful Negotiators" (Reston, VA.: Huth-waite Research Group, 1976), as reported in Ellen Raider International, Inc. (Brooklyn, N.Y.) and *Situation Management Systems*, Inc. (Plymouth, MA.), *International Negotiations: A Training Program for Corporate Executives and Diplomats* (1982).

haven't played there before. The union negotiator was only trying to be helpful," Apple notes. "The lesson learned here? When in doubt, ask for clarification."

If the communication pattern is from high-context countries, such as Japan, China, Saudi Arabia, Greece, or Spain, listening is even more challenging for Americans. In these cultures the message is embedded in the context of what is being said. Mike McMahon, a former managing director for National Semiconductor's Singapore plant, found Singaporeans reluctant to respond directly to questions. He notes, "I had to listen very carefully to figure out what was really on their minds."[4]

Here are some additional tips for effective listening:

- Limit your own talking.
- Concentrate on what TOS is saying.
- Maintain eye contact (but don't stare).
- Paraphrase and summarize TOS's remarks.
- Avoid jumping to conclusions. Be postjudicial, not prejudicial, regarding what TOS is saying.
- Watch for nonverbal cues.
- Listen for emotions.
- Ask for clarification: Assume differences, not similarities, if you are unsure of meaning.
- Don't interrupt.
- Pause for understanding; don't immediately fill the voids of silence.

Some of the rituals of international negotiating serve dual purposes of entertainment and information gathering. Foster Lin, director of the Taiwanese Far East Trade Service Office in Chicago, considers formal Taiwanese banquets and other entertainment as a prime opportunity to gain information on one's negotiating counterpart. Says Lin, "Entertainment demonstrates courtesy toward our foreign guests. It also helps us find out more about the individual person. Is this someone we can trust and want to do business with?" Such occasions can help you as well. Careful listening in this "offstage" time, away from the formal negotiating sessions, can give you another side to the negotiators. Use this time to gather additional data on your counterpart.

A key part of listening relates to body language. TOS may encode messages, making sophisticated, cogent arguments. However, one thing almost always happens during a moment of insecurity or deception: body movements change (e.g., the person literally squirms in his or her seat or blinks more rapidly). Also, be aware of the impact of your own nonverbal behavior. For example, if your gestures are quite expressive and TOS is from Sweden and quite reserved, tone it down a bit. Alternatively, if your facial and arm gestures are unexpressive and you are meeting a Brazilian who is very expressive, loosen up a bit—smile and use expressive hand and arm gestures.

WORLD-CLASS TIPS: FIVE POSITIVE THINGS YOU CAN DO WITHOUT SAYING A WORD

1. **Smile!**   It's a universal lubricant that can help you open the content of the negotiation. A genuine smile says very loudly, "I'd appreciate doing business with you."
2. **Dress appropriately and groom well**   Shined shoes, combed hair, clean nails, and clothes appropriate for the occasion show that you respect yourself and your counterpart. It also communicates that you are worthy of your counterpart's business.
3. **Lean forward**   This communicates interest and attention in almost every culture.
4. **Use open gestures**   Crossed arms in front of your chest may be viewed as disinterest or resistance on your part. More open gestures send a signal that you are open to your counterpart's ideas.
5. **Take every opportunity to nod your head**   Don't you like it when people agree with you? Let TOS know that you are listening by this simple action.

STRATEGY 6: BUILD SOLID RELATIONSHIPS

Stay away from value issues, which are full of potential land mines. When is the last time you won an argument on politics? On religion? That's right; you never have and you never will. Discussion of subjects such as politics, religion, race, and the role of women in the workplace will not help build a relationship with your negotiating counterpart, even if the other person brings up the subject or there is potential agreement. No matter what our particular view on these subjects, we tend to think that we have God, truth, and light on our side.

The personal relationship you develop with your counterpart provides the basis, or context, for the content portion of the negotiation. In many cultures it is the quality of the relationship more than the work accomplished that counts. There is more emphasis on building a solid personal relationship in some cultures than others. In Brazil, Japan, Greece, Spain, and the Czech Republic, for example, a strong personal relationship almost surely precedes any deal. In other countries, such as Germany and Switzerland, the content portion of the negotiation usually precedes any substantial relationship building. In most cases, a strong relationship is critical to even short-term success. In all cases, it is critical to long-term success.

Be a pleasure to do business with. Even if you don't agree on the content part of the negotiation, you want TOS to have a positive view of you when they see you coming.

WORLD-CLASS TIPS: FIFTEEN STATEMENTS THAT WILL HELP BUILD SOLID RELATIONSHIPS (OR AT LEAST KEEP YOU OUT OF DEEP SOUP)

1. "I'm very pleased to meet you."
2. "Could you tell me more about your proposal?"
3. "I have a few more questions I'd like to ask you."
4. "We might be able to consider X if you could consider Y."
5. "Let me try to summarize where we stand now in our discussion."
6. "I'm very happy to see you again."
7. "Could you tell me more about your concerns?"
8. "Let me tell you where I have a concern."
9. "I feel disappointed that we haven't made more progress."
10. "I really appreciate the progress that we've made."
11. "Thank you."
12. "Can I answer any more questions about our organization or proposal?"
13. "What would it take for us to close this deal?"
14. "I've enjoyed doing business with you."
15. "I haven't talked to you since we signed the contract. I just wanted to follow up with you to see how things are working out."

Even when you mean well, there are some terms and phrases that carry negative overtones. One study found that skilled negotiators used only 2.3 irritating words and phrases per hour in face-to-face negotiations, compared with 10.8 "irritators" per hour for average negotiators. Irritators included such phrases as "generous offer," "fair price," and "reasonable arrangement."[3] Exhibit 3 is a "dirty word list" that details other phrases that tend to upset others, regardless of the culture involved.

There's another word that should be taken out of your business vocabulary: negotiate. Yes, we use it when discussing the subject, but in real-life situations, all kinds of images come to mind when you tell someone, "Let's negotiate this deal." There's the feeling that something manipulative is about

These Words:	May Provoke These Reactions:
You always/You never …	I always, I never? Perhaps I often or seldom behave in that way, but not always or never.
What you need to understand …	I'll let you know if I need to understand it.
Be reasonable …	I didn't think I was being unreasonable. (Have you ever met anyone in your whole life who told you, "I don't tend to be very reasonable, and I just thought I'd let you know?")
Calm down!	If they were calm, they won't be after you tell them this!
Needless to say …	Then why are you saying it?
Obviously …	You've somehow cornered the market on what is and is not obvious?
The fact of the matter is …	You know what is factual and I don't?
You can't tell me …	You bet I can tell you—that is, if you'll just listen!
Listen …	I may choose to listen, but I don't want to be directed to do so.
As you know … Most people would …	Maybe I do and maybe I don't. Are you suggesting that I'm some kind of oddball if I don't happen to agree with you?

EXHIBIT 3   Words and phrases to avoid.

to happen. Instead, say something like, "Let's work out something that is good for both of us" or "Let's discuss the concerns you have."

Reaching a deadlock or impasse is a common and often frustrating experience. This can happen even when both parties are bargaining in good faith and are trying hard to reach an agreement. When you reach an impasse with TOS, take steps to break the deadlock and yet keep the relationship strong. The following list of World-Class Tips provides some helpful methods.

WORLD-CLASS TIPS: SEVENTEEN WAYS TO BREAK DEADLOCKS AND YET KEEP THE RELATIONSHIPS

1. Recap the discussion to ensure there really is a deadlock.
2. Emphasize mutual interests.
3. Stress the cost of not agreeing and situations you want to avoid.
4. Reach an agreement in principle, postponing difficult parts of the agreement.
5. Try to find out if the problem is based on something TOS isn't telling you.

6. Change the type of contract.
7. Change contract specifications or terms.
8. Add options to the contract.
9. Hold informal discussions in a different setting.
10. Make concessions that are contingent upon settling all of the issues.
11. Form a joint study committee.
12. Change a team member or team leader.
13. Discuss how both you and TOS might respond to a hypothetical solution, without committing either party to a course of action.
14. Tell a funny story.
15. Take a recess.
16. Consider setting a deadline for resolution. Deadlines create a sense of urgency and encourage action.
17. Be patient.

Keep in mind that both the tone and the content of the current negotiation will impact future negotiations with TOS. This is true even if you don't successfully conclude the current negotiation; sometimes you are really setting the stage for the next one. It's like arguing with the umpire in American baseball. Why do baseball managers do it? They never prevail. Aside from pleasing the crowd, the manager argues with the umpire for one simple reason—not for this call, but for the next call! So, too, in your negotiations, put markers in TOS's mind for the next time you sit down to do business. Leave him or her with two thoughts: (1) you're a good person for TOS to do business with and (2) here are some expectations to keep in mind.

STRATEGY 7: MAINTAIN PERSONAL INTEGRITY

A few years ago a businessman came up to me before I was about to make a speech on negotiations. He said that he was a good Christian and, as such, didn't know if he should stay for the speech since he assumed I'd be talking about scheming ways to manipulate other people. I told him that while I didn't know whether or not he should stay, negotiators who use manipulative, scheming, hidden agendas do not do very well in negotiations. He seemed somewhat shocked but relieved by my response.

Personal integrity is absolutely critical for your effectiveness as a world-class negotiator. My conviction on this point is not related to religion but to pragmatism. There are two reasons why personal integrity and trust are vital. The first reason has to do with information. No one tells you anything of importance if he or she doesn't trust you.* If you are not viewed as trustworthy, people will tell you only what they must tell you because of your position or title. For example, if you are trusted, after a negotiating session TOS may ask for some confidential "whisper time." She may confide in you as follows:

> TOS: *Look, I know we've been pressing for A, B, C, and D in there. But, off the record, what we're really interested in is only C and D.*
> You: *But you've been really pushing hard for A and B.*
> TOS: *I know. But if you can find a way to give us C and D, we've got a deal.*

This is a rich disclosure. This is the stuff that will make you successful, not because you are technically brilliant, but because you are trusted. Risky, key data are shared with you only if your personal integrity is unquestioned.

---

* Herb Cohen talks about this effectively in his video *Persuasive Negotiating.*

Personal integrity is vital to building your negotiating strength for a second reason: *Issues of trust are the most difficult relationship problems to repair.* In fact, these are often irreparable. With some hard work, some skill, and a little luck, other types of relationship problems can be healed, but the trust issue hardly ever gets fixed. Think of the people you really don't trust in your professional or personal life. Is there *anything* they can do to repair the relationship and get back in your good graces? If you are like most people, the answer is "nothing."

American negotiators sometimes try to resolve issues of trust by formalizing the intent of the parties in an ironclad contract. We then hold TOS to the contract, regardless of how much we trust them. In many cultures, however, it is the person or the relationship that your counterpart trusts, not a piece of paper. Making and keeping contractual commitments is not a high priority for many of your international counterparts. Much of this view relates to the relative uncertainty felt by those from other cultures compared with Americans. Malaysians, for example, prefer to have exit clauses in their contracts in case things don't work out. They feel little control over future business events or even their country as a whole and want provisions for a respectable withdrawal should future circumstances make their compliance impossible.[6] In much of the Arab world, negotiators stress mutual trust and see themselves doing business with "the man" rather than a company or a contract.[7] In Britain, there are strong legal precedents but less reliance on formalized contracts than in the United States. Tom Wilson, a British management consultant, observes, "Detailed legal contracts are seldom the order of the day. The British feel aggrieved when outsmarted by clever contract language. Besides," he adds, "a legal decision will not enforce that for which there is no will to perform."

Building trust can be a long process, particularly in global negotiating, and it can be harmed in subtle ways. This is why you should avoid excessive use of phrases such as "to be honest with you ... " (are you not normally honest?), "to tell you the truth ... " (are you not normally truthful?), and "frankly ... " (are you not usually candid?). Though TOS may not be conscious of why he or she doesn't trust you, too many of these phrases lead to a conclusion that you are not trustworthy, even if you are honest.

If you are viewed as trustworthy by TOS, protect this aspect of the negotiation at all costs. Remember, *lose the deal if you must, but keep the trust.* This will be vital for your next negotiation with TOS.

STRATEGY 8: CONSERVE CONCESSIONS

Concessions give valuable information about you, your style, and your resolve. How you use them sets the tone, not only for a current negotiation, but for future negotiations as well. Your current concession pattern teaches TOS how to treat you in the future.

Let's say you're in Budapest, involved in a tough negotiation with the Hungarians. You have traded data with them and made logical defenses of your negotiating position for five long meetings. The negotiation seems to be going nowhere. This particular negotiation is price-sensitive, and in the first meeting, you quoted $80 per unit for your product. The Hungarians have offered you $20. You know that building a good relationship is important in any negotiation. They haven't budged from the $20 since the first meeting.

In order to break the logjam, you show your good faith in working out this negotiation by making a counteroffer of $45. This, you think, shows that you mean business in resolving this issue and that you are acting in good faith. Besides, your "really asking" price is $40, and you will certainly have gone more than halfway. The Hungarians will surely do the same, and you can all conclude the session, have some vodka, and go home.

It may not work out this way. In fact, in the case related above, you can bet you are about to get clobbered. Like many negotiators, you might feel that making a concession will create goodwill or soft up TOS. Unfortunately, a much more likely scenario is that such a concession will suggest weakness on your part, make your counterpart greedy, or even make your counterpart suspicious. You must therefore be extremely careful in making concessions.

WORLD-CLASS TIPS: TEN GUIDELINES ON MAKING CONCESSIONS

1. Don't be the first to make a concession on an important issue.
2. Never accept the first offer.
3. Make TOS reduce a high initial demand; don't honor a high demand by making a counteroffer.
4. Make small concessions. Lower the expectation of TOS.
5. When you make concessions, make them slowly (like wine, they improve with time).
6. Make TOS feel good by making concessions of low value to you but of perceived high value to TOS.
7. Defer concessions on matters that are important to you.
8. Make contingent concessions (i.e., get something in return, or concede only on the condition that all issues be settled).
9. Celebrate the concessions you get. Don't feel guilty.
10. Don't feel that you must reciprocate every concession made to you.

The number of initial concessions differs among cultures. One study found that Japanese negotiators made fewer initial concessions per half-hour bargaining session (6.5) than did negotiators from the United States (7.1) or Brazil (9.4).[8] As a rule, the fewer the concessions, the better.

Also, beware when TOS asks for a concession on the grounds of "fairness." Whenever your counterparts tell you that they want you to make a concession because their offer to you has been very "fair" or "reasonable," don't believe them. More often than not, this is a manipulative tactic to make you feel guilty.

STRATEGY 9: MAKE PATIENCE AN OBSESSION

Since almost every stage of a global negotiation tends to take longer than the domestic, patience is not only a virtue, but a necessity. Patience serves three vital functions: (1) It facilitates getting information from TOS, (2) it builds the relationship by sending out signals of courtesy, and (3) it increases your chances of effective concession making. Patience is linked to concession behavior because impatient negotiators tend to make both more counterproposals and more concessions. Skilled negotiators make fewer counterproposals than do less skilled negotiators.[9]

Patience may also be one of TOS's negotiating tactics, since TOS tries to wear you down with their patience. They are counting on your becoming anxious and making concessions that you otherwise wouldn't make. Don't be a victim. Take these countermeasures:

*   Give yourself plenty of time.
*   Relax and make yourself comfortable.
*   Prepare your own people back home for a long negotiation.
*   Recognize that it may be tougher on TOS than on you.
*   Consider setting a deadline.

Patience, as important as it is, can be hard work. One manager from an American oil company illustrates this point in the Pacific Rim: "Negotiating in Indonesia is like drinking a thousand cups of tea—very challenging and very slow." Ted Cline, who has negotiated many large contracts in the Middle East, stresses the importance of persistence. "I tell my people: If you beat your head on the wall, it will get bloody. But if you keep constant pressure on the wall, some day it will fall down."

JUST-IN-TIME MANAGEMENT

I was in the small Central American country of Belize to address a management conference. I was scheduled to speak at 9:00 A.M., so I was ready to go about 8:00 A.M., waiting for my hosts in the hotel lobby. They weren't there. 8:15—no one. 8:30—nobody. 8:45—nope. I checked with the front desk to make sure I had set my watch to the correct time zone. 9:00—9:15—still no one. Now I'm getting out my letter of invitation, thinking, "Could this be my worst nightmare? Could I be in the wrong country on the wrong date? At about 9:20 my hosts showed up, and we drove to the hotel where the conference was being held. After a short discussion about my flight, the weather, and related items, I said, "It's about 9:30. Wasn't I on the agenda for 9:00 A.M.?"

No response.

"I'm just curious, but if it's about 9:35, aren't we late for the conference?" I persisted.

"Oh no, Mr. Acuff," one of my hosts said jovially. "Nothing here in Belize starts at the time on the agenda. We'll be quite early. The conference won't start for another hour or so."

"Thank you," I said, relieved. My life was good again.

STRATEGY 10: BE CULTURALLY LITERATE AND ADAPT THE NEGOTIATING PROCESS TO THE HOST COUNTRY ENVIRONMENT

By acquiring insight into the culture of TOS, as well as into your own cultural predispositions, you can bridge the cultural gap to become a more effective negotiator. You can be empathetic with TOS only if you understand the culture and environment in which TOS operates. Every step of the negotiating process must be seen through the lens of the host-country culture. Increasing your cultural IQ pays off in every step of the negotiating process, from the initial planning and greeting TOS right down to setting the stage for future business.

Cultural savvy takes many forms. Witness, for example, a supplier of oilfield technology that sent a program administrator to resolve the snags associated with a Russian joint venture. Despite the progress on technical details, the Russians continued to be very standoffish. Only later did the firm learn that sending a midlevel manager with the title of program administrator was an insult to the Russians, who felt that anyone with such a lowly title was unlikely to have the authority to negotiate a substantial deal, and that sending a midlevel manager was disrespectful of them. Such title and rank considerations are important to Russian negotiators. In this particular case, the firm's vice-president of international projects relates that now, when the program administrator travels to Russia, his title is revised to "managing director of special projects." The vice-president notes, "The title change makes the Russians feel like they are dealing with the right level of person, and all it costs us are new business cards."

Moira Crean, manager of contracts administration for MasterCard International, finds that cultural savvy takes the form of sensitivity to age in mainland China. "Age," she explains, "can be a key aspect in a big negotiation. Our Chinese partners have been known to dismiss a young person—let's say, a 35-year-old vice president—and say, 'Send over the old guy.'"

Even concession making must be seen through a cultural perspective. Exhibit 4 illustrates different perceptions of your good intentions. The reaction to a large concession may range from pleasure (a U.S. negotiator) to dismay (a Swiss negotiator).

If you just remember the following two guidelines, you will not only be culturally literate, but you will be a superb global negotiator.

Negotiators From	Likely Reaction
United States	"I gotcha."
Netherlands	"I cannot trust you."
Japan	"This has hurt the harmony."
Switzerland	"This person did not prepare well."
Saudi Arabia	"This is how business is done."

EXHIBIT 4   How a large concession from you might be perceived by negotiators from different countries.

1. Adopt the Platinum Rule

Most of us grew up with the Golden Rule or something similar: "Do unto others as *you* would that they do unto you." This works well when we are surrounded by people like us–whoever "us" might be. We know how to treat the other person because of shared backgrounds and traits. With our international counterparts, the Golden Rule is no longer very helpful, because how you want to be treated may indeed be very different from how Chin, Suresh, Ivan, Miguel, Mohanuned, Isobella, or Isa wants to be treated. Instead, adopt what I call the Platinum Rule: "Do unto others as *they* would have done unto them." You might be comfortable with a firm handshake, with being direct and open, and with getting right down to business. But if the culture of TOS encourages other behaviors and your cultural savvy enables you to engage in them, you will be ahead of the competition. As you increase your comfort zone with others, so too will you increase your negotiating effectiveness.

Is there a place for common courtesy? You bet, as long as such courtesy isn't defined only on your terms. If common courtesy means a smile upon greeting or not interrupting others, this works almost anywhere. If it means inviting TOS to lunch, picking up the tab, complimenting TOS about his or her office, extending a firm handshake, or providing a gift as a token of your appreciation, then your courtesy may be another person's idea of irritating behavior. Tact has been called intelligence of the heart. In global business affairs, tact includes knowledge of the host-country culture.

2. Conduct Yourself as an Effective Foreigner

The idea is not to go native,[10] but to be culturally savvy while remaining a foreigner. Don't worry about minor gaffes in the many rituals and customs associated with every culture. If your handshake is a little too firm in Rio de Janeiro, or you can't remember that phrase you learned in Polish, it is not the end of the world. TOS will normally give you an A for effort even if the details of the execution need a little work. Be culturally savvy, but also be authentic. If the sight of fish eyes makes you squeamish in Singapore, if it means you're going to spend an hour being sick in the bathroom, don't eat the fish eyes.

MIDDLE EAST BUSINESS PRACTICES 101: WHEN COMPLIMENTS ARE COSTLY

The Labour Minister for the United Arab Emirates was in my office to help negotiate an end to a work stoppage by the local Dubai construction workers. The meeting went well until we finished our discussions. While walking with His Highness to the door of my office, I mentioned that he had a beautiful briefcase (mine was in a general state of disrepair). As I reached the door I noticed that he was no longer walking with me. I turned around to see His Highness emptying the contents of his briefcase on my desk.

(continued)

"Did you lose something?" I asked, trying to be helpful.

"No, no," he replied. "I want you to have," he added, as he presented his briefcase to me. "This is for you. You are my friend."

After profusely apologizing, I convinced him that I really couldn't accept the briefcase.

The lesson learned? In that part of the world, don't go around complimenting people on their possessions. You just might end up with them.

NOTES

[1] N. Rackham, "The Behavior of Successful Negotiators" (Reston, VA: Huthwaite Research Group, 1976), as reported in Ellen Raider International, Inc. (Brooklyn, NY) and Situation Management Systems, Inc. (Plymouth, MA), *International Negotiations: A Training Program for Corporate Executives and Diplomats* (1982).

[2] Ibid.

[3] See P. Sperber, *Fail-Safe Business Negotiating: Strategies and Tactics for Success* (Upper Saddle River, NJ: Prentice-Hall, 1983), 40–41; and R. J. Lewicki and J. A. Litterer, *Negotiation* (Homewood, IL: Richard D. Irwin, 1985), 75–79.

[4] F. L. Acuff, "What It Takes to Succeed in Overseas Assignment," *National Business Employment Weekly* (August 25, 1991): 17–18.

[5] Rackham, "The Behavior of Successful Negotiators."

[6] N. J. Adler, *International Dimensions of Organizational Behavior* (Cincinnati: South-West, 1997), 209.

[7] P. R. Harris and R. T. Moran, *Managing Cultural Differences*, 2nd ed. (Houston: Gulf Publishing, 1987), 474.

[8] John Graham, "The Influence of Culture on Negotiations," *Journal of International Business Studies, XVI*, no. 1 (Spring 1985): 81–96.

[9] Rackham, "The Behavior of Successful Negotiators," 180.

[10] Adler, *International Dimensions*, 187.

CHAPTER 12

MANAGING DIVERSITY

MYTHS ABOUT DIVERSITY: WHAT MANAGERS NEED TO KNOW ABOUT CHANGES IN THE U.S. LABOR FORCE
   Judith T. Friedman
   Nancy DiTomaso

GENDER GAP IN THE EXECUTIVE SUITE: CEOS AND FEMALE EXECUTIVES REPORT ON BREAKING THE GLASS CEILING
   Belle Rose Ragins
   Bickley Townsend
   Mary Mattis

CULTURAL CONSTRAINTS IN MANAGEMENT THEORIES
   Geert Hofstede

BEYOND SOPHISTICATED STEREOTYPING: CULTURAL SENSEMAKING IN CONTEXT
   Joyce S. Osland
   Allan Bird

Although the United States with its waves of immigrants has always had a multicultural workforce, the last decade has brought much more emphasis on understanding the differences people bring to work and the need to incorporate an appreciation of these differences into the way we manage and work with others. Globalization and labor migration has resulted in more and more work contact with people from other cultures. The definition of diversity, however, extends beyond cultural background to include differences resulting from thinking styles, working styles, age, functional disciplines, years of service, religious beliefs, sexual orientation, marital status, physical appearance/abilities, education, and gender. This chapter deals with both domestic diversity within the United States and cross-cultural diversity.

The first article, "Myths About Diversity," is a carefully researched argument that explores common misconceptions about U.S. minorities in the workplace. Judith Friedman, sociology professor, and Nancy DiTomaso, organization management professor, have amassed a wealth of demographic data to produce a more accurate picture of workforce participation and the progress of minority groups. The second article, "Gender Gap in the Executive Suite: CEOs and Female Executives Report on Breaking the Glass Ceiling," provides a clearer understanding of the barriers women face in advancing to the highest levels of corporations. Belle Rose Ragins is a business professor while Bickley Townsend and Mary Mattis are both Ph.D.s who work for Catalyst, a non-profit research and consulting firm that specializes in gender issues in business and the professions. Their large-scale study of both CEOs and high-ranking women in their companies reveals clear discrepancies in the way both groups view the glass ceiling (the invisible barrier to advancement based on attitudinal or organizational bias) and organizational efforts to combat this problem.

The third article is written by Geert Hofstede, an internationally famous scholar whose groundbreaking study of IBM employees has been a major influence on the field of international management since 1980. In "Cultural Constraints in Management Theories," Hofstede notes that *management* is conceptualized differently around the world and warns that theories of management reflect cultural values and cannot therefore be applied in other countries. Hofstede is best known for identifying five cultural dimensions that explain differences in national culture.

The last article, "Beyond Sophisticated Stereotyping: Cultural Sensemaking in Context," also sounds a cautionary warning. This time, however, the caveat is directed against using bipolar cultural dimensions, like those identified by Hofstede, to stereotype whole cultures. Joyce Osland and Allan Bird are business professors and consultants who spent many years working overseas. As a result, they became intrigued by the paradoxical aspects of culture and devised a sensemaking model that takes context into consideration and begins to capture greater cultural complexity.

MYTHS ABOUT DIVERSITY: WHAT MANAGERS NEED TO KNOW ABOUT CHANGES IN THE U.S. LABOR FORCE*

Judith T. Friedman
Nancy DiTomaso

Despite recent concerns about labor force diversity, there are widespread misunderstandings about current labor force trends. These misunderstandings have implications. Managers rely on information about likely changes in their customer base and likely changes in the U.S. labor force as they develop business and marketing strategies and personnel policies. Misinformation can mean poor strategies and poor personnel policies. Thus *American Demographics* identifies possibly overlooked markets, such as Asians and African Americans living in suburbs, and it runs articles that explain basic demographic concepts. Similarly, a recent *Fortune* article pointed to the "power of demographics" in forming investment strategies and identifying business opportunities.[1]

This article describes recent trends in U.S. labor force composition, as well as likely future changes in U.S. labor force composition and growth. The discussion centers on nine widespread myths. Myths 1 and 2 deal with the extent to which the U.S. labor force—and the U.S. population—are becoming more diverse. Myths 3 to 6 focus on one source of labor force diversity, immigration. Myths 7 to 9 then connect the economic situation of African Americans with immigration and with diversity efforts. Many of these myths involve exaggerating small changes.

MYTHS 1 AND 2: TRENDS IN THE DIVERSITY OF THE U.S. LABOR FORCE

MYTH NO. 1: LABOR FORCE DIVERSITY WILL INCREASE DRAMATICALLY OVER THE NEXT DECADE AS THE UNITED STATES FACES A SIZABLE DECLINE IN THE PERCENTAGE OF THE LABOR FORCE THAT CONSISTS OF NON-HISPANIC WHITE MALES

Articles in the business press repeatedly assert that white males (or native-born white males) will constitute a small fraction of all those who enter the U.S. workforce over the next few years. These articles

*Reprinted with permission from *California Management Review* 38, no. 4 (Summer 1996): 54–75.

usually cite *Workforce 2000*, an influential Hudson Institute report.[2] *Business Week* provides one example: "By the year 2000, the study projected, only 15 percent of the people entering the workforce would be American-born white males, compared with 47 percent in 1987."[3]

This quote also illustrates one common definition of labor force diversity: the U.S. labor force becomes more diverse whenever the percentage of native-born white males declines.[4] Thus *any* change in the U.S. labor force that reduces the percentage of native-born white males creates greater diversity.

If native-born white males were becoming a small percentage of all new labor force entrants, managers would find the mix of job applicants changing dramatically. Further, if native-born white males became a small percentage of labor force entrants while the U.S. labor force continued to grow, the percentage of native-born white males in the *total* U.S. labor force would decline at an unprecedented rate. However, neither change is occurring. There is—and there will be—no *dramatic* decline in the percentage of native-born white males.

U.S. Department of Labor counts and projections show what actually is going on. Using these figures means using Census labor force categories. The Census provides a long time-series of figures for two broad race/ethnic categories: white and non-white. For recent years, the Census provides a four-category breakdown: non-Hispanic white, non-Hispanic African American, Hispanic, and Asian and other. Considering gender as well, this provides eight categories.[5]

TABLE 1   Changes in the Distribution of the U.S. Labor Force by Subgroup, 1994 to 2005 (Numbers in Thousands, Percents in Parentheses)

Labor Force Subgroup	1994	New Entrants	Leavers	2005	Net Additions	Change in %
Non-Hispanic White Men	54,306 (41.4)	12,937 (32.9)	10,814 (46.4)	56,429 (38.4)	2,123 (13.2)	−3.0
Non-Hispanic White Women	46,157 (35.2)	13,122 (33.4)	7,363 (31.6)	51,916 (35.3)	5,759 (35.9)	0.1
Non-Hispanic African American Men	6,981 (5.3)	2,314 (5.9)	1,512 (6.5)	7,783	802 (5.0)	0.0
Non-Hispanic African American Women	7,323 (5.6)	2,557 (6.5)	1,271 (5.5)	8,609 (5.9)	1,286 (8.0)	0.3
Hispanic Men	7,210 (5.5)	3,321 (8.4)	1,039 (4.5)	9,492 (6.5)	2,282 (14.2)	1.0
Hispanic Women	4,764 (3.6)	2,765 (7.0)	690 (3.0)	6,838 (4.6)	2,074 (12.9)	1.0
Asian and Other Men	2,317 (1.8)	1,148 (2.9)	326 (1.4)	3,139 (2.1)	822 (5.1)	0.3
Asian and Other Women	1,994 (1.5)	1,180 (3.0)	274 (1.2)	2,900 (2.0)	906 (5.6)	0.5
Totals	131,051 (99.9)	39,343 (100)	23,289 (100.1)	147,106 (100.1)	16,054 (99.9)	0.0*

*Does not add up to zero due to rounding error.

Source: H. N. Fullerton. Jr., "The 2005 Labor Force: Growing, but Slowly." *Monthy Labor Review* (November 1995): 41, as corrected in "Errata," *Monthy Labor Review* (March 1996) 38.

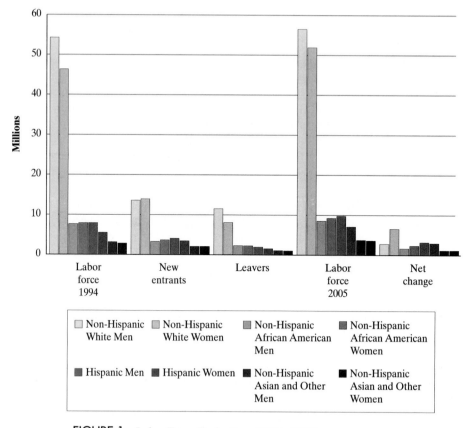

FIGURE 1   **Labor Force Projection, 1994 to 2005**
(Current Workers + New Entrants − Leavers = New Workforce)
Source: Fullerton, *Monthly Labor Review* (November 1995).

Even with eight categories, non-Hispanic white males constitute the largest single category of U.S. workers in 1994 and continue to be the largest category projected for 2005 (see Table 1 and Figure 1). In 1994, the U.S. labor force had 54 million non-Hispanic white males. They comprised 41 percent of the total labor force. (Non-Hispanic white women were the second largest category, at 35 percent.) Department of Labor projections for 2005 show the non-Hispanic white male category growing by two million. *Because other categories are expected to grow faster*, the percentage of non-Hispanic white males drops a bit, to a projected 38 percent in 2005.[6]

This projected decline of only three percent takes on clearer meaning when put into historical perspective. To show this, we must switch to the broader white/non-white categories. Each year, the percentage of the labor force that consists of white men is larger than the percentage that consists of non-Hispanic white men, as most Hispanics are classified as white. The proportion of the labor force that consists of white males has been declining for many decades. The solid line in Figure 2 traces the actual decline over slightly more than half a century—from 1940, when white males constituted 69 percent of the U.S. labor force, to 1990, when they constituted 47 percent, and then to 1994, at 46 percent. As the line shows, the overall trend is a long, slow decline in the percentage who are white males. Projections show this slow decline continuing. By 2005, white males are expected to be 44 percent of the U.S. labor force.[7]

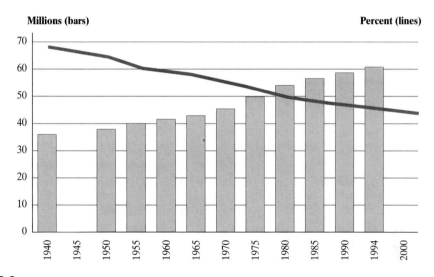

FIGURE 2   **Trends in Number and Percent of White Men in Labor Force, 1940 to 1994 and Estimate for 2005**
Source: 1940 and 1950. U.S. Buireau of the Census, U.S. Census of Population; 1955-1985. Handbook of Labor Statistics, 1989; 1990. U.S. of the Census, Current Population Reports; 1994 and estimate for 2005. Fullerton, 1995.

The *cumulative* change in the percentage who are white males over these 65 years is dramatic. Neither the recent change—nor the change predicted for the next decade—is dramatic. Further, the recent change and the predicted change involve a *slowing* of the long-term trend. The *number* of non-Hispanic white males in the U.S. labor force continues to increase. Indeed, these projections show non-Hispanic white males will remain the largest *single* race-ethinic/gender category in the U.S. labor force for the foreseeable future (see Figure 1).

Why the Misunderstanding?   The myth of dramatically increasing diversity apparently stems from the way the frequently cited report, *Workforce 2000*, presented labor force projections. *Workforce 2000* uses the term *new entrants* for a category that would be more accurately labeled *net additions*.[8] Understandably, readers assumed that a category called *new entrants* included *all* those entering the labor force. The net additions during a time period, however, are a *subset* of all new entrants. Net additions are only those new entrants who do not *replace* someone leaving the labor force, perhaps through retirement. Thus readers thought the report described total change, where the report actually described marginal change.[9]

The composition of all new entrants to a labor force and the composition of net new additions can differ markedly. Differences will develop when one category of adults predominates, numerically, for many years, and then other, numerically smaller, categories begin to grow more rapidly. The historically dominant category will have many entrants *and* many leavers, while the growing categories will have an increasing number of entrants, but few leavers. Thus members of the historically large category remain a large proportion of *all* entrants, while becoming a small proportion of net additions.

This is the case in the United States today. The vast majority of non-Hispanic white male adults are in the labor force, so the age structure of this labor force category resembles that of the total population. Members of the earliest baby-boom cohorts are reaching age 50. Younger members of the current labor force come from the smaller "baby bust" cohorts, but those just now entering the labor force include people from the slightly larger birth cohorts that followed the "bust."

Retirement is a major reason that non-Hispanic white males leave the labor force. These men have been retiring at earlier ages, lowering the labor force participation rates for males age 55 and older. Department of Labor projections assume that this small downward trend in the labor force participation of older non-Hispanic white males will continue.

Projections for 1994-2005 show 11 million leavers among non-Hispanic white males; this is 20 percent of the 1994 count of such males. The projections also show 13 million non-Hispanic white males *entering* the labor force in this time period. The vast majority of these 13 million entrants will "replace" a non-Hispanic white male who leaves the labor force.[10] With 11 million leaving, only two million (of the 13 million) new entrants remain for the count of "net additions." (Two million also is the net growth for this category.)

Compare this with the projections for Hispanic men and for "Asian and other" men. Entrants in both categories include more immigrants. Immigration (plus, for Hispanics, somewhat higher fertility) means a lower median age.[11] Immigration and age structure both lower the ratio of leavers to entrants. Projections for 1994-2005 show a ratio (leavers to entrants) of .31 for Hispanic men and .28 for Asian (and other) men, but .65 for non-Hispanic African American men and .84 for non-Hispanic white men.

Fullerton's medium projections for new entrants and for leavers in the period 1994-2005 show non-Hispanic white men constituting a third of *all* new entrants, but close to half (46 percent) of all leavers. These figures would mean that non-Hispanic white men are just 13 percent of the "*net* additions." Since the total number of net additions is small relative to the number in the total labor force, the "net additions" will have little impact on the composition of the total labor force of 2005. These projections show the percent non-Hispanic white males declining by just three percent between 1994 and 2005, to a projected 38 percent.[12]

Non-Hispanic white men are *not* going to be a small part of the future U.S. labor force, and they are *not* going to be a small part of those who enter the U.S. labor force in future years. The proportion of the U.S. labor force that consists of people other than Non-Hispanic white males is increasing, and in this sense the U.S. labor force continues a slow shift toward greater diversity. The business press has exaggerated the pace of this change, and it has failed to recognize that the current change is part of a long-term trend.

Myth No. 2: The U.S. labor force will become more diverse as the proportion female increases

Increasing gender diversity accounts for most of the increase in U.S. labor force diversity through the past century. The percentage of those in the U.S. labor force who are white women has increased rather steadily over more than a century, as all increasing percentage of all adult women have entered the paid labor force. The percentage who are African American women also has increased, but at a slower rate, because a much larger proportion of all African American women were in the labor force a century ago.

The pace of the increase in women's labor force participation (and hence in the proportion of the labor force that is female) did accelerate shortly after World War II, in part because the Depression had slowed the long-term increase. The increase in women's labor force participation then slowed markedly in the late 1980s, and Department of Labor projections assume a still-smaller increase in the near future.[13]

The 46 million non-Hispanic white women who were in the 1994 U.S. labor force comprised 35 percent of the total. Women in all racial/ethnic categories together composed 46 percent of the total 1994 labor force (Table 1). The 52 million non-Hispanic white women projected for the labor force of 2005 will be, again, 35 percent of the total. Similarly, non-Hispanic African American women were six percent of the 1994 labor force, and these projections show them as six percent of the 2005 labor force. The two other categories for women, Hispanic and Asian (and other), are growing through immigration. Overall, these projections show a two percent increase in the percent of the labor force that is female by 2005 (Table 1).

Since the increase in gender diversity is essentially over, further increases in labor force diversity must have other sources. Immigration has been a second important source of diversity. The declining importance of women's increasing labor force participation means that immigration may be a larger source of increasing diversity in the near future than it has been in the recent past.

The increasing importance of immigration to labor force diversity, then, involves the declining importance of another source of diversity, gender diversity. As the pace of women's movement into the labor force slows, changes related to immigration become more visible. As the changes from immigration become more visible, it becomes easy to exaggerate the *scale* of change involved. Here, myths about labor force change parallel myths about change in the total U.S. population.

MYTHS 3 THROUGH 6: THE EFFECTS OF IMMIGRATION

Immigration patterns, and myths about these patterns, take on still greater importance when they are repeated in debates over changes in federal immigration laws. Here, groups that represent organizations hiring immigrants stress economic benefits and dismiss ideas about any negative consequences. Conversely, those arguing for limits on immigration emphasize a range of plausible negative consequences. In making their arguments, both groups necessarily rely on estimates of current illegal immigration and on projections of overall future immigration (legal and illegal). They also rely on estimates of immigrants' use of public services, estimates of their tax payments, and evidence about the kinds of jobs that immigrants fill—and create. Thus evaluating the evidence means looking at the quality of the available numbers, and it means comparing so-called positive and negative effects.

MYTH NO. 3: IMMIGRATION IS PRODUCING A MARKED CHANGE IN THE COMPOSITION OF THE TOTAL U.S. POPULATION AND IN THE COMPOSITION OF THE TOTAL U.S. LABOR FORCE. NON-HISPANIC WHITES ARE BECOMING A MINORITY

Certainly the U.S. population (and its labor force) are becoming more diverse. The percentage of non-Hispanic whites is declining, while the percentage who are non-Hispanic African Americans remains rather constant. Population projections show the percentage of the total U.S. *population* that is non-Hispanic white declining from 73 percent in 1996 to 70 percent in 2005, 64 percent in 2020, and 53 percent in 2050.[14] These projections also show the *number* of non-Hispanic whites in the population increasing over the next four decades (to at least 2035), and then decreasing slightly (Figure 3). The faster growth of *other* categories accounts for the declining percent.

Turning this around, the percentage of the U.S. population that is Hispanic is expected to increase from 10.5 percent in 1996 to 16.3 percent in 2020 and 24.5 percent in 2050. The percentage that is Asian is expected to increase from 3.4 percent in 1996 to 5.7 percent in 2020 and 8.2 percent in 2050.

These changes may appear sizable, but they occur over a great many years, and they depend upon numerous assumptions, including assumptions about future immigration. Further, these assumptions become increasingly important as the projections move into the future.

Labor force projections to 2005 show immigration producing a modest increase in the diversity of the U.S. labor force, as the faster growth of the Hispanic and the Asian (and other) adult populations means a small reduction in the proportion non-Hispanic white.

The *number* of Hispanics in the *labor force* is expected to increase by 36 percent between 1994 and 2005, and the number of Asians (and other) is expected to increase by 40 percent (Table 1). The small initial numbers of Hispanics and of Asians (arid others), relative to the number of natives, means, however, that this rapid proportional growth will make rather little difference in the composition of the

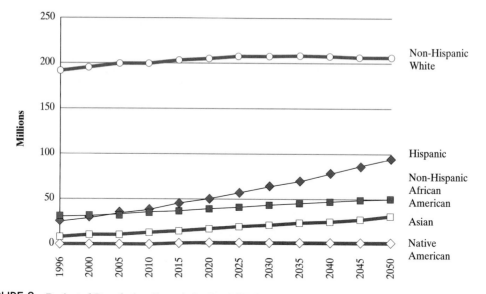

FIGURE 3 **Projected Population Growth for Racial/Ethnic Groups, 1996 to 2050 (July 1 figures)**
Source: *Current Population Reports*, Series P25-1130, 1996.

labor force. Hispanics made up nine percent of the 1994 U.S. labor force, and these projections show them as 11 percent of the 2005 labor force (an increase of two percent over 12 years). Asians (and others) made up three percent of the 1994 labor force, and these projections show them as four percent of the 2005 labor force (Table 1).

Why the Misunderstanding? Perhaps the baby boom experience accounts for part of the exaggeration in the number of immigrants likely to enter the U.S. labor force. As those in the baby boom cohorts (born 1946-1964) have aged, the bulge they produced in U.S. age structure has moved upward. Members of the initial baby boom cohorts are approaching age 50. Smaller birth cohorts followed the boom, but the number of annual births began to increase again when those in the large baby boom cohort began to have children.

The baby boom created an unprecedented increase in the number of people reaching labor force age. The smaller cohorts that followed meant a decline, for a few years, in the number reaching labor force age (16). In the total U.S. population, the number of people age 16 to 24 declined for the period 1982 to 1993. This slowing, in turn, meant that population (and labor force) growth through immigration became more visible. The drop in young native-born entrants is over, however. Population projections show the number of people age 16 to 24 increasing from 32.5 million to 37 million between 1994 and 2005.[15]

California provides a second reason for exaggerated ideas about the impact of immigration. Both the percentage who are Hispanic and the percentage who are Asian are increasing much faster in California than they are in the entire nation.

MYTH NO. 4: CALIFORNIA IS A MODEL OF THE U.S. FUTURE

California has had large Hispanic and Asian populations for a long time, and California is a major destination for Hispanic and Asian immigrants. It is no longer, however, a major destination for native-born white and African American migrants. California is one of just six states that grew primarily from

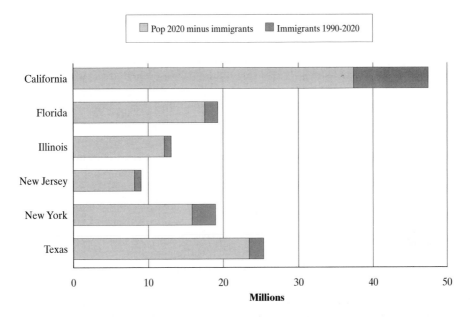

FIGURE 4 **Estimated Population in 2020 and Estimated Number Who Are Immigrants Added 1990 to 2020, for the Six States with Largest Numbers of Immigrants***

*These six states account for 41% of the estimated population for 2020, but account for 79% of the estimated immigration between 1990 and 2020. The average percent of the 2020 population accounted for by immigrants during this period in these six states is 14%; in the other 44 states it is 2.5%. The California proportion is 22%.

Source: U.S. Bureau of the Census, *Current Population Reports*, Series P25-1111.

immigration during the 1980s.[16] These are unusual patterns, and there is no reason to expect other states to follow this pattern.

It is essential to recognize that California's experience with immigration is unique. California's urbanized areas, especially Los Angeles and San Francisco, stand out as destinations for Hispanic and Asian immigrants. In 1990, a third of all U.S. foreign-born residents lived in California, and over 22 percent of California's residents were foreign-born. Projections of future immigration to each state show this pattern continuing (Figure 4).[17]

California has become the center of "anti-diversity" politics. Recent California initiatives have sought to limit illegal immigrants' access to public services and to rescind or modify affirmative action policies perceived to primarily benefit African Americans. In this, too, commentators have perceived California as a model for the nation. The concentration of immigrants in California (and a few other states) undoubtedly contributed to recent anti-immigrant politics. Fiscal issues provide one reason: concentrations of immigrants mean concentrated demands on the public services that are financed by local and state governments in the United States. Any shift of services away from the federal level will only increase these fiscal pressures on local governments that experience substantial immigration.[18] While it is possible that extensive immigration can erode political support for immigration, concentrations of immigrants also can facilitate political organization that benefits immigrants. Although California's population does have an increasing proportion of Hispanics and an increasing proportion of Asians, there is no reason to expect the nation to mirror California. The belief that immigration is making a marked change in the U.S. population and its labor force involves additional myths about the recent immigrants to the United States.

MYTH NO. 5A: THE UNITED STATES IS A MAGNET FOR SKILLED FOREIGN WORKERS

U.S. immigration patterns reflect U.S. immigration policy. This policy changes through time. It now involves three different sets of rules: those for legal immigration, those for humanitarian admissions, and those that affect illegal entry. These three sets of rules have generated three distinct immigration streams.[20]

The Immigration and Nationality Act Amendments of 1965 set the stage for major changes in the patterns of legal immigration to the United States. By removing the former strict limits on Asian immigration, this legislation permitted a shift in ethnic composition away from the historic European bias. At the same time, family reunification preferences involved an attempt to preserve the existing ethnic mix. This legislation also may have planted the seeds for the increase in the number of illegal immigrants, because it placed the first limits on Western Hemisphere countries (notably Mexico).[21]

Patterns of immigration to the United States reflect more than U.S. immigration policy, of course. The decision to immigrate involves individuals' calculations of their prospects in their native country and in various destination countries. U.S. policies can specify who can come, but they cannot determine who, among those permitted in, does come. Thus, U.S. policy can welcome the highly skilled, but the decision of highly skilled people to immigrate also involves (among other things) the economic return that they can get, in various countries, for their years in school.

Before the 1965 immigration legislation, the U.S. had become a relatively less-attractive destination for highly skilled immigrants. European immigrants have tended to be highly educated. By 1965, the immigration slots allotted to many European countries regularly were going unfilled. Canada and Australia have been relatively more attractive destinations, and immigrants to these countries have fared better, over time, in the labor forces of their adopted countries.[22] The percentage of all immigrants to the United States who come from Europe only recently began to increase a bit.[23]

David North argues that difficulty in attracting skilled immigrants is one reason for the practice of enticing skilled immigrants to the United States by paying their way to attend U.S. graduate schools,[24] indeed, foreign science and engineering students who stay in the United States after completing their education (most of them at university expense) are a major source of skilled immigrants. The proportion of these students who stay is increasing,[25] but these students remain a small percentage of all recent immigrants to the United States.

MYTH NO. 5B: RECENT IMMIGRANTS TO THE UNITED STATES ARE PREDOMINATELY UNSKILLED

Whatever the intentions of those writing the 1965 (and later) immigration legislation, the overall stream of immigrants changed in ethnic composition and in skill mix after 1965. If we use formal education to measure skill, it is the *variation* in education that stands out. Comparisons of adults who arrived in the United States between 1980 and 1990 with native-born adults illustrate this. The proportion with a college degree is higher among the recent immigrants than among native-born adults *and* the proportion with little formal education is higher among the recent immigrants than among native-born adults.[26] This variation in immigrants' education involves the three distinct streams of immigrants. Legal immigrants are, if anything, somewhat better educated than the native-born population, while low levels of education predominate among the much smaller number of illegal immigrants.

Attempts to change the skill mix of immigrants by changing public policy must consider the policies that affect *each* immigration stream (legal, humanitarian, illegal). Further, it is important to recognize that current policies have several goals. The goals behind the public policies that now shape legal immigration include unifying the families of U.S. citizens, but family unification can mean admitting less-educated relatives. If a change in the family-unification policy makes the United States less attractive to highly skilled people, it will not have the desired impact.

Concern with the skill levels of recent immigrants stems, in part, from a belief that the United States population only benefits from skilled immigrants. Is this true?

MYTH NO. 5C: THE NATIVE-BORN U.S. POPULATION
BENEFITS ONLY FROM SKILLED IMMIGRANTS

The inclusive phrasing—"the U.S. population"—makes this idea difficult to evaluate. Narrower questions are more meaningful. Which segments of the "native-born" population, if any, benefit from a stream of unskilled immigrants? We limit this discussion to economic benefits, even though other benefits from diversity are at least as important.

Benefits from any kind of immigration are distributed unevenly. Flows of unskilled workers can provide low-cost child care, and they can lower the cost of services such as restaurant meals, lawn care, and cleaning services. This situation can increase the quality of life for the people who can afford such services,[27] a largely non-Hispanic white group. A pool of unskilled workers to supply these services also makes it easier for others to participate in the labor force. Employers who hire substantial numbers of low-skill workers also benefit from flows of unskilled immigrants. Case studies of labor markets that have substantial populations of unskilled workers find immigrants concentrated in certain low-wage industries, such as apparel manufacture and restaurants.[28]

Indirect effects of this low-paid labor force may, of course, be more diffused. While low-wage labor may translate into lower market prices for everyone, any calculation of indirect effects must also bring in the shared costs of low wages, such as public subsidies for the health care of people not covered by employee health insurance or the cost of educating the children of immigrants. Even if only certain segments of the native-born population gain economic benefits from immigration, possibly negative consequences of immigration are spread over a large proportion of the native-born population.

MYTH NO. 6: NEGATIVE ECONOMIC IMPACTS
FROM IMMIGRATION ARE WIDESPREAD

Numerous econometric studies compare the employment and the earnings of native-born workers in labor markets that differ in the extent of recent immigration. Such comparisons require statistical "control" of other labor market factors that could account for these differences. Reviewing this work, Michael Fix and Jeffrey S. Passel of The Urban Institute conclude that the aggregate data show "no overall effect" of immigration on wages or on jobs.[29]

Fix and Passel note that it is easy to overlook the various positive economic effects of immigration, and hence to overemphasize the negative effects.[30] In areas with substantial immigration, for example, immigrants set up businesses that serve other immigrants and hire other immigrants. Jobs in these immigrant-owned businesses would not exist without the immigrants, and these businesses have multiplier effects that ripple out of the immigrant community.

Analyses of 1990 Census data suggest another, less-benign, reason for these findings. During the 1980s, just six states grew primarily through immigration (California, New York, Texas, New Jersey, Illinois, and Florida). Within these states, immigrants are concentrated in port of entry metropolitan areas. These ports of entry experienced net out-migration by native-born residents during the 1980s, and the out-migrants tended to be whites who had not completed college (i.e., people who would have competed with low-skilled immigrants for jobs).[31]

Immigration is having direct negative economic impacts on particular segments of the U.S. labor force. Econometric studies that focus on categories of adults most likely to "compete" for jobs with low-skilled immigrants find that immigration increases the unemployment of low-skilled workers, and it lowers their wages. These impacts are greatest for two categories of workers, African Americans and immigrants who arrived a bit earlier. These effects are concentrated in the geographical areas that have received substantial immigration, and they are most pronounced during recessions.[32]

How important, then, is immigration to the economic situation of low-skilled African Americans?

MYTHS 7-9: AFRICAN AMERICANS IN A DIVERSE LABOR FORCE

MYTH NO. 7: GREATLY REDUCED IMMIGRATION WOULD IMPROVE THE ECONOMIC PROSPECTS FOR LOW-SKILLED AFRICAN AMERICANS

Changes in the mix of jobs within the U.S. economy have especially reduced the number of jobs, and particularly the number of "good" jobs, available for men with "low skill." Studies of this typically equate skill with level of formal education. "Low skill" can mean less than a high school degree, or it can mean no more than a high school degree (i.e., high school graduate or less).

This job loss has been especially great in Frostbelt manufacturing centers. During the 1980s alone, Frostbelt cities in large metropolitan areas lost a quarter of their manufacturing jobs.[33] Decades earlier, jobs in these Frostbelt cities attracted African American job-seekers, and these cities have sizable African American populations. There are new "low-skill" jobs, but these jobs are concentrated in the Sunbelt and in Frostbelt suburbs.

National employment figures document the impact of these economic trends. In 1968–1970, roughly 80 percent of central city African American males age 16–64 (and out of school) who had less than a high school education were employed. Most held blue-collar jobs. Just over 20 years later, 1990–1992, less than half of such men were employed. This was true despite the fact that an increasing proportion of African American men this age had completed college, and hence a smaller proportion of those age 16 to 64 were seeking jobs that did not require a high school degree. Employment also declined among central city white males with little formal education, but the decline was not nearly as dramatic.[34]

The percentage of all African Americans who live in suburbs has been increasing. In 1990, nearly a third of those living in metropolitan areas lived in a suburb. This percentage is low, however, compared with other groups. Half of all Asians living in metropolitan areas, over 40 percent of all such Hispanics, and two-thirds of all such non-Hispanic whites lived in suburbs. The percentage of all African Americans who live in suburbs is increasing slowly. College-educated African Americans are most likely to move into a suburb, and the proportion with a college education is increasing. Immigrants still tend to settle first in cities, but, as the suburban percentages for Asians and Hispanics suggest, increases in social status are more likely to mean a move to a suburb.[35]

These patterns, taken together, mean that low-skilled African Americans are especially spatially isolated from low-skilled jobs. Further, in cities that are ports of entry, such as New York, Los Angeles, and San Francisco, they "compete" with immigrants for the remaining low-skilled jobs. Out-migration by low-skilled native-born whites reduces the overall competition for jobs, but it makes competition between native-born African Americans and immigrants more striking. The low levels of African American out-migration from cities with growing immigrant populations (compared with out-migration levels for the white population) itself suggests that out-migration is not an option for African Americans.[36]

African Americans can be at a disadvantage here for a variety of reasons.[37] There is evidence that many employers prefer other workers, including immigrants, over native-born African Americans, for low-skilled jobs. This becomes apparent in practices such as recruiting low-skilled workers in ways that make it difficult for qualified African Americans to hear of openings. Reasons apparently include ideas that immigrants have better work ethics—a phrase that can include the idea that immigrants are more docile employees. It is interesting to note, here, that some of this research suggests employers are more likely to hire African Americans for low-skilled jobs if their hiring procedures include some measure of applicants' job-related skills.

Perhaps more commonly, employers never actually make such decisions. Low-skilled jobs commonly are filled by word-of-mouth. One worker recommends another for an opening, or someone hears of a coming opening and applies before the opening officially exists. Here, who you know is crucial. Once a workplace hires immigrants, immigrant networks are likely to provide the new hires.[38]

Further, immigrants themselves set up new businesses, including restaurants, food stores, and beauty shops. These businesses add to the total number of low-skilled jobs in ports-of-entry. These jobs, however, go to other immigrants.[39]

What if the immigration of low-skilled adults dropped sharply? This could improve the job prospects for low-skilled African Americans in ports of entry. Unfortunately, it also could mean that some businesses now hiring low-skilled immigrants will close and that some companies might accelerate changes in production that eliminate positions for low-skilled workers. The job situation of low-skilled African Americans is, after all, not that much better in U.S. labor markets that have few immigrants.

The situation of low-skilled African Americans may seem surprising, given decades of experience with affirmative action guidelines. Certainly such policies must have made a difference.

MYTH NO. 8: AFRICAN AMERICANS HAVE BENEFITED SUBSTANTIALLY FROM DIVERSITY INITIATIVES

The myth of a coming shortage of non-Hispanic white males in the U.S. labor force suggests a further myth: African Americans, male and female, are moving rapidly into good management jobs.

An increasing number (and percentage) of African Americans have completed college, and affirmative action has been official policy for many years. The African American middle class is growing. The proportion of African Americans in all management jobs rose from three percent in 1974 to seven percent two decades later, in 1994. This is a distinct increase, but seven percent remains below the proportion of African Americans in the total U.S. labor force (10.4 percent).[40]

Figures for particular management occupations plus "management-related" professions begin to fill in necessary detail. African Americans are concentrated in a few of these occupations (Table 2). The percentage who are African American is relatively high among public officials and administrators (13 percent), administrators in education and related fields (12 percent), personnel, training, and labor relations specialists (12 percent) and inspectors and compliance officers, except construction (15 percent). Note the importance of public-sector jobs, where civil service means clear job descriptions and guidelines for promotions, as well as visibility. A case study of Los Angeles identifies the public sector as the economic niche filled by African Americans.[41]

A second pattern appears in analyses of specific professional and managerial occupations that have an increasing percentage of African American or white females. Many of these occupations are changing in ways that make them less attractive to white males. The "deterioration" can involve a loss of status, declining income, or declining opportunities for advancement. Natalie Sokoloff provides extensive documentation of this pattern for African American women (and white women) in the professions between 1960 and 1980.[42]

A third pattern involves the kinds of *private* management and management-related occupations in which African Americans are well-represented, compared with the kinds in which they are substantially

TABLE 2   Percent African American in Managerial and Professional Employment, 1994

Occupation	Percent African American
Total, 16 years and over	10.4
Managerial and professional speciality	7.1
Executive, administrative and managerial	6.8
Officials and administrators, public administration	12.7
Administrators, protective serices	4.6
Financial managers	7.0
Personnel and labor relations managers	8.9
Purchasing managers	1.7
Managers, marketing, advertising, and public relations	2.6
Administrators, education and related fields	12.2
Managers, medicine and health	5.4
Postmasters and mail superintendents	8.5
Managers, food service and lodging establishments	8.0
Managers, properties and real estate	6.3
Funeral directors	3.7
Management-related occupations	8.8
Accountants and auditors	9.0
Underwriters	3.3
Other financial officers	7.4
Management analysts	5.5
Personnel, training, and labor relations specialists	12.3
Buyers, wholesale and retail trade, except farm products	3.4
Construction inspectors	6.1
Inspectors and compliance officers, except construction	15.4

Source: U.S. Department of Labor, Bureau of Labor Statistics, *Employment and Earnings*, 42/1 (January 1995): 175.

underrepresented. In 1994, African Americans were underrepresented in all except two categories: personnel, training, and labor relations specialists; and inspectors and compliance officers (Table 2). They were substantially underrepresented as purchasing managers; managers in marketing, advertising, and public relations; management analysts; and buyers in wholesale and retail trade, and they were underrepresented as financial managers and as other financial officers.[43]

As this suggests, hiring patterns in the private sector have concentrated African Americans away from lines of communication and decision making within the corporation. This structural isolation then hinders promotions. In addition, these hiring patterns make African American executives' hold on corporate jobs fragile.[44] Structural isolation makes them vulnerable to downsizing. Further, isolation—in jobs that were created, in part, because of political pressure for affirmative action and for improved relations with the African American community—makes African American jobs vulnerable to changes in the political climate. These patterns make it less surprising to find that among male college graduates, the ratio of the African American unemployment rate to the white unemployment rate *increased* between 1968 and 1988.[45]

Studies of the economic return for additional years of education provide a broader perspective on the economic situation of African Americans who have invested in high levels of education. Reynolds Farley recently showed that African Americans still receive lower rates of return for each additional year of education than whites of the same gender.[46]

MYTH NO. 9: GREATER DIVERSITY OVERALL IN THE U.S. POPULATION WILL IMPROVE THE ECONOMIC SITUATION OF AFRICAN AMERICANS

If immigrants provide a substantial flow of low-skilled workers willing to take "dirty" jobs, they could replace African Americans at the bottom of the U.S. job hierarchy. For African Americans to benefit in this way, however, they must get better jobs as they move out of or are displaced from jobs at the bottom. Instead, they are being pushed out of the labor force altogether.

The primary ethnic/racial distinction in the United States remains that between African Americans and everyone else. "White" has been an elastic category. Its meaning has changed over the last century. The term originated as a synonym for "Anglo-American," and hence the "white" were those of English ancestry. Through time, "white" came to include Germans, the Irish, Jews, Italians, and the Polish.[47]

Semantic inclusion paralleled economic inclusion, and the parallel with economic inclusion remains today. Reynolds Farley finds that members of all white ethnic groups get higher average rates of return on each year of formal education than do African Americans and other non-white groups. Further, there is little variation in this rate of return among the white ethnic groups.[48]

As the U.S. population becomes more diverse, the term *white* may continue to expand, adding categories now growing by immigration, but still not adding African Americans. Although acknowledging that many immigrants face unpleasant, hostile, and even exploitative conditions in the United States, Andrew Hacker argues that over time, many current immigrants will be accepted as a new variant of white. Those of African ancestry, however, will remain outside the white category.[49] This exclusion is the crux of the diversity issue in the United States.

IMPLICATIONS

These nine myths about the U.S. labor force misdirect corporate business and marketing strategies, and they misdirect corporate personnel policies. Even more important, these myths direct attention away from serious problems that do exist in the U.S. economy, problems that affect corporations and their employees. The myths themselves appear to reflect underlying concerns about the supply of new workers. Will the total U.S. labor force grow fast enough? Is immigration making up for a presumed slow growth of the native-born labor force? Is the labor force becoming too "diverse" (i.e., too different from the traditional non-Hispanic white male labor force)?

The U.S. labor force will continue to grow. While its composition is changing, this change is rather slow, and there is no sharp departure from past trends. Further, the distribution of African Americans among management occupations suggests that corporations still are not taking advantage of this resource.

Concerns about slow labor force growth can mean business support for policies that increase the supply of labor, including immigration. The effectiveness of immigration for this purpose is limited, however. Making the United States a more attractive destination for people already educated abroad will not necessarily attract such people. Further, as recent experience in science and engineering points out, buying skilled labor by supporting foreign-born graduate students can, at the same time, slow changes within the United States that would attract more native-born students to these fields.

Here, we must emphasize that we are *not* arguing for reduced immigration. This argument deals only with certain economic consequences of certain immigration patterns. Any discussion of changes in immigration policy must bring in numerous additional issues. Further, the economic consequences of immigration considered here involve the *response to immigration* by those already here. The consequences of immigration for low-skilled African Americans, for example, involve the supply of immigrants *combined with* employer hiring practices for low-skilled jobs. Similarly, concentrations of immigrants in workplaces that pay less than minimum wage involve employer decisions and the enforcement of U.S. labor laws.

Within corporations, concern about slow labor force growth can lead to changes in hiring practices that draw people into the labor force. Such changes in hiring practices may have contributed to the recent growth of the African American middle-class. Through these same years, however, the economic situation of African Americans *overall* has not improved. Conditions in city public schools, persistent residential segregation, and persistent biases in hiring suggest future deterioration. Concern about slow labor force growth also can be a reason to reorganize production in ways that reduce the number of employees needed by a corporation.

Indeed, the labor force problem that the United States faces today is a shortage of steady jobs that pay enough to support the person holding the job, much less dependents. Reviewing changes into the 1990s, Lawrence Mishel and Jared Bernstein conclude that "the character of employment has decidedly shifted: a much larger proportion of the workforce is either underemployed, overemployed [working two or more jobs], low paid, or trapped in unfavorable job situations."[50] The reasons for the shift toward low-quality jobs include corporate decisions to increase the use of contingent workers and to shift work to subcontractors. Further changes in production could contribute to a shortage of jobs overall in the near future.[51]

Companies creating minimum-wage jobs without fringe benefits have been able to count on government back up, in the form of food stamps and other programs that supplement wages. As support for various public welfare programs declines, employers will have three choices, as they consider their low-end jobs: increase wages and fringe benefits for workers earning the lowest salaries; accept a workforce that does not have minimum access to medical care, housing, and even food; and/or accelerate internal changes that reduce the need for such workers. The second choice can be indirect, as corporations depend even more upon subcontractors.

A mix of contracting out and downsizing may appear to be the best solution for any one corporation. When many corporations do this at one time, however, the process erodes the social fabric of the nation.

ENDNOTES

[1] Examples from *American Demographics* include: M. Mogelonsky, "Asian-Indian Americans," *American Demographics* (August 1995): 32–39; W. P. O'Hare, W. H. Frey, and D. Fost, "Asians in the Suburbs," *American Demographics* (May 1994): 32–38; W. P. O'Hare and W. H. Frey, "Booming, Suburban, and Black," *American Demographics* (September 1992): 30–38; and B. Miller, "A Beginners Guide to Demographics," *American Demographics* (October 1995): 54–64. The Population Reference Bureau also organizes demographic information about markets. Both sources present labor force projections as well. Examples include: T. G. Exter, "In and Out of Work," *American Demographics* (June 1992): 63; H. N. Fullerton. Jr., "Labor-Force Change Exaggerated: One-Third of New Workers Will Still Be White Men," *Population Today* (May 1993): 6–7, 9. E. Schonfeld mentions the "power of demographics" in "Betting on the Boomers," *Fortune*, December 25, 1995, 78–87.

[2] W. B. Johnston and A. H. Packer, *Workforce 2000: Work and Workers for the 21st Century* (Indianapolis, IN: Hudson Institute, 1987).

[3] This quote comes from the January 31, 1994 issue, p. 54. Similarly, The *New York Times* reported that: "It [the Hudson Institute report] predicted that because of demographic changes, white men would make up just 12 to 15 percent of the people joining the workforce between 1988 and 2000" [April 20, 1995, p. D4]. There are many more examples.

[4] *Workforce 2000* identifies six categories: native-born white males and females; native-born nonwhite males and females; and immigrant males and females. Because government statistics do not distinguish people by nativity, it is not clear how the authors created this classification system.

[5] The "other" in "Asian and other" includes Pacific Islanders, American Indians, Eskimo, and Aleut. The categories "Asian" and "Hispanic" each include people with numerous national backgrounds. The U.S. Census Bureau first

used the category "Hispanic" in 1980. *Workforce 2000* apparently included U.S.-born Hispanics among native-born whites. See L. Mishel and R. A. Teixeira, *The Myth of the Coming Labor Shortage: Jobs, Skills, and Income of America's Workforce 2000*, Economic Policy Institute, Washington, DC, 1991.

[6] Information about the 1994 U.S. labor force and these labor force projections come from H. N. Fullerton, Jr., "The 2005 Labor Force: Growing, But Slowly," *Monthly Labor Review* (November 1995): 29–44 and "Errata [in Table 11]" *Monthly Labor Review* (March 1996): 38. Fullerton developed three projections using different assumptions about labor force participation rates, immigration, and so forth. We present his "medium" projection.

[7] Percentages for 1940 and 1950 come from the Census of Population. In 1940, the labor force included those age 14 and 15. Percentages for 1955 to 1994 come from the U.S. Census Bureau's Current Population Reports. Fullerton (1995) provides the estimate for 2005.

[8] The report is not entirely to blame. Numerous experts have tried to set the record straight. Examples include Fullerton (1993), "Labor Force Change Is Greatly Exaggerated." *Wall Street Journal*, September 22, 1989, B1; P. Barnum, "Misconceptions About the Future U.S. Workforce: Implications for Strategic Planning," *Human Resource Planning*, 14/3 (Fall 1991): 209–219; and N. DiTomaso and J. J. Friedman, "A Sociological Commentary on *Workforce 2000*," *The New Modern Times* ed. David B. Bills (Albany, NY: SUNY Press, 1995): 207–234.

[9] In addition, a frequently cited table juxtaposes the composition of the total 1985 labor force with the composition of net changes projected for 1985–2000. The title refers to "new entrants." *Workforce 2000* also invites misunderstanding by emphasizing "facts" and claiming that "demography is destiny" [p. 75]. DiTomaso and Friedman provide a more complete analysis of this influential report and also a discussion of population projections.

[10] The term "replace" is, of course, figurative.

[11] Young non-Hispanic white (and African American) men now in the labor force come from the relatively small "baby bust" cohorts (which began with 1965). If U.S. fertility had remained higher, these two categories would have a larger number of entrants, but about the same number of leavers. The baby boom cohorts have not yet reached retirement age. The size of the baby boom cohorts relative to more recent cohorts means the median age of those in the U.S. labor force is increasing. See Fullerton, and "The Baby Boom Hits 50," *Wall Street Journal*, October 31, 1995, B1. Even so, the U.S. labor force remains "younger" than the pre-baby-boom labor force.

[12] A hypothetical example may clarify this. Suppose only 1,000 "net additions" were added to the U.S. labor force (of 131 million) between 1994 and 2005, and suppose that *none* of the 1,000 were non-Hispanic, white men. Every non-Hispanic, white male who enters the labor force "replaces" a non-Hispanic, white male who leaves (a number expected to be about 11 million). The increment of 1,000 people makes virtually no difference in the overall distribution of a labor force of 131 million, and it makes virtually no difference to the relative representation of the 11 million non-Hispanic, white male new entrants. In this hypothetical example, non-Hispanic, white men would be the same proportion of the labor force in 2005 as in 1994, even though they were not included *at all* among net new entrants during this period.

[13] Fullerton, 37.

[14] All population projections (including those in Fullerton) come from U.S. Bureau of the Census, "Population Projections of the U.S., by Age, Sex, Race, and Hispanic Origin: 1995 to 2050," *Current Population Reports*, Series P-25-1130 (November 1995, released February 1996). These population projections separate Asians and Pacific Islanders from American Indians, Eskimo, and Aleut.

[15] Fullerton, 32 and 37. These projections begin with 1994, and they use the category "Asian and other," which combines Asians and Pacific Islanders with American Indians, Eskimo, and Aleut.

[16] See pages 285–286 in W. H. Frey, "The New Geography of Population Shifts" *State of the Union: America in the 1990s*, Vol. 2, *Social Trends*, R. Farley, ed. (New York, NY: Russell Sage Foundation, 1995): 271–336.

[17] Frey: also, p. 227–229 in B. R. Chiswick and T. A. Sullivan, "The New Immigrants," *State of the Union: America in the 1990s. Vol. 2, Social Trends* R. Farley, ed. (New York, NY: Russell Sage Foundation, 1995): 211–270.

[18] M. Fix and J. S. Passel review research on the fiscal impacts of immigration in *Immigration and Immigrants: Setting the Record Straight* (Washington, D.C. The Urban institute, 1994). When all levels of government are considered together, immigrants "generate significantly more in taxes paid than they cost in services received" [p. 57].

[19] A recent *New York Times* article illustrates some of these points (D. Carvajal "For Immigrant Maids, Not a Job but Servitude," February 25, 1996, 1, 37). She describes domestic workers who are isolated in suburban homes. Immigrant organizations in New York City and on Long Island are finding ways to reach them.

[20] Fix and Passel, 3.

[21] Fix and Passel, 10.

[22] See G. Borjas, *Friends or Strangers* (New York, NY: Basic Books, 1990), 37.

[23] See E. Funkhouser and S. J. Trejo, "The Labor Market Skills of Recent Male Immigrants: Evidence from the Current Population Survey." *Industrial and Labor Relations Review 48* (July 1995): 792–811.

[24] *Soothing the Establishment: The Impact of Foreign-Born Scientists and Engineers on America* (Lanham, MD: University Press of America, Inc., 1995).

[25] M. G. Finn and L. A. Pennington, "Foreign Nationals Who Receive Science or Engineering Ph.D.s from U.S. Universities: Stay Rates and Characteristics of Stayers," unpublished paper, October 1994.

[26] Fix and Passel, 32–34; J. S. Passel and M. Fix, "Myths about Immigrants," *Foreign Policy* (Summer 1994), 151–160; Chiswick and Sullivan.

[27] Borjas, 221–223; Carvajal, 234–236; R. Waldinger and M. Bozorgmehr, eds., (*Ethnic Los Angeles*, New York, NY: Russell Sage Foundation, 1996), Chapter 15.

[28] Waldinger and Bozorgmehr; J. R. Logan, R. D. Alba, and T. L. McNulty, "Ethnic Economics in Metropolitan Regions: Miami and Beyond," *Social Forces 72* (March 1994): 691–724; P. Kwong, *The New Chinatown* (New York, NY: Hill and Wang, 1987); "New York: The Empire City," in R. J. S. Ross and K. C. Trachte, *Global Capitalism: The New Leviathan* (Albany, NY: SUNY Press, 1990) 156–169.

[29] Fix and Passel include an extensive review of the research on immigration-related labor market effects. Appendix B provides a concise summary of each study. Borjas reviews the economic literature.

[30] Fix and Passel, 52–54.

[31] See Frey, 285–289; R. K. Filer, "The Effects of Immigrant Arrivals on Migratory Patterns of Native Workers," *Immigration and the Workforce: Economic Consequences for the U.S. and Source Areas*, eds.,G. J. Borjas and R. B. Freeman (Chicago, IL: University of Chicago Press, 1992) 245–269.

[32] M. E. Enchautegui, "The Effects of Immigration on the Wages and Employment of African American Males," Working Paper, Program for Research on Immigration Policy, Urban Institute, PRIP-UI-25, May 1993; Fix and Passel, 50; G. J. Borjas, "Immigrants, Minorities, and Labor Market Competition," *Industrial and Labor Relations 40* (1987): 382–392; G. DeFreitas, "Hispanic Immigration and Labor Market Segmentation," *Industrial Relations 27* (1988): 195–214; J. G. Altonji and D. Card, "The Effects of Immigration on the Labor Market Outcomes of Less-skilled Natives," *Immigration, Trade, and the Labor Market*, eds., J. M. Abowd and R. B. Freeman (Chicago, IL: University of Chicago Press, 1991), 201–234; F. D. Bean, M. A. Fossett, and K. T. Park, "Labor Market Dynamics and the Effects of Immigration on African Americans," *African Americans, Immigration, and Race Relations*, ed., Gerald Jaynes, (New Haven, CT: Yale University, 1993); Waldinger and Bozorgmehr; and Filer.

[33] See page 222 of J. D. Kasarda, "Industrial Restructuring and the Changing Location of Jobs," *State of the Union: America in the 1990s, V. 1: Economic Trends,* ed., R. Farley (New York, NY: Russell Sage Foundation, 1995), 215–267. The percent is for central counties of metropolitan areas with populations of 750,000 or more.

[34] Kasarda, 256–258. Also, see J. Bound and H. J. Holzer, "Industrial Shifts, Skills Levels, and the Labor Market for White and Black Males," *The Review of Economics and Statistics 75* (August 1993): 387–396.

[35] Frey, 287–289, 314–325.

[36] Filer.

[37] K. M. Neckerman and J. Kirschenman, "Hiring Strategies, Racial Bias, and Inner-City Workers," *Social Problems 38* (November 1991): 433–447: J. Kirschenman and K. M. Neckerman, "'We'd Love to Hire Them, But ...': The Meaning of Race for Employers," *The Urban Underclass,* eds., C. Jencks and P. E. Peterson (Washington, DC: The Brookings Institution, 1991) 203–232; Kasarda, 265; J. Kirschenman, P. Moss, and C. Tilly, "Employer Screening Methods and Racial Exclusion," Russell Sage Foundation Working Paper 77, October 1995; Waldinger and Bozorgmehr.

[38] Waldinger and Bozorgmehr. Also, G. P. Green, L. M. Tigges, and I. Browne, "Social Resources, Job Search, and Poverty in Atlanta," *Research in Community Sociology 5* (Greenwich, CT: JAI Press, Inc., 1995) 161–182.

[39] Kasarda, 258; J. Kaufman, "Immigrants' Businesses Often Refuse to Hire African Americans in Inner City," *Wall Street Journal*, June 6, 1995, A1.

[40] U.S. Department of Labor, *Employment and Earnings* (Washington, DC: U.S. Government Printing Office, January 1995), Table 11; "Employed Persons by Detailed Occupation, Sex, Race, and Hispanic Origin," 175; Bureau of the Census, "The Social and Economic Status of the Black Population in the United States, 1974." *Current Population Reports,* Special Studies Series P-23, No. 54 (Washington, DC: U.S. Government Printing Office, 1974) Table 50.

[41] Waldinger and Bozorgmehr.

[42] N. J. Sokoloff, *African American Women and White Women in the Professions: Occupational Segregation by Race and Gender, 1960–1980* (New York, NY: Routledge, 1992). Case studies of public relations and of bank managers show similar patterns for all women. See B. Reskin and P. Roos, *Job Queues, Gender Queues* (Philadelphia, PA: Temple University Press, 1990).

[43] N. DiTomaso and S. A. Smith, "Race and Ethnic Minorities and White Women in Management: Changes and Challenges," *Women and Minorities in American Professions,* eds., J. Tang and E. Smith (Albany, NY: SUNY Press); U.S. Department of Labor.

[44] S. M. Collins, "The Making of the African American Middle Class," *Social Problems, 30/4* (1983): 369–382; S. M. Collins, "The Marginalization of African Americans Executives," *Social Problems 36* (1989): 317–331; S. M. Collins, "Blacks on the Bubble: the Vulnerability of Black Executives in White Corporations," *The Sociological Quarterly 34* (1993): 429–447; S. M. Nkomo and T. Cox, Jr., "Factors Affecting the Upward Mobility of Black Managers in Private Sector Organizations," *The Review of Black Political Economy 18* (Winter 1990): 39–58.

[45] F. D. Wilson, M. Tienda, and L. Wu, "Race and Unemployment: Labor Market Experiences of Black and White Men, 1968–1988," *Work and Organizations 22* (August 1995): 245–270.

[46] R. Farley, "Black, Hispanics, and White Ethnic Groups: Are Blacks Uniquely Disadvantaged?" *Sources: Notable Selections in Race and Ethnicity,* eds. A. Aguirre, Jr., and D. V. Baker (Guilford, CT: The Dushkin Publishing Group, 1995) 209–217. Hispanics and Native Americans also have relatively low levels of education and low rates of return for each additional year of school. Asians receive lower rates of return for each additional year of education, but their high levels of education bring tip average incomes. For Asians, see also H. O. Duleep and S. Sanders, "Discrimination at the Top: American, Born Asian and White Men," *Industrial Relations 31* (Fall 1992): 416–432.

[47] A. Hacker, *Two Nations: African American and White, Separate, Hostile, Unequal* (New York, NY: Ballantine Books, 1992); T. W. Allen, *The Invention of the White Race* (London: Verso, 1994); D. R. Roediger, *The Wages of Whiteness: Race and the Making of the American Working Class* (London: Verso, 1991).

[48] Farley.

[49] Hacker 103. Until recently, official statistics counted Hispanics as white. This change involved requests for separate information, rather than a change in perception.

[50] L. Mishel and J. Bernstein, *The State of Working America, 1994–95* (Washington, D.C.: Economic Policy Institute, 1994) 203. M. B. Gittleman and D. R. Howell document declines in the quality of low-skill jobs in "Changes in the Structure and Quality of Jobs in the U.S.: Effects by Race and Gender, 1973–1990," *Industrial and Labor Relations Review 48* (April 1995): 420–440.

[51] See discussion in J. Rifkin, *The End of Work* (New York, NY: G.P. Putnam's Sons, 1995).

GENDER GAP IN THE EXECUTIVE SUITE: CEOS AND FEMALE EXECUTIVES REPORT ON BREAKING THE GLASS CEILING*

Belle Rose Ragins
Bickley Townsend
Mary Mattis

Executive Overview

While business organizations are struggling to hold on to their best and brightest women, the persistence of the glass ceiling makes this difficult. Dismantling the glass ceiling requires an accurate understanding of the overt and subtle barriers to advancement faced by women, and the strategies used to overcome these barriers. A large-scale, national survey of Fortune 1000 CEOs

*Reprinted with permission from *Academy of Management Executive 12*, no. 1 (1998): 28–42.

and the highest-ranking, most successful women in their companies identified key career strate-
gies used by the women in their rise to the top, and the barriers to advancement they faced in
their firms. A startling finding of the study was the disparity in the perceptions of chief executive
officers and the high-ranking women in their firms. The Fortune 1000 CEOs had vastly different
perceptions of the organizational and environmental barriers faced by their female employees, and
in their companies' progress towards equality in the workplace.

Women currently constitute nearly half of the U.S. labor force, and occupy a significant and growing proportion of entry and mid-level managerial positions. In 1972 women held 17 percent of managerial positions, and this proportion swelled to 42.7 percent in 1995.[1] Although women are flooding the managerial pipeline, they have been stymied in their entrance to top-level positions; currently, less than five percent of executive positions are held by women.[2] Of greater concern is the lack of progress on this front. The proportion of top level positions in *Fortune 1000* companies held by women increased from .5 percent in 1979 to only 2.9 percent in 1989,[3] and only four of the *Fortune 1000* CEO positions are held by women. A 1995 census revealed that while women accounted for 10 percent of corporate officers, they represented just 2.4 percent of the highest ranks of corporate leadership, and held 1.9 percent of the most highly compensated officer positions in *Fortune 500* companies.[4]

This lack of progress has been attributed to the glass ceiling, an invisible barrier to advancement based on attitudinal or organizational bias.[5] The glass ceiling appears to be pervasive in corporate America; over 92 percent of executive women report its existence.[6] The glass ceiling is costly, not only in terms of lost productivity among workers who feel blocked in their careers, but also in terms of turnover costs, which are estimated to average 150 percent of managers' annual salaries.[7] Eighty percent of female middle-level managers in one study reported leaving their last organization because of the glass ceiling,[8] and other studies indicate that many leave to start their own competing business.[9]

Increasingly, individuals in many organizations are recognizing the importance of shattering the glass ceiling and removing barriers that prevent women from utilizing their full potential.[10] However, the fact that the glass ceiling has remained virtually intact over the last 10 years indicates that these efforts have been largely ineffectual. Dismantling the glass ceiling requires three key pieces of information. First, it is critical to understand the barriers women face in their advancement. Second, it is instructive to understand the career strategies used by women who successfully overcame the barriers to advancement. Finally, it is vital that corporate leaders have an accurate and complete understanding of the barriers and organizational climate faced by their female employees. Commitment to breaking the glass ceiling, while important, is not sufficient; for change to occur, CEOs must also have a clear understanding of the subtle and overt barriers women face in their advancement.

To obtain information about these issues, Catalyst undertook the first large-scale, national study of women executives and CEOs of *Fortune 1000* companies. We surveyed 1,251 executive women who hold titles of vice president or above in *Fortune 1000* companies and all of the *Fortune 1000* CEOs. Surveys were returned by 461 female executives and 325 CEOs.[11] We also conducted indepth, follow-up telephone interviews with 20 female executives and 20 CEOs.[12]

Our study addressed women's advancement from the perspective of women who have actually advanced to senior levels of leadership in the nation's largest companies. These trailblazers are in the best position to provide inside information on the types of obstacles encountered on the road to senior management. By sharing the personal and career strategies used for effectively navigating through those obstacles, this breakthrough generation of female executives can provide critical information for future generations of female managers coming up through the ranks. Of equal significance, by juxtaposing CEOs' perspectives on barriers to advancement with the perspective of female executives, we can assess for the first time whether CEOs understand the subtle and complex organizational barriers faced by their female employees.

STRATEGIES FOR BREAKING THE GLASS CEILING: HOW WOMEN DO IT

The female executives in this large national study were presented with a list of 13 possible career strategies that may contribute to the advancement of women to senior management and were asked to rate the importance of each strategy to their own career advancement.[13] As shown in Table 1, nine career strategies emerged as central to the advancement of these successful female executives. In particular, four of these strategies stand out as key to their career success. These are consistently, exceeding performance expectations (rated critical by 77 percent); developing a style with which male managers are comfortable (61 percent); seeking out difficult or challenging assignments (50 percent), and having influential mentors (37 percent).[14] We interviewed female executives from this national sample to learn more about career strategies used by these female pioneers.

PERFORMANCE IS THE BOTTOM LINE

Superior performance is expected of all executives, but it may be particularly important for women. Consistently exceeding performance expectations was the top-ranking strategy used by these successful female executives, and an overwhelming 99 percent of the respondents reported that this strategy was critical or fairly important. These women reported that they had to prove their ability repeatedly, and needed to overperform in order to counter negative assumptions in a predominantly male business environment. These successful female executives reported that they were often not viewed as credible, and that they had to prove themselves and reestablish their credibility in each new work situation. One survey respondent advised:

> *Do the best you possibly can at every assignment no matter how trivial. Always go the extra mile. It is not enough to be willing, you have to do it, even if no one is looking.*

How do successful corporate women demonstrate superior performance? Follow-up interviews revealed two particular strategies: work harder than your peers; and develop unique skills and expertise.

TABLE 1   Women's Career Advancement Strategies

Strategy	Critical	Fairly Important	Not Important	Did Not Use
Consistently exceed performance expectations	77%	22%	1%	0%
Develop style that men are comfortable with	61%	35%	3%	1%
Seek difficult or high visibility assignments	50%	44%	2%	4%
Have an influential mentor	37%	44%	9%	9%
Network with influential colleagues	28%	56%	9%	6%
Gain line management experience	25%	29%	11%	33%
Move from one functional area to another	23%	34%	20%	22%
Initiate discussion regarding career aspirations	15%	47%	25%	12%
Be able to relocate	14%	22%	17%	45%
Upgrade educational credentials	12%	33%	24%	29%
Change companies	12%	24%	23%	39%
Develop leadership out-side office	11%	41%	29%	18%
Gain international experience	5%	19%	24%	51%

In describing their high-performance track records, successful female executives emphasized the importance of sheer hard work and stamina. In interviews, executive women described workdays that begin at 4:00 A.M. with several hours of pre-dawn reading before the children awake, late-night business calls and faxes to homes fully teleconnected to the office, and travel schedules and after-hours business obligations that keep them away from home several evenings a week.

But the interviews indicated that while hard work was important, the performance bar may be placed higher for women than for men. One survey respondent advised: "Be willing to work much harder than male peers."

Besides sheer hard work, developing specialized expertise is another effective means for women to become known as high performers. Some successful women executives made a point of developing unique skills so as to become indispensable; others built their expertise by gaining external recognition:

> *I think you have to have a specialty ... and you have to do it better than anybody else can conceivably know how to do it.*
>
> —Corporate controller, consumer products company.

Beyond Performance: Walking the Fine Line

For women, being a star performer, even outperforming their male peers, is not enough to break through the glass ceiling. Fully 96 percent of the executive women in our study identify a second factor, unrelated to performance, as critical or fairly important to their career success. That key factor involves developing a professional style with which male managers are comfortable. These successful executives had to adapt to a predominantly male culture and environment, and deal with the phenomenon often referred to as the male managerial model, in which models for successful managers incorporate masculine styles and characteristics.[15] This male managerial model places women in a double bind: if their managerial styles are feminine, they run the risk of not being viewed as effective managers, but if they adopt masculine styles viewed as appropriate for managerial roles, they may be criticized for not being feminine.

One successful woman executive points out the double-behavioral standard:

> *... the guys can yell at each other all the time, shake hands and walk out the door, and it's perfectly comfortable for them—but on the rare occasion that I raise my voice, it's not accepted in the same way.*
>
> —Personnel director, retail organization.

Another interviewee reported that she had to learn:

> *how to interact with men who had never dealt with women before, and how to be heard, and how to get past what you looked like, and what sex you were, and into what kind of brain you had .... I had to learn how to offer opinions in a way that they could be heard because I wasn't necessarily given the right to have an opinion.*
>
> —Vice president, consumer products company

These restrictions on behaviors were listed by two other survey respondents in an ironic litany of don'ts for female executives:

> *Don't be attractive. Don't be too smart. Don't be assertive. Pretend you're not a woman. Don't be single. Don't be a mom. Don't be a divorcee.*
> *Do not make waves. Do not disagree and be correct (kiss of death!). [Working] longer, harder, smarter means nothing if you have a mind of your own and express your own ideas and opinions.*

Women in managerial positions are forced to develop managerial styles that are not masculine or feminine, but are acceptable to male colleagues, supervisors and subordinates. This is a daunting challenge that is not faced by their male counterparts.

Not only must women walk a fine line, they must also be concerned with making their male colleagues comfortable with their very presence:

> *With 13 men on the management committee, and I'm the only woman ... it was very awkward at first. But it's been over two years now, and what I have found is that they are never truly comfortable because it's not a hundred percent men. And that's not because they don't like me, or they don't like the fact that a woman's there. It's that there's always that certain guard that what they might say in a roomful of men will be taken wrong when a woman is there.*
> —Senior Vice President, health care organization.

In short, not only must women exceed performance expectations, they must also find the appropriate way to perform that will not threaten their male peers or make them uncomfortable.

Some CEOs acknowledge the challenges women face in fitting into the corporate culture and creating a comfort level with male managers. As one CEO notes:

> *I don't think it has anything to do with competency. I think it's just that our society has certain norms that have been built in—wives being uncomfortable with women working in the same office as their husbands, things of that nature .... The men might not articulate it that way. But I believe that sociologically, we are where we are through no deliberate intent.*

Although the intention may not be deliberate, the spillover of cultural expectations of women's roles into the corporate boardroom creates a unique set of challenges for women seeking leadership positions.

THE IMPORTANCE OF STRETCH ASSIGNMENTS

Seeking out difficult or highly visible assignments was the third critical success factor identified by the women executives in our study. Half of those surveyed deemed it critical, and fully 94 percent regarded it as important to their career progression. Key assignments have been found to be related to differential career tracking for men and women and are pivotal for three reasons.[16] First, stretch assignments provide professional growth and learning challenges. Second, they serve as grooming exercises for career tracks leading to executive positions. Finally, highly visible assignments provide critical access to key decision-makers and influential mentors in the company. As one interviewee points out:

> *When I first came to the company, I was assigned certain very specific, very important high-profile projects, which gave me the opportunity to work on matters that were very important to the company .... They involved contact with the handful of senior people and gave me the opportunity, as a relative newcomer with good credentials but not a lot of prior exposure, to develop their trust and their confidence and their sense that when given an assignment I could get it done.*
> —General counsel, media company.

While undertaking these assignments is an important prerequisite for gaining access to highpower career tracks, women encounter gender-related barriers to gaining this career milestone. Many of the women in our study reported that they often had to explicitly signal their willingness to take on unusual or challenging assignments, since otherwise managers may assume they are not interested. Several CEOs underscored the importance of this point:

> *There's been an assumption on the part of men that opportunities everywhere are open to them, whereas there might be a perception that a woman might not want to move, because of personal*

interests of one kind or another ... Managers are reluctant to talk about these things today, for what-
ever reason ... I think it's more incumbent on a woman to come forward and say how free she is
to do things.

This suggests that the burden of obtaining these key assignments falls largely on the woman. Unlike their male counterparts, who may be approached by senior management and offered key assignments, women must first independently recognize the importance of these assignments and then
convince others that they are both motivated and able to fill these assignments. The women who successfully reached the executive suite in our study did not wait for potentially career-enhancing opportunities to come to them; they actively took charge of their own careers by overcoming gender-related
expectations and seeking visible assignments that promoted their mobility.

MENTORING IS MANDATORY

A full 91 percent of the female executives surveyed reported having a mentor sometime in the course
of their careers, and 81 percent saw their mentor as being either critical or fairly important in their career advancement. Additionally, nearly all of the 20 female executives who were personally interviewed identified at least one senior man who was instrumental in their development and advancement.

I think it's the single most critical piece to women advancing career-wise. In my experience you
need somebody to help guide you and ... go to bat for you. And I'm not saying someone to take
care of you because you're a woman. I'm saying, because you are a woman, you need somebody
to fight some of your battles in the male environment.

—Vice president/corporate secretary, utility company

The importance of mentoring has been documented in other studies. Individuals with mentors receive more promotions, have more career mobility, and advance at a faster rate than those lacking
mentors.[17] Additionally, both male and female executives in other studies overwhelmingly report the
presence of a mentor sometime during the course of their careers.[18]

While mentors are important for everyone, they are particularly critical for women seeking to
break through the glass ceiling. Influential male mentors, with preestablished networks and credibility, can sponsor their female protégés into senior management circles, and provide inside information
usually obtained in the old boy networks. Mentors also can buffer women from adverse forces in the
organization, and help them navigate through the challenging and changing political terrain. These
buffering functions were pointed out by one interviewee:

I think mentoring is very important for career advancement because you have somebody who is
there for you, will defend you, will reinforce the decisions that you make with others .... (Mentors)
help you understand the organization, to understand the players, to understand the personalities.
And they did that for me, but more importantly, whenever I had a problem, they'd stand up for me
because they believed in me, and that's invaluable. It's something I could not have done for my-
self, and if I hadn't had that, I don't think that I could have made it because I do think women have
different issues in that regard, at least women who were starting their careers 20 years ago.

—Executive vice president, insurance company

While a few women executives had female mentors, the scarcity of women in senior management
limited their supply. Yet those who were fortunate enough to have both male and female mentors point
out the differential strengths associated with each of these key relationships. While male mentors are
more influential in organizations and can provide greater access to inner power circles, female mentors were better able to identify and empathize with the barriers faced by women in organizations.

Many of the interviewees recounted that exclusionary corporate environments and performance pressures led to erosion of self-esteem and self-confidence during the early career years. Mentors were viewed as instrumental for counteracting chilly corporate climates and building self-esteem. In particular, female mentors were identified as better able than male mentors to identify and address self-esteem issues and concerns.

One interviewee pointed out that some male mentors

don't understand what you're up against. Or what you may be confronting, or the attitudes that some people, some men, may have, particularly a young woman coming into a meeting with a responsible job .... But I think that's overcome if they really are a good mentor, helping you understand the male perspective and the male world.

—Executive vice president, insurance company

A key function of mentors is that they build their protégé's self-confidence and professional identity.[19] These functions are critical for women; many of the women in our study reported that lack of support and isolation depleted their self-esteem and self-confidence.

Because of the important role mentoring played in their own careers, many of the senior women interviewed felt an obligation to mentor others, especially women. Over half of the women interviewed reported being mentors, and nearly all of them reported mentoring other women in their organizations. These female mentors recognize the need for mentoring as a benefit both to promising young managers and to the company. They also feel a need to give back to younger generations of women.

The most important lesson for women ... is to learn that they're not in competition for each other for a short list of jobs ... it changed in my head back in the early 1980's, when I realized that was just a sexist attitude in the environment to begin with, and so (I) began mentoring in the sense of networking with other women and building a team environment with other women ....

—Vice president, chemical company

This comment mirrors the finding of other empirical research, which has found no support for the idea that women become inaccessible "queen bees" once they obtain high-ranking positions in organizations.[20]

In sum, these pioneering women relied on career strategies that were adaptive, proactive, and characterized by hard work. They attributed their success to consistently exceeding performance expectations, developing a style with which male managers feel comfortable, seeking out challenging and visible assignments, and obtaining the support of an influential mentor.

These career strategies are not independent, and may in fact build upon one another. For example, exceptional and visible job performance increases the likelihood of being selected by a mentor.[21] Mentors, in turn, provide their protégés with coaching and visible assignments, which improves their job performance and places their protégés on the fast track to advancement.[22] By developing a managerial style with which male managers feel comfortable, these women may also have improved their chances of getting selected by a male mentor. Existing research indicates that while women are as likely as men to obtain a mentor, women need to overcome greater barriers to getting a mentor than men, and that key barriers involve the mentor's reluctance to assume a mentoring role for fear that the relationship would be misconstrued as romantic in nature.[23] These women may have developed the political savvy to not only recognize this barrier, but also overcome it by managing their image and the perception of others. Finally, mentors provide feedback that shapes their protégés' management style. This is particularly critical for women, who need to develop a managerial style that is not only effective, but effective for their gender.[24] While male mentors may help female protégés develop acceptable styles, female mentors may be better suited for this task. Although most of the female executives interviewed lacked access to a female mentor, they recognized that women may be better able to share tried and true strategies for walking the fine line, and reported making it a point to share their hard-earned strategies with their female protégés.

WHITE NOISE IN THE EXECUTIVE SUITE: DIVERGENT PERSPECTIVES ON BARRIERS TO ADVANCEMENT

The executive women in these *Fortune 1000* companies overcame gender-related barriers in order to break through the glass ceiling. An important question is whether their CEOs understood the barriers these women faced in their advancement. CEOs need accurate perceptions to develop effective solutions. We presented the female executives and CEOs in our survey with 10 possible barriers to advancement, and asked them to select the three factors they considered to be the most significant in preventing women from advancing to the highest level of corporate leadership. What we found was both startling and revealing. Survey responses, as well as the follow-up interviews, revealed a marked gender gap in perspectives. Although the women and men in our study were all successful executives and were describing essentially the same corporate environment, they viewed this environment in different ways.

What's Holding Women Back? CEOs Blame Lack of Experience

An interesting finding in this study is the degree of consensus among male CEOs as to the key factors preventing women from advancing to corporate leadership. As shown in Figure 1, a decisive 82 percent point to lack of general management or line experience as the most crucial barrier holding women back.[25] A second critical barrier, according to almost two-thirds of CEOs (64 percent), is that women have not been in the pipeline long enough—that is, the executive talent pool has included few women until recently.

In an interview, one CEO explained:

> *My class from business school had 7 women in it, out of 650. So, there is a pipeline issue. And it'll take another five to eight years before the number of 45-year-old women ready for senior management jobs is balanced with the number of men.*

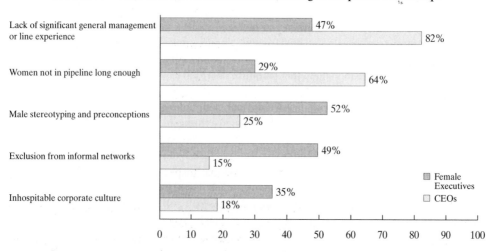

FIGURE 1   **What Prevents Women from Advancing to Corporate Leadership?**

However, some CEOs contend that time alone will not solve the problem. As one CEO points out:

It's not that women haven't been in the pipeline long enough; it's what they have done while they are in the pipeline.

Some CEOs attributed women's lack of experience in line management functions to women's self-selection or lack of understanding of the importance of these experiences; others see company practices as in part responsible:

I think that, without question, some women have chosen not to pursue certain tracks that, for one reason or another, might be more attractive to men. I think that the larger reason is probably that we, the men of the organization, have built in credentials that we measure people against and, for one reason or another, that probably are biased against women.
I think many women have been held back because they haven't been prepared to make the same sacrifices as perhaps men are ... they're not apt to move or relocate. Their families are all there.

One CEO recognized the more subtle dynamics that prevent women from obtaining key job assignments:

In the case of women, we use the lack of specific training for a job as a reason not to open the jobs to them, when we are more ready to bring men into jobs for which they are not specifically trained. That kind of discrimination or stereotyping is much subtler and more difficult to get at.

Our study also revealed a profound disparity between the kinds of experience CEOs identify as critical to advancement and the experience of most corporate women today. The majority (82 percent) of CEOs pointed to women's lack of general management/line experience with profit and loss responsibility as a key deterrent to their advancement. Only 47 percent of the female executives saw this as a critical barrier to women's advancement. Moreover, the executive women were far less likely than the male CEOs to believe that women have not been in the pipeline long enough; only 29 percent of the women reported this as a key barrier, compared to 64 percent of the CEOs. Clearly, most of the women in our study would disagree with the argument that it is simply a matter of time until female executives catch up with their male counterparts.

Women Point to Corporate Culture

The women executives surveyed had a profoundly different view of the barriers women face in breaking the glass ceiling. The women were more than twice as likely as the CEOs to consider inhospitable work environments as a barrier to women's advancement: 52 percent of the women executives cited "male stereotyping and preconceptions of women" as a top factor holding women back, compared with 25 percent of CEOs; 49 percent of women identified "exclusion from informal networks," compared with 15 percent of CEOs; and inhospitable corporate culture was identified by 35 percent of women, but only 18 percent of CEOs.

One interviewee pointed to the tenacious nature of stereotypes by describing a situation where, despite her impressive credentials and achievements, she was still assumed to be a secretary in a business meeting:

I was 43 years old and I was the highest ranking woman on the ... staff, and this guy thinks I'm somebody's secretary. I mean I was at Harvard. I was a fellow at Harvard ....

—Executive vice president, transportation company

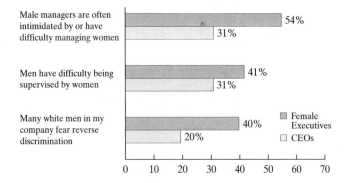

FIGURE 2   **Men's Attitudes Toward Women in the Workplace: Female Executives' and CEOs' Views**

Another emphasized the exclusionary climate by her comment:

You'd want for once in your life to walk into a room where people are talking that they contin-ue to talk and you don't feel that you're listening in on something you're not supposed to be lis-tening in on.

—Vice president, high technology company

These successful female executives describe corporate cultures that are inhospitable and exclu-sionary, environments with white noise—constant background static that is distracting, debilitating, and a constant reality for many of these female executives, but that is often not heard by their male bosses.

In order to probe these environmental issues in more depth, our survey also included items as-sessing male managers' attitudes and behaviors. Again, the CEOs and executive women in our study sharply differed in their perceptions. As shown in Figure 2, executive women were significantly more likely than CEOs to agree or strongly agree that men have difficulty either supervising or being su-pervised by women.

Twice as many women executives as CEOs (40 percent versus 20 percent) believe that white men in their companies are concerned with reverse discrimination, presumably because of workforce di-versity initiatives. To the extent that these concerns are significant, they fuel fears of a quota system and can undermine corporate efforts to achieve greater diversity in leadership.

Another striking difference in the opinions of male CEOs and female executives is the impor-tance ascribed to politics and style. Women were more apt than men to identify women's lack of aware-ness of organizational politics and ineffective leadership style as factors holding women back. While these factors ranked fairly low in both executive women's and CEO's ratings, the fact that substantially more women singled them out as obstacles suggests that female executives regard the issue of cultur-al fit and acceptance as a greater challenge for women than do top male executives. As one female ex-ecutive noted:

To understand what was going on politically—for lack of a better word—was irreplaceable in making career progress and every bit as important as the actual assignments that I had.

—Vice president, consumer products company.

One reason that male CEOs may not perceive style as being an important impediment to women's advancement is that it was not an issue for them in their own advancement. As discussed earlier, a key career strategy used by these successful female executives was the development of a managerial style that made male coworkers comfortable. It is unlikely that the CEOs in this study had to develop an adaptive style in order to make their female coworkers comfortable. This is illustrated by one CEO's comment: "I'm 56 years old and it's never happened in my career that I have reported to a woman."

IMPLICATIONS OF DUAL PERSPECTIVES

Why would such a dramatic difference be found between the men's and women's perception of the environment they share? One interpretation of the data is that there are dual environments—one for men that is designed to foster their advancement, one for women that presents subtle, but significant obstacles to their advancement.

The CEOs in this study were logical in their approach, and viewed the problem of women's advancement in terms of what they can see and what they can count: the number of women in the pipeline and their years of experience. They have no way of understanding the corporate environment faced by their female employees because it is an environment that they do not currently experience, nor did they face in their rise to the top. As members of the majority, they were in environments designed by and for men, and presumably geared to being responsive to their needs and advancement. The problem is that CEOs are the critical change agent in most organizations, and if they do not understand the nature of the problem, it is nearly impossible for them to develop effective solutions.

THE PROBLEM DEFINES THE SOLUTION

The divergence in perceptions of the cause of the problem conceivably may lead to a marked divergence in proposed solutions. The CEOs viewed the major impediment to women's advancement as lack of experience and time in the pipeline. The logical solution to this barrier may be to fill the pipeline with women and then passively wait for their advancement. This pipeline approach assumes that time will take care of the problem, and that if women do not advance it is because they are unwilling or unable to do so. The burden for change therefore lies with the individual woman. The underlying assumption in the pipeline approach is that the playing field is level all the way up to the corporate suite, and it is therefore up to the individual women to perform effectively and make the right choices to obtain corporate leadership positions. The organization's role in addressing this problem is passive once there are enough women in the pipeline. Proponents of this approach are perplexed that while women are flooding into the managerial pipeline, and advancing as quickly as their male counterparts, few break through to the top leadership positions in organizations.[26]

The female executives in our study present a very different assessment of the problem. These women sharply disagreed with the CEOs, and pointed to an exclusionary corporate culture as the primary barrier for women's advancement. In contrast to the CEOs, these women identified a playing field that was not level, but represented more of an obstacle course for women. Under this culture perspective, the problem does not lie with the individual women, but with attitudes and subtle barriers in the organization which foster an inhospitable corporate culture.

This culture perception may call for one of two solutions. The first solution is to change the corporate culture. This requires an active, planned intervention, which is clearly at odds with the pipeline approach of passively letting time handle the problem. The second solution is for the individual woman to adapt to the culture. Indeed, this is the approach that was consistently reported by these female executives. As discussed earlier, these women used career strategies that involved outperforming their male peers and developing adaptive management styles that made their male peers comfortable. While this solution may work for a select group of women who are both willing and able to adapt to an inhospitable corporate climate, it may not be an effective solution for the next generation of talented female employees aspiring to corporate leadership positions.

While this group of successful female executives adapted to inhospitable corporate cultures, this approach is definitely at odds with current perspectives on diversity in organizations and does not represent an effective, long-term solution to the problem. Diversity experts observe that organizations are most effective when active measures are taken to adapt corporate cultures to the needs of an increasingly diverse workforce, rather than placing the entire burden of change on the minority employee.[27] Increasingly, it is recognized that by expecting minorities to adapt to the dominant culture, organizations fail to capitalize on the innovative and creative outcomes of a diverse workforce.

The view as to who is responsible for change, the individual woman or the organization, yielded contradictory results in our study. While both the CEOs (80 percent) and female executives (76 percent) strongly agreed or agreed with the statement that it is the company's responsibility to change to meet the needs of management women, 73 percent of the female executives and 61 percent of the CEOs in our study also strongly agreed or agreed with the statement that it is up to women to change to fit the corporate culture. These conflicting responses may reflect recent and incomplete shifts in attitudes regarding diversity and responsibility for organizational change.

IS THE SOLUTION WORKING? IT DEPENDS ON WHOM YOU ASK

It is reasonable to ask whether any of the solutions described above are working. Are these *Fortune 1000* organizations making headway in removing promotional roadblocks and providing more opportunities for women? The answer depends on who is asked. As displayed in Figure 3, the CEOs were more than twice as likely as the executive women to say that opportunities for women in their companies improved greatly over the past five years. The female executives were more pessimistic about the change; 15 percent of the women reported no change in opportunities, compared with only 2 percent of the CEOs. Once again, we found a sharp divergence in the perception of the same organizational environment.

Are these female executives accurate in their perceptions, or are they being overly-pessimistic in their appraisal of women's opportunities in their organizations? While it can be argued that women who break through the glass ceiling are probably best equipped to assess its density, no definitive answer to this question can be found. Existing studies reveal limited progress in women achieving corporate

FIGURE 3 Opportunities for Women to Advance to Senior Leadership in Your Company Compared to Five Years Ago

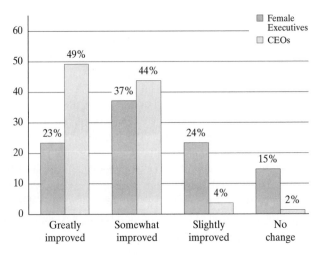

leadership positions.[28] Whatever the reality, the perception that there are limited opportunities for advancement is sufficient for turnover decisions and reduced career aspirations among talented female employees. The barriers do not have to be real to be effective.

A salient finding of our study is that the majority of CEOs surveyed apparently are unaware of the corporate environment faced by their female employees. As pointed out earlier, women were nearly twice as likely as CEOs to point to inhospitable corporate cultures as a barrier to women's advancement. CEOs, on the other hand, are more than twice as likely as women to report great improvement in the opportunities for women to advance in their corporations. How can these CEOs be so out of touch with the workplace experiences of nearly half of their workforce?

VOICES FROM THE TOP: SOME CEOs GET IT, OTHERS NEED WORK

We explored these issues further in our interviews with 20 male CEOs and found four themes underlying their perceptions of the corporate climate faced by the women in their organizations. Each theme represents a continuum on which CEOs varied, and the themes illuminated underlying assumptions that may have contributed to the differing perceptions of the CEOs and the female executives who worked for them.

Gender-Blind Treatment Results in Gender-Blind Outcomes

The first theme is the view that organizations need to treat men and women exactly the same. This perspective assumes a level playing field in the organization. Gender-blind treatment is therefore expected to result in gender-blind outcomes. One CEO explains:

> *I think companies have to be gender-blind. Period. Whatever they do for men, they do for women. We're gender blind and that's the only thing that's going to work.*

The assumption that the same career strategy is equally effective for men and women is not supported by the findings of our study; the female executives in our study attributed their success to developing a managerial style appropriate for their gender, which is clearly a gender-typed career strategy. CEOs who hold a gender-blind perspective may be reluctant to develop special career development programs aimed at helping women and other minorities navigate through the potentially non-level playing field in their organizations.

Some CEOs did not share the gender-blind perspective. These CEOs recognized that organizational climates are not always supportive to women and minorities, and that gender-blind policies do not necessarily result in gender-blind outcomes. Some of these CEOs acknowledged the potential resistance and stereotyping women may encounter from male managers. Some recognized the subtle, exclusionary nature of many organizational cultures, and applied this perspective to their view of diversity and corporate culture. In contrast, other CEOs maintained that since organizations treat everyone the same, individuals should therefore adapt to the organization.

Gender Generalizations: All Women are Alike and They are all Very Different from Men

The second theme that emerged from the CEO interviews was that CEOs varied on the extent to which they used group stereotypes to view individual women. Some saw men and women as being very different, whereas others saw them as nearly the same.

Some generalizations about gender differences had negative connotations:

> *Everyone has (career) slumps. I think that a greater percentage of women, when they have a slump, will look at the option of dropping out of the workforce. Most men wouldn't see it as an option.*

If a woman wants to be as assertive as men, she can get just as much air time. In many cases she can do better than a man. But sometimes mentally their knees buckle in an area where they are toe to toe .... If they want to be forceful, they are just as good.
I'd say there is a gender bias that there's less tough, aggressive women than men.

Some CEOs rejected the notion of group generalizations and focused instead on individual differences within groups:

I find that the women in our company have the same range of ambition as the men, ranging from people who are fiercely ambitious and want to rise high and go far, to people who want to lead balanced lives and are pretty happy with what they're doing.
    You can make a lot of generalizations about men and women, but when you get down to it, you've got to deal with specific people. Whether they're male or female, they don't necessarily fit the stereotype .... Some women we have around here aren't collaborative at all. They're extremely competitive people.

Other CEOs not only recognize individual differences, but also recognize that any gender differences in behaviors are often overshadowed by gender-neutral behaviors that emerge in response to position and responsibility:

Whether you're male or female, by the time you get to a senior management position, you've learned a different style of leadership anyway.

How do group generalizations relate to CEO perceptions of corporate climate? Existing research indicates a reciprocal relationship between group stereotyping and exclusionary corporate climates for women.[29] Group stereotyping leads to the dual perception that all women are alike, and they are all very different from men. This perception is amplified when women are in the numerical minority.[30] This results in a situation where men are treated on the basis of their individual characteristics, whereas women are automatically shunted into group categories, and are treated on the basis of those categories. This creates dual environments in organizations: one for women, and one for men, a distinction that is further fueled by group stereotypes. So male CEOs may assume that women do not want stretch assignments because of lack of aggressiveness or family demands, or they may place women in team leadership positions because of gender stereotypes that women are less competitive and more nurturing than men, and are therefore more likely to put their own needs aside for the good of the group. In either case, the challenge that is faced by women, but not their male counterparts, is to prove to their male colleagues that they are individuals and that they should be evaluated on the basis of their individual characteristics, rather than their group membership. In order to meet this challenge, women may expend considerable energy developing impression management strategies to project an image that runs counter to gender-role expectations.

Consciousness Raising in the Executive Suite: The Impact of Personal Experience

The third theme that emerged from the CEO interviews was the degree to which the CEOs were conscious of the exclusionary climate faced by their female employees. Many of the CEOs recognized that their own personal experiences influenced their awareness of gender issues, as well as issues faced by other minorities in their organizations. While most of the CEOs were white males, one CEO reflected on his own experience of being targeted for stereotyping and discrimination:

I'm Jewish. There weren't any Jewish people going into banking and there were no Jewish officers of banks. I was asked a lot, "Why are you doing this? There aren't any examples of Jews having succeeded in banking." I answered that it was because nobody had tried.

This CEO went on to relate how his background influenced his views of diversity in organizations:

People would ask, what is it like to go to school with blacks? I would think about how I would sit in class and not know the answers to questions and a black person would. So I would look at people as individuals. If you give them the same chances to perform and development experiences, you see race and religion and gender don't have much to do with success. This leads me to the conclusion that you can succeed by doing things differently.

Some CEOs observed that their early experiences interacting with competent women resulted in their casting aside gender-role stereotypes and generalizations:

Let me just say that I have been around very capable women all my working life. I certainly have never doubted the competency and capabilities of women in decision-making roles ... So I have seen women all my life be very effective in very difficult situations.
I have women friends who got MBAs and have gone on to run major companies.

Other CEOs reported that they become cognizant of gender issues through direct experiences with family members, most notably, their daughters. These direct, personal experiences were instrumental in raising the CEOs' consciousness and awareness of gender issues in organizations:

I have five girls, no sons .... One interesting issue is my two youngest daughters, one of whom is in grad school, the other's going to start this year—they're both into women's issues. That's what they want to do as a career, work on women's issues .... You talk about politics. I catch it if I don't think the way they do on those issues. Those things have certainly had an impact.

I have a couple of career-minded daughters. I would like them to have the opportunity to go as far as their abilities will take them.

...I would stand my three daughters against most males I know and they would compete very well.

Some of the CEOs interviewed recognized that they do not automatically become sensitive to these environmental issues because it is not part of their daily experience in their organizations. These CEOs sought to increase their awareness of gender issues through experiential training. It is important for CEOs to recognize that while feedback from female employees may increase their sensitivity to gender issues, it is often quite difficult for women to give this feedback without invitation. Personal experiences allow CEOs to understand the corporate climate faced by their female and minority employees. Whether the experience is directly aimed at the CEO or vicariously observed through others, it generally shatters the assumption that discrimination does not exist in their organization.

The Mantle for Change   The final theme revealed from the CEO interviews was the CEOs' responsibility for making change occur in their organizations. The CEOs' role in the change process may involve a range of actions from actively mentoring and grooming women for high-ranking positions to providing a more flexible workplace and a corporate culture that relishes diversity. Whatever the nature of the change, for change to be effective, it must come from the top.

While many of the CEOs interviewed recognized their responsibility for taking the mantle of change, some also recognized the potential risks involved with making change happen. One CEO elaborated:

I really had to ... take some chances in promoting women into roles that exposed them to high risk—and me as well. I had to run those risks to demonstrate that women could, in fact, handle these particular high-sensitivity, high-visibility jobs. So having done that, that's continued to open opportunities for women because there's no longer an artificial barrier to such promotions.

Other CEOs were reluctant to take the mantle of change, partly because of fears that the intervention would be viewed as an affirmative action gesture:

...holding managers accountable for developing women. I really dislike that. I think that could really backfire on you. I feel about that like I feel about affirmative action. People who weren't qualified were force-fed into it to match some sort of artificial goal.

Some CEOs did not take on the mantle of change because they believed that change did not need to occur. However, while these CEOs maintained that their organizations were gender-blind, they still expected women to help other women, thereby inferring that their corporate culture may not be as blind as they would like it to be.

Still other CEOs take the more benign approach that change needs to occur from a grass-roots level. Instead of active intervention, these CEOs hope that change will be initiated by women and other minorities in their organizations. Their role in the change process would therefore be to support the change, but not initiate it. However, one problem with giving the mantle for change to women and minorities is that these employees are vulnerable to backlash, and typically lack the power to sustain the change over time.

The themes that emerged from these interviews were connected. CEOs who were sensitized to the dual environments in their organizations did not assume a level playing field between the genders; they understood the exclusionary climate women face and they therefore did not advocate gender-blind policies and programs. CEOs who were sensitized to women's experiences were also more likely to emphasize individual differences between women, rather than using broad-based group generalizations to categorize their female employees. These CEOs also recognized their role in changing the inhospitable corporate climates faced by their female employees. In short, they attempted to hear the white noise in their organizations.

BRIDGING THE GENDER GAP

How do we bridge the gender gap and sensitize CEOs to the corporate climate faced by their female employees? Most CEOs do not understand the experience of being a minority in their organization since they themselves are in the majority. However, some recognize this disparity, and that the playing field is not perceived as being level by their female employees. This understanding is often obtained by direct, personal experiences with female colleagues and family members, most notably daughters. In the business world, it may be obtained by working with women as fellow members of corporate boards.[31] Other interventions that may raise CEO awareness include diversity training, focus groups featuring women, cross-gender mentoring, discussions with other CEOs, inclusion of gender and diversity issues in executive education, and other educational approaches using a variety of media.

Many organizational interventions aimed at breaking the glass ceiling that have been identified elsewhere are also supported by our study.[32] For example, organizations need to track women into direct line experience positions with profit and loss responsibility, minimize gender bias by using objective performance appraisal systems, facilitate effective mentoring relationships, promote work/life balance by implementing flexible workplace policies, and make managers responsible for the career development and tracking of their female employees. As pointed out by the Gordon and Whelan article in this issue, organizations also need to address the specific career needs of midlife women by offering flexible job designs and specialized career path programs.

Our study adds one more intervention to this list: raising the consciousness of chief executive officers and other senior officers slated for those top positions. In fact, this intervention may be the key underlying factor behind effective implementation of all of the other interventions listed above; effective implementation requires top management commitment. Organizations need the support and guidance of top management if women are to break through the glass ceiling. For this to occur, the gender gap must be bridged.

ENDNOTES

[1] U.S. Department of Labor, "Employed Persons By Occupation, Race and Sex," *Employment and Earnings* (Washington, DC: Department of Labor, January 1996): 171.

[2] Korn/Ferry International *Decade of the Executive Woman* (New York: Korn/Ferry International Federal Glass Ceiling Commission, 1995); *Good For Business: Making Full Use of the Nation's Human Capital* (Washington, DC: U.S. Government).

[3] Korn/Ferry International, *Korn/Ferry International's Executive Profile: A Decade of Change in Corporate Leadership* (New York: Korn/Ferry International and UCLA Graduate School of Management).

[4] Catalyst, *Census of Women Corporate Officers and Top Earners* (New York, NY: Catalyst, 1996).

[5] A. Morrison, R. P. White, and E. Van Velsor. *Breaking the Glass Ceiling: Can Women Reach the Top of America's Largest Corporations?* (Reading, MA: Addison-Wesley, 1998).

[6] Korn-Ferry International, 1995.

[7] J. D. Phillips, and B. Reisman, *Turnover and Return on Investment Models for Family Leave Parental Leave and Productivity: Current Research,* eds., D. E. Friedman, E. Galinsky, and V. Plowden (New York: Families and Work Institute): 33–53.

[8] Department of Industry, Labor and Human Relations, *Report of the Governor's Task Force on the Glass Ceiling Commission* (Madison, WI: State of Wisconsin, 1993).

[9] C. G. Brush, "Research on Women Business Owners: Past Trends, New Perspectives and Future Directions." *Entrepreneurship: Theory and Practice 16* (1992): 5–30.

[10] An alternative reason for the persistence of the glass ceiling is that stated intentions to break the ceiling may not reflect real intentions; some individuals may benefit from maintaining the status quo.

[11] The response rates for the female executive and CEO samples were 36.8 percent and 33 percent. On average, the female executives were 45 years old, earned an annual salary of $248,000, and were highly educated: almost two-thirds have postgraduate degrees. Seventy-two percent of the women were married, and almost two-thirds (64 percent) have children. Only nine percent identify themselves as other than Caucasian, and these women of color earned an average annual salary of $229,000. Eight-one percent of the women were within two reporting levels of the CEO, and 44 percent report directly to the CEO or are only one level from the CEO. More than 60 percent held staff positions. The largest number held the title of vice president (54 percent) or senior vice president (19 percent); survey respondents also included a significant number of even more senior executives, such as president, executive vice president, chief financial officer and general counsel.

[12] A sample of 40 women was randomly drawn from the survey mailing list, and 20 of these women participated in a telephone interview. Among the CEOs completing the survey, 50 respondents noted in a separate postcard their interest in participating in a follow-up interview, and 22 of these were randomly selected to participate. Complete interview data were collected from 20 CEOs. The semi-structured interviews were taped, transcribed, and analyzed using a variant of thematic and componential analyses.

[13] We used earlier studies, based on interviews with small groups of hand-picked female executives, as a launching point for the development of this list of strategies. We refer the reader to ground-breaking studies by Morrison, White, and Van Velsor (1988) and L. Mainiero, "Getting Anointed for Advancement: The Case of Executive Women," *Academy of Management Executive 8* (1994): 53–67. Our study extends these studies by asking a large sample of female executives to prioritize the specific strategies used in their advancement.

[14] We also asked the female executives to prioritize among the list of 13 strategies by selecting the top three strategies that were most important. The same four strategies were picked as the most important strategies for advancement: consistently exceeding performance expectations (ranked in the top three by 74 percent of the sample); seeking out difficult or challenging assignments (51 percent); developing a style with which male managers are comfortable (48 percent); and having influential mentors (39 percent).

[15] L. Putnam and J. S. Heinen, "Women in Management: The Fallacy of the Trait Approach," *MSU Business Topics* (Summer 1976): 47–53. O. C. Brenner, J. Tomkiewicz, and V. E. Schein, "The Relationship Between Sex Role Stereotypes and Requisite Management Characteristics Revisited," *Academy of Management Journal 32* (1989): 662–669. See also research by Fagenson (1990) and Ely (1995) which suggests that women's gender identity is influenced by rank and numerical representation in organizations: E. A. Fagenson, "Perceived Masculine and Feminine Attributes Examined as a Function of Individuals' Sex and Level in the Organizational Power Hierarchy:

A Test of Four Theoretical Perspectives," *Journal of Applied Psychology 75* (1990): 204–211; R. Ely, "The Power in Demography: Women's Social Constructions of Gender Identity at Work," *Academy of Management Journal 38* (1995): 589–634.

[16] P. Tharenou, S. Latimer, and D. Conroy, "How Do You Make It to the Top? An Examination of Influences on Women's and Men's Managerial Advancement," *Academy of Management Journal 37* (1994): 899–931. P. J. Ohlott, M. N. Ruderman, and C. D. McCauley, "Gender Differences in Managers' Developmental Job Experiences," *Academy of Management Journal 37* (1994): 46–67. B. Ragins, and E. Sundstrom, "Gender and Power in Organizations: A Longitudinal Perspective." *Psychological Bulletin 105* (1989): 51–88.

[17] G. F. Dreher and R. A. Ash, "A Comparative Study of Mentoring Among Men and Women in Managerial, Professional, and Technical Positions," *Journal of Applied Psychology 75*: (1990): 539–546. E. A. Fagenson, "The Mentor Advantage: Perceived Career/Job Experiences of Protégés vs. Non-Protégés, *Journal of Organizational Behavior 10* (1989): 309–320. T. A. Scandura, "Mentorship and Career Mobility: An Empirical Investigation," *Journal of Organizational Behavior 13* (1990): 169–174.

[18] B. R. Ragins and T. A. Scandura, "Gender Differences in Expected Outcomes of Mentoring Relationships," *Academy of Management Journal 37* (1994): 957–971. Korn/Ferry International, 1993.

[19] K. E. Kram, *Mentoring at Work* (Glenview, IL: Scott, Foresman and Company, 1985).

[20] The queen bee syndrome contends that successful women are unwilling to help others at lower ranks. This popularized idea is tenacious, but empirically refuted. In a study of female and male executives, Belle Ragins and Terri Scandura found that women were as likely as men to be mentors, and mentored protégés of the same gender with greater frequency. B. R. Ragins and T. A. Scandura, "Gender Differences in Expected Outcomes of Mentoring Relationships," *Academy of Management Journal 37* (1994): 957–971. G. Staines, C. Travis, and T. E. Jayerante, "The Queen Bee Syndrome." *Psychology Today 7*, no. 8 (1973): 55–60.

[21] J. D. Olian, S. J. Carroll, and C. M. Giannantonio, "Mentor Reactions to Protégés: An Experiment with Managers," *Journal of Vocational Behavior 43* (1993): 266–278.

[22] Kram, 1995.

[23] B. R. Ragins and J. Cotton, "Easier Said Than Done: Gender Differences in Perceived Barriers to Gaining a Mentor," *Academy of Management Journal 34* (1991): 939–951.

[24] B. R. Ragins, "Barriers to Mentoring: The Female Manager's Dilemma," *Human Relations 42* (1989): 1–22. B. R. Ragins, "Diversified Mentoring Relationships in Organizations: A Power Perspective," *Academy of Management Review 22* (1997): 482–521. Kram, 1985.

[25] Research on career paths of male executives indicates that line positions with profit and loss responsibility were more likely to be used than staff positions in obtaining executive positions. Korn/Ferry International 1990 and Korn/Ferry International, *Korn/Ferry International's Executive Profile: A Survey of Corporate Leaders in the Eighties* (New York: Korn/Ferry International, 1986).

[26] Korn/Ferry International, 1993. For more discussion on pipeline issues see L. K. Stroh, J. M. Brett, and A. H. Reilly, "All the Right Stuff: A Comparison of Female and Male Managers' Career Progression," *Journal of Applied Psychology 77* (1992): 251–260, and A. B. Antal, and D. N. Izraeli, "A Global Comparison of Women in Management: Women Managers in Their Homelands and as Expatriates," *Women in Management: Trends, Issues and Challenges in Managerial Diversity,* ed. E. A. Fagenson (Newbury Park: Sage, 1993): 52–96.

[27] T. Cox, "The Multicultural Organization," *Academy of Management Executive 5* (1991): 34–47.

[28] Korn/Ferry International, 1993.

[29] Ely, 1995.

[30] R. M. Kanter, *Men and Women of the Corporation* (New York: Basic Books, 1977).

[31] Catalyst, *Women on Corporate Boards: The Challenge of Change* (New York, NY: Catalyst, 1993). Catalyst, *1995 Catalyst Census of Female Board Directors of the* Fortune 500 (New York, NY: Catalyst, 1995).

[32] M. C. Mattis, "Dismantling the Glass Ceiling, Pane by Pane," *The Human Resources Professional* (Fall 1990): 5–8. Department of Industry, Labor and Human Relations, 1993. Catalyst, 1993. Catalyst, *Women in Corporate Management, Model Programs for Development and Mobility* (New York, NY: Catalyst, 1991).

CULTURAL CONSTRAINTS IN MANAGEMENT THEORIES*

Geert Hofstede

Lewis Carroll's *Alice in Wonderland* contains the famous story of Alice's croquet game with the Queen of Hearts.

> *Alice thought she had never seen such a curious croquet-ground in all her life: it was all ridges and furrows; the balls were live hedgehogs, the mallets live flamingoes, and the soldiers had to double themselves up and to stand on their hands and feet, to make the arches.*

You probably know how the story goes: Alice's flamingo mallet turns its head whenever she wants to strike with it; her hedgehog ball runs away; and the doubled-up soldier arches walk around all the time. The only rule seems to be that the Queen of Hearts always wins.

Alice's croquet playing problems are good analogies to attempts to build culture-free theories of management. Concepts available for this purpose are themselves alive with culture, having been developed within a particular cultural context. They have a tendency to guide our thinking toward our desired conclusion.

As the same reasoning may also be applied to the arguments in this article, I better tell you my conclusion before I continue—so that the rules of my game are understood. In this article we take a trip around the world to demonstrate that there are no such things as universal management theories.

Diversity in management *practices* as we go around the world has been recognized in U.S. management literature for more than 30 years. The term *comparative management* has been used since the 1960s. However, it has taken much longer for the U.S. academic community to accept that not only practices but also the validity of *theories* may stop at national borders, and I wonder whether even today everybody would agree with this statement.

An article I published in *Organizational Dynamics* in 1980 entitled "Do American Theories Apply Abroad?" created more controversy than I expected. The article argued, with empirical support, that generally accepted U.S. theories like those of Maslow, Herzberg, McClelland, Vroom, McGregor, Likert, Blake, and Mouton may not or only very partly apply outside the borders of their country of origin—assuming they do apply within those borders. Among the requests for reprints, a larger number were from Canada than from the United States.

MANAGEMENT THEORISTS ARE HUMAN

Employees and managers are human. Employees as humans was "discovered" in the 1930s, with the Human Relations school. Managers as humans was introduced in the late 1940s by Herbert Simon's "bounded rationality" and elaborated in Richard Cyert and James March's *Behavioral Theory of the Firm* (1963, and recently re-published in a second edition). My argument is that management scientists, theorists, and writers are human too: They grew up in a particular society in a particular period, and their ideas cannot help but reflect the constraints of their environment.

The issues explored here were presented by Dr. Hofstede, the Foundation for Administrative Research Distinguished International Scholar, at the 1992 Annual Meeting of the Academy of Management. Las Vegas, Nevada, August 11, 1992.

*Reprinted with permission from the *Academy of Management Executive 7*, no. 1 (1993): 81–93.

The idea that the validity of a theory is constrained by national borders is more obvious in Europe, with all its borders, than in a huge borderless country like the United States. Already in the sixteenth century Michel de Montaigne, a Frenchman, wrote a statement which was made famous by Blaise Pascal about a century later "Vérite en-deça des Pyrenées, erreur au-delà"—There are truths on this side of the Pyrenées which are falsehoods on the other.

FROM DON ARMADO'S LOVE TO TAYLOR'S SCIENCE

According to the comprehensive ten-volume *Oxford English Dictionary* (1971), the words *manage*, *management*, and *manager* appeared in the English language in the sixteenth century. The oldest recorded use of the word *manager* is in Shakespeare's "Love's Labour's Lost," dating from 1588, in which Don Adriano de Armado, "a fantastical Spaniard," exclaims (Act I, scene ii, 188):

> *"Adieu, valour! rust, rapier! be still, drum! for your manager is in love; yea, he loveth."*

The linguistic origin of the word is from Latin *manus*, hand, via the Italian *maneggiare*, which is the training of horses in the *manege*; subsequently its meaning was extended to skillful handling in general, like of arms and musical instruments, as Don Armado illustrates. However, the word also became associated with the French *menage*, household, as an equivalent of *husbandry* in its sense of the art of running a household. The theatre of present-day management contains elements of both *manege* and *menage* and different managers and cultures may use different accents.

The founder of the science of economics, the Scot Adam Smith, in his 1776 book The *Wealth of Nations*, used *manage*, *management* (even *bad management*) and *manager* when dealing with the process and the persons involved in operating joint stock companies (Smith, V.i.e.). British economist John Stuart Mill (1806-1873) followed Smith in this use and clearly expressed his distrust of such hired people who were not driven by ownership. Since the 1880s the word "management" appeared occasionally in writings by American engineers, until it was canonized as a modern science by Frederick W. Taylor in *Shop Management* in 1903 and in *The Principles of Scientific Management* in 1911.

While Smith and Mill used *management* to describe a process and *managers* for the persons involved, *management* in the American sense—which has since been taken back by the British—refers not only to the process but also to the managers as a class of people. This class (1) does not own a business but sells its skills to act on behalf of the owners and (2) does not produce personally but is indispensable for making others produce, through motivation. Members of this class carry a high status and many American boys and girls aspire to the role. In the United States, the manager is a cultural hero.

Let us now turn to other parts of the world. We will look at management in its context in other successful modern economies: Germany, Japan, France, Holland, and among the Overseas Chinese. Then we will examine management in the much larger part of the world that is still poor, especially South-East Asia and Africa, and in the new political configurations of Eastern Europe, and Russia in particular. We will then return to the United States via mainland China.

Germany   The manager is not a cultural hero in Germany. If anybody, it is the engineer who fills the hero role. Frederick Taylor's *Scientific Management* was conceived in a society of immigrants—where large numbers of workers with diverse backgrounds and skills had to work together. In Germany this heterogeneity never existed.

Elements of the mediaeval guild system have survived in historical continuity in Germany until the present day. In particular, a very effective apprenticeship system exists both on the shop floor and in the office, which alternates practical work and classroom courses. At the end of the apprenticeship the worker receives a certificate, the *Facharbeiterbrief*, which is recognized throughout the country. About two thirds of the German worker population holds such a certificate and a corresponding occupational pride. In fact, quite a few German company presidents have worked their way up from the ranks through an apprenticeship. In comparison, two thirds of the worker population in Britain have no occupational qualification at all.

The highly skilled and responsible German workers do not necessarily need a manager, American-style, to "motivate" them. They expect their boss or *Meister* to assign their tasks and to be the expert in resolving technical problems. Comparisons of similar German, British, and French organizations show the Germans as having the highest rate of personnel in productive roles and the lowest both in leadership and staff roles.

Business schools are virtually unknown in Germany. Native German management theories concentrate on formal systems. The inapplicability of American concepts of management was quite apparent in 1973 when the U.S. consulting firm of Booz, Allen, and Hamilton, commissioned by the German Ministry of Economic Affairs, wrote a study of German management from an American view point. The report is highly critical and writes among other things that "Germans simply do not have a very strong concept of management." Since 1973, from my personal experience, the situation has not changed much. However, during this period the German economy has performed in a superior fashion to the United States in virtually all respects, so a strong concept of management might have been a liability rather than an asset.

Japan   The American type of manager is also missing in Japan. In the United States, the core of the enterprise is the managerial class. The core of the Japanese enterprise is the permanent worker group; workers who for all practical purposes are tenured and who aspire at life-long employment. They are distinct from the non-permanent employees—most women and subcontracted teams led by gang bosses, to be laid off in slack periods. University graduates in Japan first join the permanent worker group and subsequently fill various positions, moving from line to staff as the need occurs while paid according to seniority rather than position. They take part in Japanese-style group consultation sessions for important decisions, which extend the decision-making period but guarantee fast implementation afterwards. Japanese are to a large extent controlled by their peer group rather than by their manager.

Three researchers from the East-West Center of the University of Hawaii, Joseph Tobin, David Wu, and Dana Danielson, did an observation study of typical preschools in three countries: China, Japan, and the United States. Their results have been published both as a book and as a video. In the Japanese preschool, one teacher handled 28 four-year-olds. The video shows one particularly obnoxious boy, Hiroki, who fights with other children and throws teaching materials down from the balcony. When a little girl tries to alarm the teacher, the latter answers "What are you calling me for? Do something about it!" In the U.S. preschool, there is one adult for every nine children. This class has its problem child too, Glen, who refuses to clear away his toys. One of the teachers has a long talk with him and isolates him in a corner, until he changes his mind. It doesn't take much imagination to realize that managing Hiroki 30 years later will be a different process from managing Glen.

American theories of leadership are ill-suited for the Japanese group-controlled situation. During the past two decades, the Japanese have developed their own *PM* theory of leadership, in which *P* stands for performance and *M* for maintenance. The latter is less a concern for individual employees than for maintaining social stability. In view of the amazing success of the Japanese economy in the past 30 years, many Americans have sought the secrets of Japanese management hoping to copy them.

France   The manager, U.S. style, does not exist in France either. In a very enlightening book, unfortunately not yet translated into English, the French researcher Philippe d'Iribarne (1989) describes the results of in-depth observation and interview studies of management methods in three subsidiary plants of the same French multinational: in France, the United States, and Holland. He relates what he finds to information about the three societies in general. Where necessary, he goes back in history to trace the roots of the strikingly different behaviors in the completion of the same tasks. He identifies three kinds of basic principles (*logiques*) of management. In the United States, the principle is the *fair contract* between employer and employee, which gives the manager considerable prerogatives, but within its limits. This is really a labor *market* in which the worker sells his or her labor for a price. In France, the principle is the *honor* of each class in a society which has always been and remains extremely stratified, in which superiors behave as superior beings and subordinates accept and expect this, conscious of their own lower level in the national hierarchy but also of the honor of their own class. The French do not think in terms of managers versus nonmanagers but in terms of *cadres* versus *noncadres*; one becomes cadre by attending the proper schools and one remains it forever, regardless of their actual task, cadres have the privileges of a higher social class, and it is very rare for a non-cadre to cross the ranks.

The conflict between French and American theories of management became apparent in the beginning of the twentieth century, in a criticism by the great French management pioneer Henri Fayol (1841-1925) on his U.S. colleague and contemporary Frederick W. Taylor (1856-1915). The difference in career paths of the two men is striking. Fayol was a French engineer whose career as a *cadre supérieur* culminated in the position of Président-Directeur-Général of a mining company. After his retirement he formulated his experiences in a pathbreaking text on organization: *Administration industrielle et générale*, in which he focused on the sources of authority. Taylor was an American engineer who started his career in industry as a worker and attained his academic qualifications through evening studies. From chief engineer in a steel company he became one of the first management consultants. Taylor was not really concerned with the issue of authority at all; his focus was on efficiency. He proposed to split the task of the first-line boss into eight specialisms, each exercised by a different person; an idea which eventually led to the idea of a matrix organization.

Taylor's work appeared in a French translation in 1913, and Fayol read it and showed himself generally impressed but shocked by Taylor's "denial of the principle of the Unity of Command" in the case of the eight-boss system.

Seventy years later André Laurent, another of Fayol's compatriots, found that French managers in a survey reacted very strongly against a suggestion that one employee could report to two different bosses, while U.S. managers in the same survey showed fewer misgivings. Matrix organization has never become popular in France as it has in the United States.

Holland   In my own country, Holland or as it is officially called, the Netherlands, the study by Philippe d'Iribarne found the management principle to be a need for *consensus* among all parties, neither predetermined by a contractual relationship nor by class distinctions, but based on an open-ended exchange of views and a balancing of interests. In terms of the different origins of the word *manager*, the organization in Holland is more *menage* (household) while in the United States it is more *menege* (horse drill).

At my university, the University of Limburg at Maastricht, every semester we receive a class of American business students who take a program in European Studies. We asked both the Americans and a matched group of Dutch students to describe their ideal job after graduation, using a list of 22 job characteristics. The Americans attached significantly more importance than the Dutch to earnings, advancement, benefits, a good working relationship with their boss, and security of employment. The Dutch attached more importance to freedom to adopt their own approach to the job, being consulted by their boss in his or her decisions, training opportunities, contributing to the success of their organization, fully using their skills and abilities, and helping others. This list confirms d'Iribarne's findings of a contractual employment relationship in the United States, based on earnings and career opportunities, against a consensual relationship in Holland. The latter has centuries-old roots; the Netherlands were the first republic in Western Europe (1609-1810), and a model for the American republic. The country has been and still is governed by a careful balancing of interests in a multi-party system.

In terms of management theories, both motivation and leadership in Holland are different from what they are in the United States. Leadership in Holland presupposes modesty, as opposed to assertiveness in the United States. No U.S. leadership theory has room for that. Working in Holland is not a constant feast, however. There is a built-in premium on mediocrity and jealousy, as well as time-consuming ritual consultations to maintain the appearance of consensus and the pretense of modesty. There is unfortunately another side to every coin.

The Overseas Chinese Among the champions of economic development in the past 30 years we find three countries mainly populated by Chinese living outside the Chinese mainland: Taiwan, Hong Kong, and Singapore. Moreover, Overseas Chinese play a very important role in the economies of Indonesia, Malaysia, the Philippines, and Thailand, where they form an ethnic minority. If anything, the little dragons—Taiwan, Hong Kong, and Singapore—have been more economically successful than Japan, moving from rags to riches and now counted among the world's wealthy industrial countries. Yet very little attention has been paid to the way in which their enterprises have been managed. *The Spirit of Chinese Capitalism* by Gordon Redding (1990), the British dean of the Hong Kong Business School, is an excellent book about Chinese business. He bases his insights on personal acquaintance and in-depth discussions with a large number of Overseas Chinese businesspeople.

Overseas Chinese American enterprises lack almost all characteristics of modern management. They tend to be small, cooperating for essential functions with other small organizations through networks based on personal relations. They are family-owned, without the separation between ownership and management typical in the West, or even in Japan and Korea. They normally focus on one product or market, with growth by opportunistic diversification; in this, they are extremely flexible. Decision making is centralized in the hands of one dominant family member, but other family members may be given new ventures to try their skills on. They are low-profile and extremely cost-conscious, applying Confucian virtues of thrift and persistence. Their size is kept small by the assumed lack of loyalty of non-family employees, who, if they are any good, will just wait and save until they can start their own family business.

Overseas Chinese prefer economic activities in which great gains can be made with little manpower, like commodity trading and real estate. They employ few professional managers, except their sons and sometimes daughters who have been sent to prestigious business schools abroad, but who upon return continue to run the family business the Chinese way.

The origin of this system, or—in the Western view—this lack of system, is found in the history of Chinese society, in which there were no formal laws, only formal networks of powerful people guided by general principles of Confucian virtue. The favors of the authorities could change daily, so nobody could be trusted except one's kinfolk—of whom, fortunately, there used to be many, in an extended family structure. The Overseas Chinese way of doing business is also very well adapted to their position in the countries in which they form ethnic minorities, often envied and threatened by ethnic violence.

Overseas Chinese businesses following this unprofessional approach command a collective gross national product of some 200 to 300 billion U.S. dollars, exceeding the GNP of Australia. There is no denying that it works.

MANAGEMENT TRANSFER TO POOR COUNTRIES

Four-fifths of the world population live in countries that are not rich but poor. After World War II and decolonization, the stated purpose of the United Nations and the World Bank has been to promote the development of all the world's countries in a war on poverty. After 40 years it looks very much like we are losing this war. If one thing has become clear, it is that the export of Western—mostly American—management practices and theories to poor countries has contributed little to nothing to their development. There has been no lack of effort and money spent for this purpose: students from poor countries have been trained in this country, and teachers and Peace Corps workers have been sent to the poor countries. If nothing else, the general lack of success in economic development of other countries should be sufficient argument to doubt the validity of Western management theories in non-Western environments.

If we examine different parts of the world, the development picture is not equally bleak, and history is often a better predictor than economic factors for what happens today. There is a broad regional pecking order with East Asia leading. The little dragons have passed into the camp of the wealthy; then follow South-East Asia (with its Overseas Chinese minorities), Latin American (in spite of the debt crisis), South Asia, and Africa always trails behind. Several African countries have only become poorer since decolonization.

Regions of the world with a history of large-scale political integration and civilization generally have done better than regions in which no large-scale political and cultural infrastructure existed, even if the old civilizations had decayed or been suppressed by colonizers. It has become painfully clear that development cannot be pressure-cooked; it presumes a cultural infrastructure that takes time to grow. Local management is part of this infrastructure; it cannot be imported in package form. Assuming, that with so-called modern management techniques and theories outsiders can develop a country has proven a deplorable arrogance. At best, one can hope for a dialogue between equals with the locals, in which the Western partner acts as the expert in Western technology and the local partner as the expert in local culture, habits, and feelings.

Russia and China   The crumbling of the former Eastern bloc has left us with a scattering of states and would-be states of which the political and economic future is extremely uncertain. The best predictions are those based on a knowledge of history, because historical trends have taken revenge on the arrogance of the Soviet rulers who believed they could turn them around by brute power. One obvious fact is that the former bloc is extremely heterogeneous, including countries traditionally closely linked with the West by trade and travel, like Czechia, Hungary, Slovenia, and the Baltic states, as well as others with a Byzantine or Turkish past; some having been prosperous, others always extremely poor.

The industrialized Western world and the World Bank seem committed to helping the ex-Eastern bloc countries develop, but with the same technocratic neglect for local cultural factors that proved so unsuccessful in the development assistance to other poor countries. Free market capitalism, introduced by Western-style management, is supposed to be the answer from Albania to Russia.

Let me limit myself to the Russian republic, a huge territory with some 140 million inhabitants, mainly Russians. We know quite a bit about the Russians as their country was a world power for several hundreds of years before communism, and in the nineteenth century it has produced some of the greatest writers in world literature. If I want to understand the Russians—including how they could so long support the Soviet regime—I tend to re-read Lev Nikolayevich Tolstoy. In his most famous novel *Anna Karenina* (1876) one of the main characters is a landowner, Levin, whom Tolstoy uses to express his own views and convictions about his people. Russian peasants used to be serfs; serfdom had been abolished in 1861, but the peasants, now tenants, remained as passive as before. Levin wanted to break this passivity by dividing the land among his peasants in exchange for a share of the crops; but the peasants only let the land deteriorate further. Here follows a quote:

> *(Levin) read political economy and socialistic works ... but, as he had expected, found nothing in them related to his undertaking. In the political economy books—in (John Stuart) Mill, for instance, whom he studied first and with great ardour, hoping every minute to find an answer to the questions that were engrossing him—he found only certain laws deduced from the state of agriculture in Europe; but he could not for the life of him see why these laws, which did not apply to Russia, should be considered universal .... Political economy told him that the laws by which Europe had developed and was developing her wealth were universal and absolute. Socialist teaching told him that development along those lines leads to ruin. And neither of them offered the smallest enlightenment as to what he, Levin, and all the Russian peasants and landowners were to do with their millions of hands and millions of acres, to make them as productive as possible for the common good.*

In the summer of 1991, the Russian lands yielded a record harvest, but a large share of it rotted in the fields because no people were to be found for harvesting. The passivity is still there, and not only among the peasants. And the heirs of John Stuart Mill (whom we met before as one of the early analysts of *management*) again present their universal recipes which simply do not apply.

Citing Tolstoy, I implicitly suggest that management theorists cannot neglect the great literature of the countries they want their ideas to apply to. The greatest novel in the Chinese literature is considered Cao Xueqin's *The Story of the Stone*, also known as *The Dream of the Red Chamber* which appeared around 1760. It describes the rise and fall of two branches of an aristocratic family in Beijing, who live in adjacent plots in the capital. Their plots are joined by a magnificent garden with several pavillions in it, and the young, mostly female members of both families are allowed to live in them. One day the management of the garden is taken over by a young woman, Tan-Chun, who states:

> *I think we ought to pick out a few experienced trust-worthy old women from among the ones who work in the Garden—women who know something about gardening already—and put the upkeep of the Garden into their hands. We needn't ask them to pay us rent; all we need ask them for is an annual share of the produce. There would be four advantages in this arrangement. In the first place, if we have people whose sole occupation is to look after trees and flowers and so on, the condition of the Garden will improve gradually year after year and there will be no more of those long periods of neglect followed by bursts of feverish activity when things have been allowed to get out of hand. Secondly there won't be the spoiling and wastage we get at present. Thirdly the women themselves will gain a little extra to add to their incomes which will compensate them for the hard work they put in throughout the year. And fourthly, there's no reason why we shouldn't use the money we should otherwise have spent on nurserymen, rockery specialists, horticultural cleaners and so on for other purposes.*

As the story goes on, the capitalist privatization—because that is what it is—of the Garden is carried through, and it works. When in the 1980s Deng Xiaoping allowed privatization in the Chinese villages, it also worked. It worked so well that its effects started to be felt in politics and threatened the existing political order, hence the knockdown at Tienanmen Square of June 1989. But it seems that the forces of privatization are getting the upper hand again in China. If we remember what Chinese entrepreneurs are able to do once they have become Overseas Chinese, we shouldn't be too surprised. But what works in China—and worked two centuries ago—does not have to work in Russia, not in Tolstoy's days and not today. I am not offering a solution; I only protest against a naive universalism that knows only one recipe for development, the one supposed to have worked in the United States.

A THEORY OF CULTURE IN MANAGEMENT

Our trip around the world is over and we are back in the United States. What have we learned? There is something in all countries called *management*, but its meaning differs to a larger or smaller extent from one country to the other, and it takes considerable historical and cultural insight into local conditions to understand its processes, philosophies, and problems. If already the word may mean so many different things, how can we expect one country's theories of management to apply abroad? One should be extremely careful in making this assumption, and test it before considering it proven. Management is not a phenomenon that can be isolated from other processes taking place in a society. During our trip around the world we saw that it interacts with what happens in the family, at school, in politics, and government. It is obviously also related to religion and to beliefs about science. Theories of management always had to be interdisciplinary, but if we cross national borders they should become more interdisciplinary than ever.

Cultural differences between nations can be, to some extent, described using first four, and now five, bipolar *dimensions*. The position of a country on these dimensions allows us to make some predictions on the way their society operates, including their management processes and the kind of theories applicable to their management.

As the word *culture* plays such an important role in my theory, let me give you my definition, which differs from some other very respectable definitions. Culture to me is *the collective programming of the mind which distinguishes one group or category of people from another*. In the part of my work I am referring to now, the category of people is the nation.

Culture is a *construct*, that means it is "not directly accessible to observation but inferable from verbal statements and other behaviors and useful in predicting still other observable and measurable verbal and nonverbal behavior." It should not be reified; it is an auxiliary concept that should be used as long as it proves useful but bypassed where we can predict behaviors without it.

The same applies to the *dimensions* I introduced. They are constructs too that should not be reified. They do not "exist"; they are tools for analysis which may or may not clarify a situation. In my statistical analysis of empirical data the first four dimensions together explain 49 percent of the variance in the data. The other 51 percent remain specific to individual countries.

The first four dimensions were initially detected through a comparison of the values of similar people (employees and managers) in 64 national subsidiaries of the IBM Corporation. People working for the same multinational, but in different countries, represent very well-matched samples from the populations of their countries, similar in all respects except nationality.

The first dimension is labelled *Power Distance*, and it can be defined as the degree of inequality among people which the population of a country considers as normal: from relatively equal (that is, small power distance) to extremely unequal (large power distance). All societies are unequal, but some are more unequal than others.

The second dimension is labelled *Individualism*, and it is the degree to which people in a country prefer to act as individuals rather than as members of groups. The opposite of individualism can be called *Collectivism*, so collectivism is low individualism. The way I use the word it has no political connotations. In collectivist societies a child learns to respect the group to which it belongs, usually the family, and to differentiate between in-group members and out-group members (that is, all other people). When children grow up they remain members of their group, and they expect the group to protect them when they are in trouble. In return, they have to remain loyal to their group throughout life. In individualist societies, a child learns very early to think of itself as "I" instead of as part of "we". It expects one day to have to stand on its own feet and not to get protection from its group any more; and therefore it also does not feel a need for strong loyalty.

The third dimension is called *Masculinity* and its opposite pole *Femininity*. It is the degree to which tough values like assertiveness, performance, success, and competition, which in nearly all societies are associated with the role of men, prevail over tender values like the quality of life, maintaining warm personal relationships, service, care for the weak, and solidarity, which in nearly all societies are more associated with women's roles. Women's roles differ from men's roles in all countries; but in tough societies, the differences are larger than in tender ones.

The fourth dimension is labelled *Uncertainty Avoidance*, and it can be defined as the degree to which people in a country prefer structured over unstructured situations. Structured situations are those in which there are clear rules as to how one should behave. These rules can be written down, but they can also be unwritten and imposed by tradition. In countries which score high on uncertainty avoidance, people tend to show more nervous energy, while in countries which score low, people are more easy-going. A (national) society with strong uncertainty avoidance can be called rigid; one with weak uncertainty avoidance, flexible. In countries where uncertainty avoidance is strong a feeling prevails of "what is different, is dangerous." In weak uncertainty avoidance societies, the feeling would rather be "what is different, is curious."

The fifth dimension was added on the basis of a study of the values of students in 23 countries carried out by Michael Harris Bond, a Canadian working in Hong Kong. He and I had cooperated in another study of students' values which had yielded the same four dimensions as the IBM data. However, we wondered to what extent our common findings in two studies could be the effect of a Western bias introduced by the common Western background of the researchers: remember Alice's croquet game. Michael Bond resolved this dilemma by deliberately introducing an Eastern bias. He used a questionnaire prepared at his request by his Chinese colleagues, the *Chinese Value Survey* (CVS), which was translated from Chinese into different languages and answered by 50 male and 50 female students in each of 23 countries in all five continents. Analysis of the CVS data produced three dimensions significantly correlated with the three IBM dimensions of power distance, individualism, and masculinity. There was also a fourth dimension, but it did not resemble uncertainty avoidance. It was composed, both on the positive and on the negative side, from items that had not been included in the IBM studies but were present in the Chinese Value Survey because they were rooted in the teachings of Confucius. I labelled this dimension: *Long-term* versus *Short-term Orientation*. On the long-term side one finds values oriented towards the future, like thrift (saving) and persistence. On the short-term side one finds values rather oriented towards the past and present, like respect for tradition and fulfilling social obligations.

Table 1 lists the scores on all five dimensions for the United States and for the other countries we just discussed. The table shows that each country has its own configuration on the four dimensions. Some of the values in the table have been estimated based on imperfect replications or personal impressions. The different dimension scores do not "explain" all the differences in management I described earlier. To understand management in a country, one should have both knowledge of and empathy with the entire local scene. However, the scores should make us aware that people in other countries may think, feel, and act very differently from us when confronted with basic problems of society.

TABLE 1   Cultural Dimension Scores for Ten Countries

	PD	ID	MA	UA	LT
United States	40L	91H	62H	46L	29L
Germany	35L	67H	66H	65M	31M
Japan	54M	46M	95H	92H	80H
France	68H	71H	43M	86H	30*L
Netherlands	38L	80H	14L	53M	44M
Hong Kong	68H	25L	57H	29L	96H
Indonesia	78H	14L	46M	48L	25*L
West Africa	77H	20L	46M	54M	16L
Russia	95*H	50*M	40*L	90*H	10*L
China	80*H	20*L	50*M	60*M	118H

PD = Power Distance; ID = Individualism; MA = Masculinity; UA = Uncertainty Avoidance;
LT = Long-Term Orientation; H = top third, M = medium third, L = bottom third (among 53
countries and regions for the first four dimensions; among 23 countries for the fifth)

*estimated

IDIOSYNCRACIES OF AMERICAN MANAGEMENT THEORIES

In comparison to other countries, the U.S. culture profile presents itself as below average on power distance and uncertainty avoidance, highly individualistic, fairly masculine, and short-term oriented. The Germans show a stronger uncertainty avoidance and less extreme individualism; the Japanese are different on all dimensions, least on power distance; the French show larger power distance and uncertainty avoidance, but are less individualistic and somewhat feminine; the Dutch resemble the Americans on the first three dimensions, but score extremely feminine and relatively long-term oriented; Hong Kong Chinese combine large power distance with weak uncertainty avoidance, collectivism, and are very long-term oriented; and so on.

The American culture profile is reflected in American management theories. I will just mention three elements not necessarily present in other countries: the stress on market processes, the stress on the individual, and the focus on managers rather than on workers.

The Stress on Market Processes   During the 1970s and 1980s it has become fashionable in the United States to look at organizations from a "transaction costs" viewpoint. Economist Oliver Williamson has opposed "hierarchies" to "markets." The reasoning is that human social life consists of economic transactions between individuals. We found the same in d'Iribarne's description of the U.S. principle of the contract between employer and employee, the labor market in which the worker sells his or her labor for a price. These individuals will form hierarchical organizations when the cost of the economic transactions (such as getting information, finding out whom to trust etc.) is lower in a hierarchy than when all transactions would take place on a free market.

From a cultural perspective the important point is that the "market" is the point of departure or base model, and the organization is explained from market failure. A culture that produces such a theory is likely to prefer organizations that internally resemble markets to organizations that internally resemble more structured models, like those in Germany of France. The ideal principle of control in organizations in the market philosophy is competition between individuals. This philosophy fits a society that combines a not-too-large power distance with a not-too-strong uncertainty avoidance and individualism; besides the United States, it will fit all other Anglo countries.

The Stress on the Individual   I find this constantly in the design of research projects and hypotheses; also in the fact that in the United States, psychology is clearly a more respectable discipline in management circles than sociology. Culture however is a collective phenomenon. Although we may get our information about culture from individuals, we have to interpret it at the level of collectivities. There are snags here known as the "ecological fallacy" and the "reverse ecological fallacy." None of the U.S. college textbooks on methodology I know deals sufficiently with the problem of multilevel analysis.

Culture can be compared to a forest, while individuals are trees. A forest is not just a bunch of trees: it is a symbiosis of different trees, bushes, plants, insects, animals, and micro-organism, and we miss the essence of the forest if we only describe its most typical trees. In the same way, a culture cannot be satisfactorily described in terms of the characteristics of a typical individual. There is a tendency in the U.S. management literature to overlook the forest for the trees and to ascribe cultural differences to interactions among individuals.

A striking example is found in the otherwise excellent book *Organizational Culture and Leadership* by Edgar H. Schein (1985). On the basis of his consulting experience he compares two large companies, nicknamed "Action" and "Multi." He explains the differences in culture between these companies by the group dynamics in their respective boardrooms. Nowhere in the book are any conclusions drawn from the fact that the first company is an American-based computer firm, and the second a Swiss-based pharmaceutics firm. This information is not even mentioned. A stress on interactions among individuals obviously fits a culture identified as the most individualistic in the world, but it will not be so well understood by the four-fifths of the world population for whom the group prevails over the individual.

One of the conclusions of my own multilevel research has been that culture at the national level and culture at the organizational level—corporate culture—are two very different phenomena and that the use of a common term for both is confusing. If we do use the common term, we should also pay attention to the occupational and the gender level of culture. National cultures differ primarily in the fundamental, invisible values held by a majority of their members, acquired in early childhood, whereas organizational cultures are a much more superficial phenomenon residing mainly in the visible practices of the organization, acquired by socialization of the new members who join as young adults. National cultures change only very slowly if at all; organizational cultures may be consciously changed, although this isn't necessarily easy. This difference between the two types of culture is the secret of the existence of multinational corporations that employ, as I showed in the IBM case, employees with extremely different national cultural values. What keeps them together is a corporate culture based on common practices.

The Stress on Managers Rather than Workers   The core element of a work organization around the world is the people who do the work. All the rest is superstructure, and I hope to have demonstrated to you that it may take many different shapes. In the U.S. literature on work organization, however, the core element, if not explicitly then implicitly, is considered the manager. This may well be the result of the combination of extreme individualism with fairly strong masculinity, which has turned the manager into a culture hero of almost mythical proportions. For example, he—not really she—is supposed to make decisions all the time. Those of you who are or have been managers must know that this is a fable. Very few management decisions are just "made" as the myth suggests it.

Managers are much more involved in maintaining networks; if anything, it is the rank-and-file work-er who can really make decisions on his or her own, albeit on a relatively simple level.

An amusing effect of the U.S. focus on managers is that in at least 10 American books and arti-cles on management I have been misquoted as having studied IBM managers in my research, where-as the book clearly describes that the answers were from IBM employees. My observation may be biased, but I get the impression that compared to 20 or 30 years ago less research in this country is done among employees and more on managers. But managers derive their raison d'être from the people managed: Culturally, they are the followers of the people they lead, and their effectiveness depends on the latter. In other parts of the world, this exclusive focus on the manager is less strong, with Japan as the supreme example.

CONCLUSION

This article started with *Alice in Wonderland*. In fact, the management theorist who ventures outside his or her own country into other parts of the world is like Alice in Wonderland. He or she will meet strange beings, customs, ways of organizing or disorganizing and theories that are clearly stupid, old-fashioned or even immoral—yet they may work, or at least they may not fail more frequently than corresponding theories do at home. Then, after the first culture shock, the traveller to Wonderland will feel enlightened, and may be able to take his or her experiences home and use them advantageously. All great ideas in science, politics, and management have travelled from one country to another, and been enriched by foreign influences. The roots of American management theories are mainly in Eu-rope: with Adam Smith, John Stuart Mill, Lev Tolstoy, Max Weber, Henri Fayol, Sigmund Freud, Kurt Lewin and many others. These theories were re-planted here and they developed and bore fruit. The same may happen again. The last thing we need is a Monroe doctrine for management ideas.

Beyond sophisticated stereotyping: Cultural sensemaking in context*

Joyce S. Osland
Allan Bird

If U.S. Americans are so individualistic and believe so deeply in self-reliance, why do they have the highest percentage of charitable giving in the world and readily volunteer their help to community projects and emergencies?

In a 1991 survey, many Costa Rican customers preferred automatic tellers over human tellers be-cause "at least the machines are programmed to say 'good morning' and 'thank you.'"[1] Why is it that so many Latin American cultures are noted for warm interpersonal relationships and a cultural script of simpatía (positive social behavior),[2] while simultaneously exhibiting seeming indifference as ser-vice workers in both the private and public sectors?

Based on Hofstede's[3] value dimension of Uncertainty Avoidance, the Japanese have a low toler-ance for uncertainty while Americans have a high tolerance. Why then do the Japanese intentionally incorporate ambiguous clauses in their business contracts, which are unusually short, while Americans dot every *i*, cross every *t*, and painstakingly spell out every possible contingency?

*Reprinted with permission from the *Academy of Management Executive 14*, no. 1 (2000): 65–77.

Many people trained to work in these cultures found such situations to be paradoxical when they first encountered them. These examples often contradict and confound our attempts to neatly categorize cultures. They violate our conceptions of what we think particular cultures are like. Constrained, stereotypical thinking is not the only problem, however. The more exposure and understanding one gains about any culture, the more paradoxical it often becomes. For example, U.S. Americans are individualistic in some situations (e.g., "the most comprehensive of rights and the right most valued is the right to be left alone"[4]) and collectivist in others (e.g., school fundraising events).

Long-term sojourners and serious cultural scholars find it difficult to make useful generalizations since so many exceptions and qualifications to the stereotypes, on both a cultural and individual level, come to mind. These cultural paradoxes are defined as situations that exhibit an apparently contradictory nature.

Surprisingly, there is little mention of cultural paradoxes in the management literature.[5] Our long-term sojourns as expatriates (a combined total of 22 years), as well as our experience in teaching cross-cultural management, preparing expatriates to go overseas, and doing comparative research, has led us to feel increasingly frustrated with the accepted conceptualizations of culture. Thus, our purpose is to focus attention on cultural paradoxes, explain why they have been overlooked and why they exist, and present a framework for making sense of them. Our intent is to initiate a dialogue that will eventually provide teachers, researchers, and people who work across cultures with a more useful way to understand culture.

A look at the comparative literature reveals that cultures are described in somewhat limited terms.[6] There are 22 dimensions commonly used to compare cultures, typically presented in the form of bipolar continua, with midpoints in the first examples, as shown in Table 1. These dimensions were developed to yield greater cultural understanding and allow for cross-cultural comparisons. An unanticipated consequence of using these dimensions, however, is the danger of stereotyping entire cultures.

TABLE 1   Common Cultural Dimensions

Subjugation to nature	Harmony	Mastery of nature
Past	Present	Future
Being	Containing and controlling	Doing
Hierarchical relationships	Group	Individualistic
Private space	Mixed	Public
Evil human nature	Neutral or mixed	Good
Human nature as changeable		Human nature as unchangeable
Monochronic time		Polychronic time
High-context language		Low-context language
Low uncertainty avoidance		High uncertainty avoidance
Low power distance		High power distance
Short-term orientation		Long-term orientation
Individualism		Collectivism
Masculinity		Femininity
Universalism		Particularism
Neutral		Emotional
Diffuse		Specific
Achievement		Ascription
Individualism		Organization
Inner-directed		Outer-directed
Individualism (competition)		Group-organization (collusion)
Analyzing (reductivist)		Synthesizing (larger, integrated wholes)

Sources: Kluckhohn and Strodtbeck (1961); Hall and Hall (1990); Hofstede (1980); Parsons and Shils (1951); Trompenaars and Hampden Turner (1993); Trompenaars (1994). The dimensions are bipolar continua, with the first six containing midpoints.

SOPHISTICATED STEREOTYPING

In many parts of the world, one hears a generic stereotype for a disliked neighboring ethnic group—"The (fill in the blank) are lazy, dirty thieves, and their women are promiscuous." This is a low-level form of stereotyping, often based on lack of personal contact and an irrational dislike of people who are different from oneself. Professors and trainers work very hard to dispel such stereotypes. Rarely, however, do we stop to consider whether we are supplanting one form of stereotyping for another. For example, when we teach students and managers how to perceive the Israelis using Hofstede's[7] cultural dimensions, they may come to think of Israelis in terms of small power distance, strong uncertainty avoidance, moderate femininity, and moderate individualism. The result is to reduce a complex culture to a shorthand description they may he tempted to apply to all Israelis. We call this sophisticated stereotyping, because it is based on theoretical concepts and lacks the negative attributions often associated with its lower-level counterpart. Nevertheless, it is still limiting in the way it constrains individuals' perceptions of behavior in another culture.

Do we recommend against teaching the cultural dimensions shown in Table 1 so as to avoid sophisticated stereotyping? Not at all. These dimensions are useful tools in explaining cultural behavior. Indeed, cultural stereotypes can be helpful—provided we acknowledge their limitations. They are more beneficial, for example, in making comparisons between cultures than in understanding the wide variations of behavior within a single culture. Adler[8] encourages the use of "helpful stereotypes," which have the following limitations: They are consciously held, descriptive rather than evaluative, accurate in their description of a behavioral norm, the first best guess about a group prior to having direct information about the specific people involved, and modified based on further observations and experience. As teachers, researchers, and managers in cross-cultural contexts, we need to recognize that our original characterizations of other cultures are best guesses that we need to modify as we gain more experience.

For understandable, systemic reasons, business schools tend to teach culture in simple-minded terms, glossing over nuances and ignoring complexities. An examination of the latest crop of organizational behavior and international business textbooks revealed that most authors present only Hofstede's cultural dimensions, occasionally supplemented by Hall's theory of high- and low-context cultures.[9] Although these disciplines are not charged with the responsibility of teaching culture in great depth, these are the principal courses in many curricula where business students are exposed to cross-cultural concepts. Another handicap is that many business professors do not receive a thorough grounding in culture in their own disciplines and doctoral programs. One could further argue that we are joined in this conspiracy to give culture a quick-and-dirty treatment by practitioners and students who are looking for ways to simplify and make sense of the world.

The limitations of sophisticated stereotyping become most evident when we confront cultural paradoxes. This is the moment we realize our understanding is incomplete, misleading, and potentially dangerous. Perhaps because cultural paradoxes reveal the limitations in our thinking, they are often left unmentioned, even though virtually anyone with experience in another culture can usually identify one or two after only a moment's reflection.

WHY DON'T WE KNOW MORE ABOUT CULTURAL PARADOXES?

With one exception,[10] the cross-cultural literature contains no mention or explanation of cultural paradoxes. This absence can be explained by:

- Homegrown perceptual schemas that result in cultural myopia
- Lack of cultural experience that leads to misinterpretation and failure to comprehend the entire picture
- Cultural learning that plateaus before complete understanding is achieved
- Western dualism that generates theories with no room for paradox or holistic maps

- Features of cross-cultural research that encourage simplicity over complexity
- A between-culture research approach that is less likely to capture cultural paradoxes than a within-culture approach.

PERCEPTUAL SCHEMAS

When outsiders look at another culture, they inevitably interpret its institutions and customs using their own lenses and schemas; cultural myopia and lack of experience prevent them from seeing all the nuances of another culture.

In particular, a lack of experience with the new culture creates difficulties for new expatriates trying to make sense of what they encounter. The situation is analogous to putting together a jigsaw puzzle. Though one may have the picture on the puzzle box as a guide, making sense of each individual piece and understanding where and how it fits is exceedingly difficult. As more pieces are put into place, however, it is easier to see the bigger picture and understand how individual pieces mesh. Similarly, as one acquires more and varied experiences in the new culture, one can develop an appreciation for how certain attitudes and behaviors fit the puzzle and create an internal logic of the new culture.

The danger with sophisticated stereotyping is that it may lead individuals·to think that the number of shapes that pieces may take is limited and that pieces fit together rather easily. As Barnlund notes: "Rarely do the descriptions of a political structure or religious faith explain precisely when and why certain topics are avoided or why specific gestures carry such radically different meanings according to the context in which they appear."[11]

Expatriates and researchers alike tend to focus first on cultural differences and make initial conclusions that are not always modified in light of subsequent evidence.[12] Proactive learning about another culture often stops once a survival threshold is attained, perhaps because of an instinctive inclination to simplify a complex world. This may lead us to seek black-and-white answers rather than tolerate the continued ambiguity that typifies a more complete understanding of another culture.

One of the best descriptions of the peeling away of layers that characterizes deeper cultural understanding is found in a fictionalized account of expatriate life written by an expatriate manager, Robert Collins.[13] He outlines ascending levels on a Westerner's perception scale of Japanese culture that alternate, in daisy-petal-plucking fashion, between seeing the Japanese as significantly different or not really that different at all:

> The initial Level on a Westerner's perception scale clearly indicates a "difference" of great significance. The Japanese speak a language unlike any other human tongue ... they write the language in symbols that reason alone cannot decipher. The airport customs officers all wear neckties, everyone is in a hurry, and there are long lines everywhere.
>
> Level Two is represented by the sudden awareness that the Japanese are not different at all. Not at all. They ride in elevators, have a dynamic industrial/trade/financial system, own great chunks of the United States, and serve cornflakes in the Hotel Okura.
>
> Level Three is the "hey, wait a minute" stage. The Japanese come to all the meetings, smile politely, nod in agreement with everything said, but do the opposite of what's expected. And they do it all together. They really are different.
>
> But are they? Level Four understanding recognizes the strong group dynamics, common education and training, and the general sense of loyalty to the family—which in their case is Japan itself. That's not so unusual, things are just organized on a larger scale than any social unit in the West. Nothing is fundamentally different.
>
> Level Five can blow one's mind, however. Bank presidents skipping through streets dressed as dragons at festival time; single ladies placing garlands of flowers around huge, and remarkably

graphic, stone phallic symbols; Ministry of Finance officials rearranging their bedrooms so as to sleep in a "lucky" direction; it is all somewhat odd. At least, by Western standards. There is something different in the air.

And so on. Some Westerners, the old Japan hands, have gotten as far as Levels 37 or 38.[14]

The point of Collins's description is that it takes time and experience to make sense of another culture. The various levels he describes reflect differing levels of awareness as more and more pieces of the puzzle are put into place. Time and experience are essential because culture is embedded in the context. Without context it makes little sense to talk about culture. Yet just as its lower-order counterpart does, sophisticated stereotyping tends to strip away or ignore context. Thus, cognitive schemas prevent sojourners and researchers from seeing and correctly interpreting paradoxical behavior outside their own cultures.

THEORETICAL LIMITATIONS

Another reason for the inattention to cultural paradoxes stems from the intersection between cognitive schemas and theory. Westerners have a tendency to perceive stimuli in terms of dichotomies and dualisms rather than paradoxes or holistic pictures.[15] The idea of paradox is a fairly recent wrinkle on the intellectual landscape of management theorists[16] and has not yet been incorporated into cultural theories in a managerial context.

Cross-cultural research is generally held to be more difficult than domestic studies. Hofstede's[17] work represented a major step forward and launched a deluge of studies utilizing his dimensions. Hundreds of studies have used one or more of Hofstede's dimensions to explore similarities and differences across cultures regarding numerous aspects of business and management. However, Hofstede himself warned against expecting too much of these dimensions and of using them incorrectly. For example, he defended the individualism-collectivism dimension as a useful construct, but then went on to say: "This does not mean, of course, that a country's Individual Index score tells all there is to be known about the backgrounds and structure of relationship patterns in that country. It is an abstraction that should not be extended beyond its limited area of usefulness."[18]

When we fail to specify under what conditions a culture measures low or high on any of the common cultural dimensions, or to take into consideration the impact of organizational culture, it misleads rather than increases our understanding of comparisons of culture and business practices. Such an approach prevents rather than opens up opportunities for learning and exploration.

A final explanation for the failure to address cultural paradoxes can be traced to the emic/etic distinction commonly used in the cultural literature. An emic perspective looks at a culture from within its boundaries, whereas an etic perspective stands outside and compares two or more cultures. To make between-culture differences more prominent, the etic approach minimizes the inconsistencies within a culture. Most cultural approaches in management adopt a between-culture approach, playing down the within-culture differences that expatriates must understand in order to work successfully in the host country.

Anthropologist Claude Levi-Strauss warned that explanation does not consist of reducing the complex to the simple, but of substituting a more intelligible complexity for one that is less intelligible.[19] In failing to acknowledge cultural paradoxes or the complexity surrounding cultural dimensions, we may settle for simplistic, rather than intelligently complex, explanations.

SOURCES OF PARADOX IN CULTURAL BEHAVIOR

Behavior that looks paradoxical to an expatriate in the initial stages of cultural awareness may simply reflect the variance in behavioral norms for individuals, organizational cultures, subcultures, as well as generational differences and changing sections of the society. In addition, expatriates may also form microcultures[20] with specific members of the host culture. The cultural synergy of such microcultures may not be reflective of the national culture. These false paradoxes need to be discarded before more substantive paradoxes can be evaluated.

Based on an analysis of all the paradoxes we could find, we have identified six possible explanations for cultural behaviors that appear truly paradoxical. They are:

- The tendency for observers to confuse individual with group values
- Unresolved cultural issues
- Bipolar patterns
- Role differences
- Real versus espoused values
- Value trumping, a recognition that in specific contexts certain sets of values take precedence over others.

Confusing individual with group values is exemplified by the personality dimension labeled allocentrism versus idiocentrism, which is the psychological, individual-level analog to the individualism-collectivism dimension at the level of culture.[21] Allocentric people, those who pay primary attention to the needs of a group, can be found in individualistic cultures, and idiocentric people, those who pay more attention to their own needs than to the needs of others, in collectivist cultures. What we perceive as cultural paradox may not reflect contradictions in cultural values, but instead may reveal the natural diversity within any culture that reflects individual personality and variation.

Unresolved cultural issues are rooted in the definition of culture as a learned response to problems. Some paradoxes come from problems for which there is no clear, happy solution. Cultures may manifest a split personality with regard to an unresolved problem.[22] As a result, they shuttle back and forth from one extreme to the other on a behavioral continuum. U.S. Americans, for example, have ambivalent views about sex, and, as one journalist recently noted: "Our society is a stew of prurience and prudery."[23] Censorship, fears about sex education, and sexual taboos coexist uncomfortably with increasingly graphic films and TV shows and women's magazines that never go to press without a feature article devoted to sex. This melange is more than a reflection of a diverse society that has both hedonists and fundamentalists with differing views of sex; both groups manifest inconsistent behaviors and attitudes about sex, signaling an enduring cultural inability to resolve this issue.

Bipolar patterns make cultural behavior appear paradoxical because cultural dimensions are often framed, perhaps inaccurately, as dualistic, either-or continua. Cultures frequently exhibit one of these paired dimensions more than the other, but it is probable that both ends of the dimensions are found in cultures—but only in particular contexts. For example, in Latin America, ascribed status, derived from class and family background, is more important than its polar opposite, achieved status, which is based on talent and hard work. When it comes to professional soccer, however, achieved status trumps class and ascription.

Often some groups and roles appear to deviate from cultural stereotypes. For example, in the United States, autocratic behavior is frequently tolerated in CEOs, even though the United States is characterized as an egalitarian culture. Such behavior may also be an example of a high power distance context in a low power distance culture: We accept that CEOs possess an unequal degree of power and that they will behave in a different manner than most U.S. Americans.

There is also a difference between real versus espoused values. All cultures express preferences for ideal behaviors—for what should be valued and how people should act. Nevertheless, people do not always act consistently with ideal behaviors and values. For example, U.S. Americans may simultaneously pay lip service to the importance of equality (an espoused value), while trying to acquire more power or influence for themselves (a real value).

A final possible explanation of cultural paradoxes derives from a holistic, contextual view of culture in which values co-exist as a constellation, but their salience differs depending on the situation.

Using the Gestalt concept of figure-ground, at times a particular value becomes dominant (figure), while in other circumstances, this same value recedes into the background (ground).[24] In India, for example, collectivism is figural when individuals are expected to make sacrifices for their families or for the larger society—such as Hindu sons who postpone marriage until their sisters marry, or daughters who stay single to care for their parents. In other circumstances, however, collectivism fades into the background and individualism comes to the fore and is figural when Indians focus more upon self-realization—for example, elderly men who detach themselves from their family to seek salvation.[25] Taking the figure-ground analogy a step further, depending on the context, one cultural value might trump another, lessening the influence another value normally exerts.[26] For example, we find it useful to view culture as a series of card games in which cultural values or dimensions are individual cards. Depending on the game, previous play, and the hand one is dealt, players respond by choosing specific cards that seem most appropriate in a given situation. Sometimes a particular card trumps the others; in another round, it does not. In a given context, specific cultural values come into play and have more importance than other values. To a foreigner who does not understand enough about the cultural context to interpret why or when one value takes precedence over another, such behavior looks paradoxical. Members of the culture learn these nuances more or less automatically. For example, children learn in what context a socially acceptable white lie is more important than always telling the truth. A true understanding of the logic of another culture includes comprehending the interrelationships among values, or how values relate to one another in a given context.

A MODEL OF CULTURAL SENSEMAKING

To make sense of cultural paradoxes and convey a holistic understanding of culture, we propose a model of cultural sensemaking. The model shown in Figure 1 helps explain how culture is embedded in context.[27] Cultural sensemaking is a cycle of sequential events:

- **Indexing Context**   The process begins when an individual identifies a context and then engages in indexing behavior, which involves noticing or attending to stimuli that provide cues about the situation. For example, to index the context of a meeting with a subordinate, we consider characteristics such as prior events (recent extensive layoffs), the nature of the boss-subordinate relationship within and without work (golfing partner), the specific topic under discussion (employee morale), and the location of the interaction (boss's office).
- **Making Attributions**   The next step is attribution, a process in which contextual cues are analyzed in order to match the context with appropriate schema. The matching process is moderated

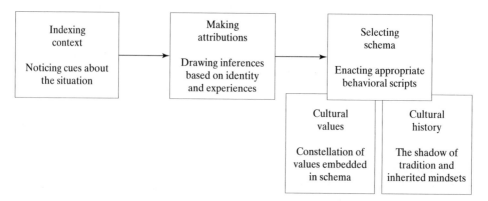

FIGURE 1   **Cultural Sensemaking Model**

or influenced by one's social identity (e.g., ethnic or religious background, gender, social class, organizational affiliation) and one's history (e.g., experiences and chronology). A senior U.S. American manager who fought against the Japanese in World War II will make different attributions about context and employ different schema when he meets with a Japanese manager than will a Japanese-American manager of his generation, or a junior U.S. manager whose personal experience with Japan is limited to automobiles, electronics, and sushi.

- **Selecting Schema**   Schemas are cultural scripts, "a pattern of social interaction that is characteristic of a particular cultural group."[28] They are accepted and appropriate ways of behaving, specifying certain patterns of interaction. From personal or vicarious experience, we learn how to select schema. By watching and working with bosses, for example, we develop scripts for how to act when we take on that role ourselves. We learn appropriate vocabulary and gestures, which then elicit a fairly predictable response from others.

- **The Influence of Cultural Values**   Schemas reflect an underlying hierarchy of cultural values. For example, people working for U.S. managers who have a relaxed and casual style and who openly share information and provide opportunities to make independent decisions will learn specific scripts for managing in this fashion. The configuration of values embedded in this management style consists of informality, honesty, equality, and individualism. At some point, however, these same managers may withhold information about a sensitive personnel situation because privacy, fairness, and legal concerns would trump honesty and equality in this context. This trumping action explains why the constellation of values related to specific schema is hierarchical.

- **The Influence of Cultural History**   When decoding schema, we may also find vestiges of cultural history and tradition. Mindsets inherited from previous generations explain how history is remembered.[29] For example, perceptions about a colonial era may still have an impact on schemas, particularly those involving interactions with foreigners, even though a country gained its independence centuries ago.

SOME ILLUSTRATIONS OF SENSEMAKING

Sensemaking involves placing stimuli into a framework that enables people "to comprehend, understand, explain, attribute, extrapolate, and predict."[30] Let's analyze each of the cultural paradoxes presented in the introduction using the sensemaking model. In the United States, when a charity requests money, when deserving people are in need, or when disaster hits a community (indexing contexts), many U.S. Americans (e.g., religious, allocentric people making attributions) respond by donating their money, goods, or time (selecting schema). The values underlying this schema are humanitarian concern for others, altruism,[31] and collectivism (cultural values). Thus, individualism (a sophisticated stereotype) is moderated by a communal tradition that has its roots in religious and cultural origins (cultural history).

Fukuyama[32] writes that U.S. society has never been as individualistic as its citizens thought, because of the culture's relatively high level of trust and resultant social capital. The United States "has always possessed a rich network of voluntary associations and community structures to which individuals have subordinated their narrow interests."[33] Under normal conditions, one should take responsibility for oneself and not rely on others. However, some circumstances and tasks can overwhelm individual initiative and ingenuity. When that happens, people should help those in need, a lesson forged on the American frontier (cultural history). To further underscore the complexity of culture, in the same contexts noted above, the tax code and prestige associated with philanthropy (cultural history) may be the primary motivations for some citizens (e.g., idiocentric, upwardly ambitious people making attributions) to act charitably (selecting schema), but the value underlying the schema would be individualism.

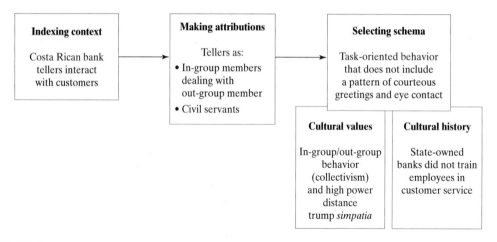

FIGURE 2   **Making Sense of Paradoxical Behavior: Seemingly Indifferent Customer Service in a Culture Characterized by Positive, Warm Relations**

The Costa Rican example is illustrated in Figure 2. When bank tellers interact with clients (indexing context) many of them (e.g., members of various in-groups, civil servants making attributions) do not greet customers and make eye contact, but concentrate solely on their paperwork (selecting schema). The values that underlie this schema are in-group-out-group behavior[34] and power (cultural values). In collectivist cultures such as Costa Rica, members identify strongly with their in-group and treat members with warmth and cooperation. In stark contrast, out-group members are often treated with hostility, distrust, and a lack of cooperation. Customers are considered as strangers and out-group members who do not warrant the special treatment given to in-group members (family and friends). One of the few exceptions to simpatía and personal dignity in Costa Rica, and Latin America generally, is rudeness sometimes expressed by people in positions of power.[35] In this context, the cultural value of high power distance (the extent to which a society accepts the fact that power in institutions and organizations is distributed unequally)[36] trumps simpatía. Whereas simpatía lessens the distance between people, the opposite behavior increases the distance between the powerful and the powerless. Unlike many other contexts in Costa Rica, bank telling does not elicit a cultural script of simpatía, and state-owned banks did not have a history of training employees in friendly customer service (cultural history) at this time.

In the third cultural example, when Japanese business people make contracts (indexing context), they (e.g., business people making attributions) opt for ambiguous contracts (selecting schema). The dominant value underlying this schema is collectivism (cultural value). In this context, collectivism is manifested as a belief that those entering into agreement are joined together and share something in common; thus, they should rely on and trust one another. Collectivism trumps high uncertainty avoidance (sophisticated stereotype) in this context, but uncertainty avoidance is not completely absent. Some of the uncertainty surrounding the contract is dealt with upstream in the process by carefully choosing and getting to know business partners, and by using third parties. An additional consideration is that many Japanese like flexible contracts, because they have a greater recognition of the limits of contracts and the difficulties of foreseeing all contingencies (cultural history). Even though U.S. Americans are typically more tolerant of uncertainty (sophisticated stereotype), they value pragmatism and do not like to take unnecessary risks (cultural values). If a deal falls through, they rely on the legal system for a resolution (cultural history).

WORKING FROM A SENSEMAKING APPROACH

Sophisticated stereotypes are useful in the initial stages of making sense of complex behaviors within cultures. However, rather than stereotyping cultures somewhere along a continuum, we can advance understanding by thinking in terms of specific contexts that feature particular cultural values that then govern behavior. Geertz maintains that "culture is best seen not as complexes of concrete behavior patterns—customs, usages, traditions, habit clusters—as has by and large been the case up to now, but as a set of control mechanisms—plans, recipes, rules, instructions (what computer engineers call *programs*)—for the governing of behavior."[37]

Understanding the control mechanisms within a culture requires the acquisition of attributional knowledge, the awareness of contextually appropriate behavior.[38] This is in contrast to factual knowledge and conceptual knowledge. Factual knowledge consists of descriptions of behaviors and attitudes. For example, it is a fact that Japanese use small groups extensively in the workplace. Conceptual knowledge consists of a culture's views and values about central concerns. Sophisticated stereotyping operates in the realm of conceptual knowledge. This category of knowledge is an organizing tool, but it is not sufficient for true cultural understanding. Knowing that the Japanese are a communal society (conceptual knowledge) does not explain the noncommunal activities that exist in Japanese organizations or when the Japanese will or will not be communal. For example, why are quality control circles used in some work settings and not in others? Factual and conceptual knowledge about Japanese culture cannot answer that question; only attributional knowledge can.

Managers can acquire attributional knowledge from personal experience, vicariously from others' experience, and from cultural mentoring. The personal experience method involves carefully observing how people from another culture act and react, and then formulating and reformulating hypotheses and cultural explanations for the observed behavior. When expatriates test their hypotheses and find them valid, they form schemas about specific events in the host culture.

One can learn vicariously by reading about other cultures, but the best form of vicarious learning is via cultural assimilator exercises.[39] These are critical incidents of cross-cultural encounters, accompanied by alternative explanations for the behavior of people from the foreign culture. After choosing what they perceive as the most likely answer, trainees then read expert opinions relating why each answer is adequate or inadequate. These opinions are validated by cross-cultural experts and include information about the relative importance of cultural dimensions or context-specific customs in the culture in question.

A cultural mentor can be viewed as a hybrid of vicarious and personal acquisition of attributional knowledge—a sort of live cultural assimilator. Cultural mentors are usually long-term expatriates or members of the foreign culture. The latter are often helpful souls who have lived abroad themselves and understand the challenge of mastering another culture or people not totally in step with their own culture.[40] "They interpret the local culture for expatriates and guide them through its shoals, as well as providing them with the necessary encouragement when it feels like the expatriates will never 'break the code' of another culture and fit in comfortably."[41] Reading an explanation from a book or working through a series of cultural assimilators is different from receiving an explanation of an experience the expatriate has personally lived through and now wishes to understand. Cultural mentors can correct inaccurate hypotheses about the local culture. Expatriates who had cultural mentors overseas have been found to fare better than those who did not have such mentors: They were more fluent in the foreign language; they perceived themselves as better adapted to their work and general living conditions abroad; they were more aware of the paradoxes of expatriate life, indicating a higher degree of acculturation and understanding of the other culture; and they received higher performance appraisal ratings from both their superiors and themselves.[42]

In spite of the benefits of mentoring, few multinationals formally assign a cultural mentor to their expatriates. Yet another way of developing an expatriate's attributional knowledge is to provide more training in the host country rather than relying solely an predeparture culture "inoculations."

Admittedly, there are trade-offs to developing attributional knowledge. The acquisition of cultural knowledge takes a good deal of time and energy, which is not available to all managers. Nor is it reasonable to expect employees who work with people from various cultures on a daily basis to master each culture. Nevertheless, organizing the knowledge they do acquire as context-specific schemas can speed up cultural learning and prevent confusion and errors in making sense of cultural paradoxes.

If we accept that cultures are paradoxical, then it follows that learning another culture occurs in a dialectical fashion—thesis, antithesis, and synthesis. Thesis entails a hypothesis involving a sophisticated stereotype; antithesis is the identification of an apparently oppositional cultural paradox. Synthesis involves making sense of contradictory behavior—understanding why certain values are more important in certain contexts. Behavior appears less paradoxical once the foreigner learns to index contexts and match them with the appropriate schemas in the same way that members of the host culture do. Collins's description of the Westerner's Perception Scale in comprehending Japanese culture[43] illustrates one form of dialectical culture learning, an upwardly spiraling cycle of cultural comprehension.

USING THE MODEL

Because this cultural sensemaking model provides a more complex way of understanding culture, it has clear implications for those who teach culture, for those who work across cultures, and for organizations that send expatriates overseas.

TEACHING ABOUT CULTURAL UNDERSTANDING

Sophisticated stereotyping should be the beginning of cultural learning, not the end, as is so often the case when teaching or learning about culture. Recognition of a more complex, holistic, sensemaking model of culture allows us to respond more effectively when students or trainees provide examples of paradoxes that seem to contradict cultural dimensions. The model also requires a somewhat different teaching approach. We have developed a sequential method that has been effective in our teaching:

- **Help students understand the complexity of their own culture**   To acquaint students with the vast challenge of comprehending culture, we begin with a thorough understanding of the internal logic of one's own culture and its socioeconomic, political, and historical roots. We add complexity by pointing out paradoxes as well as identifying regional, ethnic, religious, organizational, and individual variations in behavior. For example, when Thai students describe their culture as friendly, we ask the following series of questions: "Are all Thais friendly? Are Thais always friendly? Under what circumstances would Thais not exhibit friendly behavior? Why?"
- **Give students cultural dimensions and values as well as sophisticated stereotypes as basic tools**   These dimensions, including the values listed in Table 1, can then be used to explain contrasting behavior from two or more different cultures (e.g., what can sample obituaries from the United States and Mexico reveal about cultural values? What is the typical response of businesses in both countries when a member of an employee's family dies?). Students practice recognizing cultural dimensions in cross-cultural dialogues and cases and learn sophisticated stereotypes. This helps them gain conceptual knowledge about different cultures so they can make between-culture distinctions.
- **Develop students' skills in cultural observation and behavioral flexibility**   One of the difficulties expatriates confront in making sense of a new culture is the contradiction between the expected culture, the sophisticated stereotype taught in predeparture training or gleaned from others,

and the manifest culture, the one actually enacted in a situation.[44] To help students become skilled at observing and decoding other cultures, teach them to think more like anthropologists and give them practice in honing observational and interpretive skills. To help students develop the behavioral flexibility needed to adapt to unanticipated situations, role-playing and videos of cross-cultural interactions can be used.

- **Have students do an in-depth study or experience with one culture**   To go beyond sophisticated stereotypes, students learn the internal logic and cultural history of a single culture. They acquire attributional knowledge from cultural mentors and/or cultural immersion, in addition to extensive research.

- **Focus on learning context-appropriate behavior in other cultures and developing cultural hypotheses and explanations for paradoxical behavior**   Once students have mastered the preceding steps, the emphasis changes to learning schemas for different contexts. For example, student teams are instructed to deliberately demonstrate incorrect behavior; they ask others to point out the mistakes and then replay the scene using correct behavior. To model the crucial behavior of asking for help in understanding cultural mysteries,[45] students use cultural mentors to explain situations they choose to learn about (e.g., "How do managers in _____ encourage employees to perform at high levels? Why does that work for them?") The variation in the mentors' answers ("Some managers are successful doing this while others ... ") and the qualified answers ("This seems to work unless ... ; it depends on ... ") helps students develop more complex understandings of the other culture. To highlight the message of moving beyond cultural stereotypes, use language that focuses on forming and testing hypotheses about contextual behavior: "What are your hypotheses about why a French employee behaves this way in this situation? How can you find out if these hypotheses are correct?"

SENSEMAKING FOR INDIVIDUALS WORKING ACROSS CULTURES

After the training program, and once on assignment in a new culture, this cultural sensemaking approach has other practical implications.

- **Approach learning another culture more like a scientist who holds conscious stereotypes and hypotheses in order to test them**   One of the key differences between managers who were identified by their fellow MBA students as the "most internationally effective" and the "least internationally effective" is that the former changed their stereotypes of other nationalities as they interacted with them while the latter did not.[46]

- **Seek out cultural mentors and people who possess attributional knowledge about cultures**   Perhaps one of the basic lessons of cross-cultural interaction is that tolerance and effectiveness result from greater understanding of another culture. Making sense of a culture's internal logic and decoding cultural paradoxes is easiest with the aid of a willing and knowledgeable informant.

- **Analyze disconfirming evidence and instances that defy cultural stereotypes**   Even people with a great deal of experience in another culture can benefit from analyzing cultural paradoxes. For instance, the question, "In what circumstances do Latin Americans fail to exhibit *simpatía*?" led to a more complex cultural understanding for one of the authors, who had already spent nine curious years in that region. Once expatriates can function reasonably well in another culture, it is easy for them to reach plateaus in their cultural understanding and mistakenly assume that they comprehend the entire puzzle. This presents a danger when expatriates inadvertently pass on inaccurate information about the local culture, or make faulty, and even expensive, business decisions based on partial understandings.

- **Learn cultural schemas that will help you be effective**   Knowing how to act appropriately in specific cross-cultural settings results in self-confidence and effectiveness. One cannot memorize all the rules in another culture, but understanding the values that underlie most schemas can often prevent us from making serious mistakes.

How Multinational Organizations Can Use the Sensemaking Model

The cultural sensemaking model also has practical implications for multinational organizations.

- **Use cognitive complexity as a selection criterion for expatriates and people in international positions** Avoid black-and-white thinkers in favor of people who exhibit cognitive complexity, which involves the ability to handle ambiguity and multiple viewpoints. This skill is better suited to a thesis-antithesis approach to understanding the paradoxical nature of culture.
- **Provide in-country cultural training for expatriates that goes beyond factual and conceptual knowledge** Predeparture cultural training is complemented by on-site training, which has the advantage of good timing. In-country culture training takes place when expatriates are highly motivated to find answers to real cultural dilemmas and when they are ready for greater complexity.[47]
- **Gauge the cultural knowledge possessed by expatriates within a country** The accuracy and depth of one's cultural understanding is not always linked to the time one has spent in another country; it depends on the degree of involvement with the other culture as well as cultural curiosity and desire to learn. Nevertheless, when companies determine the optimum length of overseas assignments, they should consider how much time is generally necessary to function effectively in a particular culture. If a firm's expatriates stay abroad for only two years, it is less likely that a deep understanding of the culture will be shared among them than if they were to stay for longer periods. As long as the longer-term expatriates do not stop at a low-level plateau of cultural learning, mixing short-term (2-3 years) with. longer-term expatriates (6-7 years) with permanent expatriates could produce more shared organizational learning about the culture. It is also essential to recognize that expatriates working for the same organization may he at different levels of cultural understanding.
- **Act like learning organizations with regard to cultural knowledge** Multinationals benefit from formal mechanisms to develop a more complex understanding of the cultures where they do business through such methods as cultural mentors and in-country cultural training. There should also be mechanisms for sharing cultural knowledge. For example, having returned expatriates give formal debriefing sessions in which they report what they learned in their assignment increases the company's collective cultural knowledge and eases the expatriates' transition home by helping them make sense of a highly significant experience.[48]

ENDNOTES

[1] This was one of the findings of a class research project on the acceptance of ATMs by Dr. Osland's graduate students at INCAE's (Central American Institute of Business Administration) Banking Program in 1991.

[2] J. C. Triandis, G. Marin, J. Lisansky, and H. Betancourt, "Simpatía as a Cultural Script of Hispanics," *Journal of Personality and Social Psychology 47*, no. 6 (1984): 1363–1375.

[3] G. Hofstede, *Culture's Consequences: International Differences in Work Related Values* (Beverly Hills: Sage, 1980).

[4] *Olmstead v. United States*, 277 U.S. 438, 478 (1928) (J. Brandeis, dissenting).

[5] The descriptions of cultural metaphors in *Understanding Global Cultures: Metaphorical Journeys Through 17 Countries* (Thousand Oaks, CA: Sage, 1994) by Martin Gannon and his associates, contain passing references to paradoxes, but do not address the issue directly.

[6] T. Parsons and E. Shils, *Toward a General Theory of Action* (Cambridge: Harvard University Press, 1951); F. Kluckhohn and F. L. Strodtbeck, *Variations in Value Orientations* (Evanston, IL: Row, Peterson, 1961); Hofstede; H. C. Triandis, "Dimensions of Cultural Variations as Parameters of Organizational Theories," *International Studies of Management and Organization 12,* no. 4 (1982): 139–169; S. Ronen and O. Shenkar, "Clustering Countries

on Attitudinal Dimensions: A Review and Synthesis," *Academy of Management Review 10* (1985): 435–454; E. T. Hall and M. R. Hall, *Understanding Cultural Differences* (Yarmouth, ME: Intercultural Press, 1990); A. P. Fiske, "The Four Elementary Forms of Sociality: Framework For a Unified Theory of Social Relations," *Psychological Review 99*, no. 4 (1992): 689–723; S. Schwartz, "Universals in the Content and Structure of Values: Theoretical Advances and Empirical Tests in 20 Countries," *Advances in Experimental Social Psychology*, ed. M. Zanna (New York, NY: Academic Press, 1992): 1–66. F. Trompenaars and C. Hampden Turner, *The Seven Cultures of Capitalism* (New York: Doubleday, 1993).

[7] Hofstede.

[8] N. Adler. *International Dimensions of Organizational Behavior*, 3rd ed. (Cincinnati: South-Western, 1997): 75–76.

[9] Hall and Hall.

[10] Gannon.

[11] D. Barnlund, *Public and Private Self in Japan and the United States* (Yarmouth, ME: Intercultural Press, 1975): 6.

[12] J. S. Osland, *The Adventure of Working Abroad: Hero Tales from the Global Frontier* (San Francisco: Jossey-Bass, 1995).

[13] R. J. Collins, *Max Danger: The Adventures of an Expat in Tokyo* (Rutland, VT: Charles E. Tuttle Co, 1987).

[14] Ibid, 14–15.

[15] R. C. Tripathi, "Aligning Development to Values in India." *Social Values and Development: Asian Perspectives*, eds. H. S. Sinha and R. Kao (New Delhi: Sage, 1988): 315–333; J. Wilbur, *A Brief History of Everything* (New York: Shambala 1995).

[16] R. Quinn and K. S. Cameron, eds. *Paradox and Transformation* (Cambridge, MA: Ballinger, 1988); K. K. Smith and D. N. Berg, *Paradoxes of Group Life* (San Francisco: Jossey-Bass, 1987).

[17] Hofstede.

[18] G. Hofstede, In U. Kim, H. S. Triandis, C. Kâgitçibasi, S. Choi, and G. Yoon, eds., *Individualism and Collectivism* (Thousand Oaks. CA: Sage, 1994): XI.

[19] C. Levi-Strauss, *La Pensée Sauvage* (Paris: Adler's Foreign Books, Inc., 1962).

[20] G. Fontaine, *Managing International Assignments: The Strategy for Success* (Upper Saddle River, NJ: Prentice Hall, 1989).

[21] H. C. Triandis, R. Bontempo, M. J. Villareal, M. Asai, and N. Lucca, "Individualism and Collectivism: Cross-Cultural Perspectives on Self-Ingroup Relationships," *Journal of Personality and Social Psychology 54* (1998): 323–338.

[22] G. Bateson, *Steps to an Ecology of Mind* (London: Paladin Books, 1973).

[23] J. Haught, "What Does Sex Have To Do with It?" *Oregonian*, December 29, 1993, D7.

[24] Tripathi, Marin et. al.

[25] Ibid.

[26] A. Bird, J. S. Osland, M. Mendenhall, and S. Schneider, "Adapting and Adjusting to Other Cultures: What We Know But Don't Always Tell," *Journal of Management Inquiry 8* (1999): 152–165.

[27] Context is also embedded in culture, so one could argue that the entire model is situated within the broader culture. For simplicity's sake, however, we chose to focus only on the sensemaking that occurs in deciphering cultural paradoxes.

[28] Triandis, Marin, et. al.

[29] G. Fisher, *Mindsets: The Role of Culture and Perception in International Relations* (Yarmouth, ME: Intercultural Press, 1997).

[30] W. H. Starbuck and F. J. Milliken, "Executives' Personal Filters: What They Notice and How They Make Sense," *The Executive Effect: Concepts and Methods for Studying Top Managers*, ed. D. Hambrick (Greenwich, CT: JAI Press, 1988): 51.

[31] Barnlund.

[32] F. Fukuyama, *Trust* (New York: Penguin Books, 1996).

[33] Ibid., 29.

[34] Triandis, et al.

[35] J. S. Osland, S. De Franco, and A. Osland, "Organizational Implications of Latin American Culture: Lessons for the Expatriate Manager," *Journal of Management Inquiry 8*, no. 2 (1999): 219–234.

[36] Hofstede, *Culture's Consequences*.

[37] C. Geertz, *The Interpretation of Cultures* (New York: HarperCollins Basic Books, 1973): 44.

[38] A. Bird, S. Heinbuch, R. Dunbar, and M. McNulty, "A Conceptual Model of the Effects of Area Studies Training Programs and a Preliminary Investigation of the Model's Hypothesized Relationships," *International Journal of Intercultural Relations 17*, no. 4 (1993): 415–436.

[39] The original cultural assimilators were developed by Harry Triandis at the University of Illinois. A recent collection is found in *Intercultural Interactions: A Practical Guide* by R. Brislin, K. Cushner, C. Cherrie, and M. Yong (Thousand Oaks, CA: Sage, 1986 and 1996—second edition).

[40] Osland, *Working Abroad*.

[41] Ibid., 68.

[42] Ibid., 74.

[43] Collins.

[44] J. Schermerhorn Jr. and M. H. Bond, "Cross-Cultural Leadership Dynamics in Collectivism and High Power Distance Settings," *Leadership and Organization Development Journal 18*, no. 4 (1997): 187–193.

[45] On occasion we have heard frustrated cross-cultural trainers grumble that some expatriates view seeking out cultural explanations with the same disdain they reserve for stopping to ask for driving directions.

[46] I. Ratiu, "Thinking Internationally: A Comparison of How International Students Learn," *International Studies of Management and Organization 13* (1983): 139–150.

[47] Bird, Osland, et al.

[48] Osland, *Working Abroad*.

This section of the Reader focuses on the knowledge and essential skills required of effective leaders, managers, team leaders, and self-leaders.

CHAPTER 13

LEADERSHIP

WHAT MAKES A LEADER?
Daniel Goleman

WHY DOES VISION MATTER?
Burt Nanus

SUPERLEADERSHIP: BEYOND THE MYTH OF HEROIC LEADERSHIP
Charles C. Manz
Henry P. Sims, Jr.

Leadership is one of the most frequently researched topics in organizational behavior, which makes it difficult to choose among the thousands of articles written on this subject. Our conceptions or schemas of what constitutes a good leader vary from culture to culture and can also change over time within the same culture.

Emotional intelligence is a fairly recent addition to our knowledge about leaders, which explains why we chose "What Makes a Leader?" by Daniel Goleman, co-chairman of the Consortium for Research on Emotional Intelligence in Organizations at Rutgers University. Based on research findings, Goleman argues that emotional intelligence (self-awareness, self-regulation, motivation, empathy, and social skill) is indispensable for effective leadership.

The second article is a classic by Burt Nanus, an educator, author, and consultant who has written widely on leadership. In "Why Does Vision Matter?" Nanus explains the role of vision and its effect on organizations. He compares organizations with visions to those without visions.

Our third choice was "Superleadership: Beyond the Myth of Heroic Leadership," a popular article by Charles Manz and Henry Sims, Jr., business professors and consultants. Manz and Sims describe four types of leadership, which gives you some sense of changing expectations of leaders over time. The authors promote the idea of SuperLeaders who encourage their followers to become self-leaders by utilizing seven steps.

WHAT MAKES A LEADER?*

Daniel Goleman

Every businessperson knows a story about a highly intelligent, highly skilled executive who was promoted into a leadership position only to fail at the job. And they also know a story about someone

---

*Reprinted with permission from the *Harward Business Review* (November-December 1998): 73–102.

with solid—but not extraordinary—intellectual abilities and technical skills who was promoted into a similar position and then soared.

Such anecdotes support the widespread belief that identifying individuals with the "right stuff" to be leaders is more art than science. After all, the personal styles of superb leaders vary: some leaders are subdued and analytical; others shout their manifestos from the mountaintops. And just as important, different situations call for different types of leadership. Most mergers need a sensitive negotiator at the helm, whereas many turnarounds require a more forceful authority.

I have found, however, that the most effective leaders are alike in one crucial way: they all have a high degree of what has come to be known as *emotional intelligence*. It's not that IQ and technical skills are irrelevant. They do matter, but mainly as "threshold capabilities"; that is, they are the entry-level requirements for executive positions. But my research, along with other recent studies, clearly shows that emotional intelligence is the sine qua non of leadership. Without it, a person can have the best training in the world, an incisive, analytical mind, and an endless supply of smart ideas, but he still won't make a great leader.

In the course of the past year, my colleagues and I have focused on how emotional intelligence operates at work. We have examined the relationship between emotional intelligence and effective performance, especially in leaders. And we have observed how emotional intelligence shows itself on the job. How can you tell if someone has high emotional intelligence, for example, and how can you recognize it in yourself? In the following pages, we'll explore these questions, taking each of the components of emotional intelligence—self-awareness, self-regulation, motivation, empathy, and social skill—in turn.

EVALUATING EMOTIONAL INTELLIGENCE

Most large companies today have employed trained psychologists to develop what are known as "competency models" to aid them in identifying, training, and promoting likely stars in the leadership firmament. The psychologists have also developed such models for lower-level positions. And in recent years, I have analyzed competency models from 188 companies, most of which were large and global and included the likes of Lucent Technologies, British Airways, and Credit Suisse.

In carrying out this work, my objective was to determine which personal capabilities drove outstanding performance within these organizations, and to what degree they did so. I grouped capabilities into three categories: purely technical skills like accounting and business planning; cognitive abilities like analytical reasoning; and competencies demonstrating emotional intelligence such as the ability to work with others and effectiveness in leading change.

To create some of the competency models, psychologists asked senior managers at the companies to identify the capabilities that typified the organization's most outstanding leaders. To create other models, the psychologists used objective criteria such as a division's profitability to differentiate the star performers at senior levels within their organizations from the average ones. Those individuals were then extensively interviewed and tested and their capabilities were compared. This process resulted in the creation of lists of ingredients for highly effective leaders. The lists ranged in length from 7 to 15 items and included such ingredients as initiative and strategic vision.

When I analyzed all this data, I found dramatic results. To be sure, intellect was a driver of outstanding performance. Cognitive skills such as big-picture thinking and long-term vision were particularly important. But when I calculated the ratio of technical skills, IQ, and emotional intelligence as ingredients of excellent performance, emotional intelligence proved to be twice as important as the others for jobs at all levels.

Moreover, my analysis showed that emotional intelligence played an increasingly important role at the highest levels of the company, where differences in technical skills are of negligible importance.

In other words, the higher the rank of a person considered to be a star performer, the more emotional intelligence capabilities showed up as the reason for his or her effectiveness. When I compared star performers with average ones in senior leadership positions, nearly 90 percent of the difference in their profiles was attributable to emotional intelligence factors rather than cognitive abilities.

Other researchers have confirmed that emotional intelligence not only distinguishes outstanding leaders but can also be linked to strong performance. The findings of the late David McClelland, the renowned researcher in human and organizational behavior, are a good example. In a 1996 study of a global food and beverage company, McClelland found that when senior managers had a critical mass of emotional intelligence capabilities, their divisions outperformed yearly earnings goals by 20 percent. Meanwhile, division leaders without that critical mass underperformed by almost the same amount. McClelland's findings, interestingly, held as true in the company's U.S. divisions as in its divisions in Asia and Europe.

In short, the numbers are beginning to tell us a persuasive story about the link between a company's success and the emotional intelligence of its leaders. And just as important, research is also demonstrating that people can, if they take the right approach, develop their emotional intelligence. (See the box on page 375 titled "Can Emotional Intelligence Be Learned?")

The Five Components of Emotional Intelligence at Work

	Definition	**Hallmarks**
Self-Awareness	The ability to recognize and understand your moods, emotions, and drives, as well as their effect on others	Self-confidence Realistic self-assessment Self-deprecating sense of humor
Self-Regulation	The ability to control or redirect disruptive impulses and moods The propensity to suspend judgment—to think before acting	Trustworthiness and integrity Comfort with ambiguity Openness to change
Motivation	A passion to work for reasons that go beyond money or status A propensity to pursue goals with energy and persistence	Strong drive to achieve Optimism, even in the face of failure Organizational commitment
Empathy	The ability to understand the emotional makeup of other people Skill in treating people according to their emotional reactions	Expertise in building and retaining talent Cross-cultural sensitivity Service to clients and customers
Social Skill	Proficiency in managing relationships and building networks An ability to find common ground and build rapport	Effectiveness in leading change Persuasiveness Expertise in building and leading teams

SELF-AWARENESS

Self-awareness is the first component of emotional intelligence—which makes sense when one considers that the Delphic oracle gave the advice to "know thyself" thousands of years ago. Self-awareness means having a deep understanding of one's emotions, strengths, weaknesses, needs, and drives. People with strong self-awareness are neither overly critical nor unrealistically hopeful. Rather, they are honest—with themselves and with others.

People who have a high degree of self-awareness recognize how their feelings affect them, other people, and their job performance. Thus a self-aware person who knows that tight deadlines bring out the worst in him plans his time carefully and gets his work done well in advance. Another person with high self-awareness will be able to work with a demanding client. She will understand the client's impact on her moods and the deeper reasons for her frustration. "Their trivial demands take us away from the real work that needs to be done," she might explain. And she will go one step further and turn her anger into something constructive.

Self-awareness extends to a person's understanding of his or her values and goals. Someone who is highly self-aware knows where he is headed and why; so, for example, he will be able to be firm in turning down a job offer that is tempting financially but does not fit with his principles or long-term goals. A person who lacks self-awareness is apt to make decisions that bring on inner turmoil by treading on buried values. "The money looked good so I signed on," someone might say two years into a job, "but the work means so little to me that I'm constantly bored." The decisions of self-aware people mesh with their values; consequently, they often find work to be energizing.

How can one recognize self-awareness? First and foremost, it shows itself as candor and an ability to assess oneself realistically. People with high self-awareness are able to speak accurately and openly—although not necessarily effusively or confessionally—about their emotions and the impact they have on their work. For instance, one manager I know of was skeptical about a new personal-shopper service that her company, a major department-store chain, was about to introduce. Without prompting from her team or her boss, she offered them an explanation: "It's hard for me to get behind the rollout of this service," she admitted, "because I really wanted to run the project, but I wasn't selected. Bear with me while I deal with that." The manager did indeed examine her feelings; a week later, she was supporting the project fully.

Such self-knowledge often shows itself in the hiring process. Ask a candidate to describe a time he got carried away by his feelings and did something he later regretted. Self-aware candidates will be frank in admitting to failure—and will often tell their tales with a smile. One of the hallmarks of self-awareness is a self-deprecating sense of humor.

Self-awareness can also be identified during performance reviews. Self-aware people know—and are comfortable talking about—their limitations and strengths, and they often demonstrate a thirst for constructive criticism. By contrast, people with low self-awareness interpret the message that they need to improve as a threat or a sign of failure.

Self-aware people can also be recognized by their self-confidence. They have a firm grasp of their capabilities and are less likely to set themselves up to fail by, for example, overstretching on assignments. They know, too, when to ask for help. And the risks they take on the job are calculated. They won't ask for a challenge that they know they can't handle alone. They'll play to their strengths.

Consider the actions of a mid-level employee who was invited to sit in on a strategy meeting with her company's top executives. Although she was the most junior person in the room, she did not sit there quietly, listening in awestruck or fearful silence. She knew she had a head for clear logic and the skill to present ideas persuasively, and she offered cogent suggestions about the company's strategy. At the same time, her self-awareness stopped her from wandering into territory where she knew she was weak.

Despite the value of having self-aware people in the workplace, my research indicates that senior executives don't often give self-awareness the credit it deserves when they look for potential leaders. Many executives mistake candor about feelings for "wimpiness" and fail to give due respect to employees who openly acknowledge their shortcomings. Such people are too readily dismissed as "not tough enough" to lead others.

In fact, the opposite is true. In the first place, people generally admire and respect candor. Further, leaders are constantly required to make judgment calls that require a candid assessment of capabilities—their own and those of others. Do we have the management expertise to acquire a competitor?

CAN EMOTIONAL INTELLIGENCE BE LEARNED?

For ages, people have debated if leaders are born or made. So too goes the debate about emotional intelligence. Are people born with certain levels of empathy, for example, or do they acquire empathy as a result of life's experiences? The answer is both. Scientific inquiry strongly suggests that there is a genetic component to emotional intelligence. Psychological and developmental research indicates that nurture plays a role as well. How much of each perhaps will never be known, but research and practice clearly demonstrate that emotional intelligence can be learned.

One thing is certain: emotional intelligence increases with age. There is an old-fashioned word for the phenomenon: *maturity*. Yet even with maturity, some people still need training to enhance their emotional intelligence. Unfortunately, far too many training programs that intend to build leadership skills—including emotional intelligence—are a waste of time and money. The problem is simple: they focus on the wrong part of the brain.

Emotional intelligence is born largely in the neuro-transmitters of the brain's limbic system, which governs feelings, impulses, and drives. Research indicates that the limbic system learns best through motivation, extended practice, and feedback. Compare this with the kind of learning that goes on in the neocortex, which governs analytical and technical ability. The neocortex grasps concepts and logic. It is the part of the brain that figures out how to use a computer or make a sales call by reading a book. Not surprisingly—but mistakenly—it is also the part of the brain targeted by most training programs aimed at enhancing emotional intelligence. When such programs take, in effect, a neocortical approach, my research which the Consortium for Research on Emotional Intelligence in Organizations has shown they can even have a negative impact on people's job performance.

To enhance emotional intelligence, organizations must refocus their training to include the limbic system. They must help people break old behavioral habits and establish new ones. That not only takes much more time than conventional training programs, it also requires an individualized approach.

Imagine an executive who is thought to be low on empathy by her colleagues. Part of that deficit shows itself as an inability to listen; she interrupts people and doesn't pay close attention to what they're saying. To fix the problem, the executive needs to be motivated to change, and then she needs practice and feedback from others in the company. A colleague or coach could be tapped to let the executive know when she has been observed failing to listen. She would then have to replay the incident and give a better response; that is, demonstrate her ability to absorb what others are saying. And the executive could be directed to observe certain executives who listen well and to mimic their behavior.

With persistence and practice, such a process can lead to lasting results. I know one Wall Street executive who sought to improve his empathy—specifically his ability to read people's reactions and see their perspectives. Before beginning his quest, the executive's subordinates were terrified of working with him. People even went so far as to hide bad news from him. Naturally, he was shocked when finally confronted with these facts. He went home and told his family—but they only confirmed what he had heard at work. When their opinions on any given subject did not mesh with his, they, too, were frightened of him.

(continued)

Enlisting the help of a coach, the executive went to work to heighten his empathy through practice and feedback. His first step was to take a vacation to a foreign country where he did not speak the language. While there, he monitored his reactions to the unfamiliar and his openness to people who were different from him. When he returned home, humbled by his week abroad, the executive asked his coach to shadow him for parts of the day, several times a week, in order to critique how he treated people with new or different perspectives. At the same time, he consciously used on-the-job interactions as opportunities to practice "hearing" ideas that differed from his. Finally, the executive had himself videotaped in meetings and asked those who worked for and with him to critique his ability to acknowledge and understand the feelings of others. It took several months, but the executive's emotional intelligence did ultimately rise, and the improvement was reflected in his overall performance on the job.

It's important to emphasize that building one's emotional intelligence cannot—will not—happen without sincere desire and concerted effort. A brief seminar won't help; nor can one buy a how-to manual. It is much harder to learn to empathize—to internalize empathy as a natural response to people—than it is to become adept at regression analysis. But it can be done. "Nothing great was ever achieved without enthusiasm," wrote Ralph Waldo Emerson. If your goal is to become a real leader, these words can serve as a guidepost in your efforts to develop high emotional intelligence.

Can we launch a new product within six months? People who assess themselves honestly—that is, self-aware people—are well suited to do the same for the organizations they run.

SELF-REGULATION

Biological impulses drive our emotions. We cannot do away with them—but we can do much to manage them. Self-regulation, which is like an ongoing inner conversation, is the component of emotional intelligence that frees us from being prisoners of our feelings. People engaged in such a conversation feel bad moods and emotional impulses just as everyone else does, but they find ways to control them and even to channel them in useful ways.

Imagine an executive who has just watched a team of his employees present a botched analysis to the company's board of directors. In the gloom that follows, the executive might find himself tempted to pound on the table in anger or kick over a chair. He could leap up and scream at the group. Or he might maintain a grim silence, glaring at everyone before stalking off.

But if he had a gift for self-regulation, he would choose a different approach. He would pick his words carefully, acknowledging the team's poor performance without rushing to any hasty judgment. He would then step back to consider the reasons for the failure. Are they personal—a lack of effort? Are there any mitigating factors? What was his role in the debacle? After considering these questions, he would call the team together, lay out the incident's consequences, and offer his feelings about it. He would then present his analysis of the problem and a well-considered solution.

Why does self-regulation matter so much for leaders? First of all, people who are in control of their feelings and impulses—that is, people who are reasonable—are able to create an environment of trust and fairness. In such an environment, politics and infighting are sharply reduced and productivity is high. Talented people flock to the organization and aren't tempted to leave. And self-regulation has a trickle-down effect. No one wants to be known as a hothead when the boss is known for her calm approach. Fewer bad moods at the top mean fewer throughout the organization.

Second, self-regulation is important for competitive reasons. Everyone knows that business today is rife with ambiguity and change. Companies merge and break apart regularly. Technology transforms work at a dizzying pace. People who have mastered their emotions are able to roll with the changes, when a new change program is announced, they don't panic; instead, they are able to suspend judgment, seek out information, and listen to executives explain the new program. As the initiative moves forward, they are able to move with it.

Sometimes they even lead the way. Consider the case of a manager at a large manufacturing company. Like her colleagues, she had used a certain software program for five years. The program drove how she collected and reported data and how she thought about the company's strategy. One day, senior executives announced that a new program was to be installed that would radically change how information was gathered and assessed within the organization. While many people in the company complained bitterly about how disruptive the change would be, the manager mulled over the reasons for the new program and was convinced of its potential to improve performance. She eagerly attended training sessions—some of her colleagues refused to do so—and was eventually promoted to run several divisions, in part because she used the new technology so effectively.

I want to push the importance of self-regulation to leadership even further and make the case that it enhances integrity, which is not only a personal virtue but also an organizational strength. Many of the bad things that happen in companies are a function of impulsive behavior. People rarely plan to exaggerate profits, pad expense accounts, dip into the till, or abuse power for selfish ends. Instead, an opportunity presents itself, and people with low impulse control just say yes.

By contrast, consider the behavior of the senior executive at a large food company. The executive was scrupulously honest in his negotiations with local distributors. He would routinely lay out his cost structure in detail, thereby giving the distributors a realistic understanding of the company's pricing. This approach meant the executive couldn't always drive a hard bargain. Now, on occasion, he felt the urge to increase profits by withholding information about the company's costs. But he challenged that impulse—he saw that it made more sense in the long run to counteract it. His emotional self-regulation paid off in strong, lasting relationships with distributors that benefited the company more than any short-term financial gains would have.

The signs of emotional self-regulation, therefore, are not hard to miss: a propensity for reflection and thoughtfulness; comfort with ambiguity and change; and integrity—an ability to say no to impulsive urges.

Like self-awareness, self-regulation often does not get its due. People who can master their emotions are sometimes seen as cold fish—their considered responses are taken as a lack of passion. People with fiery temperaments are frequently thought of as "classic" leaders—their outbursts are considered hallmarks of charisma and power. But when such people make it to the top, their impulsiveness often works against them. In my research, extreme displays of negative emotion have never emerged as a driver of good leadership.

MOTIVATION

If there is one trait that virtually all effective leaders have, it is motivation. They are driven to achieve beyond expectations—their own and everyone else's. The key word here is *achieve*. Plenty of people are motivated by external factors such as a big salary or the status that comes from having an impressive title or being part of a prestigious company. By contrast, those with leadership potential are motivated by a deeply embedded desire to achieve for the sake of achievement.

If you are looking for leaders, how can you identify people who are motivated by the drive to achieve rather than by external rewards? The first sign is a passion for the work itself—such people seek out creative challenges, love to learn, and take great pride in a job well done. They also display an unflagging energy to do things better. People with such energy often seem restless with the status quo. They are persistent with their questions about why things are done one way rather than another; they are eager to explore new approaches to their work.

A cosmetics company manager, for example, was frustrated that he had to wait two weeks to get sales results from people in the field. He finally tracked down an automated phone system that would beep each of his salespeople at 5 P.M. every day. An automated message then prompted them to punch in their numbers—how many calls and sales they had made that day. The system shortened the feedback time on sales results from weeks to hours.

That story illustrates two other common traits of people who are driven to achieve. They are forever raising the performance bar, and they like to keep score. Take the performance bar first. During performance reviews, people with high levels of motivation might ask to be "stretched" by their superiors. Of course, an employee who combines self-awareness with internal motivation will recognize her limits—but she won't settle for objectives that seem too easy to fulfill.

And it follows naturally that people who are driven to do better also want a way of tracking progress—their own, their team's, and their company's. Whereas people with low achievement motivation are often fuzzy about results, those with high achievement motivation often keep score by tracking such hard measures as profitability or market share. I know of a money manager who starts and ends his day on the Internet, gauging the performance of his stock fund against four industry-set benchmarks.

Interestingly, people with high motivation remain optimistic even when the score is against them. In such cases, self-regulation combines with achievement motivation to overcome the frustration and depression that come after a set-back or failure. Take the case of another portfolio manager at a large investment company. After several successful years, her fund tumbled for three consecutive quarters, leading three large institutional clients to shift their business elsewhere.

Some executives would have blamed the nosedive on circumstances outside their control; others might have seen the setback as evidence of personal failure. This portfolio manager, however, saw an opportunity to prove she could lead a turn-around. Two years later, when she was promoted to a very senior level in the company, she described the experience as "the best thing that ever happened to me; I learned so much from it."

Executives trying to recognize high levels of achievement motivation in their people can look for one last piece of evidence: commitment to the organization. When people love their job for the work itself, they often feel committed to the organizations that make that work possible. Committed employees are likely to stay with an organization even when they are pursued by headhunters waving money.

It's not difficult to understand how and why a motivation to achieve translates into strong leadership. If you set the performance bar high for yourself, you will do the same for the organization when you are in a position to do so. Likewise, a drive to surpass goals and an interest in keeping score can be contagious. Leaders with these traits can often build a team of managers around them with the same traits. And of course, optimism and organizational commitment are fundamental to leadership—just try to imagine running a company without them.

EMPATHY

Of all the dimensions of emotional intelligence, empathy is the most easily recognized. We have all felt the empathy of a sensitive teacher or friend; we have all been struck by its absence in an unfeeling coach or boss. But when it comes to business, we rarely hear people praised, let alone rewarded, for their empathy. The very word seems unbusinesslike, out of place amid the tough realities of the marketplace.

But empathy doesn't mean a kind of "I'm okay, you're okay" mushiness. For a leader, that is, it doesn't mean adopting other people's emotions as one's own and trying to please everybody. That would be a nightmare—it would make action impossible. Rather, empathy means thoughtfully considering employees' feelings—along with other factors—in the process of making intelligent decisions.

For an example of empathy in action, consider what happened when two giant brokerage companies merged, creating redundant jobs in all their divisions. One division manager called his people together and gave a gloomy speech that emphasized the number of people who would soon be fired. The manager of another division gave his people a different kind of speech. He was upfront about his own worry and confusion, and he promised to keep people informed and to treat everyone fairly.

The difference between these two managers was empathy. The first manager was too worried about his own fate to consider the feelings of his anxiety-stricken colleagues. The second knew intuitively what his people were feeling, and he acknowledged their fears with his words. Is it any surprise that the first manager saw his division sink as many demoralized people, especially the most talented, departed? By contrast, the second manager continued to be a strong leader, his best people stayed, and his division remained as productive as ever.

Empathy is particularly important today as a component of leadership for at least three reasons: the increasing use of teams; the rapid pace of globalization; and the growing need to retain talent.

Consider the challenge of leading a team. As anyone who has ever been a part of one can attest, teams are cauldrons of bubbling emotions. They are often charged with reaching a consensus—hard enough with two people and much more difficult as the numbers increase. Even in groups with as few as four or five members, alliances form and clashing agendas get set. A team's leader must be able to sense and understand the viewpoints of everyone around the table.

That's exactly what a marketing manager at a large information technology company was able to do when she was appointed to lead a troubled team. The group was in turmoil, overloaded by work and missing deadlines. Tensions were high among the members. Tinkering with procedures was not enough to bring the group together and make it an effective part of the company.

So the manager took several steps. In a series of one-on-one sessions, she took the time to listen to everyone in the group—what was frustrating them, how they rated their colleagues, whether they felt they had been ignored. And then she directed the team in a way that brought it together: she encouraged people to speak more openly about their frustrations, and she helped people raise constructive complaints during meetings. In short, her empathy allowed her to understand her team's emotional makeup. The result was not just heightened collaboration among members but also added business, as the team was called on for help by a wider range of internal clients.

Globalization is another reason for the rising importance of empathy for business leaders. Cross-cultural dialogue can easily lead to miscues and misunderstandings. Empathy is an antidote. People who have it are attuned to subtleties in body language; they can hear the message beneath the words being spoken. Beyond that, they have a deep understanding of the existence and importance of cultural and ethnic differences.

Consider the case of an American consultant whose team had just pitched a project to a potential Japanese client. In its dealings with Americans, the team was accustomed to being bombarded with questions after such a proposal, but this time it was greeted with a long silence. Other members of the team, taking the silence as disapproval, were ready to pack and leave. The lead consultant gestured them to stop. Although he was not particularly familiar with Japanese culture, he read the client's face and posture and sensed not rejection but interest—even deep consideration. He was right: when the client finally spoke, it was to give the consulting firm the job.

Finally, empathy plays a key role in the retention of talent, particularly in today's information economy. Leaders have always needed empathy to develop and keep good people, but today the stakes are higher. When good people leave, they take the company's knowledge with them.

That's where coaching and mentoring come in. It has repeatedly been shown that coaching and mentoring pay off not just in better performance but also in increased job satisfaction and decreased turnover. But what makes coaching and mentoring work best is the nature of the relationship. Outstanding coaches and mentors get inside the heads of the people they are helping. They sense how to give effective feedback. They know when to push for better performance and when to hold back. In the way they motivate their protégés, they demonstrate empathy in action.

In what is probably sounding like a refrain, let me repeat that empathy doesn't get much respect in business. People wonder how leaders can make hard decisions if they are "feeling" for all the people who will be affected. But leaders with empathy do more than sympathize with people around them: they use their knowledge to improve their companies in subtle but important ways.

SOCIAL SKILL

The first three components of emotional intelligence are all self-management skills. The last two, empathy and social skill, concern a person's ability to manage relationships with others. As a component of emotional intelligence, social skill is not as simple as it sounds. It's not just a matter of friendliness, although people with high levels of social skill are rarely mean-spirited. Social skill, rather, is friendliness with a purpose: moving people in the direction you desire, whether that's agreement on a new marketing strategy or enthusiasm about a new product.

Socially skilled people tend to have a wide circle of acquaintances, and they have a knack for finding common ground with people of all kinds—a knack for building rapport. That doesn't mean they socialize continually; it means they work according to the assumption that nothing important gets done alone. Such people have a network in place when the time for action comes.

Social skill is the culmination of the other dimensions of emotional intelligence. People tend to be very effective at managing relationships when they can understand and control their own emotions and can empathize with the feelings of others. Even motivation contributes to social skill. Remember that people who are driven to achieve tend to be optimistic, even in the face of setbacks or failure. When people are upbeat, their "glow" is cast upon conversations and other social encounters. They are popular, and for good reason.

Because it is the outcome of the other dimensions of emotional intelligence, social skill is recognizable on the job in many ways that will by now sound familiar. Socially skilled people, for instance, are adept at managing teams—that's their empathy at work. Likewise, they are expert persuaders—a manifestation of self-awareness, self-regulation, and empathy combined. Given those skills, good persuaders know when to make an emotional plea, for instance, and when an appeal to reason will work better. And motivation, when publicly visible, makes such people excellent collaborators; their passion for the work spreads to others, and they are driven to find solutions.

But sometimes social skill shows itself in ways the other emotional intelligence components do not. For instance, socially skilled people may at times appear not to be working while at work. They seem to be idly schmoozing—chatting in the hallways with colleagues or joking around with people who are not even connected to their "real" jobs. Socially skilled people, however, don't think it makes sense to arbitrarily limit the scope of their relationships. They build bonds widely because they know that in these fluid times, they may need help someday from people they are just getting to know today.

For example, consider the case of an executive in the strategy department of a global computer manufacturer. By 1993, he was convinced that the company's future lay with the Internet. Over the course of the next year, he found kindred spirits and used his social skill to stitch together a virtual community that cut across levels, divisions, and nations. He then used this de facto team to put up a corporate Web site, among the first by a major company. And, on his own initiative, with no budget or formal status, he signed up the company to participate in an annual Internet industry convention. Calling on his allies and persuading various divisions to donate funds, he recruited more than 50 people from a dozen different units to represent the company at the convention.

Management took notice: within a year of the conference, the executive's team formed the basis for the company's first Internet division, and he was formally put in charge of it. To get there, the executive had ignored conventional boundaries, forging and maintaining connections with people in every corner of the organization.

Is social skill considered a key leadership capability in most companies? The answer is yes, especially when compared with the other components of emotional intelligence. People seem to know intuitively that leaders need to manage relationships effectively; no leader is an island. After all, the leader's task is to get work done through other people, and social skill makes that possible. A leader who cannot express her empathy may as well not have it at all. And a leader's motivation will be useless if he cannot communicate his passion to the organization. Social skill allows leaders to put their emotional intelligence to work.

It would be foolish to assert that good-old-fashioned IQ and technical ability are not important ingredients in strong leadership. But the recipe would not be complete without emotional intelligence. It was once thought that the components of emotional intelligence were "nice to have" in business leaders. But now we know that, for the sake of performance, these are ingredients that leaders "need to have."

It is fortunate, then, that emotional intelligence can be learned. The process is not easy. It takes time and, most of all, commitment. But the benefits that come from having a well-developed emotional intelligence, both for the individual and for the organization, make it worth the effort.

Why Does Vision Matter?*

Burt Nanus

Max DePree, CEO of the brilliantly successful Herman Miller Company, says, "The first responsibility of a leader is to define reality."[1] The reality of an organization has many dimensions:

- How it grew to its current size. The challenges it faced and overcame. The decisions that proved right and those that proved costly.
- Its character and culture. Its traditions and rituals. The way it conducts its business. Its organizational structure.
- The challenges and prospects facing it. Product obsolescence. Emerging opportunities. New production processes.
- Its competitive advantages and limitations. Its distinctive competence. Its resource base. Competitive threats.
- The skills and knowledge of its workers and managers. Its capacity for training and development.
- The trends in the outside world that affect it. New technologies. Possible government regulations. Changes in the needs and wants of customers.

All these factors converge to help an effective leader define a sense of direction or vision. A vision is "a realistic, credible, attractive future for the organization."[2] A vision is a beckoning symbol of all that is possible for the organization—a shining destination, a distinctive path that no other organization is likely to have, even one that may be in the very same business.

---

*Reprinted with permission from *Leading the Way to Organizational Renewal* by Burt Nanus. Copyright © 1996 by Productivity Press, P.O. Box 13390, Portland, OR 97213–6868.

LEADERS AND VISIONS

As the main person setting direction, the leader points the way. He or she champions a particular image of what is possible, desirable, and intended for the future of the enterprise. "Let's go this way," says the leader. "Together we'll be able to realize our own deepest desires for meaning, accomplishment, and self-fulfillment. Here's where the action is. Here's where we can make our unique contributions. On this path lie the glittering prizes. Follow me."

Such an image has great power. As deBono said, "The sense of direction urges action. The sense of direction shapes the action. The sense of direction allows the value of the action to be satisfied: has it got me nearer my goal? The sense of direction allows all judgments and decisions to be made more easily: does this help me toward my goal or hinder me?"[3]

Think of some of the great leaders of history: Jefferson, Lincoln, Gandhi, Henry Ford. We see them as great mainly because their unique visions powered great efforts and accomplishments. These leaders were captivated by their dreams. They were obsessed with the need to turn dreams into reality. They were able to infect others with enthusiasm and commitment to their visions. Eventually, a critical mass shared the dream, and the vision became a reality that motivated behavior. It became a target and plans were made for achieving it. Actions followed plans, and people were able to live the dream.

THE POWER OF A VISION

Why is vision so powerful? The key reason is that it grabs attention. It provides focus. Every organization has lots of ways to go. The outside world pulls it in every direction. Each has its own attractions. Yet, no organization can be all things to all people—not General Motors, not IBM, not even the United States of America. So amidst all the chaos and conflicting pressures, the vision compels an organization to remember what's really important and where it intends to go. With focus, other benefits follow:

- **Vision creates meaning for everyone in the organization** It cuts through confusion and makes the world understandable. It helps explain why things are being done the way they are, why some things are considered good and rewarded while others are not. Once they see the big picture, people can see how their own jobs relate to it. They can look at their own skills and interests and see if there's a future for them in the organization.
- **Vision provides a worthwhile challenge** It stretches people by showing them a joint accomplishment that they can be a part of. It generates pride in being part of a team with a useful goal. It makes people feel important. It goads them on to higher levels of commitment and performance.
- **Vision is energizing** It provides something to believe in. It is exhilarating and exciting. Shared aspirations lead to commitment, which energizes people. It provides the spark that ignites the engine of change. It encourages risk-taking, experimentation. It inspires new ways to think, behave, act, and learn.
- **Vision brings the future into the present** When one imagines what can be and gives it a name, it becomes real right now. Real enough to become a beacon. Real enough to change perceptions and attitudes. Real enough to change today's decisions. Real enough to define what is essential and filter out distractions. Real enough to concentrate, resources and decisions where they truly matter.
- **Vision creates a common identity** People work together with a sense of common ownership and common destiny. A common identity fosters cooperation and promotes synergy. It aligns people's energies in a common direction.

In short, vision is the main tool leaders use to lead from the front. Effective leaders don't push or pressure their followers. They don't boss them around or manipulate them. They are out front showing the way. The vision allows leaders to inspire, attract, align, and energize their followers—to empower them by encouraging them to become part of a common enterprise dedicated to achieving the vision.

	Organization Without Vision	Organizations With Shared Vision
Primary thrust	Problem-driven	Opportunity-driven
Worldview	Stability	Change
Information systems based on:	Past performance	Progress toward goals
Decision making	Tactical	Strategic
Performance measures	Short-term results	Long-term results
Control mechanism	Habit, fear	Peer group pressure
Planning style	Reactive	Proactive

FIGURE 1   Organizations With and Without Vision

Contrast all this with organizations that lack vision (see Figure 1).

If they're well managed, they may still operate reasonably well, at least in the short run. They may have a certain momentum. The products may get out the door on time. The bills get paid. Orders continue to come in. But there's no energy. No excitement. No sense of going somewhere. No sense of progress or renewal. None of the extra effort that people will invest only if they are committed to something challenging and worthwhile.

In the worst situations, organizations without a shared vision begin to stagnate. Managers can't agree on priorities. They are less willing to take risks. Forces for the status quo, always strong, may be unopposed. The initiative for innovation slowly erodes. Workers worry about their prospects for the future. Conflicts become difficult to resolve. Schedules begin to slip.

Eventually, the organization is less able to serve its customers or clients. Revenues erode. Staff may be laid off, further weakening morale and the ability to serve customers. The downward spiral may end up in total failure unless a new leader can be found who can give the organization a new sense of direction.

NOTES

[1] M. DePree, *Leadership Is an Art* (New York: Doubleday, 1989) 9.
[2] B. Nanus, *Visionary Leadership* (San Francisco: Jossey-Bass, 1992) 8.
[3] L. deBono, *Tactics—The Art and Science of Success* (Boston: Little, Brown, 1984) 4.

SUPERLEADERSHIP: BEYOND THE MYTH OF HEROIC LEADERSHIP*

Charles C. Manz
Henry P. Sims, Jr.

When most of us think of leadership, we think of one person doing something to another person. This is "influence," and a leader is someone who has the capacity to influence another. Words like *charismatic* and *heroic* are sometimes used to describe a leader. The word *leader* itself conjures up visions

*Reprinted, by permission of the publisher, from *Organizational Dynamics, 19*, no. 4. (Spring 1991) 18–35.

of a striking figure on a rearing white horse who is crying "Follow me!" The leader is the one who has either the power or the authority to command others.

Many historical figures fit this mold: Alexander, Caesar, Napoleon, Washington, Churchill. Even today, the turnaround of Chrysler Corporation by Lee Iacocca might be thought of as an act of contemporary heroic leadership. It's not difficult to think of Iacocca astride a white horse, and he is frequently thought of as "charismatic."

But is this heroic figure of the leader the most appropriate image of the organizational leader of today? Is there another model? We believe there is. In many modern situations, *the most appropriate leader is the one who can lead others to lead themselves*. We call this powerful new kind of leadership *SuperLeadership*.

Our viewpoint represents a departure from the dominant and, we think, incomplete view of leadership. Our position is that true leadership comes mainly from within a person, not from outside. At its best, external leadership provides a spark and supports the flame of the true inner leadership that dwells within each person. At its worst, it disrupts this internal process, causing damage to the person and the constituencies he or she serves.

Our focus is on a new form of leadership that is designed to facilitate the self-leadership energy within each person. This perspective suggests a new measure of a leader's strength—one's ability to maximize the contributions of others through recognition of their right to guide their own destiny, rather than the leader's ability to bend the will of others to his or her own. The challenge for organizations is to understand how to go about bringing out the wealth of talent that each employee possesses. Many still operate under a quasi-military model that encourages conformity and adherence rather than one that emphasizes how leaders can lead others to lead themselves.

WHY IS SUPERLEADERSHIP AN IMPORTANT PERSPECTIVE?

This SuperLeadership perspective is especially important today because of several recent trends facing American businesses. First, the challenge to U. S. corporations from world competition has pressured companies to utilize more fully their human resources. Second, the workforce itself has changed a great deal in recent decades—for instance, "baby boomers" have carried into their organization roles elevated expectations and a need for greater meaning in their work lives.

As a consequence of these kinds of pressures, organizations have increasingly experimented with innovative work designs. Widespread introduction of modern management techniques, such as quality circles, self-managed work teams, Japanese business practices, and flatter organization structures, has led to the inherent dilemma of trying to provide strong leadership for workers who are being encouraged and allowed to become increasingly self-managed. The result is a major knowledge gap about appropriate new leadership approaches under conditions of increasing employee participation. The SuperLeadership approach is designed to meet these kinds of challenges.

Before presenting specific steps for becoming a SuperLeader, it is useful to contrast SuperLeadership with other views of leadership.

Viewpoints on what constitutes successful leadership in organizations have changed significantly over time. A simplified historical perspective on different approaches to leadership is presented in Figure 1. As it suggests, four different types of leader can be distinguished: the "strong man," the "transactor," the "visionary hero," and the "SuperLeader."

The strong-man view of leadership is perhaps the earliest dominant form in our culture. The emphasis with this autocrat view is on the strength of the leader. We use the masculine noun purposely because when this leadership approach was most prevalent it was almost a completely male-dominated process.

	Strong Man	**Transactor**	**Visionary Hero**	**SuperLeader**
Focus	Commands	Rewards	Visions	Self-leadership
Type of power	Position/ authority	Rewards	Relational/ inspirational	Shared
Source of leader's wisdom and direction	Leader	Leader	Leader	Mostly followers (self-leaders) and then leaders
Followers' response	Fear-based compliance	Calculative compliance	Emotional commitment based on leader's vision	Commitment based on ownership
Typical leader behaviors	Direction/ command	Interactive goal setting	Communication of leader's vision	Becoming an effective self-leader
	Assigned goals	Contingent personal reward	Emphasis on leader's values	Modeling self-leadership
	Intimidation	Contingent material reward	Exhortation	Creating positive thought patterns
	Reprimand	Contingent reprimand	Inspirational persuasion	Developing self-leadership through reward & constructive reprimand
				Promoting self-leading teams
				Facilitating a self-leader leadership culture

FIGURE 1

The strong-man view of leadership still exists today in many organizations (and is still widely reserved for males), although it is not as highly regarded as it once was.

The strong-man view of leadership creates an image of a John Wayne type who is not afraid to "knock some heads" to get followers to do what he wants done. The expertise for knowing what should be done rests almost entirely in the leader. It is he who sizes up the situation and, based on some seemingly superior strength, skill, and courage, delivers firm commands to the workers. If the job is not performed as commanded, inevitably some significant form of punishment will be delivered by the leader to the guilty party. The focus is on the leader whose power stems primarily from his position in the organization. He is the primary source of wisdom and direction-strong direction. Subordinates simply comply.

One would think that the day of the strong-man leader has passed, but one apparently managed to work his way up the corporate hierarchy at Kellogg Co. This venerable Battle Creek cereal maker terminated its president in an unusual action. Accounts printed in the *Wall Street Journal* described this person as "abrasive and often unwilling to listen, ... very abrupt ... more inclined to manage without being questioned." He was known for deriding unimpressive presentations as a "CE"—career ending—performance. As another example, we suspect that the majority of employees at Eastern Airlines would describe former CEO Frank Lorenzo as a prototypical strong man.

The second view of leadership is that of a *transactor*.

As time passed in our culture, the dominance of the strong-man view of leadership lessened somewhat. Women began to find themselves more frequently in leadership positions. With the development of knowledge of the power of rewards (such as that coming from research on behavior modification), a different view of influence began to emerge. With this view, the emphasis was increasingly placed on a rational exchange approach (exchange of rewards for work performed) in order to get workers to do their work. Even Taylor's views on scientific management, which still influence significantly many organizations in many industries, emphasized the importance of providing incentives to get workers to do work.

With the transactor type of leader, the focus is on goals and rewards; the leader's power stems from the ability to provide rewards for followers doing what the leader thinks should be done. The source of wisdom and direction still rests with the leader. Subordinates will tend to take a calculative view of their work. "I will do what he (or she) asks as long as the rewards keep coming."

Perhaps one of the most prototypical (and successful) transactor organizations in the world today is Pepsico. *Fortune* described the company with phrases like "... boot camp ... sixty-hour weeks, ... back breaking standards that are methodically raised." Those who can't compete are washed out. Those who do compete successfully are rewarded very handsomely—first-class air travel, fully loaded company cars, stock options, bonuses that can hit 90 percent of salary. Those who are comfortable and effective in this culture receive the spoils. Those who are not comfortable tend to leave early in their career.

Perhaps the ultimate transactor leader is Chairman Larry Phillips-Van Heusen, manufacturer of shirts, sweaters, and casual shoes. Phillips has set up a scheme whereby the 11 senior executives will each earn a $1 million bonus if the company's earnings per share grow at a 35 percent compound annual rate during the four years ending in January 1992. Not surprisingly, company executives are actively absorbed in striving to meet this goal.

The next type of leader, which probably represents the most popular view today, is that of the visionary hero. Here the focus is on the leader's ability to create highly motivating and absorbing visions. The leader represents a kind of heroic figure who is somehow able to create an almost larger-than-life vision for the workforce to follow. The promise is that if organizations can just find those leaders that are able to capture what's important in the world and wrap it up into some kind of purposeful vision, then the rest of the workforce will have the clarifying beacon that will light the way to the promised land.

With the visionary hero, the focus is on the leader's vision, and the leader's power is based on followers' desire to relate to the vision and to the leader himself or herself. Once again, the leader represents the source of wisdom and direction. Followers, at least in theory, are expected to commit to the vision and the leader.

The notion of the visionary hero seems to have received considerable attention lately, but the idea has not gone without criticism. Peter Drucker, for example, believes that charisma becomes the undoing of leaders. He believes they become inflexible, convinced of their own infallibility, and slow to really change. Instead, Drucker suggests that the most effective leaders are those not afraid of developing strength in their subordinates and associates.

The final view of leadership included in our figure represents the focus of this article—the SuperLeader. We do not use the word *Super* to create an image of a larger-than-life-figure who has all the answers and is able to bend others' wills to his or her own. On the contrary, with this type of leader, the focus is largely on the followers. Leaders become "super"—that is, can possess the strength and wisdom of many persons—by helping to unleash the abilities of the "followers" (self-leaders) that surround them.

The focus of this leadership view is on the followers who become self-leaders. Power is more evenly shared by leaders and followers. The leader's task becomes largely that of helping followers to develop the necessary skills for work, especially self-leadership, to be able to contribute more fully to the organization. Thus, leaders and subordinates (that are becoming strong self-leaders) together represent the source of wisdom and direction. Followers (self-leaders), in turn, experience commitment and ownership of their work.

SEVEN STEPS TO SUPERLEADERSHIP

For the SuperLeader, the essence of the challenge is to lead followers to discover the potentialities that lie within themselves. How can a SuperLeader lead others to become positive effective self-leaders? How can a SuperLeader lead others to lead themselves?

We will present seven steps to accomplish these ends. As we will see, some of the elements included in the other leadership views summarized above are a part of SuperLeadership (for instance, the use of rewards) but as Figure 1 indicates, the focus of the leadership process and the basis of power and the relationship of the SuperLeader with followers are very different.

STEP 1—BECOMING A SELF-LEADER

Before learning how to lead others, it is important—make that essential—to first learn how to lead ourselves. Consequently, the first step to becoming a SuperLeader is to become an effective self-leader.

In a taped interview from the historical files of Hewlett-Packard, David Packard, co-founder of Hewlett-Packard, described how, as a young man, he used a daily schedule as a strategy to organize his own efforts. "I was resolved that I was going to have everything organized so, when I was a freshman, I had a schedule set for every day ... what I was going to do every hour of the day ... and times set up in the morning to study certain things .... You did have to allocate your time ..." At a very young age, David Packard was developing the self-leadership skills that became so critical to his later success as an executive.

Self-leadership is the influence we exert on ourselves to achieve the self-motivation and self-direction we need to perform. The process of self-leadership consists of an array of behavioral and cognitive strategies for enhancing our own personal effectiveness.

Self-leadership is also the essence of effective followership. As one Ford Motor Co. executive exclaimed to us, "We started participative management, but we didn't know what that meant for the subordinate!" What are the responsibilities of the follower? How does he or she behave in a participative management situation? Developing self-leadership skills is the answer to this question. From a SuperLeadership perspective, effective followers are leaders in their own right—they are skilled at leading themselves.

We will address two classes of self-leadership strategies. The first focuses mainly on effective behavior and action—"behavioral focused strategies"; the second focuses on effective thinking and feeling—"cognitive focused strategies." A summary of these strategies is provided in Figure 2.

Behavioral Focused Strategies   These self-leadership actions are designed to help individuals organize and direct their own work lives more effectively. Specifically, these strategies include self-observation, self-goal setting, cue management, self-reward, constructive self-punishment or self-criticism, and rehearsal.

The necessity for self-observation, for example, was dramatically brought forward at Harley Davidson, when the American motorcycle manufacturer instituted a Just-in-Time employee involvement program. Management had to train workers to use statistical tools to monitor and control the quality of their own work—an effective prerequisite for helping employees to design and conduct their own self-observation system. The Harley story is a resounding success. This is one American company that has been extraordinarily successful in dealing with the Japanese incursion into their markets.

Each of these strategies, with the exception of self-criticism, when practiced consistently and effectively, has been found to be significantly related to higher performance. While self-criticism can at times serve a useful purpose, it tends to have a demoralizing and destructive impact when overused.

Behavior-Focused Strategies

Self-Observation—observing and gathering information about specific behavior that you have targeted for change

Self-Set Goals—setting goals for your own work efforts

Management of Cues—arranging and altering cues in the work environment to facilitate your desired personal behaviors

Rehearsal—physical or mental practice of work activities before you actually perform them

Self-Reward—providing yourself with personally valued rewards for completing desirable behaviors

Self-Punishment/Criticism—administering punishments to yourself for behaving in undesirable ways

Cognitive-Focused Strategies

Building Natural Rewards into Tasks—self-redesign of where and how you do your work to increase the level of natural rewards in your job. Natural rewards that are part of rather than separate from the work (*i.e.*, the work, like a hobby, becomes the reward) result from activities that cause you to feel:

    a sense of competence

    a sense of self-control

    a sense of purpose

Focusing Thinking on Natural Rewards—purposely focusing your thinking on the naturally rewarding features of your work

Establishment of Effective Thought Patterns—establishing constructive and effective habits or patterns in your thinking (e.g., a tendency to search for opportunities rather than obstacles embedded in challenges) by managing your:

    beliefs and assumptions

    mental imagery

    internal self-talk

FIGURE 2   Self-Leadership Strategies

Nevertheless, constructive self-criticism can sometimes send a signal to others that we are ready to accept responsibility for our own actions—and that we are sometimes human and make a mistake. Basketball coach John Thompson of Georgetown University was ejected from a game when he protested too vigorously to game officials. Later he commented, "It was probably my fault more than the officials' fault. I have respect for all three of those men. I probably let my competitive juices overflow ... I made a mistake." Thompson's willingness to recognize some of his own flaws is one reason he is so widely respected.

Cognitive-Focused Strategies   In addition to behaviorally focused strategies, we can help ourselves to become more effective through the application of self-leadership strategies that promote effective thinking.

First, effective self-leaders can both physically and mentally redesign their own tasks to make them more naturally rewarding; that is, they can create ways to do tasks so that significant natural reward value is obtained from the enjoyment of doing the job itself. Natural rewards are derived from performing tasks in a way that allows us to experience (1) a sense of competence, (2) a sense of self-control, and (3) a sense of purpose. An example of this notion is embodied in the reply of a young girl featured in a recent news story who was asked why she had made a rock collection, and why she had tried to understand all about rocks. She replied, "Because it makes me feel good in my mind."

Other cognitive strategies help us by establishing constructive and effective habits or patterns of thinking—such as "opportunity thinking" as opposed to "obstacle thinking." For example, by studying and managing our beliefs and assumptions, we can begin to develop the ability to find opportunities in each new work challenge. Until managers began to believe that employees could be important participating partners in the success of American industry, much opportunity for progress was being wasted.

In summary, it's important to remember that if we want to lead others to be self-leaders, we must first practice self-leadership ourselves. If you want to lead somebody, the first critical step is to lead yourself.

STEP 2—MODELING SELF-LEADERSHIP

Once we have mastered self-leadership ourselves, the next step is to demonstrate these skills to subordinate employees; that is, our own self-leadership behaviors serve as a model from which others can learn. As Max DePree, chairman of Herman Miller, the office furniture maker, says, "It's not what you preach, but how you behave."

Modeling can be used to develop subordinate self-leadership on a day-to-day basis in two ways. The first use is to establish new behaviors—specifically self-leadership behaviors. The main point is that an employee can learn an entirely new behavior, especially self- leadership, without actually performing it. Executives that are self-starters and well-organized are likely to have subordinates who, in turn, are self-starters and well-organized. Executives, in particular, have a special responsibility to serve as the kind of self-leadership example that they wish subordinate employees to emulate.

The second use involves strengthening the probability of previously learned self-leadership behaviors. Self-leadership behaviors can be enhanced through observation of positive rewards received by others for desired behaviors. We observed, for example, an older woman react with delight when presented with a special achievement award for developing a new inspection procedure at Tandem Computer. She had developed this procedure using her own initiative—she had acted as a self-leader.

This incident served as a symbolic model for other employees at Tandem. Management made it clear that initiating the development of innovative cuing strategies (the inspection procedure) is desirable and that these types of actions are encouraged and rewarded. The hope and intention are that other employees will perceive innovative behavior to be desirable and potentially rewarding. Over time, the objective is to encourage and stimulate widespread incidents of innovative self-leadership.

The lesson from the Tandem incident is straightforward. Employees learn from and are motivated when they see rewards given to others for the performance of self-leadership behaviors. Public recognition to enhance a self-leadership model can be a powerful motivating force for others to initiate self-leadership actions.

Many learn the art of self-leadership from senior executives whom they admire and respect. The book *Eisenhower: Portrait of a Hero* by Peter Lyon (Little Brown, 1974) suggests that General Dwight Eisenhower formulated his own self-leadership style under the guidance of General George Marshall. "What General Marshall wanted most ... were senior officers who would take the responsibility for action in their own areas of competence without coming to him for the final decision; officers who in their turn would have enough sense to delegate the details of their decisions to their subordinates." Learning to lead from those above him, Ike later carried this sense of delegation and control into his own military leadership style.

Sometimes a model of self-leadership can be inspiring. Who can forget the image of Jimmy Carter as he humbly went about building low-cost housing with his own hammer and nails. The sight of a former U.S. President actually engaging in a relatively minor self-leadership behavior had more influence than anything he could have said. Carter seems to be garnering more admiration as a former president than he acquired as a president.

STEP 3—ENCOURAGING SELF-SET GOALS

Goal setting, in general, has been one of the most actively investigated aspects of employee behavior and performance. Several general principles have been derived from this extensive research.

First, virtually any kind of goal setting seems to be better than none at all. The mere existence of a goal serves to focus employee attention and energy. This is one of the most pervasive findings of all organizational psychological research. Further, specific goals seem to be better than ambiguous or "fuzzy" ones. Also, in general, more difficult goals result in higher performance—provided the goals are accepted by the employee.

Last but not least, many believe that participation in setting goals will also enhance performance. The logic is that if an employee sees the goal as his or her own, the employee is more likely to give the effort required to attain the goal. Of course, the idea of participation is very closely connected with the essence of SuperLeadership.

Since the main aim of the SuperLeader is to improve the performance of subordinates through the development of their own self-leadership capabilities, employee self-goal setting is a key element. An important point to note is that goal setting is a learned behavior; that is, it is a skill or sequence of actions that an employee can develop over a period of time, not an innate behavior that every new employee brings to the job. Since self-goal setting is something to be learned, the role of the SuperLeader is to serve as a model, coach, and teacher. The SuperLeader helps employees learn to effectively set specific challenging goals for themselves.

Among the more interesting and extreme examples of institutionalized self-set goals is the "Research Fellows" program at IBM. These high-status, high-performing scientists make their own decisions about how substantial resources will be allocated. Obviously, IBM believes its investment in the self-leadership capabilities of these eminent scientists will pay off in the long run. Other organizations would do well to learn from their example.

These ideas also have currency at the level of the shop floor. In a *Business Week* article (August 21, 1989), Alvin K. Allison, leader of a team of mechanics at Monsanto's Greenwood, South Carolina plant, says, "I knew 20 years ago that I could direct my own job, but nobody wanted to hear what I had to say." Today, Allison is a part of the upside-down revolution that seems to be driving dramatic improvements in quality and productivity at the Greenwood plant.

STEP 4—CREATE POSITIVE THOUGHT PATTERNS

Constructive thought patterns are an important element in successful self-leadership. Part of the SuperLeader role is to transmit positive thought patterns to subordinates. Especially important is the process of facilitating positive self-expectation in subordinates.

Sometimes, but especially in the early stages of a new job, employees do not have adequate natural habits of constructive thinking about themselves. They have doubts and fears—a general lack of confidence in themselves. At this stage, the actions of the SuperLeader are critical: His or her positive comments must serve as a temporary surrogate for the employee's own constructive thought patterns. As indicated in a *Fortune* article (March 26, 1990), Jack Welch, CEO of General Electric, thinks this issue is critical: "We need to drive self-confidence deep into the organization .... We have to undo a 100-year-old concept and convince our managers that their role is not to control people and stay 'on top' of things but rather to guide, energize, and excite."

The notion of constructing positive thought patterns may also be particularly critical when things are not going well. In the book *Joe Paterno: Football My Way* by Hyman and White (Collier, 1971), the very successful football coach emphasized that enhancing self-esteem is an important part of the equation: "When the staff is down ... when the squad is down ... when they are starting to doubt themselves ... then it's gotta be a positive approach. The minute I have the feeling they have doubts concerning ... [their] ability to do it ... then I immediately want to jump in there and ... talk about how good the kids are and what a great job they've done." He emphasizes confidence and pride: "A coach must be able to develop three things [in a team member] ... pride, poise, and confidence in himself."

The SuperLeader creates productive thought patterns by carefully expressing confidence in the employee's ability to extend his or her present level of competence. Support and encouragement are necessary. In many ways, this expression of confidence is the essence of the "guided-participation" phase in which SuperLeaders teach each employee to lead himself or herself. We discuss this phase later in this article.

This SuperLeadership behavior is well founded in the results of research on the self-fulfilling prophecy: If a person believes something can be done, that belief makes it more likely that it *will* be done. Perhaps the SuperLeader plays "Professor Higgins" to an employee's "Eliza." Most of all, through expressions of confidence, the SuperLeader helps to create productive patterns of thinking—new constructive thought habits.

Step 5—Develop Self-Leadership Through Reward and Constructive Reprimand

One of the SuperLeader's most potent strategies in developing employee self-leadership is reward and reinforcement. For the most part, conventional viewpoints about using organizational rewards tend to focus on so-called extrinsic rewards as a means of reinforcing performance. One example is incentive pay systems.

We are basically in sympathy with this behavioral-management viewpoint and generally believe that material rewards should be used to reinforce desirable job-related behaviors. However, rewards take on a new perspective when seen through the eyes of the SuperLeader. If the purpose of the Super-Leader is to lead others to self-leadership, then an essential ingredient is to teach employees how to reward themselves and to build natural rewards into their own work. The SuperLeader attempts to construct a reward system that emphasizes self-administered and natural rewards and, in a comparative sense, de-emphasizes externally administered rewards. Thus the focus shifts from material types of rewards to a stronger emphasis on natural rewards that stem more from the task itself and on self-administration of rewards.

This usually means that people need to have the freedom to do their jobs in the ways they most value and can thrive in; that is, in the ways that they find most naturally rewarding. In the book *Our Story So Far* (3M Co., 1977), William McKnight, former CEO of 3M Company during perhaps 3M's most critical years in becoming an organizational success story, was quoted on the need for employees to do their jobs the way they want to do them. He stated, "Those men and women to whom we delegate authority and responsibility, if they are good people, are going to want to do their jobs in their own way. These are characteristics we want and should be encouraging."

In addition, a new type of reprimand is appropriate to develop employee self-leadership. We know that reprimand, in the short term, can keep somebody's nose to the grindstone, but the effectiveness of this mode of behavior is limited. Author Ken Blanchard was quoted in the *Minneapolis Star and Tribune* (May 27, 1987) as saying, "Most managers can get things done when they are around to nag and push. However, the real test of leadership is when management isn't present ... which is about 70 percent of the time."

From a behavioral viewpoint, reprimand *should* be easy to understand. When an employee does something wrong, the manager provides a contingent aversive consequence, and the undesirable employee behavior *should* be reduced or eliminated. However, the long-term efficacy of reprimand is much more complex and leaves much to be desired. Most of all, a complex and sometimes confusing set of emotions typically accompanies reprimand, sometimes even leading to aggressive and disruptive behavior.

Reprimand is usually the opposite of what needs to be done to develop productive thought patterns in others. One objective of the SuperLeader is to encourage constructive self-confidence as an important part of the transition to self-leadership, but reprimand induces guilt and depression and diminishes self-confidence. On the other hand, if a SuperLeader treats a mistake as a learning opportunity, then employee self-esteem can be enhanced. After all, one sign of self-confidence is an individual objectively realizing that he has "made every mistake in the book" and has the experience and confidence to handle surprising situations.

We do recognize that reprimand is sometimes a necessary element in a SuperLeader's repertoire of behaviors, especially with careless or chronic underperformers. The most important lesson to remember is that the careless use of reprimand can be very discouraging to employees who are in their transition to self-leadership. The main focus should be to treat a mistake as a learning opportunity, to provide positive acceptance of the *person* despite the mistake, and to remember how the opportunity to make mistakes was a critical element in the SuperLeader's own development. Following these tips will result in a *constructive* feedback process that is more effective than the traditional use of reprimand and that positively influences employee self-leadership and long-term effectiveness.

Step 6—Promote Self-Leadership Through Teamwork

One of the more interesting examples of self-leadership systems is the team-oriented system at Volvo. Volvo has considerable experience with team assembly concepts, which were pioneered at its Kalmar plant. Further, the automobile assembly approach has been completely scrapped in the design of the new $315 million plant at Uddevalla. The key organizational philosophy at this plant is the work team, and the technical system has been designed to match the team concept. As Peter Gyllenhammar, Volvo's CEO, says, "I want the people in a team to be able to go home at night and really say, 'I built that car.'"

In the United States, the self-managing team concept has had a slow but steady start. More recent media interest seems to indicate that the team idea is about to take off. The dramatic success of the team approach at the GM-Toyota joint venture in Fremont, California has been instructive to the U.S. automobile industry in general. In our own research, we have documented the leader characteristics that are necessary to make a team effort successful, the core of which are the basic principles of SuperLeadership.

Top-management teams are also important, as represented by this quote that appeared in *Fortune* (August, 1987) from Tom Watson, Jr., former CEO of IBM: "My most important contribution to IBM was my ability to pick strong and intelligent men and then hold the team together . . . ."

One of the more interesting indicators of a self-leadership culture is the presence of quite a few teams. The types of teams (not all work groups are called teams) include product teams, top-executive teams, ad hoc teams, and shop-floor self-managing teams. Of course, teams require a good deal of self-leadership at the group level to function correctly.

> *Teamwork is important at Hewlett-Packard when it comes to the precision timing and integration required for successful new product release. At H-P, a committee called "board of directors" serves to drive the process to completion. Representatives from every department involved in the project serve on these committees.*

Step 7—Facilitate a Self-Leadership Culture

A major factor in developing SuperLeadership is the challenge of designing an integrated organizational culture that is conducive to high performance. Organizations will find it difficult to obtain initiative and innovation from employees without providing a pervasive environment that facilitates those elements of self-leadership.

For the most part, we focus on the one-on-one relationship between a SuperLeader and an employee: How can an executive lead that employee to lead himself or herself? For an organization, however, the best results derive from a total integrated system that is deliberately intended to encourage, support, and reinforce self-leadership *throughout* the system. Most of all, this is an issue that addresses the question of how top executives can create self-leadership cultures.

One company that has shown demonstrable results of an effort to develop a self-leadership culture is Xerox Corporation, winner of the Malcolm Baldrige National Quality Award. The award recognized companies that attain preeminent leadership in quality control. At Xerox, the quality effort includes plant-level employee "family groups" that work with little direct supervision. But most of all, the award recognizes the effort of Xerox to build a total quality culture based on bottom-up employee involvement.

At another company, Dana Corporation, highly visible symbolic acts were instrumental in turning the organizational culture around. One of Rene McPherson's first concerns was to indicate the importance of giving discretion to make decisions down through the ranks. The most famous story is about one of his first actions: eliminating the procedures manual. According to one account, the procedures manual had risen to a height of 22.5 inches. McPherson was said to have dumped it in a wastebasket and replaced it with a one-page policy statement.

Rene McPherson used the following metaphor to describe his philosophy of a decentralized self-leadership culture at Dana as reported in an article in *Management Review* entitled "Hell Week—Or How Dana Makes its Managers Money Conscious" (1984). "You can control a business in one of two ways. You can institute a kind of martial law, with troops stationed in each hamlet or village standing guard; or you can sit back and let each village be self-governing . . . . What we are after is to help that person [the division manager] to be [his own] . . . manager." McPherson said of his division managers, "We didn't tell the guys what they were gonna do–they came in and told us!"

Through his radical change in culture, McPherson has left a meaningful legacy for Dana Corporation. He transformed a top-heavy, bureaucratic, sluggish organization into one of the most successful and competitive manufacturing businesses in the United States today. Self-leadership was a key ingredient: Rene McPherson demonstrated a special capacity to lead others to lead themselves.

SuperLeadership at the top requires the creation of positive organizational cultures within which self-leadership can flourish. Such environments consist of a host of factors, some observable and concrete, others more subtle and symbolic. Culture becomes particularly important when it comes to balancing the needs of individualism with the needs for organized, coordinated effort. As Peter Drucker put it in the July 3, 1989 issue of *Fortune* ". . . it is important to build up the oboist as an oboist, but it is even more important to build up the oboist's pride in the performance of the orchestra . . . it puts a tremendous premium on having very clear goals and a very clear and demanding mission for the enterprise." Over-reaching organizational values that support self-leadership are perhaps the most important factor.

Ford Motor Company, for example, has developed a set of guidelines that is widely circulated throughout the corporation and known as its "Mission, Values and Guiding Principles." Among other things, they identify employee involvement and teamwork as Ford's "core human values."

In addition, training and development efforts that equip employees with both task-performance and self-leadership capabilities are important means of stimulating cultures based on leading others to lead themselves. Thus the SuperLeader's challenge is not limited to direct one-on-one leadership; the SuperLeader must also foster an integrated world in which self-leadership can survive and grow; in which self-leadership becomes an exciting, motivating, and accepted way of life. At lower levels, the challenge for aspiring SuperLeaders is to develop subcultures within their own control that stimulate the unique self-leadership strengths of subordinates.

THE TRANSITION TO SELF-LEADERSHIP

Three basic assumptions underlie our ideas on self-leadership. First, everyone practices self-leadership to some degree, but not everyone is an effective self-leader. Second, self-leadership can be learned, and thus is not restricted to people who are "born" to be self-starters or self-motivated. And third, self-leadership is relevant to executives, managers, and all employees—that is, to everyone who works.

Few employees are capable of highly effective self-leadership the moment they enter a job situation. Especially at the beginning, the SuperLeader must provide orientation, guidance, and direction.

The need for specific direction at the beginning stages of employment stems from two sources. First, the new employee is unfamiliar with the objectives, tasks, and procedures of his or her position. He or she will probably not yet have fully developed task capabilities. But more pertinent, the new employee may not yet have an adequate set of self-leadership skills. For the SuperLeader, the challenge lies in shifting employees to self-leadership. Thus the role of the SuperLeader becomes critical: He or she must lead others to lead themselves.

Throughout the entire process of leading others to lead themselves, aspects of SuperLeadership are involved that do not necessarily represent a distinct step but that are nevertheless quite important. For example, *encouragement* of followers to exercise initiative, take on responsibility, and to use self-leadership strategies in an effective way to lead themselves, is an important feature that runs through the entire process. Also, a feature we call *guided participation* is very important to Super-Leadership. This involves facilitating the gradual shifting of followers from dependence to independent self-leadership through a combination of initial instruction, questions that stimulate thinking about self-leadership (e.g., What are you shooting for? ... what is your goal. How well do you think you're doing?), and increasing participation of followers.

Consider the goal setting process as an example of how the transition to self-leadership unfolds. Teaching an employee how to set goals can follow a simple procedure: First, an employee is provided with a model to emulate; second, he or she is allowed guided participation; and finally, he or she assumes the targeted self-leadership skill, which in this case is goal setting. Once again modeling is an especially key element in learning this skill. Because of their formal position of authority, Super-Leaders have a special responsibility to personally demonstrate goal setting behavior that can be emulated by other employees. Furthermore, goals need to be coordinated among the different levels of the hierarchy. Subordinate goals, even those that are self-set, need to be consistent with superior and organizational goals.

A SuperLeader takes into account the employee's time and experience on the job, as well as the degree of the employee's skill and capabilities. For a new employee, whose job-related and self-leadership skills may yet be undeveloped, an executive may wish to begin with assigned goals, while modeling self-set goals for himself or herself. Within a short period of time, the SuperLeader endeavors to move toward interactive goals. Usually the best way to accomplish this is by "guided participation," which includes asking the employee to propose his or her own goals. At this stage, the SuperLeader still retains significant influence over goal setting, actively proposing and perhaps imposing some of the goals. Usually, this is the give and take that is typical of the traditional MBO approach.

Finally, for true self-leadership to develop and flourish, the SuperLeader will deliberately move toward employee self-set goals. In this situation, the SuperLeader serves as a source of information and experience, as a sounding board, and as the transmitter of overall organizational goals. In the end, in a true self-leadership situation, the employee is given substantial latitude to establish his or her own goals.

We have found that sharing goal setting with subordinates is frequently one of the most difficult transitions for traditional leaders to understand and accept on their road to effective SuperLeadership. Often, an executive is reluctant to provide the full opportunity for a subordinate to lead himself or herself because it seems the executive is losing control.

One of the most interesting aspects of Coach Joe Paterno is his ability to be introspective about this dilemma of overcontrol and undercontrol. Hyman and White quoted him as follows: "It's difficult" he candidly admits "for me to handle people in the way I think they want to be handled ... because I have a tendency to want *complete control* .... In the early part of my career ... I would plot every offensive and defensive move we would use in a ball game and try to devise the game play by myself ... I felt that I had to have input in everything that went on every minute of the day and every day of the week." Paterno seems destined to deal with the classic dilemma between his natural "hands on" activist leadership style and the behaviors required of a SuperLeader. There seems to be a conflict between his emotional self, which has a strong desire to control—perhaps over-control—the situation, versus his intellectual self, which realizes the necessity and benefit of providing more opportunity for his assistant coaches. The "natural" self says, "Hey, I gotta get in there and do it myself," while the intellectual self says, "I have to stand back and give them an opportunity to do it." In the end, the important thing, he says, "is still keeping control but knowing when you don't have to have control."

Good leaders intuitively understand the effects on performance of "knowing where they are going." During subordinate employees' critical transition from traditional external leadership to self-leadership, previous dependency on superior authority needs to be unlearned. In its place, employees must develop a strong sense of confidence in their own abilities to set realistic and challenging goals on their own.

Frequently this transition is not very smooth, leaving the employee wondering why "the boss" is not providing more help, and the executive biting his lip to avoid telling the employee to do the "right thing." Employees need to have some latitude in making mistakes during this critical period.

Reprimand takes on special importance during the critical transition phase, when the superior-subordinate relationship is very delicate. Careless use of reprimand can seriously set back the employee's transition to self-leadership. The issue becomes especially salient when employees make mistakes—sometimes serious mistakes. In our experience, during the transition to self-leadership, some mistakes are inevitable and should be expected as an employee reaches out. The way the SuperLeader responds to the mistakes can ensure or thwart a successful transition. Again, in 3M's historical book *Our Story So Far*, former CEO William McKnight commented on the issue this way, "Mistakes will be made, but if a person is essentially fight, the mistakes he or she makes are not as serious in the long run as the mistakes management will make if it is dictatorial and undertakes to tell those under its authority exactly how they must do their job . . . . Management that is destructively critical when mistakes are made kills initiative and it is essential that we have many people with initiative if we're going to grow."

Andrew Grove, CEO of chip maker Intel Corporation, discussed the issue of how to react when an employee seems to be making a mistake. Reacting too soon or too harshly can result in a serious setback in efforts to develop employee self-leadership. According to Grove, the manager needs to consider the degree to which the error can be tolerated or not. For example, if the task is an analysis for internal use, the experience the employee receives may be well worth some wasted work and delay. However, if the error involves a shipment to a customer, the customer should not bear the expense of boosting the employee further down the learning curve.

Sometimes the SuperLeader might *deliberately* hold back goals or decisions that, at other times, in other places, he or she would be more than willing to provide. Self-led employees must learn to stand on their own.

Once through this critical transition phase, the effects on the self-led employee's performance can be remarkable. Effectively leading themselves produces a motivation and psychological commitment that energizes employees to greater and greater achievements. SuperLeaders who have successfully unleashed the power of self-led employees understand the ultimate reward and satisfaction of managing these individuals.

SUPERLEADERSHIP: A COMPREHENSIVE FRAMEWORK

It should be clear by now that we are addressing a different approach to leadership, radically unlike many of the classic stereotypes of strong leadership. Most of all, we believe that SuperLeadership is a process that can be *learned*, that is not restricted to a few "special" individuals that are born with an unusual capability. Granted, some seem to have more to learn than others, but the potential for SuperLeadership seems to be almost universal.

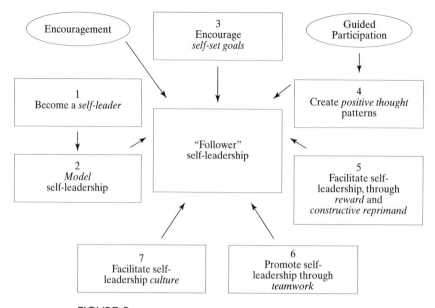

FIGURE 3   **The Seven-Step Process of SuperLeadership**

Figure 3 is a representation of the separate components of SuperLeadership, brought together in an organized framework with self-leadership at the core. The logic is that each SuperLeadership component is of central importance to the development of the self-leadership system within each employee. The potential payoffs include increased employee performance and innovation flowing from enhanced commitment, motivation, and employee capability.

It seems clear that an essential ingredient to SuperLeadership is a boundless optimism about the potential of ordinary people to accomplish extraordinary things. In the March 26, 1990 issue of *Fortune*, Max DePree, Herman Miller chairman, put it this way: "Take a 33-year-old man who assembles chairs. He's been doing it several years. He has a wife and two children. He knows what to do when the children have earaches, and how to get them through school. He probably serves on a volunteer board, and when he comes to work we give him a supervisor . . . . He doesn't need one." This positive viewpoint of man in general is a fairly common characteristic of SuperLeaders. They seem to have unlimited faith that, if given the opportunity to perform, most people will come through for them.

SuperLeadership is not all that unusual if we just know where to look for it. The Peace Corps, for example, has been an organization in the business of producing SuperLeaders for years, even though they don't use the term. Consider the young woman, Patty, who organizes health education events for the women and children of a third-world community. Eventually, the community decides itself to build community latrines, and within a year, 15 latrines have been constructed. Health improves. Now, building latrines doesn't sound much like the stuff of leadership, but this young Peace Corps volunteer was indeed a SuperLeader by leading others to lead themselves to accomplish something of critical importance to all those who were involved.

It's all too easy to underestimate the capability of seemingly ordinary people. Lincoln Electric, the highly successful welding manufacturer, found some special capabilities among its employees when its sales were sagging in 1982. Faced with a no-layoff policy, management asked its factory workers for some help. Fifty of their production workers volunteered to help out in sales.

After a quickie sales training course, the former production workers started calling on body shops all over the country. They concentrated on small shops that would be able to use the company's Model

SP200, a small welder. The end of the story is that their efforts brought in $10 million in new sales and established the small arc welder as one of Lincoln's best-selling items.

Lincoln Electric was relying on the idea of the self-fulfilling prophecy. Like real SuperLeaders, they were willing to take a risk on people; and the risk frequently becomes self-fulfilling. Lincoln carries this philosophy throughout all parts of the organization. As one example, it manages to produce the lowest cost, highest quality welders in the industry with a supervisor to worker ratio of 1 to 100. Yes, that's right—one supervisor for every 100 workers. Clearly, this would not be possible unless every employee was considered to be a true self-leader. At Lincoln, every employee is evaluated on the ability to work without supervision.

Ideally, the SuperLeader comes to be surrounded by strong people—self-leaders in their own right—who pursue exceptional achievement because they love to. The SuperLeader's strength is greatly enhanced since it is drawn from the strength of many people who have been encouraged to grow, flourish, and become important contributors. The SuperLeader becomes "Super" through the talents and capabilities of others. As self-leadership is nurtured, the power for progress is unleashed. In the March 26, 1990 issue of *Fortune*, Colgate-Palmolive CEO Ruben Mark put it this way: "I see business moving away from the authoritarian approach and toward a shared decision-making approach . . . making partnership with our own people."

SuperLeadership offers the most viable mechanism for establishing exceptional self-leading followers. True excellence can be achieved by facilitating the self-leadership system that operates within each person—by challenging each person to reach deep inside for the best each has to offer. Employee compliance is not enough. Leading others to lead themselves is the key to tapping the intelligence, the spirit, the creativity, the commitment, and most of all the tremendous unique potential of each individual.

To us, the message is clear: Excellence is achievable, but only if leaders are dedicated to tapping the vast potential within each individual. Most of all, this does not mean that more so-called charismatic or transformational leaders are needed to influence followers to comply with and carry out the vision of the leader. Rather, the vision itself needs to reflect and draw upon the vast resources contained within individual employees.

The currently popular notion that excellent leaders need to be visionary and charismatic may be a trap if taken too far. Wisdom on leadership for centuries has warned us about this potential trap. Remember what Abraham Lincoln said, "You cannot help men permanently by doing for them what they could and should do for themselves." Remember, also, the timeless words, "Give a man a fish and he will be fed for a lifetime."

It is time to transcend the notion of leaders as heroes and to focus instead on leaders as heromakers. Is the spotlight on the leader, or on the achievements of the followers? To discover this new breed of leader, look not at the leader but at the followers. SuperLeaders have SuperFollowers that are dynamic self-leaders. The SuperLeader leads others to lead themselves. Perhaps this spirit was captured most succinctly by Lao-tzu, a sixth-century B.C. Chinese philosopher, when he wrote the following:

A leader is best
When people barely know he exists,
Not so good when people obey and acclaim him.
Worse when they despise him.
But of a good leader, who talks little,
When his work is done, his aim fulfilled,
They will say:
We did it ourselves.

CHAPTER 14
ORGANIZATIONAL CULTURE

UNCOVERING THE LEVELS OF CULTURE
Edgar H. Schein

THREE CULTURES OF MANAGEMENT: THE KEY TO ORGANIZATIONAL LEARNING
Edgar. H. Schein

EVOLUTION AND REVOLUTION AS ORGANIZATIONS GROW
Larry E. Greiner

Organizational culture greatly influences the way people behave at work. Ever since this discovery was made, scholars and managers alike have been interested in learning how to create, manage, and maintain productive and healthy organizational cultures.

Edgar Schein, management professor emeritus, has contributed much of our current knowledge about organizational culture. The first selection, "Uncovering the Levels of Culture," is a chapter from his book, *Organizational Culture and Leadership*, considered a classic in its field. Schein defines organizational culture and explains how it works.

Schein and others have also noted the presence and importance of subcultures and occupational cultures. The second article, "Three Cultures of Management: The Key to Organizational Learning," is also written by Schein. He provides an answer to a question that has plagued many managers and organizational consultants—why organizations fail to learn and innovate. Schein points to organizational subcultures that arise within and across organizations that fail to act in concert.

The final article is an updated classic by Larry Greiner, management and organization professor. In "Evolution and Revolution as Organizations Grow," Greiner outlines five phases organizations go through as they develop and grow. According to Greiner, leaders should understand where their organization is in this developmental scheme, in part because each phase requires a different type of leadership and organizational emphasis.

~⟩

UNCOVERING THE LEVELS OF CULTURE*

Edgar H. Schein

The culture of a group can now be defined as

A pattern of shared basic assumptions that the group learned as it solved its problems of external adaptation and internal integration, that has worked well enough to be considered valid and,

---

*Excerpted with permission from *Organizational Culture and Leadership* (San Francisco, CA: Jossey-Bass, 1997): 16–27.

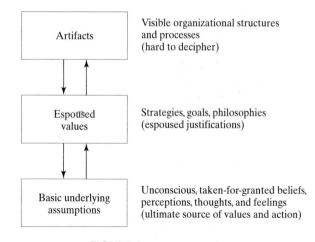

FIGURE 1   **Levels of Culture**

*therefore, to be taught to new members as the correct way to perceive, think, and feel in relation
to those problems.*

The purpose of this chapter is to show that culture can be analyzed at several different levels, where
the term level refers to the degree to which the cultural phenomenon is visible to the observer. Some
of the confusion of definition of what culture really is results from not differentiating the levels at
which it manifests itself. These levels range from the very tangible overt manifestations that one can
see and feel to the deeply embedded, unconscious basic assumptions that I am defining as the essence
of culture. In between we have various espoused values, norms, and rules of behavior that members
of the culture use as a way of depicting the culture to themselves and others.

Many other culture researchers prefer the concept of "basic values" for describing the deepest
levels. As I will try to show with later examples, my preference is for "basic assumptions" because these
tend to be taken for granted and are treated as nonnegotiable. Values can be and are discussed, and people can agree to disagree about them. Basic assumptions are so taken for granted that someone who
does not hold them is viewed as crazy and automatically dismissed. The levels at which culture can
be analyzed are shown in Figure 1.

ARTIFACTS

At the surface we have the level of *artifacts*, which includes all the phenomena that one sees, hears,
and feels when one encounters a new group with an unfamiliar culture. Artifacts would include the visible products of the group such as the architecture of its physical environment, its language, its technology and products, its artistic creations, and its style as embodied in clothing, manners of address,
emotional displays, myths and stories told about the organization, published lists of values, observable
rituals and ceremonies, and so on. For purposes of cultural analysis this level also includes the visible
behavior of the group and the organizational processes into which such behavior is made routine.

The most important point about this level of the culture is that it is easy to observe and very difficult to decipher. The Egyptians and the Maya both built highly visible pyramids, but the meaning of
pyramids in each culture was very different—tombs in one and temples as well as tombs in the other.
In other words, the observer can describe what she sees and feels but cannot reconstruct from that
alone what those things mean in the given group, or whether they even reflect important underlying
assumptions.

On the other hand, one school of thought argues that one's own response to physical artifacts such as buildings and office layouts can lead to the identification of major images and root metaphors that reflect the deepest level of the culture (Gagliardi, 1990). This would be especially true if the organization one is deciphering is in the same larger culture as the researcher. The problem is that symbols are ambiguous, and one can only test one's insight into what something might mean if one has also experienced the culture at the level of its values and the level of its basic assumptions.

It is especially dangerous to try to infer the deeper assumptions from artifacts alone because one's interpretations will inevitably be projections of one's own feelings and reactions. For example, when one sees a very informal, loose organization, one may interpret that as inefficient if one's own background is based on the assumption that informality means playing around and not working. Alternatively, if one sees a very formal organization, one may interpret that to be a sign of lack of innovative capacity if one's own experience is based on the assumption that formality means bureaucracy and formalization.

Every facet of a group's life produces artifacts, creating the problem of classification. In reading cultural descriptions, one often notes that different observers choose to report on different sorts of artifacts, leading to noncomparable descriptions. Anthropologists have developed classification systems, but these tend to be so vast and detailed that cultural essence becomes difficult to discern.

If the observer lives in the group long enough, the meanings of artifacts gradually become clear. If, however, one wants to achieve this level of understanding more quickly, one can attempt to analyze the espoused values, norms, and rules that provide the day-to-day operating principles by which the members of the group guide their behavior. This kind of inquiry takes us to the next level of cultural analysis.

ESPOUSED VALUES

All group learning ultimately reflects someone's original values, someone's sense of what ought to be as distinct from what is. When a group is first created or when it faces a new task, issue, or problem, the first solution proposed to deal with it reflects some individual's own assumptions about what is right or wrong, what will work or not work. Those individuals who prevail, who can influence the group to adopt a certain approach to the problem, will later be identified as "leaders" or founders, but the group as a group does not yet have any shared knowledge because it has not yet taken a common action in response to the new problem. Therefore, whatever is proposed can only have the status of a value from the point of view of the group, no matter how strongly the proponent may believe that he or she is uttering absolute proven truth. Until the group has taken some joint action and its members have together observed the outcome of that action, there is not as yet a shared basis for determining what is factual and real.

For example, in a young business if sales begin to decline, a manager may say, "We must increase advertising" because of her belief that advertising always increases sales. The group, never having experienced this situation before, will hear that assertion as a statement of that manager's values: "She believes that when one is in trouble it is a *good* thing to increase advertising." What the leader initially proposes, therefore, cannot have any status other than a value to be questioned, debated, challenged, and tested.

If the manager convinces the group to act on her belief and if the solution works and if the group has a shared perception of that success, then the perceived value that advertising is "good" gradually starts a process of *cognitive transformation*. First, it will be transformed into a *shared value or belief* and, ultimately, into a *shared assumption* (if action based on it continues to be successful). If this transformation process occurs—and it will occur only if the proposed solution continues to work, thus implying that it is in some larger sense "correct" and must reflect an accurate picture of reality—group members will tend to forget that originally they were not sure and that the proposed course of action was at an earlier time debated and confronted.

Not all values undergo such transformation. First of all, the solution based on a given value may not work reliably. Only values that are susceptible to physical or social validation and that continue to work reliably in solving the group's problems will become transformed into assumptions. Second, value domains dealing with the less controllable elements of the environment or with aesthetic or moral matters may not be testable at all. In such cases consensus through social validation is still possible, but it is not automatic.

By social validation I mean that certain values are confirmed only by the shared social experience of a group. Such values typically involve the group's internal relations, where the test of whether they work or not is how comfortable and anxiety-free members are when they abide by them. Social validation also applies to those broader values that involve relationships to the environment but in a nontestable fashion, such as religion, ethics, and aesthetics.

In these realms the group learns that certain such values, as initially promulgated by prophets, founders, and leaders, work in the sense of reducing uncertainty in critical areas of the group's functioning. And as they continue to work, they gradually become transformed into nondiscussable assumptions supported by articulated sets of beliefs, norms, and operational rules of behavior. The derived beliefs and moral/ethical rules remain conscious and are explicitly articulated because they serve the normative or moral function of guiding members of the group in how to deal with certain key situations and in training new members in how to behave. A set of values that becomes embodied in an ideology or organizational philosophy thus can serve as a guide and as a way of dealing with the uncertainty of intrinsically uncontrollable or difficult events.

Values at this conscious level will predict much of the behavior that can be observed at the artifactual level. But if those values are not based on prior learning, they may also reflect only what Argyris and Schön (1978) have called *espoused values*, which predict well enough what people will say in a variety of situations but which may be out of line with what they will actually *do* in situations where those values should, in fact, be operating. Thus, a company may say that it values people and has high quality standards for its products, but its record in that regard may contradict what it says.

If the espoused values are reasonably congruent with the underlying assumptions, then the articulation of those values into a philosophy of operating can be helpful in bringing the group together, serving as a source of identity and core mission. But in analyzing values one must discriminate carefully between those that are congruent with underlying assumptions and those that are, in effect, either rationalizations or only aspirations for the future. Often such lists of values are not patterned, sometimes they are even mutually contradictory, and often they are inconsistent with observed behavior. Large areas of behavior are often left unexplained, leaving us with a feeling that we understand a piece of the culture but still do not have the culture as such in hand. To get at that deeper level of understanding, to decipher the pattern, and to predict future behavior correctly, we have to understand more fully the category of basic assumptions.

BASIC ASSUMPTIONS

When a solution to a problem works repeatedly, it comes to be taken for granted. What was once a hypothesis, supported only by a hunch or a value, comes gradually to be treated as a reality. We come to believe that nature really works this way. Basic assumptions, in this sense, are different from what some anthropologists call dominant value orientations in that such dominant orientations reflect the preferred solution among several basic alternatives, but all the alternatives are still visible in the culture, and any given member of the culture could, from time to time, behave according to variant as well as dominant orientations (Kluckhohn and Strodtbeck, 1961).

Basic assumptions, in the sense in which I want to define the concept, have become so taken for granted that one finds little variation within a cultural unit. In fact, if a basic assumption is strongly held in a group, members will find behavior based on any other premise inconceivable. For example, a group whose basic assumption is that the individual's rights supersede those of the group members will find it inconceivable that members would commit suicide or in some other way sacrifice themselves to the group even if they had dishonored the group. In a capitalist country, it is inconceivable that one might design a company to operate consistently at a financial loss or that it does not matter whether or not a product works. Basic assumptions, in this sense, are similar to what Argyris has identified as *theories-in-use*, the implicit assumptions that actually guide behavior, that tell group members how to perceive, think about, and feel about things (Argyris, 1976; Argyris and Schön, 1974).

Basic assumptions, like theories-in-use, tend to be those we neither confront nor debate and hence are extremely difficult to change. To learn something new in this realm requires us to resurrect, reexamine, and possibly change some of the more stable portions of our cognitive structure, a process that Argyris and others have called double-loop learning or frame breaking (for example, Argyris, Putnam, and Smith, 1985; Bartunek and Moch, 1987). Such learning is intrinsically difficult because the reexamination of basic assumptions temporarily destabilizes our cognitive and interpersonal world, releasing large quantities of basic anxiety.

Rather than tolerating such anxiety levels we tend to want to perceive the events around us as congruent with our assumptions, even if that means distorting, denying, projecting, or in other ways falsifying to ourselves what may be going on around us. It is in this psychological process that culture has its ultimate power. Culture as a set of basic assumptions defines for us what to pay attention to, what things mean, how to react emotionally to what is going on, and what actions to take in various kinds of situations. Once we have developed an integrated set of such assumptions, which might be called a thought world or mental map, we will be maximally comfortable with others who share the same set of assumptions and very uncomfortable and vulnerable in situations where different assumptions operate either because we will not understand what is going on, or, worse, misperceive and misinterpret the actions of others (Douglas, 1986).

The human mind needs cognitive stability. Therefore, any challenge to or questioning of a basic assumption will release anxiety and defensiveness. In this sense, the shared basic assumptions that make up the culture of a group can be thought of at both the individual and group levels as psychological cognitive *defense mechanisms* that permit the group to continue to function. Recognizing this connection is important when one thinks about changing aspects of a group's culture, for it is no easier to do that than to change an individual's pattern of defense mechanisms. In either case the key is the management of the large amounts of anxiety that accompany any relearning at this level.

To understand how unconscious assumptions can distort data, consider the following example. If we assume, on the basis of past experience or education, that other people will take advantage of us whenever they have an opportunity, we expect to be taken advantage of and then interpret the behavior of others in a way that coincides with those expectations. We observe people sitting in a seemingly idle posture at their desks and interpret their behavior as loafing rather than thinking out an important problem. We perceive absence from work as shirking rather than doing work at home.

If this is not only a personal assumption but one that is shared and thus part of the organization's culture, we will discuss with others what to do about our "lazy" work force and institute tight controls to ensure that people are at their desks and busy. If employees suggest that they do some of their work at home, we will be uncomfortable and probably deny the request because we will assume that at home they would loaf (Bailyn, 1992; Perin, 1991).

In contrast, if we assume that everyone is highly motivated and competent, we will act in accordance with that assumption by encouraging people to work at their own pace and in their own way. If someone is discovered to be unproductive in the organization, we will assume that there is a mismatch between the person and the job assignment, not that the person is lazy or incompetent. If the employee wants to work at home, we will perceive that as evidence of wanting to be productive even if circumstances require him to be at home.

In both cases there is the potential for distortion. The cynical manager will not perceive how highly motivated some of the subordinates really are, and the idealistic manager will not perceive that there are subordinates who are lazy and who are taking advantage of the situation. As McGregor (1960) noted several decades ago, such assumption sets in the human area become the basis of whole management and control systems that perpetuate themselves because if people are treated consistently in terms of certain basic assumptions, they come eventually to behave according to those assumptions in order to make their world stable and predictable.

Unconscious assumptions sometimes lead to ridiculously tragic situations, as illustrated by a common problem experienced by American supervisors in some Asian countries. A manager who comes from an American pragmatic tradition takes it for granted that solving a problem always has the highest priority. When that manager encounters a subordinate who comes from a different cultural tradition, in which good relationships and protecting the superior's "face" are assumed to have top priority, the following scenario can easily result.

The manager proposes a solution to a given problem. The subordinate knows that the solution will not work, but his unconscious assumption requires that he remain silent because to tell the boss that the proposed solution is wrong is a threat to the boss's face. It would not even occur to the subordinate to do anything other than remain silent or even reassure the boss that they should go ahead and take the action if the boss were to inquire what the subordinate thought.

The action is taken, the results are negative, and the boss, somewhat surprised and puzzled, asks the subordinate what he would have done. When the subordinate reports that he would have done something different, the boss quite legitimately asks why the subordinate did not speak up sooner. This question puts the subordinate in an impossible bind because the answer itself is a threat to the boss's face. He cannot possibly explain his behavior without committing the very sin he is trying to avoid in the first place—namely, embarrassing the boss. He might even lie at this point and argue that what the boss did was right and only "bad luck" or uncontrollable circumstances prevented it from succeeding.

From the point of view of the subordinate, the boss's behavior is incomprehensible because it shows lack of self-pride, possibly causing the subordinate to lose respect for that boss. To the boss the subordinate's behavior is equally incomprehensible. The boss cannot develop any sensible explanation of the subordinate's behavior that is not cynically colored by the assumption that the subordinate at some level just does not care about effective performance and therefore must be gotten rid of. It never occurs to the boss that another assumption such as "one never embarrasses a superior" is operating and that to the subordinate that assumption is even more powerful than "one gets the job done."

If assumptions such as these operate only in an individual and represent her idiosyncratic experience, they can be corrected more easily because the person will detect that she is alone in holding a given assumption. The power of culture comes about through the fact that the assumptions are shared and therefore mutually reinforced. In these instances probably only a third party or some cross-cultural education could help to find common ground whereby both parties could bring their implicit assumptions to the surface. And even after they have surfaced, such assumptions would still operate, forcing the boss and the subordinate to invent a whole new communication mechanism that would permit each to remain congruent with her or his culture—for example, agreeing that before any decision is made and before the boss has stuck her neck out, the subordinate will be asked for suggestions and for factual data that will not be face threatening. Note that the solution must keep each cultural assumption intact. One cannot in these instances simply declare one or the other cultural assumption "wrong." One has to find a third assumption to allow them both to retain their integrity.

I have dwelled on this example to illustrate the potency of implicit, unconscious assumptions and to show that such assumptions often deal with fundamental aspects of life—the nature of time and space; human nature and human activities; the nature of truth and how one discovers it; the correct way for the individual and the group to relate to each other; the relative importance of work, family, and self-development; the proper role of men and women; and the nature of the family.

We do not develop new assumptions about each of these areas in every group or organization we join. Each member of a new group will bring her or his own cultural learning from prior groups, but as the new group develops its own shared history, it will develop modified or brand-new assumptions in critical areas of its experience. Those new assumptions make up the culture of that particular group.

Any group's culture can be studied at these three levels—the level of its artifacts, the level of its values, and the level of its basic assumptions. If one does not decipher the pattern of basic assumptions that may be operating, one will not know how to interpret the artifacts correctly or how much credence to give to the articulated values. In other words, the essence of a culture lies in the pattern of basic underlying assumptions, and once one understands those, one can easily understand the other more surface levels and deal appropriately with them.

SUMMARY AND CONCLUSIONS

Though the essence of a group's culture is its pattern of shared, taken-for-granted basic assumptions, the culture will manifest itself at the levels of observable artifacts and shared espoused values, norms, and rules of behavior. It is important to recognize in analyzing cultures that artifacts are easy to observe but difficult to decipher and that values may only reflect rationalizations or aspirations. To understand a group's culture, one must attempt to get at its shared basic assumptions and one must understand the learning process by which such basic assumptions come to be.

Leadership is originally the source of the beliefs and values that get a group moving in dealing with its internal and external problems. If what a leader proposes works and continues to work, what once was only the leader's assumption gradually comes to be a shared assumption. Once a set of shared basic assumptions is formed by this process, it can function as a cognitive defense mechanism both for the individual members and for the group as a whole. In other words, individuals and groups seek stability and meaning. Once these are achieved, it is easier to distort new data by denial, projection, rationalization, or various other defense mechanisms than to change the basic assumption. As we will see, culture change, in the sense of changing basic assumptions is, therefore, difficult, time consuming, and highly anxiety provoking. This point is especially relevant for the leader who sets out to change the culture of the organization.

The most central issue for leaders, therefore, is how to get at the deeper levels of a culture, how to assess the functionality of the assumptions made at each level, and how to deal with the anxiety that is unleashed when those levels are challenged.

ENDNOTES

Argyris, C. *Integrating the Individual and the Organization* (New York: Wiley, 1976).

Argyris, C. and D. A. Schön, *Theory in Practice: Increasing Professional Effectiveness* (San Francisco: Jossey-Bass, 1974).

Argyris, C. and D. A. Schön, *Organizational Learning* (Reading, MA: Addison-Wesley, 1978).

Argyris, C., R. Putnam, and D. M. Smith, *Action Science* (San Francisco: Jossey-Bass, 1985).

Bailyn, L., "Changing the Conditions of Work: Implications for Career Development," *Career Development in the 1990's: Theory and Practice*, D. H. Montross and C. J. Shinkman (Springfield, IL: Thomas, 1992).

Bartunek, J., and M. K. Moch, "First Order, Second Order, and Third Order Change and Organization Development Interventions: A Cognitive Approach," *Journal of Applied Behavioral Science 23* (1987): 483–500.

Douglas, M., *How Institutions Think* (Syracuse, NY: Syracuse University Press, 1986).

Gagliardi, P. (ed.), *Symbols and Artifacts: Views of the Corporate Landscape* (New York: de Gruyter, 1990).

Kluckhohn, F. R., and F. L. Strodtbeck, *Variations in Value Orientations* (New York: Harper & Row, 1961).

McGregor, D. M., *The Human Side of Enterprise* (New York: McGraw-Hill, 1960).

Perin, C., "The Moral Fabric of the Office," S. Bacharach, S. R. Barley, and P. S. Tolbert (eds.), *Research in the Sociology of Organizations* (special volume on the professions) (Greenwich, CT: JAI Press, 1991).

THREE CULTURES OF MANAGEMENT: THE KEY TO ORGANIZATIONAL LEARNING*

Edgar H. Schein

Why do organizations fail to *learn how to learn* and therefore remain competitively marginal? In this article, I try to explain why organizational innovations either don't occur or fail to survive and proliferate. Some typical explanations revolve around vague concepts of "resistance to change," or "human nature," or failures of "leadership." I propose a more fundamental reason for such learning failures, derived from the fact that, in every organization, there are three particular cultures among its subcultures, two of which have their roots *outside* the organization and are therefore more fundamentally entrenched in their particular assumptions. Every organization develops an internal culture based on its operational success, what I call the *operator culture*. But every organization also has, in its various functions, the designers and technocrats who drive the core technologies. I call this the *engineering culture*; their fundamental reference group is their worldwide occupational community. Every organization also has its executive management, the CEO and his or her immediate subordinates—what I call the *executive culture*. CEOs, because of the nature of their jobs and the structure of the capital markets, also constitute a worldwide occupational community in the sense that they have common problems that are unique to their roles.

These three cultures are often not aligned with each other, and it is this lack of alignment that causes the failures of organizational learning that I will discuss. The question is whether we have misconceived the initial problem by focusing on organizational learning, when, in fact, it is the executive and engineering communities that must begin their own learning process if we are to meet the challenges of the twenty-first century.

ORGANIZATIONS DON'T LEARN; INNOVATIONS DON'T LAST OR DIFFUSE

The ability to create new organizational forms and processes, to innovate in both the technical and organizational arenas, is crucial to remaining competitive in an increasingly turbulent world. But this kind of organizational learning requires not only the invention of new forms but also their adoption and diffusion to the other relevant parts of the organization and to other organizations in a given industry. Organizations still have not learned how to manage that process. The examples of successful organizational learning we have seen either tend to be short-run adaptive learning—doing better at what

---

*Reprinted with permission from the *Sloan Management Review* (Fall 1996): 9–20.

we are already doing—or, if they are genuine innovations, tend to be isolated and eventually subverted and abandoned.

For example, a new product development team in a large auto company worked with the MIT Organizational Learning Center to develop a capacity for learning. By using various techniques derived from "action science," systems dynamics, and organization development, the team created high levels of openness between hierarchical levels and increased communication and trust among its members.[1] This openness and trust permitted team members to reveal engineering design problems as they arose instead of waiting until they had solutions, as prior tradition in this company had dictated.[2]

Early identification of those problems was crucial in order to avoid later interactive effects that would require costly, complex redesigns. For example, changing the chassis design might increse weight, which might require a different tire design, which, in turn, might cause more internal noise, and so on. By revealing such problems early, the team could view the whole car more systemically and could therefore speed up redesign.

However, the pileup of early problems caused upper-level managers to make a false attribution. They considered the team to be "out of control" and ordered it to get itself back under control. The team realized that higher management did not understand the value of early problem identification and continued to use its new learning, assuming that the ultimate results would speak for themselves. The team was able to complete the design well ahead of schedule and with considerably lower costs, but, contrary to expectations, higher managers never understood the reasons for these notable results nor gave the team credit for having learned a new way of solving problems. Instead, higher managers gave themselves credit for having gotten the team "under control." They did not consider the team to be particularly innovative and disbanded it. They subsequently encouraged several of its members and leaders to take early retirement as part of the company's general downsizing program.

In another example, an insurance company decided to move toward the paperless office.[3] Top management hired a manager to implement the new system, mandated a schedule, and provided whatever resources the manager needed to accomplish the task. In order to use the new system, employees had to learn complex new computer routines to replace their familiar work with paper. Because the company was also under financial pressure, it had instituted a number of productivity programs that caused line managers to insist that all the daily work continue to be performed even while the learning of the new system was supposed to take place. The new manager was equally insistent that the system be implemented on schedule, causing employees to short-circuit certain routines, to learn only the rudiments of the new system, and even to misrepresent the degree to which they were now working without paper.

The new manager, based on partial and incorrect information, declared that the system was implemented "on schedule" and was given public credit for this achievement. However, the result was that the employees did not learn the new system well enough to make it more productive than the old paper system. In fact, productivity was lower with the new system because it was so imperfectly implemented.

In a third example, a company decided to introduce automatic machine tools into its production process.[4] The idea originated with the engineers who saw an opportunity to do some "real" engineering. The engineers and the vendors developed a proposal based on technical elegance but found that middle management would not push the proposal up to executive management unless it was rewritten to show how it would reduce costs by cutting labor. No accurate figures were available, so the team more or less invented the numbers to justify the purchase of the expensive new machines.

As the proposal worked its way up the hierarchy, the labor union got wind of the project and insisted that it would not go along unless management guaranteed that no jobs would be lost and that all the present operators would be retrained. This not only delayed the project, but, when the machines were finally installed, the production process proved to be much less effective and much more costly than had been promised in the proposal. The engineers were highly disappointed that their elegant solution had, from their point of view, been subverted and that all the operators that were to have been replaced had merely been retrained and kept on jobs that the engineers considered superfluous.

Beyond these three specific cases, the history of organizational development, change, innovation, and learning shows over and over that certain lessons seem not to take hold. Since the Hawthorne studies of the 1920s, it has been recognized that employee involvement increased both productivity and motivation. Lewin, Argyris, McGregor, Likert, and many others showed how managers who treated people as adults, who involved them appropriately in the tasks that they were accountable for, and who created conditions so employees could obtain good feedback and monitor their own performance were more effective than those who did not.[5]

Programs such as the National Training Labs' sensitivity training groups and Blake's managerial grid were, for several decades, touted as the solution to all our productivity problems, just as the human relations and participatory management programs of the forties had promised.[6] Yet these and other similar programs have come and gone, and it is not at all clear what organizations learned from them or why these innovations have disappeared, only to be reinvented under new labels such as empowerment, self-managed groups, and servant leadership.

The lesson of these and similar cases is complicated. On the one hand, we can say that this is just normal life in organizations. It is just politics or just human nature. Or we can say that these projects and programs were mismanaged, by either the project teams or the executive managers above them. Or we can say that all these human-relations-oriented programs were misguided in the first place. However, I have begun to see deeper phenomena at work here.

The deeper issue is that in most organizations, there are three different major occupational cultures that do not really understand each other very well and that often work at cross-purposes. These cultures cut across organizations and are based on what have been described as "occupational communities."[7]

THE CONCEPT OF CULTURE AND OCCUPATIONAL COMMUNITIES

A culture is a set of basic tacit assumptions about how the world is and ought to be that a group of people share and that determines their perceptions, thoughts, feelings, and, to some degree, their overt behavior.[8] Culture manifests itself at three levels: the level of deep tacit assumptions that are the essence of the culture, the level of espoused values that often reflect what a group wishes ideally to be and the way it wants to present itself publicly, and the day-to-day behavior that represents a complex compromise among the espoused values, the deeper assumptions, and the immediate requirements of the situation. Overt behavior alone cannot be used to decipher culture because situational contingencies often make us behave in a manner that is inconsistent with our deeper-values and assumptions. For this reason, one often sees "inconsistencies" or "conflicts" in overt behavior or between behavior and espoused values. To discover the basic elements of a culture, one must either observe behavior for a very long time or get directly at the underlying values and assumptions that drive the perceptions and thoughts of the group members.

For example, many organizations espouse "teamwork" and "cooperation," but the behavior that the incentive and control systems of the organization reward and encourage is based more on a shared tacit assumption that only individuals can be accountable and that the best results come from a system of individual competition and rewards. If the external situation demands teamwork, the group will develop some behavior that looks, on the surface, like teamwork by conducting meetings and seeking consensus, but members will continue to share the belief that they can get ahead by individual effort and will act accordingly when rewards are given out. I have heard many executives tell their subordinates that they expect them to act as a team but remind them in the same sentence that they are all competing for the boss's job!

CULTURES AND SUBCULTURES

Cultures arise within organizations based on their own histories and experiences. Starting with the founders, those members of an organization who have shared in its successful growth have developed assumptions about the world and how to succeed in it, and have taught those assumptions to new members of the organization.[9] Thus IBM, Hewlett-Packard, Ford, and any other company that has had several decades of success will have an organizational culture that drives how its members think, feel, and act.

Shared assumptions also typically form around, the functional units of the organization. They are often based on members' similar educational backgrounds or similar organizational experiences, what we often end up calling "stove pipes" or "silos." We all know that getting cross-functional project teams to work well together is difficult because the members bring their functional cultures into the project and, as a consequence, have difficulty communicating with each other, reaching consensus, and implementing decisions effectively. The difficulty of communication across these boundaries arises not only from the fact that the functional groups have different goals, but also from the more fundamental issue that the very meaning of the words they use will differ. The word "marketing" will mean product development to the engineer, studying customers through market research to the product manager, merchandising to the salesperson, and constant change in design to the manufacturing manager. When they try to work together, they will often attribute disagreement to personalities and fail to notice the deeper, shared assumptions that color how each function thinks.

Another kind of subculture, less often acknowledged, reflects the common experiences of given levels within a hierarchy. Culture arises through shared experiences of success. If first-line supervisors discover ways of managing their subordinates that are consistently successful, they gradually build up shared assumptions about how to do their job that can be thought of as the "culture of first-line supervision." In the same way, middle management and higher levels will develop their own shared assumptions and, at each level, will teach those assumptions to newcomers as they get promoted. These hierarchically based cultures create the communication problems associated with "selling senior management on a new way of doing things," or "getting budget approval for a new piece of equipment," or "getting a personnel requisition through." As each cultural boundary is crossed, the proposal has to be put into the appropriate language for the next higher level and has to reflect the values and assumptions of that level. Or, from the viewpoint of the higher levels, decisions have to be put into a form that lower levels can understand, often resulting in "translations" that actually distort and sometimes even subvert what the higher levels wanted.

So far, I have focused on the cultures that arise within organizations from the unique experiences of its members. But "occupational communities" also generate cultures that cut across organizations.[10] For example, fishermen around the world develop similar world-views, as do miners, as do the members of a particular industry based on a particular technology. In these cases, the shared assumptions derive from a common educational background, the requirements of a given occupation such as the licenses that have to be obtained to practice, and the shared contact with others in the occupation. The various functional cultures in organizations are, in fact, partly the result of membership in broader cross-organizational occupational communities. Salespeople the world over, accountants, assembly line workers, and engineers share some tacit assumptions about the nature of their work regardless of who their particular employer is at any given time.

Such similar outlooks across organizations also apply to executive managers, particularly CEOs. CEOs face similar problems in all organizations and in all industries throughout the world. Because executives are likely to have, somewhere in their history, some common education and indoctrination, they form a common worldview—common assumptions about the nature of business and what it takes to run a business successfully.

THREE CULTURES OF MANAGEMENT

The learning problems that I have identified can be directly related to the lack of alignment among three cultures, two of which are based on occupational communities—(1) the culture of engineering, (2) the culture of CEOs, and (3) the culture of operators—and the shared assumptions that arise in the "line units" of a given organization as it attempts to operate efficiently and safely. To understand how these three cultures interact, let us examine their shared assumptions.

THE OPERATOR CULTURE

The culture of operators is the most difficult to describe because it evolves locally in organizations and within operational units (see "Assumptions of the Operator Culture"). Thus we can identify an operator culture in the nuclear plant, the chemical complex, the auto manufacturing plant, the airplane cockpit, and the office, but it is not clear what elements make this culture broader than the local unit. To focus on this issue, we must consider that the operations in different industries reflect the broad technological trends in those industries. At some fundamental level, how one does things in a given industry reflects the core technologies that created that industry. And, as those core technologies themselves evolve, the nature of operations changes. For example, as Zuboff has persuasively argued, information technology has made manual labor obsolete in many industries and replaced it with conceptual tasks.[11] In a chemical plant, the worker no longer walks around observing, smelling, touching, and manipulating. Instead he or she sits in a control room and infers the conditions in the plant from the various indexes that come up on the computer screen.

ASSUMPTIONS OF THE OPERATOR CULTURE

- Because the action of any organization is ultimately the action of people, the success of the enterprise depends on people's knowledge, skill, learning ability, and commitment.
- The required knowledge and skill are "local" and based on the organization's core technology.
- No matter how carefully engineered the production process is or how carefully rules and routines are specified, operators must have the capacity to learn and to deal with surprises.
- Most operations involve interdependencies between separate elements of the process; hence, operators must be able to work as a collaborative team in which communication, openness, mutual trust, and commitment are highly valued.

The operator culture is based on human interaction, and most line units learn that high levels of communication, trust, and teamwork are essential to getting the work done efficiently. Operators also learn that no matter how clearly the rules are specified as to what is supposed to be done under different operational conditions, the world is to some degree unpredictable and one must be prepared to use one's own innovative skills. If the operations are complex, as in a nuclear plant, operators learn that they are highly interdependent and must work together as a team, especially when dealing with unanticipated events. Rules and hierarchy often get in the way in unpredicted conditions. Operators become highly sensitive to the degree to which the production process is a system of interdependent functions, all of which must work together to be efficient and effective. These points apply to all kinds of "production processes," whether a sales function, a clerical group, a cockpit, or a service unit.

The tragedy of most organizations is that the operators know that, to get the job done effectively, they must adhere to the assumptions stated above, but that neither the incentive system nor the day-to-day management system may support those assumptions. Operators thus learn to subvert what they know to be true and "work to rule," or use their learning ability to thwart management's efforts to improve productivity. To understand why this happens, we must examine how two other major cultures operate in organizations.

THE ENGINEERING CULTURE

In all organizations, one group represents the basic design elements of the technology underlying the work of the organization and has the knowledge of how that technology is to be utilized. This occupational community cuts across nations and industries and can best be labeled the "engineering culture."[12] A colleague who works for a company driven by the engineering culture told me that in the parking lot of his company, signs say, "Maximum Speed Limit: 5.8 Miles Per Hour." Although this culture is most visible in traditional engineering functions, it is also evident among the designers and implementers of all kinds of technologies—information technology, market research, financial systems, and so on. The shared assumptions of this community are based on common education, work experience, and job requirements (see "Assumptions of the Engineering Culture").

Engineers and technocrats of all persuasions are attracted to engineering because it is abstract and impersonal. Their education reinforces the view that problems have abstract solutions and that those solutions can, in principle, be implemented in the real world with products and systems free of human foibles and errors. Engineers, and I use this term in the broadest sense, are designers of products and systems that have utility, elegance, permanence, efficiency, safety, and maybe, as in the case of architecture, even aesthetic appeal, but they are basically designed to require standard responses from their human operators, or, ideally, to have no human operators at all.

In the design of complex systems such as jet aircraft or nuclear plants, the engineer prefers a technical routine to ensure safety rather than relying on a human team to manage the possible contingencies. Engineers recognize the human factor and design for it, but their preference is to make things as automatic as possible. Safety is built into the designs themselves.

ASSUMPTIONS OF THE ENGINEERING CULTURE

- Engineers are proactively optimistic that they can and should master nature.
- Engineers are stimulated by puzzles and problems and are pragmatic perfectionists who prefer "people free" solutions.
- The ideal world is one of elegant machines and processes working in perfect precision and harmony without human intervention.
- Engineers are safety oriented and overdesign for safety.
- Engineers prefer linear, simple cause-and-effect, quantitative thinking.

When I asked an Egyptian Airlines pilot whether he preferred Russian or U.S. planes, he answered immediately that he liked the U.S. planes because the Russian planes have only one or two back-up systems, while the U.S. planes have three back-up systems. In a similar vein, during a landing at the Seattle airport, I overhead two engineers saying to each other that the cockpit crew was totally unnecessary. A computer could easily fly and land the plane.

In other words, a key theme in the culture of engineering is the preoccupation with designing humans out of the systems rather than into them. For example, the San Francisco Bay Area Rapid Transit (BART) uses totally automated trains. But the customers, not the operators, objected to this degree of automation, forcing management to put human operators on each train even though they had nothing to do except to reassure people by their presence.

In the earlier example of the company introducing automated machines tools into production processes, the engineers were very disappointed that the operations of the elegant machine they were purchasing would be constrained by the presence of more operators than necessary, by a costly retraining program, and by management-imposed policies that had nothing to do with "real engineering." In my own research on information technology, I found that engineers fundamentally wanted the operators to adjust to the language and characteristics of the particular computer system being implemented and were quite impatient with the operators' "resistance to change." From the viewpoint of the users—the operators—not only was the language arcane, but they did not consider the systems useful for solving the operational problems.[13]

Both operators and engineers often find themselves out of alignment with a third critical culture, the culture of executives.

THE EXECUTIVE CULTURE

The "executive culture" is the set of tacit assumptions that CEOs and their immediate subordinates share worldwide. This executive worldview is built around the necessity to maintain an organization's financial health and is preoccupied with boards, investors, and the capital markets. Executives may have other preoccupations, but they cannot get away from having to worry about and manage the financial survival and growth of their organization.[14] (See "Assumptions of the Executive Culture.")

What I have identified as the executive culture applies particularly to CEOs who have risen through the ranks and been promoted to their jobs. Founders of organizations or family members appointed to these levels have different assumptions and often have a broader focus.[15] The promoted CEO, especially, adopts the exclusively financial viewpoint because of the nature of the executive career. As managers rise in the hierarchy, as their level of responsibility and accountability grows, they not only have to become more preoccupied with financial matters, but also find that it becomes harder to observe and influence the basic work of the organization. They discover that they have to manage from afar, and that discovery inevitably forces them to think in terms of control systems and routines that become increasingly impersonal. Because accountability is always centralized and flows to the top of organizations, executives feel an increasing need to know what is going on, while recognizing that it is harder to get reliable information. That need for information and control drives them to develop elaborate information systems alongside the control systems and to feel increasingly alone in their position atop the hierarchy.

ASSUMPTIONS OF THE EXECUTIVE CULTURE

FINANCIAL FOCUS

- Executives focus on financial survival and growth to ensure returns to shareholders and to society.
- Financial survival is equivalent to perpetual war with one's competitors.

SELF-IMAGE: THE EMBATTLED LONE HERO

- The economic environment is perpetually competitive and potentially hostile, so the CEO is isolated and alone, yet appears omniscient, in total control, and feels indispensable.
- Executives cannot get reliable data from subordinates so they must trust their own judgement.

(continued)

HIERARCHICAL AND INDIVIDUAL FOCUS

- Organization and management are intrinsically hierarchical; the hierarchy is the measure of status and success and the primary means of maintaining control.
- The organization must be a team, but accountability has to be individual.
- The willingness to experiment and take risks extends only to those things that permit the executive to stay in control.

TASK AND CONTROL FOCUS

- Because the organization is very large, it becomes depersonalized and abstract and, therefore, has to be run by rules, routines (systems), and rituals ("machine bureaucracy").
- The inherent value of relationships and community is lost as an executive rises in the hierarchy.
- The attraction of the job is the challenge, the high level of responsibility, and the sense of accomplishment (not the relationships).
- The ideal world is one in which the organization performs like a well-oiled machine, needing only occasional maintenance and repair.
- People are a necessary evil, not an intrinsic value.
- The well-oiled organization does not need people, only activities that are contracted for.

Paradoxically, throughout their careers, managers have to deal with people and recognize intellectually that people ultimately make the organization run. First-line supervisors, especially, know very well how dependent they are on people. However, as managers rise in the hierarchy, two factors cause them to become more "impersonal." First, they become increasingly aware that they are no longer managing operators, but other managers who think like they do, thus making it not only possible but also likely that their thought patterns and worldview will increasingly diverge from the worldview of the operators. Second, as they rise, the units they manage grow larger and larger until it becomes impossible to personally know everyone who works for them. At some point, they recognize that they cannot manage all the people directly and, therefore, have to develop systems, routines, and rules to manage "the organization." They increasingly see people as "human resources" to be treated as a cost rather than a capital investment.

The executive culture, thus, has in common with the engineering culture a predilection to see people as impersonal resources that generate problems rather than solutions. In other words, both the executive culture and the engineering culture view people and relationships as means to the end of efficiency and productivity, not as ends in themselves. If we must have human operators, so be it, but let's minimize their possible impact on the operations and their cost to the enterprise.

DYSFUNCTIONAL INTERACTIONS AMONG THE THREE CULTURES

In many industries, there is enough initial alignment among the needs of the task as defined by the operators, the needs of the engineers for reliable and efficient operations, and the needs of the executives for minimizing costs and maximizing profits so that there are no problems. But when organizations attempt to learn in a generative way, when they attempt to reinvent themselves because the technologies and environmental conditions have changed drastically, these three cultures collide, and we see frustration, low productivity, and the failure of innovations to survive and diffuse.

For example, in their research on nuclear plants, Carroll and Perin found that plant operators understood very well the interdependencies and interactions of all the systems.[16] They lived in an environment that had its own ecology in which interdependence was visible and in which the management of interdependencies through teamwork was crucial to safety and productivity. But one or two levels above the plant, management saw only specific technical and financial issues, driven very much by the outside forces of the Nuclear Regulatory Agency and their own worldview as executives, a view that could best be described as a "machine bureaucracy," while the operators' worldview could better be described as a "sociotechnical system."

The plants were different in how they operated, but each developed its own concept of how to improve its operations. Such improvement plans often required additional allocations of money for training and plant redesign, and also often required bending some formal rules and procedures mandated by the industry and the government. When such requirements were articulated, the engineering community, focused primarily on finding standard solutions to problems, preferably solutions free of human intervention, and executive management focused primarily on money and cost control. The lack of alignment among the three cultures often led to inaction and the continuation of practices that were viewed as less efficient or effective.

In some situations, like that in an airplane cockpit, the executive and operator cultures can collide in a drastically dysfunctional way. Blake's research has shown that some airline crashes are due to communication failures in the cockpit resulting from obsession with rank and hierarchy.[17] For example, in one crash a few miles short of the runway, the flight recorder revealed that the flight engineer had shouted for several minutes that they were running out of gas, while the pilot, functioning as the CEO, continued to circle and tried to fix a problem with the landing gear. When this situation was run in a simulator, the same phenomenon occurred; the pilot was so busy with his operational task and so comfortable in his hierarchical executive position that he literally did not hear critical information that the flight engineer shouted at him. Only when the person doing the shouting was a fellow pilot of equal or higher rank did the pilot pay attention to the information. In other words, the hierarchy got in the way of solving the problem. The engineering solution of providing more warning lights or sounds would not have solved the problem either, because the pilot could easily rationalize them as computer or signal malfunctions.

At the boundary between the engineering and executive cultures, other conflicts and problems of communication arise. In my research on executive views of information technology (IT) contrasted with the views of IT specialists with an engineering mentality, the IT specialists saw information as discrete, packageable, and electronically transmittable, while executives saw information as holistic, complex, imprecise, and dynamic.[18] Whereas the IT specialist saw networking as a way of eliminating hierarchy, executives saw hierarchy as intrinsic to organizational control and coordination. Whereas IT specialists saw the computer and expert systems as the way to improve management decision making, executives saw the computer as limiting and distorting thinking by focusing only on the kinds of information that can be packaged and electronically transmitted. And if executives did buy into IT implementations for reasons of cost reduction and productivity, they often mandated it in a way that made it difficult for the operators to learn to use the systems effectively because insufficient time and resources were devoted to the relearning process itself, as the earlier insurance company example showed.

Of course, the way in which technology is used is influenced by the values and goals imposed by the executive culture, as some of my examples have shown. And those values are sometimes more stable than the technological possibilities, causing technologies like information technology to be underutilized from the viewpoint of the engineering culture.[19] In the earlier example, the engineers were thwarted by the executive culture, and the solution that resulted from union pressure reflected the executives' short-run financial fears.

The lack of alignment among the executive, engineering, and operator cultures can be seen in other industries such as health care in which the needs of the primary care physicians (the operators) to do health maintenance and illness prevention conflicts with the engineering desire to save life at all costs and the executive desire to minimize costs no matter how this might constrain either the engineers or the operators.

In education, the same conflicts occur between teachers who value the human interaction with students and the proponents of sophisticated computerized educational systems on the one hand and the cost constraints imposed by school administrators on the other hand. If the engineers win, money is spent on computers and technologically sophisticated classrooms. If the administrators win, classes become larger and undermine the classroom climate. In either case, the operators—the teachers—lose out, and human innovations in learning are lost.

IMPLICATIONS OF THE THREE CULTURES

There are several important points to note about the three cultures. First, the executive and engineering cultures are worldwide occupational communities that have developed a common worldview based on their education, their shared common technology, and their work experience. This means that even if an executive or engineer in a given organization learns to think like an operator and becomes more aligned with the operator culture, his or her eventual replacement will most probably return the organization to where it was. The field of organization development is replete with examples of innovative new programs that did not survive executive succession. In other words, the executive's or the engineer's reference group is often *outside* the organization in his or her peer group, whose definition of "best practice" may differ sharply from what is accepted *inside* the organization. Executives and engineers learn more from each other than from their subordinates.

Second, each of the three cultures is "valid" from its viewpoint, in the sense of doing what it is supposed to. Executives are supposed to worry about the financial health of their organization, and engineers are supposed to innovate toward the most creative people-free solutions. To create alignment among the three cultures, then, is not a case of deciding which one has the right viewpoint, but of creating enough mutual understanding among them to evolve solutions that will be understood and implemented. Too often in today's organizational world, either the operators assume that the executives and engineers don't understand, so they resist and covertly do things their own way, or executives and/or engineers assume that they need to control the operators more tightly and force them to follow policies and procedure manuals. In either case, effectiveness and efficiency will suffer because there is no common plan that everyone can understand and commit to.

Third, both the executive and engineering cultures are primarily task focused and operate on the implicit assumption that people are the problem, either as costs or as sources of error. In the case of the engineers, the assumption is already implicit in their education and training. The ultimately elegant solution is one that always works and works automatically, in other words, without human intervention. In the case of the executives, the situation is more complex. Either executives have come from the engineering culture where people were not important in the first place, or they learned as they were promoted and began to feel responsible for hundreds of people that they had to think in terms of systems, routines, rules, and abstract processes for organizing, motivating, and controlling. And as they became chief executives accountable to the financial markets and their stockholders, they learned to focus more and more on the financial aspects of the organization. The gradual depersonalization of the organization and the perception that employees are mostly a cost instead of a capital investment is thus a learned occupational response.

It is not an accident that chief executives tend to band together and form their own culture because they come to believe that no one except another chief executive really understands the lonely warrior role. With that sense of aloneness come related assumptions about the difficulty of obtaining valid information and the difficulty of ensuring that subordinates down the line will understand and implement what they are asked to do, leading ultimately to fantasies of spying on their own organizations like the

Caliph of Baghdad who donned beggar's clothes to mingle among the people and find out what they were really thinking. Even though the CEO's immediate subordinates are humans, increasingly the chief executive sees them as part of a larger system that must be managed impersonally by systems and rules. CEOs often feel strongly about not fraternizing with subordinates because, if the organization gets into trouble, those subordinates are often the first to be sacrificed as evidence of "fixing" things.

Fourth, the engineering and executive cultures may agree on the assumption that people are a problem, but they disagree completely on how to make organizations work more effectively. Executives recognize that their world is one of imperfect information, of constant change, and of short-run coping while attempting to maintain a strategic focus. Engineers seek elegant permanent solutions that are guaranteed to work and be safe under all circumstances and, therefore, typically produce solutions that cost much more than the executives believe they can afford. So the executives and the engineers constantly battle about how good is good enough and how to keep costs down enough to remain competitive.

What is most problematic is that we have come to accept the conflict between engineering and management as "normal," leading members of each culture to devalue the concerns of the other rather than looking for integrative solutions that will benefit both. A few creative companies have sent engineers to talk to customers directly to acquaint them with business realities and customer needs. Some executives aware of this conflict involve themselves from time to time in operations and product development so they do not lose touch with the realities and strengths of the other cultures. But this kind of remedy deals only with the organizational level. The dilemma of twenty-first century learning is broader.

THE DILEMMA OF TWENTY-FIRST CENTURY LEARNING

Organizations will not learn effectively until they recognize and confront the implications of the three occupational cultures. Until executives, engineers, and operators discover that they use different languages and make different assumptions about what is important, and until they learn to treat the other cultures as valid and normal, organizational learning efforts will continue to fail. Powerful innovations at the operator level will be ignored, subverted, or actually punished; technologies will be grossly underutilized; angry employees will rail against the impersonal programs of reengineering and downsizing; frustrated executives who know what they want to accomplish will feel impotent in pushing their ideas through complex human systems; and frustrated academics will wonder why certain ideas like employee involvement, sociotechnical systems analyses, high-commitment organizations, and concepts of social responsibility continue to be ignored, only to be reinvented under some other label a few decades later.

First, we must take the concept of culture more seriously than we have. Instead of superficially manipulating a few priorities and calling that "culture change," we must recognize and accept how deeply embedded the shared, tacit assumptions of executives, engineers, and employees are. We have lived in this industrial system for more than a century and have developed these assumptions as an effective way to deal with our problems. Each culture can justify itself historically, and each has contributed to the success of the industrial system that has evolved.

Second, we must acknowledge that a consequence of technological complexity, globalism, and universal transparency is that some of the old assumptions no longer work. Neither the executives nor the engineers alone can solve the problems that a complex sociotechnical system like a nuclear plant generates. We must find ways to communicate across the cultural boundaries, first, by establishing some communication that stimulates mutual understanding rather than mutual blame.

Third, we must create such communication by learning how to conduct cross-cultural "dialogues." Recently, the concept of "dialogue" has substantially improved our understanding of human thought and communication and promises to make some understanding across cultural boundaries possible.[20] If people from the different cultures will sit in a room together, which is hard enough, they must reflectively listen to themselves and to each other, which is even harder. Fortunately, the understanding of what it takes to create effective dialogues is itself coming to be better understood.

The engineering and executive cultures I have described are not new. What is new is that the operator culture in all industries has become much more complex and interdependent, which has thrown it more out of alignment with the other two cultures. The implication is that each community will have to learn how to learn and evolve some new assumptions. We have directed our efforts primarily at the operational levels of organizations and viewed the executive and engineering cultures as problems or obstructions, partly because they do not sufficiently consider the human factor. Yet these cultures have evolved and survived and have strengths as well as weaknesses.

The key to organizational learning may be in helping executives and engineers learn how to learn, how to analyze their own cultures, and how to evolve those cultures around their strengths. These communities may learn in different ways, and we will have to develop appropriate learning tools for each community. Learning may have to be structured along industry lines through consortia of learners rather than along individual organizational lines.[21] And business and engineering education itself will have to examine whether the assumptions of academics are evolving at a sufficient rate to deal with current realities.

We are a long way from having solved the problems of organizational learning, but thinking about occupational communities and the cultures of management will begin to structure these problems so that solutions for the twenty-first century will be found.

REFERENCES

[1] C. Argyris, R. Putnam, and D. Smith, *Action Science* (San Francisco: Jossey-Bass, 1985); P. Senge, *The Fifth Discipline* (New York: Doubleday, 1990); and R. Beckhard and R. T. Harris, *Organizational Transitions: Managing Complex Change, 2nd ed.* (Reading, MA: Addison-Wesley, 1987).

[2] G. L. Roth and A. Kleiner, "The Learning Initiative at the Auto Company Epsilon Program" (Cambridge, MA: MIT Organizational Learning Center, working paper 18.005, 1996).

[3] G. L. Roth, "In Search of the Paperless Office" (Cambridge, MA: MIT, Ph.D. dissertation, 1993).

[4] R. J. Thomas, *What Machines Can't Do* (Berkeley, CA: University of California Press, 1994).

[5] D. M. McGregor, *The Human Side of Enterprise* (New York: McGraw-Hill, 1960).

[6] E. H. Schein and W. G. Bennis, *Personal and Organizational Change Through Group Methods: The Laboratory Approach* (New York: John Wiley, 1965); and R. R. Blake, J. S. Mouton, and N. A. McCanse, *Change by Design* (Reading, MA: Addison-Wesley, 1989).

[7] J. Van Maanen and S. R. Barley, "Occupational Communities: Culture and Control in Organizations," *Research in Organizational Behavior*, vol. 6 (eds.) B. M. Staw and L. L. Cummings, (Greenwich, CT: JAI Press, 1984).

[8] E. H. Schein, *Organizational Culture and Leadership*, 2nd ed. (San Francisco: Jossey-Bass, 1992a).

[9] E. H. Schein, "The Role of the Founder in the Creation of Organizational Culture," *Organizational Dynamics* (Summer 1983): 13–28.

[10] Van Maanen and Barley (1984).

[11] S. Zuboff, *In the Age of the Smart Machine: The Future of Work* (New York: Basic Books, 1988).

[12] G. Kunda, *Engineering Culture: Control and Commitment in a High-Tech Corporation* (Philadelphia: Temple University Press, 1992).

[13] E. H. Schein, "The Role of the CEO in the Management of Change: The Case of Information Technology," *Transforming Organizations*, T.A. Kochan and M. Useem (eds.), (New York: Oxford University Press, 1992b).

[14] G. Donaldson and J. W. Lorsch, *Decision Making at the Top* (New York: Basic Books, 1983).

[15] Schein, 1983.

[16] J. Carroll and C. Perin, "Organizing and Managing for Safe Production: New Frameworks, New Questions, New Actions" (Cambridge, MA: MIT Center for Energy and Environmental Policy Research, Report NSP 95-005, 1995).

[17] Blake et al. (1989).

[18] Schein (1992a, 1992b).

[19] L. Thurow, *The Future of Capitalism* (New York: William Morrow, 1996).

[20] W. N. Isaacs, "Taking Flight: Dialogue, Collective Thinking, and Organizational Learning," *Organizational Dynamics* (Winter 1993): 24–39; and E. H. Schein, "On Dialogue, Culture, and Organizational Learning" *Organizational Dynamics* (Winter 1993): 40–51.

[21] E. H. Schein, "Building the Learning Consortium" (Cambridge, MA: MIT Organizational Learning Center, working paper 10.005, 1995).

EVOLUTION AND REVOLUTION AS ORGANIZATIONS GROW*

Larry E. Greiner

Key executives of a retail store chain hold on to an organizational structure long after it has served its purpose because the structure is the source of their power. The company eventually goes into bankruptcy.

A large bank disciplines a "rebellious" manager who is blamed for current control problems, when the underlying causes are centralized procedures that are holding back expansion into new markets. Many young managers subsequently leave the bank, competition moves in, and profits decline.

The problems at these companies are rooted more in past decisions than in present events or market dynamics. Yet management, in its haste to grow, often overlooks such critical developmental questions as, Where has our organization been? Where is it now? and What do the answers to these questions mean for where it is going? Instead, management fixes its gaze outward on the environment and toward the future, as if more precise market projections will provide the organization with a new identity.

In stressing the force of history on an organization, I have drawn from the legacies of European psychologists who argue that the behavior of individuals is determined primarily by past events and experiences, rather than by what lies ahead. Extending that thesis to problems of organizational development, we can identify a series of developmental phases through which companies tend to pass as they grow. Each phase begins with a period of evolution, with steady growth and stability, and ends with a revolutionary period of substantial organizational turmoil and change—for instance, when centralized practices eventually lead to demands for decentralization. The resolution of each revolutionary period determines whether or not a company will move forward into its next stage of evolutionary growth.

A MODEL OF HOW ORGANIZATIONS DEVELOP

To date, research on organizational development has been largely empirical, and scholars have not attempted to create a model of the overall process. When we analyze the research, however, five key dimensions emerge: an organization's age and size, its stages of evolution and revolution, and the growth rate of its industry. The graph "How Companies Grow" shows how these elements interact to shape an organization's development.

---

*Reprinted with permission from *Harvard Business Review* (May-June, 1998): 55–65.

HOW COMPANIES GROW

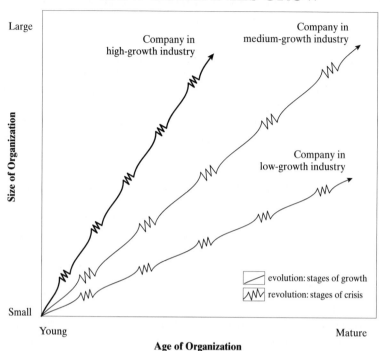

Age of the Organization

The most obvious and essential dimension for any model of development is the life span of an organization (represented on the graph as the horizontal axis). History shows that the same organizational practices are not maintained throughout a long life span. This demonstrates a most basic point: management problems and principles are rooted in time. The concept of decentralization, for example, can describe corporate practices at one period but can lose its descriptive power at another.

The passage of time also contributes to the institutionalization of managerial attitudes. As these attitudes become rigid and eventually outdated, the behavior of employees becomes not only more predictable but also more difficult to change.

Size of the Organization

This dimension is depicted on the chart as the vertical axis. A company's problems and solutions tend to change markedly as the number of its employees and its sales volume increase. Problems of coordination and communication magnify, new functions emerge, levels in the management hierarchy multiply, and jobs become more interrelated. Thus, time is not the only determinant of structure; in fact, organizations that do not become larger can retain many of the same management issues and practices over long periods.

Stages of Evolution

As organizations age and grow, another phenomenon emerges: prolonged growth that we can term the *evolutionary period*. Most growing organizations do not expand for two years and then contract for one; rather, those that survive a crisis usually enjoy four to eight years of continuous growth without a major economic setback or severe internal disruption. The term *evolution* seems appropriate for describing these quiet periods because only modest adjustments appear to be necessary for maintaining growth under the same overall pattern of management.

Stages of Revolution   Smooth evolution is not inevitable or indefinitely sustainable; it cannot be assumed that organizational growth is linear. *Fortune*'s "500" list, for example, has had considerable turnover during the last 50 years. In fact, evidence from numerous case histories reveals periods of substantial turbulence interspersed between smoother periods of evolution.

We can term the turbulent times *periods of revolution* because they typically exhibit a serious upheaval of management practices. Traditional management practices that were appropriate for a smaller size and earlier time no longer work and are brought under scrutiny by frustrated top-level managers and disillusioned lower-level managers. During such periods of crisis, a number of companies fall short. Those that are unable to abandon past practices and effect major organizational changes are likely either to fold or to level off in their growth rates.

The critical task for management in each revolutionary period is to find a new set of organizational practices that will become the basis for managing the next period of evolutionary growth. Interestingly enough, those new practices eventually sow the seeds of their own decay and lead to another period of revolution. Managers therefore experience the irony of seeing a major solution in one period become a major problem in a later period.

Growth Rate of the Industry   The speed at which an organization experiences phases of evolution and revolution is closely related to the market environment of its industry. For example, a company in a rapidly expanding market will have to add employees quickly; hence, the need for new organizational structures to accommodate large staff increases is accelerated. Whereas evolutionary periods tend to be relatively short in fast-growing industries, much longer evolutionary periods occur in mature or slow-growing industries.

Evolution can also be prolonged, and revolutions delayed, when profits come easily. For instance, companies that make grievous errors in a prosperous industry can still look good on their profit-and-loss statements; thus, they can buy time before a crisis forces changes in management practices. The aerospace industry in its highly profitable infancy is an example. Yet revolutionary periods still occur, as one did in aerospace when profit opportunities began to dry up. By contrast, when the market environment is poor, revolutions seem to be much more severe and difficult to resolve.

PHASES OF GROWTH

With the foregoing framework in mind, we can now examine in depth the five specific phases of evolution and revolution. As shown in the graph "The Five Phases of Growth," each evolutionary period is characterized by the dominant management style used to achieve growth; each revolutionary period is characterized by the dominant management problem that must be solved before growth can continue. The pattern presented in the chart seems to be typical for companies in industries with moderate growth over a long period; companies in faster-growing industries tend to experience all five phases more rapidly, whereas those in slower-growing industries encounter only two or three phases over many years.

THE FIVE PHASES OF GROWTH

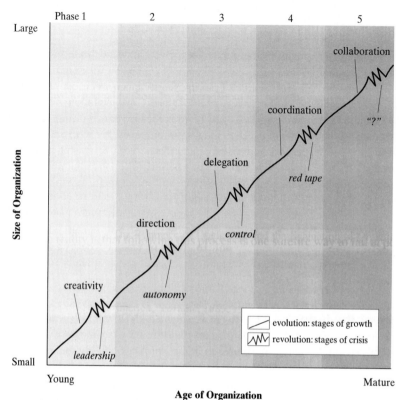

It is important to note that each phase is at once a result of the previous phase and a cause for the next phase. For example, the evolutionary management style in Phase 3 is delegation, which grows out of and becomes the solution to demands for greater autonomy in the preceding Phase 2 revolution. The style of delegation used in Phase 3, however, eventually provokes a revolutionary crisis that is characterized by attempts to regain control over the diversity created through increased delegation.

For each phase, managers are limited in what they can do if growth is to occur. For example, a company experiencing an autonomy crisis in Phase 2 cannot return to directive management for a solution; it must adopt a new style—delegation—in order to move forward.

Phase 1: Creativity   In the birth stage of an organization, the emphasis is on creating both a product and a market. The following are the characteristics of the period of creative evolution:

- The founders of the company are usually technically or entrepreneurially oriented, and they generally disdain management activities; their physical and mental energies are absorbed entirely by making and selling a new product.
- Communication among employees is frequent and informal.
- Long hours of work are rewarded by modest salaries and the promise of ownership benefits.
- Decisions and motivation are highly sensitive to marketplace feedback; management acts as customers react.

All the foregoing individualistic and creative activities are essential for a company to get off the ground. But as the company grows, those very activities become the problem. Larger production runs require knowledge about the efficiencies of manufacturing. Increased numbers of employees cannot be managed exclusively through informal communication, and new employees are not motivated by an intense dedication to the product or organization. Additional capital must be secured, and new accounting procedures are needed for financial control. The company's founders find themselves burdened with unwanted management responsibilities. They long for the "good old days" and try to act as they did in the past. Conflicts among harried leaders emerge and grow more intense.

At this point, a *crisis of leadership* occurs, which is the onset of the first revolution, Who will lead the company out of confusion and solve the managerial problems confronting it? Obviously, a strong manager is needed—one who has the necessary knowledge and skills to introduce new business techniques. But finding that manager is easier said than done. The founders often resist stepping aside, even though they are probably temperamentally unsuited to the job. So here is the first critical choice in an organization's development: to locate and install a strong business manager who is acceptable to the founders and who can pull the organization together.

Phase 2: Direction   Those companies that survive the first phase by installing a capable business manager usually embark on a period of sustained growth under able, directive leadership. Here are the characteristics of this evolutionary period:

- A functional organizational structure is introduced to separate manufacturing from marketing activities, and job assignments become increasingly specialized.
- Accounting systems for inventory and purchasing are introduced.
- Incentives, budgets, and work standards are adopted.
- Communication becomes more formal and impersonal as a hierarchy of titles and positions grows.
- The new manager and his or her key supervisors assume most of the responsibility for instituting direction; lower-level supervisors are treated more as functional specialists than as autonomous decision-making managers.

Although the new directive techniques channel employees' energy more efficiently into growth, they eventually become inappropriate for controlling a more diverse and complex organization. Lower-level employees find themselves restricted by a cumbersome and centralized hierarchy. They have come to possess more direct knowledge about markets and machinery than do their leaders at the top; consequently, they feel torn between following procedures and taking initiative on their own.

Thus, the second revolution emerges from a *crisis of autonomy*. The solution adopted by most companies is to move toward more delegation. Yet it is difficult for top-level managers who previously were successful at being directive to give up responsibility to lower-level managers. Moreover, the lower-level managers are not accustomed to making decisions for themselves. As a result, numerous companies flounder during this revolutionary period by adhering to centralized methods, while lower-level employees become disenchanted and leave the organization.

Phase 3: Delegation   The next era of growth evolves from the successful application of a decentralized organizational structure. It exhibits these characteristics:

- Much greater responsibility is given to the managers of plants and market territories.
- Profit centers and bonuses are used to motivate employees.
- Top-level executives at headquarters limit themselves to managing by exception based on periodic reports from the field.
- Management often concentrates on acquiring outside enterprises that can be lined up with other decentralized units.
- Communication from the top is infrequent and usually occurs by correspondence, telephone, or brief visits to field locations.

The delegation phase allows companies to expand by means of the heightened motivation of managers at lower levels. Managers in decentralized organizations, who have greater authority and incentives, are able to penetrate larger markets, respond faster to customers, and develop new products.

A serious problem eventually emerges, however, as top-level executives sense that they are losing control over a highly diversified field operation. Autonomous field managers prefer to run their own shows without coordinating plans, money, technology, and personnel with the rest of the organization. Freedom breeds a parochial attitude.

Soon, the organization falls into a *crisis of control*. The Phase 3 revolution is under way when top management seeks to regain control over the company as a whole. Some top-management teams attempt a return to centralized management, which usually fails because of the organization's newly vast scope of operations. Those companies that move ahead find a new solution in the use of special coordination techniques.

Phase 4: Coordination   The evolutionary period of the coordination phase is characterized by the use of formal systems for achieving greater coordination and by top-level executives taking responsibility for the initiation and administration of these new systems. For example:

* Decentralized units are merged into product groups.
* Formal planning procedures are established and intensively reviewed.
* Numerous staff members are hired and located at headquarters to initiate companywide programs of control and review for line managers.
* Capital expenditures are carefully weighed and parceled out across the organization.
* Each product group is treated as an investment center where return on invested capital is an important criterion used in allocating funds.
* Certain technical functions, such as data processing, are centralized at headquarters, while daily operating decisions remain decentralized.
* Stock options and company wide profit sharing are used to encourage employees to identify with the organization as a whole.

All these new coordination systems prove useful for achieving growth through the more efficient allocation of a company's limited resources. The systems prompt field managers to look beyond the needs of their local units. Although these managers still have a great deal of decision-making responsibility, they learn to justify their actions more carefully to a watchdog audience at headquarters.

A lack of confidence, however, gradually builds between line and staff, and between headquarters and the field. The many systems and programs introduced begin to exceed their usefulness. A *red-tape crisis* is in full swing. Line managers, for example, increasingly resent direction from those who are not familiar with local conditions. And staff people, for their part, complain about uncooperative and uninformed line managers. Together, both groups criticize the bureaucratic system that has evolved. Procedures take precedence over problem solving, and innovation dims. In short, the organization has become too large and complex to be managed through formal programs and rigid systems. The Phase 4 revolution is under way.

Phase 5: Collaboration   The last observable phase emphasizes strong interpersonal collaboration in an attempt to overcome the red-tape crisis. Where Phase 4 was managed through formal systems and procedures, Phase 5 emphasizes spontaneity in management action through teams and the skillful confrontation of interpersonal differences. Social control and self-discipline replace formal control. This transition is especially difficult for the experts who created the coordination systems as well as for the line managers who relied on formal methods for answers.

The Phase 5 evolution, then, builds around a more flexible and behavioral approach to management. Here are its characteristics:

- The focus is on solving problems quickly through team action.
- Teams are combined across functions to handle specific tasks.
- Staff experts at headquarters are reduced in number, reassigned, and combined into interdisciplinary teams that consult with, not direct, field units.
- A matrix-type structure is frequently used to assemble the right teams for the appropriate problems.
- Formal control systems are simplified and combined into single multipurpose systems.
- Conferences of key managers are held frequently to focus on major problems.
- Educational programs are used to train managers in behavioral skills for achieving better teamwork and conflict resolution.
- Real-time information systems are integrated into daily decision-making processes.
- Economic rewards are geared more to team performance than to individual achievement.
- Experimenting with new practices is encouraged throughout the organization.

What will be the revolution in response to this stage of evolution? Many large U.S. companies are now in the Phase 5 evolutionary stage, so the answer is critical. Although there is little clear evidence regarding the outcome, I imagine that the revolution arising from the *"?"* crisis will center around the psychological saturation of employees who grow emotionally and physically exhausted from the intensity of teamwork and the heavy pressure for innovative solutions.

My hunch is that the Phase 5 revolution will be solved through new structures and programs that allow employees to periodically rest, reflect, and revitalize themselves. We may even see companies with dual organizational structures: a habit structure for getting the daily work done and a reflective structure for stimulating new perspective and personal enrichment. Employees could move back and forth between the two structures as their energies dissipate and are refueled.

One European organization has implemented just such a structure. Five reflective groups have been established outside the company's usual structure for the purpose of continuously evaluating five task activities basic to the organization. The groups report directly to the managing director, although their findings are made public throughout the organization. Membership in each group includes all levels and functions in the company, and employees are rotated through the groups every six months.

Other concrete examples now in practice include providing sabbaticals for employees, moving managers in and out of hot-spot jobs, establishing a four-day workweek, ensuring job security, building physical facilities for relaxation during the workday, making jobs more interchangeable, creating an extra team on the assembly line so that one team is always off for reeducation, and switching to longer vacations and more flexible work hours.

The Chinese practice of requiring executives to spend time periodically on lower-level jobs may also be worth a nonideological evaluation. For too long, U.S. management has assumed that career progress should be equated with an upward path toward title, salary, and power. Could it be that some vice presidents of marketing might just long for, and even benefit from, temporary duty in field sales?

IMPLICATIONS OF HISTORY

Let me now summarize some important implications for practicing managers. The main features of this discussion are depicted in the table "Organizational Practices in the Five Phases of Growth," which shows the specific management actions that characterize each growth phase. These actions are also the solutions that ended each preceding revolutionary period.

In one sense, I hope that many readers will react to my model by seeing it as obvious and natural for depicting the growth of an organization. To me, this type of reaction is a useful test of the model's validity.

But at a more reflective level, I imagine some of these reactions come more from hindsight than from foresight. Experienced managers who have been through a developmental sequence can identify that sequence now, but how did they react when in the midst of a stage of evolution or revolution? They can probably recall the limits of their own developmental understanding at that time. Perhaps they resisted desirable changes or were even swept emotionally into a revolution without being able to propose constructive solutions. So let me offer some explicit guidelines for managers of growing organizations to keep in mind.

Organizational Practices in the Five Phases of Growth

Category	Phase 1	Phase 2	Phase 3	Phase 4	Phase 5
Management Focus	Make and sell	Efficiency of operations	Expansion of market	Consolidation of organization	Problem solving and innovation
Organizational Structure	Informal	Centralized and functional	Decentralized and geographical	Line staff and product groups	Matrix of teams
Top-Management Style	Individualistic and entrepreneurial	Directive	Delegative	Watchdog	Participative
Control System	Market results	Standards and cost centers	Reports and profit centers	Plans and investment centers	Mutual goal setting
Management Reward Emphasis	Ownership	Salary and merit increases	Individual bonus	Profit sharing and stock options	Team bonus

Know where you are in the developmental sequence. Every organization and its component parts are at different stages of development. The task of top management is to be aware of the stages; otherwise, it may not recognize when the time for change has come, or it may act to impose the wrong solution.

Leaders at the top should be ready to work with the flow of the tide rather than against it; yet they should be cautious because it is tempting to skip phases out of impatience. Each phase produces certain strengths and learning experiences in the organization that will be essential for success in subsequent phases. A child prodigy, for example, may be able to read like a teenager, but he cannot behave like one until he matures through a sequence of experiences.

I also doubt that managers can or should act to avoid revolutions. Rather, these periods of tension provide the pressure, ideas, and awareness that afford a platform for change and the introduction of new practices.

Recognize the limited range of solutions. In each revolutionary stage, it becomes evident that the stage can come to a close only by means of certain specific solutions; moreover, these solutions are different from those that were applied to the problems of the preceding revolution. Too often, it is tempting to choose solutions that were tried before but that actually make it impossible for the new phase of growth to evolve.

Management must be prepared to dismantle current structures before the revolutionary stage becomes too turbulent. Top-level managers, realizing that their own managerial styles are no longer appropriate, may even have to take themselves out of leadership positions. A good Phase 2 manager facing Phase 3 might be wise to find a position at another Phase 2 organization that better fits his or her talents, either outside the company or with one of its newer subsidiaries.

Finally, evolution is not an automatic affair; it is a contest for survival. To move ahead, companies must consciously introduce planned structures that not only solve a current crisis but also fit the next phase of growth. That requires considerable self-awareness on the part of top management as well as great interpersonal skills in persuading other managers that change is needed.

Realize that solutions breed new problems. Managers often fail to recognize that organizational solutions create problems for the future, such as when a decision to delegate eventually causes a problem of control. Actions in the past determine much of what will happen to a company in the future.

An awareness of this effect should help managers evaluate company problems with a historical understanding instead of pinning the blame on a current development. Better yet, it should place managers in a position to predict problems and thereby to prepare solutions and coping strategies before a revolution gets out of hand.

Top management that is aware of the problems ahead could well decide not to expand the organization. Managers may, for instance, prefer to retain the informal practices of a small company, knowing that this way of life is inherent in the organization's limited size, not in their congenial personalities. If they choose to grow, they may actually grow themselves out of a job and a way of life they enjoy.

And what about very large organizations? Can they find new solutions for continued evolution? Or are they reaching a stage when the government will act to break them up because they are too large?

Clearly, there is still much to learn about processes of development in organizations. The phases outlined here are merely five in number and are still only approximations. Researchers are just beginning to study the specific developmental problems of structure, control, rewards, and management style in different industries and in a variety of cultures.

One should not, however, wait for conclusive evidence before educating managers to think and act from a developmental perspective. The critical dimension of time has been missing for too long from our management theories and practices. The intriguing paradox is that by learning more about history, we may do a better job in the future.

REVOLUTION IS STILL INEVITABLE

I wrote the first draft of this article while I was felled by a bad leg during a ski vacation in Switzerland. At the time, the business world was buzzing with numerous faddish techniques. Perhaps it was the size and height of the mountains that made me feel that there were deeper and more powerful forces at work in organizations.

Four basic points still seem valid about the model. First, we continue to observe major phases of development in the life of growing companies, lasting anywhere from 3 to 15 years each. Although scholars debate the precise length and nature of these phases, everyone agrees that each phase contains its own unique structure, systems, and leadership. The growth rate of the industry seems to determine the phases length.

Second, transitions between developmental phases still do not occur naturally or smoothly, regardless of the strength of top management. All organizations appear to experience revolutionary difficulty and upheaval, and many of these organizations falter, plateau, fail, or get acquired rather than grow further. IBM before Lou Gerstner and General Electric before Jack Welch both suffered badly at the end of the fourth phase of coordination, when sophisticated management systems evolved into rigid bureaucracies.

Third, the logic of paradox underlying the model continues to ring true, although it often haunts and confuses the managerial psyche. Managers have difficulty in understanding that an organizational solution introduced by them personally in one phase eventually sows the seeds of revolution.

Fourth, the greatest resistance to change appears at the top because revolution often means that units under each senior executive will be eliminated or transformed. That is why we so often see new chief executives recruited from the outside and why senior managers frequently leave

(continued)

companies. Executives depart not because they are "bad" managers but because they just don't fit with where the company needs to go.

As for the differences that I have observed since the article's original publication, there is obviously much more "death" in the life of organizations today. Few organizations make it through all the phases of growth. If they don't fail, as most do in the initial phase of creativity and entrepreneurship, they often get acquired by companies that are in a later phase.

The phases are not as cleanly marked off as I depicted them. The vestiges of one phase remain as new approaches are introduced. Such overlaps are most notable in the case of the first phase entrepreneur hanging on when professional management is added in the second phase of direction.

There are also miniphases within each evolutionary stage. the delegation phase, for example, does not typically begin with the complete decentralization of the entire organization into multiple product units, as the article implies. Usually one product group is launched, and then others are added over time. Also, as delegation—or *decentralization*, as I now prefer to call this phase—advances, senior managers at the corporate office are not as hands-off as I depicted them. The addition of multiple product or geographic units over time requires a sophisticated level of involvement by senior management to review strategies, evaluate results, and communicate the organization's values—but not to micro-manage the units under them.

I would change some of the things I said about the fifth phase of collaboration. My original description of this phase suggests that the entire organization is turned into a matrix of teams. I now see the matrix as confined largely to senior management, where the heads of geographic areas, product lines, and functional disciplines collaborate as a team in order to ensure that their decisions are coordinated and implemented across global markets. The most significant change in this phase occurs when the previously bureaucratic Phase 4 control-oriented staff and systems are replaced by a smaller number of consulting staff experts who help facilitate, rather than control, decisions.

My speculation that "psychological saturation" is the crisis ending Phase 5 now seems wrong. Instead, I think the crisis is one of realizing that there is no internal solution, such as new products, for stimulating further growth. Rather, the organization begins to look outside for partners or for opportunities to sell itself to a bigger company.

A sixth phase may be evolving in which growth depends on the design of extra-organizational solutions, such as creating a holding company or a network organization composed of alliances and cross-ownership. GE may have developed a similar model in which a periphery of companies is built around a core "money" company or bank (GE Capital) that attracts capital, earns high returns, and feeds the growth of other units.

I doubt that the advancement of information technology has made much of a difference in the basic aspects of the model. Information technology appears useful as a tool that evolves in different forms to fit each phase. For example, the Phase 2 functional organizational structure requires data that reflect revenue and cost centers, whereas Phase 3 decentralization needs data that measure profit center performance.

I wrote the article mainly about industrial and consumer goods companies, not about knowledge organizations or service businesses, which had yet to come into prominence. After recently studying a number of consulting, law, and investment firms, our research team found that those organizations also experience evolution and revolution as they grow.

In the first, entrepreneurial phase, the professional service firm pursues and tests a variety of market paths. The phase ends with the partners arguing about whether or not to stay together to concentrate on one partner's vision for the future. In the second phase, the firm focuses on one major service and eventually finds itself with a debate among the partners about whether to continue focusing on the current practice or to open another office or add additional services. A third phase of geographic or service expansion typically ends with a struggle over ownership: how much equity are the original partners willing to share with the younger partners who led the expansion and brought in new clients? The fourth phase involves institutionalizing the firm's name, reputation, and its standard way of operating, and ends in a crisis of cultural conformity in the face of which the firm must restore innovation and flexibility.

Finally, as a strong caveat, I always remind myself and others that the "ev and rev" model depicted in this article provides only a simple outline of the broad challenges facing a management concerned with growth. It is not a cookie-cutter solution or panacea. The rate of growth, the effective resolution of revolutions, and the performance of the company within phases still depend on the fundamentals of good management: skillful leadership, a winning strategy, the heightened motivation of employees, and a deep concern for customers.

CHAPTER 15

DECISION MAKING

TWO DECADES OF RESEARCH ON PARTICIPATION: BEYOND BUZZ WORDS
AND MANAGEMENT FADS
Victor H. Vroom

HOW PEOPLE REALLY MAKE DECISIONS
Gary Klein

Decision making is more than coming up with a good judgment; managing the process of making the decision is equally important. Most supervisors and managers can point to at least one decision-making debacle in their early career caused by failing to include key players or seek out all the relevant information from the right sources. Managers and leaders also seem to struggle with the question of who should make decisions.

Victor Vroom, management professor and consultant, has devoted many years to answering this question. He and his colleagues developed a contingency theory called the leadership-participation model, which is summarized in the first article, "Two Decades of Research on Participation: Beyond Buzz Words and Management Fads." This model assumes that different decision situations require different types of leadership. As with so many contingency theories, the profile of an effective leader or manager is one who is capable of analyzing the context and choosing from various styles the one that is most appropriate.

The rational decision making process has always been popular among business people, especially in the United States where rationality is highly valued. Intuitive decision-making has traditionally received less respect and attention. There is a trend, however, toward acknowledging the contributions of intuitive decision making and acknowledging that rational and intuitive decision making are complementary.

In our opinion, the most important contribution to understanding intuitive decision making in recent years is Gary Klein's book, *Sources of Power: How People Make Decisions*. Klein, chief scientist at Klein Associates, Inc., and his colleagues studied and observed decision makers in action in order to see "How People Really Make Decisions." This excerpt, taken from several chapters in his book, explains the recognition-primed decision model, which takes most of the mystery out of intuitive decision making.

Two Decades of Research on Participation: Beyond Buzz Words and Management Fads*

Victor H. Vroom

Management may be an ancient practice, yet fads and fashions abound in our attempts to systemize the management process. Twenty years of research has enabled the author to make considerable progress in "separating the bedrock from the hucksterism." In the process, he has discovered truths that may surprise even the most experienced manager.

Management has been described as an ancient practice but a new academic discipline. It has been more than six thousand years since the Egyptians faced the monumental task of constructing the pyramids, a task that would be monumental even by today's standards. However, efforts to construct and test theories about management are relatively recent undertakings that have occurred largely within the last century. It is perhaps reflective of the "newness" of intellectual traditions surrounding management that some would argue that the term *theory* is far too dignified to convey the spirit of the fads and fashions that characterize many of our current attempts to systematize the management process. The task of separating the bedrock from the hucksterism appears, at times, to be like searching for the proverbial needle in the haystack.

One of the perennial debates in the managerial literature concerns the appropriateness or effectiveness of participative management. The scientific management of Frederick Winslow Taylor, which dominated management thought in the early part of this century and which viewed workers as inherently lazy and incapable of exercising judgment and discretion, seems gradually to have given way to a view of management that stresses human capability and the need to move from control to commitment. The "buzz words" of contemporary management include *empowerment*, *self-managing work teams*, and *total quality management*. For the time being, participative management is the "victor," in theory if not always in practice. We must ask, however, whether the current focus on worker involvement is the final answer or merely another perturbation of the ever swinging pendulum.

The relative effectiveness of various forms and degrees of participation in decision making is a subject that we have been studying at Yale for almost two decades. We are convinced that "the bedrock" lies in a situational view of participation (i.e., that the most appropriate degree of participation must depend on the circumstances surrounding the participative act). Expressed in this simple way, our assertion approaches a truism. To be testable and meaningful, we must specify the nature of this situational dependency.

MATCHING THE DECISION PROCESS WITH THE SITUATIONAL DEMANDS

Let us begin with an elemental situation that will provide the foundation for our analysis. We assume that a manager is confronted with a problem or decision that falls within his or her area of freedom and the resolution of which has effects on a group of other persons. (We shall refer to this group as "direct reports," although the usefulness of the analysis that follows is not dependent on any particular hierarchical relationship between the manager and group.)

Table 1 shows a set of five decision processes, each varying in the degree to which the group has an opportunity to participate in the decision-making process.

---

*Reprinted from *Yale Management*, Spring 1993 by permission from Victor H. Vroom, © Victor H. Vroom. Tables 1 and 2 and Figure 1 reprinted by permission from Victor H. Vroom and Arthur G. Jago, © Victor H. Vroom and Arthur G. Jago, 1987.

TABLE 1   Decision Processes

The way in which a manager reaches a decision affects the degree to which his/her direct reports have the opportunity to participate in that decision (adapted from Vroom and Jago, 1988).

AI   You reach a decision alone, employing whatever facts you have at hand.

AII   You reach a decision alone, but first seek some specific data from those who report to you. You are not obliged to tell them about the nature of the situation you face. You seek only relevant facts from them—not their advice or counsel.

CI   You consult one-on-one with those who report to you, describing the problem to each and asking for the person's advice and recommendations. However, the final decision is yours alone.

CII   You consult with those who report to you in a meeting (or portion thereof) devoted to the situation. You receive their advice and recommendations in this meeting, but the task of resolving any differences of opinions and of choosing one or more options is yours alone.

GII   You devote a meeting (or portion thereof) to a discussion of the situation and identification and consideration of possible decisions. Avoiding voting, the group attempts to concur on a decision. You coordinate the meeting, facilitate the dialogue, protect minority viewpoints, and make sure all important factors are considered. Above all, you take care to ensure that your ideas are not given any greater weight than those of others simply because of your position.

Using the terminology of Table 1, one can ask both normative and descriptive questions. The normative questions are "should" questions. If we define our goal as maximizing the likely effectiveness of the manager's choice, our task is to define the circumstances under which each alternative would be preferred. The decision process is the independent variable and components of decision effectiveness become dependent variables.

Descriptive questions are "would" questions. The decision processes are dependent variables and characteristics of the manager and his or her situation become independent variables. From a descriptive standpoint, one can ask how decision processes vary with such factors as culture, the nature of the organization, and the gender of the manager.

For 20 years, I have been working with associates in the development of a normative model of the participative process. The latest version of this model was developed in collaboration with Professor Arthur Jago of the University of Houston. The Vroom-Jago model makes use of the decision processes shown in Table 1 and seeks to provide guidance in matching the process with situational demands. This model is driven by a set of four equations which purport to model what is known about the effects of participation on four conceptually and empirically separable outcomes of the participation process. These outcomes are: (1) the quality of decisions made, (2) the amount of commitment to decisions; (3) the length of time required to make the decisions and, (4) the amount of growth or development of the group or team. The evidence is abundant that the decision process used affects each of these outcomes. Thus, the degree to which one involves one's direct reports in the making of a decision will have consequences for the quality of the decision as well as one's commitment to it, the time required to make it, and the team's subsequent learning.

The evidence is also supportive of a situational view of each of these four relationships. Sometimes consensus-seeking impairs decision quality; sometimes consensus-seeking increases it. In general, increasing participation results in a greater degree of commitment and greater development, while consuming a greater amount of time. However, there are circumstances under which one's direct reports would commit equally to an autocratically made decision and circumstances under which consensus-seeking would not be expected to increase the value of the human resources in the teams (and might even damage the team's ability to function collaboratively in the future). Finally, the effects of participation on time, while seemingly invariant in direction, will vary in magnitude from one

TABLE 2   Situational Factors in the Vroom-Jago Model

Following are the key factors affecting the decision process.

QR: Quality Requirement   How important is the technical quality of this decision?

CR: Commitment Requirement   How important is it that those who report to you are committed to the decision?

LI: Leader Information   Do you have the knowledge, or is it readily available in on-hand manuals or documents, to reach a sound decision?

ST: Problem Structure   Is the problem well structured?

CP: Commitment Probability   Are you confident that those who report to you would commit themselves to a decision that you would reach alone?

GC: Goal Congruence   Do those who report to you share the organizational goals to be attained in solving this problem?

CO: Subordinate Conflict   Are those who report to you likely to be in disagreement over the nature of the problem or over the alternatives that each might wish or recommend?

SI: Subordinate Information   Do those who report to you collectively have the knowledge to reach a technically sound solution?

TC: Time Constraint   Does a critically severe time constraint limit your ability to involve subordinates?

GD: Geographical Dispersion   Are the costs involved in bringing together geographically dispersed subordinates prohibitive?

MT: Motivation-Time   How important is it to you to minimize the time it takes to make the decision?

MD: Motivation-Development   How important is it to you to maximize the opportunities for subordinate development?

Source: Adapted from Vroom and Jago, 1988

situation to another. While groups take longer to make decisions, the degree to which they do so will depend on such factors as the amount of conflict surrounding the issue and the degree to which the problem is unstructured.

In addition, we argue that the importance of each of these four decision outcomes—quality, commitment, time, and group development—will vary from one situation to another. In some situations the analytical dimension is nonexistent (i.e., decision quality is not an issue). In other situations decision quality is paramount. Similarly, the importance of commitment, time, and development may vary from one decision problem to another.

Table 2 lists the situational factors in the Vroom-Jago model. Each is expressed in the form of a question that pertains both to the decision problem that is faced and the social context within which that problem is embedded.

The answers to four of the questions (QR, CP, MT, and MD) provide weights for the four decision outcomes by establishing upper bounds for the values of each outcome. Answers to the remaining eight questions are used in one or more of the equations to predict the relative amounts of each outcome that can be expected to be achieved by each decision process. All questions except TC and GD are answered on five-point scales.

USING THE MODEL:
TWO APPROACHES FOR MANAGERS

Managers interested in studying the intricacies of these equations may do so (see Vroom and Jago, p. 231). However, solving four equations for each of five decision processes and summing the 20 integers into the 5 values deemed to be reflective of the relative effectiveness of the 5 decision processes can be a very time-consuming process. As a practical matter, the Vroom-Jago model is best used on a personal computer. Jago's programming skill has produced an expert system that is called MPO (Managing Participation in Organizations). The program requires only 256K of memory and runs on any IBM-compatible computer. MPO runs in either novice or experienced user mode, and managers who have used it describe the program as very user friendly. To use MPO, a manager is asked to think of a specific decision problem with which he or she is faced and then to answer the 12 questions in Table 2. (Help screens are provided with each question to aid novice users in reaching a common understanding both of each question and of the alternative levels of response to it. When all questions have been answered, the screen indicates the model's choice of a decision process as well as the optimal choice were each of the four underlying criteria considered alone.

On request, additional information is available about the problem and the tradeoffs that it poses among the four decision outcomes. For example, bar graphs depicting the predicted success of each process are available, along with sensitivity of the model's recommendation to the relative importance placed on short-range considerations (e.g., time) and longer range consequences (e.g., development).

MPO has been extremely useful both as a classroom teaching device and as a managerial tool. Twice each year, I offer a three- to four-day course on leadership and decision-making for executives who come from all parts of the country and sometimes, all parts of the world. A central focus of the course has been the "what and when" of the effective use of groups for decision making. MPO is used in the classroom to analyze cases furnished by participants. Additionally, the MPO system is given to participants at the conclusion of the course as a reminder of many of the more important contingencies involved in selecting the most effective decision process.

I also use MPO in a graduate course entitled Managerial Leadership, which I teach each year for a mixed set of students from the Schools of Management, Law, Forestry, Epidemiology and Health, and Drama. Students are given a copy of MPO on a floppy disk and are asked to use it in the analysis of several cases from their own experience. Each student writes a paper comparing the model's prescription with their behavior and discusses the implications of the differences.

While the Vroom-Jago model is too new to have been subject to much validation, the data that is available is very supportive of both its usability and validity. It doesn't consider all relevant situational factors and is certainly no guarantee of successful decisions, however it does appear to be a useful and important step toward effective decision making. Furthermore, the model helps to put the current focus on empowerment and participation in a useful perspective that includes both its costs and benefits.

In addition to the computer-based method for using the Vroom-Jago model, we have developed a decision tree version. The decision tree representation of the equations requires three simplifying assumptions. First, we must assume that there are no "shades of grey." The decision tree can be used only when the status of situational factors is clear cut, and only when yes/no answers exist. A second useful (although not absolutely necessary) assumption is that there are no critically severe time constraints and that subordinates are not geographically dispersed. This assumption restricts the applicability of the model by eliminating its use in some clearly defined but relatively infrequent situations.

The final simplifying assumption is that the importance of time and development is known and fixed. A set of 25 different and relatively simple decision trees can be drawn corresponding to the combinations of 5 values of MT (Management − Time) and 5 values of MD (Motivation − Development) . To illustrate, in Figure 1 we depict what we call the time-driven decision tree, representing the case where MT −5 and MD −1 (i.e., time is very important and development is unimportant).

To use a decision tree, a manager selects a problem that is within his or her area of freedom and, in addition, has potential effects on an identifiable group of others, namely the direct reports. The tree is entered from the extreme left at "State the Problem," and the question asked pertains to attribute QR (How important is the technical quality of the decision?). The manager's answer ("High" or "Low") leads to a node signifying the next question. The process continues until an endpoint is encountered designating the recommended process.

QR Quality requirement: How important is the technical quality of this decision?

CR Commitment requirement: How important is subordinate commitment to the decision?

LI Leaders information: Do you have sufficient information to make a high-quality decision?

ST Problem structure: Is the problem well structured?

CP Commitment probability: If you were to make the decision by yourself, is it reasonably certain
                               that your subordinate(s) would be committed to the decision?

GC Goal congruence: Do subordinates share the organizational goals to be attained
                               in solving this problem?

SC Subordinate conflict: Is conflict among subordinates over preferred solutions likely?

SI Subordinate information: Do subordinates have sufficient information to make
                               a high-quality decision?

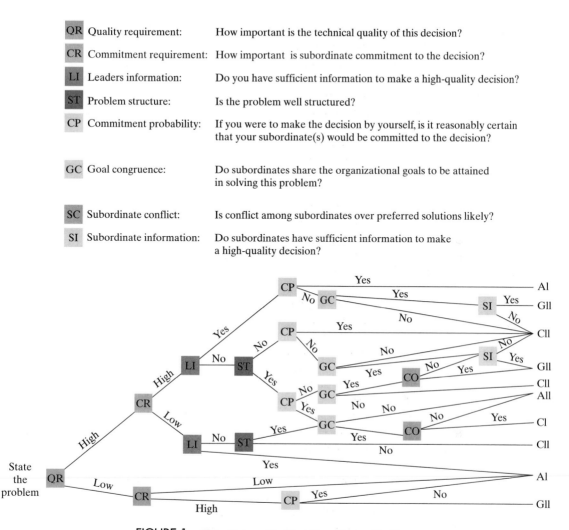

FIGURE 1   **Time-Driven Decision Tree-Group Problems**

The reader should be reminded that the particular decision tree shown in Figure 1 places no value on the long-range outcome of team development. Accordingly, it is the most autocratic of the decision trees that might have been depicted.

Before leaving the discussion of normative issues, I would like to describe an extension of the model to cover individual problems, namely those decision problems that affect not an entire group or team but rather a single other person such as a single direct report. Where the team is not involved, use of processes such as CII and GII appears inadvisable. These processes unilaterally bring together an entire group to discuss or decide an issue pertinent to only one person. In some instances these processes may constitute an invasion of privacy; in others they could be a waste of time.

There are, however, two other processes that we have labeled GI (joint decision making) and DI (delegation) that are potentially applicable. GI involves an attempt to reach consensus (through negotiation or problem solving) between the manager and the affected other. DI is more applicable in the case where the affected other is in a subordinate role. This process involves delegating or empowering the subordinate to make the decision. We have developed models to include appropriate choices of decision processes on individual problems. MPO contains these models and, in addition, there are decision tree versions to cover the kinds of special cases discussed earlier.

AUTOCRATIC OR PARTICIPATIVE MANAGEMENT: THE SITUATION DETERMINES THE STYLE

So far in this discussion, we have been concerned with the normative issues related to what forms and degrees of participation are likely to be most effective in different situations. We have also conducted research on the descriptive question of the circumstances when managers do, in fact, involve their direct reports in decision making. While we have used several different research methods in studying this question, most of what follows is based on one method, called a problem set—a set of 30 or 54 cases each depicting a manager faced with a decision problem. The cases are carefully constructed so that each situational factor (Table 2) is varied independently of other factors. In training programs, managers spend several hours working with the cases, putting themselves in the position of the manager in each case and indicating what they would do in that position. Most data has been collected in conjunction with management development programs in which each manager ultimately receives an individual computer-based analysis of his or her choices showing how they compare with one another and how they compare with the model.

One of the most robust findings from this line of investigation has been the weakening of support for the popular notion that the decision to involve others in decision making is directly controlled by a generalized personality trait. The tempting categorization of people as autocratic or participative or as varying in amount of a trait with these terms as anchors does not do justice to the data. Approximately 10 percent of the variance in behavior on standardized cases can be explained by the trait concept.

In fact, it is more meaningful to talk about autocratic or participative situations than autocratic or participative individuals since about three times as much variance is explicable by situational factors than by a general disposition to behave participatively or autocratically.

A participative situation is likely to have the following elements:

• The problem or decision is important to the organization.
• The manager is not an expert in the area of the problem, and his/her direct reports are experts.
• The problem is unstructured, thereby requiring creativity and ingenuity.
• The direct reports will be involved in the execution of the solution to the problem, and their commitment will be beneficial to their effectiveness in that role.
• The nature of the relationship between the manager and direct reports makes their commitment to his/her own solution unlikely.
• Direct reports would be unlikely to disagree about which solution would be most effective.

As these elements are removed one by one from the situation, behavior of the typical manager becomes progressively more autocratic. I do not wish to imply that managers' behavior can be understood as some linear combination of situational factors. Both managers and the normative model behave configurally [i.e., they respond to particular combinations (or patterns) among factors]. This concept can be illustrated by a simple interaction that is built into the normative model. The model responds to conflict or disagreement among team members by recommending more participative processes (such as CII and GII) when there is a shared goal but recommends less participation in the absence of a shared goal. Thus, conflict and goal congruence are treated together, with the joint pattern of these variables dictating behavior. While both the model and managers show evidence of configurality, the model makes more use of pattern combinations, particularly more complex combinations, than do managers.

So far we have talked about *typical* managers and have implicitly assumed that all managers respond similarly to situational factors. In fact, there are marked individual differences—in both direction and magnitude—in how managers deal with each of the situational factors listed above. We estimate that about 20 percent of the variance in participative behavior can be thought of as differences in how managers interpret and respond to particular situational factors. For example, while most managers are more participative on more important decisions, one-fifth are likely to involve others more on insignificant "cosmetic" issues. In the same vein, while most managers are conflict averse (i.e., respond to conflict or disagreement among others by using more autocratic methods) a minority of about 10-15 percent show exactly the opposite tendency (which we term "conflict confronting").

Both our normative and our descriptive work points to the importance of viewing the act of involving others in decision making *in relation to the situation*. Normatively, participation cannot be specified as either functional or dysfunctional without respect to the situation. Descriptively, the meaning and perceived consequences of participative decision making vary markedly with the situation in which the participation is embedded.

There are some purposes, however, for which it is illuminating to aggregate across a set of situations and talk about how the managers behave in these situations. When we do this, we are holding situations constant and ignoring variability among them. For example, we have asked whether there is any evidence of a change in the use of participative methods over the roughly two decades in which we have been collecting data. Holding situations constant by means of the kind of standardized set of situations that we discussed earlier, we find a sharp increase in the incidence of participative methods over this period. We believe that this increase reflects real differences in the culture of organizations brought about by changes in the labor force and the complexities of the environments in which organizations operate.

We have also done research on differences in participation across levels in the organizational hierarchy. Once again, we have held situations constant by employing a large number of standard decision situations. The evidence points to a higher incidence of participative practices as one ascends the organizational hierarchy.

Among the many other findings that we have examined in this vein are gender differences. By comparing the responses of female managers with a matched group of males from the same organizations, we have found women to be more participative than their male counterparts. This difference between men and women is consistent with differences in the pressures that each group encounters in carrying out its responsibilities. Our research suggests that when a manager is perceived as participative, the reactions of close associates generally are positive and are unaffected by whether the manager is male or female. However, women who are perceived to be autocratic tend to elicit much more negative reactions from others than do men who are perceived to be autocratic. Authoritarian behavior on the part of men may be viewed as a sign of decisiveness, but the same behavior on the part of women may be seen as inappropriate and violating the cultural stereotype of feminine behavior.

Early in our research program, we discovered great interest among managers in the program's findings. With few modifications, our data collection procedures could be reconfigured into a leadership development program. My earliest thoughts on this subject were described in an article I wrote called "Can Leaders Learn How to Lead?" (Vroom 1976). The concept was later elaborated in the Vroom and Jago work (Chapter 13). Integral to our approach has been the use of computerized analyses of managers' behavior on sets of standardized cases to help each manager become aware of his or her model of participation and of its similarity to or differences from the Vroom-Jago model. The goal of training is not to "program" managers to behave like the model but rather to develop a greater awareness of alternatives and to help managers make more informed judgments about the consequences of those alternatives.

Most managers have been making decisions for such a long period of time that the processes can become automatic or habituated. Habits reduce the need to make choices and enable one to act quickly. We don't have to think when we brush our teeth or tie our shoes. However, habits have another property that can be troublesome. At best, they reflect the learning environment at the time the habit was formed. If the environment remains constant, they are likely to continue to be effective. But if the environment changes markedly, habit patterns have to be re-evaluated.

Managers do not live in an unchanging world. They change jobs, change organizations, move from one country to another, or move from public sector to private or vice versa. Such changes bring with them new challenges, new opportunities, and new situational demands on leadership and management style. Old approaches need to be re-thought and new habits substituted for old.

While mobility requires change, it is by no means the only cause of change. Deregulation, global markets, and new tax laws have brought massive changes in the way in which corporations must be structured and managed. Managerial leadership no longer means maintaining the status quo. Old habits must be discarded if one is to respond to today's challenges and opportunities.

To meet these challenges, managers must have the capability to be both participative and autocratic, and to know when to employ each. They must be capable of identifying situational demands and of selecting or designing appropriate ways of dealing with them. Finally, they must have the skills necessary to implement their choices.

Our experience in working with managers over the last 15 years suggests that training focused on models of participation—both descriptive and normative—builds these critical components of leadership.

REFERENCES

V. H. Vroom, "Can Leaders Learn How to Lead?" *Organizational Dynamics 4* (1976) 17–28.
V. H. Vroom and A. G. Jago, *The New Leadership: Managing Participation in Organizations* (Upper Saddle River, NJ: Prentice Hall, 1988).

How People Really Make Decisions*

Gary Klein

During the past 25 years, the field of decision making has concentrated on showing the limitations of decision makers—that is, that they are not very rational or competent. Books have been written documenting human limitations and suggesting remedies: training methods to help us think clearly, decision support systems to monitor and guide us, and expert systems that enable computers to make the decisions and avoid altogether the fallible humans.

This book was written to balance the others and takes a different perspective. Here I document human strengths and capabilities that typically have been downplayed or even ignored.

In 1985, I did my first study of how firefighters make life-and-death decisions under extreme time pressure. That project led to others—with pilots, nurses, military leaders, nuclear power plant operators, chess masters, and experts in a range of other domains. A growing number of researchers have moved out of the laboratory, to work in the area of naturalistic decision making—that is, the study of how people use their experience to make decisions in field settings. We try to understand how people handle all of the typical confusions and pressures of their environments, such as missing information, time constraints, vague goals, and changing conditions. In doing these studies, my research team and I have slept in fire stations, observed intensive care units, and ridden in M-1 tanks, U.S. Navy AEGIS cruisers, Blackhawk helicopters, and AWACS aircraft. We have learned a lot about doing field research.

Instead of trying to show how people do not measure up to ideal strategies for performing tasks, we have been motivated by curiosity about how people do so well under difficult conditions. We all have areas in which we can use our experience to make rapid and effective decisions, from the mundane

*Execerpted with permission from *Sources of Power: How People Make Decisions* (Cambridge, MA: MIT Press, 1998): 1–35.

level of shopping to the high-stakes level of fire-fighting. Shopping in a supermarket does not seem like an impressive skill until you contrast an experienced American shopper to a recent immigrant from Russia. Moving to the other extreme of high-stakes decisions, an example is a fireground commander working under severe time pressure while in charge of a crew at a multiple-alarm fire at a four-story apartment building. Our research concentrated on this high-stakes world. The fireground commanders seemed to be making effective decisions.

EXAMPLE 1.1

THE TORN ARTERY

My research assistant, Chris Brezovic, and I are sitting in a fire station in Cleveland on a Saturday afternoon in the summer of 1985. We slept only a few hours in the station the night before since we had been up late interviewing the commander during that shift. He was going to stay up all night catching up on his work. We were assigned beds on the second floor. I was told to be ready to get down the stairs and onto the truck no more than 25 seconds after an alarm sounded. (No, we did not slide down the pole, although the station still had one. Too many firefighters had broken ankles that way, so they no longer used the pole.) I even slept with my eyeglasses on, not wanting to waste precious seconds fumbling with them. There was only one call, at around 3:00 in the morning. The horn suddenly began blaring, we all jumped out of bed, ran down the flight of stairs, pulled on our coats and boots, and climbed onto the trucks within the time limit. The fire was pretty small—a blaze in a one-car garage.

Chris and I are feeling a little sleepy that next afternoon when the alarm comes in at 3:21 P.M. for the emergency rescue team. Three minutes later, the truck is driving up to a typical house in a residential neighborhood. It is summer, and young women in bikinis who had been tanning themselves on their lawns are running over to their neighbor's yard.

When we pull to a stop, we see a man laying face down in a pool of blood, his wife crouching over him. As the emergency rescue team goes to work, the woman quickly explains that her husband had been standing on a ladder doing some home repair. He slipped, and his arm went through a pane of glass. He reacted foolishly by pulling his arm out and, in doing so, sliced open an artery. The head of the rescue team, Lieutenant M, later told us that the man had lost two units of blood. If he lost four units, he would be dead. Watching his life leak out of his arm, the man is going into shock.

The first decision facing Lieutenant M is to diagnose the problem. As he ran to the man, even before listening to the wife, he made his diagnosis. He can see from the amount of blood that the man has cut open an artery, and from the dishcloths held against the man's arm he can tell which artery. Next comes the decision of how to treat the wound. In fact, there is nothing to deliberate over. As quickly as possible, Lieutenant M applies firm pressure. Next, he might examine whether there are other injuries, maybe neck injuries, which might prevent him from moving the victim. But he doesn't bother with any more examination. He can see the man is minutes from death, so there is no time to worry about anything else.

Lieutenant M has stopped the bleeding and directs his crew to move the man on a stretcher and to the truck. He assigns the strongest of his crew to the hardest stretcher work, even though the crew member has relatively little experience. Lieutenant M decides that the man's strength is important for quick movement and thinks the crew member has enough training that he will not drop the stretcher as it is maneuvered in through the back of the rescue truck.

(continued)

On the way to the hospital, the crew puts inflatable pants on the victim. These exert pressure on the man's legs to stabilize his blood pressure. Had the crew put the pants on the man before driving, they would have wasted valuable time. When we reach the hospital I look down at my watch: 3:31 P.M. Only 10 minutes has elapsed since the original alarm.

This example shows decision making at a very high level. Lieutenant M handled many decision points yet spent little time on any one of them. He drew on his experience to know just what to do. Yet merely saying that he used his experience is not an answer. The challenge is to identify how that experience came into play.

We have found that people draw on a large set of abilities that are sources of power. The conventional sources of power include deductive logical thinking, analysis of probabilities, and statistical methods. Yet the sources of power that are needed in natural settings are usually not analytical at all—the power of intuition, mental simulation, metaphor, and storytelling. The power of intuition enables us to size up a situation quickly. The power of mental simulation lets us imagine how a course of action might be carried out. The power of metaphor lets us draw on our experience by suggesting parallels between the current situation and something else we have come across. The power of storytelling helps us consolidate our experiences to make them available in the future, either to ourselves or to others. These areas have not been well studied by decision researchers.

This book examines some recent findings that have emerged from the field of naturalistic decision making. It also describes how research can be done outside the laboratory setting by studying realistic tasks and experienced people working under typical conditions. Features that help define a naturalistic decision-making setting are time pressure, high stakes, experienced decision makers, inadequate information (information that is missing, ambiguous, or erroneous), ill-defined goals, poorly defined procedures, cue learning, context (e.g., higher-level goals, stress), dynamic conditions, and team coordination (Orasanu and Connolly 1993).

Soelberg's course on decision making at the MIT Sloan School of Management taught students how to perform the classical decision analysis method we can call the rational choice strategy. The decision maker:

1. Identifies the set of options.
2. Identifies the ways of evaluating these options.
3. Weights each evaluation dimension.
4. Does the rating.
5. Picks the option with the highest score.

For his Ph.D. dissertation, Soelberg studied the decision strategies his students used to perform a natural task: selecting their jobs as they finished their degrees. He assumed that they would rely on the rational choice strategy. He was wrong. His students showed little inclination toward systematic thinking. Instead they would make a gut choice. By interviewing his students, Soelberg found he could identify their favorite job choice and predict their ultimate choice with 87 percent accuracy—up to three weeks before the students themselves announced their choice.

Soelberg had trained his students to use rational methods, yet when it was time for them to make a rational and important choice, they would not do it. Soelberg was also a good observer, and he tried to capture the students' actual decision strategies.

What did the students do during this time? If asked, they would deny that they had made a decision yet. For them, a decision was just what Soelberg had taught: a deliberated choice between two or more options. To feel that they had made such a decision, they had to go through a systematic process of evaluation. They selected one other candidate as a comparison, and then tried to show that their favorite was as good as or better than the comparison candidate on each evaluation dimension. Once they had shown this to their satisfaction (even if it meant fudging a little or finding ways to beef up their favorite), then they would announce as their decision the gut favorite that Soelberg had identified much earlier. They were not actually making a decision; they were constructing a justification.

We hypothesized that the fireground commanders would behave in the same way. We thought this hypothesis—that instead of considering lots of options they would consider only two—was daring. Actually, it was conservative. The commanders did not consider two. In fact, they did not seem to be comparing any options at all. This was disconcerting, and we discovered it at the first background discussion we had with a fireground commander, even before the real interviews. We asked the commander to tell us about some difficult decisions he had made.

"I don't make decisions," he announced to his startled listeners. "I don't remember when I've ever made a decision."

For researchers starting a study of decision making, this was unhappy news. Even worse, he insisted that fireground commanders never make decisions. We pressed him further. Surely there are decisions during a fire—decisions about whether to call a second alarm, where to send his crews, how to contain the fire.

He agreed that there were options, yet it was usually obvious what to do in any given situation. We soon realized that he was defining the making of a decision in the same way as Soelberg's students— generating a set of options and evaluating them to find the best one. We call this strategy of examining two or more options at the same time, usually by comparing the strengths and weaknesses of each, *comparative evaluation*. He insisted that he never did it. There just was no time. The structure would burn down by the time he finished listing all the options, let alone evaluating them.

We sought to explain two puzzles: how the commanders could reliably identify good options and how they could evaluate an option without comparing it to any others.

Our results turned out to be fairly clear. It was not that the commanders were *refusing* to compare options; rather, they did not have to compare options. I had been so fixated on what they were not doing that I had missed the real finding: that the commanders could come up with a good course of action from the start. That was what the stories were telling us. Even when faced with a complex situation, the commanders could see it as familiar and know how to react.

The commanders' secret was that their experience let them see a situation, even a nonroutine one, as an example of a prototype, so they knew the typical course of action right away. Their experience let them identify a reasonable reaction as the first one they considered, so they did not bother thinking of others. They were not being perverse. They were being skillful. We now call this strategy *recognition-primed decision making*.

EXAMPLE 1.2

THE OVERPASS RESCUE

A lieutenant is called out to rescue a woman who either fell or jumped off a highway overpass. She is drunk or on drugs and is probably trying to kill herself. Instead of falling to her death, she lands on the metal supports of a highway sign and is dangling there when the rescue team arrives.

The lieutenant recognizes the danger of the situation. The woman is semiconscious and lying bent over one of the metal struts. At any moment, she could fall to her death on the pavement below. If he orders any of his team out to help her, they will be endangered because there is no way to get a good brace against the struts, so he issues an order not to climb out to secure her.

(continued)

Two of his crew ignore his order and climb out anyway. One holds onto her shoulders and the other to her legs.

A hook-and-ladder truck arrives. The lieutenant doesn't need their help in making the rescue, so tells them to drive down to the highway below and block traffic in case the woman does fall. He does not want to chance that the young woman will fall on a moving car.

Now the question is how to pull the woman to safety.

First, the lieutenant considers using a rescue harness, the standard way of raising victims. It snaps onto a person's shoulders and thighs. In imagining its use, he realizes that it requires the person to be in a sitting position or face up. He thinks about how they would shift her to sit up and realizes that she might slide off the support.

Second, he considers attaching the rescue harness from the back. However, he imagines that by lifting the woman, they would create a large pressure on her back, almost bending her double. He does not want to risk hurting her.

Third, the lieutenant considers using a rescue strap—another way to secure victims, but making use of a strap rather than a snap-on harness. However, it creates the same problems as the rescue harness, requiring that she be sitting up or that it be attached from behind. He rejects this too.

Now he comes up with a novel idea: using a ladder belt—a strong belt that firefighters buckle on over their coats when they climb up ladders to rescue people. When they get to the top, they can snap an attachment on the belt to the top rung of the ladder. If they lose their footing during the rescue, they are still attached to the ladder so they won't plunge to their death.

The lieutenant's idea is to get a ladder belt, slide it under the woman, buckle it from behind (it needs only one buckle), tie a rope to the snap, and lift her up to the overpass. He thinks it through again and likes the idea, so he orders one of his crew to fetch the ladder belt and rope, and they tie it onto her.

In the meantime, the hook-and-ladder truck has moved to the highway below the overpass, and the truck's crew members raise the ladder. The firefighter on the platform at the top of the ladder is directly under the woman shouting, "I've got her. I've got her." The lieutenant ignores him and orders his men to lift her up.

At this time, he makes an unwanted discovery: ladder belts are built for sturdy firefighters, to be worn over their coats. This is a slender woman wearing a thin sweater. In addition, she is essentially unconscious. When they lift her up, they realize the problem. As the lieutenant put it, "She slithered through the belt like a slippery strand of spaghetti."

Fortunately, the hook-and-ladder man is right below her. He catches her and makes the rescue. There is a happy ending.

Now the lieutenant and his crew go back to their station to figure our what had gone wrong. They try the rescue harness and find that the lieutenant's instincts were right: neither is usable.

Eventually they discover how they should have made the rescue. They should have used the rope they had tied to the ladder belt. They could have tied it to the woman and lifted her up. With all the technology available to them, they had forgotten that you can use a rope to pull someone up.

This rescue helped us see several important aspects of decision making. First, the lieutenant's deliberations about options took him only about a minute. That may seem too short, but if you imagine going through it in your mind, a minute is about right.

Second, the decision maker looked at several options yet never compared any two of them. He thought of the options one at a time, evaluated each in turn, rejected it, and turned to the next most typical rescue technique. We can call this strategy a *singular evaluation approach*, to distinguish it from comparative evaluation. Singular evaluation means evaluating each option on its own merits, even if we cycle through several possibilities.

Distinguishing between comparative and singular evaluation strategies is not difficult. When you order from a menu, you probably compare the different items to find the one you want the most. You are performing a comparative evaluation because you are trying to see if one item seems tastier than the others. In contrast, if you are in an unfamiliar neighborhood and you notice your car is low on gasoline, you start searching for service stations and stop at the first reasonable place you find. You do not need the best service station in town.

The difference between singular and comparative evaluation is linked to the research of Herbert Simon, who won a Nobel Prize for economics. Simon (1957) identified a decision strategy he calls *satisficing*: selecting the first option that works. Satisficing is different from optimizing, which means trying to come up with the best strategy. Optimizing is hard, and it takes a long time. Satisficing is more efficient. The singular evaluation strategy is based on satisficing. Simon used the concept of satisficing to describe the decision behavior of businesspeople. The strategy makes even more sense for fireground commanders because of their immense time pressure.

Our model of recognitional decision making was starting to fit together. The experienced fireground commanders could judge a situation as prototypical and know what to do. If their first choice did not work out, they might consider others—not to find the best but to find the first one that works.

But there was still the second puzzle. If they did not compare one course of action to another, how did they evaluate the options? All of the evaluation procedures we knew about required contrast: looking at the degree to which each option satisfies each criterion, weighing the importance of the criteria, tabulating the results, and finding the best option. If the commanders did not compare options, how did they know that a course of action was any good?

The answer lies in the overpass rescue story. To evaluate a single course of action, the lieutenant imagined himself carrying it out. Fireground commanders use the power of mental simulation, running the action through in their minds. If they spot a potential problem, like the rescue harness not working well, they move on to the next option, and the next, until they find one that seems to work. Then they carry it out. As the example shows, this is not a foolproof strategy. The advantage is that it is usually better than anything else they can do.

Before we did this study, we believed that novices impulsively jumped at the first option they could think of, whereas experts carefully deliberated about the merits of different courses of action. Now it seemed that it was the experts who could generate a single course of action, while novices needed to compare different approaches.

In one case we studied commanders who had no experience with the type of incident they faced. This helped us to see better what is required for proficient decision making.

EXAMPLE 1.3

THE CHRISTMAS FIRE

Dotted around the Midwest are oil tank farms: large complexes of storage tanks filled with oil piped in from the Texas and Oklahoma fields and held at these farms before being pumped to specific points in the Midwest. This incident took place at a tank farm. The pipeline field at this farm had 20 tanks, each 45 feet high and 100 feet in diameter and each with a capacity of more than 60,000 barrels of oil.

(continued)

On Christmas night in the middle of a bitterly cold winter, one of the tanks bursts open. The oil comes pouring out—a bad enough situation—and then ignites. A large oil tank instantly turns into a giant torch and sets fire to another tank. Most of the big power lines of the tanks are down and burning. The telephone lines are also on fire. Burning oil has spilled into a ditch, and fierce winds push the fire along.

The setting is a rural farm community crisscrossed with underground oil pipes. If the flames spread, they can conceivably set the whole town on fire.

The fire departments of the surrounding townships report to the call. These departments are staffed by volunteer firefighters who are used to putting out barn fires and garage fires, and maybe a house fire or two in a year. Now they are looking at a wall of flames 50 to 100 feet high. They have never seen anything like it before in their lives. As one commander described it to us, "Our heads turned to stone."

As they watch, one of the two burning tanks ruptures. A wave of crude oil rides over the highway and engulfs a new tank, number 91, which is filled with oil. A man from the pipeline company tells the fireground commanders that if the fire comes any farther south, it will reach a 20-inch propane gas line. The oil is following gravity northward, "creepin' like a little monster" toward a large chemical plant.

Because of the cold, everyone is bundled up, many wearing face masks. The crews have trouble recognizing if someone is from their own district. It is hard to tell who the commanders are. Worse, there is no source of water in the area. Foam is needed to put out oil fires, but the commanders can locate only a thousand gallons.

In short, they have no resources for fighting the fire and no understanding of what to do. They are afraid the fire will spread to the other tanks. They wonder if they should evacuate the town. They are bewildered.

For two days, they remain uncertain about how to proceed. A commander of one of the fire departments orders a trench to be built to contain the oil. A different commander's idea is to pipe the oil out of tank 91. But no one can tell if the lines are still working, and no one wants to take a chance of leaking oil into a field where the fire might spread. A third commander calls the power company to turn off the electricity to the downed power lines, but the power company does not comply right away. Each department goes off in a different direction.

Eventually the power company turns off power in the early morning of the second day. Crews can approach tank 91. The plan is to spray foam down onto the fire, if they can get enough foam. It is freezing cold and windy. Where should they position the ladder truck? Should a firefighter, carrying a hose, climb up a ladder to the rim of tank 91? The dikes around the tank make it hard to get close, and the field around the dikes has dangerous ravines. Eventually a ladder truck gets near tank 91, and firefighters spray foam onto the rim of the oil tank. The wind just blows the foam away, and suddenly the origination point fire, in a nearby tank, starts to boil up menacingly. Fearing an eruption, the commander evacuates his men.

Sometime during the second day, one of the chiefs asks a person working at the oil company if all the pipes leading into the complex have been turned off. The reply is that no one knows, since the tangle of pipelines is so confusing. Spurred on by the question, the plant personnel start tracing all the incoming pipelines and find a source of fuel: a large 22-inch pipe that has been pumping new oil directly into one of the burning tanks. During the second day, they get all the pipes turned off.

On the third day, the volunteer fire chiefs finally take organized action: they choose not to try to do anything. They let the fire burn while they devote all their energies to planning. One of the fireground commanders later told us that this was their first effective decision.

Here is how they go about planning. They ask themselves what their options are, and what the advantages and disadvantages are of each. Finally, in the confusion of a runaway oil fire, we find the strongest example of deliberative decision making—by chiefs who are essentially baffled about what is happening: they try rising up a tower to get a man above the rim of a tank to spray foam down onto the fire. Near the rim, he sees cracks with crude oil coming through. The pumps start spraying foam, and the command is given to start the water truck cycle. Because of earlier delays, the water truck freezes up before it can be used. Then the foam pump starts to malfunction, so they give up and call the firefighter down.

Next they try rigging up a nozzle to spray the foam down, but the high winds sweep it away, and the heat cooks it off. They order more foam from a nearby U.S. Air Force base, but the different foams that arrive are incompatible. Finally, they give up, abandon their pride, and call in some consultants. They call in the team of "Boots and Coots," former colleagues of Red Adair, a world-famous fighter of oil well fires.

Boots and Coots arrive, look briefly at the scene, and say that they will need a great deal more foam. "We don't have that much foam," the volunteer fireground commanders argue. "Of course not," Boots and Coots answer. "We've already ordered it. It will be here tomorrow."

From that point on, under the direction of the experts, the fire operations go smoothly. The entire fire is extinguished within the next two days. Although no one is seriously injured, the cost of the fire is estimated at $10 to $15 million.

From this episode we learn that there are times for deliberating about options. Usually these are times when experience is inadequate and logical thinking is a substitute for recognizing a situation as typical. Although the commanders in this case study had been firefighters for a long time, they had no experience with a fire this large. Deliberating about options makes a lot of sense for novices, who have to think their way through the decision. It is what I do when I have to buy a house or a car. I have to start from scratch, identifying features I might want, looking at the choices.

DEFINING THE RECOGNITION-PRIMED DECISION MODEL

The recognition-primed decision (RPD) model fuses two processes: the way decision makers size up the situation to recognize which course of action makes sense, and the way they evaluate that course of action by imagining it.

Figure 1 shows the basic strategy, as variation 1. Decision makers recognize the situation as typical and familiar—a typical garage fire, or apartment building fire, or factory fire, or search-and-rescue job—and proceed to take action. They understand what types of *goals* make sense (so the priorities are set), which cues are important (so there is not an overload of information), what to expect next (so they can prepare themselves and notice surprises), and the *typical ways of responding* in a given situation. By recognizing a situation as typical, they also recognize a *course of action* likely to succeed. The recognition of goals, cues, expectancies, and actions is part of what it means to recognize a situation.

Some situations are more complex, as shown by variations 2 and 3 in Figure 1. Variation 2 occurs when the decision maker may have to devote more attention *to diagnosing* the situation, since the information may not clearly match a typical case or may map onto more than one typical case. The decision maker may need to gather more information in order to make a diagnosis. Another complication is that the decision maker may have misinterpreted the situation but does not realize it until some

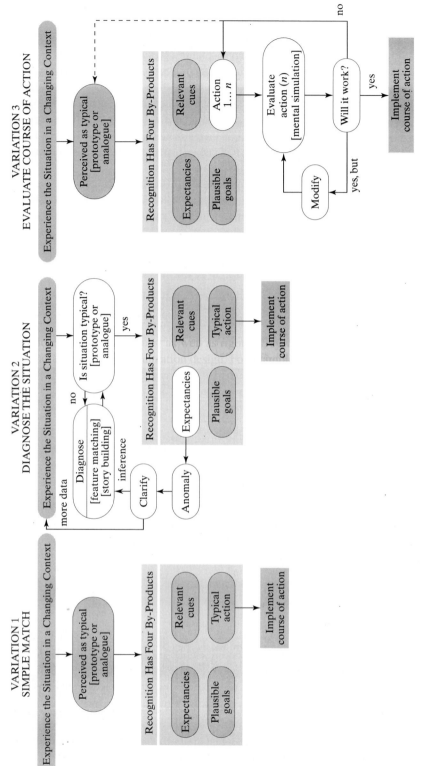

FIGURE 1   Integrated Version of Recognition-Primed Decision Model

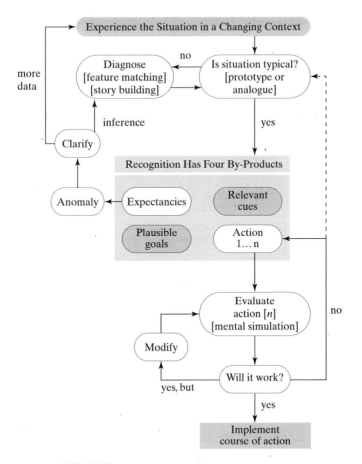

FIGURE 2   **Recognition-Primed Decision Model**

expectancies have been violated. At these times, decision makers will respond to the anomaly or ambiguity by checking which interpretation best matches the features of the situation. They may try to build a story to account for some of the inconsistencies.

Variation 3 explains how decision makers evaluate single options by imagining how the course of action will play out. A decision maker who anticipates difficulties may need to *adjust* the course of action, or maybe *reject* it and look for another option.

One way to think about these three variations is that variation 1 is basically an "if . . . then" reaction, an antecedent followed by the rule-based response. The expertise is in being able to recognize when the antecedent condition has been met. Variation 2 takes the form "if (???) . . . then," with the decision maker deliberating about the nature of the situation. Variation 3 takes the form if . . . then (???), as the decision maker ponders the outcome of a reaction. Figure 2 shows an integrated version of all three variations.

THE THEORETICAL IMPORTANCE OF THE RPD MODEL

Recognitional decision making can be contrasted with the more classical approaches. Perhaps the most widely known of these models stems from the work of Janis and Mann (1977), who warned that people try to avoid making decisions because of the stress of carrying out the analysis. Janis and Mann offered these prescriptions for making better decisions:

- Thoroughly canvas a wide range of options.
- Survey a full range of objectives.
- Carefully weigh the costs, risk, and benefits of each option.
- Intensively search for new information in evaluating options.
- Assimilate all new information.
- Reexamine the positive and negative consequences of each option.
- Carefully plan to include contingencies if various risks occur.

Janis and Mann probably did not intend this advice for time-pressured situations, but the RPD model predominates even when time is sufficient for comparative evaluations. Yet in one form or another, Janis and Mann's prescriptive advice is held up as an ideal of rationality and finds its way into most courses on cognitive development. The advice is more helpful for beginners than for experienced decision makers. In most applied settings, beginners are not going to be put in a position to make critical decisions.

The prescriptions of Janis and Mann are an example of the rational choice strategy that we had encountered: define the evaluation dimensions, weight each one, rate each option on each dimension, multiply the weightings, total up the scores, and determine the best option—that is, unless you do not have all the data you need, or are not sure how to do the ratings, or disagree with the weights, or run out of time before you have finished.

There are advantages to the rational choice strategy:

- It should result in reliable decisions (that is, the same result each time for the same analysis).
- It is quantitative.
- It helps novices determine what they do not know.
- It is rigorous; it does not leave anything out.
- It is a general strategy, which could apply in all sorts of situations.

The problem is that the assumptions of the rational choice strategy are usually too restrictive. Rarely is there the time or the information needed to make this type of strategy work. Furthermore, if we cannot trust someone to make a big judgment, such as which option is best, why would we trust all of the little judgments that go into the rational choice strategy. Clearly this method is not going to ensure that novices make good choices, and it usually is not helpful for experienced decision makers. It can be useful in working with teams, to calibrate everyone's grasp of the strengths and weaknesses of different options.

THE POWER OF INTUITION

Intuition depends on the use of experience to recognize key patterns that indicate the dynamics of the situation. Because patterns can be subtle, people often cannot describe what they noticed, or how they judged a situation as typical or atypical. Therefore, intuition has a strange reputation. Skilled decision makers know that they can depend on their intuition, but at the same time they may feel uncomfortable trusting a source of power that seems so accidental.

Bechara, Damasio, Tranet, and Damasio (1997) found that intuition has a basis in biology. They compared patients who were brain damaged to a group of normal subjects. The brain-damaged subjects lacked intuition, an emotional reaction to anticipated consequences of good and bad decisions. In the normal subjects, this system seemed to be activated long before they were consciously aware that they had made a decision.

For the first formal interview that I did in our first research project with firefighters, I was trying to find some difficult incident where my interviewee, a fireground commander, had to make a tough decision. He could think of only one case, years ago, where he said his extrasensory perception (ESP) had saved the day. I tried to get him to think of a different incident because the one he had in mind was too old, because he was only a lieutenant then, not a commander, and because I do not have much interest in ESP. But he was determined to describe this case, so I finally gave up and let him tell his story.

EXAMPLE 1.4

THE SIXTH SENSE

It is a simple house fire in a one-story house in a residential neighborhood. The fire is in the back, in the kitchen area. The lieutenant leads his hose crew into the building, to the back, to spray water on the fire, but the fire just roars back at them.

"Odd," he thinks. The water should have more of an impact. They try dousing it again, and get the same results. They retreat a few steps to regroup.

Then the lieutenant starts to feel as if something is not right. He doesn't have any clues; he just doesn't feel right about being in that house, so he orders his men out of the building—a perfectly standard building with nothing out of the ordinary.

As soon as his men leave the building, the floor where they had been standing collapses. Had they still been inside, they would have plunged into the fire below.

"A sixth sense," he assured us, and part of the makeup of every skilled commander. Some close questioning revealed the following facts:

• He had no suspicion that there was a basement in the house.
• He did not suspect that the seat of the fire was in the basement, directly underneath the living room where he and his men were standing when he gave his order to evacuate.
• But he was already wondering why the fire did not react as expected.
• The living room was hotter than he would have expected for a small fire in the kitchen of a single-family home.
• It was very quiet. Fires are noisy, and for a fire with this much heat, he would have expected a great deal of noise.

The whole pattern did not fit right. His expectations were violated, and he realized he did not quite know what was going on. That was why he ordered his men out of the building. With hindsight, the reasons for the mismatch were clear. Because the fire was under him and not in the kitchen, it was not affected by his crew's attack, the rising heat was much greater than he had expected, and the floor acted like a baffle to muffle the noise, resulting in a hot but quiet environment.

This incident helped us understand how commanders make decisions by recognizing when a typical situation is developing. In this case, the events were not typical, and his reaction was to pull back, regroup, and try to get a better sense of what was going on. By showing us what happens when the cues do not fit together, this case clarified how much firefighters rely on a recognition of familiarity and prototypicality. By the end of the interview, the commander could see how he had used the available information to make his judgment. (I think he was proud to realize how his experience had come into play. Even so, he was a little shaken since he had come to depend on his sixth sense to get him through difficult situations, and it was unnerving for him to realize that he might never have had ESP.)

This is one basis for what we call *intuition*: recognizing things without knowing how we do the recognizing. In the simple version of the RPD model, we size the situation up and immediately know how to proceed: which goals to pursue, what to expect, how to respond. We are drawn to certain cues and not others because of our situation awareness. (This must happen all the time. Try to imagine going through a day without making these automatic responses.)

There may be other aspects of intuition than the one I have been describing. I do know that the firefighters' experience enables them to recognize situations quickly.

Many people think of intuition as an inborn trait—something we are born with. I am not aware of any evidence showing that some people are blessed with intuition, and others are not. My claim in this chapter is that intuition grows out of experience.

We should not be surprised that the commander in this case was not aware of the way he used his experience. Rather than giving him specific facts from memory, the experience affected the way he saw the situation. Another reason that he could not describe his use of experience was that he was reacting to things that were not happening rather than to things that were. A third reason that he was unaware of his use of experience was that he was not drawing on his memory for any specific previous experience. A large set of similar incidents had all blended together.

Described in this way, intuition does not sound very mysterious. In fact, the simple version of the RPD model is a model of intuition.

Intuition is an important source of power for all of us. Nevertheless, we have trouble observing ourselves use experience in this way, and we definitely have trouble explaining the basis of our judgments when someone else asks us to defend them. Therefore, intuition has a bad reputation compared with a judgment that comes from careful analysis of all the relevant factors and shows each inference drawn and traces the conclusion in a clear line to all of the antecedent conditions. In fact, research by Wilson and Schooler (1991) shows that people do worse at some decision tasks when they are asked to perform analyses of the reasons for their preferences or to evaluate all the attributes of the choices.

Intuition is not infallible. Our experience will sometimes mislead us, and we will make mistakes that add to our experience base. Imagine that you are driving around in an unfamiliar city, and you see some landmark, perhaps a gas station, and you say, "Oh, now I know where we are," and (despite the protests of your spouse, who has the map) make a fateful turn and wind up on an unescapable entrance ramp to the highway you had been trying to avoid. As you face the prospect of being sent miles out of your way, you may lamely offer that the gas station you remembered must have been a different one: "I thought I recognized it, but I guess I was wrong."

PRACTICAL IMPLICATIONS

- Be sensitive to when you need to compare options and when you do not. For many tasks, we are novices, and the rational choice method helps us when we lack the expertise to recognize situations. Sometimes we may need to use formal methods to look at wide array of alternatives. Other times we may judge that we should rely on our expertise to look in greater depth at a smaller set of alternatives—maybe the first one considered.

- The part of intuition that involves pattern matching and recognition of familiar and typical cases can be trained. The ideas set forth in this chapter imply that we do not make someone an expert through training in formal methods of analysis. Quite the contrary is true, in fact: we run the risk of slowing the development of skills. If the purpose is to train people in time-pressured decision making, we might require that the trainee make rapid responses rather than ponder all the implications. If we can present many situations an hour, several hours a day, for days or weeks, we should be able to improve the trainee's ability to detect familiar patterns. The design of the scenarios is critical, since the goal is to show many common cases to facilitate a recognition of typicality along with different types of rare cases so trainees will be prepared for these as well.

We can summarize the key features of the RPD model in comparison to the standard advice given to decision makers. The RPD model claims that with experienced decision makers:

- The focus is on the way they assess the situation and judge it familiar, not on comparing options.
- Courses of action can be quickly evaluated by imagining how they will be carried out, not by formal analysis and comparison.
- Decision makers usually look for the first workable option they can find, not the best option.
- Since the first option they consider is usually workable, they do not have to generate a large set of options to be sure they get a good one.
- They generate and evaluate options one at a time and do not bother comparing the advantages and disadvantages of alternatives.
- By imagining the option being carried out, they can spot weaknesses and find ways to avoid these, thereby making the option stronger. Conventional models just select the best, without seeing how it can be improved.
- The emphasis is on being poised to act rather than being paralyzed until all the evaluations have been completed.

ENDNOTES

A. Bechara, H. Damasio, D. Tranel, and A. R. Damasio, "Deciding Advantageously Before Knowing The Advantageous Strategy," *Science* 275 (1997): 1293–1295.

I. L. Janis and L. Mann, *Decision Making: A Psychological Analysis of Conflict, Choice, and Commitment* (New York: Free Press, 1977).

J. Orasann and T. Connolly, "The Reinvention of Decision Making," *Decision Making in Action: Models and Methods*, eds. G. Klein, J. Orasanu, R. Calderwood, and C. E. Zsambok (Norwood, NJ: Ablex, 1993): 3–20.

H. A. Simon, *Models of Man: Social and Rational* (New York: Wiley 1957).

P. O. Soelberg, "Unprogrammed Decision Making," *Industrial Management Review 8* (1967): 19–29.

T. D. Wilson and J. W. Schooler, "Thinking Too Much: Introspection Can Reduce the Quality of Preferences and Decisions," *Journal of Personality and Social Psychology 60* (1991): 181–192.

CHAPTER 16

POWER AND INFLUENCE

THE NECESSARY ART OF PERSUASION
Jay A. Conger

INFLUENCE WITH AUTHORITY: THE USE OF ALLIANCES, RECIPROCITY, AND EXCHANGE TO ACCOMPLISH WORK
Allan R. Cohen
David L. Bradford

The command-and-control management style, which was more prevalent in the past, went hand in hand with an autocratic approach to using power and influence. In the current work environment, however, people in positions of authority are expected to earn the respect of their subordinates, explain the rationale for their decisions and orders, and focus on commitment rather than control with their employees. Furthermore, many employees work in cross-disciplinary teams—their influence efforts are more often directed horizontally at peers rather than vertically up or down a hierarchy. These changes have resulted in the need for a broader range of skills relating to power and influence. Power is defined as the capacity to influence the behavior of others, while influence is the process by which people successfully persuade others to follow their advice, suggestions, or orders.

In "The Necessary Art of Persuasion," Jay Conger, organizational behavior professor and consultant, reframes persuasion as a negotiating and learning process that results in a shared solution to problems. After observing and studying various types of leaders with effective persuasion skills, Conger was able to distinguish between common persuasion mistakes and the four steps that result in effective persuasion.

Allan Cohen and David Bradford, management professors and consultants, perceived early on that many employees have to influence people whom they do not supervise. Their classic article, "Influence Without Authority: The Use of Alliances, Reciprocity, and Exchange to Accomplish Work," explains the different "currencies" we can use to influence others and the exchange process of mutual influence.

THE NECESSARY ART OF PERSUASION*

Jay A. Conger

If there ever was a time for businesspeople to learn the fine art of persuasion, it is now. Gone are the command-and-control days of executives managing by decree. Today businesses are run largely by cross-functional teams of peers and populated by baby boomers and their Generation X offspring, who show little tolerance for unquestioned authority. Electronic communication and globalization have further eroded the traditional hierarchy, as ideas and people flow more freely than ever around organizations and as decisions get made closer to the markets. These fundamental changes, more than a decade in the making but now firmly part of the economic landscape, essentially come down to this: work today gets done in an environment where people don't just ask "What should I do?" but "Why should I do it?"

TWELVE YEARS OF WATCHING AND LISTENING

The ideas behind this article spring from three streams of research. For the last 12 years as both an academic and as a consultant, I have been studying 23 senior business leaders who have shown themselves to be effective change agents. Specifically, I have investigated how these individuals use language to motivate their employees, articulate vision and strategy, and mobilize their organizations to adapt to challenging business environments.

Four years ago, I started a second stream of research exploring the capabilities and characteristics of successful cross-functional team leaders. The core of my database comprised interviews with and observations of 18 individuals working in a range of U.S. and Canadian companies. These were not senior leaders as in my earlier studies but low- and middle-level managers. Along with interviewing the colleagues of these people, I also compared their skills with those of other team leaders—in particular, with the leaders of less successful cross-functional teams engaged in similar initiatives within the same companies. Again, my focus was on language, but I also studied the influence of interpersonal skills.

The similarities in the persuasion skills possessed by both the change-agent leaders and effective team leaders prompted me to explore the academic literature on persuasion and rhetoric, as well as on the art of gospel preaching. Meanwhile, to learn how most managers approach the persuasion process, I observed several dozen managers in company meetings, and I employed simulations in company executive-education programs where groups of managers had to persuade one another on hypothetical business objectives. Finally, I selected a group of 14 managers known for their outstanding abilities in constructive persuasion. For several months, I interviewed them and their colleagues and observed them in actual work situations.

To answer this why question effectively is to persuade. Yet many businesspeople misunderstand persuasion, and more still underutilize it. The reason? Persuasion is widely perceived as a skill reserved for selling products and closing deals. It is also commonly seen as just another form of manipulation—devious and to be avoided. Certainly, persuasion can be used in selling and deal-clinching situations, and it can be misused to manipulate people. But exercised constructively and to its full potential, persuasion supersedes sales and is quite the opposite of deception. Effective persuasion becomes a negotiating and

---

* Reprinted with permission from *Harvard Business Review* (May-June 1998) 85–95.

learning process through which a persuader leads colleagues to a problem's shared solution. Persuasion does indeed involve moving people to a position they don't currently hold, but not by begging or cajoling. Instead, it involves careful preparation, the proper framing of arguments, the presentation of vivid supporting evidence, and the effort to find the correct emotional match with your audience.

Effective persuasion is a difficult and time-consuming proposition, but it may also be more powerful than the command-and-control managerial model it succeeds. As AlliedSignal's CEO Lawrence Bossidy said recently, "The day when you could yell and scream and beat people into good performance is over. Today you have to appeal to them by helping them see how they can get from here to there, by establishing some credibility, and by giving them some reason and help to get there. Do all those things, and they'll knock down doors." In essence, he is describing persuasion—now more than ever, the language of business leadership.

Think for a moment of your definition of persuasion. If you are like most businesspeople I have encountered (see "Twelve Years of Watching and Listening"), you see persuasion as a relatively straightforward process. First, you strongly state your position. Second, you outline the supporting arguments, followed by a highly assertive, data-based exposition. Finally, you enter the deal-making stage and work toward a "close." In other words, you use logic, persistence, and personal enthusiasm to get others to buy a good idea. The reality is that following this process is one surefire way to fail at persuasion (See "Four Ways Not to Persuade").

What, then, constitutes effective persuasion? If persuasion is a learning and negotiating process, then in the most general terms it involves phases of discovery, preparation, and dialogue. Getting ready to persuade colleagues can take weeks or months of planning as you learn about your audience and the position you intend to argue. Before they even start to talk, effective persuaders have considered their positions from every angle. What investments in time and money will my position require from others? Is my supporting evidence weak in any way? Are there alternative positions I need to examine?

Dialogue happens before and during the persuasion process. Before the process begins, effective persuaders use dialogue to learn more about their audience's opinions, concerns, and perspectives. During the process, dialogue continues to be a form of learning, but it is also the beginning of the negotiation stage. You invite people to discuss, even debate, the merits of your position, and then to offer honest feedback and suggest alternative solutions. That may sound like a slow way to achieve your goal, but effective persuasion is about testing and revising ideas in concert with your colleagues' concerns and needs. In fact, the best persuaders not only listen to others but also incorporate their perspectives into a shared solution.

Persuasion, in other words, often involves—indeed, demands—compromise. Perhaps that is why the most effective persuaders seem to share a common trait: they are open-minded, never dogmatic. They enter the persuasion process prepared to adjust their viewpoints and incorporate others' ideas. That approach to persuasion is, interestingly, highly persuasive in itself. When colleagues see that a persuader is eager to hear their views and willing to make changes in response to their needs and concerns, they respond very positively. They trust the persuader more and listen more attentively. They don't fear being bowled over or manipulated. They see the persuader as flexible and are thus more willing to make sacrifices themselves. Because that is such a powerful dynamic, good persuaders often enter the persuasion process with judicious compromises already prepared.

FOUR ESSENTIAL STEPS

Effective persuasion involves four distinct and essential steps. First, effective persuaders establish credibility. Second, they frame their goals in a way that identifies common ground with those they intend to persuade. Third, they reinforce their positions using vivid language and compelling evidence. And fourth, they connect emotionally with their audience. As one of the most effective executives in our research commented, "The most valuable lesson I've learned about persuasion over the years is that there's just as much strategy in how you present your position as in the position itself. In fact, I'd say the strategy of presentation is the more critical."

FOUR WAYS NOT TO PERSUADE

In my work with managers as a researcher and as a consultant, I have had the unfortunate opportunity to see executives fail miserably at persuasion. Here are the four most common mistakes people make:

1. They Attempt to Make Their Case with an Up-Front, Hard Sell   I call this the John Wayne approach. Managers strongly state their position at the outset, and then through a process of persistence, logic, and exuberance, they try to push the idea to a close. In reality, setting out a strong position at the start of a persuasion effort gives potential opponents something to grab onto—and fight against. It's far better to present your position with the finesse and reserve of a lion tamer, who engages his "partner" by showing him the legs of a chair. In other words, effective persuaders don't begin the process by giving their colleagues a clear target in which to set their jaws.

2. They Resist Compromise   Too many managers see compromise as surrender, but it is essential to constructive persuasion. Before people buy into a proposal, they want to see that the persuader is flexible enough to respond to their concerns. Compromises can often lead to better, more sustainable shared solutions.

By not compromising, ineffective persuaders unconsciously send the message that they think persuasion is a one-way street. But persuasion is a process of give-and-take. Kathleen Reardon, a professor of organizational behavior at the University of Southern California, points out that a persuader rarely changes another person's behavior or viewpoint without altering his or her own in the process. To persuade meaningfully, we must not only listen to others but also incorporate their perspectives into our own.

3. They Think the Secret of Persuasion Lies in Presenting Great Arguments
In persuading people to change their minds, great arguments matter. No doubt about it. But arguments, per se, are only one part of the equation. Other factors matter just as much, such as the persuader's credibility and his or her ability to create a proper, mutually beneficial frame for a position, connect on the right emotional level with an audience, and communicate through vivid language that makes arguments come alive.

4. They Assume Persuasion is a One-Shot Effort   Persuasion is a process, not an event. Rarely, if ever, is it possible to arrive at a shared solution on the first try. More often than not, persuasion involves listening to people, testing a position, developing a new position that reflects input from the group, more testing, incorporating compromises, and then trying again. If this sounds like a slow and difficult process, that's because it is. But the results are worth the effort.

Establish Credibility   The first hurdle persuaders must overcome is their own credibility. A persuader can't advocate a new or contrarian position without having people wonder, Can we trust this individual's perspectives and opinions? Such a reaction is understandable. After all, allowing oneself to be persuaded is risky, because any new initiative demands a commitment of time and resources. Yet even though persuaders must have high credibility, our research strongly suggests that most managers overestimate their own credibility—considerably.

In the workplace, credibility grows out of two sources: expertise and relationships. People are considered to have high levels of expertise if they have a history of sound judgment or have proven themselves knowledgeable and well informed about their proposals. For example, in proposing a new product idea, an effective persuader would need to be perceived as possessing a thorough understanding of the product—its specifications, target markets, customers, and competing products. A history of prior successes would further strengthen the persuader's perceived expertise. One extremely successful executive in our research had a track record of 14 years of devising highly effective advertising campaigns. Not surprisingly, he had an easy time winning colleagues over to his position. Another manager had a track record of seven successful new-product launches in a period of five years. He, too, had an advantage when it came to persuading his colleagues to support his next new idea.

On the relationship side, people with high credibility have demonstrated—again, usually over time—that they can be trusted to listen and to work in the best interests of others. They have also consistently shown strong emotional character and integrity; that is, they are not known for mood extremes or inconsistent performance. Indeed, people who are known to be honest, steady, and reliable have an edge when going into any persuasion situation. Because their relationships are robust, they are more apt to be given the benefit of the doubt. One effective persuader in our research was considered by colleagues to be remarkably trustworthy and fair; many people confided in her. In addition, she generously shared credit for good ideas and provided staff with exposure to the company's senior executives. This woman had built strong relationships, which meant her staff and peers were always willing to consider seriously what she proposed.

If expertise and relationships determine credibility, it is crucial that you undertake an honest assessment of where you stand on both criteria before beginning to persuade. To do so, first step back and ask yourself the following questions related to expertise: How will others perceive my knowledge about the strategy, product, or change I am proposing? Do I have a track record in this area that others know about and respect? Then, to assess the strength of your relationship credibility, ask yourself, Do those I am hoping to persuade see me as helpful, trustworthy, and supportive? Will they see me as someone in sync with them—emotionally, intellectually, and politically—on issues like this one? Finally, it is important to note that it is not enough to get your own read on these matters. You must also test your answers with colleagues you trust to give you a reality check. Only then will you have a complete picture of your credibility.

In most cases, that exercise helps people discover that they have some measure of weakness, either on the expertise or on the relationship side of credibility. The challenge then becomes to fill in such gaps.

In general, if your area of weakness is on the expertise side, you have several options:

- First, you can learn more about the complexities of your position through either formal or informal education and through conversations with knowledgeable individuals. You might also get more relevant experience on the job by asking, for instance, to be assigned to a team that would increase your insight into particular markets or products.
- Another alternative is to hire someone to bolster your expertise—for example, an industry consultant or a recognized outside expert, such as a professor. Either one may have the knowledge and experience required to support your position effectively. Similarly, you may tap experts within your organization to advocate your position. Their credibility becomes a substitute for your own.
- You can also utilize other outside sources of information to support your position, such as respected business or trade periodicals, books, independently produced reports, and lectures by experts. In our research, one executive from the clothing industry successfully persuaded his company to reposition an entire product line to a more youthful market after bolstering his credibility with articles by a noted demographer in two highly regarded journals and with two independent market-research studies.

- Finally, you may launch pilot projects to demonstrate on a small scale your expertise and the value of your ideas.

As for filling in the relationship gap:

- You should make a concerted effort to meet one-on-one with all the key people you plan to persuade. This is not the time to outline your position but rather to get a range of perspectives on the issue at hand. If you have the time and resources, you should even offer to help these people with issues that concern them.
- Another option is to involve like-minded coworkers who already have strong relationships with your audience. Again, that is a matter of seeking out substitutes on your own behalf.

For an example of how these strategies can be put to work, consider the case of a chief operating officer of a large retail bank, whom we will call Tom Smith. Although he was new to his job, Smith ardently wanted to persuade the senior management team that the company was in serious trouble. He believed that the bank's overhead was excessive and would jeopardize its position as the industry entered a more competitive era. Most of his colleagues, however, did not see the potential seriousness of the situation. Because the bank had been enormously successful in recent years, they believed changes in the industry posed little danger. In addition to being newly appointed, Smith had another problem: his career had been in financial services, and he was considered an outsider in the world of retail banking. Thus he had few personal connections to draw on as he made his case, nor was he perceived to be particularly knowledgeable about marketplace exigencies.

As a first step in establishing credibility, Smith hired an external consultant with respected credentials in the industry who showed that the bank was indeed poorly positioned to be a low-cost producer. In a series of interactive presentations to the bank's top-level management, the consultant revealed how the company's leading competitors were taking aggressive actions to contain operating costs. He made it clear from these presentations that not cutting costs would soon cause the bank to fall drastically behind the competition. These findings were then distributed in written reports that circulated throughout the bank.

Next, Smith determined that the bank's branch managers were critical to his campaign. The buy-in of those respected and informed individuals would signal to others in the company that his concerns were valid. Moreover, Smith looked to the branch managers because he believed that they could increase his expertise about marketplace trends and also help him test his own assumptions. Thus, for the next three months, he visited every branch in his region of Ontario, Canada—135 in all. During each visit, he spent time with branch managers, listening to their perceptions of the bank's strengths and weaknesses. He learned firsthand about the competition's initiatives and customer trends, and he solicited ideas for improving the bank's services and minimizing costs. By the time he was through, Smith had a broad perspective on the bank's future that few people even in senior management possessed. And he had built dozens of relationships in the process.

Finally, Smith launched some small but highly visible initiatives to demonstrate his expertise and capabilities. For example, he was concerned about slow growth in the company's mortgage business and the loan officers' resulting slip in morale. So he devised a program in which new mortgage customers would make no payments for the first 90 days. The initiative proved remarkably successful, and in short order Smith appeared to be a far more savvy retail banker than anyone had assumed.

Another example of how to establish credibility comes from Microsoft. In 1990, two product-development managers, Karen Fries and Barry Linnett, came to believe that the market would greatly welcome software that featured a "social interface." They envisioned a package that would employ animated human and animal characters to show users how to go about their computing tasks.

Inside Microsoft, however, employees had immediate concerns about the concept. Software programmers ridiculed the cute characters. Animated characters had been used before only in software for children, making their use in adult environments hard to envision. But Fries and Linnett felt their proposed product had both dynamism and complexity, and they remained convinced that consumers would eagerly buy such programs. They also believed that the home-computer software market—largely untapped at the time and with fewer software standards—would be open to such innovation.

Within the company, Fries had gained quite a bit of relationship credibility. She had started out as a recruiter for the company in 1987 and had worked directly for many of Microsoft's senior executives. They trusted and liked her. In addition, she had been responsible for hiring the company's product and program managers. As a result, she knew all the senior people at Microsoft and had hired many of the people who would be deciding on her product.

Linnett's strength laid in his expertise. In particular, he knew the technology behind an innovative tutorial program called PC Works. In addition, both Fries and Linnett had managed Publisher, a product with a unique help feature called Wizards, which Microsoft's CEO, Bill Gates, had liked. But those factors were sufficient only to get an initial hearing from Microsoft's senior management. To persuade the organization to move forward, the pair would need to improve perceptions of their expertise. It hurt them that this type of social-interface software had no proven track record of success and that they were both novices with such software. Their challenge became one of finding substitutes for their own expertise.

Their first step was a wise one. From within Microsoft, they hired respected technical guru Darrin Massena. With Massena, they developed a set of prototypes to demonstrate that they did indeed understand the software's technology and could make it work. They then tested the prototypes in market research, and users responded enthusiastically. Finally, and most important, they enlisted two Stanford University professors, Clifford Nass and Bryon Reeves, both experts in human-computer interaction. In several meetings with Microsoft senior managers and Gates himself, they presented a rigorously compiled and thorough body of research that demonstrated how and why social-interface software was ideally suited to the average computer user. In addition, Fries and Linnett asserted that considerable jumps in computing power would make more realistic cartoon characters an increasingly malleable technology. Their product, they said, was the leading edge of an incipient software revolution. Convinced, Gates approved a full product-development team, and in January 1995, the product called BOB was launched. BOB went on to sell more than half a million copies, and its concept and technology are being used within Microsoft as a platform for developing several Internet products.

Credibility is the cornerstone of effective persuading; without it, a persuader won't be given the time of day. In the best-case scenario, people enter into a persuasion situation with some measure of expertise and relationship credibility. But it is important to note that credibility along either lines can be built or bought. Indeed, it must be, or the next steps are an exercise in futility.

Frame For Common Ground   Even if your credibility is high, your position must still appeal strongly to the people you are trying to persuade. After all, few people will jump on board a train that will bring them to ruin or even mild discomfort. Effective persuaders must be adept at describing their positions in terms that illuminate their advantages. As any parent can tell you, the fastest way to get a child to come along willingly on a trip to the grocery store is to point out that there are lollipops by the cash register. That is not deception. It is just a persuasive way of framing the benefits of taking such a journey. In work situations, persuasive framing is obviously more complex, but the underlying principle is the same. It is a process of identifying shared benefits.

Monica Ruffo, an account executive for an advertising agency, offers a good example of persuasive framing. Her client, a fast-food chain, was instituting a promotional campaign in Canada; menu items such as a hamburger, fries, and cola were to be bundled together and sold at a low price. The strategy made sense to corporate headquarters. Its research showed that consumers thought the company's products were higher priced than the competition's, and the company was anxious to overcome this perception. The franchisees, on the other hand, were still experiencing strong sales and were far more concerned about the short-term impact that the new, low prices would have on their profit margins.

A less experienced persuader would have attempted to rationalize headquarters' perspective to the franchisees—to convince them of its validity. But Ruffo framed the change in pricing to demonstrate its benefits to the franchisees themselves. The new value campaign, she explained, would actually improve franchisees' profits. To back up this point, she drew on several sources. A pilot project in Tennessee, for instance, had demonstrated that under the new pricing scheme, the sales of french fries and drinks—the two most profitable items on the menu—had markedly increased. In addition, the company had rolled out medium-sized meal packages in 80 percent of its U.S. outlets, and franchisees' sales of fries and drinks had jumped 26 percent. Citing research from a respected business periodical, Ruffo also showed that when customers raised their estimate of the value they receive from a retail establishment by 10 percent, the establishment's sales rose by 1 percent. She had estimated that the new meal plan would increase value perceptions by 100 percent, with the result that franchisee sales could be expected to grow 10 percent.

Ruffo closed her presentation with a letter written many years before by the company's founder to the organization. It was an emotional letter extolling the values of the company and stressing the importance of the franchisees to the company's success. It also highlighted the importance of the company's position as the low-price leader in the industry. The beliefs and values contained in the letter had long been etched in the minds of Ruffo's audience. Hearing them again only confirmed the company's concern for the franchisees and the importance of their winning formula. They also won Ruffo a standing ovation. That day, the franchisees voted unanimously to support the new meal-pricing plan.

The Ruffo case illustrates why—in choosing appropriate positioning—it is critical first to identify your objective's tangible benefits to the people you are trying to persuade. Sometimes that is easy. Mutual benefits exist. In other situations, however, no shared advantages are readily apparent—or meaningful. In these cases, effective persuaders adjust their positions. They know it is impossible to engage people and gain commitment to ideas or plans without highlighting the advantages to all the parties involved.

At the heart of framing is a solid understanding of your audience. Even before starting to persuade, the best persuaders we have encountered closely study the issues that matter to their colleagues. They use conversations, meetings, and other forms of dialogue to collect essential information. They are good at listening. They test their ideas with trusted confidants, and they ask questions of the people they will later be persuading. Those steps help them think through the arguments, the evidence, and the perspectives they will present. Oftentimes, this process causes them to alter or compromise their own plans before they even start persuading. It is through this thoughtful, inquisitive approach they develop frames that appeal to their audience.

Consider the case of a manager who was in charge of process engineering for a jet engine manufacturer. He had redesigned the work flow for routine turbine maintenance for airline clients in a manner that would dramatically shorten the turnaround time for servicing. Before presenting his ideas to the company's president, he consulted a good friend in the company, the vice president of engineering, who knew the president well. This conversation revealed that the president's prime concern would not be speed or efficiency but profitability. To get the president's buy-in, the vice president explained, the new system would have to improve the company's profitability in the short run by lowering operating expenses.

At first this information had the manager stumped. He had planned to focus on efficiency and had even intended to request additional funding to make the process work. But his conversation with the vice president sparked him to change his position. Indeed, he went so far as to change the work-flow design itself so that it no longer required new investment but rather drove down costs. He then carefully documented the cost savings and profitability gains that his new plan would produce and presented this revised plan to the president. With his initiative positioned anew, the manager persuaded the president and got the project approved.

Provide Evidence   With credibility established and a common frame identified, persuasion becomes a matter of presenting evidence. Ordinary evidence, however, won't do. We have found that the most effective persuaders use language in a particular way. They supplement numerical data with examples, stories, metaphors, and analogies to make their positions come alive. That use of language paints a vivid word picture and, in doing so, lends a compelling and tangible quality to the persuader's point of view.

Think about a typical persuasion situation. The persuader is often advocating a goal, strategy, or initiative with an uncertain outcome. Karen Fries and Barry Linnett, for instance, wanted Microsoft to invest millions of dollars in a software package with chancy technology and unknown market demand. The team could have supported its case solely with market research, financial projections, and the like. But that would have been a mistake, because research shows that most people perceive such reports as not entirely informative. They are too abstract to be completely meaningful or memorable. In essence, the numbers don't make an emotional impact.

By contrast, stories and vivid language do, particularly when they present comparable situations to the one under discussion. A marketing manager trying to persuade senior executives to invest in a new product, for example, might cite examples of similar investments that paid off handsomely. Indeed, we found that people readily draw lessons from such cases. More important, the research shows that listeners absorb information in proportion to its vividness. Thus it is no wonder that Fries and Linnett hit a home run when they presented their case for BOB with the following analogy:

> *Imagine you want to cook dinner and you must first go to the supermarket. You have all the flexibility you want—you can cook anything in the world as long as you know how and have the time and desire to do it. When you arrive at the supermarket, you find all these overstuffed aisles with cryptic single-word headings like "sundries" and "ethnic food" and "condiments." These are the menus on typical computer interfaces. The question is whether salt is under condiments or ethnic food or near the potato chip section. There are surrounding racks and wall spaces, much as our software interfaces now have support buttons, tool bars, and lines around the perimeters. Now after you have collected everything, you still need to put it all together in the correct order to make a meal. If you're a good cook, your meal will probably be good. If you're a novice, it probably won't be.*
>
> *We [at Microsoft] have been selling under the supermarket category for years, and we think there is a big opportunity for restaurants. That's what we are trying to do now with BOB: pushing the next step with software that is more like going to a restaurant, so the user doesn't spend all of his time searching for the ingredients. We find and put the ingredients together. You sit down, you get comfortable. We bring you a menu. We do the work, you relax. It's an enjoyable experience. No walking around lost trying to find things, no cooking.*

Had Fries and Linnett used a literal description of BOB's advantages, few of their highly computer-literate colleagues at Microsoft would have personally related to the menu-searching frustration that BOB was designed to eliminate. The analogy they selected, however, made BOB's purpose both concrete and memorable.

A master persuader, Mary Kay Ash, the founder of Mary Kay Cosmetics, regularly draws on analogies to illustrate and "sell" the business conduct she values. Consider this speech at the company's annual sales convention:

> *Back in the days of the Roman Empire, the legions of the emperor conquered the known world. There was, however, one band of people that the Romans never conquered. Those people were the followers of the great teacher from Bethlehem. Historians have long since discovered that one of*

the reasons for the sturdiness of this folk was their habit of meeting together weekly. They shared their difficulties, and they stood side by side. Does this remind you of something? The way we stand side by side and share our knowledge and difficulties with each other in our weekly unit meetings. I have so often observed when a director or unit member is confronted with a personal problem that the unit stands together in helping that sister in distress. What a wonderful circle of friendships we have. Perhaps it's one of the greatest fringe benefits of our company.

Through her vivid analogy, Ash links collective support in the company to a courageous period in Christian history. In doing so, she accomplishes several objectives. First, she drives home her belief that collective support is crucial to the success of the organization. Most Mary Kay salespeople are independent operators who face the daily challenges of direct selling. An emotional support system of fellow salespeople is essential to ensure that self-esteem and confidence remain intact in the face of rejection. Next she suggests by her analogy that solidarity against the odds is the best way to stymie powerful oppressors—to wit, the competition. Finally, Ash's choice of analogy imbues a sense of a heroic mission to the work of her sales force.

You probably don't need to invoke the analogy of the Christian struggle to support your position, but effective persuaders are not afraid of unleashing the immense power of language. In fact, they use it to their utmost advantage.

Connect Emotionally   In the business world, we like to think that our colleagues use reason to make their decisions, yet if we scratch below the surface we will always find emotions at play. Good persuaders are aware of the primacy of emotions and are responsive to them in two important ways.

First, they show their own emotional commitment to the position they are advocating. Such expression is a delicate matter. If you act too emotional, people may doubt your clearheadedness. But you must also show that your commitment to a goal is not just in your mind but in your heart and gut as well. Without this demonstration of feeling, people may wonder if you actually believe in the position you're championing.

Perhaps more important, however, is that effective persuaders have a strong and accurate sense of their audience's emotional state, and they adjust the tone of their arguments accordingly. Sometimes that means coming on strong, with forceful points. Other times, a whisper may be all that is required. The idea is that whatever your position, you match your emotional fervor to your audience's ability to receive the message.

Effective persuaders seem to have a second sense about how their colleagues have interpreted past events in the organization and how they will probably interpret a proposal. The best persuaders in our study would usually canvass key individuals who had a good pulse on the mood and emotional expectations of those about to be persuaded. They would ask those individuals how various proposals might affect colleagues on an emotional level—in essence, testing possible reactions. They were also quite effective at gathering information through informal conversations in the hallways or at lunch. In the end, their aim was to ensure that the emotional appeal behind their persuasion matched what their audience was already feeling or expecting.

To illustrate the importance of emotional match-making in persuasion, consider this example. The president of an aeronautics manufacturing company strongly believed that the maintenance costs and turnaround time of the company's U.S. and foreign competitors were so much better than his own company's that it stood to lose customers and profits. He wanted to communicate his fear and his urgent desire for change to his senior managers. So one afternoon, he called them into the boardroom. On an overhead screen was the projected image of a smiling man flying an old-fashioned biplane with his scarf blowing in the wind. The right half of the transparency was covered. When everyone was seated, the president explained that he felt as this pilot did, given the company's recent good fortune. The organization, after all, had just finished its most successful year in history. But then with a deep sigh, he announced that his happiness was quickly vanishing. As the president lifted the remaining portion of the sheet, he revealed an image of the pilot flying directly into a wall. The president then faced his audience and in a heavy voice said, "This is what I see happening to us." He asserted that the company was headed for a crash if people didn't take action fast. He then went on to lecture the group about the steps needed to counter this threat.

The reaction from the group was immediate and negative. Directly after the meeting, managers gathered in small clusters in the hallways to talk about the president's "scare tactics." They resented what they perceived to be the president's overstatement of the case. As the managers saw it, they had exerted enormous effort that year to break the company's records in sales and profitability. They were proud of their achievements. In fact, they had entered the meeting expecting it would be the moment of recognition. But to their absolute surprise, they were scolded.

The president's mistake? First, he should have canvassed a few members of his senior team to ascertain the emotional state of the group. From that, he would have learned that they were in need of thanks and recognition. He should then have held a separate session devoted simply to praising the team's accomplishments. Later, in a second meeting, he could have expressed his own anxieties about the coming year. And rather than blame the team for ignoring the future, he could have calmly described what he saw as emerging threats to the company and then asked his management team to help him develop new initiatives.

Now let us look at someone who found the right emotional match with his audience: Robert Marcell, head of Chrysler's small-car design team. In the early 1990s, Chrysler was eager to produce a new subcompact—indeed, the company had not introduced a new model of this type since 1978. But senior managers at Chrysler did not want to go it alone. They thought an alliance with a foreign manufacturer would improve the car's design and protect Chrysler's cash stores.

Marcell was convinced otherwise. He believed that the company should bring the design and production of a new subcompact in-house. He knew that persuading senior managers would be difficult, but he also had his own team to contend with. Team members had lost their confidence that they would ever again have the opportunity to create a good car. They were also angry that the United States had once again given up its position to foreign competitors when it came to small cars.

Marcell decided that his persuasion tactics had to be built around emotional themes that would touch his audience. From innumerable conversations around the company, he learned that many people felt as he did—that to surrender the subcompact's design to a foreign manufacturer was to surrender the company's soul and, ultimately, its ability to provide jobs. In addition, he felt deeply that his organization was a talented group hungry for a challenge and an opportunity to restore its self-esteem and pride. He would need to demonstrate his faith in the team's abilities.

Marcell prepared a 15-minute talk built around slides of his hometown, Iron River, a now defunct mining town in Upper Michigan, devastated, in large part, by foreign mining companies. On the screen flashed recent photographs he had taken of his boarded-up high school, the shuttered homes of his childhood friends, the crumbling ruins of the town's ironworks, closed churches, and an abandoned railroad yard. After a description of each of these places; he said the phrase, "We couldn't compete"—like the refrain of a hymn. Marcell's point was that the same outcome awaited Detroit if the production of small cars was not brought back to the United States. Surrender was the enemy, he said, and devastation would follow if the group did not take immediate action.

Marcell ended his slide show on a hopeful note. He spoke of his pride in his design group and then challenged the team to build a "made-in-America" subcompact that would prove that the United States could still compete. The speech, which echoed the exact sentiments of the audience, rekindled the group's fighting spirit. Shortly after the speech, group members began drafting their ideas for a new car.

Marcell then took his slide show to the company's senior management and ultimately to Chrysler Chairman Lee Iacocca. As Marcell showed his slides, he could see that Iacocca was touched. Iacocca, after all, was a fighter and a strongly patriotic man himself. In fact, Marcell's approach was not too different from Iacocca's earlier appeal to the U.S. Congress to save Chrysler. At the end of the show, Marcell stopped and said, "If we dare to be different, we could be the reason the U.S. auto industry survives. We could be the reason our kids and grandkids don't end up working at fast-food chains." Iacocca stayed on for two hours as Marcell explained in greater detail what his team was planning. Afterward, Iacocca changed his mind and gave Marcell's group approval to develop a car, the Neon.

With both groups, Marcell skillfully matched his emotional tenor to that of the group he was addressing. The ideas he conveyed resonated deeply with his largely Midwestern audience. And rather than leave them in a depressed state, he offered them hope, which was more persuasive than promising doom. Again, this played to the strong patriotic sentiments of his American-heartland audience.

No effort to persuade can succeed without emotion, but showing too much emotion can be as unproductive as showing too little. The important point to remember is that you must match your emotions to your audience's.

THE FORCE OF PERSUASION

The concept of persuasion, like that of power, often confuses and even mystifies businesspeople. It is so complex—and so dangerous when mishandled—that many would rather just avoid it altogether. But like power, persuasion can be a force for enormous good in an organization. It can pull people together, move ideas forward, galvanize change, and forge constructive solutions. To do all that, however, people must understand persuasion for what it is—not convincing and selling but learning and negotiating. Furthermore, it must be seen as an art form that requires commitment and practice, especially as today's business contingencies make persuasion more necessary than ever.

Unfortunately, while many have written about power theoretically, there have been few empirical examinations of power and its use. Most of the work has taken the form of case studies. Michel Crozier's *The Bureaucratic Phenomenon* (University of Chicago Press, 1964) is important because it describes a group's source of power as control over critical activities and illustrates how power is not strictly derived from hierarchical position. J. Victor Baldridge's *Power and Conflict in the University* (John Wiley & Sons, 1971) and Andrew Pettigrew's study of computer purchase decisions in one English firm (*Politics of Organizational Decision Making*, Tavistock, 1973) both present insights into the acquisition and use of power in specific instances. Our work has been more empirical and comparative, testing more explicitly the ideas presented in this article. The study of university decision making is reported in articles in the June 1974, pp. 135–151, and December 1974, pp. 453–473, issues of the *Administrative Science Quarterly*, the insurance firm study in J. G. Hunt and L. L. Larson's collection, *Leadership Frontiers* (Kent State University Press, 1975), and the study of hospital administrator succession will appear in 1977 in the *Academy* of *Management Journal*.

INFLUENCE WITHOUT AUTHORITY:
THE USE OF ALLIANCES, RECIPROCITY, AND EXCHANGE TO ACCOMPLISH WORK*

Allan R. Cohen
David L. Bradford

Bill Heatton is the director of research at a $250 million division of a large west coast company. The division manufactures exotic telecommunications components and has many technical advancements

*Reprinted, by permission of the publisher, from *Organizational Dynamics*, Winter 1989. © 1989 American Management Association, New York. All rights reserved.

to its credit. During the past several years, however, the division's performance has been spotty at best; multimillion dollar losses have been experienced in some years despite many efforts to make the division more profitable. Several large contracts have resulted in major financial losses, and in each instance the various parts of the division blamed the others for the problems. Listen to Bill's frustration as he talks about his efforts to influence Ted, a colleague who is marketing director, and Roland, the program manager who reports to Ted.

> *Another program is about to come through. Roland is a nice guy, but he knows nothing and never will. He was responsible for our last big loss, and now he's in charge of this one. I've tried to convince Ted, his boss, to get Roland off the program, but I get nowhere. Although Ted doesn't argue that Roland is capable, he doesn't act to find someone else. Instead, he comes to me with worries about my area.*
>
> *I decided to respond by changing my staffing plan, assigning to Roland's program the people they wanted. I had to override my staff's best judgment about who should be assigned. Yet I'm not getting needed progress reports from Roland, and he's never available for planning. I get little argument from him, but there's no action to correct the problem. That's bad because I'm responding but not getting any response.*
>
> *There's no way to resolve this. If they disagree, that's it. I could go to a tit-for-tat strategy, saying that if they don't do what I want, we'll get even with them next time. But I don't know how to do that without hurting the organization, which would feel worse than getting even!*
>
> *Ted, Roland's boss, is so much better than his predecessor that I hate to ask that he be removed. We could go together to our boss, the general manager, but I'm very reluctant to do that. You've failed in a matrix organization if you have to go to your boss. I have to try hard because I'd look bad if I had to throw it in his lap.*
>
> *Meanwhile, I'm being forceful, but I'm afraid it's in a destructive way. I don't want to wait until the program has failed to be told it was all my fault.*

Bill is clearly angry and frustrated, leading him to behave in ways that he does not feel good about. Like other managers who very much want to influence an uncooperative co-worker whom they cannot control, Bill has begun to think of the intransigent employee as the enemy. Bill's anger is narrowing his sense of what is possible; he fantasizes revenge but is too dedicated to the organization to actually harm it. He is genuinely stuck.

Organizational members who want to make things happen often find themselves in this position. Irrespective of whether they are staff or line employees, professionals or managers, they find it increasingly necessary to influence colleagues and superiors. These critical others control needed resources, possess required information, set priorities on important activities, and have to agree and cooperate if plans are to be implemented. They cannot be ordered around because they are under another area's control and can legitimately say no because they have many other valid priorities. They respond only when they choose to. Despite the clear need and appropriateness of what is being asked for (certainly as seen by the person who is making the request), compliance may not be forthcoming.

All of this places a large burden on organizational members, who are expected not only to take initiatives but also to respond intelligently to requests made of them by others. Judgment is needed to sort out the value of the many requests made of anyone who has valuable resources to contribute. As Robert Kaplan argued in his article "Trade Routes: The Manager's Network of Relationships" (*Organizational Dynamics*, Spring 1984), managers must now develop the organizational equivalent of "trade routes" to get things done. Informal networks of mutual influence are needed. In her book, *The Change Masters* (Simon & Schuster, 1983), Rosabeth Moss Kanter showed that developing and implementing all kinds of innovations require coalitions to be built to shape and support new ways of doing business.

A key current problem, then, is finding ways to develop mutual influence without the formal authority to command. A peer cannot "order" a colleague to change priorities, modify an approach, or implement a grand new idea. A staff member cannot "command" his or her supervisor to back a proposal, fight top management for greater resources, or allow more autonomy. Even Bill Heatton, in dealing with Roland (who was a level below him in the hierarchy but in another department), could not dictate that Roland provide the progress reports that Bill so desperately wanted.

EXCHANGE AND THE LAW OF RECIPROCITY

The way influence is acquired without formal authority is through the "law of reciprocity"—the almost universal belief that people should be paid back for what they do, that one good (or bad) deed deserves another. This belief is held by people in primitive and not-so-primitive societies all around the world, and it serves as the grease that allows the organizational wheel to turn smoothly. Because people expect that their actions will be paid back in one form or another, influence is possible.

In the case of Bill Heatton, his inability to get what he wanted from Roland and Ted stemmed from his failure to understand fully how reciprocity works in organizations. He therefore was unable to set up mutually beneficial exchanges. Bill believed that be had gone out of his way to help the marketing department by changing his staffing patterns, and he expected Roland to reciprocate by providing regular progress reports. When Roland failed to provide the reports, Bill believed that Ted was obligated to remove Roland from the project. When Ted did not respond, Bill became angry and wanted to retaliate. Thus Bill recognized the appropriateness of exchange in making organizations work. However, he did not understand how exchange operates.

Before exploring in detail how exchange can work in dealing with colleagues and superiors, it is important to recognize that reciprocity is the basic principle behind all organizational transactions. For example, the basic employment contract is an exchange ("an honest day's work for an honest day's pay"). Even work that is above and beyond what is formally required involves exchange. The person who helps out may not necessarily get (or expect) immediate payment for the extra effort requested, but some eventual compensation is expected.

Think of the likely irritation an employee would feel if his or her boss asked him or her to work through several weekends, never so much as said thanks, and then claimed credit for the extra work. The employee might not say anything the first time this happened, expecting or hoping that the boss would make it up somehow. However, if the effort were never acknowledged in any way, the employee, like most people, would feel that something important had been violated.

Exchanges enable people to handle the give-and-take of working together without strong feelings of injustice arising. They are especially important during periods of rapid change because the number of requests that go far beyond the routine tends to escalate. In those situations, exchanges become less predictable, more free-floating, and spontaneous. Nevertheless, people still expect that somehow or other, sooner or later, they will be (roughly) equally compensated for the acts they do above and beyond those that are covered by the formal exchange agreements in their job. Consequently, some kind of "currency" equivalent needs to be worked out, implicitly if not explicitly, to keep the parties in the exchange feeling fairly treated.

CURRENCIES: THE SOURCE OF INFLUENCE

If the basis of organizational influence depends on mutually satisfactory exchanges, then people are influential only insofar as they can offer something that others need. Thus power comes from the ability to meet others' needs.

A useful way to think of how the process of exchange actually works in organizations is to use the metaphor of "currencies." This metaphor provides a powerful way to conceptualize what is important to the influencer and the person to be influenced. Just as many types of currencies are traded in the world

Inspiration-Related Currencies

Vision	Being involved in a task that has larger significance for the unit, organization, customers, or society.
Excellence	Having a chance to do important things really well.
Moral/Ethical Correctness	Doing what is "right" by a higher standard than efficiency.

Task-Related Currencies

Resources	Lending or giving money, budget increases, personnel, space, and so forth.
Assistance	Helping with existing projects or undertaking unwanted tasks.
Cooperation	Giving task support, providing quicker response time, approving a project, or aiding implementation.
Information	Providing organizational as well as technical knowledge.

Position-Related Currencies

Advancement	Giving a task or assignment that can aid in promotion.
Recognition	Acknowledging effort, accomplishment, or abilities.
Visibility	Providing chance to be known by higher-ups or significant others in the organization.
Reputation	Enhancing the way a person is seen.
Importance/Insiderness	Offering a sense of importance, of "belonging."
Network/Contacts	Providing opportunities for linking with others.

Relationship-Related Currencies

Acceptance/Inclusion	Providing closeness and friendship.
Personal support	Giving personal and emotional backing.
Understanding	Listening to others' concerns and issues.

Personal-Related Currencies

Self-Concept	Affirming one's values, self-esteem, and identity.
Challenge/Learning	Sharing tasks that increase skills and abilities.
Ownership/Involvement	Letting others have ownership and influence.
Gratitude	Expressing appreciation or indebtedness.

EXHIBIT 1   Commonly Traded Organizational Currencies

financial market, many types are "traded" in organizational life. Too often people think only of money or promotion and status. Those "currencies," however, usually are available only to a manager in dealing with his or her employees. Peers who want to influence colleagues or employees who want to influence their supervisors often feel helpless. They need to recognize that many types of payments exist, broadening the range of what can be exchanged.

Some major currencies that are commonly valued and traded in organizations are listed in Exhibit 1. Although not exhaustive, the list makes evident that a person does not have to be at the top of an organization or have hands on the formal levers of power to command multiple resources that others may value.

Part of the usefulness of currencies comes from their flexibility. For example, there are many ways to express gratitude and to give assistance. A manager who most values the currency of appreciation could be paid through verbal thanks, praise, a public statement at a meeting, informal comments to his peers, and/or a note to her boss. However, the same note of thanks seen by one person as a sign of appreciation may be seen by another person as an attempt to brownnose or by a third person as a cheap way to try to repay extensive favors and service. Thus currencies have value not in some abstract sense but as defined by the receiver.

Although we have stressed the interactive nature of exchange, "payments" do not always have to be made by the other person. They can be self-generated to fit beliefs about being virtuous, benevolent, or committed to the organization's welfare. Someone may respond to another person's request because it reinforces cherished values, a sense of identity, or feelings of self-worth. The exchange is interpersonally stimulated because the one who wants influence has set up conditions that allow this kind of self-payment to occur by asking for cooperation to accomplish organizational goals. However, the person who responds because "it is the right thing to do" and who feels good about being the "kind of person who does not act out of narrow self-interest" is printing currency (virtue) that is self-satisfying.

Of course, the five categories of currencies listed in Exhibit 1 are not mutually exclusive. When the demand from the other person is high, people are likely to pay in several currencies across several categories. They may, for example, stress the organizational value of their request, promise to return the favor at a later time, imply that it will increase the other's prestige in the organization, and express their appreciation.

ESTABLISHING EXCHANGE RATES

What does it take to pay back in a currency that the other party in an exchange will perceive as equivalent? In impersonal markets, because everything is translated into a common monetary currency, it generally is easy to say what a fair payment is. Does a ton of steel equal a case of golfclubs? By translating both into dollar equivalents, a satisfactory deal can be worked out.

In interpersonal exchanges, however, the process becomes a bit more complicated. Just how does someone repay another person's willingness to help finish a report? Is a simple thank-you enough? Does it also require the recipient to say something nice about the helper to his or her boss? Whose standard of fairness should be used? What if one person's idea of fair repayment is very different from the other's?

Because of the natural differences in the way two parties can interpret the same activity, establishing exchanges that both parties will perceive as equitable can be problematic. Thus it is critical to understand what is important to the person to be influenced. Without a clear understanding of what that person experiences and values, it will be extremely difficult for anyone to thread a path through the minefield of creating mutually satisfactory exchanges.

Fortunately, the calibration of equivalent exchanges in the interpersonal and organizational worlds is facilitated by the fact that approximations will do in most cases. Occasionally, organizational members know exactly what they want in return for favors of help, but more often they will settle for very rough equivalents (providing that there is reasonable goodwill).

THE PROCESS OF EXCHANGE

To make the exchange process effective, the influencer needs to (1) think about the person to be influenced as a potential ally, not an adversary, (2) know the world of the potential ally, including the pressures as well as the person's needs and goals, (3) be aware of key goals and available resources that may be valued by the potential ally, and (4) understand the exchange transaction itself so that win-win outcomes are achieved. Each of these factors is discussed below.

POTENTIAL ALLY, NOT ADVERSARY

A key to influence is thinking of the other person as a potential ally. Just as many contemporary organizations have discovered the importance of creating strategic alliances with suppliers and customers, employees who want influence within the organization need to create internal allies. Even though each party in an alliance continues to have freedom to pursue its own interests, the goal is to find areas of mutual benefit and develop trusting, sustainable relationships. Similarly, each person whose cooperation is needed inside the organization is a potential ally. Each still has self-interests to pursue, but those self-interests do not preclude searching for and building areas of mutual benefit.

Seeing other organizational members as potential allies decreases the chance that adversarial relationships will develop—an all-too-frequent result (as in the case of Bill Heatton) when the eager influencer does not quickly get the assistance of cooperation needed. Assuming that even a difficult person is a potential ally makes it easier to understand that person's world and thereby discover what that person values and needs.

THE POTENTIAL ALLY'S WORLD

We have stressed the importance of knowing the world of the potential ally. Without awareness of what the ally needs (what currencies are valued), attempts to influence that person can only be haphazard. Although this conclusion may seem self-evident, it is remarkable how often people attempt to influence without adequate information about what is important to the potential ally. Instead, they are driven by their own definition of "what should be" and "what is right" when they should be seeing the world from the other person's perspective.

For example, Bill Heatton never thought about the costs to Ted of removing Roland from the project. Did Ted believe he could coach Roland to perform better on this project? Did Ted even agree that Roland had done a poor job on the previous project, or did Ted think Roland had been hampered by other departments' shortcomings? Bill just did not know.

Several factors can keep the influencer from seeing the potential ally clearly. As with Bill Heatton, the frustration of meeting resistance from a potential ally can get in the way of really understanding the other person's world. The desire to influence is so strong that only the need for cooperation is visible to the influencer. As a result of not being understood, the potential ally digs in, making the influencer repeat an inappropriate strategy or back off in frustration.

When a potential ally's behavior is not understandable ("Why won't Roland send the needed progress reports?"), the influencer tends to stereotype that person. If early attempts to influence do not work, the influencer is tempted to write the person off as negative, stubborn, selfish, or "just another bean counter/whiz kid/sales-type" or whatever pejorative label is used in that organizational culture to dismiss those organizational members who are different.

Although some stereotypes may have a grain of truth, they generally conceal more than they reveal. The actuary who understands that judgment, not just numbers, is needed to make decisions disappears as an individual when the stereotype of "impersonal, detached number machine" is the filter through which he or she is seen. Once the stereotype is applied, the frustrated influencer is no longer likely to see what currencies that particular potential ally actually values.

Sometimes, the lack of clear understanding about a potential ally stems from the influencer's failure to appreciate the organizational forces acting on the potential ally. To a great extent, a person's behavior is a result of the situation in which that person works (and not just his or her personality). Potential allies are embedded in an organizational culture that shapes their interests and responses. For example, one of the key determinants of anyone's behavior is likely to be the way the person's performance is measured and rewarded. In many instances, what is mistaken for personal orneriness is merely the result of the person's doing something that will be seen as good performance in his or her function.

The salesperson who is furious because the plant manager resists changing priorities for a rush order may not realize that part of the plant manager's bonus depends on holding unit costs down—a task made easier with long production runs. The plant manager's resistance does not necessarily reflect his or her inability to be flexible or lack of concern about pleasing customers or about the company's overall success.

Other organizational forces that can affect the potential ally's behavior include the daily time demands on that person's position; the amount of contact the person has with customers, suppliers, and other outsiders; the organization's information flow (or lack of it); the style of the potential ally's boss; the belief and assumptions held by that person's co-workers; and so forth. Although some of these factors cannot be changed by the influencer, understanding them can be useful in figuring out how to frame and time requests. It also helps the influencer resist the temptation to stereotype the noncooperator.

SELF-AWARENESS OF THE INFLUENCER

Unfortunately, people desiring influence are not always aware of precisely what they want. Often their requests contain a cluster of needs (a certain product, arranged in a certain way, delivered at a specified time). They fail to think through which aspects are more important and which can be jettisoned if necessary. Did Bill Heatton want Roland removed, or did he want the project effectively managed? Did he want overt concessions from Ted, or did he want better progress reports?

Further, there is a tendency to confuse and intermingle the desired end goal with the means of accomplishing it, leading to too many battles over the wrong things. In *The Change Masters*, Kanter reported that successful influencers in organizations were those who never lost sight of the ultimate objective but were willing to be flexible about means.

Sometimes influencers underestimate the range of currencies available for use. They may assume, for example, that just because they are low in the organization they have nothing that others want. Employees who want to influence their boss are especially likely not to realize all of the supervisor's needs that they can fulfill. They become so caught up with their feelings of powerlessness that they fail to see the many ways they can generate valuable currencies.

In other instances, influencers fail to be aware of their preferred style of interaction and its fit with the potential ally's preferred style. Everyone has a way of relating to others to get work done. However, like the fish who is unaware of the water, many people are oblivious of their own style of interaction or see it as the only way to be. Yet interaction style can cause problems with potential allies who are different.

For example, does the influencer tend to socialize first and work later? If so, that style of interaction will distress a potential ally who likes to dig right in to solve the problem at hand and only afterward chat about sports, family, or office politics. Does the potential ally want to be approached with answers, not problems? If so, a tendency to start influence attempts with open-ended, exploratory problem solving can lead to rejection despite good intentions.

NATURE OF THE EXCHANGE TRANSACTION

Many of the problems that occur in the actual exchange negotiation have their roots in the failure to deal adequately with the first three factors outlined above. Failure to treat other people as potential allies, to understand a potential ally's world, and to be self-aware are all factors that interfere with successful exchange. In addition, some special problems commonly arise when both parties are in the process of working out a mutually satisfactory exchange agreement.

- **Not knowing how to use reciprocity**   Using reciprocity requires stating needs clearly without "crying wolf," being aware of the needs of an ally without being manipulative, and seeking mutual gain rather than playing "winner takes all." One trap that Bill Heatton fell into was not being able to "close on the exchange." That is, he assumed that if he acted in good faith and did his part, others would automatically reciprocate. Part of his failure was not understanding the other party's world; another part was not being able to negotiate cleanly with Ted about what each of them wanted. It is not even clear that Ted realized Bill was altering his organization as per Ted's requests, that Ted got what he wanted, or that Ted knew Bill intended an exchange of responses.

• **Preferring to be right rather than effective**   This problem is especially endemic to professionals of all kinds. Because of their dedication to the "truth" (as their profession defines it), they stubbornly stick to their one right way when trying to line up potential allies instead of thinking about what will work given the audience and conditions. Organizational members with strong technical backgrounds often chorus the equivalent of "I'll be damned if I'm going to sell out and become a phone salesman, trying to get by on a shoeshine and smile." The failure to accommodate to the potential ally's needs and desires often kills otherwise sound ideas.

• **Overusing what has been successful**   When people find that a certain approach is effective in many situations, they often begin to use it in many situations, they often begin to use it in places where it does not fit. By overusing the approach, they block more appropriate methods. Just as a weight lifter becomes muscle-bound from overdeveloping particular muscles at the expense of others, people who have been reasonably successful at influencing other people can diminish that ability by overusing the same technique.

For example, John Brucker, the human resources director at a medium-size company, often cultivated support for new programs by taking people out to fancy restaurants for an evening of fine food and wine. He genuinely derived pleasure from entertaining, but at the same time he created subtle obligations. One time, a new program he wanted to introduce required the agreement of William Adams, head of engineering. Adams, an old-timer, perceived Brucker's proposal as an unnecessary frill, mainly because he did not perceive the real benefits to the overall organization. Brucker responded to Adams's negative comments as he always did in such cases—by becoming more friendly and insisting that they get together for dinner soon. After several of these invitations, Adams became furious. Insulted by what he considered to be Brucker's attempts to buy him off, he fought even harder to kill the proposal. Not only did the program die, but Brucker lost all possibility of influencing Adams in the future. Adams saw Brucker's attempts at socializing as a sleazy and crude way of trying to soften him up. For his part, Brucker was totally puzzled by Adams' frostiness and assumed that he was against all progress. He never realized that Adams had a deep sense of integrity and a real commitment to the good of the organization. Thus Brucker lost his opportunity to sell a program that, ironically, Adams would have found valuable had it been implemented.

As the case above illustrates, a broad repertoire of influence approaches is needed in modern organizations. Johnny-one-notes soon fall flat.

THE ROLE OF RELATIONSHIPS

All of the preceding discussion needs to be conditioned by one important variable: the nature of the relationship between both parties. The greater the extent to which the influencer has worked with the potential ally and created trust, the easier the exchange process will be. Each party will know the other's desired currencies and situational pressures, and each will have developed a mutually productive interaction style. With trust, less energy will be spent on figuring out the intentions of the ally, and there will be less suspicion about when and how the payback will occur.

A poor relationship (based on previous interactions, on the reputation each party has in the organization, and/or on stereotypes and animosities between the functions or departments that each party represents) will impede an otherwise easy exchange. Distrust of the goodwill, veracity, or reliability of the influencer can lead to the demand for "no credit; cash up front," which constrains the flexibility of both parties.

The nature of the interaction during the influencer process also affects the nature of the relationship between the influencer and the other party. The way that John Brucker attempted to relate to William Adams not only did not work but also irreparably damaged any future exchanges between them.

Few transactions within organizations are one-time deals. (Who knows when the other person may be needed again or even who may be working for him or her in the future?) Thus in most exchange situations two outcomes matter: success in achieving task goals and success in improving the relationship so that the next interaction will be even more productive. Too often, people who want to be influential focus only on the task and act as if there is no tomorrow. Although both task accomplishment and an improved relationship cannot always be realized at the same time, on some occasions the latter can be more important than the former. Winning the battle but losing the war is an expensive outcome.

INCONVERTIBLE CURRENCIES

We have spelled out ways organizational members operate to gain influence for achieving organizational goals. By effectively using exchange, organizational members can achieve their goals and at the same time help others achieve theirs. Exchange permits organizational members to be assertive without being antagonistic by keeping mutual benefit a central outcome.

In many cases, organizational members fail to acquire desired influence because they do not use all of their potential power. However, they sometimes fail because not all situations are amenable to even the best efforts at influencing. Not everything can be translated into compatible currencies. If there are fundamental differences in what is valued by two parties, it may not be possible to find common ground, as illustrated in the example below.

The founder and chairman of a high-technology company and the president he had hired five years previously were constantly displeased with one another. The president was committed to creating maximum shareholder value, the currency he valued most as a result of his M.B.A. training, his position, and his temperament. Accordingly, he had concluded that the company was in a perfect position to cash in by squeezing expenses to maximize profits and going public. He could see that the company's product line of exotic components was within a few years of saturating its market and would require massive, risky investment to move to sophisticated end-user products.

The president could not influence the chairman to adopt this direction, however, because the chairman valued a totally different currency, the fun of technological challenge. An independently wealthy man, the chairman had no interest in realizing the $10 million or so he would get if the company maximized profits by cutting research and selling out. He wanted a place to test his intuitive, creative research hunches, not a source of income.

Thus the president's and chairman's currencies were not convertible into one another at an acceptable exchange rate. After they explored various possibilities but failed to find common ground, they mutually agreed that the president should leave—on good terms and only after a more compatible replacement could be found. Although this example acknowledges that influence through alliance, currency conversion, and exchange is not always possible, it is hard to be certain that any situation is hopeless until the person desiring influence has fully applied all of the diagnostic and interpersonal skills we have described.

Influence is enhanced by using the model of strategic alliances to engage in mutually beneficial exchanges with potential allies. Even though it is not always possible to be successful, the chances of achieving success can be greatly increased. In a period of rapid competitive, technological, regulative, and consumer change, individuals and their organizations need all the help they can get.

CHAPTER 17

EMPOWERMENT AND COACHING

PUTTING PEOPLE FIRST FOR ORGANIZATIONAL SUCCESS
Jeffrey Pfeffer
John F. Veiga

INTELLECTUAL CAPITAL = COMPETENCE × COMMITMENT
Dave Ulrich

MANAGEMENT DIALOGUES: TURNING ON THE MARGINAL PERFORMER
John R. Schermerhorn, Jr.
William L. Gardner
Thomas N. Martin

By this point, you have read several references in different articles about the growing obsolescence of the command-and-control management style. Managers with this mentality conceive of their job as making decisions, giving orders, and ensuring that subordinates obey. A more effective approach is high involvement (high performance or high commitment) management, which focuses on employee commitment and empowerment. Empowerment is defined as granting employees, the autonomy to assume more responsibility within an organization and strengthening their sense of effectiveness. Managers empower employees by sharing power, information, and the responsibility to manage their own work as much as possible.

The first two articles in this chapter show us what high involvement management looks like in action. In "Putting People First for Organizational Success," Jeffrey Pfeffer and John Veiga report on research conclusions that investing in employees by utilizing a high involvement management approach results in the increased economic performance of businesses. Pfeffer, organizational behavior professor and business speaker, and Veiga, management professor, identify the seven key management practices linked to successful firms.

In a relatively recent development, intellectual capital has come to be seen as part of a company's competitive advantage. In his article, "Intellectual Capital = Competence × Commitment," Dave Ulrich, well-known human resources professor and consultant, explains the importance of intellectual capital and presents a list of practical suggestions for increasing employee competence and commitment. He also includes a list of symptoms to help recognize burnout.

While the first two articles in this section focus on system-level management practices, the third article returns us to the perennial micro-level problem of how to handle and coach poorly performing employees. "Management Dialogues: Turning on the Marginal Performer," written by management professors John Schermerhorn, Jr., William Gardner, and Thomas Martin, provides blow-by-blow advice for dealing with performance problems. Reading this article will prepare you for the inevitable job interview question, "What would you do if you had an employee who wasn't doing an acceptable job?" Don't miss the reference to the attribution errors discussed in Chapter 8.

Putting people first
for organizational success*

Jeffrey Pfeffer
John Veiga

Over the past decade or so, numerous rigorous studies conducted both within specific industries and in samples of organizations that cross industries have demonstrated the enormous economic returns obtained through the implementation of what are variously called high involvement, high performance, or high commitment management practices. Furthermore, much of this research serves to validate earlier writing on participative management and employee involvement. But even as these research results pile up, trends in actual management practice are, in many instances, moving in a direction exactly opposite to what this growing body of evidence prescribes. Moreover, this disjuncture between knowledge and management practice is occurring at the same time that organizations, confronted with a very competitive environment, are frantically looking for some magic elixir that will provide sustained success, at least over some reasonable period of time.

Rather than putting their people first, numerous firms have sought solutions to competitive challenges in places and means that have not been very productive treating their businesses as portfolios of assets to be bought and sold in an effort to find the right competitive niche, downsizing and outsourcing in a futile attempt to shrink or transact their way to profit, and doing a myriad of other things that weaken or destroy their organizational culture in efforts to minimize labor costs.

SHOW ME THE EVIDENCE

Though we could go on at length about a company like Apple as a case in point (see "The Apple Story"), executives frequently say, "don't just give me anecdotes specifically selected to make some point. Show me the evidence!" Fortunately, there is a substantial and rapidly expanding body of evidence, some of it quite methodologically sophisticated, that speaks to the strong connection between how firms manage their people and the economic results achieved. This evidence is drawn from studies of the five-year survival rates of initial public offerings; studies of profitability and stock price in large samples of companies from multiple industries; and detailed research on the automobile, apparel, semiconductor, steel manufacturing, oil refining, and service industries. It shows that substantial gains, on the order of 40 percent, can be obtained by implementing high performance management practices.[1]

According to an award-winning study of the high performance work practices of 968 firms representing all major industries, "a one standard deviation increase in use of such practices is associated with a ... 7.05 percent decrease in turnover and, on a per employee basis, $27,044 more in sales and $18,641 and $3,814 more in market value and profits, respectively."[2] Yes, you read those results correctly. That's an $18,000 increase in stock market value per *employee*! A subsequent study conducted on 702 firms in 1996 found even larger economic benefits: "A one standard deviation improvement in the human resources system was associated with an increase in shareholder wealth of $41,000 per employee"[3]—about a 14 percent market value premium.

---

*Reprinted with permission from the *Academy of Management Executive 13*, no. 2 (May 1999): 37–48.

THE APPLE STORY

Most accounts of Apple Computer's history have stressed either strategic mistakes, such as not licensing the Macintosh operating system, or leadership issues, such as the succession to CEO by John Sculley and others. However, the Apple story also illustrates rather poignantly the negative case of what happens when a firm whose success derives fundamentally from its people fails to put people first.

Apple was founded in 1976 by Stephen Wozniak and Stephen Jobs in Jobs's garage. Their vision was to bring the power of the computer to the individual user. The Macintosh operating system, introduced in 1984, was (and many would maintain, still is) a leading technology in terms of ease of use. Apple launched the desktop publishing movement, and the company's emphasis on networks and connectivity among machines was also ahead of its time.

Apple was a company largely built on a unique culture. The Macintosh design team worked in a separate building with a pirate flag flying over it. The company built a cult-like commitment among its employees. People were recruited to Apple with the idea that they would be helping to change the world. Apple was more than a company; it was a cause. Its strategy of being an innovator in designing user-friendly personal computers that would make people more productive required a highly talented, creative, and innovative workforce. When it took actions that resulted in the loss of that workforce, its ability to implement its business strategy and to regain market leadership was irreparably harmed.

Not all of Apple's problems can be traced to how it handled its people. Even though its competitive advantage lay in its operating system, employing a mouse and a graphical user interface, the company consistently failed to license the operating system to other manufacturers, thereby limiting its share of the personal computer market. Because its culture emphasized technological innovation, Apple would occasionally introduce products, such as the Newton personal digital assistant that were either far ahead of their time or had some remaining hardware or software bugs, or both, thus occasionally suffering commercial flops. But, a case can be made that its handling of its people made both its technical and market problems and its recovery from them much worse.

In the beginning, the *Apple Employee Handbook* espoused the importance of people to the firm's success and spelled out many of the company's cherished cultural traditions, such as management accessibility and open communication, mementos of significant company events, celebrations of important life events of employees, and bagels and cream cheese on Friday mornings. After John Sculley laid off 20 percent of its workforce to cut costs when sales did not meet expectations in 1985, Apple maintained that its responsibility to its employees was not to give them any security or a career with a progression of jobs, but rather simply to provide a series of challenging job assignments that would permit them to learn and develop so as to be readily employable. In a booming local job market, this encouraged people to develop talent and skills at Apple and then to use them elsewhere. Apple's shift in emphasis to an individualistic culture could also be seen in the language used to talk about employees, who were characterized as A, B, or C players. Apple wanted to attract and retain more As and get rid of the Cs.

In 1991, about 10 percent of the workforce was laid off. In 1993, Michael Spindler replaced Sculley and continued the cost cutting by laying off 2,500 people, about 14 percent of the workforce. In 1997, another round of layoffs affected almost a third of the remaining people. More damaging than the layoffs themselves was the way they occurred in waves over time, making people unsure of their futures and tempting the best people to leave. Salaries, which had been excellent to attract the best people, were cut, as were many of the amenities that had made working at the company special. Because they feared losing jobs when a project was over, many people slowed their progress substantially. The loss of key technical and marketing personnel made the firm's prospects even worse.

The pathologies of Apple Computer are all too common. A company initially having problems with its profits, costs, or share price, takes quick action to raise profits and lower costs. Since employee costs are typically the most quickly and easily changed, the following actions are common: training is curtailed; pay may be frozen or cut; promotions are held up; the use of part-time or temporary help increases; and people are laid off or forced to work reduced hours. These measures logically and inevitably reduce motivation, satisfaction, and loyalty to the company. Rather than focus on their jobs, employees spend time discussing rumors and sharing complaints with coworkers. Cutting training cuts skill and knowledge development and dissemination. Attention focused on unhappiness at work can create a climate in which accidents and poor customer service flourish. Poor service, high accident rates, and increased turnover and absenteeism adversely affect sales, profits, and costs. So the cycle continues.

In the short run, some firms may be able to cut costs and thereby increase profits. In some cases, cuts can be made in ways that do not damage the viability of the organization. And, of course, Apple's obituary has yet to be written. While employees admit that Apple was in a death spiral, the recent return of Stephen Jobs and Apple's introduction of the iMac suggest to some that a rebirth is possible.

Indeed, as Stephen Jobs told *Fortune*,[A] "Innovation has nothing to do with how many R&D dollars you have .... It's not about money. It's about the people you have, how you are led, and how much you get it."

[A]D. Kirkpatrick, "The Second Coming of Apple," *Fortune*, November 9, 1998, 90.

Are these results unique to firms operating in the United States? No. Similar results were obtained in a study of more than 100 German companies operating in 10 industrial sectors. The study found "a strong link between investing in employees and stock market performance. Companies which place workers at the core of their strategies produce higher long-term returns to shareholders than their industry peers."[4]

One of the clearest demonstrations of the causal effect of management practices on performance comes from a study of the five-year survival rate of 136 non-financial companies that initiated their public offering in the U.S. stock market in 1988.[5] By 1993, some five years later, only 60 percent of these companies were still in existence. The empirical analysis demonstrated that with other factors such as size, industry, and even profits statistically controlled, both the value the firm placed on human resources—such as whether the company cited employees as a source of competitive advantage—and how the organization rewarded people—such as stock options for all employees and profit sharing—were significantly related to the probability of survival. Moreover, the results were substantively important. As shown in Figure 1, the difference in survival probability for firms one standard deviation above and one standard deviation below the mean (in the upper 16 percent and the lower 16 percent of all firms in the sample) on valuing human resource was almost 20 percent. The difference in survival depending on where the firm scored on rewards was even more dramatic, with a difference in five-year survival probability of 42 percent between firms in the upper and lower tails of the distribution.

How can such substantial benefits in profits, quality, and productivity occur? Essentially, these tremendous gains come about because high performance management practices provide a number of important sources for enhanced organizational performance. Simply put, people work harder because of the increased involvement and commitment that comes from having more control and say in their work; people work

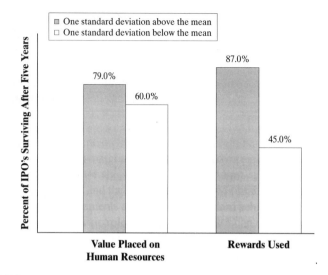

FIGURE 1   **Probability of an Initial Public Offering Firm's Surviving Five Years**
Source: Based on information from T. Welbourne and A. Andrews, "Predicting Performance of
Initial Public Offering Firms: Should HRM Be in the Equation?" *Academy of Management Journal*
39 (1996): 910–911.

smarter because they are encouraged to build skills and competence; and people work more responsibly because more responsibility is placed in hands of employees farther down in the organization. These practices work not because of some mystical process, but because they are grounded in sound social science principles that have been shown to be effective by a great deal of evidence. And, they make sense.

SEVEN PRACTICES OF SUCCESSFUL ORGANIZATIONS

Based on these various studies, related literature, and personal observation and experience, a set of seven dimensions emerge that seem to characterize most, if not all, of the systems producing profits through people. Let's take a look at each one briefly.

EMPLOYMENT SECURITY

Most research on the effects of high performance management systems has incorporated employment security as an important dimension. Indeed, "one of the most widely accepted propositions ... is that innovations in work practices or other forms of worker-management cooperation or productivity improvement are not likely to be sustained over time when workers fear that by increasing productivity they will work themselves out of their jobs."[6]

The idea of providing employment security in today's competitive world seems somehow anachronistic or impossible and very much at odds with what most firms seem to be doing. But employment security is fundamental to the implementation of most other high performance management practices. For example, when General Motors wanted to implement new work arrangements in its innovative Saturn plant in the 1990s, it guaranteed its people job security except in the most extreme circumstances. When New United Motors Manufacturing, Inc. (NUMMI) was formed to operate the Fremont automobile assembly plant, it offered its people job security. How else could it ask for flexibility and cooperation in becoming more efficient and productive?

Many additional benefits follow from employment assurances besides workers' free contribution of knowledge and their efforts to enhance productivity. One advantage to firms is the decreased likelihood that they will lay off employees during downturns. How is this a benefit to the firm? In the absence of some way of building commitment to retaining the workforce—either through pledges about employment security or through employment obligations contractually negotiated with a union— firms may lay off employees too quickly and too readily at the first sign of financial difficulty. This constitutes a cost for firms that have done a good job selecting, training, and developing their work- force because layoffs put important strategic assets on the street for the competition to employ. Herb Kelleher, the CEO of Southwest Airlines, summarized this argument best when he wrote:

> *Our most important tools for building employee partnership are job security and a stimulating work environment … Certainly there were times when we could have made substantially more profits in the short-term if we had furloughed people, but we didn't. We were looking at our employees' and our company's longer-term interests … [A]s it turns out, providing job security imposes addi- tional discipline, because if your goal is to avoid layoffs, then you hire very sparingly. So our commitment to job security has actually helped us keep our labor force smaller and more productive than our competitors'.*[7]

SELECTIVE HIRING

Companies serious about obtaining profits through people will expend the effort needed to ensure that they recruit the right people in the first place. This requires several things. First, the organization needs to have a large applicant pool from which to select. In 1993, for example, Southwest Airlines received about 98,000 job applications, interviewed 16,000 people, and hired 2,700. In 1994, applications in- creased to more than 125,000 for 4,000 hires. Some organizations see processing this many job inquiries as an unnecessary expense. Southwest sees it as a necessary first step.

Second, the organization needs to be clear about what are the most critical skills and attributes need- ed in its applicant pool. At Southwest, applicants for flight attendant positions are evaluated on the basis of initiative, judgment, adaptability, and their ability to learn. These attributes are assessed in part from interview questions that evoke specific instances of these attributes. For instance, to assess adaptabil- ity, interviewers ask, "Give an example of working with a difficult co-worker. How did you handle it?"[8] To measure initiative, one question asks, "Describe a time when a co-worker failed to pull their weight and what you did about it."

Third, the skills and abilities sought need to be carefully considered and consistent with the par- ticular job requirements and the organization's approach to its market. Enterprise Rent-A-Car is today the largest car rental company in the United States, and it has expanded at a rate of between 25 and 30 percent a year for the past 11 years. It has grown by pursuing a high customer service strategy and em- phasizing sales of rental car services to repair garage customers. In a low-wage, often unionized, and seemingly low-employee-skill industry, virtually all of Enterprise's people are college graduates. But these people are hired primarily for their sales skills and personality and for their willingness to provide good service, not for their academic performance. Brian O'Reilly interpolates Enterprise's reasoning:

> *The social directors make good sales people, able to chat up service managers and calm down someone who has just been in a car wreck … The Enterprise employees hired from the caboose end of the class have something else going for them … a chilling realization of how unforgiving the job market can be.*[9]

Fourth, organizations should screen primarily on important attributes that are difficult to change through training and should emphasize qualities that actually differentiate among those in the appli- cant pool. Southwest rejected a top pilot from another airline who did stunt work for movie studios because he was rude to a receptionist. Southwest believes that technical skills are easier to acquire than a teamwork and service attitude. Ironically, many firms select for specific, job-relevant skills that, while important, are easily acquired. Meanwhile, they fail to find people with the right attitudes, values, and cultural fit—attributes that are harder to train or change and that are quite predictive of turnover and performance.

One MBA job applicant reported that interviewers at PeopleSoft, a producer of human resource management software, asked very little about personal or academic background, except about learning experiences from school and work. Rather, the interviews focused mostly on whether she saw herself as team-oriented or as an individual achiever, what she liked to do outside school and work, and her philosophy on life. The specific question was "Do you have a personal mission statement? If you don't, what would it be if you were to write it today?" Moreover, the people interviewing the applicant presented a consistent picture of the values that were shared among employees at PeopleSoft. Such a selection process is more likely to produce cultural fit. A great deal of research evidence shows that the degree of cultural fit and value congruence between job applicants and their organizations significantly predicts both subsequent turnover and job performance.[10]

SELF-MANAGED TEAMS AND DECENTRALIZATION AS BASIC ELEMENTS OF ORGANIZATIONAL DESIGN

Numerous articles and case examples, as well as rigorous, systematic studies, attest to the effectiveness of teams as a principle of organization design. For example, Honeywell's defense avionics plant credits improved on-time delivery—reaching 99 percent in the first quarter of 1996 as compared with below 40 percent in the late 1980s—to the implementation of teams.[11] Perhaps one of the greatest payoffs from team-based organizations is that teams substitute peer-based control for hierarchical control of work. Team-based organizations also are largely successful in having all of the people in the firm feel accountable and responsible for the operation and success of the enterprise, not just a few people in senior management positions. This increased sense of responsibility stimulates more initiative and effort on the part of everyone involved. In addition, and perhaps most importantly, by substituting peer for hierarchical control, teams permit removal of layers of hierarchy and absorption of administrative tasks previously performed by specialists, avoiding the enormous costs of having people whose sole job it is to watch people who watch other people do the work.

The tremendously successful natural foods grocery store chain, Whole Foods Markets, organized on the basis of teams, attributes much of its success to that arrangement. Between 1991 and 1996, the company enjoyed sales growth of 864 percent and net income growth of 438 percent as it expanded, in part through acquisitions as well as through internal growth, from 10 to 68 stores. In its 1995 annual report, the company's team-oriented philosophy is clearly stated.

> *Our growing information systems capability is fully aligned with our goal of creating a more intelligent organization—one which is less bureaucratic, elitist, hierarchical, and authoritarian and more communicative, participatory, and empowered. The ultimate goal is to have all team members contributing their full intelligence, creativity, and skills to continuously improving the company ... Everyone who works at Whole Foods Market is a team member. This reflects our philosophy that we are all partners in the shared mission of giving our customers the very best in products and services. We invest in and believe in the collective wisdom of our team members. The stores are organized into self-managing work teams that are responsible and accountable for their own performance.*[12]

Teams also permit employees to pool their ideas to come up with better and more creative solutions to problems. Teams at Saturn and at the Chrysler Corporation's Jefferson North plant, for example, "provide a framework in which workers more readily help one another and more freely share their production knowledge—the innumerable 'tricks of the trade' that are vital in any manufacturing process."[13]

Team-based organizations are not simply a made-only-in-America phenomenon. Consider, for example, Vancom Zuid-Limburg, a joint venture in the Netherlands that operates a public bus company. This company has enjoyed very rapid growth in ridership and has been able to win transport concessions by offering more services at the same price as its competitors. The key to this success lies in its use of self-managed teams and the consequent savings in management overhead.

> *Vancom is able to [win transport contracts] mainly because of its very low overhead costs ... [O]ne manager supervises around 40 bus drivers ... This management-driver ratio of 1 in 40 substantially differs from the norm in this sector. At best, competitors achieve a ratio of 1 in 8. Most of this difference can be attributed to the self-managed teams. Vancom ... has two teams of around 20 drivers. Each team has its own bus lines and budgeting responsibilities ... Vancom also expects each individual driver to assume more responsibilities when on the road. This includes customer service (e.g., helping elderly persons board the bus), identifying problems (e.g., reporting damage to a bus stop), and active contributions (e.g., making suggestions for improvement of the services).*[14]

COMPARATIVELY HIGH COMPENSATION CONTINGENT ON ORGANIZATIONAL PERFORMANCE

It is often argued that high compensation is a consequence of organizational success, rather than its progenitor, and that high compensation (compared with the average) is possible only in certain industries that either face less competition or have particularly highly educated employees. But neither of these statements is correct. Obviously, successful firms can afford to pay more, and frequently do so, but high pay can also produce economic success.

When John Whitney assumed the leadership of Pathmark, a large grocery store chain in the eastern United States in 1972, the company had about 90 days to live, according to its banks, and was in desperate financial shape. Whitney looked at the situation and discovered that 120 store managers in the chain were paid terribly. Many of them made less than the butchers, who were unionized. He decided that the store managers were vital to the chain's success and its ability to accomplish a turnaround. Consequently, he gave the store managers a substantial raise-about 40 to 50 percent. Whitney attributes the subsequent success of the chain to the store managers' focusing on improving performance instead of worrying and complaining about their pay.

The idea that only certain jobs or industries can or should pay high wages is belied by the example of many firms. Home Depot has been successful and profitable, and its stock price has shown exceptional returns. Even though the chain emphasizes everyday low pricing as an important part of its business strategy and operates in a highly competitive environment, it pays its staff comparatively well for the retail industry, hires more experienced people with building industry experience, and expects its sales associates to provide a higher level of individual customer service.

Contingent compensation also figures importantly in most high performance work systems. Such compensation can take a number of different forms, including gain sharing, profit sharing, stock ownership, pay for skill, or various forms of individual or team incentives. Wal-Mart, AES Corporation, Southwest Airlines, Whole Foods Markets, Microsoft, and many other successful organizations encourage share ownership. When employees are owners, they act and think like owners. However, little evidence suggests that employee ownership, by itself, affects organizational performance. Rather, employee ownership works best as part of a broader philosophy or culture that incorporates other practices. Merely putting in ownership schemes without providing training, information sharing, and delegation of responsibility will have little effect on performance. Even if people are more motivated by their share ownership, they don't necessarily have the skills, information, or power to do anything with that motivation.

EXTENSIVE TRAINING

Training is often seen as a frill in many U.S. organizations, something to be reduced to make profit goals in times of economic stringency. Studies of firms in the United States and the United Kingdom consistently provide evidence of inadequate levels of training and training focused on the wrong things: specialist skills rather than generalist competence and organizational culture. This is the case in a world in which we are constantly told that knowledge and intellectual capital are critical for success. Knowledge and skill *are* critical—and too few organizations act on this insight. Training is an essential component of high performance work systems because these systems rely on frontline employee skill and initiative to identify and resolve problems, to initiate changes in work methods, and to take responsibility for quality. All of this requires a skilled and motivated workforce that has the knowledge and capability to perform the requisite tasks.

Training can be a source of competitive advantage in numerous industries for firms with the wisdom to use it. The Men's Wearhouse, an off-price specialty retailer of men's tailored business attire and accessories, went public in 1991. Its 1995 annual report noted that it had achieved compounded annual growth rates in revenues and net earnings of 32 and 41 percent, respectively, and that the value of its stock had increased by approximately 400 percent. The company attributes its success to how it treats its people and particularly to the emphasis it has placed on training, an approach that separates it from many of its competitors. The company built a 35,000 square foot training center in Fremont, California, its headquarters. In 1994, some 600 "clothing consultants" went through Suits University, and that year the company added Suits High and Selling Accessories U.[15] During the winter, experienced store personnel come back to headquarters in groups of about 30 for a three- or four-day retraining program.

While training is an investment in the organization's staff, in the current business milieu it virtually begs for some sort of return-on-investment calculations. But such analyses are difficult, if not impossible, to carry out. Successful firms that emphasize training do so almost as a matter of faith and because of their belief in the connection between people and profits. Even Motorola does a poor job of measuring its return on training. Although the company has been mentioned as reporting a $3 return for every $1 invested in training, an official from Motorola's training group said that she did not know where these numbers came from and that the company is notoriously poor at evaluating its $170 million investment in training. The firm mandates 40 hours of training per employee per year, and believes that the effects of training are both difficult to measure and expensive to evaluate. Training is part and parcel of an overall management process and is evaluated in that light.

REDUCTION OF STATUS DIFFERENCES

The fundamental premise of high performance management systems is that organizations perform at a higher level when they are able to tap the ideas, skill, and effort of all of their people. In order to help make all organizational members feel important and committed, most high commitment management systems attempt to reduce the status distinctions that separate individuals and groups and cause some to feel less valued. This is accomplished in two principle ways—symbolically, through the use of language and labels, physical space, and dress, and substantively, in the reduction of the organization's degree of wage inequality, particularly across levels.

At NUMMI, everyone wears the same colored smock; executive dining rooms and reserved parking don't exist. At Kingston Technology, a private firm manufacturing add-on memory modules for personal computers, the two cofounders sit in open cubicles and do not have private secretaries.[16] Status differences are also reduced, and a sense of common fate developed, by limiting the difference in compensation between senior management and other employees. Herb Kelleher, who earns about $500,000 per year as the CEO of Southwest, including base and bonus, has been on the cover of *Fortune* magazine with the headline, "Is He America's Best CEO?" In 1995, when Southwest negotiated a five-year wage freeze with its pilots in exchange for stock options and occasional profitability bonuses, Kelleher agreed to freeze his base salary at $395,000 for four years. Sam Walton, the founder and chairman of Wal-Mart, was one of the most underpaid CEOs in the United States. Kelleher and Walton weren't poor; each owned stock in his company. But stock ownership was also encouraged for their employees. Having an executive's fortune rise and fall together with those of the other employees differs dramatically from providing large bonuses and substantial salaries for executives even as the stock price languishes and people are being laid off.

SHARING INFORMATION

Information sharing is an essential component of high performance work systems. The sharing of information on such things as financial performance, strategy, and operational measures conveys to the organization's people that they are trusted. John Mackey, the chief executive of Whole Foods Markets, states, "If you're trying to create a high-trust organization ... an organization where people are all-for-one and one-for-all, you can't have secrets."[17] Whole Foods shares detailed financial and performance information with every employee, including individual salary information. Every Whole Foods store has a book that lists the previous year's salary and bonus of all 6,500 employees.[18]

Even motivated and trained people cannot contribute to enhancing organizational performance if they don't have information on important dimensions of performance and training on how to use and interpret that information. The now famous case of Springfield ReManufacturing Corporation (SRC) illustrates this point. On February 1, 1983, SRC was created when the plant's management and employees purchased an old International Harvester plant in a financial transaction that consisted of about $100,000 in equity and $8.9 million in debt, an 89-1 debt-to-equity ratio that has to make this one of the most leveraged of all buy-outs. Jack Stack, the former plant manager and now chief executive, knew that if the plant was to succeed, all employees had to do their best, and had to share all their wisdom and ideas for enhancing the plant's performance. Stack came up with a system called "open-book management," that has become so popular that SRC now makes money by running seminars on it. When General Motors canceled an order in 1986 that represented about 40 percent of Springfield's business for the coming year, the firm averted a layoff by providing its people with information on what had happened and letting them figure out how to grow the company and achieve the productivity improvements that would obviate layoffs. SRC has since enjoyed tremendous financial success. In 1983, its first year of operation, sales were about $13 million. By 1992, sales had increased to $70 million and the number of employees had grown from 119 to 700. The original equity investment of $100,000 was worth more than $23 million by 1993. No one who knows the company, and certainly not Jack Stack or the other managers, believes this economic performance could have been achieved without a set of practices that enlisted the cooperation and ingenuity of all of the firm's people. The system and philosophy of open-book management took a failing International Harvester plant and transformed it into a highly successful, growing business.

IT ALL SEEMS SO EASY

How difficult can it be to increase the level of training, to share information and plans with people, to reorganize work into teams, to upgrade hiring practices, and to do all the other things described above? It is easy to form the ideas that are the foundation for people-centered management. But, if it were actually easy to implement those ideas, other airlines would have been able to copy Southwest, other grocery stores would be as successful as Whole Foods Markets, other power producers would be as profitable and efficient as AES, other retailers would have achieved the same record of growth and profitability as the Men's Wearhouse. Implementing these ideas in a systematic, consistent fashion remains rare enough to be an important source of competitive advantage for firms in a number of industries. Why is this so?

MANAGERS ARE ENSLAVED BY SHORT-TERM PRESSURES

Because achieving profits through people takes time to accomplish, an emphasis on short-term financial results will not be helpful in getting organizations to do the right thing. Short-term financial pressures and measurements abound. Many organizations provide raises and bonuses based on annual results. Ask senior managers how long it takes to change an organization's culture, and it's extremely unlikely that you will hear, "a year or less." But that is the time horizon of the evaluation process. Taking actions with payoffs that will occur beyond the time for which you will be measured on your performance is difficult and risky.

A second pressure occurs when organizations seek to create shareholder value by increasing stock price. The time horizon for evaluating stock market returns is again often quite short, often a year or less. Mutual fund and other institutional money managers are themselves frequently evaluated on a quarterly or at most an annual basis; they often invest in stocks for only a short time and have high portfolio turnover, so it is little surprise that they, in turn, put pressure on organizations for short-term, quick results.

A third pressure is that the immediate drives out the long-term. Today's pressing problems make it difficult to focus on actions aimed at building a better organization for the future. Managerial career processes contribute to this short-term pressure. When and where managers are hired for an indefinite period and careers are embedded in a single organization, it makes sense for those individuals to take a long-term view. But movements by managers across organizations have increased dramatically at nearly all organizational levels. Individuals trying to build a track record that will look good on the external labor market aren't likely to take a longer-term view of building organizational competence and capabilities. Stephen Smith has argued that the typical career system facing managers today encourages "managerial opportunism." He suggests that "managers are rewarded ... for appropriating the ideas of their subordinates or for improving the bottom line in the short run and then moving on to other positions before the long-term implications of the strategies they have adopted make themselves felt."[19]

ORGANIZATIONS TEND TO DESTROY COMPETENCE

Organizations often inadvertently destroy wisdom and competence or make it impossible for wisdom, knowledge, and experience to benefit the firm. Management practices that require programs and ideas to be explained and reviewed in groups are a major culprit.

That formal planning and evaluation, and particularly the use of financial criteria, destroy competence is consistent with the results of research on innovation. Experts on organizational management have acquired the ability to see and understand things that are not evident to novices. An expert advertising executive moves quickly and creatively to come up with a good advertising campaign; an expert in production management understands the dynamics of both the human and mechanical elements of the production system and can accurately and quickly diagnose problems and figure out appropriate action; an expert in management or leadership has a good grasp of the principles of human motivation, great intuition, and the ability to read people and situations. But in any domain of expertise, by definition, some portion of the expert's knowledge and competence must be tacit, not readily articulated or explainable, irreducible to a formula or recipe. If that were not the case, then the expert knowledge would be codified and novices could do about as well as experts at the task in question, given access to the same formulas or insights.

But if expert knowledge has a substantial component of tacit knowledge, it will be impossible for experts to present the real basis of their judgments and decisions. Experts are more likely to rely on those factors and evidence that are available and accessible to all. In so doing, they lose virtually all the benefits of their expertise. Forced to explain decisions to a wider audience, the experts will have to rely on the same data and decision processes as anyone else. Thus, the organization will have created a decision process in which its experts behave like novices, and will have lost the benefits of the experts' wisdom and competence.

Consider the following example. Bob Scott, associate director of the center for Advanced Study in the Behavioral Sciences at Stanford, had to give a talk about the center's management to an outside group interested in establishing an interdisciplinary, social-science research center. As he was giving the talk, he recalled thinking, "If we actually managed the center this way, it would be a disaster." It was not possible for him to articulate his expertise, to explain his tacit knowledge. Suppose that instead of a group of curious outsiders, his audience had been a governing board or oversight body that would hold Scott and his colleagues accountable for following and implementing the ideas he expressed? They might have been forced to manage in ways that could seriously degrade the organization's operations.

MANAGERS DON'T DELEGATE ENOUGH

Relying on the tacit knowledge and expertise of others requires trust and the willingness to let them do what they know how to do. Using self-managing teams as an organizing principle requires permitting the teams to actually manage themselves. At NUMMI, teams were given real responsibility and were listened to, while at the General Motors Van Nuys, California, plant, a culture of hierarchical control meant that team members were frequently told to be quiet and supervisors exercised the same control they had before the institution of teams.

Even though employee participation is associated with enhanced economic performance, organizations frequently fail to introduce it, and it remains fragile even when it is implemented. At least some of this resistance derives from two social psychological processes: first, belief in the efficacy of leadership, that is, the "faith in supervision" effect; and second, a self-enhancement bias. The faith in supervision effect means that observers tend to believe that the greater the degree of supervisor involvement and control, the better the work produced. In one study, for instance, identical company performance was evaluated more positively when the leadership factors accounting for the performance were made more apparent.[20] The self-enhancement bias is a pervasive social psychological phenomenon. Researchers have found that "one of the most widely documented effects in social psychology is the preference of most people to see themselves in a self-enhancing fashion. As a consequence, they regard themselves as more intelligent, skilled, ethical, honest, persistent, original, friendly, reliable, attractive, and fair-minded than their peers or the average person ... On the job, approximately 90 percent of managers and workers rate their performances as superior to their peers."[21] It is no wonder then that such a bias would lead supervisors to evaluate more positively the work they have been involved in creating.

Both of these processes contribute to the same prediction: work performed under more oversight and control will be perceived as better than the identical work performed with less oversight. This effect will be particularly strong for the person doing the supervision. In a real work setting, these social psychological processes would, of course, be counterbalanced by pressures to achieve results and by the knowledge that participation and empowerment may be helpful in improving performance. Nonetheless, these beliefs may be significant factors hindering the use of high performance work practices and the participation and delegation they imply.

PERVERSE NORMS ABOUT WHAT CONSTITUTES GOOD MANAGEMENT

Two norms about what constitutes good management are simultaneously growing in acceptance and are enormously perverse in their implications. The first is the idea that good managers are mean or tough, able to make such difficult choices as laying off thousands of people and acting decisively. The second is that good management is mostly a matter of good analysis, a confusion between math and management. The two views are actually related, since an emphasis on analysis takes one away from such issues as motivation, commitment, and morale, and makes it more likely that one can and will act in a tough fashion.

An article in *Newsweek* stated that "firing people has gotten to be trendy in corporate America ... Now you fire workers—especially white collar workers—to make your corporate bones ... Wall Street and Big Business have been in perfect harmony about how in-your-face capitalism is making America great."[22] *Fortune* magazine regularly runs an article entitled "America's Toughest Bosses." Does one want to appear on that list, especially since many of those on it do not last very long in their jobs, having been "fired—in part, for being too mean"?[23] Little evidence exists that being a mean or tough boss is necessarily associated with business success. "Financial results from these bosses' companies vary from superb to pathetic. The median return on shareholder's equity over the past five years for 7 of the 10 companies for which data are available ranged from 7.3 percent ... to 18.1 percent ... That compares with the median for the *Fortune 500* of 13.8 percent."[24] Nonetheless, *Fortune* predicts that "toughness ... will probably become more prevalent. Most nominees for this list rose to prominence in industries shaken by rapid change ... As global competition heats up and turmoil rocks more industries, tough management should spread. So look for more bosses who are steely, super demanding, unrelenting, sometimes abusive, sometimes unreasonable, impatient, driven, stubborn, and combative."[25]

The belief that the good manager is a skilled analyst also has questionable merit and validity. The belief first arose after World War II with the emergence of Robert McNamara and systems analysis in the Defense Department. It spread to operations research and mathematical analysis in such business schools as Carnegie Mellon and such businesses as the Ford Motor Company. The emphasis on mathematical elegance and analysis as cornerstones for effective management implicitly derogates the importance of emotion, leadership, and building a vision. It represents an attempt to substitute data and analytical methods for judgment and common sense. Emphasizing analytical skills over interpersonal, negotiating, political, and leadership skills inevitably leads to errors in selection, development, and emphasis on what is important to an organization.

A ONE-IN-EIGHT CHANCE

Firms often attempt piecemeal innovations. It is difficult enough to change some aspect of the compensation system without having to also be concerned about training, recruitment and selection, and how work is organized. Implementing practices in isolation may not have much effect, however, and, can actually be counterproductive. Increasing the firm's commitment to training activities won't accomplish much unless changes in work organization permit these more skilled people to actually implement their knowledge. If wages are comparatively low and incentives are lacking, the better-trained people may simply depart for the competition. Employment security can be counterproductive unless the firm hires people who fit the culture and unless incentives reward outstanding performance.

Implementing work teams will not accomplish much unless the teams receive training in specific technical skills and team processes, and are given financial and operating performance goals and information.

Implementing and seeing results from many of these practices takes time. It takes time to train and upgrade workers' skills and even more time to see the economic benefits of this training in reduced turnover and enhanced performance. It takes time to share operating and financial information with people, and to be sure that they understand and know how to use it. Even more time is needed before suggestions and insights can provide business results. It certainly requires time for employees to believe in employment security and for that belief to generate trust and produce higher levels of innovation and effort. Consequently, a long-term view of a company's development and growth is at least useful, if not absolutely essential, to implementation of high performance organizational arrangements.

One must bear in mind that one-half of organizations won't believe the connection between how they manage their people and the profits they earn. One-half of those who do see the connection will do what many organizations have done—try to make a single change to solve their problems, not realizing that the effective management of people requires a more comprehensive and systematic approach. Of the firms that make comprehensive changes, probably only about one-half will persist with their practices long enough to actually derive economic benefits. Since one-half times one-half times one-half equals one-eighth, at best 12 percent of organizations will actually do what is required to build profits by putting people first. Don't like these odds? Well, consider this: almost every other source of organizational success—technology, financial structure, competitive strategy—can be initiated in a short period of time. How many other sources of competitive advantage have a one-in-eight chance of success?

In the end, the key to managing people in ways that lead to profits, productivity, innovation, and real organizational learning ultimately lies in the manager's perspective. When managers look at their people, do they see costs to be reduced? Do they see recalcitrant employees prone to opportunism, shirking, and free riding, who can't be trusted and who need to be closely controlled through monitoring, rewards, and sanctions? Do they see people performing activities that can and should be contracted out to save on labor costs? Or, do they see intelligent, motivated, trustworthy individuals—the most critical and valuable strategic assets their organizations can have? When they look at their people, do they see them as the fundamental resources on which their success rests and the primary means of differentiating themselves from the competition? With the right perspective, anything is possible. With the wrong one, change efforts and new programs become gimmicks, and no army of consultants, seminars, and slogans will help.

ENDNOTES

[1] J. Pfeffer, *The Human Equation: Building Profits by Putting People First* (Boston, MA: Harvard Business School Press, 1998) Chapter 2.

[2] M. A. Huselid, "The Impact of Human Resource Management Practices on Turnover, Productivity, and Corporate Financial Performance," *Academy of Management Journal 38* (1995): 647.

[3] M. A. Huselid and B. E. Becker, "The Impact of High Performance Work Systems, Implementation Effectiveness, and Alignment with Strategy on Shareholder Wealth," Unpublished paper, Rutgers University, New Brunswick, NJ (1997): 18–19.

[4] L. Blimes, K. Wetzker, and P. Xhonneux, "Value in Human Resources," *Financial Times*, February 1997, 10.

[5] T. Welbourne and A. Andrews, "Predicting Performance of Initial Public Offering Firms: Should HRM Be in the Equation?" *Academy of Management Journal 39* (1996): 891–919.

[6] R. M. Locke, "The Transformation of Industrial Relations: A Cross-National Review," *The Comparative Political Economy of Industrial Relations* eds. Kirsten S. Wever and Lowell Turner (Madison, WI: Industrial Relations Research Association, 1995) 18–19.

[7] H. Kelleher, "A Culture of Commitment," *Leader to Leader 1* (1997): 23.

[8] Southwest Airlines, *Case S-OB-28* (Palo Alto, CA: Graduate School of Business, Stanford University, 1994): 29.

[9] B. O'Reilly, "The Rent-A-Car Jocks Who Made Enterprise #1," *Fortune,* 1996, 128.

[10] See, for instance, C. A. O'Reilly, J. A. Chatman, and D. F. Caldwell, "People and Organizational Culture: A Profile Comparison Approach to Assessing Person-Organization Fit," *Academy of Management Journal 34* (1991): 487–516; and J. A. Chatman, "Managing People and Organizations: Selection and Socialization in Public Accounting Firms," *Administrative Science Quarterly 36* (1991): 459–484.

[11] "Work Week," *Wall Street Journal,* May 28, 1996, Al.

[12] Whole Foods Market, Inc., *1995 Annual Report,* Austin, TX: 3,17.

[13] H. Shaiken, S. Lopez, and I. Mankita, "Two Routes to Team Production: Saturn and Chrysler Compared," *Industrial Relations 36* (1997): 31.

[14] M. Van Beusekom, *Participation Pays! Cases of Successful Companies with Employee Participation* (The Hague: Netherlands Participation Institute, 1996) 7.

[15] Men's Wearhouse, *1994 Annual Report,* Fremont, CA: 3.

[16] "Doing the Right Thing," *The Economist 20* (1995): 64.

[17] C. Fishman, "Whole Foods Teams," *Fast Company,* April/May 1996, 106.

[18] Ibid., 105.

[19] E. Appelbaum and R. Batt, *The New American Workplace* (Ithaca, NY: ILR Press, 1994): 147.

[20] J. R. Meindl and S. B. Ehrlich, "The Romance of Leadership and the Evaluation of Organizational Performance," *Academy of Management Journal 30* (1987): 91–109.

[21] Ibid.

[22] A. Sloan, "The Hit Men," *Newsweek,* 1996, 44–45.

[23] B. Dumaine, "America's Toughest Bosses," *Fortune,* 1993, 39.

[24] S. Flax, "The Toughest Bosses in America," *Fortune,* 1989, 19.

[25] P. Nulty, "America's Toughest Bosses," *Fortune,* 1989, 54.

Intellectual Capital = Competence × Commitment*

Dave Ulrich

In the ongoing debate about where managers should focus their attention, something has been missing: a focus on intellectual capital. Intellectual capital—the commitment and competence of workers—is embedded in how each employee thinks about and does work and in how an organization creates policies and systems to get work done. It has become a critical issue for six reasons:

First, intellectual capital is a firm's only appreciable asset. Most other assets (building, plant, equipment, machinery, and so on) begin to depreciate the day they are acquired. Intellectual capital must grow if a firm is to prosper. A manager's job is to make knowledge productive, to turn intellectual capital into customer value.

Second, knowledge work is increasing, not decreasing. James Brian Quinn has observed that the service economy is growing directly in service industries such as retail, investments, information, and food and indirectly in traditional manufacturing industries like autos, durable goods, and equipment.[1] As the service economy grows, the importance of intellectual capital increases. Service generally comes from relationships founded on the competence and commitment of individuals.

Third, employees with the most intellectual capital have essentially become volunteers, because the best employees are likely to find work opportunities in a number of firms.[2] This does not mean that employees work for free, but that they have choices about where they work and, therefore, essentially volunteer in a particular firm. Volunteers are committed because of their emotional bond to a firm;

---

*Reprinted with permission from *Sloan Management Review* (Winter 1998): 15–26.

they are less interested in economic return than in the meaning of their work. Employees with this mind-set can easily leave for another firm.

Fourth, many managers ignore or depreciate intellectual capital. In the aftermath of downsizing, increased global competition, customers' higher requirements, fewer management layers, increased obligations, and pressures exacted from almost every other modern management practice, employees' work lives have not always changed for the better. In a recent workshop with 60 high-potential managers from a successful global company, we discussed careers. Of these managers (mostly in their thirties and early forties), 50 percent did not think that they would stay with the company long enough to retire, not because of lack of opportunity but because of the enormous stress and high demands. Within this group, 90 percent personally knew someone who had voluntarily left the company in the past six months because of the increased workload. When a group member shared these issues with an executive, he was told that a job at the company was a good one, there were backups for anyone who did not want to work hard, and discussions of work-life balance were not useful for business results.

Fifth, employees with the most intellectual capital are often the least appreciated. Some studies have correlated front-line employees' attitudes to a firm with customers' attitudes to the same firm.[3] For example, my opinion of McDonald's, Sears, or Ford relates to the service I get at the local establishment. At a time when companies are investing millions to train executives to think strategically and act globally, my impressions are likely to come from employees who serve me when I buy food, clothes, or cars. In many firms, these employees are transient and not committed or competent to answer my questions or meet my needs. As a result, the overall image of the organization falls.

Sixth, current investments in intellectual capital are misfocused. Under the name "corporate citizenship," many senior executives talk about work-family issues. This seems to imply that after you have done all the real business, then you spend time on employees' citizenship concerns. Intellectual capital is the most important business issue. Douglas Ivester, president and COO of Coca-Cola, recently said, "People are our defining assets." He added that in leveraging human and intellectual capital, he staked his career on creating a learning culture throughout his company.

How do you increase intellectual capital without creating the perception that it's a social agenda not related to real business challenges? In this article, I offer tools for creating the competence and commitment that increase intellectual capital.

WHAT IS INTELLECTUAL CAPITAL?

While many agree that intellectual capital matters, few can explicitly quantify it. This lack of definition leaves the concept relevant, timely, and important—but vague. While there has been research on the concept, I propose a simple, yet measurable and useful definition: intellectual capital $-$ competence $\times$ commitment.[4] This equation suggests that within a unit, employees' overall competence should rise but that competence alone does not secure intellectual capital. Firms with high competence but low commitment have talented employees who can't get things done. Firms with high commitment but low competence have less talented employees who get things done quickly. Both are dangerous. Intellectual capital requires both competence and commitment. Because the equation multiplies rather than adds, a low score on either competence or commitment significantly reduces overall intellectual capital.

We can assess competence and commitment at the firm, unit, or individual level. For example, a restaurant chain may measure the intellectual capital of each restaurant. It can derive such an establishment index from the average skill level of restaurant employees (competence) times the average retention of the same employees (commitment). This intellectual capital index would likely predict other positive outcomes, for example, customer loyalty, productivity, and profitability.

Or an employee might document his or her growth in intellectual capital by assessing the increase of knowledge, skill, or ability within a time frame and by evaluating commitment to the organization's goals and purposes. Such personal assessments can be accumulated into a collective assessment of the intellectual capital within a unit.

TOOLS FOR INCREASING COMPETENCE

There are two primary challenges in increasing competence: First, competencies must align with business strategy. Competence in the absence of strategy is like acting without an audience. The audience gives the act focus and energy. Customers help a firm focus a strategy; then the firm aligns competencies to deliver strategy. Second, competencies need to be generated through more than one mechanism. There are five tools for increasing competence within a unit (firm, site, business, or plant): buy, build, borrow, bounce, and bind. Appropriately using all five ensures a stable flow of competence.

BUY

Managers can go outside the unit to replace current talent with higher quality talent. Buying involves staffing and selection from the entry level to the officer level. A classic example of buying to increase competence is similar to sports teams that pursue free agents and spend millions of dollars searching for new talent to lead them to victory.

Many executives seeking to rapidly transform their firms have relied on buying new talent. Larry Bossidy replaced 90 of the top 120 executives at Allied Signal by hiring some people from inside the company but many from outside. This signaled a shift in the firm's culture and direction. When Al Dunlop went to Sunbeam, he brought his own management team and completely replaced the previous one. Buying new talent brings new ideas, breaks old cultural roadblocks, and creates intellectual capital by shaking up the firm.

A buy strategy works when talent is available and accessible, but the risks are also great. The firm may not find external talent that is better or more qualified than internal talent. It may alienate qualified internal employees who resent management carpetbaggers. It may not integrate diverse external talent into a workable team that knows the business. Teams that invest in free agents often do not win championships in sports for which teamwork is required.

BUILD

By building, managers invest in the current workforce to make it stronger and better. As employees must find new ways to think about and do work, many firms, such as Motorola and General Electric, have invested heavily in helping them learn new technical and managerial skills. Some learning occurs in formal training programs and centers; much more occurs in structured on-the-job experiences. In either case, managers build intellectual capital by investing in employee learning in which inquiry is coupled with action, new ideas replace the old, and behavior changes.

A build strategy for intellectual capital works when senior managers ensure that development is more than an academic exercise, when training is tied to business results not theory, when action learning occurs, and when systemic learning from job experience occurs. The risk of a build strategy is in spending enormous money and time on training for its own sake, not for building intellectual capital.

BORROW

In borrowing, managers invest in outside vendors who bring in ideas, frameworks, and tools to make the organization stronger. Effectively used consultants or outsourcing partners may share knowledge, create new knowledge, and design work in ways that people too close to the work would not have done.

Many firms are learning to use consultants, not become dependent on them. This approach requires adapting, not adopting, consultants' models, because each firm has different ways to apply those ideas.

Knowledge must transfer into the client organization so that the consultants essentially "work themselves out of a job." The firm must unravel the consultants' processes and tools so that employees can replicate and deploy them afterward. Borrowing means less focus on studies and more on recrafting processes with consultant input. Successful use of a consultant means "leasing to own" the consultant's knowledge versus renting.

Borrowing also has risks. It may mean spending large amounts of capital and time with little return. The firm may become dependent on a consultant without a transfer of knowledge into the firm. It may use answers from another setting without adaptation. However appropriately used, borrowing competence is a viable way to secure intellectual capital.

BOUNCE

Managers must remove those individuals who fail to perform to standard. Sometimes people who were once qualified have failed to develop new skills and are unqualified for current work practices. At other times, individuals are simply incapable of changing, learning, and adapting. A firm should systematically and courageously remove the bottom percentiles in performance. Managers must make difficult personnel decisions decisively. Those who stay or leave should know why and what is expected of them. A fair, equitable process must meet legal requirements.

Bouncing also has risks. Downsizing may become a panacea. Bouncing may lose the wrong individuals and demoralize those who stay. Difficult personnel decisions may be based on perception, not fact, and management credibility will suffer as a result.

BIND

Retaining employees is critical at all levels. Keeping senior managers who have vision, direction, and competence is important, and retaining technical, operational, and hourly workers also matters because investments made in individual talent often take years to pay back.

A large bank was frustrated with its credit training program because, after three years of formal classroom training coupled with tailored job assignments, it often lost its loan officers to other banks. The bank had a buy-and-build strategy, but it was creating intellectual capital for competitors by not retaining those in whom it had invested.

Another firm facing high labor costs decided that instead of focusing on the 7 percent to 10 percent of employees it might have to let go, it would focus on the 20 percent to 25 percent it could not afford to let go. The managers began to identify the critical employees, interview them to find out how to keep them, and then shape individual contracts with them so they would not leave. The firm was able to retain the important employees and increase intellectual capital.

All managers use some version of buy, build, borrow, bounce, and bind. By selecting and integrating these tools, managers can increase competence (see "Tools for Increasing Competence").

COMMITMENT VERSUS BURNOUT

One trap in creating intellectual capital is to focus only on competence. Just having more competent employees who are not committed to doing good work is like trying to win a team sport with an all-star team. While the individual players may be talented, they do not perform as a team.

Building commitment involves engaging employees' emotional energy and attention. It is reflected in how employees relate to each other and feel about a firm. In many cases, the competitive pressures that require more employee commitment actually reduce it. Competition demands more of employees; they must be more global, more customer responsive, more flexible, more learning-oriented, more team driven, more productive, and so on. These demands require committed employees who give their emotional, intellectual, and physical energy to the firm's success. Unfortunately, many managers do not deal with increased employee demands effectively. They continue to expect more and more of employees, creating not commitment but stress and burnout. Employees may become depressed and experience various symptoms (see "Symptoms of Employee Burnout").

Theory and research from literature on teenage depression provides a framework for understanding employee stress, burnout, or lack of commitment. Research has found that depression occurs when the social, physical, cognitive, and affective demands on teenagers exceed their resources to cope.[5] These demands have comparable characteristics: First, they are inevitable and affect every adolescent regardless of social status. Trying to avoid them is impossible. Second, they cannot be denied or discounted. Third, the demands are cognitive; they are perceived in the expectations set by parents, teachers, peers, and themselves.

TOOLS FOR INCREASING COMPETENCE

Buy: Acquire new talent by hiring individuals from outside the firm or from elsewhere within the firm.

Build: Train or develop talent through formal job training, job rotation, job assignment, and action learning.

Borrow: Form partnerships with people outside the firm (for example, consultants, vendors, customers, or suppliers) to find new ideas.

Bounce: Remove individuals with low or sub-par performance.

Bind: Retain the most talented employees.

SYMPTOMS OF EMPLOYEE BURNOUT

Don't feel recognized or appreciated for their work; don't know how to celebrate success.

Feel that their lives are out of balance, with too much energy focused on work and not enough on personal and family issues.

Lament how good work used to be.

Feel that no matter how much they do, it is never enough.

Feel unable to control the amount or quality of work they are asked to do or the resources required to do it.

Incur stress-related health care costs.

Feel that their bosses are out of touch with reality or don't care.

Are embarrassed to discuss personal issues at work (hobbies, family, and so on).

Become short-tempered and argue about trivial issues.

Have lowered morale and talk about being burned out by stress and pressure.

Spend time thinking about protecting their own careers more than serving customers.

Rebel by merely following the rules and doing only what they are told.

Talk about disagreements and concerns in informal settings rather than through formal channels of communication.

Quit having fun at work and talk about how difficult work is; don't see what's in it for them to work harder.

Have difficulty making commitments to get work done.

Feel that they have little chance of real career progression or that their careers are out of their control.

Feel caught in a rut or routine and overwhelmed by all they have to do just to keep up.

Are cynical about new corporate initiatives and see programs as just another way to make them work harder.

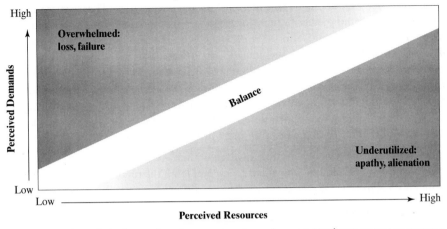

Depression or lack of commitment occurs when demands are greater than resources or resources are greater than demands.

FIGURE 1   **Teenage Depression or Employee Lack of Commitment**

Resources are the energy-providing activities that help individuals cope with demands. At its simplest level, depression occurs when a teenager feels he or she just can't cope with it all. It is not demand alone, but the inability to cope that causes the depression (see Figure 1). Many resources are available to increase the ability to cope with demands, for example, supportive parents or family, cognitive ability, success in some activities, and so on.

Like teenagers, employees may also feel that the demands on them exceed their resources or ability to cope. A lack of commitment does not come from the demands (because competitiveness requires that employee demands *must* be high) but from the imbalance of demands and resources. By listening to employees and having exit interviews, surveys, and employee activities, a company can find evidence of employee depression and lack of commitment. To reduce depression and increase commitment, the company needs to appropriately balance demands and resources, so aspirations (demands) slightly exceed resources.[6] Once demands and resources are balanced, employees can contribute. They are committed to improve and competent enough to make the right improvements. Their intellectual capital increases.

HOW TO FOSTER COMMITMENT

A company can foster commitment in three ways. *First*, it can reduce demands. Employees can find ways to do less so that they stay in balance. *Second*, it can increase resources. Employees can find new resources to accomplish work. *Third*, it can turn demands into resources.

REDUCE DEMANDS

Employees have many demands of varying importance. Helping them separate legitimate from groundless demands and then removing the unnecessary ones may balance their lives.

Prioritize   Prioritization can eliminate some demands. The old adage, "Everything worth doing is worth doing well," may become, "Everything worth doing is worth overdoing," as Steve Kerr of GE notes.[7] Some managers may think that if one high-performing team works best for decision A, then every employee should participate in high-performing teams for all decisions. Or, if a training program works for one group of employees, all employees must go through the program. These processes overwhelm employees. Setting priorities means that some activities are worth doing well; others should be let go.

At General Electric, a change effort, "Work Out," began by getting rid of work that did not add value.[8] The assumption was that work accumulates like the clutter in closets or attics. Things just pile up without much rationale or reasoning. Cleaning closets means discarding items that you don't use anymore. Cleaning out work systems means discarding work processes that are not adding value. At GE, this meant filtering reports, approvals. procedures, measures, and meetings (the elements of bureaucracy) by asking: Is there a customer who gets value from this work? If not, we can discard the work. Some other questions for assessing, the value of work are:

- Who uses the report? How is the information used to improve decision making? How accurate and up-to-date is it? How much time do people spend preparing the report?
- How often does someone not give approval for something? If someone always signs a requisition (for example, for a tuition waiver or travel approval under a certain amount), then the signature is more a bureaucratic requirement than an added value. Who is ultimately responsible? Does the approval process focus on this person?
- Who uses the measures tracked? Are the behaviors reinforced by measurement of those we should increase? Are we measuring what is easy or what is important? How costly are the measures? Are we collecting lead or lag data?
- Why hold this meeting? What if we do not have this meeting? What is the return on the amount of time for those who attend? Are we using the meeting for communication or for decision making?
- How many steps are in this process? Can we streamline the steps and get things done more quickly?

Focus   Employee demands may be too high because they are unfocused. A company can encourage focus by ending many initiatives and doing only a few critical activities. Unfortunately, quality, innovation, empowerment, attention to customers, team building, productivity, and so on are all necessary. Who is willing to forgo innovation to accomplish productivity? High-demand organizations must win on many dimensions.

Focus requires weaving multiple initiatives into overarching themes. In some ways, it matters less what the theme is and more that there is one. For example. George Fisher, CEO at Eastman Kodak, has selected quality as an important theme. CEO Arthur Martinez has concentrated on making Sears a compelling place to work, shop, and invest. Irv Hockaday, Hallmark CEO, has focused on product leadership. Steve Kerr of GE suggests that integrative themes are like locomotives pulling multiple, varied train cars. The individual box cars (initiatives) may change, but the locomotive pulls them together in the same direction.

Reengineer   There is much advice about how to reengineer work.[9] In terms of employee commitment, reengineering processes reduce demands by streamlining, automating, and simplifying work. When complex processes are simplified, some employee demands are eliminated.

For Dale Carnegie management training programs, the process time from concept to delivery of a new program was about six months. After serious reengineering work during which managers examined the decision points for new programs, the steps for creating materials, and the necessary activities, they were able to reduce the cycle time for a new program to 20 days.

Camco, the General Electric Appliance business unit in Canada, reengineered its distribution system so that customer orders could immediately be turned into products. Instead of building to inventory, it began to build to order. This significantly reduced the inventory cost, removed many activities from the work process, and shifted employee focus to high-value-added work.

Even with priority setting, focusing and reengineering, demands on employees will continue to increase. Regardless of how many demands are removed or reduced, competition continues.

INCREASE RESOURCES

Not all demands can be reduced. Business demands accompany a firm's desire to compete in tough markets. Walking away from competition would, in many cases, equate to failure. Demands will inevitably be high in globally competitive firms. Resources represent the value practices and actions the company takes to respond to demands. Certain resources may counterbalance demands (see "Tools for Developing Commitment").

Control   In a classic experiment, management gave employees a lever that controlled how fast they could operate an assembly line. Originally afraid that employees would take advantage of the situation and slow down the process, management was surprised that employees actually worked faster when they felt in control of their work.

Many companies have learned the value of sharing control with employees as a way to let them decide how to cope with increased demands. A hotel chain wanted each of its maids to clean 19 rooms per day, an increase of one room per day. Rather than merely raising the standard, management experimented by creating high-performing work teams of five maids who were responsible for cleaning 95 rooms per day (the new standard). The hotel gave the team complete control over how it could organize to get the work done on time and within quality standards. The team members decided that four of them would go to work, while the fifth would stay home with the children of all five. This approach gave management what it wanted (increased productivity and continued quality) and employees what they wanted (flexibility and autonomy).

TOOLS FOR DEVELOPING COMMITMENT

Control: Enable employees to control decisions on how they do their work.

Strategy or Vision: Offer employees a vision and direction that commits them to working hard.

Challenging Work: Provide employees with stimulating work that develops new skills.

Collaboration and Teamwork: Form teams to get work done.

Work Culture: Establish an environment of celebration, fun, excitement, and openness.

Shared Gains: Compensate employees for work accomplished.

Communication: Candidly and frequently share information with employees.

Concern for People: Ensure that each individual is treated with dignity and that differences are openly shared.

Technology: Give employees the technology to make their work easier.

Training and Development: Ensure that employees have the skills to do their work well.

Control can involve work schedules. Flex-time and flex-hours have helped many firms maintain employee commitment. Giving employees control over how to meet the demands partly led to Microsoft's success. In its early days, the computer programmers faced enormous pressures and demands to prepare thousands of lines of code for the operating system. These programmers had no time clock and no one monitoring their work; they controlled their own schedules.

The location of work can also be an issue of control. Arthur Andersen Consulting lets employees live where they want as long as they can fly to meet with clients. Rather than traveling four days a week, then coming into the office for that day, the consultants may spend the fifth day working from home or wherever they choose. This autonomy and control does not mean standards are any less rigorous, merely that employees control where they work.

In sharing power and giving up control, managers implicitly trust that their employees have the skills and motivation to do a good job. Sharing control demonstrates trust and builds employee commitment. Managers may use control as a resource by creatively and flexibly answering: Where is work done? How is work done? What work is done? When is work done? Who does what work? As long as employees understand and are committed to the goals, they can share the way goals are accomplished.

Strategy or Vision   Employees who feel personally committed to a strategy or vision are more likely to work hard. If you ask employees to think of an occasion when they faced enormously high demands (tough schedule, demanding customer, and so on) and how they felt in working toward that goal, almost inevitably they discuss feeling committed from having a common vision. Employee commitment often comes from a leader who shares a clear vision that passionately communicates agenda and intent. Many executives articulate visions or directions that give employees resources and add to their resolve to cope with increased demand.

When George Fisher became chairman of Eastman Kodak, one employee commented that, while Kodak had been engaged in quality, improvement, and efficiency efforts for years, Fisher was really serious about it. This employee felt that, while the language was the same, the passion and dedication were new. He also reported that many employees were excited and energized by the new leadership dedication.

Challenging Work   Boring work is draining; lots of boring work is deadly. Asking employees to do increasing amounts of boring work is self-defeating. There are numerous ways to make work challenging.

Baxter Healthcare connects employees directly to customers. The criterion of effectiveness is customers' perceptions of Baxter's work. For example, Frank LaFasto, vice president of human resources, spends much time building teams with hospitals that are Baxter customers. His hard work is immediately challenging and has direct customer payback.

Amgen, a leading biotech firm, is constantly searching for new genes and biotechnology to turn into products. It asks its scientists to do more work in research and applications and reduce product introduction time. The scientists are continually stimulated by extensive technical support, up-to-date laboratories, and extremely challenging work. They know they are working on cutting-edge research that will add value to science as well as to Amgen's portfolio.

Collaboration and Teamwork   Teams often turn individual efforts into extraordinary successes. Studies and cases of high-performing teams show that teams can often leverage individual talents into collective achievements.[10] When faced with high demands, teams solve problems better than isolated individuals can.

The demands for creating the Boeing 777 air frame were exceptional: it had to be completed (from design to delivery) in less time than previous models, be produced at less cost, meet customer needs, please pilots, and be more fuel efficient than any other aircraft. These demands were not easily met. More than 200 teams participated in the 777's design, engineering, manufacture, and assembly. This program redefined not only the Boeing fleet but the process for delivering air frames.

Teams often are accused of slow decision making. In many cases, the opposite is true. In high-demand situations, in which solutions are not readily available, teams can focus and rapidly resolve an issue. For example, Hallmark faced increased competition from American Standard and other brands. Hallmark executives had to rethink how work was accomplished. Under the leadership of CEO Irv Hockaday, they developed a product leadership strategy in which they defined distinct brands and products distributed to its different, diverse outlets. Creating this strategy changed many assumptions and processes that already had been reengineered at Hallmark. Most important was the formation of the North American Management Team (NAMT) composed of nine senior executives. Meeting regularly, they struggled to make the strategy work. They exerted peer pressure and, under Hockaday's leadership, made disciplined, rigorous, tough, and rapid decisions to execute the product leadership strategy. The NAMT improved both decision making and strategy implementation by being focused on the strategy and rigorous in decision making.

Teams can be formal corporate bodies such as Hallmark's NAMT or task forces such as the hundreds of Boeing 777 teams. They can also be less formal support groups in which individuals find emotional and intellectual support. At Coopers & Lybrand, a host of informal, collegial teams helped employees find outlets for their demands and provided arenas for discussing problems and finding creative solutions outside the formal hierarchy. Support groups, clubs, social activities, professional associations, minority groups, and other informal teams can often serve to increase resources for employees.

Finally, collaboration may take the form of formal and informal mentor relationships. In the U.S. Army, some younger officers from the Vietnam era were disillusioned about older officers' lack of commitment to learning. The group formed a mentor program in which an officer who had previously held a position would observe the current officer in simulations or other settings. The preceding officer could not officially mentor those under his or her command, and comments—sometimes blunt, candid, off-the-record feedback on how to improve performance—were not officially recorded. This mentoring system has been credited with improving leadership quality and helping current officers cope with demands.[11]

Work Culture Imagine a competition that requires you to work very hard for a long time. Then imagine your feelings when you win an award. What if you could not celebrate your success but must quietly accept the award and then immediately prepare for the next round of competition? Does that sound like fun? Too many work settings have taken the fun out of winning. Establishing, striving for, and accomplishing goals should be energizing, exciting, and worthy of celebration.

Some companies have maintained a culture of fun. Southwest Airlines requires that employees be very serious about airline rules and regulations but also go out of their way to help passengers enjoy flying on Southwest.[12] Flight attendants sing, dance, climb into overhead bins, and entertain passengers while performing their required duties. Sam Walton's hula on Wall Street after exceeding goals was fun for employees and also showed that he would go to great (and humorous) lengths for his employees if they delivered results.

Defining a work culture can encourage employees. Harley-Davidson employees frequently wear Harley T-shirts and Levis to work. They ride their bikes to rallies and join customers in the Harley experience. Hallmark encourages creative department staffers not only to innovate with their card designs but to decorate their workstations to show their creativity and personality.

Shared Gains In a recent workshop, I spent two hours talking about all the exciting things happening in a particular company. The executives were articulating a vision, producing new and exciting products, reducing cycle times for product introduction, serving customers, and living the fantasy of the modern corporation. At the end of the discussion, a participant who had been listening quietly commented, "This is all well and good, but what's in it for me?" Great question! People working hard must be rewarded personally. Most of us are not totally altruistic and need to touch, see, and feel the rewards from what we do. For most people, compensation becomes a scorecard for success.

Companies are learning that sharing the economic gains of reaching targets helps employees stay motivated to reach increasingly difficult goals. PepsiCo has a program called Sharepower in which all employees—500,000 workers in 195 countries—who work at least 1,500 hours a year and have been with PepsiCo for one year are given stock in the company. Such gain sharing is not altruistic but increases employees' commitment. Pepsi employees try to please customers because they know the impact of customer service on future stock performance.[13]

When employees see that a particularly demanding project results in economic payback, they are likely to be more committed. When the line of sight between work and reward is clear, employees may cope better with increased demands.

Communication   Almost every employee attitude survey about communication suggests that there is not enough information sharing. Even after weeks and months of presentations on strategy, many employees do not always understand it. The fact that communication is difficult, however, does not undermine its importance as a resource.

If employees understand why a company is doing something, they will more readily accept it. Too often, managers focus on the what and not the why, making statements such as, "We are going to reorganize," "We are going to reduce cycle times," We are going to increase quality," or "We are going to reengineer." Employees may fail to grasp the principle behind the program. When employees have a knowledge of the business so that they can communicate goals to external stakeholders (for example, customers, investors, suppliers, potential employee groups, and so on), they see communication and information as resources.

When Hallmark introduced its reorganization, which would increase the demands and expectations on the entire workforce, the executive team diligently communicated to employees the changes' intent and implications. The team members held meetings of all employees at which executives explained the new organization and goals and answered questions. They prepared press releases so extended family members could understand what was happening. They summarized executive remarks in briefings and newsletters and invited employees with further questions to contact their managers. The extensive communication plan was a major resource. Employees knew not only what was happening but why and how it would affect their jobs and careers.

Communication requires symbols and words. When Sears developed its vision of becoming a compelling place to shop, work, and invest, Barbara Lehman, director of public relations, and her staff created a triangular paperweight; at the base was the balanced scorecard Sears wanted to achieve (profitability, people, and preferred supplier). Each side represented a stakeholder (customers, employees, and investors). At the chairman's conference presenting the vision, each participant received the paperweight as a symbol of the new Sears. In addition, to represent the balance required among the three stakeholders, participants got a gyroscope. These gifts, which may seem somewhat trivial, symbolized the new strategy.

Concern for People   Being busy is not an option, but a given. People confront the challenge of limited time, forging a path through many activities, and dealing with endless lists of things to do. Some companies give employees resources to cope with the demands on their time. 3Com has dedicated space in the corporate office for all the personal "errand" work that absorbs employee time. The company has leased space to a bank, laundromat, dry-cleaner, shoeshine stand, car repair (in the employee garage), travel agency, and other services. As employees use time before, during, and after work to accomplish errands more efficiently, they have more time to focus on the business. In some senior executive training programs, Cargill invites spouses and partners to candidly discuss the business's challenges so they can more fully understand demands. These inclusive events help families become more committed.

Federal Express has institutionalized grievance procedures so employees know that if they have a conflict with their manager, senior managers will hear their viewpoints. Motorola ensures that it will not terminate anyone who has been employed by the company for at least 10 years without a personal review by an executive committee member.

Technology   New technologies may be a demand (the requirement to learn how to do things differently) or a resource (the ability to do things differently). As a resource, technology can remove barriers by sharing information and simplifying work processes. Computers often can remove or replace routine, standardized transaction work. The resource of technology may also restructure work. In an internal study, AT&T found that a high percentage of work could be done remotely, through telephone, fax, and modem connections. Instead of having to face traffic, parking, and coming to work every day, employees can telecommute, thus working from remote, distributed locations. Virtual offices where boundaries are not geography, but information, are occurring more frequently.

Training and Development   Many companies invest heavily in activities to help employees cope with increased demands.[14] There are four types of such activities: First, a systematic management curriculum can help employees develop at each career level. General Electric's Crotonville Development Center prepares courses for employees from entry level through company officer level to ensure that they have the necessary skills. Second, developmental experiences such as job assignments, task forces, apprenticeships, or job rotation are based on the assumption that individuals learn from experience. Third, employees can gain competence from action learning, which occurs when teams attend training activities and work with a real problem. The result is a set of skills and the ability to apply tools and skills to a business problem. Finally, employees working in teams may enhance competencies by discussing business projects and teamwork.

TURN DEMANDS INTO RESOURCES

A company can turn a demand into a resource in several ways:

Hold Exit Interviews   Employees who are leaving may be the best source of information on what is really happening in the firm. When managers conduct exit interviews, they may see how company policies or management actions erode commitment. By collating information from exit interviews, they can change demands into commitment.

Assimilate New Managers   When managers arrive, demands on employees are often high. Employees reporting to the new manager may be unclear about his or her expectations, work style and behavior, which raises the level of stress.

General Electric has a systematic assimilation process to help employees work with new managers. Employees and the manager participate in a half-day workshop. Employees list questions they have about the new manager (for example, background, work habits, expectations, and so on). The new manager answers questions openly and candidly and shares concerns and questions about working with the group. The group in turn shares expectations about work processes such as decision making, conflict resolution, goals, and roles. Investing time up front on these issues saves time and resources as the demand of leadership focuses on discussing work relationships.

Consider Family Demands   Managers can turn work demands into resources and increase commitment by considering extended family issues. Marriott Corporation and Cargill invite spouses or partners to participate in executive development experiences where they discuss business strategies and the personal and family implications of executing the strategies. Organizations can become family-friendly by (1) inviting spouses, partners, and children on interview trips to ensure that they are comfortable with relocation, (2) establishing adequate family leave policies to help relieve employee stress, (3) providing on-site or corporate-supported child care, and (4) instituting corporate-supported family vacations, outings, and extracurricular activities. In global firms, family training has assisted both the employee and family in relocating. While not useful for all workers, this array of corporate activities with a family focus may help employees modify demands so that the family better understands and supports work requirements.

Involve Employees in Important Decisions Companies can have employees participate in decisions that affect them by sharing the context and rationale for the decisions. Employees who participate fully in decision making—from framing, collecting information, generating alternatives, making recommendations, and implementing and acting on the decision—have an increased sense of control and commitment. In hiring decisions, if employees screen a potential supervisor, they become more committed to the supervisor eventually hired. In product decisions, when employees can gives opinions on product introductions, they are more committed to the new product. In relocations, if employees have a voice in the placement of a new plant or facility, they will be more committed. When employees discuss strategy, they become more committed to implementing it.

Managers should decide who should receive information, who should be involved in task forces to generate information about a decision, who should help draft and implement recommendations, and who should follow up on decisions. All are important elements of involvement and can turn decisions that may be sources of employee demands into an engagement of resources.

Intellectual capital comes from employees' competence and commitment. Both must exist together for intellectual capital to grow. Leaders interested in investing, leveraging, and expanding intellectual capital should raise standards, set high expectations, and demand more of employees. They must also provide resources to help employees meet high demands. Employees will become engaged and flourish, and the organization's intellectual capital will become its defining asset.

REFERENCES

[1] J. B. Quinn, *Intelligent Enterprise* (New York: Free Press, 1992).

[2] P. F. Drucker, "Toward the New Organization," *Leader to Leader* (San Francisco: Jossey-Bass 1997) 6–8; and D. E. Bowen and C. Siehl, "The Future of Human Resource Management: March and Simon (1958) Revisited," *Human Resource Management Journal 36*, no. 1 (1997): 57–64.

[3] D. Ulrich, R. Halbrook, D. Meder, and M. Stuchlik, "Employee and Customer Attachment: Synergies for Competitive Advantage," *Human Resource Planning 4* (1991): 89–102; B. Schneider and D. E. Bowen, *Winning the Service Game* (Cambridge, MA: Harvard University Press, 1995); B. Schneider and D. E. Bowen, "Employee and Customer Perceptions of Service in Banks: Replication and Extension," *Journal of Applied Psychology 70*, no. 6 (1985): 423–433; and B. Fromm and L. Schlesinger, *The Real Heroes of Business and Not a CEO among Them* (New York: Doubleday, 1993).

[4] J. B. Quinn, "Leveraging Intellect" *Academy of Management Executive 10*, no. 1 (1996): 7–27; H. Saint-Onge, "Tacit Knowledge: The Key to the Strategic Alignment of Intellectual Capital," *Strategy and Leadership 2* (March-April 1996): 10–14; and T. Stewart, *Intellectual Capital* (New York: Doubleday/Currency, 1997).

[5] W. Ulrich. "Identification and Referral of Depressed Secondary School Students" (Ann Arbor, Michigan: University of Michigan, doctoral dissertation, 1989).

[6] The argument that aspirations should exceed resources is made in: G. Hamel and C. K. Prahalad, *Competing for the Future* (Boston: Harvard Business School Press, 1994).

[7] S. Kerr, personal conversation.

[8] Work Out has been described in a number of publications; this discussion is based on my experience and work with General Electric.

[9] M. Hammer and J. Champy, *Reengineering the Corporation* (New York: HarperBusiness, 1993).

[10] C. Larson and F. LaFasto, *Teamwork* (Newbury, CA: Sage Publications, 1989); S. Mohrman, S. Cohen, and A. Mohrman, Jr., *Designing Team-Based Organizations: New Forms of Knowledge Work* (San Francisco: Jossey-Bass, 1995); and J. R. Katzenbach and D. Smith, *The Wisdom of Teams* (Boston: Harvard Business School Press, 1993).

[11] This example comes from a speech by Thurgood Marshall in 1992 on leadership in the military model that he presented to General Electric employees charged with developing GE leaders.

[12] B. P. Sunoo, "How Fun Flies at Southwest Airlines." *Personnel Journal* (June 1995): 37–41.

[13] D. Anfuso, "PepsiCo Shared Power and Wealth with Workers," *Personnel Journal* (June 1995): 42–49.

[14] For a review of trends in development and learning, see: D. Ulrich and H. Greenfield, "From Training and Development to Development and Learning," *American Journal of Management Development 1*, no. 2 (1995): 11–22.

MANAGEMENT DIALOGUES:
TURNING ON THE MARGINAL PERFORMER*

John R. Schermerhorn, Jr.
William L. Gardner
Thomas N. Martin

Bob is an employee in the R&D laboratory of a large high-technology firm. He was hired by the lab supervisor, Fred, after a thorough recruitment and selection process. Both men were enthusiastic about the appointment. Bob had excellent technical credentials, was glad to be hired by the lab, and really liked Fred. Fred was confident in Bob's abilities and sure that Bob was just the person the lab needed. He passed by Bob's work station during Bob's first day on the job. Here's the way things started off:

Fred: *Hi, Bob. First full day on the job, I see?*
Bob: *Yes, and I'm ready to go to work.*
Fred: *Good. I just thought I'd stop by first thing to say hi and remind you we're expecting good results. You'll be pretty much on your own here, so it will be your responsibility to stay on top of things.*
Bob: *Well, that shouldn't be a problem.*
Fred: *I hope not. But if you hit any snags, don't be afraid to call me.*
Bob: *All right.*
Fred: *Good enough, Bob. See you later.*

Everything seemed in order with this brief but positive exchange between a manager and his new employee. The two men talked easily with each other. Fred quite specifically reminded Bob of his expectations and pledged his support. Bob expressed confidence in his ability to fulfill Fred's expectations, and he acknowledged the offer of support.

But six months later, things had changed dramatically. For example, consider one of Bob's typical workdays. He arrived late for work and looked at the clock, which read 8:55. "Little late this morning," he thought to himself. "Oh well, no big deal. Fred's not around anyway." Later in the day he noted that he had "come up short again" in his work. "But not too bad," he said. "This ought to be enough to keep Fred off my back." Finally, just before quitting time he considered getting a jump on the next day's schedule. But after thinking just a moment, he concluded, "Ah, why sweat it? I'll do it tomorrow."

People like Bob show up in most work sites. Although they initially seem capable and highly motivated, they become marginal performers—workers who do just enough to get by. Many frustrated managers simply consider these people unfortunate employment mistakes that must be tolerated. By contrast, we believe managers can "turn around" many marginal performers and thereby produce large productivity gains for their organization. Such *high-performance management* gets the best from each and every individual contributor.

Let's go back to the opening vignette to determine what went wrong in Fred and Bob's relationship and what could have been done about it. Why did Bob, a capable and motivated person, become a marginal performer? What could Fred have done to turn the situation around so that Bob's high-performance potential would have been realized?

---

*Reprinted, by permission of publisher, from *Organizational Dynamics*, Spring 1990. © 1990 American Management Association, New York. All rights reserved.

A COMPREHENSIVE APPROACH
TO INDIVIDUAL PERFORMANCE

The answers can be found in a management framework based on what we call the *individual performance equation*: *Performance = Ability × Support × Effort*. Central to the equation is the principle that high levels of work performance result from the combination of a person's job-related abilities, various forms of organizational support, and individual work efforts. The multiplication signs indicate that all three factors must exist for high performance to occur. Take any one or more away, and performance will be compromised. High-performance management starts with the following implications of the individual performance equation.

1. Performance Begins with Ability Individual abilities are the skills and other personal characteristics we use in a job. For someone to perform well, he or she must have the skills and abilities required to complete the work. If the person lacks the requisite baseline abilities, it will be very difficult for even extraordinary effort and support to produce high performance.

Because ability is a prerequisite for performance, it is the first factor to consider when searching for explanations of marginal work. Initially, managers must determine whether employees have the skills and aptitudes necessary to succeed. The best way to ensure that they do is to develop selection procedures that properly match individual talents and job demands. In cases where employees lack essential skills, managers should use training and development programs to help them acquire these skills. The manager may also consider replacing or reassigning personnel to achieve a better match of individual abilities with job requirements.

In addition, as Victor Vroom's expectancy theory of motivation points out, individuals must believe in their abilities if they are to exhibit high performance. A person may have the right abilities but may fail to develop the expectation that by using these skills, he or she will achieve the desired performance levels. Thus part of a manager's job is to help build self-confidence among the individual contributors—to help them realize that they have the abilities required to meet high-performance expectations.

2. Performance Requires Support The second but frequently overlooked high-performance factor is support. Even the most hard-working and highly capable individuals will be unable to maximize their performance if they do not have the necessary support.

In searching for the causes of marginal performance, managers need to examine two major dimensions of support. First, they must ask if they have done their part to create a physical work setting that supplies employees with broad opportunities to fully use their abilities. A supportive work environment provides appropriate technologies, tools, facilities, and equipment; offers adequate budgets; includes clearly defined task goals; gives autonomy without the burden of too much red tape and other performance obstacles; and pays a market-competitive base wage or salary. Deficiencies in these areas impose situational constraints that too often frustrate employees' performance efforts.

Second, managers must give proper attention to the social aspects of the work environment. Recent research into job stress, for example, suggests that social support is critical for sustained high performance. Emotional support from a person's supervisor and co-workers, as well as from non-job sources (i.e., spouse, family, and friends), can have long-term positive effects on job performance. Indeed, empathy can help a worker better handle such work stresses as skill underutilization, high workloads, and role ambiguity.

A manager's responsibility thus includes providing every individual contributor with the maximum opportunity to perform at a high level. This advice echoes Robert House's path-goal theory of leadership. Path-goal theory suggests that effective managers use various management styles—directive, supportive, achievement oriented, and participative—as necessary to ensure that employees have clear "paths" as they seek to accomplish their goals. That is, good managers use leadership behaviors that maximize the amount of situational support available to others.

3. Performance Involves Effort Effort is the final, and perhaps most commonly emphasized, individual performance factor. Here, effort refers to the amount of energy (physical and/or mental) a person applies to perform a task. In other words, it represents someone's willingness to work hard.

Effort is necessary to achieve high-performance results. Capable, well-supported, but uninspired employees are no more likely to succeed than are hard-working persons who lack ability and/or support. Yet unlike the other performance factors, which are subject to direct managerial control, the decision to exert or withhold one's effort rests solely with the individual contributor. To understand why employees sometimes decide *not* to work as hard as possible, it is again useful to consider Vroom's expectancy theory of motivation. According to this perspective, the motivation to work is the product of expectancy, instrumentality, and valence: *Expectancy* is the individual's assessment of the likelihood that his or her work effort will lead to task performance; *instrumentality* is the individual's belief that a given level of performance will lead to certain work outcomes; and *valence* is the value the person attaches to these outcomes. If the level of any one of these factors is low, motivation is likely to suffer. To avoid motivational deficits, managers are advised to make sure individual contributors see clear linkages between how hard they work, their performance results, and their rewards.

BOB, THE MARGINAL PERFORMER

Let's return to the opening vignette and begin to apply the individual performance equation. All three elements of the equation—ability, support, and effort—appear to exist. Fred set the stage for Bob's high performance by (1) hiring a technically competent person, (2) indicating his intention to provide support, and (3) encouraging Bob to work hard and use his ability to good advantage. Our first clues as to what went wrong are found in a conversation that took place after Bob had been on the job about a month.

Fred happened to pass by Bob's area and noticed Bob was working hard. He thought to himself how fortunate he was to have a dependable go-getter like Bob in his department. Bob noticed Fred approaching and wondered whether Fred would mention his good performance from the past week.

> Fred: *Hi, Bob. It sure is good weather, wouldn't you say?*
> Bob: *Yes, it sure is.*
> Fred: *I was just passing through the building on another matter. While I'm here, I thought I'd show you some new schedule changes.*
> Bob: *Oh yes, Darlene (the project manager) told me all about them. Say, how'd we end up last week anyway?*
> Fred: *Pretty good, pretty good. If you have any questions about those schedule changes, just call the project manager. Well, I've got to run. See you later, Bob.*

In this interaction Bob obviously wanted Fred's praise. What he got was a lukewarm "Pretty good, pretty good" followed by "I've got to run." Fred passed up a perfect opportunity to recognize directly Bob's accomplishments. From an expectancy theory perspective, this oversight could prove costly. Bob's expectation was probably quite high—he had already shown he could do the job when he wanted to. The valence he attached to possible work outcomes, such as praise, also was probably high. But Bob's instrumentality may have become low because he sensed little or no relationship between performing well and receiving the desired supervisory recognition. The positive reinforcement he both desired and needed was just not there. As a result, his motivation to work hard was reduced.

Things could have gotten better if the motivational dynamics had improved in later interactions between Fred and Bob. Unfortunately, as we'll now see, they didn't. Several weeks later while reading the weekly lab reports, Fred noticed a decline in Bob's performance. This was a serious problem, so Fred decided to chat with Bob right away. Bob had met high performance standards in the past and should still have been able to reach them. When Fred stopped by Bob's work station, they engaged in the following conversation.

> Fred: *Hi, Bob, how's it going?*
> Bob: *Pretty good.*
> Fred: *Say, I wanted to check with you about your performance figures for the past couple of weeks. They've been down a little, you know.*
> Bob: *Well, I got stuck on a couple of things that threw me off. But I think I'm back on track now.*
> Fred: *The only reason I'm bringing it up is that you've busted the charts in the past. I know you can do it when you put your mind to it. You're one of our top performers. I figured if you were off on the numbers there must be a reason.*
> Bob: *Well, I'm sure my performance results will be back up this week.*
> Fred: *Okay, good, Bob, Take care now.*

Reviewing this interaction, Fred thought it had been right to let Bob know he wasn't happy with his performance. But in this developing scheme, we have an indication that the only time Bob got the desired personal attention from Fred was when he did poorly. As social-learning theorists will tell us, Bob was essentially "learning" through reinforcement to work below his actual performance potential. By giving attention only when Bob turned in marginal, rather than high, performance, Fred was positively reinforcing the wrong behaviors and neglecting critical opportunities to positively reinforce the right ones. As long as this pattern continued, Bob was likely to remain a marginal performer. And, as we will see, a manager's frustrations with this situation can all too easily lead him or her to adopt ever more punitive approaches.

A few weeks later Fred noted that Bob's performance still wasn't back up to standard. While he was not the worst performer in the lab, he surely could have been doing a lot better; Bob's past record was proof positive. Being even more concerned now, Fred went to Bob's work area to discuss things with him.

> Fred: *Bob, I want to talk to you.*
> Bob: *Hi, Fred, what's on your mind?*
> Fred: *Your lousy performance, that's what! Your output has been down again for the past two weeks. Look, Bob, I know you can hit the numbers, but you're just not putting out. I need someone in here who can get the job done. If it is not you, I'll get someone else. I hope I won't have to do that. Now let's get to it?*
> Bob: *(No response.)*

Theorists advise us that Fred's threats reveal a number of shortcomings. For example, behaviors targeted for punishment frequently receive positive reinforcement from another source—like peers and coworkers or even the supervisor's inadvertent actions. For another, managers who use punishment often come to be viewed negatively by the recipients of the punishment. At the very least, then, we can expect that Fred had set the stage for potentially irreparable damage to his working relationship with Bob! Unfortunately, Fred made a common mistake. He focused only on what the employee might have been doing wrong while overlooking other possible causes for the marginal performance.

One thing is clear from the above episode. Fred was telling Bob that it was *Bob's* responsibility to find out what had gone wrong over the past couple of weeks, then take steps to correct it. Implicitly he was also attributing Bob's marginal performance to one or more things that might be wrong—

with Bob! Unfortunately, Fred made a common mistake: He focused only on what the employee might have been doing wrong while overlooking other possible causes for the marginal performance.

ATTRIBUTION ERRORS IN PERFORMANCE MANAGEMENT

Take a look at the data in Exhibit 1. It summarizes how managers from the health care and banking industries responded to two questions: (1) "What is the most frequent cause of poor performance by your employees?" and 2) "What is the most frequent cause of poor performance by yourself?" The exhibit shows quite different patterns of responses: When employees' performance deficiencies were at issue, the managers tended to attribute the problem to employees' lack of ability and/or effort; when the manager's own performance deficiencies were at issue, the problem was overwhelmingly viewed as a lack of outside support. But, we must ask, if managers need better support to achieve higher performance, doesn't the same hold true for their employees?

Responses such as these are of no great surprise to those familiar with an area of management research known as attribution theory. When dealing with marginal performers like Bob, the theory predicts that managers like Fred are more likely to "attribute" any performance problems to some deficiency within the individual—that is, to a lack of ability or lack of effort—rather than to a deficiency in the work situation, like a lack of organizational or managerial support. Given that Bob was considered technically competent when he was hired (thus satisfying the ability factor), Fred probably assumed that Bob's reduced performance resulted from a lack of motivation (a problem with the effort factor).

Managers who view performance problems in such a manner will spend valuable time and money trying to find ways to increase their employees" motivation directly and immediately. When these initial efforts fail, the threatening and punitive approach that Fred used in the last episode is likely to follow.

The fact that employees tend to attribute deficiencies in their performance to external causes, such as inadequate support, rather than to the internal causes their managers favor further complicates such situations. Bob, for example, is more likely to attribute his mediocre performance to a lack of supervisory recognition (an external cause) than to his own laziness (an internal cause)—which Fred seems to assume is the case. When such gaps between attributions exist, employees like Bob typically resent the harsh and punitive responses their managers use. On the other hand, managers get increasingly frustrated because they cannot understand the employee's failure to perform.

If this cycle of mismatched manager-employee attributions is allowed to continue, a worst-case scenario, in the form of what social psychologists call "learned helplessness," may occur. This term refers to the tendency for people who are exposed to repeated punishment or failure to believe they do not possess the skills needed to succeed at their job. As a result they become passive in their work, and they tend to remain so even after situational changes occur that make success once again possible. A

EXHIBIT 1   Marginal Performance: Attributions Given by Managers and by Employees Themselves

Number of Responses to the Question: Most common cause of poor performance by your employees?	Attribution	Number of Responses to the Question: Most common cause of poor performance by yourself?
22	Lack of Ability	2
15	Lack of Support	66
36	Lack of Effort	6

feeling that outcomes are beyond one's control, when in fact they are not, is the essence of learned helplessness. People become convinced that they are doomed to fail no matter what they do. As a consequence, employees who experience learned helplessness will usually continue to exhibit passive and maladaptive behavior long after changes (such as increased support or the arrival of a new manager) occur that make success possible.

In Bob's case, learned helplessness resulting from Fred's punitive responses may cause Bob eventually to doubt the very abilities that led to his hiring and early successes. While learned helplessness is a worst-case scenario, it exemplifies the serious complications that can arise if managers fail to address marginal performance in a constructive way. The approach that we recommend for dealing more positively with the marginal performer is outlined below.

DEALING WITH BOB—A BETTER WAY

Many marginal performers, like Bob, are aware that they are not working up to their potential—and they know why. Given a positive environment for dialogue, they are often willing and able to pinpoint the causes—both personal and situational—of their performance problems. They are also willing to assume their share of the responsibility for correcting them. Toward this end, we suggest the following managerial strategy for "turning around" a marginal performer.

- Bring the performance gap to the marginal performer's attention.
- Ask in a nonthreatening manner for an explanation.
- Describe the implications of the marginal performer's substandard work.
- Restate the original and still-desirable performance objectives.
- Offer the external support necessary for the marginal performer to improve his or her performance.
- Express confidence that the marginal performer will respond as expected.
- Agree on an appropriate time frame for jointly evaluating future performance in terms of the agreed-upon standards.
- Continue the process until it succeeds or the individual admits to an employment mismatch that can be reconciled only by a job change.

To illustrate how these steps can be followed, let's go back in time and pick up our vignette at the point where Fred first noticed that Bob's performance had dropped off. We'll assume he was prepared to adopt this more positive approach to the situation. As Fred's dialogue with Bob develops, we'll occasionally interject some discussion of his actions and Bob's responses. This will help illustrate the steps and potential benefits of the recommended approach.

Fred noticed that Bob's performance had been down for two weeks. After thinking it over, he realized that a capable person like Bob should have been consistently performing at a higher level—but he may have needed some help. Fred decided to walk to Bob's work station and talk to him about the matter at once.

> Fred: *Bob? I'd like to talk with you a bit. This last production report shows you came in below standard again the past week.*
> Bob: *Yeah, I guess I was a bit behind.*

Immediately, Fred brought the performance gap to Bob's attention. He did this politely, but specifically and face-to-face. Bob readily admitted he had fallen behind.

> Fred: *How do you feel about falling behind?*
> Bob: *Well, every time I get rolling I get hit with a schedule change. Sometimes they make sense, sometimes they don't. I'm not always clear about what to do. I didn't want to say much. So I just tried to struggle through on my own.*

In the above exchange, Fred gave Bob a chance to express his feelings without putting him on the defensive. His next step was to try to identify the causes for Bob's substandard performance. To do this, Fred asked in a nonthreatening manner for an explanation.

> Fred: *There certainly have been a lot of schedule changes lately. Which ones are giving you the most problems?*
> Bob: *Mostly the changes with the Series J designs. I'm just not clear on how to handle them.*
> Fred: *Yeah, they can be tricky. Have you asked anyone about them?*
> Bob: *Well, I realize the project manager has a lot on her mind. I just didn't want to bother her with my own problems. And ...*
> Fred: *And?*
> Bob: *Uh ... I just didn't want her to think I couldn't do the job.*

This back-and-forth talk revealed Bob's belief that his performance suffered from unclear schedule changes, something beyond his control. Fred listened to the content of Bob's message and tried to understand his feelings. He also asked Bob to clarify certain points, such as the types of schedule changes he had the most problems with and the reasons why he didn't ask for help. By remaining open-minded and avoiding common attribution errors, Fred learned a lot about the possible causes of Bob's poor performance. In fact, his active listening revealed that Bob feared he would look incompetent if he brought his problems with the design changes to the project manager's attention. Next, Fred provided Bob with some immediate support to reassure him that he was viewed as a capable and trustworthy worker.

> Fred: *You shouldn't worry about it, Bob. She thinks highly of you. In fact, she said having you here is really going to make things a lot easier. And your part of the process really counts. The project manager needs your help to meet the deadlines.*
> Bob: *Well, I thought I could work it out, even if it took extra time.*
> Fred: *I'm sure you could, Bob, with your technical skills. But on this project time counts, and there are other people here to help you when needed. It's important that you understand completely what happens when you don't make your numbers because of confusion over the schedule changes. You slow down the next process, and that compounds the schedule changes down the line. Then our standards fall off, and we risk missing the target dates. So you see, your work directly affects the overall performance of the unit.*
> Bob: *Yes, I can see where it would.*

After reassuring Bob that he was viewed as a highly capable and dependable worker, Fred made sure Bob understood the implications of his substandard work. Fred explained to Bob what happened when he slowed down on the job and stressed that his performance affected the entire project. This reminded Bob that others depended on his work being done well and on time so they could meet their performance objectives. It highlighted not only the significance of his job in general, but also the significance of high performance in that job. From the perspective of House's path-goal theory, Fred clarified the path Bob needed to follow to achieve the desired goal of high performance. But Fred wasn't finished yet.

> Fred: *Bob, before going further, let's review the performance objectives we established for you. They are ... (Fred and Bob review objectives.).*
> Bob: *Yes, Fred, they're clear to me.*
> Fred: *Well look, Bob, the next schedule change you get hit with, I want you to talk to the project manager or to me before it throws you behind. In the meantime, let's discuss ways of dealing with schedule changes for the Series J designs so that you know how to handle them. Then I'm sure your performance will be back up to the standard level where it belongs. Okay?*
> Bob: *Okay, I'll sure feel better when things are back on track.*

During this exchange Fred once again stated Bob's original and still-desired performance objectives. By doing this face-to-face, Fred reinforced the personal dimensions of their relationship, further heightened Bob's commitment to improve, and increased Bob's sense of accountability to Fred. In addition, Fred offered the support necessary for Bob to improve his performance. He urged Bob to ask for help when he ran into problems, something Bob had previously considered an unwelcome intrusion on the project manager. He further suggested that the two of them discuss how to deal with the Series J schedule changes. This was an offer of immediate help for dealing with a perceived job constraint. Finally, Fred expressed confidence that Bob would respond as expected. Bob readily agreed that he would be able to do so.

Following this discussion, Bob probably felt pretty good. Fred then made one more effort to ensure that Bob would get back on and stay on the high-performance track.

> Fred: *I feel real good about our conversation, Bob. You're a capable guy, and I know you'll be right back on top soon. Just to make sure things go okay, though, let's talk again after next week's reports are in. What do you think?*
> Bob: *I'll look forward to it. It'll give us a chance to touch base.*

Fred established an appropriate time frame and standards for evaluating Bob's future performance. By adding this control, he helped ensure that the promised improvements in productivity would become a reality. Bob was assured that Fred was interested in his ongoing performance and that productivity gains would receive attention. He also saw that a failure to obtain the desired results would require an explanation. By formally scheduling further meetings with Bob, Fred assured himself of opportunities to recognize performance improvements. If such improvements did not occur, the meetings would ensure that Bob's marginal performance would receive further attention before too much time had elapsed. At that point Fred could continue the process with Bob or, if he believed the job was a true mismatch, work with Bob to develop an alternative solution. Thus, the stage seemed set once again for Bob to become the high performer everyone expected him to be.

BROAD-BASED HIGH-PERFORMANCE MANAGEMENT

Our continuing example offers managers a starting point for developing personal and situation-specific strategies for dealing with marginal performers. Of course the exact nature of the marginal performance will vary from one person to the next. Our example has dealt with only one type—the capable individual whose work efforts have declined over time. From the individual performance equation, however, we know that marginal performance can arise from a lack of ability, effort, or support, or from some combination of these factors. To deal with the uniqueness of each situation, we suggest asking the diagnostic questions listed in Exhibit 2. The following guidelines also highlight useful actions.

TO MAXIMIZE ABILITY

The manager's task is to achieve and maintain an appropriate match between the capabilities of the marginal performer and the job he or she is asked to do. Depending on the nature of the job and the person, one of several options may be selected. In some cases the individual's abilities can be developed through training; in other cases the job may have to be changed so it better fits the individual; and in still others, individuals may have to be replaced with more capable workers. In all cases a job vacancy must be recognized for what it is—perhaps the manager's greatest opportunity to build high-performance potential into a system by hiring a person whose talents and interests match the job's requirements.

Questions to Ask About Ability

Has the individual performed at a higher level in the past?

Is the performance deficiency total, or is it confined to particular tasks?

How well do the individual's capabilities match the job's selection criteria?

Has the individual been properly trained for current task requirements?

Questions to Ask About Support

Have clear and challenging task goals been set?

Are other employees having difficulty with the same tasks?

Is the job properly designed to achieve a "best fit" with the individual's capabilities?

Do any policies and/or procedures inhibit task performance?

Is the manager providing adequate feedback?

Is the individual being fairly compensated?

Is the work environment comfortable?

Is the manager providing sufficient empathy and emotional support?

Are the individual's co-workers providing sufficient emotional support?

Has the manager actually encouraged high performance?

Questions to Ask About Effort

Does the individual lack enthusiasm for work in general? For the assigned tasks in particular?

Are individuals with similar abilities performing at higher levels?

Has the individual been properly recognized for past accomplishments?

Are rewards and incentives provided on a performance-contingent basis?

Is the individual aware of possible rewards and incentives?

Does the individual have an appropriate role model?

EXHIBIT 2   Questions Managers Can Ask When Dealing with a Marginal Performer

Earlier we noted that repeated exposure to failure and punishment can lead to learned helplessness. Because the ability deficits are more imagined than real, however, individuals suffering from learned helplessness will need help in refocusing their concerns toward other performance factors. Take, for example, the case of a newly appointed manager who inherits a team of marginal performers who had received little or no support from their previous supervisor. To restore their feelings of competence, the manager must first help them understand that any past performance problems were not due to a lack of ability. This is the first step of a "turnaround" strategy.

To Maximize Support

The manager's task here is to (1) help marginal performers secure the resources they need to achieve high levels of job performance and (2) help remove any and all obstacles that inhibit high performance. Success with this factor sometimes requires a dramatic change in the way managers view their responsibilities. Rather than simply being the person who directs and controls the work of others, an effective manager always acts to facilitate their accomplishments. This involves doing much more than telling employees what to do and then following up on them. The truly effective manager creates a supportive work environment by clarifying performance expectations, changing job designs, providing immediate feedback, fostering better interpersonal relations, and eliminating unnecessary rules, procedures, and other job constraints.

Consider again the case of the newly appointed supervisor. Support is an especially critical component of an effort to alleviate learned helplessness. Once marginal performers are convinced through attributional training that they do have the ability required to perform, they must be further persuaded that they will receive the support required to excel. The manager should engage marginal performers in dialogues that identify the types of external support needed to help them apply their abilities to best advantage. Ideally initial task assignments will then be created to produce successful experiences that further bolster employees' newfound self-confidence.

TO MAXIMIZE EFFORT

Basic principles of motivation and positive reinforcement should be applied whenever managers deal with marginal performers. First, the marginal performer should be made aware whenever his or her performance falls below standard. He or she should also be told how substandard performance adversely impacts other workers, subunits, and the organization as a whole. Immediate positive reinforcement should follow performance improvements and all above-standard achievements. Punishment should be avoided. By serving as an enthusiastic role model, a supervisor can further help marginal performers become high achievers.

For the new supervisor dealing with a group of marginal performers, strategies to correct ability and support deficits must be accompanied by assurances that high performance will lead to desired outcomes. The most powerful means of persuasion are successful experiences clearly followed by positive reinforcement—praise, recognition, and other valued rewards. It is also helpful to provide positive role models who obtain desired rewards through skilled utilization and task accomplishment.

Finally, it is important to note that managers' motivational attempts gain leverage from ability and support efforts. The key is what psychologists call the *effectance motive*, a natural motivation that occurs from feelings of self-efficacy. When people feel competent in their work, the argument goes, they can be expected to work harder at it. Competence, in turn, comes from ability and the feeling that one's skills and aptitudes are equal to the tasks at hand. Competence also comes from support and the feeling that one's work environment helps, rather than hinders, task accomplishment.

It is said that the very best motivation is that which comes from within. Thus, managers can gain additional motivational impact by investing in ability and support factors. To the extent that greater perceived ability and support enhance one's sense of competence, internal motivation is a likely consequence. Rather than concentrating only on motivational strategies designed to encourage more work effort externally, managers should make sure they take full advantage of the improved internal motivation that may be derived when ability and support factors are addressed.

A VAST POOL OF RESOURCES

Marginal performers present significant challenges to their managers—but they also represent a vast pool of human resources with the potential to offer major productivity gains to their organizations. To capitalize on this potential, managers must be committed to working with marginal performers to identify the causes of their problems and take positive actions to move them toward greater accomplishments. The individual performance equation can provide managers with the insight they need to tap the true potential of the marginal performer. Specifically, it directs a manager's attention toward three major factors that influence individual performance—the often neglected support factor as well as the more commonly recognized ability and effort factors. Guided by this action framework, managers can take advantage of every interaction and every conversation with marginal performers to pursue their turnaround strategies. In the final analysis, the foundations for high-performance management rest with the managers themselves. To achieve the desired results, managers must:

- **Recognize that marginal performers are potential sources of major productivity gains for organizations**   At the very least, they must be considered just as important as any other human resource within the organization.
- **Recognize the need to implement positive turnaround strategies for dealing with marginal performers**   Systematic and well-considered attention, rather than outright neglect and even punishment, is the order of the day—every day of a manager's workweek.
- **Be ready to accept at least partial responsibility for the fact that a subordinate has become a marginal performer**   Many workers learn to be marginal performers from the way they are treated in the workplace—they don't start out to be that way. Bob, for one, sure didn't.

ACKNOWLEDGMENT

The case setting for this article was developed from a vignette presented in Wilson Learning Corporation's instructional video "Dealing with the Marginal Performer" (*Building Leadership Skills*, New York: Wiley, 1986) and examined in William L. Gardner's accompanying instructor's guide. The initial four dialogues reported here are loosely adapted from the video. We are indebted to Wilson Learning Corporation and John Wiley & Sons for allowing us to build upon this case framework.

CHAPTER 18
PERFORMANCE APPRAISAL

ON THE FOLLY OF REWARDING A, WHILE HOPING FOR B
Steven Kerr

TEAM PERFORMANCE APPRAISAL
Leigh Thompson

Developing employees, reinforcing good performance, providing feedback, and following up on un-acceptable performance are all components of high involvement management and performance appraisal. Leaders and managers usually have the overall responsibility for ensuring that their organization's performance appraisal system accomplishes its purpose. The responsibility for evaluating the performance of subordinates, however, is now more likely to be shared with people throughout the organizational hierarchy. Due to the use of peer evaluations, reverse evaluations (subordinates evaluating bosses), multirater evaluations (by subordinates, colleagues, supervisors, and sometimes customers), companies that are serious about doing appraisals will have had to develop the necessary skill-set in a much larger group of employees.

Leaders and managers need the skills to analyze the impact of their organization's performance appraisal system and avoid the design flaws that Steven Kerr describes in an updated version of his classic article, "On the Folly of Rewarding A, While Hoping for B." Kerr, vice president of corporate management development at GE, contends that many systems foster the wrong behavior by using rewards incorrectly. A failure to understand social reinforcement theory invariably results in dysfunctional behavior at work.

Kerr noted that a common management folly is hoping for teamwork but rewarding individual behavior. In "Team Performance Appraisal," Leigh Thompson, provides the answer to this problem with cogent advice on evaluating and rewarding team performance. Thompson, a management professor and consultant, lists various types of measurement and pay used with teams. She outlines the steps involved in setting up 360-degree feedback programs commonly used with teams. Thompson also warns readers about likely sources of rater and ratee bias in team performance appraisal. This selection is an excerpt from Thompson's book *Making the Team: A Guide for Managers*.

≈⌐

ON THE FOLLY OF REWARDING A, WHILE HOPING FOR B*

Steven Kerr

Whether dealing with monkeys, rats, or human beings, it is hardly controversial to state that most organisms seek information concerning what activities are rewarded, and then seek to do (or at least

*Reprinted with permission from the *Academy of Management Executive 9*, no. 1 (February 1995): 7–14.

pretend to do) those things, often to the virtual exclusion of activities not rewarded. The extent to which this occurs of course will depend on the perceived attractiveness of the rewards offered, but neither operant nor expectancy theorists would quarrel with the essence of this notion.

Nevertheless, numerous examples exist of reward systems that are fouled up in that the types of behavior rewarded are those which the rewarder is trying to discourage, while the behavior desired is not being rewarded at all.

FOULED-UP SYSTEMS

IN POLITICS

Official goals are "purposely vague and general and do not indicate ... the host of decisions that must be made among alternative ways of achieving official goals and the priority of multiple goals ..."[1] They usually may be relied on to offend absolutely no one, and in this sense can be considered high acceptance, low quality goals. An example might be "All Americans are entitled to health care." Operative goals are higher in quality but lower in acceptance, since they specify where the money will come from, and what alternative goals will be ignored.

The American citizenry supposedly wants its candidates for public office to set forth operative goals, making their proposed programs clear, and specifying sources and uses of funds. However, since operative goals are lower in acceptance, and since aspirants to public office need acceptance (from at least 50.1 percent of the people), most politicians prefer to speak only of official goals, at least until after the election. They of course would agree to speak at the operative level if "punished" for not doing so. The electorate could do this by refusing to support candidates who do not speak at the operative level. Instead, however, the American voter typically punishes (withholds support from) candidates who frankly discuss where the money will come from, rewards politicians who speak only of official goals, but hopes that candidates (despite the reward system) will discuss the issues operatively.

IN WAR

If some oversimplification may be permitted, let it be assumed that the primary goal of the organization (Pentagon, Luftwaffe, or whatever) is to win. Let it be assumed further that the primary goal of most individuals on the front lines is to get home alive. Then there appears to be an important conflict in goals—personally rational behavior by those at the bottom will endanger goal attainment by those at the top.

But not necessarily! It depends on how the reward system is set up. The Vietnam war was indeed a study of disobedience and rebellion, with terms such as *fragging* (killing one's own commanding officer) and *search and evade* becoming part of the military vocabulary. The difference in subordinates' acceptance of authority between World War II and Vietnam is reported to be considerable, and veterans of the Second World War were often quoted as being outraged at the mutinous actions of many American soldiers in Vietnam.

Consider, however, some critical differences in the reward system in use during the two conflicts. What did the GI in World War II want? To go home. And when did he get to go home? When the war was won! If he disobeyed the orders to clean out the trenches and take the hills, the war would not be won and he would not go home. Furthermore, what were his chances of attaining his goal (getting home alive) if he obeyed the orders compared to his chances if he did not? What is being suggested is that the rational soldier in World War II, whether patriotic or not, probably found it expedient to obey.

Consider the reward system in use in Vietnam. What did the soldier at the bottom want? To go home. And when did he get to go home? When his tour of duty was over! This was the case whether or not the war was won. Furthermore, concerning the relative chance of getting home alive by obeying orders compared to the chance if they were disobeyed, it is worth noting that a mutineer in Vietnam was far more likely to be assigned rest and rehabilitation (on the assumption that fatigue was the cause) than he was to suffer any negative consequence.

In his description of the "zone of indifference," Barnard stated that "a person can and will accept a communication as authoritative only when ... at the time of his decision, he believes it to be compatible with his personal interests as a whole."[2] In light of the reward system used in Vietnam, wouldn't it have been personally irrational for some orders to have been obeyed? Was not the military implementing a system which rewarded disobedience, while hoping that soldiers (despite the reward system) would obey orders?

In Medicine

Theoretically, physicians can make either of two types of error, and intuitively one seems as bad as the other. Doctors can pronounce patients sick when they are actually well (a type 1 error), thus causing them needless anxiety and expense, curtailment of enjoyable foods and activities, and even physical danger by subjecting them to needless medication and surgery. Alternately, a doctor can label a sick person well (a type 2 error), and thus avoid treating what may be a serious, even fatal ailment. It might he natural to conclude that physicians seek to minimize both types of error.

Such a conclusion would be wrong. It has been estimated that numerous Americans have been afflicted with iatrogenic (physician caused) illnesses.[3] This occurs when the doctor is approached by someone complaining of a few stray symptoms. The doctor classifies and organizes these symptoms, gives them a name, and obligingly tells the patient what further symptoms may be expected. This information often acts as a self-fulfilling prophecy, with the result that from that day on the patient for all practical purposes is sick.

Why does this happen? Why are physicians so reluctant to sustain a type 2 error (pronouncing a sick person well) that they will tolerate many type 1 errors? Again, a look at the reward system is needed. The punishments for a type 1 error are real: guilt, embarrassment, and the threat of a malpractice suit. On the other hand, a type 1 error (labeling a well person sick) is a much safer and conservative approach to medicine in today's litigious society. Type 1 errors also are likely to generate increased income and a stream of steady customers who, being well in a limited physiological sense, will not embarrass the doctor by dying abruptly. Fellow physicians and the general public therefore are really rewarding type 1 errors while hoping fervently that doctors will try not to make them.

A current example of rewarding type 1 errors is provided by Broward County, Florida, where an elderly or disabled person facing a competency hearing is evaluated by three court-appointed experts who get paid much more *for the same examination* if the person is ruled to be incompetent. For example, psychiatrists are paid $325 if they judge someone to be incapacitated, but earn only $125 if the person is judged competent. Court-appointed attorneys in Broward also earn more—$325 as opposed to $175—if their clients lose than if they win. Are you surprised to learn that, of 598 incapacity proceedings initiated and completed in the county in 1993, 570 ended with a verdict of incapacitation?[4]

In Universities

Society hopes that professors will not neglect their teaching responsibilities but rewards them almost entirely for research and publications. This is most true at the large and prestigious universities. Clichés such as "good research and good teaching go together" notwithstanding, professors often find that they must choose between teaching and research-oriented activities when allocating their time. Rewards for good teaching are usually limited to outstanding teacher awards, which are given to only a small percentage of good teachers and usually bestow little money and fleeting prestige. Punishments for poor teaching are also rare.

Rewards for research and publications, on the other hand, and punishments for failure to accomplish these, are common. Furthermore, publication-oriented résumés usually will be well-received at other universities, whereas teaching credentials, harder to document and quantify, are much less transferable. Consequently it is rational for university professors to concentrate on research, even to the detriment of teaching and at the expense of their students.

By the same token, it is rational for students to act based upon the goal displacement[5] which has occurred within universities concerning what they are rewarded for. If it is assumed that a primary goal of a university is to transfer knowledge from teacher to student, then grades become identifiable as a means toward that goal, serving as motivational, control, and feedback devices to expedite the knowledge transfer. Instead, however, the grades themselves have become much more important for entrance to graduate school, successful employment, tuition refunds, and parental respect, than the knowledge or lack of knowledge they are supposed to signify.

It therefore should come as no surprise that we find fraternity files for examinations, term paper writing services, and plagiarism. Such activities constitute a personally rational response to a reward system which pays off for grades rather than knowledge. These days, reward systems—specifically, the growing threat of lawsuits—encourage teachers to award students high grades, even if they aren't earned. For example:

> *When Andy Hansen brought home a report card with a disappointing C in math, his parents ... sued his teacher .... After a year and six different appeals within the school district, another year's worth of court proceedings, $4,000 in legal fees paid by the Hansens, and another $8,500 by the district ... the C stands. Now the student's father, auto dealer Mike Hansen, says he plans to take the case to the State Court of Appeals We went in and tried to make a deal: They wanted a C, we wanted an A, so why not compromise on a B?" Mike Hansen said. "But they dug in their heels, and here we are."[6]*

In Consulting

It is axiomatic that those who care about a firm's well-being should insist that the organization get fair value for its expenditures. Yet it is commonly known that firms seldom bother to evaluate a new TQM, employee empowerment program, or whatever, to see if the company is getting its money's worth. Why? Certainly it is not because people have not pointed out that this situation exists; numerous practitioner-oriented articles are written each year on just this point.

One major reason is that the individuals (in human resources, or organization development) who would normally be responsible for conducting such evaluations are the same ones often charged with introducing the change effort in the first place. Having convinced top management to spend money, say, on outside consultants, they usually are quite animated afterwards in collecting rigorous vignettes and anecdotes about how successful the program was. The last thing many desire is a formal, revealing evaluation. Although members of top management may actually hope for such systematic evaluation, their reward systems continue to reward ignorance in this area. And if the HR department abdicates its responsibility, who is to step into the breach? The consultants themselves? Hardly! They are likely to be too busy collecting anecdotal "evidence" of their own, for use on their next client.

In Sports

Most coaches disdain to discuss individual accomplishments, preferring to speak of teamwork, proper attitude, and one-for-all spirit. Usually, however, rewards are distributed according to individual performance. The college basketball player who passes the ball to teammates instead of shooting will not compile impressive scoring statistics and is less likely to be drafted by the pros. The ballplayer who hits to right field to advance the runners will win neither the batting nor home run titles, and will be offered smaller raises. It therefore is rational for players to think of themselves first, and the team second.

In Government

Consider the cost-plus contract or its next of kin, the allocation of next year's budget as a direct function of this year's expenditures—a clear-cut example of a fouled up reward system. It probably is conceivable that those who award such budgets and contracts really hope for economy and prudence in spending. It is obvious, however, that adopting the proverb "to those who spend shall more be given," rewards not economy, but spending itself.

In Business

The past reward practices of a group health claims division of a large eastern insurance company provides another rich illustration. Attempting to measure and reward accuracy in paying surgical claims, the firm systematically kept track of the number of returned checks and letters of complaint received from policyholders. However, underpayments were likely to provoke cries of outrage from the insured, while overpayments often were accepted in courteous silence. Since it was often impossible to tell from the physician's statement which of two surgical procedures, with different allowable benefits, was performed, and since writing for clarifications would have interfered with other standards used by the firm concerning percentage of claims paid within two days of receipt, the new hire in more than one claims section was soon acquainted with the informal norm: "When in doubt, pay it out!"

This situation was made even worse by the firm's reward system. The reward system called for annual merit increases to be given to all employees, in one of the following three amounts:

1. If the worker was "outstanding" (a select category, into which no more than two employees per section could be placed): 5 percent
2. If the worker was "above average" (normally all workers not "outstanding" were so rated): 4 percent
3. If the worker committed gross acts of negligence and irresponsibility for which he or she might be discharged in many other companies: 3 percent

Now, since the difference between the five percent theoretically attainable through hard work and the four percent attainable merely by living until the review date is small, many employees were rather indifferent to the possibility of obtaining the extra one percent reward. In addition, since the penalty for error was a loss of only one percent, employees tended to ignore the norm concerning indiscriminant payments.

However, most employees were not indifferent to a rule which stated that, should absences or latenesses total three or more in any six-month period, the entire four or five percent due at the next merit review must be forfeited. In this sense, the firm was *hoping* for performance, while *rewarding* attendance. What it got, of course, was attendance. (If the absence/lateness rule appears to the reader to be stringent, it really wasn't. The company counted "times" rather than "days" absent, and a ten-day absence therefore counted the same as one lasting two days. A worker in danger of accumulating a third absence within six months merely had to remain ill—away from work—during a second absence until the first absence was more than six months old. The limiting factor was that at some point salary ceases, and sickness benefits take over. This was usually sufficient to get the younger workers to return, but for those with 20 or more years' service, the company provided sickness benefits of 90 percent of normal salary, tax-free! Therefore . . . .).

Thanks to the U.S. government, even the reporting of wrongdoing has been corrupted by an incredibly incompetent reward system that calls for whistleblowing employees to collect up to 30 percent

TABLE 1   Common Management Reward Follies

We hope for ...	But we often reward ...
• Long-term growth; environmental responsibility	• Quarterly earnings
• Teamwork	• Individual effort
• Setting challenging "stretch" objectives	• Achieving goals; "making the numbers"
• Downsizing; rightsizing; delayering; restructuring	• Adding staff; adding budget; adding Hay points
• Commitment to total quality	• Shipping on schedule, even with defects
• Candor; surfacing bad news early	• Reporting good news, whether it's true or not; agreeing with the boss, whether or not (s)he's right

of the amount of a fraud without a stated limit. Thus prospective whistleblowers are encouraged to delay reporting a fraud, even to actively participate in its continuance, in order to run up the total and, thus, their percentage of the take.

I'm quite sure that by now the reader has thought of numerous examples in his or her own experience which qualify as "folly." However, just in case, Table 1 presents some additional examples well worth pondering.

CAUSES

Extremely diverse instances of systems which reward behavior A although the rewarder apparently hopes for behavior B have been given. These are useful to illustrate the breadth and magnitude of the phenomenon, but the diversity increases the difficulty of determining commonalities and establishing causes. However, the following four general factors may be pertinent to an explanation of why fouled-up reward systems seem to be so prevalent.

1. **Fascination with an "Objective" Criterion**   Many managers seek to establish simple, quantifiable standards against which to measure and reward performance. Such efforts may be successful in highly predictable areas within an organization, but are likely to cause goal displacement when applied anywhere else.

2. **Overemphasis on Highly Visible Behaviors**   Difficulties often stem from the fact that some parts of the task are highly visible while other parts are not. For example, publications are easier to demonstrate than teaching, and scoring baskets and hitting home runs are more readily observable than feeding teammates and advancing base runners. Similarly, the adverse consequences of pronouncing a sick person well are more visible than those sustained by labeling a well person sick. Team-building and creativity are other examples of behaviors which may not be rewarded simply because they are hard to observe.

3. **Hypocrisy**   In some of the instances described the rewarder may have been getting the desired behavior, notwithstanding claims that the behavior was not desired. For example, in many jurisdictions within the United States, judges' campaigns are funded largely by defense attorneys, while prosecutors are legally barred from making contributions. This doesn't do a whole lot to help judges to be "tough on crime" though, ironically, that's what their campaigns inevitably promise.

4. **Emphasis on Morality or Equity Rather than Efficiency**   Sometimes consideration of other factors prevents the establishment of a system which rewards behavior desired by the rewarder. The felt obligation of many Americans to vote for one candidate or another, for example, may impair their ability to withhold support from politicians who refuse to discuss the issues. Similarly,

the concern for spreading the risks and costs of wartime military service may outweigh the advantage to be obtained by committing personnel to combat until the war is over. The 1994 Clinton health plan, the Americans with Disabilities Act, and many other instances of proposed or recent governmental intervention provide outstanding examples of systems that reward inefficiency, presumably in support of some higher objective.

ALTERING THE REWARD SYSTEM

Managers who complain about lack of motivation in their workers might do well to consider the possibility that the reward systems they have installed are paying off for behavior other than what they are seeking. This, in part, is what happened in Vietnam, and this is what regularly frustrates societal efforts to bring about honest politicians and civic-minded managers.

A first step for such managers might be to explore what types of behavior are currently being rewarded. Chances are excellent that these managers will be surprised by what they find—that their firms are not rewarding what they assume they are. In fact, such undesirable behavior by organizational members as they have observed may be explained largely by the reward systems in use.

This is not to say that all organizational behavior is determined by formal rewards and punishments. Certainly it is true that in the absence of formal reinforcement some soldiers will be patriotic, some players will be team oriented, and some employees will care about doing their job well. The point, however, is that in such cases the rewarder is not causing the behavior desired but is only a fortunate bystander. For an organization to act upon its members, the formal reward system should positively reinforce desired behavior, not constitute an obstacle to be overcome.

POSTSCRIPT

An irony about this article's being designated a management classic is that numerous people claim to have read and enjoyed it, but I wonder whether there was much in it that they didn't know. I believe that most readers already knew, and act on in their non-work lives, the principles that underlie this article. For example, when we tell our daughter (who is about to cut her birthday cake) that her brother will select the first piece, or inform our friends before a meal that separate checks will be brought at the end, or tell the neighbor's boy that he will be paid five dollars for cutting the lawn after we inspect the lawn, we are making use of prospective rewards and punishments to cause other people to care about our own objectives. Organizational life may seem to be more complex, but the principles are the same.

Another irony attached to this "classic" is that it almost didn't see the light of day. It was rejected for presentation at the Eastern Academy of Management and was only published in the *Academy of Management Journal* because Jack Miner, its editor at the time, broke a tie between two reviewers. Nobody denied the relevance of the content, but reviewers were quite disturbed by the tone of the manuscript, and therefore its appropriateness for an academic audience. A compromise was reached whereby I added a bit of the great academic cure-all, data (Table 1 in the original article, condensed and summarized in this update), and a copy editor strangled some of the life from my writing style. In this respect, I would like to acknowledge the extremely competent editorial work performed on this update by John Veiga and his editorial staff. I am grateful to have had the opportunity to revisit the article, and hope the reader has enjoyed it also.

ENDNOTES

[1] C. Perrow, "The Analysis of Goals in Complex Organizations," *Readings on Modern Organizations*, ed. A. Etzioni (Upper Saddle River, NJ: Prentice Hall, 1969) 66.

[2] C. I. Barnard, *The Functions of the Executive* (Cambridge, MA: Harvard University Press, 1964) 165.

[3] L. H. Garland, "Studies of the Accuracy of Diagnostic Procedures," *American Journal Roentgenological, Radium Therapy Nuclear Medicine 82* (1959): 25–38; and T. J. Scheff, "Decision Rules, Types of Error, and Their Consequences in Medical Diagnosis," *Mathematical Explorations in Behavioral Science*, eds. F. Massarik and P. Ratoosh (Homewood, IL: Irwin, 1965).

[4] *Miami Herald*, May 8, 1994, 1a, 10a.

[5] Goal displacement results when means become ends in themselves and displace the original goals. See P. M. Blau and W. R. Scott, *Formal Organizations* (San Francisco, CA: Chandler, 1962).

[6] "San Francisco Examiner," reported in *Fortune*, February 7, 1994, 161.

TEAM PERFORMANCE APPRAISAL*

Leigh Thompson

Individual performance appraisal is an evaluation of a person's behaviors and accomplishments in terms of the person's work in an organization. Performance appraisals are a source of feedback, a basis for personal development, and a determination of pay. The rise of teams presents special challenges for performance appraisal. It is difficult for a supervisor to conduct a traditional performance appraisal of an individual who is serving at least part time on a team. When the individual is part of a self-managed, self-directing, self-governing team, it is virtually impossible because supervisors are rarely close enough to the teams to evaluate them. The catch-22 is that if they were, they might hinder the performance of the team. Here, we deal with the question of exactly how performance should be measured and by whom.

WHAT IS MEASURED?

A change in traditional performance appraisals, precipitated by the rise of teams, concerns what is measured in performance reviews. In many traditional control-oriented organizations, the major determinant of employees' pay is the type of work they do or their seniority. The major alternative is competency-based pay. Companies are increasingly recognizing that dynamic factors, such as competencies and skills, may be a better way to measure success than static measures, such as experience and education. In the following paragraphs, we review job-based pay, skill-based pay, and competency-based pay.

JOB-BASED PAY

Job-based pay is determined by a job evaluation system, which frequently takes a point factor approach to evaluating jobs (Lawler, 1990b). The point factor approach begins with a written job description that is scored in terms of duties. The point scores are then translated into salary levels. A key advantage of job-based pay systems is that organizations can determine what other companies are paying and can assess whether they are paying more or less than their competitors. Another advantage of job evaluation systems is that they allow for centralized control of an organization's pay system.

SKILL-BASED PAY

To design a skill-based pay system, a company must identify those tasks that need to be performed in the organization. Next, the organization identifies skills that are needed to perform the tasks and develops tests or measures to determine whether a person has learned these skills. For this reason, it is

---

*Excerpted with permission from *Making the Team: A Guide for Managers* (Upper Saddle River, NJ: Prentice Hall, 2000): 43–58.

important to specify the skills that an individual can learn in a company. Employees need to be told what they can learn given their position in the organization and how learning skills will affect their pay. People are typically paid only for those skills that they currently can and are willing to perform. Many skill-based plans give people pay increases when they learn a new skill. One system of skill-based pay is a technical ladder, in which individuals are paid for the depth of skill they have in a particular technical specialty. Procter & Gamble started using skill-based pay in the late 1960s to support the development of work teams. In the P&G system, production employees are paid for horizontal skills and, in some cases, upwardly vertical skills. In a few cases, they are also paid for learning downwardly vertical skills, such as cleaning and routine production tasks. (For an example of how one skill-based pay plan failed to work, see "When Skill Based Pay Doesn't Work.")

WHEN SKILL-BASED PAY DOESN'T WORK

John Powenski, the HR manager at Frito Lay in Kirkwood, New York, helped to orchestrate a performance and productivity improvement at the 800-employee facility, with initially strong results. A Leadership Team, composed of manufacturing, distribution, planning, technical, and HR managers, challenged the plant to become more customer-focused, team-based, and owner-driven. Teams trained together, met to discuss production plans, and give each other 360-degree feedback. However, "All hell broke loose when we linked pay to performance," Powenski says. It was a radical departure, and employees had not been included in development of the new compensation structure. "They didn't like a peer affecting their pay and had concerns about the integrity of the whole system," Powenski notes. "We had not included the technicians in the pay restructuring, and that was a big mistake." Recognizing that the change had not been accepted, the Leadership Team returned to the previous system (Novak, 1997).

COMPETENCY-BASED PAY

Competency-based pay differs from skill-based pay in that employees prove they can use their skills. After all, it is possible for people to attain skills (e.g., training and mentoring programs) but never use them—or be ineffective when using them. For example, Volvo gives every employee in a work area a pay increase when the employees in that area prove they can operate without a supervisor (Lawler, 1992). It is important for organizations to focus on demonstrated competencies, rather than accumulated accreditations.

Competency-based pay is regarded as a much more sensible and ultimately profitable approach to use in a team-based organization. First, competency-based pay systems promote flexibility in employees: When employees can perform multiple tasks, organizations gain tremendous flexibility in using their workforce. This, of course, is the concept of cross-training. In addition to the benefits of cross-training, individuals who have several skills have an advantage in terms of developing an accurate perspective on organizational problems and challenges. When employees have an overview of the entire company, they are more committed. When they are broadly knowledgeable about the operations of an organization, they can increase their self-managing, coordinate with others, utilize organizational resources, and communicate more effectively.

However, competency-based pay systems are not perfect. An organization using a competency-based pay system typically commits to giving everyone the opportunity to learn multiple skills and then to demonstrate them; thus, the organization has to make a large investment in training and evaluation. There is a trade-off between getting the work done and skill acquisition and demonstration.

WHO DOES THE MEASURING?

The standard is the employee's supervisor, or some set of top-level persons. With the increasing use of teams, peer review is becoming more common and more necessary in organizations. Popularly known as *360-degree* or *multirater feedback* methods, the peer review procedure involves getting feedback about an employee from all sides: Top (supervisors), bottom (subordinates), coworkers, suppliers, and end-user customers or clients (see Figure 1). Typically, several people (ideally 5 to 10) participate in the evaluation, compared with a traditional review where only one person, usually a supervisor, provides feedback. Anonymity is the key to building a nonbiased feedback system, especially for peers and subordinates. Otherwise, the entire system is compromised. General Electric's CEO, Jack Welch, explains how his company does it: "Every employee is graded on a 1-5 scale by his manager, his peers, and all his subordinates in areas such as team-building, quality focus, and vision. Some people think it's bureaucratic. But it embodies our values (which come out of years of discussions with employees). And the subordinates clearly provide the best input. Peers are a little more careful, and the boss is always a little more cautious" (Hillkirk, 1993, p. 5B).

A big disadvantage of the top-down performance review is evaluation bias. The multiple data points and aggregate responses provided by 360-degree feedback make the bias of a single person less of a problem.

A second major disadvantage e of single-source evaluation is that it is easy to dismiss the information. "If my boss tells me something, I can easily ignore it," says Mark Edwards of Teams, Inc. With multiple sources, the information becomes more credible and is more difficult to discount. As Jarman (1998) puts it, "If in the course of a day you meet a disagreeable person, chances are you've met a disagreeable person. But if in the course of a day you meet five disagreeable people, chances are you're the disagreeable person" (p. D1).

As an example of how companies put 360-degree feedback in place, consider the Long Term Credit Bank of Japan, or LTCB, which bases its annual bonuses for managers in part on evaluations by their subordinates. LTCB, which previously adopted a skill-based pay system, is trying to increase the transparency of its performance evaluation methods by inviting the rank and file to grade bosses.

FIGURE 1   360-Degree Multirater Feedback

In the system, managers select a group of up to 20 subordinates, colleagues, and supervisors to grade their job performance. Of the group, as many as nine employees, including two or three who work directly under the manager, evaluate their boss. Managerial employees receive a monthly base pay plus two bonuses; over 30 percent of their bonus is based on the evaluations (Dow Jones News Service, April 14, 1998).

At Phelps Dodge, 360-degree evaluations were first administered to the company's top 180 executives worldwide, including Chairperson Douglas Yearley. The company developed a set of core competencies, such as demonstrating sound business judgment, driving for results, fostering teamwork, and creating an ownership philosophy among employees, and evaluated executives on these dimensions. Because the core competencies used to evaluate employees are part of the company's or department's mission statement, the 360-degree process helps bring performance of individual employees in line with company goals and values. In fact, companies beginning to develop 360-degree evaluations are encouraged to start with their mission statement.

In theory, the 360-degree process provides a multifaceted view of the team member. However, putting it into practice can be difficult: If the number of feedback sources is limited, raters are not guaranteed anonymity and may fear retaliation. The system is subject to abuse if members make side deals to rate one another favorably. Many people going into it are against the idea, and it takes time to make several evaluations!

However, despite its difficulties, 360-degree or multirater feedback is usually regarded to be a more fair assessment of performance than is top-down review (for an argument of how information systems [IS] can benefit from 360-degree feedback, see "Why Information Systems [IS] Need 360s"). Although team members are often best qualified to rate each other, there are some weaknesses to this approach. Team members unpopular for reasons other than performance can suffer. Team members do not always grasp the big picture in terms of organizational goals. As raters, peers can suffer from evaluation biases.

WHY INFORMATION SYSTEMS (IS) NEED 360S

Michael Schrage jokes that "whenever managers talk about 360-degree job reviews, I think of that joke about the nattering egomaniac at the cocktail party: But enough about me; let's talk about you. What do you think about me?" (Schrage, 1998, p. 33).

Schrage quite seriously goes on to argue that the key reason why IS should passionately embrace 360s is that these reviews represent the best way to promote better communication of expectations. Basically, 360s force technical people and businesspeople to communicate about something other than the tasks, specs, and deadlines at hand. Properly managed, 360s hold the promise of creating new networks of interactions around the challenge of creating productive relationships.

DEVELOPING A 360-DEGREE PROGRAM

It is impossible to develop a 360-degree evaluation program overnight. Most teams are not ready to base all of their pay on multisource performance management, especially when teams are relatively new. Most teams are hesitant to have all of their pay tied to team member evaluations; at the same time, they scoff at individual pay performance systems. The key is to set up a system of feedback that is anonymous and private and slowly build into an open feedback, public knowledge system. Often, team members will let companies know when they are ready to have pay based on their individual performance as evaluated by relevant others.

There is no standard method for 360-degree implementation. Some companies administer and develop the whole system. Some allow outside consultants to prepare and analyze feedback to ensure anonymity. For example, Groupe Schneider, an international firm, invites its managers to participate in 360-degree evaluations by choosing nine people to provide confidential evaluations. The entire evaluation is carried out by an outside consulting firm that collects and prepares all of the results, which are completely confidential. Often, the survey used to evaluate employees is developed by a cross-sectional team of company employees. In addition to specifying evaluation criteria, the group also determines the makeup of the evaluation teams and how they will be selected. This team also makes decisions on who will get to see the results of the evaluations and devises a follow-up program to ensure that employees take action on the feedback they receive.

As a start for developing 360-degree evaluation systems, consider the steps outlined in Box 1 (see Milliman et al., 1994; Hoffman, 1995).

BOX 1

THINGS TO THINK ABOUT BEFORE DEVELOPING A 360-DEGREE PROGRAM IN YOUR COMPANY

Companies should ask themselves the following questions before undertaking 360-degree evaluation programs (Hoffman, 1995; Milliman, Zawacki, Powell, and Kirksey, 1994):

- Should only the 360-degree feedback be used or should the process be combined with other appraisal systems?
- Should an outside consultant be used?
- Can a program be purchased off the shelf or should the process be customized for the organization?
- Is a computer-based or paper and pencil form best for the organization?
- How many raters should be used? (The ideal is 5 to 10; fewer than 5 limits perspectives; more than 10 makes the system too complex and time-consuming.)
- Who should do the rating?
- Who selects the raters?
- How does the organization define *peer, internal customer, supervisor, subordinate,* and so on?
- How many questions/items should be included on the form?
- Should the feedback be anonymous?
- How should employees be trained on giving and receiving constructive feedback and the nature of 360-degree feedback?

The answers to the questions in Box 1 will be different for every organization. Duplicating systems used by world-class companies is not necessarily the best approach. Each organization should develop the 360-degree system that will optimize effectiveness within its organizational design. Companies should first use a test 360-degree program that is not tied to compensation and is not public. In the beginning stages, only the employee sees all of the feedback; gradually, the supervisor is brought into the loop. Eventually, it is important to tie employee compensation to the 360-degree evaluation. Yet there is considerable variation on this. For example, at Phelps Dodge, 360-degree feedback is used as a development and training tool and not the basis for performance evaluation and pay. In contrast, Farm

Credit uses 360-degree reviews to evaluate the performances of its 68 employees and determine their compensation levels.

At Johnson & Johnson Advanced Behavioral Technology, which has many teams but still retains traditional hierarchical reporting relationships, ratees develop a list of key internal and external customers with whom they interact and then recommend 5 to 10 people to serve as raters. The supervisor has the ultimate responsibility for the appraisal. In contrast, at Digital Equipment, the ratee has the primary responsibility for selecting the raters. The Digital ratee works with the team leader to select a panel consisting of a coach and three other employees to be objective advocates. Raters are then selected at random from the ratee's team by a computer-generated system and notified by e-mail to participate in the appraisal. The random system ensures that a fair distribution of raters is created.

As companies begin to challenge old assumptions about performance appraisals, they need to be careful not to cross the line of legal liability (see Box 2). If people other than management are involved in the appraisal process, then they must be trained on the legal issues involved with discrimination law, the Americans with Disabilities Act, and other relevant legislation. Stated more eloquently:

> *The use of multiple raters is becoming more popular as many firms move toward team-based management systems. Use of multiple raters reduces the influence of idiosyncratic rating policies on personnel decisions. However, sharing ratings to arrive at a consensus is not an acceptable way of offsetting the bias of a single rater* (Loiseau v. Department of Human Resources, *1983). An important caution in the use of multiple raters as illustrated in the Hopkins case, is that illegal bias on the part of one or two raters can taint the entire process with legal discrimination. (Austin, Villanova, & Hindman, 1996, p. 283; reference to* Price Waterhouse v. Hopkins, *1989, which involved gender bias in a consensus promotion decision made by PW partners)*

BOX 2

PRESCRIPTIONS FOR LEGALLY DEFENSIBLE APPRAISAL SYSTEMS (ADAPTED FROM BERNARDIN & CASCIO, 1988)

1. Job analysis to identify important duties and tasks should precede development of a performance appraisal system.
2. The performance appraisal system should be standardized and formal.
3. Specific performance standards should be communicated to employees in advance of the appraisal period.
4. Objectives and uncontaminated data should be used whenever possible.
5. Ratings on traits such as dependability, drive, or attitude should be avoided.
6. Employees should be evaluated on specific work dimensions rather than on a single, global, or overall measure.
7. If work behaviors rather than outcomes are to be evaluated, evaluators should have ample opportunity to observe ratee performance.
8. To increase the reliability of ratings, more than one independent evaluator should be used whenever possible.
9. Behavioral documentation should be prepared for ratings.
10. Employees should be given an opportunity to review their appraisals.
11. A formal system of appeal should be available for appraisal disagreements.
12. Raters should be trained to prevent discrimination and to evaluate performance consistently.
13. Appraisals should be frequent, offered at least annually.

SOURCES OF RATER BIAS

Peers are often best qualified to evaluate a team member's performance. Lots of empirical research indicates that peer assessment is a valid and reliable evaluation procedure (Huber, Neale, and Northcraft, 1987). In addition, the team's supervisor and the team's customers or clients (either internal or external, if available) are also valuable sources of input. These information sources are valuable, but can also be biased. Raters are not perfect; below we discuss several serious sources of bias that can threaten the quality of peer evaluation.

EXTRINSIC INCENTIVES BIAS

Most managers believe that employees are primarily motivated by extrinsic incentives (e.g., job security and pay) and less motivated by intrinsic incentives (e.g., learning new things). For example, Douglas McGregor (1960) explicitly acknowledged this tendency when he described a social fault line between managers who inferred motivations incorrectly and those who inferred them correctly. He bemoaned the commonness of Theory X managers (who believe that employees dislike work, wish to avoid responsibility, and desire security above all) and the scarcity of Theory Y managers (who believe that employees like work, wish to develop their skills, and desire to participate in tasks that advance worthy organizational goals). Consider a survey of 486 prospective lawyers, who were questioned by Kaplan Educational Centers during a preparation course for the Law School Admissions Test (Lawler, Mohrman, and Ledford, 1995). The prospective lawyers were asked to describe their own motivations for pursuing a legal career and then those of their peers. Although 64 percent said that they were pursuing a legal career because it was intellectually appealing or because they had always been interested in the law, only 12 percent thought this about their peers. Instead, 62 percent thought that their peers were pursuing a legal career because of the financial rewards. Indeed, most of us have claimed that "they're only in it for the money" many more times than we have claimed "I'm only in it for the money" (Heath, 1998).

According to Frederick Taylor, "What workers want most from their employers beyond anything else is high wages" (Taylor, 1911). In contrast, McGregor (1960) and other members of the human relations school of management argued that intrinsic features motivated employees.

The extrinsic incentives bias states that people believe that others are more motivated than themselves by motivations that are situational or extrinsic, and less motivated than themselves by motivations that are dispositional or intrinsic (Heath, 1998). For example, in one survey, 74 MBA students ranked the importance of eight different motivations (benefits, pay, job security, learning new skills, praise from manager, developing skills, accomplishing something worthwhile, and feeling good about oneself) for themselves and predicted the rank order that would be provided by their classmates and by actual managers and employees (customer service representatives at Citibank; Heath, 1998). The MBA students overestimated how highly the Citibank managers would rank extrinsic incentives: They predicted that the top four incentives would be primarily extrinsic (pay, security, benefits, and praise); however, the actual Citibank employees listed only one extrinsic incentive in their top four (benefits).

If managers falsely assume that others' motives are less noble than their own, then they may fail to communicate the importance and relevance of the organization's goals (Bennis and Nanus, 1985). Corporate managers may spend too little time highlighting the satisfaction of solving customer problems; nonprofit managers may spend more time describing the joys of charity balls than the pleasures of community service. When managers fall prey to the extrinsic incentives bias, they may overlook the importance of feedback, neglect opportunities to make jobs more interesting, and underestimate the employee's desire to participate in team and organizational decisions. Managers could substantially improve their ability to understand the motivations of others if they would assume that others are motivated exactly as they are (Heath, 1998).

People work hard for a lot of different reasons. It is a mistake to think that the only thing that drives performance is monetary incentives and that people hoard effort until incentives justify greater contributions. Many managers incorrectly believe that people are primarily motivated by monetary reward. However, they view themselves as having loftier reasons. For example, most people overestimate the impact that financial reward exerts on their peers' willingness to donate blood (Miller and Ratner, 1998).

In sum, evolutionary biology, neoclassical economics, behaviorism, and psychoanalytic theory all assume that people actively and single-mindedly pursue their self-interest (Schwartz, 1986). However, organizational science research tells a different story: People often care more about the fairness of procedures they are subjected to than the material outcomes these procedures yield (Tyler, 1990); they often care more about a group's collective outcomes than about their personal outcomes (Dawes, Orbell, and van de Kragt, 1988); and their attitudes toward public policies are often shaped more by values and ideologies than the impact they have on material well-being (Sears and Funk, 1990, 1991).

HOMOGENEITY BIAS

Generally, appraisers rate appraisees who are similar to themselves more favorably than those who are different from them. This means that in general, white male superiors tend to favor white male subordinates over females and minority supervisees (cf. Kraiger and Ford, 1985).

HALO BIAS

Once we know one positive (or negative) fact about someone, we tend to perceive all other information we learn about them in line with our initial perceptions. This has several serious implications, the most obvious of which is the fact that physically attractive people are evaluated more positively than are less attractive people—even when holding constant their skills and competencies.

FUNDAMENTAL ATTRIBUTION ERROR

We tend to perceive people's behaviors as reflecting their personality rather than temporary, situational factors. This can obviously be a good thing for someone who seems to be doing well, but very problematic for a person who seems to be performing under par.

COMMUNICATION MEDIUM

Performance appraisers give poor performers substantially higher ratings when they have to give face-to-face feedback as opposed to anonymous written feedback.

EXPERIENCE EFFECT

Experienced appraisers tend to render higher quality appraisals. Thus, training and practice can reduce error in ratings (Klimoski and Inks, 1990).

RECIPROCITY BIAS

People feel a strong social obligation to return favors. Thus, a potential flaw of 360-degree programs is that they are subject to collusion: "I'll give you a good rating if you give me one." Providing for anonymous rating may reduce both biases. However, this is difficult to achieve when team size is relatively small.

BANDWAGON BIAS

People want to "jump on the bandwagon," meaning that they will want to hold the same opinion of someone as does the rest of the group.

PRIMACY AND RECENCY BIAS

People tend to be overly affected by their first impression of someone (primacy) or their most recent interaction with this person (recency).

There is no simple solution to overcoming these biases. Awareness is an important first step. We suggest that everyone in the business of providing performance evaluations be made aware of these biases. Employees in companies probably do receive some form of training on conducting performance appraisals, but hardly anyone receives training on the biases that afflict ratings. As a second step, we suggest that only objective behavior and productivity measures be used—they are less susceptible to biases than are judgment traits and attitudes. As a rule of thumb—if you can't observe it directly, then don't measure it.

SOURCES OF RATEE BIAS

In addition to the rater biases discussed earlier, the quality of a 360-degree process can be compromised by the ratees themselves. Although countless articles and books have dealt with sources of rater bias, virtually no attention has been paid to bias on the part of ratees—as if feedback, once delivered, is perfectly received by the recipient. In fact, that is not the case. The more managers know about ratee bias, the better able they will be to anticipate the impact of a performance review on the employee.

EGOCENTRIC BIAS

Most people feel underrecognized for the work they do and the value they bring to their company. This feeling is largely attributable to the human cognitive system, which is primarity egocentric in nature. In short, people give themselves greater credit than do others. This means that in a typical 360-degree evaluation, no matter how positive it may be, people will feel that they are underappreciated by others. There is no perfect solution to dealing with this. Our suggestion is that the supervisor (or person providing the feedback) should present as many facts as possible to justify the ratings and feedback.

It is important to focus on behaviors rather than attitudes when assessing others because it is more difficult to misinterpret objective information (e.g., "you've been late 18 out of the last 20 days").

INTRINSIC INTEREST

As we noted earlier, people are strongly motivated by intrinsic interest, rather than extrinsic rewards. However, this is not to say that people don't care about extrinsic rewards. Furthermore, this does not mean that intrinsic interest will always flourish. In fact, even positive feedback, if not carefully administered, may undermine intrinsic interest (Freedman, Cunningham, and Krismer, 1992). That is, employees may do something for purely intrinsic reasons, such as the joy of learning new things or expressing themselves; however, if a supervisor or a person of obvious importance praises the work and administers large extrinsic rewards for the work, this may lead the employees to believe that they are doing the work for the money (or other extrinsic rewards). In some cases, external reward may undermine intrinsic interest. For example, Kohn (1993) argues that incentive or pay-for-performance systems tend to make people less enthusiastic about their work.

We are not suggesting that companies should never offer extrinsic (e.g., pay-based) rewards to their employees. Rather, the manager should emphasize, when providing the reward, what is valued about the work and how the company views the employee. The research evidence supports this: When high effort is rewarded, people are more industrious. Just as people can be reinforced for working hard, they can be reinforced for creativity (Eisenberger and Selbst, 1994). Thus, for fabulous work effort, a supervisor or company may give the team a special cash reward or noncash recognition and clearly communicate to the team that the company values their inspiring motivation, creativity, and attention to detail. It is important to clearly indicate what is being rewarded.

SOCIAL COMPARISON

People have a basic drive to compare themselves with others. This is why students feel less value in receiving an A if they find out that everyone has received an A. Thus, supervisors must anticipate that team members will talk and compare notes, one way or another, about the feedback they receive. It is often these comparisons that drive how employees interpret feedback.

Supervisors should anticipate that social comparison will occur, and be frank about feedback to employees and team members. For example, it would be wrong to imply that an employee was the only stellar performer if, in fact, over 60 percent performed at the same level. (For this reason, it may be useful to provide information about averages and standard deviations to employees.)

FAIRNESS

People evaluate the quality of their organizational experiences by how fair they regard them to be. Whether the ultimate outcome is positive or negative, people are more likely to accept the outcome if they think the procedure has been fair. The fairness of procedures is determined by the extent to which the employee has a voice in the system among other things (Lind and Tyler, 1988). Supervisors should actively involve the employee in the performance review, because people who are invited to participate regard procedures and systems to be fairer than those who are not invited. For example, superiors may ask employees to anticipate the feedback they will receive and to suggest how to best act upon it.

Although there is no surefire way to eliminate the biases on the part of the ratee, awareness of the bias is key. A second step is to recognize that many ratee biases are driven by a need to maintain or enhance self-esteem. Thus, it is important to put evaluations in a positive light and to help employees view them as opportunities to grow, rather than marks of failure. A third step is to involve employees actively in the evaluation procedure before they receive their results. For this reason, an early planning meeting, months ahead of the evaluation, can be an ideal opportunity for teams and leaders to work together to identify and clarify goals. Finally, it is important to recognize that performance appraisals, in any form, tend to be stressful for all involved. However, they provide an opportunity for everyone to gain feedback about what otherwise might be an "undiscussable problem." Tools such as 360-degree evaluations have the power to break down the barriers of fear in the organization. However, this can only be effective if managers are trained and skilled at using the information to break down barriers instead of building new ones.

CONCLUSIONS

Many organizations promote and value teamwork yet pay people based upon individual accomplishments. Individuals operating under this system feel the tension. Just as college basketball players who feed their teammates instead of shooting will not compile impressive scoring statistics and are less likely to be drafted by the pros, managers who devote energy to organizational goals will often not forward their own career. Viewed in this sense, it is rational for team members to think of themselves first and the team second. The organization that wants otherwise had better "walk the walk"—and the walk involves serious thought about performance evaluation and compensation.

ENDNOTES

J. T. Austin, P. Villanova, and H. D. Hindman, "Legal Requirements and Technical Guidelines Involved in Implementing Performance Appraisal Systems," *Human Resources Management: Perspectives, Context, Function, and Outcomes*, 3rd ed., eds., G. Ferris & R. M. Buckley (Upper Saddle River, NJ: Prentice Hall, 1996): 283.

W. Bennis, and B. Nanus, *Leaders* (New York: Harper & Row, 1985).

H. J. Bernardin and W. F. Cascio, "Performance Appraisal and the Law," *Readings in Personnel and Human Resource Management*, 3rd ed., R. S. Schuler, S. A. Youngblood, and V. L. Huber (St. Paul, MN: West Publishing Company, 1988): 239.

R. Dawes, J. Orbell, and A. van de Kragt, "Not Me or Thee But We: The Importance of Group Identity in Eliciting Cooperation in Dilemma Situations," *Acta Psychologica 68* (1988): 83–97.

Dow Jones News Service, "Japan's LTCB Asks Workers to Grade Executives," April 14, 1998.

R. Eisenberger. and M. Selbst, "Does Reward Increase or Decrease Creativity?" *Journal of Personality and Social Psychology 49* (1994): 520–528.

J. L. Freedman, J. A. Cunningham, and K. Krismer, "Inferred Values and the Reverse Incentive Effect in Induced Compliance," *Journal of Personality and Social Psychology 62* (1992): 357–368.

C. Heath, "On the Social Psychology of Agency Relationships: Lay Theories of Motivation Overemphasize Extrinsic Rewards," Unpublished manuscript, Duke University, Durham, NC, 1998.

J. Hillkirk, "Tearing Down Walls Builds GE," *USA Today*, July 26, 1993, 5B.

R. Hoffman, "Ten Reasons You Should Be Using 360-Degree Feedback," *HR Magazine 40 (4)*, (April 1995): 82–85.

V. L. Huber, M. A. Neale, and G. B. Northcraft, "Judgment by Heuristics: Effects of Ratee and Rater Characteristics and Performance Standards on Performance-Related Judgments," *Organization Behavior and Human Decision Processes 40* (1987): 149–169.

M. Jarman, "Complete Turn-Around: 360-degree Evaluations Gaining Favor with Workers, Management." *The Arizona Republic*, April 19, 1998, D1; R. Klimoski and L. Inks, "Accountability Forces in Performance Appraisal," *Organization Behavior and Human Decision Processes 45,* no. 2, (April 1990): 194–208.

A. Kohn, "Why Incentive Plans Cannot Work," *Harvard Business Review 71* (1993): 54–63.

K. Kraiger, and J. K. Ford, "A Meta-Analysis of Ratee Race Effects in Performance Ratings," *Journal of Applied Psychology 70*(1); (February 1995): 56–65.

E. E. Lawler, *Strategic Pay: Aligning Organizational Strategies and Pay Systems* (San Francisco, CA: Jossey-Bass, 1990).

E. E. Lawler, *The Ultimate Advantage: Creating the High-Involvement Organization* (San Francisco, CA: Jossey-Bass, 1992).

E. E. Lawler, S. A. Mohrman, and G. E. Ledford, Jr., *Creating High Performance Organizations: Practices and Results of Employee Involvement and Total Quality Management in Fortune 1000 Companies* (San Francisco, CA: Jossey-Bass, 1995).

E. A. Lind and T. R. Tyler, *The Social Psychology of Procedural Justice* (New York: Plenum, 1988).

D. McGregor, *The Human Side of Enterprise* (New York: McGraw-Hill, 1960).

D. T. Miller and R. Ratner, "The Disparity Between the Actual and Assumed Power of Self-Interest," *Journal of Personality and Social Psychology 74*, no. 1 (1998): 53–62.

J. F. Milliman, R. F. Zawacki, C. Norman, L. Powell, and J. Kirksey, "Companies Evaluate Employees from All Perspectives," *Personnel Journal 73*, no. 11 (1994): 99–103.

C. J. Novak, "Proceed with Caution When Paying Teams," *HR Magazine 42*, no. 4 (April 1997). 73–78.

M. Schrage, "Why Your Department Needs to Implement 360s," *Computer World*, October 5, 1998, 33.

B. Schwartz, *The Battle for Human Nature: Science, Morality, and Modern Life* (New York: Norton, 1986).

D. O. Sears and C. L. Funk, "The Limited Effect of Economic Self-Interest on the Political Attitudes of the Mass Public" *Journal of Behavioral Economics 19*, no. 3 (1990): 247–271.

D. O. Sears and C. L. Funk, "Graduate Education in Political Psychology: Annual Meeting of International Society of Political Psychology, Washington, D.C.," *Political Psychology 12*, no. 2 (1991): 345–362.

F. W. Taylor, *Shop Management* (New York: Harper & Brothers, 1911).

T. R. Tyler, *Why People Obey the Law* (New Haven, CT: Yale University Press, 1990).

In this section of the book, we're going to make a more obvious transition from microlevel topics in organizational behavior dealing with individuals and groups to macro-level issues that effect the entire organization. In addition to a thorough grounding in the topics we have already covered, organization design and change are heavily dependent on systems thinking and analytical skills.

CHAPTER 19

ORGANIZATION DESIGN

THE ORGANIZATION OF THE FUTURE: STRATEGIC IMPERATIVES AND CORE COMPETENCIES FOR THE TWENTY-FIRST CENTURY

David A. Nadler
Michael L. Tushman

ORGANIZING IN THE KNOWLEDGE AGE: ANTICIPATING THE CELLULAR FORM

Raymond E. Mile
Charles C. Snow
John A. Mathews
Grant Miles
Henry J. Coleman, Jr.

UP THE (E)ORGANIZATION!: A SEVEN-DIMENSIONAL MODEL FOR THE CENTERLESS ENTERPRISE

Gary L. Neilson
Bruce A. Pasternack
Albert J. Viscio

Organizations cannot function at peak capacity if they are not well designed. In previous articles, you have read about system-wide efforts to influence employee commitment, motivation, and involvement. These are examples of some of the "building blocks" managers use to design an organization (such as strategy, structure, systems, type of staff, competencies, managerial style, rewards, and so forth). All the articles in this chapter are based on the assumption that a good, complementary "fit" among the various components is necessary to organizational success—with some exceptions that allow for evolution and adaptation to change.

The end of the millennium produced numerous writings and predictions about the next century. In our opinion, the best attempt at taking stock of where we are and where business needs to go is David Nadler and Michael Tushman's "The Organization of the Future: Strategic Imperatives and Core Competencies for the Twenty-First Century." Based on the changes they see in the environment, Nadler, chairman and CEO of the Delta Consulting Group Inc., and Tushman, professor and consultant, list six strategies essential for organizations of the future. Next, they identify the organizational competencies and architecture needed to carry out these strategies.

The second article, "Organizing in the Knowledge Age: Anticipating the Cellular Form," reiterates the necessity of adapting to environmental changes. The focus of authors Raymond Miles, Charles Snow, John Mathews, Grant Miles, and Henry Colemen Jr., all business professors, is identifying the structure best suited to the current environment. They provide a historical view of organizational forms, culminating with the cellular form. Based on their discussions with managers in leading-edge firms around the world, they argue that the cellular design is most appropriate for the twenty-first century. They provide examples of several companies organized in this fashion.

The newest business form, e-commerce, is forcing us to rethink organizational design. Gary Neilson, Bruce Pasternack, and Albert Viscio, vice presidents at the Booz-Allen and Hamilton consulting firm, tackle the design challenges of Internet companies in "Up the (E)Organization!" In the process, they clarify the organizational differences between the traditional businesses and e-commerce. Their example, Cicso Systems, shows how the key building blocks of organizational design fit together in an excellent e.org.

THE ORGANIZATION OF THE FUTURE: STRATEGIC IMPERATIVES AND CORE COMPETENCIES FOR THE 21ST CENTURY*

David A. Nadler
Michael L. Tushman

Poised on the eve of the next century, we are witnessing a profound transformation in the very nature of our business organizations. Historic forces have converged to fundamentally reshape the scope, strategies, and structures of large, multi-business enterprises.

Driven by new competitive demands and fueled by an abundance of capital, companies have massively rearranged their portfolios, adding and discarding businesses to sharpen their strategic focus. Those discreet and dramatic portfolio plays, characterized by the high-profile mergers and acquisitions of the past three years, have provided a constant flow of front page news. But beyond the headlines lies a more subtle story, one with greater long-term significance than the acquisitive appetites of auto makers and telecom giants. Heading into the new century, the most important business development is the pursuit of competitive advantage in an uncertain world through new approaches to organization design.

These new approaches should lead those of us concerned with the theory and practice of organizational design to reconsider those ideas still grounded in the post-War, pre-Internet world that lasted through the 1980s. As this remarkable decade draws to a close, it's appropriate to reflect on the state of organization design and to distill those timeless ideas that will guide us in designing the effective organization of the future.

Our purpose here is first to present our perspectives on the most relevant lessons of organization design. We'll then examine the challenges of the new environment and their implications for tomorrow's organizations. Next, we'll identify six new strategic imperatives that flow from this reshaped environment. We'll conclude by proposing a set of organizational challenges that encompass the most critical design issues for the organization of the future.

A PERSPECTIVE ON ORGANIZATION DESIGN

What we think of today as "organization design" began to evolve in the aftermath of World War II. Building on the research of the 1920s and 1930s and the experience of the 1940s, the notion of the "organization as machine" gave way to a more subtle perspective on the social and technical aspects of the organization. Much of our contemporary thinking can be traced to the landmark work *Organization and Environment* by Lawrence and Lorsch, (1969), which introduced several profound ideas.

*Reprinted with permission from *Organizational Dynamics* (Summer 1999): 45–59.

The first was "contingency theory"—the notion that organizations are most effective when their design characteristics match their environment. The second major idea flowed from the first; if two units of the same organization operate in different environments, each should take on different characteristics. That creates a dual demand for both "differentiation" and "integration," or the capacity to link different units within the same organization.

The twin principles of "integration and differentiation" are more relevant than ever, given the complexity of modern organizations. The new challenge is to effectively manage dramatically different businesses that overlap or even compete against one another within a single, strategically focused enterprise. What's more, there will be a growing need for integration patterns—joint ventures, alliances, etc.—that extend beyond traditional corporate boundaries.

We believe there are four core lessons of organization design that will retain their relevance in the coming decade:

1. The environment drives the strategic architecture of the enterprise, either through anticipation of, or reaction to, major changes in the marketplace. Every industry evolves through cycles of incremental change punctuated by turbulent periods of disequilibrium that call for radical or discontinuous change. The organization's capacity to understand its environment and to make the right kinds of strategic changes at the appropriate point in the cycle will determine its competitive strength.

2. Strategy drives organizational architecture, a term that describes the variety of ways in which the enterprise structures, coordinates, and manages the work of its people in pursuit of strategic objectives. Over the years, we have described this concept as the congruence model of organizational behavior (Figure 1). This model views the organization as an open system that transforms input from the external environment into output of various types. The organization, consisting of the formal and informal arrangements, the people, and the core work, is driven by an articulated strategy. The more closely each component of the organization is aligned with the others—and with the strategy—the more effective the overall performance. Consequently, effective organizations design patterns of formal and informal structures and processes best suited to their strategic objectives.

FIGURE 1

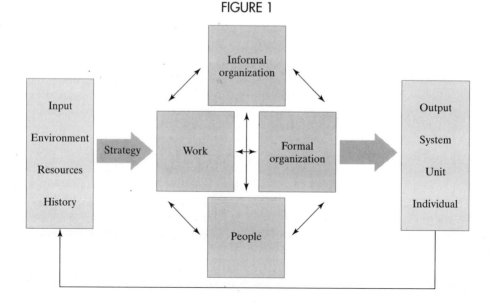

3. The relationship between strategy and organization design is reciprocal. How an enterprise is organized will influence its focus and time horizons, either encouraging or restricting its people's ability to develop creative strategies.

4. The basic dilemma of organizational design remains unchanged. This raises several questions: How do we design and manage both differentiation and integration? How do we group people, processes, and operating units in ways appropriate to their unique competitive environments and strategic requirements, while maintaining their link to the larger organization? How do we encourage both divergence and cohesion? The key to effective design requires an appreciation of the underlying duality of this challenge.

Assuming these are the relevant lessons that should continue to guide us, our task in the remainder of this paper is to address three key issues:

1. What are the key characteristics of the changing business environment? What are the critical changes that will drive new thinking in strategic and organizational architecture?
2. What are the strategic imperatives that flow from the environmental changes we've identified?
3. What organizational challenges will be created by the new strategic imperatives? How will effective organizations translate strategic imperatives into new organizational architectures and new leadership priorities?

To answer these questions, we begin by considering the historic trends that have already begun to reshape the competitive environment.

THE NEW BUSINESS ENVIRONMENT

In many ways, today's business environment has changed qualitatively since the late 1980s. The end of the Cold War radically altered the very nature of global politics and economics. In just a few short years, the triumph of capitalism has spawned a variety of trends with profound consequences: the opening of markets, true global competition, widespread industry deregulation, and an abundance of accessible capital. We have experienced both the benefits and perils of a truly global economy, with both Wall Street and Main Street feeling the pangs of economic dislocation half a world away.

At the same time, we have fully entered the information age. Startling breakthroughs in information technology have irreversibly altered the ability to conduct business unconstrained by the traditional limitations of time or space. Today, it's almost impossible to imagine a world devoid of intranets, e-mail, and laptops. With stunning speed, the Internet is profoundly changing the way we work, shop, do business, and communicate.

In less than 10 years, the changes wrought by new information technology have been phenomenal.

As a consequence, we have truly entered the post-industrial economy. We are rapidly shifting from an economy based on manufacturing and commodities to one that places the greatest value on information, services, support, and distribution. That shift, in turn, places an unprecedented premium on "knowledge workers," a new class of affluent, educated, and mobile people who view themselves as free agents in a seller's market.

Beyond the realm of information technology, the accelerated pace of technological change in virtually every industry has created entirely new businesses, wiped out others, and produced a pervasive demand for continuous innovation. New product, process, and distribution technologies provide powerful levers for creating competitive value. More companies are learning the importance of destructive technologies—innovations that hold the potential to make a product line, or even an entire business segment, virtually obsolete.

Another major trend has been the fragmentation of consumer and business markets. There's a growing appreciation that superficially similar groups of customers may have very different preferences in terms of what they want to buy and how they want to buy it. Now, new technology makes it easier, faster, and cheaper to identify and serve targeted micromarkets in ways that were physically impossible or prohibitively expensive in the past. Moreover, the trend feeds on itself, a business' ability to serve sub-markets fuels customers' appetites for more and more specialized offerings.

IMPLICATIONS OF ENVIRONMENTAL CHANGE

We all know that change has become an inherent part of business. What's more significant is the rapidly accelerating velocity of change. More specifically, the lifespan of product, process, and distribution technologies has contracted with breathtaking speed.

The critical issue is time. The rapidly increasing velocity of change warps organizational time and space, bending the very shape of the enterprise. It's not just simply a matter of doing the same things, only faster; it's more like the difference between checkers and three-dimensional chess. The massive demands imposed by time compression will force organizations to:

- Compete and innovate simultaneously in multiple venues and in overlapping time frames; and
- Find creative ways to design and implement new organizational architectures in half the time required by current processes without sacrificing the benefits traditionally associated with deliberate planning and appropriate participation.

Together, these changes in the business environment challenge our fundamental assumptions of organizational design. Historically, the purpose of organizational structures was to institutionalize stability; in the organization of the future, the goal of design will be to institutionalize change. In that sense, we stand in the midst of a profound shift in the design and purpose of organizational design.

THE NEW STRATEGIC IMPERATIVES

We believe that the changing environment we've just described creates six strategic imperatives for the organization of the future. It will be required to: increase strategic clock speed; focus portfolios, with various business models; abbreviate strategic life cycles; create "go-to-market" flexibility; enhance competitive innovation; and manage intra-enterprise cannibalism. We will describe each in turn.

1 Increase Strategic Clock Speed   From a strategic standpoint, speed is quickly becoming a critical success factor. In a strategic context, speed involves an organizational capacity to understand, anticipate, and respond appropriately to those external changes that fundamentally alter the rules of engagement and the sources of value in a given industry or business segment. Examples abound: the deregulation of telecommunications and other utilities, the emergence of new technologies such as wireless communication, the development of e-commerce, and the rise of "category killer" outlets in consumer segments such as home improvement (Home Depot) and toys (Toys "R" Us). Virtually every industry has seen vast changes in the way it designs, produces, or reaches the market with its offerings.

Timing is everything. During periods of radical, discontinuous change, the first movers enjoy significant advantages. Those who perceive the early signs of discontinuity in the environment and then rapidly fashion an appropriate new strategy are infinitely more successful than those who miss the warning signs or delay their response. Those who move slowly find they must react to competitors; those who wait too long find themselves struggling for survival.

2 Focus Portfolios, with Various Business Models   Over the past 40 years, there's been significant change in the underlying strategies that defined our large and complex business enterprises. Through the mid-1960s, the classical form or organizational architecture consisted of companies with a single dominant business design that was largely duplicated down through the pyramid of divisions and operating companies. These shared designs allowed for tight linkages and a sense of consistency.

The mid-1960s saw the rise of the conglomerate. Driven by a thirst for growth, a fundamental belief that "bigger is better," and a desire to offset the cyclical downturns in specific industries, companies diversified their portfolios in unprecedented ways. Within each corporation, there might be dozens of companies with wholly unrelated strategies and entirely different business designs. The holding company model involved only the most minimal linkages across the enterprise, with each business operating essentially as an independent agent in pursuit of financial goals dictated from above.

Now we're witnessing the emergence of the new "strategic enterprise." The changing marketplace no longer rewards unfocused growth and gross market share. Instead, companies are reshaping their portfolios in the pursuit of strategic focus, concentrating on those businesses where they can create sustainable value by applying their core competencies to provide competitive advantage. They are spinning off or selling businesses that either dilute focus, in terms of resources and managerial energy, or whose potential value cannot be leveraged within the larger enterprise. In effect, companies are breaking up and reassembling the traditional value chain.

This sharpened focus is leading companies to seek new ways to compete within a given competitive space, operating simultaneously in mature, emerging, and future segments of the same markets. Consequently, we're going to see more and more variations in business design within a single enterprise. In this context, we use the term *business design* as defined by Slywotzky and Morrison as encompassing four dimensions: which customers to pursue, how to capture value (i.e., profit), how to maintain a unique value proposition, and what scope of activities to pursue.

For example, consider the case of Lucent Technologies, a spinoff created by AT&T in 1995 from four of its businesses and much of Bell Labs. As part of AT&T, those businesses were locked in a strategic dilemma created by deregulation: In order to realize their full value, they would have to do business with AT&T's widening array of direct competitors. That created major conflicts for everyone concerned. Once Lucent became independent from AT&T, its value as a manufacturer and supplier of telecommunications equipment and systems skyrocketed; its profits more than quadrupled between 1995 and 1998, and its stock price rose from $13.50 a share in 1996 to nearly $120, adjusted for splits.

But it wasn't long before Lucent realized that it, too, would have to reshape its business design. Just a few years after the spinoff, Lucent exited the consumer business, where it lacked the front-end linkages—sales, distribution, customer base—to sufficiently leverage its back-end technology and production strengths. Instead, Lucent chose to focus exclusively on business communications. In early 1999, it acquired Ascend Communications Inc., a move that represented a $20 billion bet on data networking—a business involving substantially different technology than Lucent's traditional circuit switching. Now, the challenge for Lucent is figuring out how to manage these two different—and, in some ways, directly competing—business designs.

3 Abbreviated Strategic Life Cycles
Each industry progresses through a fairly predictable life cycle. There may be huge differences in the duration of that cycle depending upon the industry segment, but the pattern of cycles is consistent. Understanding those cycles is essential for leaders. Different stages in the cycle of industry evolution—the well-known "S-curve"—demand different strategies at various points along the curve.

But waves of change in industry leadership suggest that firms must engage in both incremental and discontinuous technical change, as well as architectural innovation—taking the same product and taking it to different markets. Thus in photolithography for disk drives, leading firms were unable to take known technologies and move to new customers. Dynamic capabilities seem to be rooted in shaping streams of different types of innovation in a given product class.

The consequences of the sweeping and rapid changes in the environment discussed earlier have had the effect of substantially shortening those evolutionary cycles for every industry. In the past, companies large and small, including AT&T, General Motors, and even IBM, could get along for a decade, and sometimes longer, without any fundamental changes in strategy. Those days are gone. Rather than thinking in terms of decades, the pace of change in the environment will require the organization of the future to significantly change its underlying strategy on a regular basis of between 18 months and 5 years, depending upon the industry. Indeed, it's not uncommon to hear executives, as they talk about strategic cycles, talk in terms of "Web years," signifying a compressed timeframe of 3 months rather than 12.

4 Create "Go-to-Market" Flexibility   The fragmentation of markets, one of the significant changes in the environment, has enormous strategic implications for organizations. In order to reach each market segment in the most effective way, companies have begun focusing more intensely than ever before on the rising demand for "go-to-market" variability. Various market segments offer widely divergent demands for the same core product or service in terms of pricing options, sales and service support, speed of delivery, customization, and so forth. Today, no organization can succeed with a "one size fits all" approach to the marketplace.

The most highly publicized changes, of course, have involved the Internet and the emergence of so-called "e-commerce"; by some accounts, sales of goods over the Internet rose from being barely measurable in 1996 to more than $4 billion during the 1998 Christmas season. Waves of change in distribution channels are coming faster all the time. It was only a few years ago that independent booksellers were wilting under the pressure of the book superstores, such as Barnes & Noble and Borders. Then, practically overnight, Amazon.com reshaped the industry, putting the leading competitors on the defensive and forcing them to follow the upstart onto the Web, despite their enormous investments in brick-and-mortar outlets.

Implicit in the notion of "go-to-market" variability is the potential it creates for conflicting internal priorities. Consider the auto industry. By some estimates, we are quickly approaching the point when more than half of all new car buyers in the United States start out by searching the Internet for information, comparing models, options, prices, and financing alternatives before they ever set foot in a showroom. What many shoppers are looking for is a vehicle's factory invoice price, the essential number that equips them to bargain knowledgeably with the local dealer. That's not good news for the dealer; but at this point, the auto companies have no choice but to cater to the demands of sophisticated customers for more and better information. At the same time, reeling from assaults by Car-Max and other high-volume used-car chains, the auto companies have to think seriously about starting their own used-car outlets—an historic shift in distribution that would put a further squeeze on profits of their own franchised dealerships.

5 Enhance Competitive Innovation   It has practically become an article of faith that innovation provides a critical source of competitive advantage. But the accepted definition of *innovation* is too narrow; we would argue that the scope of innovation must be expanded to include the full range of an organization's capabilities.

Innovation traditionally focused on products and processes. More recently, distribution has attracted attention as an area where significant innovation can lead to dramatic gains. But the combination of product, process, and distribution still fails to capture the full potential for organizational innovation.

We believe the successful organization of the future will also develop exceptional skills to innovate in two other areas: strategy development and organization design. If the most critical characteristic of the new business environment is the accelerating pace of change, then the ability to quickly and creatively develop and implement new strategies and the organization designs required to make them work will become a major source of competitive differentiation.

6 Manage Intra-Enterprise Cannibalism   What we call *purposeful cannibalism*—the need to develop and support new strategies, product lines, and distribution channels that might eventually dry up existing revenue streams—is not a new idea. Visionary business leaders have done it for years. But two elements of intra-enterprise cannibalism are new.

The first change is that cannibalism has been rare. Business historians praise Tom Watson Jr. for his foresight in developing the IBM 360, which held the potential to wipe out many of the company's best-selling product lines. His willingness to put a major revenue stream at risk was remarkable in large part because it was so uncommon. In the successful organization of the future, the idea of cannibalism will become routine, an accepted part of each company's strategy.

The other change relates, once again, to speed. In the future, it won't suffice to make one big bet each decade. The pace of innovation and the abbreviated strategic cycles will force companies to place multiple bets on an ongoing basis, acknowledging that a new product may be well on its way to obsolescence by the time it reaches the market.

Lucent Technologies' $20 billion acquisition of Ascend, which we mentioned earlier, involved more than a strategy of multiple bets on alternative technologies. There's a good chance that the newly acquired data networking strategy based on packet switching may actually displace the circuit switching technology that now provides the bulk of Lucent's profits. And before long, it's entirely possible that Lucent will have to invest in alternative packet switching strategies as new technologies come along and require new business designs.

ORGANIZATIONAL CHALLENGES

The six strategic imperatives described above create a compelling need for some new and unconventional organizational architectures. As we said earlier, organizational architecture throughout much of this century was generally viewed as a way to institutionalize and manage stability. But today, the challenge is to design organizational architectures that are flexible and adaptive, that enable the organization to perform effectively in the face of uncertainty—not just day-to-day, but in the broader context of profound discontinuous change.

In our view, the new strategic imperatives create a corresponding set of challenges for the organization of the future; to succeed, organizations will be forced to become proficient in eight core competencies.

1 Increase Organizational Clock Speed   The strategic imperative of timely anticipation and speedy response to change will require the design of organizations with the capacity to do everything faster. The ability to configure the organization in ways that ensure a constant and acute awareness of impending changes in the marketplace will become an essential capability that will separate the leaders from the laggards.

Beyond that, organizations will have to find creative ways to achieve unprecedented speed in all their operating and support processes. They'll want to significantly reduce their time to market and time to volume. They'll want to accelerate decision-making up and down the line. They'll need to substantially cut the time it takes to design and implement strategic and organizational changes. Enlightened leaders already understand that speed doesn't mean operating the same way as in the past, only faster; they know that radical improvements in speed involve doing things differently. In order to increase strategic clock speed, organizations will face three challenges.

First, senior leaders will need a much deeper understanding of the quickening cycle times in their industries. They will have to alter their assumptions about large-scale change, both in terms of the frequency and speed of major change initiatives. Once upon a time, CEOs were expected to be the stewards of stability. Through the 1980s, a CEO might expect to lead one or, in extreme cases, two episodes of radical change. Today, and in the coming decades, leaders of complex organizations should enter their jobs with the expectation that they might well be required to reinvent their organizations three, four, or even more times over the course of their tenure. That will require a fundamentally different attitude about the role of the CEO as an agent of change.

Second, successful enterprises will need to develop sensitive organizational antennae—the roles, structures, and processes that will significantly enhance their ability to detect the early warning signs of value migration. In particular, they will have to keep close watch on minor players and industry outliers, the frequent sources of major innovation. They are the ones to monitor most carefully; they are the ones most likely to employ new technologies and distribution patterns to nullify the dominant conventional business designs.

Finally, companies will need to redesign their organizational architectures in ways that encourage the "capacity to act" in response to indications of environmental change. In too many organizations, managers lack clear accountabilities, support from above, adequate resources, and sufficient information; faced with major opportunities or challenges, they freeze in their tracks. The growing demand for speed in every facet of the business will require organizations to fashion the formal structures, processes, and roles as well as the informal operating environment necessary to encourage managers throughout the enterprise to act swiftly and independently.

2 Design Structural Divergence   The changing environment is requiring enterprises to employ a variety of business designs as they develop multiple ways to achieve value within a defined competitive space. The organizational challenge will be to master the art of designed divergence—the ability to create, support, and link, where necessary, a wide variety of related businesses that use dramatically different architectures to pursue varying and sometimes conflicting strategies.

In recent years, we have argued the case for ambidextrous management—the ability to maintain superior performance in established businesses while managing innovation in targeted areas. The organization of the future will have to be more than just ambidextrous; in a sense, it will have to become polydextrous. Rather than operating, in essence, in both the present and the future, polydextrous leadership will also require an ability to coordinate businesses that are both complementary and competitive in the current marketplace (Figure 2). That will require a fundamental rethinking of the form and purpose of organizational architecture. The framework we have developed over the past 20 years, the Congruence Model, is generally synonymous with consistency. It implies that effective organizations maintain a consistent architecture with minor variations, throughout the enterprise. We now believe that the organization of the future will seek congruence at the enterprise level, providing an effective framework that successfully melds a broad array of different architectures at the business unit level and beyond. Rather than seeking blanket consistency, leaders will come to perceive internal architectural divergence as a powerful source of evolutionary strength.

The most critical issue will be to figure out the appropriate linkages across a broad range of very different businesses. The challenge involves an inherent balancing act: minimizing linkages in order to maximize the focus of independent business units while, at the same time, capitalizing on potential sources of leverage to create value from the joint ownership and management of multiple businesses. In other words, leaders will have to learn when it's best to encourage autonomy and differentiation, and how to create value through the selective use of linking structures and integrative processes.

In reality, the choices are somewhat limited. Businesses can be linked on the back end, through common technology architectures. They can be linked in the middle through infrastructure—manufacturing

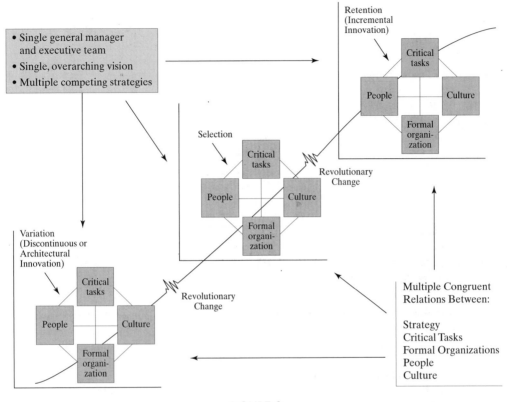

FIGURE 2

processes, supply chains, etc. And they can be linked on the front end, through shared customer relationships, distribution channels, sales and service operations, and so on (Figure 3). The more points of linkage, the more diffused the focus. So the issue is to start with a clean slate, to weigh the marginal costs and benefits of each potential linkage, and to arrive at the correct scope and intensity of linkage at each point in the value chain. Corning Inc., for example, has come to the conclusion that its various businesses—photonic devices for telecommunications, stepper lenses for photolithography (for creating

FIGURE 3

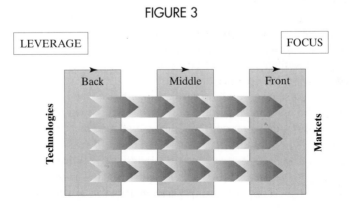

chips), ceramic substrates for catalytic converters—offer no leverage on the front end, minimal leverage in the middle, and considerable leverage on the back end, where common technologies provide innovations with applications across its businesses.

3 Promote Organizational Modularity

The growing prevalence of abbreviated strategic life cycles will require ever-faster development and implementation of appropriate organizational designs. That requirement clearly calls for both product and process innovation in the domain of organizational design. The implications may be far-reaching, indeed.

In recent decades, we have rejected the notion of "off-the-rack" organization designs. We have steadfastly argued in favor of "custom designs." Our thinking was based on two fundamental beliefs; first, that each design should be suited to the unique demands of the organization—its environment, its strategy, its people, and its culture; and second, that the very process of designing the appropriate structures, processes, systems, and roles held inherent long-term value for the organization and the individuals who took part in the process.

As valuable as it has been, it may well be time to rethink that approach. The transforming requirements of speed might well dictate situations in which there is simply not enough time to engage in a conventional organization design process. We may be approaching a time when theorists and practitioners ought to develop a set of design principles that will allow organizations to quickly select an appropriate architecture for a given strategy.

Many organizations will no longer be able to afford the luxury of spending six or nine months creating and implementing a new design; few companies will be able to wait that long to address the imminent changes in their environment. So the notion of starting each design process with a blank slate will soon become obsolete. The challenge will be to devise a streamlined process, employing modular design, that still retains some of the important benefits—the learning, insight, team-building and ownership—that we attempt to create through the customized design approach.

4 Structure Hybrid Distribution Channels

The strategic imperative for go-to-market variability will require organizations to develop different kinds of structures that will enable them to simultaneously manage different channels of distribution in order to serve highly fragmented markets. Xerox Corp.'s early 1999 restructuring—its third in less than a decade—illustrates the kind of new, creative designs that will be required by the organization of the future.

For years, Xerox basically sold a range of generic products through a sales force that called on companies, built relationships, and helped customers to learn about the features and benefits of those products. But changes in the environment battered the business design that had served Xerox so well. Early in the 1990s, Xerox reorganized into business units that focused on selling particular products to corresponding segments of the office market. But after just a few years, that design, and its later refinements, failed to keep pace with the continued fragmentation of the market. The digital office, the proliferation of small businesses and home offices, the demand for new ways to purchase and service equipment, the unique document requirements of specific industries—they all served to fragment the market for office equipment and solutions.

In many cases, companies were no longer satisfied with just "the box," a freestanding copier sitting in a side office. As the digital office became a reality, more customers demanded a networked, multi-function machine to help them solve production, distribution, and archiving problems; others wanted the software and systems design to make the whole set-up work seamlessly. And in extreme cases, they wanted Xerox not only to supply the system, but to design and operate it as well. At the other end of the spectrum was the so-called SOHO market (Small Office/Home Office), whose customers were primarily interested in products that were inexpensive, high quality, easily installed and operated, and

Strategic Imperatives	Organizational Challenges
• Increase strategic clock speed	• Increase organizational clock speed
• Focus portfolios with various business models	• Design structural divergence
• Abbreviate strategic life cycles	• Promote organizational modularity
• Create "go-to-market" flexibility	• Structure hybrid distribution channels
• Enhance competitive innovation	• Design asymmetrical research and development
• Manage intra-enterprise cannibalism	• Construct conflict management processes
	• Maintain organizational coherence
	• Develop executive teams

FIGURE 4

quickly ordered, often by phone or over the Internet. And in the middle was still a substantial conventional market, businesses that were happy to keep dealing with the traditional sales force.

Early in 1999, Xerox reconfigured the front end of the organization to focus on customer segments (Figure 5). These segments recognized the geographic distinctions markets in varying stages of economic development and the specific needs of customers in various industries. Facing these customer segments were an array of targeted operations and business groups. General Markets Operations, for example, was aimed at the lower end of the market, and consequently required the structures, processes, culture, and clock speed needed to meet the demands of the small customer. On the other hand, Industry and Solutions Operations focused on solutions rather than products, and was further segmented by industry on the principle that systems solutions in financial services and pharmaceuticals, for example, must be unique and custom-tailored.

The Xerox organization design leverages the back end of the value chain, the common technologies. It involves an uncommonly complex design on the front end, however, one that recognizes that Xerox must provide immense variety in the ways it goes to market if it is to compete successfully in a marketplace characterized by the fragmentation of sub-markets.

5 Design Metrical Research and Development   The strategic imperative of competitive innovation will require the organization of the future to design the structures and processes that guide research and development in some new and creative ways.

Today, different companies design their R&D processes in different configurations, but in the end, there tends to be a single innovation model patterned around the basic business model. That model is entirely inconsistent with the notion of design divergence. Within the same enterprise, businesses and operations with very different strategies will require dramatically different innovation streams, or processes for turning ideas into marketable products. Organizations that insist on applying a single innovation process symmetrically across the enterprise will inevitably run into trouble.

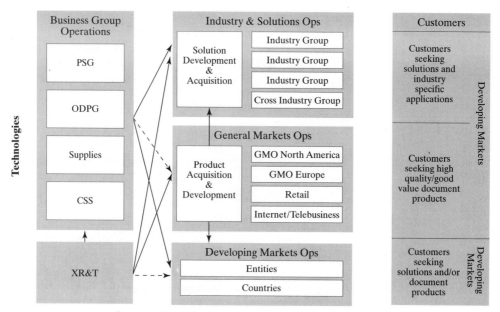

Corporate Strategic Direction, Governance & Infrastructure

FIGURE 5

The problem is that competing simultaneously in both the present and the future requires a range of R&D processes, structures, priorities, and behavior. In a mature business, the emphasis in innovation is on the right solution—the absolutely right solution. The marketplace will accept nothing less. Particularly if you're among the market leaders, you can follow a highly structured process with strictly enforced priorities, deadlines and resource allocations.

The picture is entirely different in emerging markets. There, the priorities are speed and flexibility. If you can be first to market, a roughly right solution is better than none; in the extra time it might take to find the absolutely perfect solution, the market could well pass you by. And in those early stages of product life cycle, the customer calls the shots; R&D operations need the flexibility to respond swiftly to unexpected opportunities and challenges.

Consequently, companies whose strategy requires a range of business designs cannot employ symmetrical innovation processes and hope to succeed. There will still be value in a core R&D function; allocating all R&D to the business units eliminates an important potential source of leverage. But the processes by which R&D operates in relation to each business unit—goal setting, funding mechanisms, conflict resolution, etc.—need to be customized and asymmetrical.

6 Construct Conflict Management Processes   In the past, as we've mentioned, an important role of organization design was to preserve consistancy, stability, and perhaps even a degree of harmony within the organization. But as we look to the future, organizations that use design to impose an artificial sense of stability in the face of sweeping environmental change will become their own worst enemy.

Instead, effective leaders will actually use organization design to import the conflict and competition of the marketplace into the very structure of their companies. But as the proliferation of internally competitive strategies becomes commonplace, what are the implications for organizations and their leaders?

In short, conflict management will become an essential organizational capability. Today, an extremely short list of companies—Intel usually tops the list—have established reputations for their ability to creatively manage internal conflict. What is a rare talent today will become a standard requirement before long. The successful organization of the future will need to develop the processes, cultures, and behaviors capable of accommodating and resolving conflict in ways that benefit the customer and strengthen the value proposition.

So far, we've been describing organizational challenges that directly correspond with the new strategic imperatives. There are two additional organizational challenges that apply to the full range of strategic imperatives: the changing nature of organizational coherence, and the magnified role of executive teams. Both address the issue of how to manage the organization of the future as it changes to address the growing demands of speed, variable business design, abbreviated strategic cycles, greater go-to-market variability, competitive innovation and intra-enterprise cannibalism.

7 Organizational Coherence In recent years, we've witnessed a growing recognition that values, culture, and shared goals are replacing formal structures as the glue that holds organizations together. That trend will rapidly accelerate as the result of the strategic and organizational changes we've discussed here.

As business units and operating companies become increasingly autonomous, to the point of becoming outright competitors with one another, the very nature of organizational coherence will undergo a radical transformation. Job titles, formal structures, and bureaucratic procedures will have less and less importance to people whose primary loyalty will be to their own business group and, even more narrowly, to their own professional discipline. Organizational coherence at the enterprise level will become increasingly difficult to maintain, and will rest almost entirely on a common goal and a small number of shared values—not the formal rhetorical flourishes that are the organization's espoused values, but those few values that truly embody the way people think of themselves and their enterprise.

In that context, the notions of "brand" and identity will assume growing importance within the enterprise. The dominant cultural norms—the HP Way, the feistiness of Sun Microsystems, the insistence on winning at Lucent Technologies, Intel's creative conflict, or Microsoft's self-image as the best and the brightest—these will be the understood, though not always explicit, values that will hold divergent enterprises together. The so-called "soft stuff" will, over time, become the essential stuff.

8 Executive Teams Where will the leadership come from to generate this intangible coherence while managing the tangible hardware of the enterprise? The answer will be in the executive team.

Consider the degree of complexity we're envisioning for the organization of the future. In a sense, what we're talking about is the capacity to manage paradoxes. Large organizations will have to be managed as if they were small; they'll have to be both global and local; they'll need to promote both internal conflict and overall coherence. It's virtually impossible to imagine how a single person, in the form of the CEO, could possess the staggering combination of leadership skills, managerial talent, and technical knowledge required to meet these assorted strategic and organizational challenges. It's absurd to expect that of one person.

Instead, it will fall more and more to the executive team to become the key mechanism for managing the organization of the future. That does not diminish the role of the CEO; to the contrary, the effective CEO will have to become a deft leader of the executive team, a major job in itself. It will require the combined efforts of the CEO and the executive team, working together, to truly understand and anticipate the changes in the environment. It will be up to them to make the critical strategic decision. It will require their combined efforts to understand the timing and guide the implementation of the constant refinement and tuning the complex organization will demand—redesigning the structure to add focus here or to provide more leverage there.

These sophisticated tasks will require the combined intellect of senior people who share a commitment to the common good of the enterprise. Indeed, the enormity of the challenge suggests that senior leadership will need to be expanded for certain types of work, drawing upon the skills, knowledge, and insights of people who haven't traditionally been viewed as members of the senior-level inner circle. One of the challenges for top leaders will be to determine when, how, and in what situations to make the top team more inclusive rather than less.

What is clear is that the organization of the future, in order to succeed, will become less dependent on the independent actions of disaggregated individuals. To succeed, organizations will have to develop a competency in the design and leadership of executive teams, a collective skill that will be just as important as the ability to design innovative strategies and organizational architectures.

ORGANIZING IN THE KNOWLEDGE AGE: ANTICIPATING THE CELLULAR FORM*

Raymond E. Miles
Charles C. Snow
John A. Mathews
Grant Miles
Henry J. Coleman Jr.

Since the Industrial Revolution, the U. S. economy has moved through the machine age into the information age and now stands at the threshold of the knowledge age. The locus of organizational exemplars has shifted from capital-intensive industries, such as steel and automobiles, to information-intensive industries, such as financial services and logistics, and now toward innovation-driven industries, such as computer software and biotechnology, where competitive advantage lies mostly in the effective use of human resources.

This evolution has been simultaneously powered and facilitated by the invention of a succession of new organizational forms—new approaches to accumulating and applying know-how to the key resources of the day. The contribution of each new form has been to allow firms to use their expanding, know-how to adapt to market opportunities and demands, first for standardized goods and services, then to increasing levels of product and service customization, and presently toward the expectation of continuous innovation. Certain trends visible in the coevolution of markets and organizations make it possible to predict the shape and operation of the twenty-first century organization. A number of pioneering firms are already demonstrating the organizational characteristics suggested by those trends, especially a growing reliance on entrepreneurship, self-organization, and member ownership of firm assets and resources.

THE EVOLUTION OF ORGANIZATIONAL FORMS

An organizational form is an overall logic shaping a firm's strategy, structure, and management processes into an effective whole. In each historical era, market forces pull forth new organizational forms as managers seek new ways of arranging assets and resources to produce the products and services that customers want and expect. At the same time, some companies accumulate more know-how than their present operating logic allows them to utilize. Those excess capabilities push managers to experiment

---

*Reprinted with permission from the *Academy of Management Executive 11*, no. 4 (1997): 7–24.

TABLE 1   Organizational Evolution

Historical Era	Standardization	Customization	Innovation
Organizational Form	Hierarchy	Network	Cell
Key Asset	Capital Goods	Information	Knowledge
Influential Manager	Chief Operating Officer	Chief Information Officer	Chief Knowledge Officer
Key Capability	Specialization and Segmentation	Flexibility and Responsiveness	Design Creativity

with new organizational arrangements that, in turn, stimulate the search for new markets and/or new products or services. The continuing interaction of these push-pull forces has been visible in the major eras that have characterized the U.S. economy over the past hundred-plus years (see Table 1).

ERA OF STANDARDIZATION

The era of standardization saw hierarchical forms of organization used to apply know-how primarily to the use of such physical assets as raw materials, capital equipment, and plant facilities. In the late nineteenth and early twentieth centuries, the pioneering companies of that time learned to efficiently mass produce standardized products (e.g., steel and automobiles) and services (e.g., transportation and communications).[1] The period's dominant organizational form, the functional organization, used a centrally coordinated, vertically integrated structure to manage employees in highly specialized jobs. By focusing, on limited product and service lines, firms moved down the learning curve using their accumulating know-how to produce time and cost reductions that constantly added value to employed resources and allowed the United States to mass produce its way to a position of global economic power.

EARLY CUSTOMIZATION

As illustrated in Figure 1, the era of customization actually began during the earlier period of standardized production. That is, by the middle of the twentieth century (and even before in industries such as automotive and retailing), markets had generally become more demanding, and some firms had accumulated know-how that could not be fully utilized in the production of their existing goods and services. Thus, markets pulled companies to diversify their offerings, and their underutilized know-how and resources pushed them toward new markets where expansion was possible.[2] Those forces coalesced in the invention of a new organizational form, the divisional, which allowed companies to serve related markets with differentiated goods and services. In the divisional form, know-how that accumulated in one market could be utilized by a newly created, semi-autonomous division to provide products or services to different but related markets. Corporate-level executives sought new market opportunities for the creation of new divisions and used the current revenue streams to invest know-how and resources in these new arenas. Although each division typically produced a standard product (e.g., autos at General Motors), the divisional form enabled companies to achieve limited amounts of customization (market segmentation).

The movement from standardization to customization continued into the late 1960s and 1970s, as firms adopted mixed organizational forms, such as the matrix, that allowed a dual focus on both stable and emerging market segments and clients.[3] For example, by employing, a matrix organization, an aerospace firm such as TRW could produce differentiated but standard products for the civilian and military markets in one or more divisions, while simultaneously transferring some resources from those

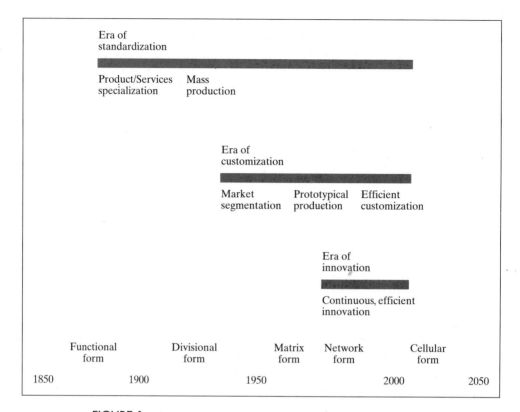

FIGURE 1   Coevolution of Economic Era and Organizational Form

units into project groups that designed and built prototypical products for space exploration. The matrix organization provided companies with a more finely grained mechanism for exploiting their know-how across a wider range of both standardized and customized products and services.

FULL, EFFICIENT CUSTOMIZATION

By the 1980s, the pull toward customization intensified as a rapidly growing number of firms around the world used their know-how to enter an increasingly deregulated global marketplace.[4] New entrants competed for customer attention with lower prices, improved quality and distribution, and seemingly endless choices among styles and models. However, many existing companies initially found it difficult to unleash their competencies and know-how to meet the new market opportunities and pressures. Divisional and matrix organizations, designed for less challenging and turbulent markets, were better suited to internal coordination needs than to rapid forays into new markets.

Once again, a new organizational form was needed in order to help firms use and extend their capabilities. The model that evolved from the late 1970s into the 1990s was the network organization.[5] The key contribution of the network form was not just its ability to rapidly respond to market demands for differentiated products and services, but to do so efficiently by extending the customization process backward and forward along the entire industry value chain, from raw materials to parts and component production, to manufacture and assembly, to distribution and final sale. In their search for flexibility and responsiveness, most traditional companies began by downsizing and then refocusing on those areas where their assets and know-how added the greatest economic value. As companies downsized and reengineered, they began to outsource non-core operations to upstream and downstream partner firms whose capabilities complemented their own. As multifirm networks proliferated, numerous potential partners around the world began to occupy points along industry value chains offering increased overall flexibility and therefore more opportunities for customization. The expanded number of competent firms kept prices in check, improved product and service quality, and pressured all firms to adopt better information and production technologies.

Most importantly from an organizational point of view, companies began to realize that success in the age of efficient customization again demanded a higher level of know-how and resource utilization than existing internal management processes allowed. Increasingly, firms turned to network structures in which empowered teams managed not only their internal work processes, but also external relationships with upstream and downstream partners. In many networks of the 1990s, it became difficult to determine where one organization ended and another began, as cross-firm teams resolved interface issues, representatives of important customers were invited to participate in new product development processes, and suppliers were given access to large firms' scheduling and accounting processes through electronic data interchange systems.

In little more than a century, the pull of market forces and the push of underutilized company know-how carried the U.S. economy through the era of mass standardization into the era of efficient customization. Throughout this period, firms faced increasingly complex market and technological environments. In response, firms themselves became more complex, by creating, new organizational means of adding economic value.

Functional firms, as shown in Table 2, primarily utilized increased operating know-how to add economic value, with only top managers providing coordination and entrepreneurial direction. The divisional form utilized operating knowledge and also developed an applied knowledge of how to invest money, people, and systems in related markets—so-called diversification know-how. In the process, divisional firms brought not only corporate managers, but an expanding group of divisional managers, into organizational and business decision processes.

Matrix organizations were designed to add value not only through the application of operating and investment know-how, but also through their adaptation capabilities—the frequent refocusing of underutilized assets on the needs of temporary projects and new market opportunities. In those organizations, top managers, division managers, and project managers all were involved in entrepreneurial and organizational decisions.

The network form allowed value to be added across as well as within firms along the value chain, combining the operational, investment, and adaptation know-how of individual firms and achieving higher levels of overall utilization through their freedom to link rapidly with numerous upstream and downstream partners. The network organization's dependence on decision-making teams, both within and across firms, dramatically increased involvement in organizational and entrepreneurial decisions in all firms at all levels.

TABLE 2   Location of Managerial Know-How in Alternative Organizational Forms

	Operational Know-how	Investment Know-how	Adaptation Know-how
Functional	Top, Middle, Lower	Top	Top
Divisional	Top, Middle, Lower	Top, Middle	Top
Matrix	Top, Middle, Lower	Top, Middle	Top, Middle
Network	Top, Middle, Lower	Top, Middle	Top, Middle, Lower
Cellular	Top, Middle, Lower	Top, Middle, Lower	Top, Middle, Lower

In sum, across this entire period of organizational evolution, certain trends are clearly evident. First, as each new organizational form was created, it brought an expectation that more and more organization members would develop the ability to self-organize around operational, market, and partnering tasks. Second, each new form increased the proportion of members who were expected to perform entrepreneurial tasks—identifying customer needs and then finding and focusing resources on them. Third, each new organizational form increased member opportunities to experience psychological ownership of particular clients, markets, customized products and services, and so on. Also, because performance measurement now occurred at more points and organizational levels, the opportunity for reward systems to promote financial ownership increased, mostly in the form of bonuses and stock-purchase plans. These key trends, we believe, can be used to forecast the main characteristics of twenty-first century organizational forms.

THE TWENTY-FIRST CENTURY: ERA OF INNOVATION

In tomorrow's business world, some markets will still be supplied with standard products and services, while other markets will demand large amounts of customization. However, the continued pull of market forces, and the push of ever-increasing know-how honed through network partnering, is already moving some industries and companies toward what amounts to a continuous process of innovation. Beyond the customization of existing designs, product and service invention is becoming the centerpiece of value-adding activity in an increasing number of firms. So-called knowledge businesses—such as design and engineering services, advanced electronics and biotechnology, computer software design, health care, and consulting—not only feed the process of innovation but feed upon it in a continuous cycle that creates more and more complex markets and environments.[6] Indeed, for companies in such businesses, both by choice and by the consequences of their choices, organizational inputs and outputs become highly unpredictable.

For example, according to the CEO of a biotechnology firm, the potential inputs to the firm are spread across hundreds and even thousands of scientists worldwide. Around each prominent researcher is a cluster of colleagues, and each cluster is a rich mix of talent held together by a set of connecting mechanisms, including shared interests, electronic mail systems, and technical conferences. Connecting devices are not coordinated by plan but rather are self-organizing, reflecting the knowledge needs and data-sharing opportunities recognized by members of the various clusters. The overall challenge of the biotechnology firm is to maintain close contact with as much of this continuously evolving knowledge field as it can. A similarly complex pattern is visible at the output interface of the firm, as myriad alliances and partnerships are formed to take partially developed products (and by-products) through the stages of final design, testing, and marketing. Clearly, a biotechnology firm that is rigidly structured will not be able to muster the internal flexibility required to match the complexity of its environment.

A NEW ORGANIZATIONAL FORM FOR A NEW ECONOMIC ERA

Similar elements of complexity are visible in a growing number of industries. In computer software, for example, there are few limits on potentially profitable product designs, and a vast array of independent designers move in and around software companies of every size. The choices firms face at both the input and output ends of their operation are thus large and constantly changing. Faced with these opportunities and projecting the evolutionary trends discussed above, one would expect the twenty-first century organization to rely heavily on clusters of self-organizing components collaboratively investing the enterprise's know-how in product and service innovations for markets that they have helped create and develop.

Such firms can best be described as cellular.[7] The cellular metaphor suggests a living adaptive organization. Cells in living organisms possess fundamental functions of life and can act alone to meet a particular need. However, by acting in concert, cells can perform more complex functions. Evolving characteristics, or learning, if shared across all cells can create a higher-order organism. Similarly, a cellular organization is made up of cells (self-managing teams, autonomous business units, etc.) that can operate alone but that can interact with other cells to produce a more potent and competent business mechanism. It is this combination of independence and interdependence that allows the cellular organizational form to generate and share the know-how that produces continuous innovation.

BUILDING BLOCKS OF THE CELLULAR FORM

In the future, complete cellular firms will achieve a level of know-how well beyond that of earlier organizational forms by combining entrepreneurship, self-organization, and member ownership in mutually reinforcing ways. Each cell (team, strategic business unit, firm) will have an entrepreneurial responsibility to the larger organization. The customers of a particular cell can be outside clients or other cells in the organization. In either case, the purpose is to spread an entrepreneurial mind-set throughout the organization so that every cell is concerned about improvement and growth. Indeed, giving each cell entrepreneurial responsibility is essential to the full utilization of the firm's constantly growing know-how. Of course, each cell must also have the entrepreneurial skills required to generate business for itself and the overall organization.

Each cell must be able to continually reorganize in order to make its expected contribution to the overall organization. Of particular value here are the technical skills needed to perform its function, the collaborative skills necessary to make appropriate linkages with other organizational units and external partner firms, and the governance skills required to manage its own activities. Application of this cellular principle may require the company to strip away most of the bureaucracy that is currently in place and replace it with jointly defined protocols that guide internal and external collaboration.

Each cell must be rewarded for acting entrepreneurially and operating in a business-like manner. If the cellular units are teams or strategic business units instead of complete firms, psychological ownership can be achieved by organizing cells as profit centers, allowing them to participate in company stock-purchase plans, and so on. However, the ultimate cellular solution is probably actual member ownership of those cell assets and resources that they have created and that they voluntarily invest with the firm in expectation of a joint return.

TOWARD THE CELLULAR ORGANIZATION

Examples of cellular organizations, in that the individual cellular principles and their interconnectedness are clearly seen, are rare. We have attempted to identify and track those companies that appear to be at the leading-edge of organizational practice, and our interviews and observations to date have uncovered one example of a complete cellular organization, Technical and Computer Graphics of Sydney, Australia. Also, The Acer Group, a rapidly-growing personal computer company, is a significant user of cellular principles on a global scale. There are many examples of companies around the world that are partial users of the cellular form, relying on one or more of its key building blocks to achieve impressive innovative capabilities.

TCG: A COMPLETE CELLULAR ORGANIZATION

Technical and Computer Graphics (TCG), a privately-held information-technology company, is perhaps the best example of the cellular approach to organizing. TCG develops a wide variety of products and services including portable and hand-held data terminals and loggers, computer graphics systems, bar-coding systems, electronic data interchange systems, and other IT products and services.

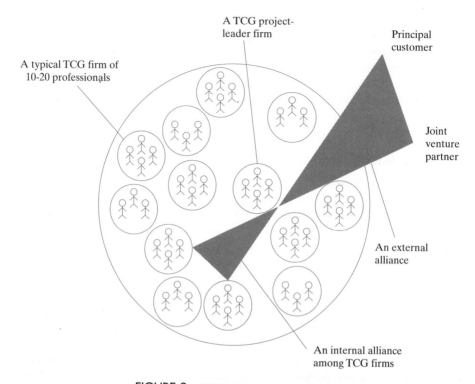

FIGURE 2   **TCG's Cellular Organization**

The 13 individual small firms at TCG are the focus of cellularity. Like a cell in a large organism, each firm has its own purpose and ability to function independently, but it shares common features and purpose with all of its sister firms. Some TCG member firms specialize in one or more product categories, while others specialize in hardware or software.

At TCG, the various firms have come into the group with existing high levels of technical and business competence. However, the operating protocol at TCG assures that systemwide competence will continue to grow. The process is called *triangulation*, and it is the means by which TCG continually develops new products and services.[8] Triangulation is a three-cornered partnership among (a) one or more TCG firms, (b) an external joint-venture partner (e.g., Hitachi) that also provides equity capital to the venture, and (c) a principal customer (e.g., Telstra, an Australian telephone company) whose large advance order wins it contractual rights as well as provides additional cash to the venture.

Each TCG firm is expected to search continually for new product and service opportunities. When a particular venture shows concrete promise, the initiating firm acts as project leader for the remainder of the venture. The first step in the triangulation process is to identify and collaborate with a joint-venture partner, a firm with expertise in the proposed technology. TCG receives partial funding for the project from the joint-venture partner, and it also gains access to technical ideas and distribution channels. Next, the project leader firm identifies an initial large customer for the new product. TCG also collaborates with the customer in the sense that it agrees to custom-design a product for that client. By working together with the joint-venture partner and the principal customer, TCG is able to efficiently develop a state-of-the-art product that is tailor-made to the principal customer's specifications.

According to TCG's governance principles, the project leader firm is also expected to search among the other TCG companies for additional partners—not only because they are needed for their technical contribution, but also because the collaboration itself is expected to enhance overall organizational know-how. The process of internal triangulation thus serves a dual purpose. It produces direct input to the project, and it helps to diffuse competence in areas such as business development, partnering, and project management. The three principles of cellularity are tightly interconnected at TCG, mutually reinforcing each other and producing a strong overall organization. First, acceptance of entrepreneurial responsibility is required for admission to the group and is increasingly enhanced by the triangulation process. Second, self-organization gives the individual firm both the ability and the freedom to reach deeply into its own know-how to create responses to a continuously evolving set of customer and partner needs. Third, each firm's profit responsibility, as well as its opportunity to own stock in other TCG firms, provides an ongoing stimulus for the growth and utilization of know-how.

To this point, TCG has pushed its version of the cellular organizational approach to a modest size (approximately 200 staff in 13 small firms). Whether TCG's particular approach can be used to propel its growth to medium or large size is not yet clear. It may well be that some modification of its self-organizing abilities and reward system may be required.

ACER: A GLOBAL CELLULAR COMPANY

An attempt to build a large-scale cellular organization is evident at the Acer Group, where cofounder Stan Shih has created a vision of a global personal computer company.[9] Shih's design, like that at TCG, calls for a federation of self-managing firms held together by mutual interest rather than hierarchical control. Shih's driving slogan is "21 in 21"—a federation of at least 21 independent firm located around the world by the twenty-first century, each operating in what Shih calls a "client-server" mode. That is, each firm, depending on the type of transaction involved, is either a client or a server of the other firms in the federation. Some firms, called Regional Business Units (RBUs), are operated primarily as marketing organizations—advertising, selling, and servicing computers according to particular national or regional needs. Other firms, called Strategic Business Units (SBUs), are primarily R&D, manufacturing, and distribution units. For the most part, RBUs are clients that receive products from servers, the SBUs. However, RBUs are required to submit on an ongoing basis short, medium, and long-term forecasts of their product needs. In this mode, the SBUs are the clients of the RBUs—depending on each RBU's knowledge of its local market to provide information that will drive product development and manufacturing.

Although each firm has a core task to perform, new product concepts can and do originate anywhere in the federation. For example, Acer America (an RBU) wanted a stylish yet affordable PC for the North American market. It contracted with Frog, an outside industrial design firm, to assist it in the development of the highly acclaimed Acer Aspire. Manufacturing was done by Acer SBUs, and the marketing campaign was jointly developed by Acer America and Acer International, another RBU based in Singapore. Other Acer units are free to borrow from the Aspire design or to create unique designs suited to their respective markets. Every new product proposal is evaluated as a business venture by the federation's partner firms.

Shih's vision for the Acer federation of companies, however, appears to go one step beyond that of TCG in terms of reinforcing both the responsibility of the individual firm for its own destiny and the responsibility of all firms for the long-term success of the total organization. At TCG, the value of each of the member firms is calculated through an internal stock market, and firms are free to leave the group if they so choose. At Acer, the firms are each jointly owned by their own management and home-country investors, with a (usually) minority ownership position held by Acer, Inc., the parent firm. Shih intends that Acer firms around the world will be listed on local stock exchanges and be free to seek capital for their own expansion. He believes that local ownership unleashes the motivation to run each business prudently.

With all Acer firms enjoying the freedom to both operate and expand, the value of their membership in the federation is the capacity of the "cells" to continue to serve one another in an increasingly competitive global marketplace. Acer has developed the competence to efficiently produce all its products for just-in-time assembly and distribution. With minimal inventories, the latest models are available at all times at every sales site.

As yet, Acer's operating protocols are not as explicitly geared to the diffusion of know-how as they are at TCG. Nevertheless, Acer's business model provides the opportunity for each firm to draw on federation partners as preferred providers or clients. Currently, Acer's worldwide training programs are being used to translate Shih's global vision into action programs at the local firm level.

PARTIAL USES OF THE CELLULAR APPROACH

Even those firms that have not yet moved to a complete cellular model appear to obtain benefits from using one or more of its three main building blocks. For example, Kyocera relied heavily on the principle of self-organization to improve its manufacturing process. Each of its cells consists of a small group of machines and a team of highly trained employees who collaborate in the production of a well-defined set of products for a specific group of customers. As opposed to the functional organization of manufacturing where machines are grouped according to task performed, and products or parts are produced through specialized batch methods, the cellular approach divides the stream of production into parallel flows, giving the members of each cell responsibility for planning their own operations, ensuring that the quality of their output meets specified performance standards, interfacing with their suppliers and customers, and responding to unusual circumstances.[10]

Oticon, the Danish hearing aid manufacturer, has carefully reengineered its organization using approaches similar to the cellular principles of self-organization and entrepreneurship. First, it dramatically and systematically removed many of the bureaucratic barriers that plagued organization members. It eliminated rules, reports, and forms, achieving in the process a paperless workplace. It reduced the need for planning and supervision by allowing employees to choose their project teams. Such volunteerism also served to stimulate entrepreneurship, as the most successful projects were those which were widely regarded as compelling ideas.[11] Thus, self-managing teams now have responsibility for both the identification and organization of new business projects.

At Semco, the Brazilian industrial-equipment manufacturer, management places great emphasis on the principles of member ownership and entrepreneurship. Work teams within all of Semco's plants have a standing invitation to take their operations outside the company and form their own business firms. If the new outside firm uses Semco equipment, the company will lease that equipment to the firm at very favorable rates. If the new firm provides a product or service desired by Semco, it can do business with its former employer. Even if the new firm later wishes to rejoin Semco, it can propose to do so, and the decision will be treated just like any other business proposal. All of these actions are encouraged because Ricardo Semler, Semco's former CEO, believes that employee ownership is the best means of achieving a competitive business. Although it is a privately held company, Semco shares almost a quarter of its profits with managers and employees.[12]

ADDING VALUE BY USING THE CELLULAR FORM

A close examination of cellularly structured firms such as TCG and Acer indicates that they also share some of the features of earlier organizational forms. Indeed, each new form, as we noted earlier, incorporates the major value-adding characteristics of the previous forms and adds new capabilities to them. Thus, the cellular form includes the dispersed entrepreneurship of the divisional form, customer responsiveness of the matrix form, and self-organizing knowledge and asset sharing of the network form.

The cellular organizational form, however, offers the potential to add value even beyond asset and know-how sharing. In its fully developed state, the cellular organization adds value through its unique ability to create and utilize knowledge. For example, knowledge sharing occurs in networks as a by-product of asset sharing rather than as a specific focus of such activity. Similarly, matrix and divisionalized firms recognize the value that may be added when knowledge is shared across projects or divisions, but they must create special-purpose mechanisms (e.g., task forces) in order to generate and share new knowledge. By contrast, as illustrated at TCG, the cellular form lends itself to sharing not only the explicit know-how that cells have accumulated and articulated, but also the tacit know-how that emerges when cells combine to design unique new customer solutions.[13] Such learning focuses not on the output of the innovation process, but on the innovation process itself: It is know-how that can be achieved and shared only by doing.

Beyond knowledge creation and sharing, the cellular form has the potential to add value through its related ability to keep the firm's total knowledge assets more fully invested than do the other organizational forms. Because each cell has entrepreneurial responsibility and is empowered to draw on any of the firm's assets for each new business opportunity, high levels of knowledge utilization across cells should be expected. Network organizations aspire to high utilization of know-how and assets, but upstream firms are ultimately dependent on downstream partners to find new product or service uses. In the cellular firm, the product/service innovation process is continuous and fully shared.

IMPLEMENTING THE CELLULAR ORGANIZATION

Many organizational variations using some or all of the cellular principles are likely to emerge in the years ahead.[14] While the direction of the evolution is clear, however, companies that attempt implementation of the complete cellular form face several significant challenges. It is certain that cellularly structured firms will not just happen. Our interviews with leaders of cellular firms make it clear that such a firm is the product of a bold managerial vision and, even more importantly, of a unique managerial philosophy.[15] The ability to envision and build the entrepreneurial, self-organizing, and ownership components of cellular organizations must be undergirded with a philosophy that emphasizes investment in human capabilities and the willingness to take substantial risks to maximize their utilization.

The first requirement is a willingness to invest in human capability that goes well beyond simply providing for current education and training. The concept of investment calls for expenditures to build the capabilities needed to respond to the future demands that will be placed on the organization, even those that cannot be easily forecast. Training to meet current needs is not an investment, because the requirement is clear, and the costs and benefits can be easily calculated. Building competencies for future needs is an investment because risk is involved—not every return can be predicted and, moreover, not everyone whose skills are enhanced will remain with the firm.

Companies such as Chaparral Steel, for example, make heavy investments in building know-how even though not all returns can be easily measured. Chaparral invests up to one-third of every member's time annually in one form or another of continuous education and skill development. Chaparral views growing know-how as the basic source of members' ability to add economic value in a highly competitive industry.[16] The competencies visible in firms such as Kyocera, Oticon, Semco, Acer, and TCG are the products of similar investments.

It is worth noting that the basic notion of achieving competitive advantage through people is far from new. In the late 1950s, Edith Penrose focused on managerial competence as the principal engine of organizational growth, and in the 1960s, Rensis Likert advocated careful accounting for investments in human resources and the costs of managerial actions that might deplete them. The 1990s have brought a renewed awareness among managers and management scholars that building know-how is the primary means by which firms create economic value.[17] The difference today, however, is that continuing investment in the competence of organization members is no longer merely an option; it is an economic must.[18]

The concept of investment always involves risk, which is usually proportional to the level of possible return. The biggest challenge facing most firms that are considering the use of a cellular form of organization is not just the investment required to build key competencies; it is the willingness to allow the levels of self-governance necessary to fully utilize that competence. For example, Oticon takes what many firms would view as an extraordinary risk in allowing members to choose their own work assignments on projects where their capabilities can be most effectively used. Others would regard the firm (cell) autonomy allowed at TCG and Acer to involve even bigger risks, since coordination is largely voluntary, and agreed-upon protocols and responsibilities are used instead of hierarchical controls.

Perhaps even more challenging than making investments and taking risks, however, is the long-term requirement for sharing with organization members the returns of their knowledge utilization. If organization members are to accept professional levels of responsibility, traditional reward schemes such as bonus plans are not likely to be sufficient. Perhaps the future structure of return-sharing will follow the philosophies expressed by Stan Shih and Ricardo Semler—that the long-run pursuit of an increasingly competent organization may require innovative mechanisms providing real ownership and profit-sharing, mechanisms that give members' intellectual capital the same rights as the financial capital supplied by stockholders.

Given the required levels of investment, risk-taking, and member ownership, many companies will not—and need not—move completely to the cellular organizational form. Firms that produce standard products or services to forecast or order may still be most productive if arranged in at least shallow hierarchies. Groups of such firms may be linked into networks for greater speed and customization. The push toward cellular approaches, as noted earlier, is appearing first in firms focused on rapid product and service innovation—unique and/or state-of-the-art offerings. However, while cellular firms are most easily associated with newer, rapidly evolving industries, the form lends itself to firms providing the design initiative in virtually any type of industry. Within a network of companies in a mature business, it is the cellularly structured firms that are likely to provide leadership in new product and service development.

CONCLUSION

Across national and regional economies, the overlapping eras of standardization, customization, and innovation will continue to evolve, and new variations of hierarchical, network, and cellular organizational forms will continue to emerge. Decades of experimentation honed the functional, divisional, matrix, and network forms, clarifying their operating logics and highlighting their costs and benefits. A similar pattern can be expected to occur with the cellular form. Throughout the evolutionary process of organizational form, one constant has been the search for ever-increasing effectiveness and efficiency in the ability to fully apply know-how to resource utilization. Firms willing to take the risks to lead this search have been and will continue to be economic leaders.

ENDNOTES

[1] For excellent accounts of the evolution of organizational forms during this period, see A. D. Chandler, Jr., *Strategy and Structure: Chapters in the History of the American Industrial Enterprise* (Cambridge, MA: The MIT Press, 1962); and P. R. Lawrence and D. Dyer, Blackwell, 1959. A new edition of this book, with a foreword by Professor Penrose, was published in 1995.

[2] A discussion of "excess managerial capacity" as the engine of corporate growth can be found in E. T. Penrose, *The Theory of the Growth of the Firm* (Oxford, England; Basil); "Generation of Self-Managing Human Systems," *Human Systems Management* 9 (1990): 57–59.

[3] For a discussion of matrix organizations, see S. M. Davis and P. R. Lawrence, *Matrix* (Reading, MA: Addison-Wesley, 1977).

[4] For a discussion of the globalization process, see M. E. Porter, ed., *Competition in Global Industries* (Boston, MA: Harvard Business School Press, 1986).

[5] The multifirm network organization was first identified and described by R. E. Miles and C. C. Snow, "Fit, Failure, and the Hall of Fame," *California Management Review 26*, no. 3 (1984): 10–28. For descriptions of the major types of network organizations used today, see R. E. Miles and C. C. Snow, *Fit, Failure, and the Hall of Fame: How Companies Succeed or Fall* (New York, NY: Free Press, 1994) chapters 7–9.

[6] S. Kauffman, *At Home in the Universe* (New York, NY: Oxford University Press, 1995).

[7] We did not invent the cellular label. The concept of cellular structures has been discussed at least since the 1960s. For a review, see J. A. Mathews, "Holonic Organisational Architectures," *Human Systems Management 15* (1996): 1–29.

[8] J. A. Mathews, "TCG R&D Networks: The Triangulation Strategy," *Journal of Industry Studies 1* (1993): 65–74.

[9] J. A. Mathews and C. C. Snow, "The Expansionary Dynamics of the Latecomer Multinational Firm: The Case of The Acer Group," *Asia Pacific Journal of Management*, forthcoming.

[10] M. Zeleny, *Amoebae: The New Renewing American Industry* (New York, NY: Free Press, 1983).

[11] L. Kolind, "Creativity at Oticon," *Fast Company*, 1996, 5–9.

[12] R. Semler, *Maverick* (New York, NY: Time Warner Books, 1993).

[13] I. Nonaka and H. Takeuchi, *The Knowledge-Creating Company: How Japanese Companies Create the Dynamics of Innovation* (New York, NY: Oxford University Press, 1995).

[14] Many of these experiments will involve various forms of strategic alliances and/or joint ventures. See A. C. Inkpen, "Creating Knowledge Through Collaboration," *California Management Review 39* (1996): 123–140.

[15] J. A. Mathews and C. C. Snow, "A Conversation with Taiwan-based Acer Group's Stan Shih on Global Strategy," *Organizational Dynamics* (Summer 1998).

[16] G. E. Forward, D. E. Beach, D. A. Gray, and J. C. Quick, "Mentofacturing: A Vision for American Industrial Excellence," *The Academy of Management Executive 5* (1991): 32–44.

[17] Penrose; R. Likert, *The Human Organization* (New York, NY: McGraw-Hill, 1967); and J. Pfeffer, *Competitive Advantage Through People* (Boston, MA: Harvard Business School Press, 1994).

[18] For an example of a firm that seriously and creatively attempted to calculate the value of its intellectual capital and other intangible assets, see L. Edvinsson and M. S. Malone, *Intellectual Capital: Realizing Your Company's True Value by Finding Its Hidden Brainpower* (New York, NY: HarperBusiness, 1997).

Up the (E) Organization!: A Seven-Dimensional Model for the Centerless Enterprise*

Gary L. Neilson
Bruce A. Pasternack
Albert J. Viscio

The Internet offers alluring opportunities for top- and bottom-line growth, yet the promise has been difficult to realize. Indeed, many companies have struggled to invest in the Internet's advantages quickly and align their operations and business models around e-commerce. Few have succeeded in becoming e-businesses-dynamic, adaptive, around-the-clock operations that can act faster and in more flexible ways.

*Reprinted with permission from *Strategy and Business 18* (First Quarter, 2000): 52–61.

True e-businesses are redefining traditional value chains and developing complex knowledge-sharing systems that connect pricing, product and design information with suppliers and customers. Examples include not only new-form competitors like eBay and Amazon.com, but also established companies like Charles Schwab, Dell and Cisco. These e-businesses incorporate four characteristics: a major revenue contribution from the Internet; a P&L focus; alignment of all processes with the Internet, and a 24/7 electronic infrastructure.

Most businesses find themselves in one of three positions along the way to becoming an e-business. At present, the great majority of companies fall into the first category—"creating brochureware." They use the Internet predominantly to provide information to prospective customers and other interested parties via a company Web site. Through this site they can extend their reach globally and begin to manage knowledge more effectively.

A second group of companies are "breaking the boundaries"—using electronic technologies and infrastructure to connect existing operations and processes through automation. They are selling goods over the Internet and shifting to a paperless order-to-delivery process. In so doing, they are starting to redefine relationships with customers and suppliers, and facilitating communications inside the company by sharing knowledge between units and tying business processes together.

If a firm uses its Web site to take orders and deliver products but does not add any capabilities such as customization or interactivity to distinguish the service from other types of direct selling, does this constitute e-commerce? If a firm develops a fully transactional Internet sales channel but does not integrate Internet technology into the rest of the firm, is this an e-business? In both cases we would say, "No."

The real potential to transform the ground rules of global commerce can be seen in the third and last category of companies, those that are "transforming the business." Such companies exploit the unique capabilities of the Internet as a computing and commerce platform to develop a distinct and dominant business on the Web. Indeed, these companies are reorganizing their business models—or creating fundamentally new businesses—to offer new value propositions to customers and shareholders. Along the way, they've changed how corporations organize themselves.

AN ORGANIZATIONAL MODEL FOR E-BUSINESS

Just as the value chain has been disintermediated, so too has the traditional organization. The Digital Age organization is no longer a single corporate entity, but rather an extended network consisting of a streamlined Global Core, market-focused business units and shared support services. The transformation to what we call an "e.org" is taking place along seven key dimensions (see Exhibit 1):

1. Organization Structure
2. Leadership
3. People and Culture
4. Coherence
5. Knowledge
6. Alliances
7. Governance

The fact that there are seven organizational dimensions retires one of the most visible relics of the command-and-control, hierarchical organization model—the org chart. A collection of boxes and reporting lines on a two-dimensional slip of paper no longer accurately captures the operating dynamics of today's extended—or "e-stended"—enterprise. It's time to label "lines and boxes" as archeological artifacts.

	1990's	E. org
Organization Structure	• Hierarchical • Command-and-control	• Centerless, networked • Flexible structure that is easily modified
Leadership	• Selected "stars" step above • Leaders set the agenda • Leaders force change	• Everyone is a leader • Leaders create environment for success • Leaders create capacity for change
People & Culture	• Long-term rewards • Vertical decision-making • Individuals and small teams are rewarded	• "Own your own career" mentality • Delegated authority • Collaboration expected and rewarded
Coherence	• Hard-wired into processes • Internal relevance	• Embedded vision in individuals • Impact projected externally
Knowledge	• Focused on internal processes • Individualistic	• Focused on customers • Institutional
Alliances	• Complement current gaps • Ally with distant partners	• Create new value and outsource uncompetitive services • Ally with competitors, customers and suppliers
Governance	• Internally focused • Top-down	• Internal and external focus • Distributed

EXHIBIT 1   E.Org Dimensions

Source: Booz-Allen and Hamilton.

ORGANIZATION STRUCTURE

In place of bureaucratic, hierarchical structures, companies should form more flexible, decentralized, team- and alliance-based organizations that enable employees to respond immediately to opportunities and competitive advantages around the globe. This new e-stended enterprise model is built around a strategic Global Core, shared-services business units, and market-facing business units.

The Global Core is a revolutionary overhaul of the old corporate center or headquarters. It is a bare-bones operation consisting solely of the CEO, his or her team, and only those services necessary to add value to the corporation-strategic leadership, corporate identity, capital-raising, management control and the ability to deploy world-class capabilities.

For example, one of the Global Core's key responsibilities is to provide strategic leadership. This is exerted through the encouragement of "out of the box" thinking and behaviors that promote it. Examples include GE's "boundaryless" corporation; ABB's "multidomestic" company; Motorola's "Six Sigma" quality methodology, and British Airways' "world's favourite airline" strategy built on customer service. Each of these removes the company's business units from a lock-step system of policy and measurement, and encourages people to use their imagination, knowledge, and common sense in pursuit of new opportunities.

Traditional overhead functions such as finance and human resources can increasingly be managed as shared services-business units providing services that are often transaction-oriented or consultative. Shared-services units operate with market dynamics by "selling" services to other business units and to the Global Core. They compete with outside vendors, and any division within the organization has the choice to buy a particular service internally or externally. Benefits are realized through economies of scale, focus of expertise, and the natural tension of market forces.

In order to compete with outside vendors and offer pricing comparable to that of other business units, shared-services units must aggressively pursue alternative delivery models to reduce costs continually and improve efficiency. The Internet enables these overhead units to form networks of shared-services units that are integrated not only with other business units, but also with suppliers and customers. These regional, national and global service networks capture world-class expertise throughout the company, while lowering overall costs.

Washington, DC-based MCI Worldcom Inc., for example, takes employee self-service and technology integration to a higher level. The company's internal on-line human resources system, known as "The Source," provides employees with more than 1,400 pages of interactive services. At the click of a mouse, employees can venture on-line to reallocate investments in their 401(k) accounts, fill out electronic W-4 tax forms, and view electronic pay stubs a week before they're paid. They can view streaming videos of managers providing briefings, check best practices within the company, and sign up for distance-learning courses directly from their desktops.

Almost every aspect of the recruiting and hiring process is automated and accessible via a single desktop interface. Systems are tightly integrated. For instance, an employee can log on to MCI's intranet and register for a training course. His or her manager is notified instantly, and the system sends an immediate confirmation back to the employee. No paperwork, no forms and no lengthy approvals. More than 55 percent of MCI employees have access to virtual course work and virtual classrooms over the company's intranet. From October 1997 through June 1999, MCI realized more than $2.8 million in total savings due to reduced travel, facility, and labor costs.

Finally, businesses should organize around natural business units (NBUs) that are agile and configured from the outside in—from the perspective of customers rather than senior management or organizational structure—to focus on unique and natural markets.

NBUs have identifiable capabilities, operations, customers, and/or competitors. They have strategic partnerships with their suppliers, even when some of those suppliers are divisions of their own corporations. Yet there are no sweetheart deals or cross-subsidies that can't be justified in economic terms.

Several of today's traditional organizations consider their Internet businesses to be NBUs and are structuring them as such. Citigroup, for example, has created e-Citi to appeal to on-line banking customers; Barnes & Noble, Inc. created Barnesandnoble.com to compete with Amazon.com in reaching readers who prefer to purchase books over the Web.

The three components of the developing organization structure need to move nimbly. The Global Core must accommodate a more complex extended enterprise and manage value from growing partnerships and alliances. Shared services need to leverage the Internet to provide a greater variety of services at substantially lower cost and with higher levels of service, sometimes by outsourcing work that cannot be provided competitively in-house. Business units must hone their unique value propositions in the rapidly evolving electronic marketplace. And the entire organization must reorient its focus to deliver speed, global reach, and superior service.

LEADERSHIP

In e-business, leadership is no longer the province of the anointed few. The process of promoting select individuals into positions of authority is a relic of a command-and-control culture that paralyzes companies trying to compete in an Internet-enabled environment. The old model of CEO as lone "star" is no longer relevant. He or she can no longer set agendas and dictate change.

In the e.org, everyone is a leader, charged with creating an environment for collective gain and success. And the mark of a leader will be to create other leaders within the organization—disciples, of a sort, who are empowered to act. These disciples, in turn, manifest their own leadership skills by translating this vision into a mandate for continued renewal. They create an environment and build management bench strength to achieve change and cascade leadership throughout the organization.

This model of cascading leadership is not a luxury; it is an imperative in a world where organizations no longer have the time for day-to-day decisions to go up and down a hierarchy, and where knowledge throughout the organization must be leveraged and shared. It's not easy. Market forces continue to rage as companies wrestle with the organizational barriers to institutionalizing this type of entrepreneurial leadership model.

British Telecommunications PLC, for example, is now developing a team of "evangelistic visionaries and mavericks," as John Swingewood, former director of B.T.'s Internet and Multimedia Services division, calls them, who are well-versed in both the breakthrough potential of Internet technology and its risks. Deregulation and competitive posturing have pushed the British telecommunications marketplace into a free-for-all, pitting B.T. against competition from a new breed of nimble up-and-comers. Assaulted on all fronts, the company must transform itself from a traditional telephone utility into a competition-minded innovator.

One of the tasks for these mavericks is to find ways for B.T. to capitalize on the research at its Advanced Technologies Research Center, and quickly find markets for the cutting-edge research conducted there. Mr. Swingewood says that B.T.'s success will depend on creating the right conditions for Digital Age leadership. As he puts it, "If the Internet has this big opportunity to sell something, it's easy for companies to figure out how to deliver it." That is, provided the company has the right culture.

PEOPLE AND CULTURE

The rapid pace and nearly infinite opportunity of e-business will test the limits of companies' people strategies and corporate culture. As digital technologies take over the more routine, administrative duties performed by employees, they will amplify the need for skilled knowledge workers in every functional group and at all levels. Unfortunately, the very same factors that accelerate demand for exceptional, versatile and motivated talent will tend to diminish a company's ability to attract and hold on to such talent. As the dot-coms hand out stock options and entrepreneurial opportunity to C.E.O.s and secretaries alike, more established companies are struggling to match these packages. Companies of all types are being held hostage by their employees.

To recruit and retain these individuals, the e.org needs to overhaul its approach to human-resources management. It needs to recognize that the basic tenets of the employment contract are no longer valid. Companies no longer offer job security, and employees no longer offer undivided commitment and loyalty. They "own their own employability," as Andrew S. Grove, chairman of the Intel Corporation, has put it.

Increasingly, employees are sharing their knowledge and unique skills with an employer in return for development opportunities. To the extent that an organization continues to offer new challenges and incentives, employees stay. Once their personal development passport has been stamped, however, employees may well move on. With this understanding in mind, companies need to anticipate and plan for their long-term needs, rather than focusing exclusively on filling today's slots.

They need to develop a culture that supports the new way of doing business—one that focuses on innovation, change management and leadership through a shared mission. Companies need to encourage intelligent risk-taking throughout the business, at all levels. In short, they need to inject starched shirts with a little entrepreneurial medicine. As Ann M. Livermore, president and CEO of the Hewlett-Packard Company's Enterprise Computing Solutions, puts it, "Try bringing the free thinkers—the rebels, the crazies—into the group so you get more diversity of thinking. And don't require them to follow procedures."

Organizations looking to respond to these shifting priorities will need to invest in people. They will need to establish a clear link between their people strategy and their corporate vision and develop a culture predicated on a people partnership. Moreover, they need to identify high performers critical to organizational success and focus on their needs—that combination of job design, career development opportunities, rewards and lifestyle that enables companies to attract and retain talent.

COHERENCE

Businesses should recognize that extracting 70 or 80 percent of their potential is not good enough; they need to be efficient at every point along the value chain to stave off the threat of disintermediation. To generate that value, employees at all levels across the company need to be ready to innovate and make good decisions quickly.

Coherence, or alignment, is what makes that possible. It is that shared sense of direction that allows a corporation to be greater than the sum of its parts. In aligned organizations, objectives are clear; roles and responsibilities are well defined and delegated, and the right things are accurately measured and rewarded.

The coherent corporation can de-emphasize a rigid organizational structure and build more flexible configurations of people, processes and systems, because the goals and objectives of the corporation are well understood. Decision-making can be accelerated and information shared. Coherence encourages every individual to drive purposefully toward a clearly communicated common goal.

This characteristic is often present in new companies, such as small Internet startups. These firms are created with a specific sense of purpose, with all employees working for a common goal and with an incentive system directly tied to the success of the enterprise. Coherence in larger companies is harder to achieve. Multiple levels and conflicting agendas can have people working at cross-purposes. Companies such as Southwest Airlines, Enron and GE have created highly coherent models due to the efforts of their CEOs to insure that the kinds of people they hire, those employees' understanding of where the company wants to go, and the means by which their contributions are rewarded, all fit into a unique system.

KNOWLEDGE

It is hard to place a value on knowledge, but to the extent that knowledge can be translated into corporate capabilities, it is precious.

Knowledge is the set of understandings used by people to make decisions or take actions that are important to the company. Part of the knowledge structure is, of course, information, a component that digital technologies have largely commoditized. But there is more to knowledge than sheer data. It is what you do with the information, how you stitch it together in unique ways with know-how, processes and market perceptions, that constitutes knowledge. And knowledge is an increasingly valuable and differentiating asset, one that will, in due time, be recorded on companies' balance sheets. More and more, companies are being seen not as a collection of businesses, but as a collection of capabilities based on highly precise knowledge.

The Internet exalts effective knowledge management, rewarding those companies that manage to translate rich data into improved customer service, increased personalization, and institutionalized best practices. As the customer's "experience" becomes the differentiated aspect of a product—while the product itself becomes a commodity—the need to create robust knowledge systems becomes all the more important. And any impediments to the free flow of knowledge in the traditional organization—the tendency to hoard your best thinking and avoid using what others have developed—must be broken down.

What does such a knowledge system look like? We see glimpses in the following:

- Cisco Systems Inc. shares knowledge with its business partners using an extranet that allows suppliers to tap directly into Cisco's manufacturing and order processes with real-time access to product logistics information and order flow (see "Focus: Cisco Systems," page 559).
- The Boeing Company's Wing Responsibility Center is a working group formed to build and maintain wings, tails and rudders for commercial and military aircraft. With an intranet, the knowledge of a worker specializing in wings for a Boeing 777 can be accessed immediately by an engineer on another project at another location.
- BP Amoco PLC uses interactive technologies to broaden collaborative employee involvement at conferences. Meetings once restricted to essential personnel are now open to thousands of employees through Internet technology, encouraging increased employee involvement.

ALLIANCES

The Internet is accelerating and intensifying the global trend toward alliances. As competitive boundaries blur in e-business, formerly disparate products, markets and geographical regions are becoming part of the same playing field. All firms are now vulnerable to the threats posed by cooperative strategies. Management must act faster and smarter with limited resources.

In this environment, successful companies need to build and deploy the critical capabilities that will enable them to gain competitive advantage, enhance customer value and drive their markets. Alliances are an excellent way to secure immediate access to those differentiating capabilities. Partners can extend their global reach, leverage their respective strengths, and bridge strategic gaps in their own capabilities.

Strategic alliances are cooperative arrangements between two or more companies where:

- A common strategy is developed in unison.
- A win-win attitude is adopted by all parties.
- The relationship is reciprocal, with each partner prepared to share specific strengths with the others, thus lending power to the enterprise.
- A pooling of resources, investment and risks occurs for mutual (rather than individual) gain.

In the new e-stended enterprise, companies will form alliances not only to bridge capabilities and geographic gaps, but also to create new value and outsource uncompetitive services. Alliances themselves will become more open and adaptable as organizations form and disband agreements with suppliers, customers, competitors, even regulators, to position themselves in a changing market. These alliances will be run more autonomously with dedicated resources and a fair degree of independent control.

The Ford Motor Company's recent alliance with CarPoint, the Microsoft Corporation's online car retailing service, is an example of how alliances will transform the consumer experience in an e-business world. Together, these two companies are developing an online build-to-order system to link consumer order configurations directly with automotive manufacturers' supply and delivery systems. This will allow consumers to order any model of car to their exact specifications on CarPoint, Ford.com and other automotive destination sites, receive immediate feedback on availability, and schedule delivery and service at their local dealership.

GOVERNANCE

Issues of governance will multiply in the e-stended enterprise of the near future. A broader concept than is generally appreciated, governance encompasses three areas—governance of the entire corporation by the board of directors, governance of intercompany alliances, and governance of intracompany entities. The traditional top-down, internally focused governance structure of the past is yielding to a more distributed model that incorporates both internal and external scrutiny.

The board of directors, while continuing its fundamental duty to safeguard shareholders' interests, should become more involved in matters of corporate governance now than it has in the past. Instead of playing a passive guardianship role, it should become an active supporter of the business.

Under this new model, the board performs an active advisory role, and also acts as a control body. It brings insights on customers from a cross-section of industries and services; it benchmarks inside knowledge with outside intelligence; it challenges the effectiveness of the CEO and top management (the role of the Global Core); and it makes sure the company is developing key business capabilities.

In terms of intracompany governance, the concept of shared services is illustrative. Shared services, such as human resources and information technology, run as autonomous business units in an internal marketplace where they serve "customers"—other business units with the power and autonomy to buy and shop elsewhere.

To govern these new business units, several organizations have set up internal governance boards. For example, AlliedSignal, Inc. (which recently merged with Honeywell Inc.) has a shared-services board that includes presidents of each sector, the CFO, the senior vice president of human resources, and the general manager of shared services. These presidents represent the key customer groups and insure alignment of shared-services policies with their needs. The corporate sponsors insure that the shared-services policies align with overall corporate objectives and the shared-services executive is there to represent the shared-services group.

Finally, along with the increased use of alliances and their rapid deployment comes an increased need for formal intercompany governance processes. Newly emerged large networks of companies, such as the Star Alliance of United Airlines, Lufthansa, Scandinavian Airlines, Thai Airways International and other regional airlines, need to have their own "organization" and governance system—potentially, a key differentiator among alliances as they compete against each other for greater market share.

Of course, successfully shifting an established organization along all seven dimensions presents its share of challenges. The path to a true e.org is far from smooth. Typically, companies move through three distinct stages.

E-aware companies feel a sense of urgency about the Internet, but view it as an IT issue. They launch a Web site with brochureware and then wonder what to do next. While "pockets of passion" emerge around the organizations, such companies have yet to develop a focused approach or strategy to address the profound shifts in structure and culture precipitated by the new medium. Still, senior management is initiating the right dialogue on leadership, behavior and people issues, and is assessing its technical skill gaps.

E-launch companies acknowledge the profound opportunity posed by the Internet and see beyond the IT issues to the business implications. They formulate a shared vision and articulate it, and the organization begins to develop some of the characteristics of the networked e.org. The CEO and senior managers of the company demonstrate new leadership behaviors, and an e-commerce point person is generally identified. Virtual communications technology facilitates the exchange of knowledge and best practices.

E.orgs have moved from Web site to mainstream. The company's vision is apparent to all and is well understood, both by employees and all external partners. An entrepreneurial culture has taken root and knowledge is shared freely throughout the organization and at all levels, facilitated by intranets and extranets. Business units seamlessly access needed resources both within and outside the company. The organization has developed a cascading leadership structure, and its people strategy is front and center. This is a true e.org, characterized by a centerless, flexible and efficient organizational structure.

FOCUS: CISCO SYSTEMS

THE PARADIGM OF AN E.ORG

Cisco Systems, Inc. may well be the best example of what we mean by an e.org. At present, Cisco does more business on-line than any other company, with electronic sales averaging more than $20 million a day. The clear market leader in the business-to-business networking hardware industry, it is the ultimate networked enterprise.

Organization Structure   Cisco maintains a strong web of strategic partnerships and systems integration with suppliers, contractors and assemblers. This network of alliances provides a flexible structure that enables the "e-stended" Cisco enterprise to shift toward new market opportunities, and away from old ones. Although it outsources functions, including a large part of its manufacturing, it also leverages its innovative human resources and IT departments as shared services to the benefit of all its business units.

Leadership   John Chambers has proven to be a strong, visionary leader, but Cisco is led by more than just a single person. The company has made more than 40 acquisitions in its short history, and many acquired companies live on as autonomous Cisco business units. But Cisco does not install new leadership for those business units; managers of the acquired companies usually have the independence to run their business units. Even more telling, Cisco's senior management is filled with executives from acquired companies. These entrepreneurial managers are not pushed out of the company; their skills as leaders are valued at all levels of Cisco.

People and Culture   Cisco's culture is straight out of the e.org textbook, and extends all the way to the company's endless search for talent. Cisco has proven to be very effective at recruiting those whom the company calls "passive" job seekers—people who aren't actively looking for a new job. The company is a recruitment innovator in the competitive Silicon Valley marketplace. The company has a Web page, for example, to connect a potential hire with a Cisco employee who works in the same sort of position. The volunteer employee "friend," and not a trained recruiter, will then call the prospect to talk about life at Cisco. This inside view of the company is an important selling tool for recruitment; it also gives employees a voice in the continued growth of the company. And Cisco's human resources ability extends to the culture of the organization and its ability to retain talent. The result? Turnover is low, at 6.7 percent annually, compared to an industry average of 18 percent. And turnover of acquired-company staff at Cisco is even lower—just 2.1 percent, compared to an industry average of more than 20 percent. (Of course, a relentlessly increasing stock price doesn't hurt.)

Coherence   Cisco is almost religious when it comes to customer focus, and the customer focus goes right to the top. CEO Chambers was reportedly late for his very first board meeting in 1994 because he was on the phone with an unhappy customer. The board excused him. Under Chambers, Cisco senior executives have their bonuses tied to customer satisfaction ratings, and the company has spared no expense developing its online service and support model to provide its customers with the industry's broadest range of hardware products, as well as related software and services. The customer focus permeates the entire organization—even to the engineering department, a group not traditionally thought of as customer oriented.

Knowledge   Cisco has leveraged the Internet to optimize every step in the value chain from sales to order-processing to customer service to manufacturing. The extent to which Cisco has tied its business partners together with shared knowledge is staggering. Web-based systems allow suppliers to tap directly into Cisco's manufacturing and order systems with real-time access to product logistics information and order flow. Cisco also shares demand forecasts, intellectual capital, electronic communication tools and volume targets. The result? Suppliers' production processes are "pulled" by Cisco's customer demand. The company's knowledge-sharing goes even further, providing online service and support to end customers; 70 percent of technical support requests are now filed electronically, generating an average customer service rating of 4+ on a 5-point scale. Cisco has saved considerable money from this online migration—an estimated $500 million a year from improved supply chain management, on-line technical support, software distribution via downloads and other Internet-enabled processes.

Alliances   It's not just knowledge that Cisco distributes electronically with its network of partners. Cisco's alliance partners are an integral component of the company's ability to serve customers, and Cisco treats them as part of the company. Indeed, half of customer orders that come in over its Web site are routed electronically to a supplier who ships directly to the customer.

Governance   Cisco's ability to grow while managing its autonomous business units and bringing together its alliance partners is indicative of its internal and external governance policies. Perhaps this is best illustrated by Cisco's acquisitions ability. The company is well known for its rapid acquisitions process, and for its ability to integrate its acquisitions quickly into the Cisco family. The Cisco integration team has the acquisitions process down to a science.

Cisco has upped the ante and established the table stakes in the industry, not only for its competitors, but also for its suppliers, by utilizing the Internet to maximum advantage. Yet its primary product, networking hardware, is not even a product that lends itself to Internet distribution. These components are not only "unbittable," they are highly specialized. Still Cisco has been able to make the sales and buying experience very "bittable," and very lucrative.

Chapter 20

Managing Change

CHANGE IS EVERYONE'S JOB: MANAGING THE EXTENDED ENTERPRISE IN A GLOBALLY CONNECTED WORLD
Rosabeth Moss Kanter

SURFING THE EDGE OF CHAOS
Richard T. Pascale

RULES OF THUMB FOR CHANGE AGENTS
Herbert A. Shepard

Managing organizational change is an art as well as an essential skill. Making a difference at work often boils down to helping your organization or department change, regardless of your position in the hierarchy. Successfully applying the knowledge and skills acquired in your study of organizational behavior requires a good understanding of how the change process works. Change efforts generally fail due to implementation problems, rather than the lack of good ideas for change. The art of organizational change involves many of the competencies mentioned throughout the *Reader*: the ability to perceive different mental maps and question their validity, the ability to understand why people and groups behave as they do and appreciate the differences among them, the ability to analyze what's really going on in organizations (including the political and informal aspects), and a thorough understanding of what distinguishes effective and ineffective employees, teams, managers, and organizations. Furthermore, successful change agents, like successful managers, have a great deal of self-awareness.

A turbulent business environment and a global economy demand swift adaptation, as Rosabeth Kanter, internationally known speaker, consultant, and management professor, argues in "Managing the Extended Enterprise in a Globally Connected World." Kanter has focused her attention on change and change masters for most of her career. After identifying global trends and their implications for businesses, Kanter provides specific suggestions for fostering innovation, knowledge exchange, and collaboration in global companies.

In recent years, organizational scholars have borrowed theories from natural science and applied, for example, the lessons of chaos theory and complexity theory to human organisms. Richard Pascale, in "Surfing the Edge of Chaos," has written a fascinating treatise on the relationship between complex adaptive systems (bee colonies, amoebae, etc.) and organizational strategy and change. Pascale, a consultant and business professor, uses the change efforts of Royal Dutch/Shell, one of his clients, to test the validity of his argument that complexity theory has lessons for human organizations. We have included his article as an example of cutting-edge thinking that has the potential to take the field of organizational behavior in new directions.

One of the first writers to capture the art of organizational change was Herb Shepard. He was an early practitioner of organizational development (OD), a specialized area of organizational behavior focused on planned change. Shepard's "Rules of Thumb for Change Agents" is a classic that contains a great deal of wisdom for both OD consultants and anyone who wants to make changes in his or her organization.

CHANGE IS EVERYONE'S JOB:
MANAGING THE EXTENDED ENTERPRISE
IN A GLOBALLY CONNECTED WORLD*

Rosabeth Moss Kanter

The Scene: High noon in Texas, the offices of the CEO of Composite Corp., a large, 100-year-old global company. Composite is officially headquartered several states away, but the CEO prefers to work from Dallas. The CEO, wearing his usual pullover sweater, enters the weekly management meeting with six of his senior executives, also casually dressed, to discuss the companies' recent successes repositioning itself at the forefront of a new technology, after selling the traditional core of the business. One wall of the conference room is a theatre-sized television screen on which status reports are being projected from a laptop computer. Another top executive, recently hired to head a major corporate staff function, joins the conversation by speakerphone; he works out of San Francisco because his wife refused to move when he was hired. Then voices check in from Los Angeles, New York, Boston, Chicago, Memphis, and around the world: Karen in London, Jose ("call me Joe") in Brazil, John in Tokyo (who calls from home because of the time difference), Rahul in Mumbai (stopping at his office after dinner with government officials), and an audience of other managers. Each office on the call is also seeing the same numbers—every-one's weekly results available to everyone else.

The Chief Technology Officer reports a full, exciting R&D pipeline in a field where knowledge is proliferating rapidly and new product life cycles declining equally rapidly. Some of the most promising projects are the result of alliances—mostly with small startups in which Composite had bought a stake, sometimes moving its people into space adjacent to the partners, but also the occasional R&D alliance with a university or a large competitor. London reports a commercial coup: Composite has teamed with a logistics company to offer a new proposition to retailers that saves everyone money across the supply chain while permitting promotions to consumers. Washington reports on the progress of an international campaign to improve literacy for poor children; Composite will donate a percentage of sales of a leading product and launch a major advertising campaign. New York reports that the product mix has been changed in the Composite store on Fifth Avenue to reflect consumer feedback.

Toward the end of the hour, there is a brief flurry of comments about the new strategic planning sessions—"Summits" involving participation from a deep diagonal slice through the organization and also key customers. Attention turns to other ways Composite is striving to become "one company." The heat rises. No one thinks global product teams are working. Knowledge-sharing is not occurring, local managers won't release their people, the best practices database has little in it and is hard to access, the pressure to make the numbers within markets drives behavior away from global synergies. The chief knowledge officer unveils plans for a worldwide tour to stimulate every region to take advantage of innovations stemming from partnerships, and he introduces, voice-to-voice, his new director of knowledge networks. The CEO ends by thanking everyone for increasing the amount of criticism and disagreement in the weekly meeting because that means that fear of hierarchy is disappearing.

I concocted my fictional company scene not as a future scenario but as a collage of today's realities. I have witnessed versions of my Composite story unfold in executive suites and boardrooms throughout

---

*Reprinted with permission of the author © 1999 Rosabeth Moss Kanter, Harvard Business School, Soldiers Field, Boston, MA 02163.

North America, Europe, and the most competitive parts of Asia and Latin America. This scene is already occurring in industries of the future—which means not only high tech and biotech but any industry that relies on knowledge and is supported by new technologies. The building blocks of twenty-first century management are in sight today in world-class companies that operate as an extended enterprise.

GLOBAL CONNECTIVITY: THE TRENDS

The defining feature of the global economy is not the flow of goods—international trade has existed for centuries—but the flow of capital, people, and information. Time and space are no longer a barrier to doing deals anywhere in the world; computer networks permit instantaneous transactions, and market watchers operate on a 24-hour basis. Consolidation in the financial sector puts control over the flow of money into fewer hands—indeed, reducing the "hands" et al, as financial transactions are electronically mediated. International mergers and acquisitions are growing, especially as many countries ease restrictions on foreign direct investment. Travel and tourism have increased dramatically. From 1960 to 1988 the real cost of international travel dropped by 60 percent; during the same period, the number of foreigners entering the Unites States on business rose by 2800 percent.

SEED GRANTS

Daily work can drive out innovation, especially innovations that cross boundaries. Line managers who are measured on the numbers have no reason to let their people participate. However, leaders can encourage innovation by offering incentives. Special funds for small grants can help the seeds of new ideas blossom. They can also help people take fast action on promising new opportunities without going through the hierarchy, bypassing a lengthy budgeting and resource allocation process. Grant funds help people pursue unexpected opportunities and incubate new initiatives without undermining local line managers.

Top management can create a modest pool of resources—a Chairman's or Executive Committee Grant Fund—as "seed money" for early stage development of transformation projects that cut across boundaries or involve cross-business unit synergies. Criteria for proposals should be clear and widely available, and a screening process should be developed. The screening team could come from the business units worldwide, and it would thus give them a chance to learn more about developments happening all over the world—so that they themselves become idea scouts and knowledge integrators.

Some proposals might involve standalone ventures; others, projects that can be embedded within business units. The seed grant helps fund the creation of a "business plan" that would then be routed back to the line organization for commitment to develop or qualify for further corporate support. In addition to direct business benefits, this has the side benefit of encouraging more people to think entrepreneurially about creative ways to approach business problems and opportunities.

Develop a very simple proposal process and format which can be widely available.

Appoint a screening team to review proposals within a short time, with a simple sign-off process for ideas that can be implemented quickly and requires little time or resources. As ideas get more elaborate, the approval process would also become so.

Encourage people to submit proposals for projects that they are willing to take responsibility.

Keep supporting the process. It often starts slowly, but then picks up momentum and eventually becomes embedded in the culture.

(continued)

> Business unit heads might want to set up their own grant fund. One incentive to do this is a Save-and-Reinvest Plan. Businesses can be encouraged to finance their own future by becoming more efficient now—an entrepreneurial incentive, like a form of departmental gain-sharing comparable to the individual gain-sharing in which individuals or teams can get in their paycheck a portion of the savings they find. In this case, the department or unit could keep a portion of cost savings as long as they have a promising innovation in which to invest it.

Intangible information-centered assets, such as proprietary technologies, brands, workforce skills, and strategic relationships, increasingly matter more than tangible assets.

For example, a Brookings Institution study shows that physical assets (property, plant, and equipment) accounted for 62.8 percent of the total market value of U.S. firms in capital-dependent manufacturing and mining industries in 1980 but dropped to only 37.9 percent of the market value of those firms by 1991. And that's manufacturing; intangible assets create nearly all of the value in service industries.

Communication Uber Alles   Information is even more mobile than capital or people and can now reach any part of the world simultaneously. One landmark was passed when CNN offered five broadcasts of the Gulf War as it happened; another when Congress put the special prosecutor's report about President Clinton on the worldwide web. The Internet makes it possible for any design, any fashion, any idea to be known anywhere in the world at the moment of launch; a New York apparel manufacturer put his spring line on the Internet and within days had five orders from Beijing. A report from Active Media shows that business-to-business marketers are eagerly adopting products allowing immediate two-way communications with customers, including net videoconferencing and workgroup products.

As global media and entertainment giants grow—Sony, Bertelsmann, Time Warner, and Disney—they seek products or concepts that travel easily over world communication channels that themselves are increasingly controlled by global giants. Communication industries on both the content and the infrastructure sides are consolidating quickly in the United States, accounting for four out of five of the largest-ever mergers through 1997: World-Com's $37 billion deal for MCI, Bell Atlantic's $25.6 billion deal for NYNEX, Disney's $19 billion acquisition of CapCities/ABC, and SBC Communications' $16.1 billion acquisition of Pacific Telesis. Bell Atlantic's proposed acquisition of GTE in 1998 for over $50 billion topped all of these.

Global Strategies   In key industries, country-by-country approaches are being replaced by global strategies. Companies are integrating their businesses across geographies. Some seek world products that can reach every part of the world at the same time, made in fewer places for bigger markets, and supported by global procurement and global marketing. Consider Gillette's shift to world products a decade ago. Like many consumer goods companies, Gillette traditionally developed products a market at a time, with gradual roll-outs around the world based on their assumption of when a market was ready for something new or more advanced. Starting with the Sensor razor in 1990, Gillette created a global product with a global launch—the same advanced product conveyed by the same advertising message available in every corner of the world within months.

Other consumer products companies are following suit. Procter & Gamble's recent reorganization is designed to ensure global simultaneity, eliminating regional business units and putting profit responsibility in the hands of seven executives responsible for global product units. New fabric care product, Febreze, launched first in the United States with expected annual sales of $150 to $200 million; if it had been launched by the new global fabric care and laundry unit, it would likely have been rolled out in other countries at the same time, generating $500 million in annual sales, new CEO Durk

Jager told the *Wall Street Journal*. Disney cartoon characters once made their way around the world at a leisurely pace, following the popularity of the films as they were gradually translated and shown. Now licensing agreements are in place with toys available everywhere even before the films are released. This sets in motion a global cascade: Global purchasing by large international companies pressures suppliers to globalize their own operations or join global networks.

While large, established companies are reinventing themselves to become more global, newer technology companies are born global. The newest technologies are inherently border-crossing, such as computers and electronic communications, and the strong American companies that develop and use them are rapidly creating alliances and networks with numerous companies in many parts of the world. Companies in new technology fields such as software, biotechnology, medical devices, or telecommunications tend to design their products with world standards in mind and partners in many places even before they are ready to ship a single item outside their home country. Sometimes this stance is propelled by their partnership with global giants; small biotech startups find willing partners in the pharmaceutical industry, in which major players such as GlaxoWellcome, Merck, and Novartis have swelled through mergers and reorganized around global product lines.

CHANGE AGENTS

Chartering a set of "change agents" from among leaders of the future is a way to build skills, create demonstrations of the value of innovation within many parts of the business, and get useful work done. This can:

Tap the energy and ambition of early-career high potential people who bring a fresh perspective to the business.
Get them working on stretch goals and promising projects that produce organizational innovations.
Build the cultural change agents of the future.

With the right training and coaching, these leaders of the future can help bring about business results today they would not be able to do in their ordinary jobs. This is a form of learning-by-doing or action learning. But in addition, the fresh eyes with which this group looks at the business can be a stimulus to change for those above them, especially for the upper middle manager group that tends to be the most conservative and bureaucratic in most companies. Their projects can serve as models for others, their skills can spread, the curriculum developed for them can be used elsewhere.

To mobilize this group:

Identify high-potential junior managers and professionals in early career stages—a diverse group from around the world.
Identify within each sector/business unit those "leverage points" or "open questions" where leaders of the future can make a difference on strategic issues that will improve execution-opportunities to execute faster, cut costs, remove barriers, or leverage the extended enterprise by taking better advantage of external alliances. This will help form the content for a Change Agent Summit and guide eventual choice of projects.
Convene the potential change agents in a global summit. Expose them to the business strategy, the strategic challenges, the views of top management, the tools for creating projects that can make a difference, and the change process.

(continued)

Link one top management "sponsor" to each "change agent." The sponsor's role is to help the change agent identity a high payoff business project opportunity outside his/her current job then help get support and resources for it within the business unit. This serves several purposes: top management "buy-in" and involvement; exposure across the generations so that top people hear from younger/newer people who can see the business with fresh eyes; assurance of support for their projects; etc.

Authorize them, with the concurrence of their bosses, to work on a short-term high-potential project (5 to 8 months). Get the bosses' support by offering them extra resources in exchange for the release time of the change agent. (Some projects might "work out" unnecessary bureaucracy and improve other people's ability to execute.)

Support them with periodic seminars with external and internal experts. Sponsors report project progress at top management meetings.

Develop metrics and assess. Spread learning. Graduate this group and start the next.

World Standards   World commercial standards inevitably follow, along with a push for even greater transparency. (Lack of transparency was one problem that ultimately caused Asia's speculative bubble to burst.) More watchdogs, with ever-more powerful analytic tools and ever-faster communication channels—securities analysts, the media, government data collectors, international trade treaty overseers, issue-oriented activists—provide data to track performance. Electronic procurement systems permit rapid comparisons among many different purveyors of goods and services. UPS and Federal Express offer software and data links that enable customers to track the status of their orders; such systems also permit customers to provide instant performance ratings. In the future it is likely that more conduct will be scrutinized, compared, and exposed along more dimensions, even when countries have different practices. New businesses are springing up to collect and disseminate these data— witness the phenomenal growth of Bloomberg business news services, available through every form of media. Casual dialogues on the Internet about experiences with particular companies, agencies, or products will become the basis for instant rating systems that accumulate and disseminate information. Management by fact will increasingly embarrass those still engaged in management by corruption or cronyism.

Inevitably, this exposure will be one more force spreading world standards. The European quality standard, ISO 9000 and beyond, became de facto world process assurance standards necessary for any organization that wanted to do business with the best industrial customers. All of these trends increase the desirability of comparative performance data, using the same metrics worldwide. Companies will measure more things about their own organizations' performance and spread those data more widely throughout the ranks in order to ensure that performance goals are met everywhere. Real-time data based on common measures will permit shifting of production from one part of the world to another (a Gillette strength) or assembling a global team to address a customer opportunity.

Going Direct   As the world becomes more globally connected, competition becomes more ferocious, and the payoff grows from creating widely known brands. Customers have more choices, and they become more informed global shoppers—whether they are large companies using electronic procurement systems to choose from the world's best suppliers or consumers buying a car through Saturn's Web site. So companies must understand customers more directly. Companies at every point in the supply chain will break out of their position to make their presence felt to end users and to get direct knowledge of consumer trends, even if they were once behind-the-scenes suppliers of invisible components. Intel changed an industry paradigm in information technology by branding a component. It sold computer chips like potato chips, hiring the same ad agencies that peddle snack foods and soft drinks to make Intel processors ("Intel Inside") more important to consumers than the maker of the computer. Similarly, Nutrasweet, a food and beverage sweetener, made its brand a driver for purchase of the main product. Manufacturers such as Rubbermaid (kitchen products), Swatch (watches), and Timberland (boots) gain direct consumer experience and contact by establishing their own stores, even when their retail customers' stores are nearby. Now the Internet makes it possible for any company anywhere to communicate and sell directly.

Collaborative Advantage   To gain strength to compete in more demanding global markets, companies collaborate (e.g., to achieve speed and quality through closer integration with suppliers and customers, to attain scale through alliances, or to redefine an industry). At Polaroid, purchasing has become "global supply chain management." Yellow Springs Instruments lists its strategic partners next to the balance sheet in its annual report. Software companies, for whom ties with independent developers, venture partners, and customers are a critical asset, dedicate senior executives and large departments solely to the management of alliances and partnerships. Companies like Disney that once licensed rights to others and stepped away now want to get more value from those arrangements, using them to gain ideas for innovation or intelligence about new country markets—or to push more Disney-branded product through those channels, with more influence over partners' businesses. Identifying the best partners early pays dividends. Johnson & Johnson brought disposable contact lenses to market first, establishing barriers to entry by locking up the best suppliers.

Collaboration gives giants access to innovation; Novartis and Monsanto look to small biotech firms, Pfizer uses contract research organizations as part of its R&D effort. Some alliance networks echo Japanese keiretsus, Korean chaebols, or the interlocking companies in Southeast Asian conglomerates, but often they are looser, with a wider range of partners and fewer permanent commitments. Collaboration also permits small companies to gain the virtues of large size; the Independent Grocers Association gives small U.S. stores some of the purchasing clout, private-label products, and market presence of large supermarket chains.

Multi-Localism   Globalization does not mean homogenization; it requires strategies and practices that accommodate to the diversity that exists across countries. Some business processes lend themselves to greater uniformity and economies of global scope, while others require local differentiation. Production processes, technologies, and supplies are more easily globalized than distribution, which has to connect with local infrastructure. Even world products and concepts reach customers in different ways depending on country conditions. For example, in its initial entry into Brazil, Wal-Mart made some obvious merchandising mistakes, such as stocking American footballs in a soccer-playing country or leaf blowers in tree-less, yard-less concrete-dominated Sao Paolo, according to the *Wall Street Journal*, and it also faced new competition (the French giant Carrefour). But the more difficult challenges involved local infrastructure. Wal-Mart had 300 deliveries per day in Sao Paolo instead of the 7 per day typical in the United States. The chain initially lacked clout with local suppliers, so it could not gain the same pricing or logistics advantages as in the United States. Its stockhandling system could not handle Brazilian pallet sizes nor could its computerized bookkeeping system address Brazil's complex taxes.

The clash of global and local ideas produces new concepts. Local companies might adapt to the presence of international competitors by creative upgrades, while foreign companies accommodate to local practices. In Lima, Peru, a local seafood restaurant in the same shopping mall with Burger King studied and adapted the foreign chain's techniques to create fast-food-style ceviche (a marinated seafood dish more popular locally than hamburgers). At the same time, McDonald's in Peru incorporated into its menu a major national soft drink, Golden Cola, because it outsells international brands.

"Global" strategy thus means multidimensional and multilocal thinking. Complicating this picture: some differentiating ties may be ethnic and tribal rather than national or regional. British Airways' "truly global" strategy includes new airplane livery and marketing campaigns featuring tribal symbols such as Highland Scottish tartan plaids or ethnic Chinese symbols. Another truth of globalization: it involves portable ethnicity recreated in outposts anywhere.

Community Embeddedness   Companies need to develop deep insider ties in particular places, value local traditions, and accommodate to local systems—even as some try to change them. Community service activities and partnerships with non-profit organizations are growing in strategic importance. United Airlines Chairman Gerald Greenwald describes his company's interest in social causes as "good for the soul and good for business." Just as public outrage can depress sales, encourage union organizing, or block permits for new facilities, public approval of a company's association with good causes can create customer and public goodwill. "Cause-related marketing" (such as AT&T's promotion with the Red Cross, Starbuck's with CARE) builds sales and identifies large companies with equally large and globally connected non-profits. Community service can also allay local concerns about foreign companies, as Japanese companies have been discovering in the United States. Some of these activities use a company's core competence to produce change, and thus contributes to innovation for the company as well as the community. IBM's Reinventing Education initiative in over 25 sites in the Unites States and four other countries deploys IBM engineers, systems integrators, and consultants in partnerships with public schools to create innovations, such as Web sites to train teachers or new voice recognition technology to teach reading.

TEACHING AND MENTORING: GLOBAL BEST PRACTICE CONTESTS

The theory behind best-practice sharing stems from an assumption that every company has people in the field with good ideas and solutions to problems that should be adopted more widely. The practical challenge: how to help people teach each other across wide organizational and geographic distances. Recognition accompanied by abundant publicity is a way to nudge a company's culture toward greater sharing of best practices. Contests generate attention and excitement. Winners can be rewarded with the chance to travel to another location to teach about their innovation, which begins the mentoring process.

Steps:

Develop contests within facilities or departments to pick successful projects involving collaboration outside of their local area and creativity in execution.

Winning teams within a facility then go to a regional "tricks of the trade show" to exhibit what they did and represent their facility/department in learning from others at the "trade show." The best of the regional trade show winners get to go to a global event. At that event the big awards are distributed, with considerable fanfare, global simulcasts, and publicity.

All winners at any level serve as global mentors—they get to travel to another facility to teach about accomplishments. For many people, the trip itself is a reward, and they take on "master" status.

To get maximum benefit from this process:

Create as much publicity as possible about the award criteria themselves before, during and after awards are handed out. Make the award important, reinforce the connection to business results and strategic goals, and communicate the values and behavior repeatedly. Among the best thing about awards is the communication opportunity.

Get every facility and function involved, and encourage awards at every level from local to global. For example, start with a contest within a facility for the team to represent that facility at a regional event. Regions pick teams to go to a global event.

Send those receiving local awards on a trip to another facility. That is a reward to them—especially for people who never get to travel. And it is also a chance to disseminate "best practices."

Develop mini-cases about how the award-winners did it. This is more important to communicate and disseminate than the mere fact of being recognized.

Make sure that the bosses and managers of the award-winners get credit. This will make them champions of the new behaviors, too. Moreover, there are important lessons to be learned about the coaching and development process. Disseminate those lessons, so other managers can feel rewarded for developing their people.

Ask award-winners for their further ideas for innovation. That is also a reward—the chance to have influence even from lower levels of the organization.

Form a network of award-winners, a kind of club to which new people are added every year. Publicize winners in the external media. Announce them in the annual report. Include a few of them where possible in customer meetings or top management conferences.

Tie awards to recognition activities already going on in the business. A culture of recognition supports high performance.

STARTING WITH A "CHAMPION"

It has been said that "collaboration is an unnatural act." It is hard enough for people to get their daily work done in numbers-driven companies facing intense competition and technological change; to take time to think about work across boundaries can be an overwhelming task. To gain the power of the entire extended enterprise of internal knowledge and external partners requires attention focused on it, facilitators ready to help encourage and improve it, and trainers able to increase skills in doing it.

Start with a "champion" for knowledge networks who is a senior manager/professional. The "director of networks" should have:

- peer credibility and many relationships that cross geographies and functions;
- deep organizational knowledge;
- diplomatic skills: can help people get along;
- imagination: can see opportunities for connections;
- openness: likes to share information and glory.

The champion's role includes tasks such as:

- finding opportunities to initiate networks;
- contact point or clearinghouse for those interested in forming networks;
- troubleshooter who looks after the health of the networks;
- helping steer networks in productive business directions;

(continued)

- helping ensure that they have tools and resources if they need them or advice about how to get them;
- tracking results, formation and dissolution;
- educating managers about the value of networks.

Tapping emerging markets, in particular, thrusts businesses into community partnerships with government, community groups, or national and international non-profit organizations. EDS, a large systems integration company, has run a Global Volunteer Day (GVD) since 1993; in India the new relationships and positive aura created by GVD were main factors in successful market entry. Lotus offered software fellowships in South Africa to black programmers through village organizations, hoping to use the resulting community partnerships to build both a staff and a market. Nortel's joint ventures in Turkey and China involve partnerships with national government ministries. First Community Bank, BankBoston's inner city bank-within-a-bank, partners with community groups to make pools of resources available for microloans too small to be otherwise profitable for the bank.

Competition For Talent   Human capital is becoming more central than financial capital. Silicon Valley is awash with investors eager to fund new ventures but is short of talent to run them. John Doerr, venture capitalist behind Netscape, has said that the product of Silicon Valley is not silicon but networking, and its scarcest resource is technical and managerial talent. The more desirable that talent, the more it will be recruited in a world labor market—especially as professionals such as engineers or Web site designers or management consultants are educated to common world standards—with global searches facilitated by information technology. Coopers & Lybrand uses the Internet to recruit for entry level accounting and auditing jobs, including on-line assessment tools in its "Springboard" system.

COLLABORATION AMBASSADORS

The extended enterprise blurs the boundary between external and internal collaboration, and many of the skills for horizontal cooperation are similar, whether the partners' home base is within the same company or outside it. The Network Champion can create a Collaboration Resource Team to support both internal and external relationships, drawn from within the business units worldwide as part-time diplomats. They should be credible professionals with line management/business experience. The team's tasks can include:

Coaching, educating, and training others in alliance and network skills;
Examining and improving the infrastructure for collaboration-communication systems, training, measures, rewards;
Serving as network troubleshooters and alliance facilitators;
Acting as ambassadors from the company to particular sets of external partners;
Monitoring the company's entire portfolio of strategic relationships to see how well they are working, the trends, the linkages among partners, the areas requiring change.

The centrality of human brainpower to future success accounts for the priority IBM has placed on improving public primary and secondary education all over the world. But IBM is not alone. In a survey of 12,000 managers in 24 countries I conducted for *Harvard Business Review*, education was the number one social priority everywhere. Education by companies is already a $55 billion industry in the United States, and it will grow elsewhere, reflecting the need for lifelong learning. In-house education is related not to company size but to market complexity and use of new workplace practices such as team-based work, cross-functional integration, and supplier partnerships—hallmarks of world class companies.

Companies will seek new ways to motivate and retain talent, including family-friendly workplace practices. Telecommuting will increase, as much to boost productivity by avoiding traffic congestion in long commutes as to help mothers work at home (as they do in U.K. software programming company FI Group). Because of their motivational value, company-sponsored community service programs will spread. Talent-hungry global consultancies already offer opportunities for their best people to work on pro bono cause-related activities. And some leading companies are hiring top executives for corporate positions who do not relocate to the corporate headquarters city.

The trends I have described support one big conclusion: To create and profit from global connectivity, change will become everyone's job.

THE ORGANIZATION OF THE FUTURE: ASPIRATIONS AND CHALLENGES

Global connectivity increases the payoff from continuous innovation and rapid, simultaneous execution. The successful twenty-first century company will empower people to innovate. The company will leverage relationships inside and outside its boundaries—the extended enterprise as the corporate version of the extended family—and encourage people to reach further, faster to gain or spread knowledge. It will:

- Connect its people and partners globally, using horizontal networks to take advantage of all of the resources in the entire extended enterprise of business units, suppliers, customers, and alliances to create value for end users;
- Craft global strategies and standards but encourage and learn from local customization and innovation, neither commanding everything from the center nor letting each unit or territory act on its own;
- Use collaborative methods—networks, cross-boundary teams, supply chain partnerships, strategic alliances—to support innovation and then spread knowledge from local innovations everywhere quickly;
- Shape a shared culture of unity that appreciates and derives strength from diversity; and
- Develop common tools and measurements to put everyone "on the same page," while also encouraging everyone to "break the mold."

Such goals are expressed by numerous companies that I visit, observe, advise, and teach. They are noble aspirations indeed—but easier said than done. Large and emerging companies alike encounter common obstacles to translating this utopian vision into practice. These typical problems are faced by companies attempting to apply the new leadership principles:

- Units performing just well enough to meet "plan," while competitors change the game with a better idea;
- Lack of money and time used as excuses for the failure to initiate projects outside mainstream orthodoxy;
- The press of too much immediate work right here, right now, driving out cooperation with distant people and groups (out of sight, out of mind);
- Lack of support by local managers for global teams, and lack of imagination about the business benefits from networks and alliances;
- Few incentives or rewards for working across boundaries, and controversy over who gets the credit anyway (transfer-pricing or evaluation issues);

- Communication overload on small matters (too many memos or e-mails) but undercommunication on big matters (major strategic priorities);
- A Tower of Babel of management languages and too few tools that truly work everywhere;
- Turf ownership provoking jealousies and conflicts (each office claims its own way works better);
- Lack of collaboration skills—so it is easier to fall back on hierarchy-knows-best command modes than to listen, persuade, modify, teach, and get buy-in.

New skills, new behaviors, and new roles are needed to support initiative and imagination, foster trust and communication, and forge the human connections that lie behind effective internal networks and external alliances. Twenty-first century leaders will spend more of their time on the culture to support innovation, knowledge exchange, and collaboration. And some people will take on new titles as idea scouts, change agents, best practice mentors, knowledge managers, network champions, and alliance ambassadors.

CREATING AN INNOVATION CULTURE

A culture for innovation begins with expectations. Rubbermaid and 3M make innovation an explicit focus, setting goals and measures for innovation, such as the percent of revenue from new products. Stretch goals and opportunities for innovation can apply to people at all levels. Wainwright Industries, a small auto supplier that won the U.S. Malcolm Baldrige National Quality Award in 1995, has made continuous improvement proposals a way of life; Wainwright factories average an amazing 1.5 implemented ideas per person per week.

In short, world-class companies expect innovation all the time, everywhere. They generate activity at three levels of a pyramid:

- At the peak, a few big bets about the future, and thus the biggest investments in product, technology, or market innovation.
- In the middle, a portfolio of promising but not-yet-proven experiments, new ventures, prototypes, or other stand-alone projects.
- At the base, a large number of operationally-embedded incremental innovations, continuous improvements, and early-stage new ideas that boost immediate revenues, take out costs, increase speed, or create a customer success.

But the pyramid is not static. Influence flows in many directions: top-down, bottom-up, or horizontally across the company. The big bets influence the domain for experimentation and provide structure for the search for incremental contributions. Sometimes modest ideas up from the bottom accumulate into a bigger force that turns into new opportunities reaching bigger bet status. Projects and ideas from one part of the organization trigger new thinking and new opportunities in another part. Special funds can provide the impetus to generate and implement new concepts. They can provide the resources to develop ideas that would otherwise languish, especially ideas that cross boundaries and thus fall outside particular line budgets (see "Seed Grants").

Making the search for innovation a part of everyone's job does not mean that people are confined to their job. Some companies encourage people to be idea scouts, looking for ideas beyond the job, the company, and the industry. I coined the term "far-afield trips" for these tours beyond conventional boundaries to encounter ideas or technologies emerging elsewhere that suggest new opportunities for the company. Creativity is stimulated by leaving familiar settings and facing the clash of perspectives and challenge to conventional wisdom that leads to break—through ideas. First-hand experience with power outages in developing countries led the head of a company making electricity-dependent photo identification cameras to see the huge potential for battery-operated cameras even in countries with reliable electricity. Some companies encourage tours of other companies, some take advantage of any way that people discover new possibilities—even on vacation on their own time in foreign countries where they see something they've never seen before. People within the company can also stimulate each other, especially through cross-fertilization of ideas by the contributions from people from different locations with different perspectives.

Leaders must create a culture that permits discussion of half-formed embryonic possibilities. The widely touted product-development firm IDEO holds open brainstorming sessions. Ocean Spray's regular, open, cross-level product development forums allowed a lower-level engineer at Ocean Spray to surface the idea for packaging innovations that led the beverage company to steal a march on its much-larger competitors by being the first to adopt the paper bottle. For some companies, their employees are also product users who can get involved in product development and offer important feedback regardless of position. Gillette tests its razors and blades on male employees who come to work unshaven and agree to use different products for each side of their faces. Xerox innovators involve Xerox employees (all of whom handle documents) in the search for document management solutions.

Customers, suppliers, and venture partners are important sources of ideas for innovation. Innovation and collaboration can work together if partners provide a new and different set of ideas that represent a window on new developments and marketplace changes. The airlines entering into the Star Alliance (Lufthansa, United, Air Canada, Varig, AllNippon, and others) have made learning from each other an explicit goal, as all seek innovation in an industry where it is sometimes hard to distinguish one carrier from another. Decades of research on industrial innovation show that users are often the primary stimulus for innovation. But when technologies change dramatically, customers sometimes join managers in resisting change, especially if established customers are too committed to old methods. For this reason, companies need to experiment with, and learn about, new ideas that take them beyond the desires or interests of current customers.

Product-developers have always focused on innovation, but in the future, many others who are not called the "creatives" will be charged with leading innovation. There will be a new role for people to serve as "change agents" with the mandate to find and lead innovation projects within many fields and functions (see "Change Agents"). And "lead sites" will take on the responsibility for developing or prototyping innovations useful in other parts of the company—field offices acting as centers for experiments on behalf of the whole. Internal new ventures focused on a new market or new technology often create concepts that are widely applicable to the mainstream. BankBoston's First Community Bank (FCB) was designed as a bank-within-a-bank to serve neglected urban constituencies in inner cities who often had limited experience with banks; the user-friendly "First Step" savings and lending products FCB developed became desirable bank-wide offerings for any newcomer to banking.

Leaders of the future will empower more people at more levels to search for new ideas, from constant operational improvements to dramatic breakthroughs.

FOSTERING KNOWLEDGE EXCHANGE

The potential for business payoffs from knowledge exchange is clear: fast transmission of strategically important information across geographies; fast customer response when there's a problem that can't be solved locally; ideas for innovation, competitor intelligence, cost-savings as solutions spread. The first challenge is to identify and recognize the "local heroes" who produce innovation and turn them into mentors helping others adopt their best practices (see "Teaching and Mentoring Across Boundaries: Global Best Practice Contests").

For learning to take place in all directions, not just top-down or from headquarters out, requires not only a communications infrastructure but also a cultural revolution in many companies. Simultaneous dissemination of information means that managers are informed at the same time as those who report to them—and in some cases, later than people below them in official rank.

Newcomers with knowledge from outside the organization can sometimes add more value than company veterans. "Kids" teach their seniors; distinguished Editor Michael Kinsley is unlearning print magazine rules and learning the Internet from Microsoft managers decades younger, as he creates a new on-line magazine *Slate*. Useful ideas might come from farflung locations once labeled "backwards"; Bell Atlantic's joint venture in Thailand taught American engineers about telecommunications technology not yet in use in the United States. Rather than holing up in headquarters bunkers, successful CEOs like Gillette's Alfred Zeien are on the road constantly to exchange ideas face-to-face in the field. The more senior the person, the greater the need for direct feedback about what's working—or not working. Sybase's top executives regularly join on-line forums tearing apart the company's products. The head of ABB's largest American units measures his managers on the number of customer complaints they surface and examine. He wants them to hear more, not fewer, complaints.

Information technology can facilitate spontaneous, instantaneous, self-organizing exchanges that bypass formal planning and formal controls. But a "soft" infrastructure of human trust is critical to mobilize people quickly to work across boundaries to seize opportunities quickly. They must be able to communicate easily and fluently with one another, know their part in the wider system, grasp the strategy, and know whom to contact elsewhere in the company with something to offer to a task at hand. Everyone should feel that they can potentially form and join networks (e.g., the factory maintenance network, the receptionists' network, the network of users of a particular supplier, the China-watchers network, the telecommuters' network, the women's network). For DuPont, networks enhance the idea generation process necessary for innovation and the knowledge transfer process necessary to solve problems or utilize best practices quickly. Its central research lab supports over 400 networks combining face-to-face meetings with electronic exchanges; they range from ad hoc exchanges to solve a particular problem to ongoing interest groups specializing in technology issues, to big teams mobilized for big strategic efforts.

The time spent on meeting with peers and communicating with them must feel productive and business results-related. This might seem obvious, but in some companies "knowledge management" involves rules and requirements, such as documenting projects in order to put them in a database—which busy professionals perceive as added work and a waste of time.

A longer-term side benefit of establishing and nurturing knowledge networks is that they facilitate horizontal relationships at middle and lower ranks—so that people know and "trust" their peers can thus "self-organize" quickly to get something done without waiting for approval from a functional, geographic, or sector hierarchy. The best networks:

- Meet face-to-face periodically and involve a mix of types of communication—supported by e-mail and electronic communication but not driven by them;
- Can cut across business units and geographies, thus giving people access to useful knowledge not locally available;
- Give something to each member useful to that person's job (reciprocity is important or else some people feel exploited by others);
- Have some joint goals (e.g., a set of projects with specific goals and measurable results) with a core group dedicating "official" time;
- Have some official status; in order to gain access to resources and management time;
- Are fluid, are organic, and have a life cycle: "sunset" as appropriate, revisit effectiveness often, make changes or dissolve;
- Feel voluntary rather than compulsory;
- Have a core of dedicated members/leaders, while others come in and out;
- Have access to tools and resources to help work together (see "Network Champions").

Knowledge exchanges are often considered frosting on the cake, something that busy people will get to someday, when they have time. So change-adept companies create occasions for exchange, whether informal lunch seminars (an Internet company has hot lunches for everyone on Wednesdays, corporate university sessions on Thursdays in the late afternoon; a software firm hosts "food for thought" brainstorming sessions), larger conferences, or internal trade fairs to show off the latest ideas. Classroom-style training courses are sometimes the least important element of the infrastructure for learning. Still, education benefits and training programs abound at change-adept companies such as Hewlett-Packard. In addition to more traditional forms of education, some companies are developing new ways to provide tools to document and pass on the benefit of experience. Skandia created software to codify learning about how to open a new office in a new country, speeding up the process of country-entry about sevenfold.

Twenty-first century managers will lead *teaching* organizations, not simply learning organizations. Skills in teaching, coaching, and mentoring will become part of everyone's job.

COLLABORATION THROUGHOUT THE EXTENDED ENTERPRISE

Collaboration comes in many forms and changes over time; sometimes it is a long-time arrangement, sometimes a temporary convenience, sometimes the starting point in a relationship that grows or wanes. Whenever there is complementary and mutual dependence for tasks of strategic importance, relationships are more stable. Supply chain partnerships linking suppliers and customers or producers and distributors tend to last the longest, involve greater commitment, and often create more value than looser affiliations. Strategic alliances and joint ventures among similar kinds of partners, in contrast, tend to be unstable. Sometimes they evolve toward closer and deeper ties, such as outright mergers, or they dissolve when they have met—or failed to meet—their goals. Sometimes they are disguised sales, with one partner eventually buying out others. Configurations of alliances are fluid and changing because each partner has multiple ties and independent interests.

Many companies will need to view their entire extended family as a whole: to identify synergies or conflicting expectations, transfer lessons across partner experiences, or see where value is increasing or declining. They will need a new cadre of cosmopolitan leaders comfortable operating in diverse cultures. Alliance directors, worldwide account managers, partner representatives, and supplier champions are among the formal titles created for cross-boundary managers. Informally, they are *integrators*, who can see beyond obvious differences between countries and cultures to find the common threads; *diplomats*, who can resolve conflicts among local ways and influence locals to accept world standards; and *cross-fertilizers*, who can bring the best from one place to another (see "Collaboration Ambassadors").

Leveraging connections requires comfort with differences. Never as fast on their feet as smaller companies, some corporate giants are learning to dance by dancing with smaller partners. Large companies like Compaq count on technological breakthroughs from smaller focused partners like Dragon Systems, an emerging world leader in voice recognition systems. Dragon, in turn, needs large partners like Digital to reach international markets. The tricky step for managers to master is how to dance with dissimilar partners without stepping on their toes. Collaboration requires interpersonal as well as organizational social sensitivity: skills in listening, self-awareness, ability to read others' signals, and a dose of humility. It requires sharing information with partners, networking between the companies at multiple organizational levels, keeping partners' interests in mind when crafting strategies, being willing to learn from those outside the firms' own walls, and respecting differences between companies and cultures.

Globalization exacerbates the need for managers to respect differences. Even a decade ago, "international" was often relegated to a separate divison, an after-thought in many companies; now it's a sensibility that ought to pervade the whole company. Managing international alliances makes cultural differences especially salient. But my research with Richard Corn on foreign acquisitions of domestic companies made clear that national cultural differences are often less important sources of problems than company style differences. Those involved in alliances and partnerships must respect diverse cultural traditions and values, whatever their source. They must deal with fuzzy social variables such as trust and reputation and use soft skills such as empathy and understanding to build relationships of mutuality. These fuzzy intangibles are increasingly recognized as having value for economies as well as businesses. The economic prosperity of nations, regions, and communities benefits from stocks of "social capital" and trust in institutions.

To be effective, leaders of the future will view differences not as obstacles to getting things done but as opportunities to gain synergy from complementary resources and skills.

THE NEXT BOTTOM LINE

The most important assets of world-class twenty-first-century companies will be what I call the 3Cs: *concepts* (ideas and technologies, driven by innovation), *competence* (skills and the ability to use them, improved by teaching and learning) and *connections* (strategic relationships, nurtured by collaboration). These soft assets rooted in human qualities—imagination, courage, creativity, sociability, diplomacy, trust—will increasingly overtake hard assets as the most important sources of a company's value. Leaders of the future will continue to have the fundamental, enduring job of mobilizing and motivating individual human talent in pursuit of collective ends. But there will be more emphasis on encouraging people to seek change, share their knowledge about it, and collaborate with other members of the extended enterprise to implement it effectively—which will stimulate further innovation, completing the circle.

As economists have learned, forecasting can be dangerous, especially about the future. It is always easier to extrapolate from past experience than to predict what will happen next. But it has also been said that the best way to predict the future is to create it. To bring my rather optimistic scenarios to pass will require enlightened leadership. The future depends on cosmopolitan leaders who are comfortable with global complexity; think horizontally; stretch to reach ever-higher standards; care about customers, end consumers, and communities; work collaboratively with partners; and truly value people, investing in their development.

Together these priorities constitute a Social Value Chain that can work like this: enlightened leaders build high-performing enterprises, excellent enterprises develop strong economies, and strong economies can produce good societies that meet people's needs. The next century can be the era that joins the dynamism of the private sector to public needs—as long as businesses see their purpose as creating both wealth and well-being.

Surfing the Edge of Chaos*

Richard T. Pascale

Treating organizations as complex adaptive systems provides powerful insights into the nature of strategic work.

---

*Reprinted from *Sloan Management Review 40* (Spring 1999): 83–94.

Every decade or two during the past one hundred years, a point of inflection has occurred in management thinking. These breakthroughs are akin to the S-curves of technology that characterize the life cycle of many industrial and consumer products: Introduction [right arrow] Acceleration [right arrow] Acceptance [right arrow] Maturity. Each big idea catches hold slowly. Yet, within a relatively short time, the new approach becomes so widely accepted that it is difficult even for old-timers to reconstruct how the world looked before.

The decade following World War II gave birth to the "strategic era." While the tenets of military strategy had been evolving for centuries, the link to commercial enterprise was tenuous. Before the late 1940s, most companies adhered to the tenet "make a little, sell a little, make a little more." After the war, faculty at the Harvard Business School (soon joined by swelling ranks of consultants) began to take the discipline of strategy seriously. By the late 1970s, the array of strategic concepts (SWOT analysis, the five forces framework, experience curves, strategic portfolios, the concept of competitive advantage) had become standard ordnance in the management arsenal. Today, a mere twenty years later, a grasp of these concepts is presumed as a threshold of management literacy. They have become so familiar that it is hard to imagine a world without them.

It is useful to step back and reflect on the scientific underpinnings to this legacy. Eric Beinhocker writes:

> The early micro-economists copied the mathematics of mid-nineteenth century, physics equation by equation. ['Atoms'] became the individual, 'force' became the economists' notion of 'marginal utility' (or demand), 'kinetic energy' became total expenditure. All of this was synthesized into a coherent theory by Alfred Marshall—known as the theory of industrial organization.[1]

Marshall's work and its underpinnings in nineteenth century physics exert a huge influence on strategic thinking to this day. From our concept of strategy to our efforts at organizational renewal, the deep logic is based on assumptions of deterministic cause and effect (i.e., a billiard ball model of how competitors will respond to a strategic challenge or how employees will behave under a new incentive scheme). And all of this, consistent with Newton's initial conceptions, is assumed to take place in a world where time, space (i.e., a particular industry structure or definition of a market), and dynamic equilibrium are accepted as reasonable underpinnings for the formulation of executive action. That's where the trouble begins. Marshall's equilibrium model offered appropriate approximations for the dominant sectors of agriculture and manufacturing of his era and are still useful in many situations. But these constructs run into difficulty in the far from equilibrium conditions found in today's service, technology, or communications-intensive businesses. When new entrants such as Nokia, Amazon.com, Dell Computer, or CNN invade a market, they succeed despite what traditional strategic thinkers would write off as a long shot.

During the 1980s and 1990s, performance improvement (e.g., total quality management, kaizen, just-in-time, reengineering) succeeded the strategic era. It, too, has followed the S-curve trajectory. Now, as it trails off, an uneasiness is stirring, a feeling that "something more" is required. In particular, disquiet has arisen over the rapidly rising fatality rates of major companies. Organizations cannot win by cost reduction alone and cannot invent appropriate strategic responses fast enough to stay abreast of nimble rivals. Many are exhausted by the pace of change, and their harried attempts to execute new initiatives fall short of expectations.

The next point of inflection is about to unfold. To succeed, the next big idea must address the biggest challenge facing corporations today—namely, to dramatically improve the hit rate of strategic initiatives and attain the level of renewal necessary for successful execution. As in the previous eras, we can expect that the next big idea will at first seem strange and inaccessible.

Here's the good news. For well over a decade, the hard sciences have made enormous strides in understanding and describing how the living world works. Scientists use the term "complex adaptive systems" ("complexity" for short) to label these theories. To be sure, the new theories do not explain everything. But the work has identified principles that apply to many living things—amoebae and ant colonies, beehives and bond traders, ecologies and economies, you and me.

For an entity to qualify as a complex adaptive system, it must meet four tests. First, it must be comprised of many agents acting in parallel. It is not hierarchically controlled. Second, it continuously shuffles these building blocks and generates multiple levels of organization and structure. Third, it is subject to the second law of thermodynamics, exhibiting entropy and winding down over time unless replenished with energy. In this sense, complex adaptive systems are vulnerable to death. Fourth, a distinguishing characteristic, all complex adaptive systems exhibit a capacity for pattern recognition and employ this to anticipate the future and learn to recognize the anticipation of seasonal chance.

Many systems are complex but not adaptive (i.e., they meet some of the above conditions, but not all). If sand is gradually piled on a table, it will slide off in patterns. If a wave in a stream is disturbed, it will repair itself once the obstruction is removed. But neither of these complex systems anticipates and learns. Only living systems cope with their environment with a predictive model that anticipates and pro-acts. Thus, when the worldwide community of strep bacteria mutates to circumvent the threat of the latest antibiotic (as it does rather reliably within three years), it is reaffirming its membership in the club of complexity.

Work on complexity originated during the mid-1980s at New Mexico's Santa Fe Institute. A group of distinguished scientists with backgrounds in particle physics, microbiology, archaeology, astrophysics, paleontology, zoology, botany, and economics were drawn together by similar questions.[2] A series of symposia, underwritten by the Carnegie Foundation, revealed that all the assembled disciplines shared, at their core, building blocks composed of many agents. These might be molecules, neurons, a species, customers, members of a social system, or networks of corporations. Further, these fundamental systems were continually organizing and reorganizing themselves, all flourishing in a boundary between rigidity and randomness and all occasionally forming larger structures through the clash of natural accommodation and competition. Molecules form cells; neurons cluster into neural networks (or brains); species form ecosystems; individuals form tribes or societies; consumers and corporations form economies. These self-organizing structures give rise to emergent behavior (an example of which is the process whereby pre-biotic chemicals combined to form the extraordinary diversity of life on earth). Complexity science informs us about organization, stability, and change in social and natural systems. "Unlike the earlier advances in hard science," writes economist Alex Trosiglio, "complexity deals with a world that is far from equilibrium, and is creative and evolving in ways that we cannot hope to predict. It points to fundamental limits to our ability to understand, control, and manage the world, and the need for us to accept unpredictability and change.[3]

The science of complexity has yielded four bedrock principles relevant to the new strategic work:

1. Complex adaptive systems are at risk when in equilibrium. Equilibrium is a precursor to death.[4]
2. Complex adaptive systems exhibit the capacity of self-organization and emergent complexity.[5] Self-organization arises from intelligence in the remote clusters (or nodes) within a network. Emergent complexity is generated by the propensity of simple structures to generate novel patterns, infinite variety, and often, a sum that is greater than the parts. (Again, the escalating complexity of life on earth is an example.)
3. Complex adaptive systems tend to move toward the edge of chaos when provoked by a complex task. Bounded instability is more conducive to evolution than either stable equilibrium or explosive instability. (For example, fire has been found to be a critical factor in regenerating healthy forests and prairies.) One important corollary to this principle is that a complex adaptive system, once having reached a temporary "peak" in its fitness landscape (e.g., a company during a golden era), must then "go down to go up" (i.e., moving from one peak to a still higher peak requires

it to traverse the valleys of the fitness landscape). In cybernetic terms, the organism must be pulled by competitive pressures far enough out of its usual arrangements before it can create substantially different forms and arrive at a more evolved basin of attraction.

4. One cannot direct a living system, only disturb it. Complex adaptive systems are characterized by weak cause-and-effect linkages. Phase transitions occur in the realm where one relatively small and isolated variation can produce huge effects. Alternatively, large chances may have little effect. (This phenomenon is common in the information industry. Massive efforts to promote a superior operating system may come to naught, whereas a series of serendipitous events may establish an inferior operating system—such as MS-DOS—as the industry standard.)

Is complexity just interesting science, or does it represent something of great importance in thinking, about strategic work? As these illustrations suggest, treating organizations as complex adaptive systems provides useful insight into the nature of strategic work. In the following pages, I will (1) briefly describe how the four bedrock principles of complexity occur in nature and (2) demonstrate how they can be applied in a managerial context. In particular, I use the efforts underway at Royal Dutch/Shell to describe an extensive and pragmatic test of these ideas.

The successes at Shell and other companies described here might be achieved with a more traditional mind-set (in much the same way as Newton's laws can be used to explain the mechanics of matter on earth with sufficient accuracy so as to not require the General Theory of Relativity). But the contribution of scientific insight is much more than descriptions of increasing accuracy. Deep theories reveal previously unsuspected aspects of reality that we don't see (the curvature of space-time in the case of relativity theory) and thereby alter the fabric of reality. This is the context for an article on complexity science and strategy. Complexity makes the strategic challenge more understandable and the task of strategic renewal more accessible. In short, this is not a polemic against the traditional strategic approach, but an argument for broadening it.

STABLE EQUILIBRIUM EQUALS DEATH

An obscure but important law of cybernetics, the law of requisite variety, states: For any system to survive, it must cultivate variety in its internal controls. If it fails to do so internally, it will fail to cope with variety successfully when it comes from an external source.[8] Here, in the mundane prose of a cybernetic axiom, is the rationale for bounded instability.

A perverse example of this axiom in action was driven home by the devastating fires that wiped out 25 percent of Yellowstone National Park in 1992. For decades, the National Park Service had imposed equilibrium on the forest by extinguishing fires whenever they appeared. Gradually, the forest floor became littered with a thick layer of debris. When a lightening strike and ill-timed winds created a conflagration that could not be contained, this carpet of dry material burned longer and hotter than normal. By suppressing natural fires for close to 100 years, the park service had prevented the forest floor from being cleansed in a natural rhythm. Now a century's accumulation of deadfall generated extreme temperatures. The fire incinerated large trees and the living components of top soil that would otherwise have survived. This is the price of enforced equilibrium.

The seductive pull of equilibrium poses a constant danger to successful established companies. Jim Cannavino, a former IBM senior executive, provides an anecdote that speaks to the hazards of resisting change. In 1993, Cannavino was asked by IBM's new CEO, Lou Gerstner, to take a hard look at the strategic planning process. Why had IBM so badly missed the mark? Cannavino dutifully examined the work product—library shelves filled with blue binders containing, 20 years of forecasts, trends, and strategic analysis.

"It all could be distilled down to one sentence," he recounts. "'We saw it coming,—PC open architecture, networking intelligence in microprocessors, higher margins in software and services than hardware; it was all there. So I looked at the operating plans. How did they reflect the shifts the strategists had projected? These blue volumes (three times as voluminous as the strategic plans) could also be summarized in one sentence: 'Nothing changed.' And the final dose of arsenic to this diet of cyanide was the year-end financial reconciliation process. When we rolled up the sector submissions into totals for the corporation, the growth opportunities never quite covered the erosion of market share. This shortfall, of course, was the tip of an iceberg that would one day upend our strategy and our primary product—the IBM 360 mainframe. But facing these fundamental trends would have precipitated a great deal of turmoil and instability. Instead, year after year, a few of our most senior leaders went behind closed doors and raised prices."[9]

While equilibrium endangers living systems, it often wears the disguise of an attribute. Equilibrium is concealed inside strong values or a coherent, close-knit social system, or within a company's well-synchronized operating system (often referred to as "organizational fit"). Vision, values, and organizational fit are double-edged swords.

Species are inherently drawn toward the seeming oasis of stability and equilibrium—and the further they drift toward this destination, the less likely they are to adapt successfully when chance is necessary. So why don't all species drift into the thrall of equilibrium and die off? Two forces thwart equilibrium and promote instability: (1) the threat of death and (2) the promise of sex.

The Darwinian process, called "selection pressures" by natural scientists, imposes harsh consequences on species entrapped in equilibrium. Most species, when challenged to adapt too far from their origins, are unable to do so and gradually disappear. But from the vantage point of the larger ecological community, selection pressures enforce an ecological upgrade, insofar as mutations that survive offer a better fit with the new environment. Natural selection exerts itself most aggressively during periods of radical change. Few readers will have difficulty identifying, these forces at work in industry today. There are no safe havens. From toothpaste to camcorders, pharmaceuticals to office supplies, bookstores to booster rockets for space payloads, soap to software, it's a Darwinian jungle out there, and it's not getting easier.

As a rule, a species becomes more vulnerable as it becomes more genetically homogeneous. Nature hedges against this condition through the reproductive process. Of the several means of reproduction that have evolved on the planet, sex is best. It is decisively superior to parthenogenesis (the process by which most plants, worms, and a few mammals conceive offspring through self-induced combination of identical genetic material).

Sexual reproduction maximizes diversity. Chromosome combinations are randomly matched in variant pairings, thereby generating more permutations and variety in offspring. Oxford's evolutionary theorist, William Hamilton, explains why this benefits a species. Enemies (i.e., harmful diseases and parasites) find it harder to adapt to the diverse attributes of a population generated by sexual reproduction than to the comparative uniformity of one produced by parthenogenesis.[10]

How does this relate to organizations? In organizations, people are the chromosomes, the genetic material that can create variety. When management thinker Gary Hamel was asked if he thought IBM had a chance of leading the next stage of the information revolution, he replied: "I'd need to know how many of IBM's top 100 executives had grown up on the west coast of America where the future of the computer industry is being created and how many were 40 years of age. If a quarter or a third of the senior group were both under 40 and possessed a west coast perspective, IBM has a chance.[11]

Here's the rub: The "exchanges of DNA" attempted within social systems are not nearly as reliable as those driven by the mechanics of reproductive chemistry. True, organizations can hire from the outside, bring seniors into frequent contact with iconoclasts from the ranks, or confront engineers and designers with disgruntled customers. But the enemy of these methods is, of course, the existing, social order, which, like the body's immune defense system, seeks to neutralize, isolate, or destroy foreign invaders. "Antibodies" in the form of social norms, corporate values, and orthodox beliefs nullify the advantages of diversity. An executive team may include divergent interests, only to engage in stereotyped listening (e.g., "There goes Techie again") or freeze iconoclasts out of important informal discussions. If authentic diversity is sought, all executives, in particular the seniors, must be more seeker than guru.

DISTURBING EQUILIBRIUM AT SHELL

In 1996, Steve Miller, age 51, became a member of Shell's committee of managing directors—the five senior leaders who develop objectives and long-term plans for Royal Dutch/Shell.[12] The group found itself captive to its hundred-year-old history. The numbing effects of tradition—a staggering, $130 billion in annual revenues, 105,000 predominantly long-tenured employees, and global operations—left Shell vulnerable. While profits continued to flow, fissures were forming beneath the surface.

Miller was appointed group managing, director of Shell's worldwide oil products business (known as "Downstream"), which accounts for $40 billion of revenues within the Shell Group. During the previous two years, the company had been engaged in a program to "transform" the organization. Yet the regimen of massive reorganization, traumatic downsizing, and senior management workshops accomplished little. Shell's earnings, while solid, were disappointing to financial analysts who expected more from the industry's largest competitor. Employees registered widespread resignation and cynicism. And the operating units at the "coal face" (Shell's term for its front-line activities within the 130 countries where Downstream does business) saw little more than business as usual.

For Steve Miller, Shell's impenetrable culture was worrisome. The Downstream business accounted for 37 percent of Shell's assets. Among the businesses in the Shell Group's portfolio, Downstream faced the gravest competitive threats. From 1992 to 1995, a full 50 percent of Shell's retail revenues in France fell victim to the onslaught of the European hypermarkets; a similar pattern was emerging in the United Kingdom. Elsewhere in the world, new competitors, global customers, and more savvy national oil companies were demanding a radically different approach to the marketplace. Having observed Shell's previous transformation efforts, Miller was convinced that it was essential to reach around the resistant bureaucracy and involve the front lines of the organization, a formidable task given the sheer size of the operation. In addition to Downstream's 61,000 full-time employees, Shell's 47,000 filling stations employed hundreds of thousands, mostly part-time, attendants and catered to more than 10 million customers every day. In the language of complexity, Miller believed it necessary to tap the emergent properties of Shell's enormous distribution system and shift the locus of strategic initiative to the front lines. He saw this system as a fertile organism that needed encouragement to, in his words, "send green shoots forth."

In an effort to gain the organization's attention (i.e., disturb equilibrium), beginning in mid-1996, Miller reallocated more than 50 percent of his calendar to work directly with front-line personnel. Miller states:

> Our Downstream business transformation program had bogged down largely because of the impasse between headquarters and the operating companies, Shell's term for its highly independent country operations. The balance of power between headquarters and field, honed during a period of relative equilibrium, had ground to a stalemate. But the forces for continuing in the old way were enormous and extended throughout the organization. We were overseeing the most decentralized operation in the world with country chief executives that had, since the 1950s, enjoyed enormous autonomy. This had been part of our success formula. Yet we were encountering a set of daunting, competitive threats that transcended national boundaries. Global customers—like British Airways or Daimler Benz—wanted to deal with one Shell contact, not with a different Shell representative in every country in which they operate. We had huge overcapacity in refining,

but each country CEO (motivated to maximize his own P&L) resisted the consolidation of refining capacity. These problems begged for a new strategic approach in which the task at the top was to provide the framework and then unleash the regional and local levels to find a path that was best for their market and the corporation as a whole.

Shell had tried to rationalize its assets through a well-engineered strategic response: directives were issued by the top and driven through the organization. But country heads successfully thwarted consolidation under the banner of host-country objections to the threatened closing of their dedicated refining capacity. Miller continues: "We were equally unsuccessful at igniting a more imaginative approach toward the marketplace. It was like the old game of telephone that we used to play when we were kids: you'd whisper a message to the person next to you, and it goes around the circle. By the time you get to the last person, it bears almost no resemblance to the message you started with. Apply that to the 61,000 people in the Downstream business across the globe, and I knew our strategic aspirations could never penetrate through to the marketplace. The linkages between directives given and actions taken are too problematic." What made sense to Miller was to fundamentally alter the conversation and unleash the emergent possibilities. Midway through the process, Miller became acquainted with core principles of living systems and adopted them as a framework to provide his organization with a context for renewal.

Miller's reports in the operating companies were saying, "Centralization will only bog us down." "They were partly right," he acknowledges. "These are big companies. Some earn several hundreds of millions a year in net income. But the alternative wasn't centralization—it was a radical chance in the responsiveness of the Downstream business to the dynamics of the marketplace—from top to bottom such that we could come together in appropriate groups, solve problems, and operate in a manner which transcended the old headquarters versus field schism. What initially seemed like a huge conflict has gradually melted away, I believe, because we stopped treating the Downstream business like a machine to be driven and began to regard it as a living system that needed to evolve."

Miller's solution was to cut through the organization's layers and barriers, put senior management in direct contact with the people at the grassroots level, foster strategic initiatives, create a new sense of urgency, and overwhelm the old order. The first wave of initiatives spawned other initiatives. In Malaysia, for example, Miller's pilot efforts with 4 initiative teams (called "action labs") have proliferated to 40. "It worked," he states, "because the people at the coal face usually know what's going on. They see the competitive threats and our inadequate response every day. Once you give them the context, they can do a better job of spotting opportunities and stepping up to decisions. In less than two years, we've seen astonishing progress in our retail business in some 25 countries. This represents around 85 percent of our retail sales volume, and we have now begun to use this approach in our service organizations and lubricant business. Results? By the end of 1997, Shell's operations in France had regained initiative and achieved double-digit growth and double-digit return on capital. Market share was increasing after years of decline." Austria went from a probable exit candidate to a highly profitable operation. Overall, Shell gained in brand-share preference throughout Europe and ranked first in share among other major oil companies. By the close of 1998, approximately 10,000 Downstream employees have been involved in this effort with audited results (directly attributed to the program) exceeding a $300 million contribution to Shell's bottom line.

SELF-ORGANIZATION AND EMERGENT COMPLEXITY

Santa Fe Institute's Stuart Kauffman is a geneticist. His lifetime fascination has been with the ordered process by which a fertilized egg unfolds into a newborn infant and later into an adult. Earlier Nobel Prize-winning work on genetic circuits had shown that every cell contains a number of "regulatory" genes that act as switches to turn one another on and off. Modern computers use sequential instructions, whereas the genetic system exercises most of its instructions simultaneously. For decades, scientists have sought to discover the governing mechanism that causes this simultaneous, nonlinear system to settle down and replicate a species.[13]

Kauffman built a simple simulation of a genetic system. His array of 100 light bulbs looked like a Las Vegas marquee. Since regulatory genes cause the cells (like bulbs) to turn on or off, Kauffman arranged for his bulbs to do just that, each independently of the other. His hypothesis was that no governing mechanism existed; rather, random and independent behavior would settle into patterns—a view that was far from self-evident. The possible combinations in Kauffman's arrangement of blinking lights was two (i.e., on and off), multiplied by itself 100 times (i.e., almost one million, trillion, trillion possibilities!).

When Kauffman switched the system on, the result was astonishing. Instead of patterns of infinite variety, the system always settled down within a few minutes to a few more or less orderly states. The implications of Kauffman's work are far-reaching. Theorists had been searching for the sequence of primordial events that could have produced the first DNA—the building block of life. Kauffman asked instead, "What if life was not just standing around and waiting until DNA happened? What if all those amino acids and sugars and gasses and solar energy were each just doing their thing like the billboard of lights?" If the conditions in primordial soup were right, it wouldn't take a miracle (like a million decks of cards falling from a balcony and all coming up aces) for DNA to randomly turn up. Rather, the compounds in the soup could have formed a coherent, self-reinforcing web of reactions and these, in turn, generated the more complex patterns of DNA.[14]

Emergent complexity is driven by a few simple patterns that combine to generate infinite variety. For example, simulations have shown that a three-pronged "crow's foot" pattern, if combined in various ways, perfectly replicates the foliage patterns of every fern on earth. Similar phenomena hold true in business. John Kao, a specialist in creativity, has observed how one simple creative breakthrough can evoke a cascade of increasing complexity.[15] "Simple" inventions such as the wheel, printing, press, or transistor lead to "complex" offshoots such as automobiles, cellular phones, electronic publishing, and computing.

The phenomenon of emergence arises from the way simple patterns combine. Mathematics has coined the term *fractals* to describe a set of simple equations that combine to form endless diversity.[16] Fractal mathematics has given us valuable insight into how nature creates the shapes we observe. Mountains, rivers, coastline vegetation, lungs, and circulatory systems are fractal, replicating a dominant pattern at several smaller levels of scale. Fractals, in effect, act like genetic algorithms enabling a species to efficiently replicate essential functions.

One consequence of emerging complexity is that you cannot see the end from the beginning. While many can readily acknowledge nature's propensity to self-organize and generate more complex levels, it is less comforting to put oneself at the mercy of this process with the foreknowledge that we cannot predict the shape that the future will take. Emerging complexity creates not one future but many.

SELF-ORGANIZATION AND EMERGENCE AT SHELL

Building on (1) the principles of complexity, (2) the fractal-like properties of a business model developed by Columbia University's Larry Seldon,[17] and (3) a second fractal-like process, the action labs, Steve Miller and his colleagues at Shell tapped into the intelligence in the trenches and channeled it into a tailored marketplace response.[18]

Miller states:

We needed a vehicle to give us an energy transfusion and remind us that we could play at a far more competitive level. The properties of self-organization and emergence make intuitive sense to me. The question was how to release them. Seldon's model gave us a sharp-edged tool to identify customer needs and markets and to develop our value proposition. This, in effect, gave our troops the 'ammunition' to shoot with—analytical distinctions to make the business case. Shell has always been a wholesaler. Yet the forecourt of every service station is an artery for commerce that any retailer would envy. Our task was to tap the potential of that real estate, and we needed both the insight and the initiatives of our front-line troops to pull it off. For a company as large as Shell, leadership can't drive these answers clown from the top. We needed to tap into ideas that were out there in the ranks—latent but ready to bear fruit if given encouragement.

At first glance, Shell's methods look pedestrian. Miller began bringing six- to eight-person teams from a half-dozen operating companies from around the world into "retailing" boot camps. The first five-day workshop introduced tools for identifying and exploiting market opportunities. It also included a dose of the leadership skills necessary to enroll others back home. Participants returned ready to apply the tools to achieve breakthroughs such as doubling net income in filling stations on the major north-south highways of Malaysia or tripling, market share of bottled gas in South Africa. As part of the discipline of the model, every intention (e.g., "to lower fuel delivery costs") was translated into "key business activities" (or KBAs). As the first group went home, six more teams would rotate in. During the next 60 days, the first group of teams used the analytical tools to sample customers, identify segments, and develop a value proposition. The group would then return to the workshop for a "peer challenge"—tough give-and-take exchanges with other teams. Then it would go back again for another 60 days to perfect a business plan. At the close of the third workshop, each action lab spent three hours in the "fishbowl" with Miller and several of his direct reports, reviewing business plans, while the other teams observed the proceedings. At the close of each session, plans were approved, rejected, amended. Financial commitments were made in exchange for promised results. (The latter were incorporated in the country's operating goals for the year.) Then the teams went back to the field for another 60 days to put their ideas into action and returned for a follow-up session.

"Week after week, team after team," continues Miller, "my six direct reports and I and our internal coaches reached out and worked directly with a diverse cross-section of customers, dealers, shop stewards, and young and mid-level professionals. And it worked. Operating company CEOs, historically leery of any 'help' from headquarters, saw their people return energized and armed with solid plans to beat the competition. The grassroots employees who participated in the program got to touch and feel the new Shell—a far more informal, give-and-take culture. The conversation down in the ranks of the organization began to change. Guerrilla leaders, historically resigned to Shell's conventional way of doing things, stepped forward to champion ingenious marketplace innovations (such as the Coca-Cola Challenge in Malaysia—a free Coke to any service-station customer who is not offered the full menu of forecourt services. It sounds trivial, but it increased volume by 15 percent). Many, if not most, of the ideas come from the lower ranks of our company who are in direct contact with the customer. Best of all, we learned together. I can't overstate how infectious the optimism and energy of these committed employees was for the many managers above them. In a curious way, these front-line employees taught us to believe in ourselves again."

As executives move up in organizations, they become removed from the work that goes on in the fields. Directives from the top become increasingly abstract as executives tend to rely on mechanical cause-and-effect linkages to drive the business: strategic guidelines, head-count controls, operational expense targets, pay-for-performance incentives, and so forth. These are the tie rods and pistons of "social engineering"—the old model of change. Complexity theory does not discard these useful devices but it starts from a different place. The living-systems approach begins with a focus on the intelligence in the nodes. It seeks to ferret out what this network sees, what stresses it is undergoing, and what is needed to unleash its potential. Other support elements (e.g., controls and rewards) are orchestrated to draw on this potential rather than to drive down solutions from above.

Miller was pioneering a very different model from what had always prevailed at Shell. His "design for emergence" generated hundreds of informal connections between headquarters and the field, resembling the parallel networks of the nervous system to the brain. It contrasted with the historical model of mechanical linkages analogous to those that transfer the energy from the engine in a car through a drive train to the tires that perform the "work."

EDGE OF CHAOS

Nothing novel can emerge from systems with high degrees of order and stability—for example, crystals, incestuous communities, or regulated industries. On the other hand, complete chaotic systems, such as stampedes, riots, rage, or the early years of the French Revolution, are too formless to coalesce. Generative complexity takes place in the boundary between rigidity and randomness.

Historically,[19] science viewed "chance" as moving from one equilibrium state (water) to another (ice). Newtonian understandings could not cope with the random, near-chaotic messiness of the actual transition itself. Ecologists and economists similarly favored equilibrium conditions because neither observation nor modeling techniques could handle transition states. The relatively inexpensive computational power of modern computers has changed all that. Nonequilibrium and nonlinear simulations are now possible. These developments, along, with the study of complexity, have enabled us to better understand the dynamics of "messiness."

Phase transitions occur in the realm near chaos where a relatively small and isolated variation can produce huge effects. Consider the example of lasers: while only a complex system and not an adaptive one, the infusion of energy into plasma excites a jumble of photons. The more the energy, the more jumbled they become. Still more and the seething mass is transformed into the coherent light of a laser beam. What drives this transition, and how can we orchestrate it? Two determinants—(1) a precise tension between amplifying and damping feedback, and (2) (unique to mankind) the application of mindfulness and intention—are akin to rudder and sail when surfing near the edge of chaos.

Two factors determine the level of excitation in a system. In cybernetics, they are known as amplifying (positive) and damping (negative) feedback.[20] Damping feedback operates like a thermostat, which keeps temperatures within boundaries with a thermocouple that continually says "too hot, too cold." Amplifying feedback happens when a microphone gets too close to a loudspeaker. The signal is amplified until it oscillates to a piercing shriek. Living systems thrive when these mechanisms are in tension.

Getting the tension right is the hard part. Business obituaries abound with examples of one or the other of these feedback systems gone amok. IT&T trader Harold Geneen or Sunbeam under "Chainsaw" Al Dunlap thrive briefly under stringent damping controls, then fade away owing to the loss of imagination and creative energy. At the opposite end, Value Jet thrives in an amplifying phase, adds more planes, departures, and staff without corresponding attention to the damping loop (operational controls, safety, reliability, and service standards).

Psychologists tell us that pain can cause us to change, and this is most likely to occur when we recontextualize pain as the means by which significant learning occurs. When the great Austro-American economist Joseph Schumpeter described the essence of free-market economies as "creative destruction," it could be interpreted as a characterization of the hazards near the edge of chaos. Enduring competitive advantage entails disrupting what has been done in the past and creating a new future.

Hewlett-Packard's printer business was one of the most successful in its portfolio. Observing a downward spiral of margins as many "me too" printers entered the market, HP reinvented its offering. Today, HP's printers are the "free razor blade"—the loss leader in a very different strategy. To maintain scale, HP abandoned its high-cost distribution system with a dedicated sales force, opting instead for mass channels, partnering, and outsourcing to lower manufacturing costs. To protect margins, it targeted its 40 biggest corporate customers and formed a partnership to deliver global business printing solutions—whether through low-cost, on-premise equipment, or networked technology. States Tim Mannon, president of HP's printer division: "The biggest single threat to our business today is staying with a previously successful business model one year too long."[21]

SHAPING, THE EDGE OF CHAOS AT SHELL

Shell moved to the edge of chaos with a multipronged design that intensified stress on all members of the Shell system.[22] First, as noted, Miller and his top team performed major surgery on their calendars and reallocated approximately half their time to teaching and coaching wave after wave of country teams. When the lowest levels of an organization were being trained, coached, and evaluated by those at the very top, it both inspired—and stressed—everyone in the system (including mid-level bosses who were not present). Second, the design, as we have seen, sent teams back to collect real data for three periods of 60 days (interspersed with additional workshop sessions). Pressure to succeed and long hours both during the workshops and back in the country (where these individuals continued to carry their regular duties along with project work) achieved the cultural "unfreezing" effects. Participants were resocialized into a more direct, informal, and less hierarchical way of working.

Miller states:

> One of the most important innovations in changing all of us was the fishbowl. The name describes what it is: I and a number of my management team sit in the middle of a room with one action lab in the center with us. The other team members listen from the outer circle. Everyone is watching as the group in the hot seat talks about what they're going to do and what they need from me and my colleagues to be able to do it. That may not sound revolutionary—but in our culture, it was very unusual for anyone lower in the organization to talk this directly to a managing director and his reports.
>
> In the fishbowl, the pressure is on to measure up. The truth is, the pressure is on me and my colleagues. The first time we're not consistent, we're dead meat. If a team brings in a plan that's really a bunch of crap, we've got to be able to call it a bunch of crap. If we cover for people or praise everyone, what do we say when someone brings in an excellent plan? That kind of straight talk is another big culture change for Shell.
>
> The whole process creates complete transparency between the people at the coal face and me and my top management team. At the end, these folks go back home and say, 'I just cut a deal with the managing director and his team to do these things.' It creates a personal connection, and it changes how we talk with each other and how we work with each other. After that, I can call up those folks anywhere in the world and talk in a very direct way because of this personal connectedness. It has completely changed the dynamics of our operations.

DISTURBING A LIVING SYSTEM

An important and distinct property of living systems is the tenuous connection between cause and effect. As most seasoned managers know, the best-laid plans are often perverted through self-interest, misinterpretation, or lack of necessary skills to reach the intended goal.

Consider the war of attrition waged by ranchers and the U.S. Fish and Wildlife Service to "control" the coyote. A cumulative total of $3 billion (in 1997 dollars) has been spent during the past 100 years to underwrite bounty hunters, field a sophisticated array of traps, introduce novel morsels of poisoned bait, and interject genetic technology (to limit fertility of females)—all with the aim of protecting sheep and cattle ranchers from these wily predators. Result? When white men first appeared in significant numbers west of the Mississippi in the early 1800s, coyotes were found in twelve western states and never seen east of the Mississippi. However, as a direct result of the aggressive programs to eliminate the coyote, the modern day coyote is 20 percent larger and significantly smarter than his predecessor. The coyote is now found in 49 of the 50 states—including suburbs of New York City and Los Angeles. How could this occur? Human intervention so threatened the coyote's survival that a significant number fled into Canada where they bred with the larger Canadian wolf. Still later, these visitors migrated south (and further north to Alaska) and, over the decades, bred with (and increased the size of) the U.S. population. The same threats to survival that had driven some coyotes into Canada drove others to adapt to climates as varied as Florida and New Hampshire. Finally, the persistent efforts to trap or hunt or poison the coyote heightened selection pressures. The survivors were extremely streetwise and wary of human contact. Once alerted by a few fatalities among their brethren, coyotes are usually able to sniff out man's latest stratagem to do them harm.

As the tale of the coyote suggests, living systems are difficult to direct because of these weak cause-and-effect linkages. The best laid efforts by man to intervene in a system, to do it harm, or even to replicate it artificially almost always miss the mark. The strategic intentions of governments in Japan, Taiwan, and Germany to replicate Silicon Valley provide one example. The cause-and-effect formula seemed simple: (1) identify a region with major universities with strong departments in such fields as microelectronics, genetics, and nuclear medicine and having a geography with climate and amenities suitable to attract professionals and (2) invest to stimulate a self-reinforcing community of interests. But these and many similar efforts have never quite reached a critical mass. The cause-and-effect relationships proved unclear.[23] A lot depends on chance. One is wiser to acknowledge the broad possibilities that flow from weak cause-and-effect linkages and the need to consider the second- and third-order effects of any bold intervention one is about to undertake.

DISTURBING A COMPLEX SYSTEM AT SHELL

In today's fast-changing environment, Shell's Steve Miller dismisses the company's old traditional approach as mechanistic. "Top-down strategies don't win ballgames," he states. "Experimentation, rapid learning, and seizing the momentum of success is the better approach."[24]

Miller observes:

We need a different definition of strategy and a different approach to generating it. In the past, strategy was the exclusive domain of top management. Today, if you're going to have a successful company, you have to recognize that the top can't possibly have all the answers. The leaders provide the vision and are the context setters. But the actual solutions about how best to meet the challenges of the moment, those thousands of strategic challenges encountered every day, have to be made by the people closest to the action—the people at the coal face.

Change your approach to strategy, and you change the way a company runs. The leader becomes a context setter, the designer of a learning experience—not an authority figure with solutions. Once the folks at the grassroots realize they own the problem, they also discover that they can help create and own the answers, and they get after it very quickly, very aggressively, and very creatively, with a lot more ideas than the old-style strategic direction could ever have prescribed from headquarters.

A program like this is a high-risk proposition, because it goes counter to the way most senior executives spend their time. I spend 50 percent to 60 percent of my time at this, and there is no direct guarantee that what I'm doing is going to make something happen down the line. It's like becoming the helmsman of a big ship when you've grown up behind the steering wheel of a car. This approach isn't about me. It's about rigorous, well-taught marketing concepts combined with a strong process design, that enable front-line employees to think like businesspeople. Top executives and front-line employees learn to work together in partnership.

People want to evaluate this against the old way, which gives you the illusion of 'making things happen.' I encountered lots of thinly veiled skepticism: 'Did your net income change from last quarter because of this chance process?' These challenges create anxiety. The temptation, of course, is to reimpose your directives and controls even though we had an abundance of proof that this would not work. Instead, top executives and lower-level employees learn to work together in partnership. The grassroots approach to strategy development and implementation doesn't happen overnight. But it does happen. People always want results yesterday. But the process and behavior that drive authentic strategic change aren't like that.

There's another kind of risk to the leaders of a strategic inquiry of this kind—the risk of exposure. You're working very closely and intensely with all levels of staff, and they get to assess and evaluate you directly. Before, you were remote from them; now, you're very accessible. If that evaluation comes up negative, you've got a big-time problem.

Finally, the scariest part is letting go. You don't have the same kind of control that traditional leadership is used to. What you don't realize until you do it is that you may, in fact, have more controls but in a different fashion. You get more feedback than before, you team more than before, you know more through your own people about what's going on in the marketplace and with customers than before. But you still have to let go of the old sense of control.

Miller's words testify to his reconciliation with the weak cause-and-effect linkages that exist in a living system. When strategic work is accomplished through a "design for emergence," it never assumes that a particular input will produce a particular output. It is more akin to the study of subatomic particles in a bubble chamber. The experimenter's design creates probabilistic occurrences that take place within the domain of focus. Period. Greater precision is neither sought nor possible.

REFERENCES

This article is drawn from R. Pascale, M. Millemann, and L. Gioja, *Surfing the Edge of Chaos: How the Smartest Companies Use the New Science To Stay Ahead* (New York: Crown, 2000).

[1] E. Beinhocker, "Strategy at the Edge of Chaos," *McKinsey Quarterly*, no. 1 (1997): 25.

[2] For an entertaining treatment of this inquiry, see: M. M. Waldrop, *Complexity* (New York: Simon & Schuster, 1992).

[3] A. Trosiglio, "Managing Complexity" (unpublished working paper, June 1995) 3; and D. Deutsch, *The Fabric of Reality* (New York: Penguin, 1997) 3–21.

[4] See S. Kauffman, *At Home in the Universe* (New York: Oxford University Press, 1995) 21; and G. Hamel and C. K. Prahalad, "Strategic Intent," *Harvard Business Review 67* (May-June 1989): 63–76.

[5] See Kauffman (1995) 205; and J. H. Holland, *Hidden Order* (Reading, MA: Addison-Wesley, 1995) 3.

[6] See Kauffman (1995) 230; and M. Gell-Mann, *The Quark and the Jaguar* (New York: Freeman, 1994) 249.

[7] See Gell-Mann (1994) 238-239; and Holland (1995) 5 and 38–39.

[8] W. Ashby, *An Introduction to Cybernetics* (New York: Wiley, 1956).

[9] R. Pascale, interviews with James Cannavino, May 1996.

[10] See Gell-Mann (1994) 64, 253; and S. J. Gould, *Full House* (New York: Crown, 1996) 138.

[11] G. Hamel, "Strategy as Revolution," *Harvard Business Review 74* (July-August 1996): 69–82.

[12] Information and quotations in this section are drawn from: R. Pascale, interviews with Steve Miller, London, The Hague, and Houston, October 1997 through February 1998.

[13] Kauffman (1995) 80–86.

[14] Waldrop (1992) 110.

[15] J. Kao, *Jamming: The Art and Discipline of Business Creativity* (New York: HarperCollins, 1997).

[16] I. Marshall and D. Zohar, *Who's Afraid of Schrodinger's Cat?* (New York: Morrow, 1997) 16, 19, 153–158.

[17] Seldon's work is unpublished. He considers it proprietary and solely for consulting purposes.

[18] Information and quotations in this section are drawn from: Pascale, interviews with Steve Miller, London, The Hague, and Houston, October 1997 through February 1998.

[19] Gell-Mann (1994) 228–230.

[20] Waldrop (1992) 138–139.

[21] R. Hof, "Hewlett Packard," *Business Week*, February 13, 1995, 67.

[22] Information and quotations in this section are drawn from: R. Pascale, interviews with Steve Miller, London, The Hague, and Houston, October 1997 through February 1998.

[23] A Saxenian, "Lessons from Silicon Valley," *Technology Review 97*, no. 5, July 1994, 42–45.

[24] Information and quotations in this section are drawn from: R. Pascale, interviews with Steve Miller, London, The Hague, and Houston, October 1997 through February 1998.

RULES OF THUMB FOR CHANGE AGENTS*

Herbert A. Shepard

The following aphorisms are not so much bits of advice (although they are stated that way) as things to think about when you are being a change agent, a consultant, an organization or community development practitioner—or when you are just being yourself trying to bring about something that involves other people.

RULE I: STAY ALIVE

This rule counsels against self-sacrifice on behalf of a cause that you do not wish to be your last.

Two exceptionally talented doctoral students came to the conclusion that the routines they had to go through to get their degrees were absurd, and decided they would be untrue to themselves to conform to an absurd system. That sort of reasoning is almost always self-destructive. Besides, their noble gesture in quitting would be unlikely to have any impact whatever on the system they were taking a stand against.

This is not to say that one should never take a stand or a survival risk. But such risks should be taken as part of a purposeful strategy of change and appropriately timed and targeted. When they are taken under such circumstances, one is very much alive.

But Rule I is much more than a survival rule. The rule means that you should let your whole being be involved in the undertaking. Since most of us have never been in touch with our whole beings, it means a lot of putting together of parts that have been divided, of using internal communications channels that have been closed or were never opened.

Staying alive means loving yourself. Self-disparagement leads to the suppression of potentials, to a win-lose formulation of the world, and to wasting life in defensive maneuvering.

Staying alive means staying in touch with your purpose. It means using your skills, your emotions, your labels and positions, rather than being used by them. It means not being trapped in other people's games. It means turning yourself on and off, rather than being dependent on the situation. It means choosing with a view to the consequences as well as the impulse. It means going with the flow even while swimming against it. It means living in several worlds without being swallowed up in any. It means seeing dilemmas as opportunities for creativity. It means greeting absurdity with laughter while

---

*Reprinted by permission of the publisher and author from the *OD Practitioner*, December 1984. Organization Development Network, Portland, Oregon.

trying to unscramble it. It means capturing the moment in the light of the future. It means seeing the environment through the eyes of your purpose.

RULE II: START WHERE THE SYSTEM IS

This is such ancient wisdom that one might expect its meaning had been fully explored and apprehended. Yet in practice the rule—and the system—are often violated.

The rule implies that one should begin by diagnosing the system. But systems do not necessarily *like* being diagnosed. Even the term *diagnosis* may be offensive. And the system may be even less ready for someone who calls himself or herself a "change agent!" It is easy for the practitioner to forget that the use of jargon which prevents laypeople from understanding the professional mysteries is a hostile act.

Starting where the system is can be called the Empathy Rule. To communicate effectively, to obtain a basis for building sound strategy, the change agent needs to understand how clients see themselves and their situation, and needs to understand the culture of the system. Establishing the required rapport does not mean that the change agent who wants to work in a traditional industrial setting should refrain from growing a beard. It does mean that, if he has a beard, the beard is likely to determine where the client is when they first meet, and the client's curiosity needs to be dealt with. Similarly, the rule does not mean that a female change agent in a male organization should try to act like one of the boys, or that a young change agent should try to act like a senior executive. One thing it does mean is that sometimes where the client is, is wondering where the change agent is.

Rarely is the client in any one place at any one time. That is, she or he may be ready to pursue any of several paths. The task is to walk together on the most promising path.

Even unwitting or accidental violations of the Empathy Rule can destroy the situation. I lost a client through two violations in one morning. The client group spent a consulting day at my home. They arrived early in the morning, before I had my empathy on. The senior member, seeing a picture of my son in the livingroom said, "What do you do with boys with long hair?" I replied thoughtlessly, "I think he's handsome that way." The small chasm thus created between my client and me was widened and deepened later that morning when one of the family tortoises walked through the butter dish.

Sometimes starting where the client is, which sounds both ethically and technically virtuous, can lead to some ethically puzzling situations. Robert Frost[A] described a situation in which a consultant was so empathetic with a king who was unfit to rule that the king discovered his own unfitness and had himself shot, whereupon the consultant became king.

Empathy permits the development of a mutual attachment between client and consultant. The resulting relationship may be one in which their creativities are joined, a mutual growth relationship. But it can also become one in which the client becomes dependent and is manipulated by the consultant. The ethical issues are not associated with starting where the system is, but with how one moves with it.

RULE III: NEVER WORK UPHILL

This is a comprehensive rule, and a number of other rules are corollaries or examples of it. It is an appeal for an organic rather than a mechanistic approach to change, for a collaborative approach to change, for building strength and building on strength. It has a number of implications that bear on the choices the change agent makes about how to use him/herself, and it says something about life.

[A] Robert Frost, "How Hard It Is To Keep From Being King When It's in You and in the Situation," *In the Clearing* (New York: Holt, Rinehart and Winston, 1962) 74–84.

COROLLARY 1: DON'T BUILD HILLS AS YOU GO

This corollary cautions against working in a way that builds resistance to movement in the direction you have chosen as desirable. For example, a program which has a favorable effect on one portion of a population may have the opposite effect on other portions of the population. Perhaps the commonest error of this kind has been in the employment of T-group training in organizations: turning on the participants and turning off the people who didn't attend, in one easy lesson.

COROLLARY 2: WORK IN THE MOST PROMISING ARENA

The physician-patient relationship is often regarded as analogous to the consultant-client relationship. The results for system change of this analogy can be unfortunate. For example, the organization development consultant is likely to be greeted with delight by executives who see in his specialty the solution to a hopeless situation in an outlying plant. Some organization development consultants have disappeared for years because of the irresistibility of such challenges. Others have wiled away their time trying to counteract the Peter Principle by shoring up incompetent managers.

COROLLARY 3: BUILD RESOURCES

Don't do anything alone that could be accomplished more easily or more certainly by a team. Don Quixote is not the only change agent whose effectiveness was handicapped by ignoring this rule. The change agent's task is an heroic one, but the need to be a hero does not facilitate team building. As a result, many change agents lose effectiveness by becoming spread too thin. Effectiveness can be enhanced by investing in the development of partners.

COROLLARY 4: DON'T OVERORGANIZE

The democratic ideology and theories of participative management that many change agents possess can sometimes interfere with common sense. A year or two ago I offered a course to be taught by graduate students. The course was oversubscribed. It seemed that a data-based process for deciding whom to admit would be desirable, and that participation of the graduate students in the decision would also be desirable. So I sought data from the candidates about themselves, and xeroxed their responses for the graduate students. Then the graduate students and I held a series of meetings. Then the candidates were informed of the decision. In this way we wasted a great deal of time and everyone felt a little worse than if we had used an arbitrary decision rule.

COROLLARY 5: DON'T ARGUE IF YOU CAN'T WIN

Win-lose strategies are to be avoided because they deepen conflict instead of resolving it. But the change agent should build her or his support constituency as large and deep and strong as possible so that she or he can continue to risk.

COROLLARY 6: PLAY GOD A LITTLE

If the change agent doesn't make the critical value decisions, someone else will be happy to do so. Will a given situation contribute to your fulfillment? Are you creating a better world for yourself and others. Or are you keeping a system in operation that should be allowed to die? For example, the public education system is a mess. Does that mean that the change agent is morally obligated to try to improve it, destroy it, or develop a substitute for it? No, not even if he or she knows how. But the change agent does need a value perspective for making choices like that.

RULE IV: INNOVATION REQUIRES A GOOD IDEA, INITIATIVE, AND A FEW FRIENDS

Little can be accomplished alone, and the effects of social and cultural forces on individual perception are so distorting that the change agent needs a partner, if only to maintain perspective and purpose.

The quality of the partner is as important as the quality of the idea. Like the change agent, partners must be relatively autonomous people. Persons who are authority-oriented—who need to rebel or need to submit—are not reliable partners: the rebels take the wrong risks and the good soldiers don't take any. And rarely do they command the respect and trust from others that is needed if an innovation is to be supported.

The partners need not be numerous. For example, the engineering staff of a chemical company designed a new process plant using edge-of-the-art technology. The design departed radically from the experience of top management, and they were about to reject it. The engineering chief suggested that the design be reviewed by a distinguished engineering professor. The principal designers were in fact former students of the professor. For this reason he accepted the assignment, charged the company a large fee for reviewing the design (which he did not trouble to examine) and told the management that it was brilliantly conceived and executed. By this means the engineers not only implemented their innovations, but also grew in the esteem of their management.

A change agent experienced in the Washington environment reports that he knows of only one case of successful interdepartmental collaboration in mutually designing funding and managing a joint project. It was accomplished through the collaboration of himself and three similarly-minded young men, one from each of four agencies. They were friends and met weekly for lunch. They conceived the project and planned strategies for implementing it. Each person undertook to interest and influence the relevant key people in his own agency. The four served one another as consultants and helped in influencing opinion and bringing the decision-makers together.

An alternative statement of Rule IV is as follows: Find the people who are ready and able to work, introduce them to one another, and work with them. Perhaps because many change agents have been trained in the helping professions, perhaps because we have all been trained to think bureaucratically, concepts like organization position, representatives or need are likely to guide the change agent's selection of those he or she works with.

A more powerful beginning can sometimes be made by finding those persons in the system whose values are congruent with those of the change agent, who possess vitality and imagination, who are willing to work overtime, and who are eager to learn. Such people are usually glad to have someone like the change agent join in getting something important accomplished, and a careful search is likely to turn up quite a few. In fact, there may be enough of them to accomplish general system change, if they can team up in appropriate ways.

In building such teamwork the change agent's abilities will be fully challenged, as he joins them in establishing conditions for trust and creativity; dealing with their anxieties about being seen as subversive; enhancing their leadership, consulting, problem-solving, diagnosing and innovating skills; and developing appropriate group norms and policies.

RULE V: LOAD EXPERIMENTS FOR SUCCESS

This sounds like counsel to avoid risk taking. But the decision to experiment always entails risk. After that decision has been made, take all precautions.

The rule also sounds scientifically immoral. But whether an experiment produces the expected results depends upon the experimenter's depth of insight into the conditions and processes involved. Of course, what is experimental is what is new to the system: it may or may not be new to the change agent.

Build an umbrella over the experiment. A chemical process plant which was to be shut down because of the inefficiency of its operations undertook a union management cooperation project to improve efficiency. which involved a modified form of profit-sharing. Such plans were contrary to company policy, but the regional vice president was interested in the experiment, and successfully concealed it from his associates. The experiment was successful; the plant became profitable. But in this case, the umbrella turned out not to be big enough. The plant was shut down anyway.

Use the Hawthorne effect. Even poorly conceived experiments are often made to succeed when the participants feel ownership. And conversely, one of the obstacles to the spread of useful innovations is that the groups to which they are offered do not feel ownership of them.

For example, if the change agent hopes to use experience-based learning as part of his/her strategy, the first persons to be invited should be those who consistently turn all their experiences into constructive learning. Similarly, in introducing team development processes into a system, begin with the best functioning team.

Maintain voluntarism. This is not easy to do in systems where invitations are understood to be commands, but nothing vital can be built on such motives as duty, obedience, security-seeking, or responsiveness to social pressure.

RULE VI: LIGHT MANY FIRES

Not only does a large monolithic development or change program have high visibility and other qualities of a good target, it also tends to prevent subsystems from feeling ownership of, and consequent commitment to the program.

The meaning of this rule is more orderly than the random prescription—light many fires—suggests. Any part of a system is the way it is partly because of the way the rest of the system is. To work towards change in one subsystem is to become one more determinant of its performance. Not only is the change agent working uphill, but as soon as he turns his back, other forces in the system will press the subsystem back towards its previous performance mode.

If many interdependent subsystems are catalyzed, and the change agent brings them together to facilitate one another's efforts, the entire system can begin to move.

Understanding patterns of interdependency among subsystems can lead to a strategy of fire-setting. For example, in public school systems, it requires collaboration among politicians, administrators, teachers, parents, and students to bring about significant innovation, and active opposition on the part of only one of these groups to prevent it. In parochial school systems, on the other hand, collaboration between the administration and the church can provide a powerful impetus for change in the other groups.

RULE VII: KEEP AN OPTIMISTIC BIAS

Our society grinds along with much polarization and cruelty, and even the helping professions compose their world of grim problems to be "worked through." The change agent is usually flooded with the destructive aspects of the situations he enters. People in most systems are impressed by one another's weaknesses, and stereotype each other with such incompetencies as they can discover.

This rule does not advise ignoring destructive forces. But its positive prescription is that the change agent be especially alert to the constructive forces which are often masked and suppressed in a problem-oriented, envious culture.

People have as great an innate capacity for joy as for resentment, but resentment causes them to overlook opportunities for joy. In a workshop for married couples, a husband and wife were discussing their sexual problem and how hard they were working to solve it. They were not making much progress, since they didn't realize that sex is not a problem, but an opportunity.

Individuals and groups locked in destructive kinds of conflict focus on their differences. The change agent's job is to help them discover and build on their commonalities, so that they will have a foundation of respect and trust which will permit them to use their differences as a source of creativity. The unhappy partners focus on past hurts, and continue to destroy the present and future with them. The change agent's job is to help them change the present so that they will have a new past on which to create a better future.

RULE VIII: CAPTURE THE MOMENT

A good sense of relevance and timing is often treated as though it were a "gift" or "intuition" rather than something that can be learned, something spontaneous rather than something planned. The opposite is nearer the truth. One is more likely to "capture the moment" when everything one has learned is readily available.

Some years ago my wife and I were having a very destructive fight. Our nine-year-old daughter decided to intervene. She put her arms around her mother and asked: "What does Daddy do that bugs you?" She was an attentive audience for the next few minutes while my wife told her, ending in tears. She then put her arms around me: "What does Mommy do that bugs you?" and listened attentively to my response, which also ended in tears. She then went to the record player and put on a favorite love song ("If Ever I Should Leave You"), and left us alone to make up.

The elements of my daughter's intervention had all been learned. They were available to her, and she combined them in a way that could make the moment better.

Perhaps it's our training in linear cause-and-effect thinking and the neglect of our capacities for imagery that makes us so often unable to see the multiple potential of the moment. Entering the situation "blank" is not the answer. One needs to have as many frameworks for seeing and strategies for acting available as possible. But it's not enough to involve only one's head in the situation; one's heart has to get involved too. Cornelia Otis Skinner once said that the first law of the stage is to love your audience. You can love your audience only if you love yourself. If you have relatively full access to your organized experience, to yourself and to the situation, you will capture the moment more often.